THE LETTERS OF GERTRUDE STEIN
AND CARL VAN VECHTEN
1913–1946

THE LETTERS OF GERTRUDE STEIN AND CARL VAN VECHTEN 1913–1946

EDITED BY

EDWARD BURNS

NEW YORK

COLUMBIA UNIVERSITY PRESS

Columbia University Press
Publishers Since 1893
New York   Chichester, West Sussex
cup.columbia.edu
Copyright © 2013 Columbia University Press

Materials in this book are published with permission from the
following copyright holders:
Letters of Gertrude Stein © 1986 the Estate of Gertrude Stein
Letters of Alice B. Toklas © 1986 Edward Burns
Letters of Carl Van Vechten © 1986 the Estate of Carl Van Vechten (by permission
of Donald Gallup, literary trustee for Carl Van Vechten)
Letters of Fania Marinoff Van Vechten © 1986 the Estate of Fania Marinoff Van
Vechten (by Joseph Solomon, executor)
Gertrude Stein's "And too. Van Vechten a sequel to One" © 1986 the
Estate of Gertrude Stein

Library of Congress Cataloging-in-Publication Data
Burns, Edward, 1944–.
The letters of Gertrude Stein and Carl Van Vechten, 1913–1946 / edited by
Edward Burns.
    p. cm.
    Includes bibliographical references and index.
    ISBN 978–0-231–06309–8 (pbk.) — ISBN 978–0-231–51901–4 (e-book)

Library of Congress Subject Data and Holding Information can be found in
the Library of Congress Online Catalog.

LCCN: 2013933742

Contents

List of Illustrations

Preface

This edition collects all of the extant correspondence between Gertrude Stein and Carl Van Vechten. For the sake of completeness I have included those letters written to or from both Alice Toklas and Fania Marinoff Van Vechten during the years covered by this correspondence, 1913–1946.

The primary manuscript location for these letters is the Collection of American Literature, Beinecke Rare Book and Manuscript Library, Yale University. Unless otherwise identified, the Stein–Van Vechten letters are from this collection. The Toklas and Marinoff letters are also from this collection.

From his gift to Yale University Library, of Stein's letters to him Van Vechten selected a few that dealt specifically with his writings and his silver wedding anniversary; these letters he presented to the New York Public Library, Rare Books and Manuscripts Division. Letters from this source are so identified in the heading for each letter.

In preparing this edition I have benefited from the transcriptions of Stein's letters prepared by Dr. Donald Gallup for the Yale Collection of American Literature. While his work has proved helpful as a reference, all the letters collected here were transcribed anew from the holograph letters. The transcriptions of the Van Vechten, Toklas, and Marinoff letters were made from photocopies of the originals.

The goal in transcribing these letters has been to remain as faithful as possible to Stein's and Van Vechten's texts. The transcriptions, therefore, retain the original punctuation (including Van Vechten's ever-present dots and dashes, which should not be construed as ellipses) or lack of punctuation; inconsistencies in the titles of books, newspapers, and articles; such compoundings as "alright" and "to-day"; Stein's idiosyncratic "x" instead of "ex," as in "xcited"; and her use of "inclosed" for "enclosed."

Misspellings, grammatical errors, repetitions, typos, and other unintended oddities that appear in the letters have been left uncorrected. Misspellings of proper names, however, are corrected in the text in brackets. Van Vechten's initial misspelling of Toklas' name has been noted and left uncorrected. I have silently added apostrophes in contractions since their absence did not follow any particular pattern. For the sake of clarity I have supplied given or family names in brackets. In instances where minor lapses prevent a clear reading of the text, I have supplied the necessary word or words in brackets. In cases where the text is nearly indecipherable, my interpretation, in brackets, is followed by a query.

I have standardized all return addresses and dates and placed them in fixed positions at the head of the letter. No distinction has been made between printed and written addresses. Interpolated addresses and parts of addresses are bracketed. Signatures appear as they appear in the letters; they have, however, been placed in a fixed position. Salutations have been separated from the body of the letter and also placed in a fixed position. All postscripts, regardless of where they appear in the letter, are placed after the closing. Van Vechten often used signs in the text to indicate a postscript and when there was more than one postscript he used numbers. To avoid confusion with my annotations, I have placed these numbers in parentheses.

Stein seldom dated her letters. Fortunately, Van Vechten kept the envelopes. The dating of almost all of Stein's letters, therefore, derives from the postmarks. Where it was possible, I corroborated the dating from internal evidence. Van Vechten was remarkably orderly, and I have not found any instance where a letter has strayed into a wrong envelope. Van Vechten sometimes only partially dated his letters, often leaving out the year. Where I have supplied a date or a part of the date, I have placed the date in brackets. Doubtful dates or those that are difficult to read are preceded by a query.

I have placed the printed descriptions of a postcard in brackets in order to distinguish it from Van Vechten's written identification of those postcards made from his own photographs.

Before Van Vechten gave Stein's letters to him to the Yale Collection of American Literature, he annotated many of them. These annotations appear in my notes except for simple identifications like "Picabia, the painter," when such information is contained in a fuller annotation that I have pre-pared.

In my notes I have not documented information acquired through conventional reference sources. Where I have used newspaper or magazine articles from the Yale Collection of American Literature and I cannot cite page numbers, I have cited YCAL as the source.

Bibliographical information on Stein's and Van Vechten's principal writings is given in separate selected bibliographies. Works which appear in newspapers or reviews are fully documented in the citation. The selected bibliography contains those works that are referred to with frequency in my notes.

I have used the following abbreviations in the text of my notes to indicate a source or to supply the location of a cross-reference:

Columbia–Cerf	Bennett Cerf Collection, Rare Book and Manuscript Library, Columbia University Libraries
Columbia–Random House	Random House Collection, Rare Book and Manuscript Library, Columbia University Libraries
Doucet, Paris	Bibliothèque littéraire Jacques Doucet, Universités de Paris
NYPL–Berg	Henry W. and Albert A. Berg Collection, New York Public Library
NYPL–Lincoln Center	Lincoln Center Library for the Performing Arts, New York Public Library
NYPL–MD	Rare Books and Manuscripts Division, New York Public Library
Texas	Humanities Research Center, University of Texas at Austin
Yale–JWJ	The James Weldon Johnson Memorial Collection of Negro Arts and Letters, Collection of American Literature, Beinecke Rare Book and Manuscript Library, Yale University

YCAL Collection of American Literature, Beinecke Rare Book and Manuscript Library, Yale University

Acknowledgments

This edition of the Stein–Van Vechten correspondence received the 1983 Ellen Knowles Harcourt Award in Biography and Memoirs awarded by Columbia University and the Alfred Harcourt Foundation. I am grateful to Columbia University President Michael I. Sovern, William Jovanovich, chairman and chief executive officer of Harcourt Brace Jovanovich, Inc., and the readers of my dissertation for this award.

The suggestion that I edit the Stein–Van Vechten correspondence was made to me by Donald Gallup, now retired as curator of the Collection of American Literature, Yale University Library. Dr. Gallup has helped me throughout my work with his wisdom, encouragement, and information. Dr. David Schoonover, the present curator of the Collection of American Literature, has been continuously kind and efficient.

In my quest for an accurate reading of the text of the letters and for information for my annotations I have had the benefit of the advice and counsel of Ulla E. Dydo and Leon Katz. They have both answered countless questions of great complexity and have generously shared with me their vast knowledge of Stein's life and her writings. My research has been aided by my meetings with Bruce Kellner, Van Vechten's very able biographer and bibliographer, and Lynn Martin, Donald Sutherland's literary executor.

I wish to acknowledge warmly the courteous cooperation given to me by the curators and staffs of The Beinecke Rare Book and Manuscript Library, Yale University; the Rare Books and Manuscripts Division, New York Public Library; The Henry W. and Albert A. Berg Collection, The New

York Public Library; the Rare Book and Manuscript Division, Columbia University Libraries; the Lincoln Center Library for the Performing Arts, New York Public Library; and the library of the Frick Collection.

I wish also to express my gratitude to those individuals, cited in the text, who graciously answered my queries or who allowed me to interview them. I owe a special debt of gratitude to Madame Joan Chapman, who over many years has given me the benefit of her extensive knowledge of Stein and Toklas, and the region around Bilignin and Belley. In the early stages of this research she invited me to her home in Chazey Bons, near Belley, and took me on visits to the various sites mentioned in these letters and in Stein's writings. She also arranged for me to meet some of the individuals still alive who knew Stein.

I am indebted to the following individuals for their assistance and kindness: Joseph Barry, Bill Betts, Lillian Feder, Lynn Kadison, Denise and Claude Laurens, Allen Mandelbaum, Richard Morrison, Eleanore and Daniel Saidenberg, John Shawcross, Ruth Z. Temple, and Isabel Wilder. This edition was prepared as a doctoral dissertation for the English Department of the Graduate Center of the City University of New York. Alfred Kazin, David Greetham, and N. John Hall were generous with their suggestions, and I gained greatly from their experience.

This edition has benefited consistently from the expert scrutiny of William Rice. His intelligence and keen observation forced me to rethink many questions in the dating of the letters and in my annotations.

Louise and Michel Leiris have made my repeated visits to Paris periods of work to be recalled with the greatest of pleasure. They have been invaluable friends. At the Galerie Louise Leiris in Paris, Maurice Jardot, Bernard Lirman, Quentin Laurens, and Jeannette Druy have given me much help and advice.

Thornton Wilder claimed that Gertrude Stein was the most inspired talker that he ever heard. For their help in recreating that voice for me (or the voice of Alice Toklas) I am grateful to the following individuals who are now dead: Thornton Wilder, Elena Genin, Sir Francis Rose, Bernard Faÿ, Donald Sutherland, Daniel-Henry Kahnweiler, Louise and Redvers Taylor, and Virginia and Harold Knapik.

For permission to quote the letters of Stein, Toklas, Van Vechten, Marinoff, and those writers whose letters are cited in the text by YCAL, I am grateful to Dr. David E. Schoonover, curator, Collection of American Literature, The Beinecke Rare Book and Manuscript Library, Yale University.

The letters of Fania Marinoff Van Vechten are printed by the permission of the Estate of Fania Marinoff Van Vechten, Joseph Solomon, Executor.

Permission to quote the letters of Carl Van Vechten has been granted by Donald Gallup, Literary Trustee for Carl Van Vechten.

Thornton Wilder's joint postcard with Stein and Toklas written to Van Vechten (postmark 27 July 1935, YCAL) and the excerpt from Wilder's letter to Elizabeth Chapman are printed by permission of Donald Gallup, Literary Executor, Estate of Thornton Wilder.

Permission to quote from Stein's letters to Bennett Cerf (Random House) has been granted by Kenneth Lohf, director of the Rare Book and Manuscript Library, Columbia University Libraries. Permission to quote from the Van Vechten–Marinoff letters in the Rare Books and Manuscripts Division of the New York Public Library has been granted by Donald Anderle, associate director of Special Collections.

A number of Van Vechten's and Marinoff's letters to Stein were previously printed (either completely or in excerpts) in *The Flowers of Friendship: Letters Written to Gertrude Stein*, edited by Donald Gallup, Knopf, 1953. For permission to reprint these letters I am grateful to Random House, Inc.—Alfred A. Knopf, Inc.

I am grateful to Calman A. Levin for permission to print the letters of Gertrude Stein.

Alice Toklas' letter to the Van Vechtens of [31 July 1946], and an excerpt from her letter to Van Vechten of 22 October 1946 are reprinted from *Staying on Alone: Letters of Alice B. Toklas*, edited by Edward Burns, by permission of Liveright Publishing Corporation. Copyright © 1973 by Liveright Publishing Corporation.

Introduction

In a writer's letters what we want to hear is how he writes. We look to letters as the fascinating real-life background of works of art. We have come to expect that letters will reveal what is hovering in the writer's creative consciousness, that they will illuminate the intimate association between the writer as a person and his work. We have been conditioned to have a highly romanticized view of a writer's life—creative energy is believed to come from tensions within the writer's psyche or between him and the outside world. Letters, intimate as a journal, are expected to reveal the heart and mind of a writer with greater frankness than any other writings.

In the Stein–Van Vechten correspondence there is very little of the rich self-scrutiny that makes Henry James's letters so interesting. There is little of the intellectual excitement that fills the Edmund Wilson–Vladimir Nabokov correspondence. Nor are there the moments of searing self-examination that we find in Melville's letters. There is none of the Olympian display of knowledge and erudition that is found in Ezra Pound's correspondence. And there is none of the literary cajoling that enhances the Sherwood Anderson–Van Wyck Brooks letters about Mark Twain.

The Stein–Van Vechten letters are at once illuminating and frustrating. They bring us into touch with the devotion that Stein and Van Vechten had for each other. They also reveal the extent to which each was fortunate in having a prosaic and calm domestic life. These letters echo their authors' literary styles but are almost totally free of literary posing. They are supple, conversational, and at times vivid and lyrical.

The major biographical works on Stein (including her own autobiographical writings) omit a great deal. Understandably the story that is told is fleshed out with famous names and leavened by winsome anecdotes, but the ordinary dross of what Stein called "daily everyday living" is largely missing. Yet this information is crucial to our understanding of her life and work. Some of this daily life may be found in these letters. What is also echoed again and again in these letters is Stein's need to be loved and appreciated and Van Vechten's need to serve and offer support. They constantly convey the forms of affection each was able to give and receive.

Each had a public persona, and much about their lives has become public knowledge. In the case of Stein aspects of her life have been distorted beyond recognition. Van Vechten, not as publicized a figure as Stein, is less subject to the distortions of celebrityhood. Reading the correspondence permits us to recover aspects of their private selves that are often lost in the rush to glamorize them.

In a lecture, "On Reading the Great Letter Writers," Thornton Wilder says that letters can be read on three levels: "the surface level, that is the *literary exercise*; the second level which I call the *profile of a personality*; and the third level, which is *news of the soul*."[1] The personalities behind these letters emerge through the accumulation of seemingly insignificant details. Wilder, wary that appreciation of a writer's correspondence is often based on a reading of a very few celebrated letters, advises us:

> The first rule in reading the great letter writers is this: *Read them in extent.*
> What we get then through reading these letters in great length is this: Gradually a face hovers between the words.
> Gradually a personality (unmistakable for any other, just as you and I are unmistakable for any other) defines itself. When one has passed the hundredth letter not only the profile of the personality is becoming clear to us but that wonderful phenomenon takes place: we hear the voice of the writer in the very word order.[2]

The Stein–Van Vechten correspondence may have limitations on its "surface level," but what we learn about the personalities and the souls of Stein and Van Vechten more than compensates for the lack of glitter.

---

1. Thornton Wilder, "On Reading the Great Letter Writers," in his *American Characteristics and Other Essays*, ed. Donald Gallup (New York: Harper & Row, 1979), p. 157. This was the Daniel S. Lamont Memorial Lecture delivered at Yale University on 4 May 1928 as "English Letters and Letter Writers."

2. Ibid., p. 154.

Present from the very beginning in these letters is the unity of voice. One never senses that either Stein or Van Vechten is posturing before a mirror. Even after each agrees to give to the Yale Collection of American Literature the letters received from the other, the voice in the letters remains constant. They never write with an eye to a larger audience. Only occasionally does one sense artifice in these letters, and this change in voice comes when each responds to the other's books. The emotional response, the support for the other's work, may be genuine, but it is often expressed in a series of elegantly turned phrases that have a hollow ring. One senses that Van Vechten, reading the person in the work, went through Stein's books for the quotable bits. Certainly Van Vechten's affection for Stein resulted in a personalized reading of her works that had little depth but expressed profound admiration. One need only look at Stein's letters to Thornton Wilder or to Wendell Wilcox to realize that she was capable of a profound understanding of writing.[3] But her responses to Van Vechten's books say very little. She often resorts to weaving mere word patterns, which are hardly a substitute for real criticism. Still, the artifice employed by each is always in the service of the friendship.

Another area of artifice is in Van Vechten's closings. Van Vechten often uses closings like "743 rosy flamingos to you both!" or "178 pink-lipped poodles to you both!" These, employed in large numbers, provoke amusement in some readers. Though present in most of his letters, they are part of his preciousness and flamboyance and have no special meaning in his relationship with Stein.

An element that initially evokes a similar response but that has special significance is the term "Woojums" in these letters.[4] It was often used by Van Vechten as a term of endearment for Stein and Toklas and other friends. Its origin may be a mixed drink described in his novel *Parties*. "Woojums," however, took on more meaning at the time of Stein's American lecture tour in 1934–35: it describes their sense of a family unit. At first glance it is easy to see the Woojumses as another facet of Van Vechten's preciousness. But the family that emerged in 1934–35 is an organic outgrowth of the role each had assumed in the other's life. Gertrude became Baby Woojums (sometimes referred to by the pronoun *he*), Alice Toklas became Mama Woojums, and Carl Van Vechten became Papa Woojums. Part of Toklas' and Van Vechten's role as parents was to look after Baby Woo-

---

3. Stein's letters to Wilder and Wilcox are in YCAL.

4. Van Vechten first used the term Woojums in a letter to Stein, 26 April [1932].

jums—Gertrude. They established among themselves a family model that reflected the emotional importance each had come to assume for the other.

Van Vechten's assumption of partial responsibility for Stein began almost as soon as they met, in 1913, when she was thirty-nine and he was thirty-three. Stein was emerging from three years of emotional upheaval. Her relationship with her brother Leo, who since their childhood had shaped her tastes and attitudes, had begun to crumble in 1910. Leo's denunciation of Picasso's cubist paintings and his rejection of the direction Gertrude's writing was taking in the revision of her novel, *The Making of Americans*, were the prime reasons for the rift that remained for the rest of their lives. In a note she made while working on *The Making of Americans* Stein crystallized the reason for the break with Leo and announced her intellectual independence:

> When Leo said that all classification was teleological I knew I was not a pragmatist. I do not believe that, I believe in reality as Cezanne or Caliban believe in it. I believe in repetition. Yes. Always and always write the hymn of repetition. [Maurice] Sterne gave me the feeling for it.[5]

The rupture with Leo and his decision to leave Paris to live in Settignano, near Florence, were eased for Gertrude by her relationship with Alice Toklas. Stein had met Toklas on 9 September 1907, the day that Toklas and her traveling companion, Harriet Levy, arrived in Paris and had gone to visit the Michael Steins. The sexual understanding between Stein and Toklas developed gradually over the ensuing months. It was not until December 1910, however, after returning from spending the summer and early fall with Gertrude in Italy, that Toklas went to live with Gertrude and Leo at 27 rue de Fleurus.

The final, painful act of separation between brother and sister came in 1913 when they divided the art works that they had collected. Except for seeing him on a Paris street in 1931, an otherwise undocumented incident described in "She Bowed to Her Brother," there is no indication that she and Leo ever saw each other again.[6]

With Leo gone, Alice Toklas became the central figure in Stein's life. She assumed the role of principal validator of Stein's emotional and author-

5. Quoted in Leon Katz, "Weininger and *The Making of Americans*," *Twentieth Century Literature, Gertrude Stein Issue*, 24, No. 1 (Spring 1978), 22.

6. Stein's "She Bowed to Her Brother," in her *Portraits and Prayers* (New York: Random House, 1934), pp. 236–40.

ial needs. She freed Stein from all domestic disorder, and it was her devotion that allowed Stein to follow the regular and imperturbable course in which writing was the great priority. Stein needed what every writer needs—praise, reassurance, and the courage that comes from encouragement. In public Stein exuded a fierce individuality and an uncompromising attitude toward her writing. In private, as in these letters, she needed to know that what she was doing really mattered—even if it was not readily accepted, appreciated, or understood by a large audience. In addition to being lover, housekeeper, cook, gardener, typist, and editor, Toklas served as a one-woman chorus of affirmation.

Van Vechten could not, of course, give Stein the day-to-day support that Toklas did. His encouragement came from the steady stream of his letters. He also frequently referred to her in his essays and introduced her in some of his novels. Tirelessly, he placed many of her shorter works in magazines and sought to secure book publication for the typescripts that Stein entrusted to him. Van Vechten became her de facto literary agent and adviser. He served as go-between with publishers, as proofreader, general protector, and overseer for many of her works. In one of her last statements Stein paid tribute to Van Vechten's loyalty.

> Carl was one of the earliest ones that made me be certain. . . . It was Carl who arranged for the printing of *Tender Buttons*, he knew and what a comfort it was that there was the further knowing of the printed page. . . . Carl wrote to me and I wrote to him and he always knew, and it was always a comfort.[7]

Despite his admiration for Stein, Van Vechten did not have a firm grasp on what her writing was about. Certainly he lacked the rigorous powers of intellectual perception and imagination that made Thornton Wilder's later response to her work so crucial for Stein. What Van Vechten did bring to his relationship with the unknown Stein was an intuitive, subtle grasp of her uncertainty and vulnerability. His response was unfailing loyalty. He understood that Stein had a powerful vision, and he supported her with a constant, ringing, and committed yes.

Stein's role in Van Vechten's life is not so easily described. She was one of the few who helped shape his interests and attitudes. When he met Stein, he recognized her orphic quality, which, not always discernible in

---

7. Stein's "A Message from Gertrude Stein," in her *Selected Writings of Gertrude Stein*, ed., intro., and notes Carl Van Vechten (1946; rpt. New York: The Modern Library, 1962), p. [vii].

her writings, was apparent to all those who met and spoke with her. Van Vechten immediately recognized Stein as an artist of extraordinary originality. She retained this position for him throughout his life.

Mabel Dodge had introduced Van Vechten to the writings of Gertrude Stein (she left copies of Stein's *Portrait of Mabel Dodge at the Villa Curonia* on a table in the entrance hall of her Fifth Avenue apartment) and then, via a letter of introduction which Van Vechten presented to Stein in May 1913, to Stein herself. She also presented Van Vechten to many of the active participants in New York's intellectual life. It was at Mabel Dodge's "evenings" (the idea for them was first suggested to her by Lincoln Steffens) that Van Vechten made the acquaintance of, among others: Max Eastman, Emma Goldman, Big Bill Haywood, Walter Lippmann, Marsden Hartley, Charles Demuth, Amy Lowell, Margaret Sanger, and Edwin Arlington Robinson. In spite of the differences they were to have over the years of their friendship, Van Vechten never failed to acknowledge the key role that Dodge played in his education.

For all her gifts as a hostess and animator of a major New York salon, Mabel Dodge was only a limited participant in the artistic and literary revolution that was being shaped in the years just before World War I. In Gertrude Stein, Van Vechten found a major participant in that movement. She and her brother Leo were at the center of a significant segment of French cultural life prior to World War I, and Stein, even in their very few meetings, undoubtedly instilled in Van Vechten an enthusiasm for modernism.

Van Vechten's championship of Stein, his unceasing efforts to get her work published, became one of the fundamental elements in his life. He assumed the role of unabashed publicist, keen on elevating Stein's reputation, soon after his return from Europe in August 1913. It was Van Vechten who suggested to the enterprising young poet and publisher Donald Evans that his publishing firm, Claire Marie, print something of Stein's. Stein eventually sent Evans the text of *Tender Buttons*, a volume radically different from anything he had published before. The response to this book was almost entirely negative and derisive. It did, however, fall into the hands of a number of young people, aspiring writers and musicians who became her champions. *Tender Buttons* was both Sherwood Anderson's and Virgil Thomson's introduction to Stein's writing.

In all his efforts for Stein, Van Vechten was efficient and expeditious. The idea of personal glory or reward was totally absent from his efforts. The outstanding quality in his character was the enthusiasm with which he offered his patience, knowledge, admiration, and loyalty. He was for Stein, as he was for so many others, an indispensable ally. He labored and gave because he believed in her importance. Only once, in 1937, when there was a question of illustrating Stein's *Everybody's Autobiography* with photographs, did they have a misunderstanding. Stein proposed photographs other than those of Van Vechten, who was hurt by the proposal. Stein's letters and her draft of a telegram to him indicate that she understood she had offended him. She apologized and consented to use only his photographs.

Stein and Van Vechten were both products of the age before the telephone, when letters were an integral part of human intercourse. They were both indefatigable letter writers, as the sheer numbers collected or deposited in various public or university libraries attest. That each maintained an active creative output, engaged in a varied social life, and maintained a steady correspondence with friends, family, social acquaintances, admiring readers, and publishing contacts is indeed remarkable. For Van Vechten letters were a natural part of his immensely diverse social life and of his personal endeavors, including the collections of music, pictures, and documents that he assembled and then donated to various libraries. Van Vechten wrote letters to impart information, to express thanks, and to cajole people into action for a friend or a cause.

For Stein letter writing had a different importance. In addition to being a vehicle for exchanging news, letters were a vital part of her need to keep in touch. This need had little to do with her living in Paris and therefore craving news of the United States. Indeed, Stein deplored the use of the word expatriate. She always claimed that living in France allowed her to appreciate and love her own country the more, not separate herself from it. Her correspondence with friends allowed her to remain an American. Writing for Stein was a lonely, emotionally draining experience. Letters allowed her to continue writing literature. The letters she received gave her support, and those she wrote offered her a respite from the tension of composition.

While this correspondence is remarkable in its range, there are some curious omissions. In Stein's letters to Van Vechten certain crucial figures and events in her life are either omitted or mentioned only in passing. Although Picasso is a major presence in Stein's life from 1906 until her death, we are offered no insights into this complex man and her relationship with him. Her immense grasp of his importance is in her work, not in her letters. It is striking, too, that to Van Vechten she does not mention Ernest Hemingway to any great extent. Indeed, if one were to base a biography of Stein on her letters to Van Vechten, the only documentary evidence that she knew Hemingway would come from a draft of a review of Hemingway's *Three Stories and Ten Poems* and a draft of a letter about the review and about her portrait of Hemingway that appears on the verso of Van Vechten's letter to Stein of 3 September 1923. The other mention of Hemingway comes in a letter to Van Vechten postmarked 25 November 1938, in which Stein tells of meeting Hemingway on a street in Paris.

Stein had completed her novel *The Making of Americans* in October 1911. For years she sought in vain to have it published. Van Vechten was one of several friends to make efforts toward publication. After much anguish and vexation, it was the young Ernest Hemingway who succeeded in convincing Ford Madox Ford, then editor of the *Transatlantic Review*, to publish portions of the novel.

> Ford alleges he is delighted with the stuff and is going to call on you. I told him it took you 4 ½ years to write it and that there are six volumes.
> He is going to publish the 1st installment in the April No. going to press the 1st part of March. He wondered if you would accept 30 francs a page (his magazine page) and I said I thought I could get you to. (Be haughty but not too haughty.) I made it clear it was a remarkable scoop for his magazine obtained only through my obtaining genius.[8]

Not only did Hemingway arrange for the publication of portions of the novel, but he also helped Stein to correct the galley proofs. The publication in the *Transatlantic Review* led Robert McAlmon to undertake an edition of the complete novel. Stein's silence about Hemingway is tantalizing, and is perhaps deliberate.

One matter never discussed or hinted at in these letters is their homosexuality. Although the two did not hide their sexual preferences, sexual innuendo and gossip never enter into their letters. They wrote copiously but never indiscreetly.

Stein and Van Vechten almost never indulge in literary gossip. Where gossip does surface, it is in their remarks about Mabel Dodge. Stein had all but broken with Dodge by 1914, the war having provided a convenient means of ending a friendship that was already badly strained. Dodge attributed the

---

8. Ernest Hemingway, Letter to Gertrude Stein, 17 February 1924, in *Ernest Hemingway: Selected Letters, 1917–1961*, ed. Carlos Baker (New York: Charles Scribner's Sons, 1981), p.111.

break with Stein to Toklas' sexual jealousy of her (Dodge had four husbands and numerous lovers, and had occasional involvements with women):

> But one day at lunch, Gertrude, sitting opposite me in Edwin [Dodge]'s chair, sent me such a strong look over the table that it seemed to cut across the air to me in a band of electrified steel—a smile traveling across on it—powerful— Heaven! I remember it *now* so keenly!
>
> At that Alice arose hastily and ran out of the room onto the terrace. Gertrude gave a surprised glance after her and, as she didn't return, got up and followed after. . . . From that time on Alice began to separate Gertrude from me.[9]

Whatever the actual circumstances, it is clear from the Dodge-Stein correspondence (YCAL, not all of Stein's letters have survived) that after the 1912 visit alluded to by Dodge, they rarely saw one another. Stein refused Dodge's invitation to visit the Villa Curonia in 1913 and in 1914. From what we know of Stein's sense of propriety and privacy it is easy to see her bristle at Dodge's broadcasting of her sexual adventures and her attempts to draw Stein into the scandal involving her divorce from Edwin Dodge.

Van Vechten's relationship with Dodge became stormy in August 1914. Van Vechten, along with Neith Boyce Hapgood and two of her children with their nurse, were visiting with Dodge at Villa Curonia when World War I broke out. Mrs. Hapgood insisted on returning to the United States. Van Vechten, who wanted to marry Fania Marinoff, also decided to leave. Dodge, who was waiting for the arrival of her lover, John Reed, resented being left alone. She could understand Mrs. Hapgood's reasons for wanting to return, but she considered Van Vechten's departure unacceptable. Although Dodge and Van Vechten saw each other after 1914 and continued to correspond with each other, the intense friendship was never recaptured. Through mutual friends, including Muriel Draper and Mina Loy, both of whom saw Dodge regularly, Van Vechten and Stein were kept informed about Dodge. Dodge's marriages, particularly to the full-blooded Pueblo Indian Antonio Lujan (later changed to Luhan), her stormy relationship with D. H. Lawrence, and her volumes of memoirs all became grist for a gossip mill between Stein and Van Vechten, which at times during the 1920s and 1930s was wickedly insidious.

One final incident reveals a great deal about the nature of Stein's

---

9. Mabel Dodge Luhan, *European Experiences* (New York: Harcourt, Brace and Company, 1935); pp. 332–33.

omissions in these letters. One evening in late April 1932, while showing the writer Louis Bromfield some of her unpublished manuscripts, Stein came upon the manuscript of her early novel *Q.E.D.* (not published until 1950 and then under the title *Things As They Are*). Stein said later that she had forgotten about the existence of this 1903 work, and Toklas had never seen it or even suspected its existence. Van Vechten did not know of it. Stein gave the novel to Bromfield and to her agent William A. Bradley to read. Because of its lesbian content, they both advised against publication.

Toklas recognized in the the novel a thinly disguised lesbian love triangle in which Stein was one of the participants. In fact, the novel was Stein's faithful portrayal of her abortive love affair with May Bookstaver (later Mrs. Charles Knoblauch). What made the revelation of the affair with May Bookstaver so painful for Toklas was that Stein had never admitted to it. When Toklas pieced it together, she became furious and a strain entered their relationship that threatened to destroy it. Yet nothing of this crisis surfaces in the letters.

In October 1934 Stein and Toklas arrived in New York still very ill at ease, especially as Stein was returning to the scene of the Bookstaver affair and might see the many friends who knew of it. None of this did Van Vechten know or even suspect while he traveled with them, entertained them, and introduced them in America. Although Stein had enormous confidence in Van Vechten, the effect of the Bookstaver discovery on her life with Toklas was not known to him. It was not until years after Stein's death that Toklas told him the complete story of her own jealousy.[10]

As is commonly and resignedly recognized, the bulk of Stein's written work is what Virgil Thomson called it: "hermetic." The wall that even her best critics come up against in much of her work is simply this: they have difficulty with her prose style, and they cannot discern the subject matter of her compositions. Though much of her work remains opaque, these letters occasionally give us a direct clue as to the source or inspiration for Stein's writing.

One such instance comes when Stein writes Van Vechten that she has written a play, *A List*, and that it was inspired by a play of Avery Hop-

---

10. I am grateful to Dr. Leon Katz and Dr. Ulla Dydo for the details of the Stein-Toklas dispute.

wood's. Although Van Vechten writes several times asking which play of Hopwood's she had read, Stein never replies. Some hints of how Stein "used" or "absorbed" the play *(Our Little Wife)* occur in letters Stein wrote to Edmund Wilson, who considered publishing Stein's play in *Vanity Fair* (see Stein to Van Vechten, postmark 6 July 1923, note 3).

Another instance where Stein hints at what she tried to achieve in a work is when she writes to Van Vechten, in a letter postmarked 25 March 1936, that in her play *Listen to Me* she "tried to make it like my memories of the Kirafly brothers and the Lion tamer." (In a letter to Bennett Cerf, ? March 1936, Columbia-Random House, Stein adds the name "Wilson" to a similar statement about "the Lion Tamer.") Such tantalizing clues as to what hovered in Stein's mind as she composed these plays give the reader some assistance in approaching these works.

Stein's writing is almost always based on her experiences. To unlock the intricate and complex rhetorical structures in her work requires an immense knowledge of the details of her life. Some of those details, perfunctorily mentioned or only alluded to in passing, are in her correspondence. Once in a while a small, seemingly insignificant detail or phrase can shed unexpected light on a composition.

Gertrude Stein is often seen as the willful creator of her own myth. Statements such as "Think of the Bible and Homer think of Shakespeare and think of me," [11] "I am one of the masters of English prose," [12] and "I have been the creative literary mind of the century" [13] are often cited as examples of her bravura personality with its penchant for self-praise. The Stein revealed in these letters gives balance to that view. They follow the agonizingly slow progress toward public recognition of her work. They record her optimism at every opportunity to be published and her despair when her writings are turned down. Throughout these struggles it is the patience and support of Van Vechten that bolster her. Van Vechten sums up his relationship with Stein in a letter written to Toklas on 28 July 1946: "Those who knew her only through the greatness of her work will never know how great she could also be in friendship."

Thornton Wilder was responsible for persuading Stein to deposit her

---

11. Gertrude Stein, *The Geographical History of America or The Relation of Human Nature to the Human Mind* (New York: Random House, 1936), p. 81.

12. Gertrude Stein, *Everybody's Autobiography* (New York: Random House, 1937), p. 114.

13. Ibid., p. 23.

manuscripts and correspondence in the Yale University Library. Wilder also persuaded many of Stein's friends to give her letters to them to Yale. In a letter he wrote to Elizabeth Chapman on 29 November 1956, Wilder characterizes one aspect of Stein's letters:

> Gertrude consciously saved her intellectual energy. . . . Very rarely did she put into a letter the full strength of her mind. We should not regret this, because she gave to the world in her books what she definitely abstained from giving to her friends in correspondence. . . . Instead in the letters we get the dear, spontaneous, often rollicking charm.[14]

Stein's correspondence with Van Vechten has other, far wider, dimensions than Wilder saw in the correspondence with Mrs. Chapman (the former Bobsy Goodspeed). The Stein–Van Vechten letters are of interest as documents of cultural history. They are also significant for the light they shed on the personality of each correspondent. They are rich in biographical detail; they help to clarify the chronology of Stein's writings; and they chronicle Van Vechten's varied careers: music and dance critic, essayist, novelist, photographer, participant in the Harlem Renaissance, and promoter of various causes.

The subject matter of the letters is most commonly taken from Stein's daily concerns, from the events, people, landscape, and objects at hand. Even public figures about whom she sometimes writes are observed not from a public vantage point, but from a private and intimate one, having to do with flashes of insight into personality. Since these letters often bring to light the nearby objects and people and places that were grist for Stein's writing, their importance for an understanding of her work is immense.

14. Thornton Wilder, Letter to Elizabeth Chapman, 29 November 1956, YCAL.

The Letters

❦

To Carl Van Vechten

[30 May 1913]   27 rue de Fleurus
                                                               [Paris]

My dear Van Vechten

Will you dine with us to-morrow Saturday evening at 7.30. Let me know immediately

Yours sincerely
Gertrude Stein.[1]

1. On verso in Van Vechten's hand, "J. Bronon 95 ave. de Villiers Tel. Wagram 13–55." I cannot identify the name.

❦

To Gertrude Stein

[31 May] 1913   American Express Co.
Saturday   11 rue Scribe, Paris

Dear Miss Stein,

I'll dine with you with pleasure this evening.

Sincerely,
Carl Van Vechten

❧

To Gertude Stein

[1–4 June 1913]   American Express Co.
                                                   11 rue Scribe, Paris

Dear Miss Stein,

I've just been invited to the premiere of *Kovanchina* on Thursday night.[1] Can we change our rendez-vous to another day? [Pitts] Sanborn is going away on Friday for the day and as I want to bring him over perhaps we had better not name a day until later.[2] I'll send you a petit bleu and if you are not free you can let me know.

I want so much to read the plays[3] and Sanborn wants to see those extraordinary Picasso drawings.[4]

Sincerely,
Carl Van Vechten

1. Modest Mussorgsky's opera *Khovanshchina* had its premiere on 5 June 1913 (delayed from 30 May). The opera was presented by Diaghilev as part of the *Saison Russe* at the newly opened (2 April 1913) Théâtre des Champs-Elysées.

2. John Pitts Sanborn (1879–1941), music critic, novelist, and essayist. Sanborn and Van Vechten had traveled to Europe together. Sanborn served as music editor for the *New York Globe*, the *New York Evening Mail*, and the *New York World-Telegram* during his career as a journalist. In the summers of 1912–16 and 1919–20 Sanborn also contributed to a number of the new literary reviews including *The Trend* and *Others*.

3. Van Vechten is probably referring to Stein's plays *What Happened*, *A Five Act Play* and *White Wines*. Stein, who had begun to write plays only a few months earlier, had been showing these plays to a number of her friends (see Florence Bradley to Stein [? June 1913], YCAL).

4. In a letter to Fania Marinoff (postmark 2 June 1913, NYPL-MD) Van Vechten wrote about his first visit to Stein's apartment and of the Picassos he saw there:

> Last night I had dinner at Gertrude Stein's. She is a wonderful personality. I wish you could meet her. You will sometime. She spoke of you. . . . She lives in a place hung with Picassos and she showed me some more sketches of his including men with erect Tom-Tom's much bigger than mine.

Stein's collection included a large number of Picasso drawings, including some in a satiric vein that showed nude men.

꙳

To Gertrude Stein

[7 June] 1913   American Express Co.
Saturday   11 rue Scribe, Paris

Dear Miss Stein,

May I bring [Pitts] Sanborn over tomorrow—Sunday—afternoon—
say at 4 o'clock? If this is convenient for you will you let me know at 47 Rue
de Trévise where I seem to be for the moment![1]

Sincerely,
Carl Van Vechten

1. Van Vechten was staying at the Pax-Hôtel.

꙳

To Carl Van Vechten

[postmark: 7 June 1913]   27 rue de Fleurus
                                            [Paris]

My dear Van Vechten,

To-morrow afternoon suits, will xpect you and [Pitts] Sanborn about
four

Sincerely yours
Gertrude Stein.

To Gertrude Stein
Calling card: Carl Van Vechten

[? June 1913]   [Paris]

Miss Stein—

I'm so sorry to have missed you. If you can see me will you write me at the American Express Co?

Yours
C. V. V.

To Carl Van Vechten

[postmark: 20 June 1913]   27 rue de Fleurus
[Paris]

My dear Van Vechten

I am sorry to have missed you. I have heard nothing more from Mabel [Dodge][1] and I am afraid of not seeing her as we have to be in Céret on the 28th and so leave here the 27th.[2] Do let me know what you know. I am going out of town Saturday and Sunday, will be glad to see you any time after that

Sincerely yours
Gertrude Stein

1. Van Vechten and Stein had been discussing the anticipated arrival of Mabel Dodge. Since his arrival in Paris, Van Vechten had received only one letter from Dodge, in which she said that she might sail on 19 June but was not sure (Van Vechten to Marinoff, postmark 8 June 1913, NYPL-MD). Stein's only information about Dodge's plans had been a letter she received May–June 1913, "Just a word to say you & Alice must come to spend *July* at Villa as I will be there only for July. I leave here June 19—& go at once to Florence" (Dodge to Stein [May–June 1913], YCAL). Not having definite information about her arrival plans, Van Vechten left for London on 20 June (Van Vechten to Marinoff, 22 June [1913], NYPL-MD).

This letter, addressed to Van Vechten at the American Express Office in Paris, was forwarded to him at the American Express Office in London.

2. In mid-March Picasso and his mistress, Eva Gouel (also known as Marcelle Humbert), had arrived in Céret, a small town in the French side of the Pyrénées. Stein and Toklas intended to stop there on their way to Spain in early July. They changed their plans, however, after Picasso wrote to them on 10 June (YCAL):

> . . . Je suis bien content de vous voir bientot. Merci il faudrait que vous avancerez votre voyage de quelque jours pour etre ici le jour de ma fete le 29 juin jour de la Saint Paul. Il y aura une grande course de toros aux arena de Ceret.

Picasso became ill (it was later diagnosed as a mild case of typhoid) and decided to return to Paris. He wrote to Stein, "Je rentre a Paris demain et nous irons voir le meme jour de l'arrive" (Picasso to Stein, 19 June 1913, YCAL). When she wrote Van Vechten of her plans to leave for Céret, Stein had not yet received this letter from Picasso.

To Gertrude Stein
[Telegram]

[postmark: 28 June 1913]   London

WHERE IS MABEL DODGE I AM AT LONDOUN [i.e., Loudoun] HO-TEL SURREY STREET LONDON

CARL VAN VECHTEN

To Carl Van Vechten
[Post office telegraph]

[postmark: 28 June 1913]   Paris

MABEL DODGE IS AT HOTEL PAS DE CALAIS RUE SAINTS PÈRES PARIS[1]

GERTRUDE STEIN

1. Dodge had arrived in Paris on 26 June (Dodge to Stein, postmark 27 June 1913, YCAL). Van Vechten arrived back in Paris on 30 June and wrote to Fania Marinoff about his plans:

. . . Mike [i.e., Mabel Dodge] is here with two boys. She doesn't know yet what she is going to do but thinks she'll go to Florence later. Her motor is broken, she leaves for England tomorrow with the two boys—John Reed and Bobby Jones—and she will stay there for a couple of weeks. (Van Vechten to Marinoff, 30 June [1913], NYPL-MD)

The plan to go to England was quickly dropped (Dodge to Stein [1 July 1913], YCAL). Dodge sent her son, John Evans, and his nurse, Miss Galvin, to Florence by train, and on 6 July she, Van Vechten, Reed, and Jones left by car for Florence (postcard, Dodge, Van Vechten, Reed, and Jones to Stein, "So this is Fountainbleau," postmark 6 July 1913, YCAL).

To Gertrude Stein

[? October 1913]   Hotel Longacre
                                                  157 West 47 Street
                                                  [New York]

Dear Miss Stein—

I did so want to print one of your new plays in my paper and Mabel [Dodge] was going to write one of her fascinating introductions—but Miss [Florence] Bradley wouldn't let us have one—at least not now.[1]

I am sending you my interview with George Moore[2]—which is absolutely stenographic and which, I fear, won't interest you much, and I am sending Miss Taklos[3] the pictures of Fania Marinoff, which she asked for. . . . These are totally inadequate but the best at hand.[4]

New York is madly interested in Hamlet just now. Even Hutch[ins Hapgood] is writing articles about him. There are two theatres giving *Hamlet* now.[5] Mike [i.e., Mabel Dodge] and I have devised a plan for [Robert de la] Condamine to play the part—with Aubrey Beardsley costumes![6]

Otherwise there are no booms. I hope all goes to your liking and wish I could drop in upon you. Please remember me to Miss Taklos.

Sincerely,
Carl Van Vechten

I seem to be living at the Hotel Longacre, 157 W. 47 St.

---

1. When he returned to New York in August 1913, Van Vechten resigned from the *New York Times*, where he had been a staff reporter and then assistant music critic since October 1906.

He then joined the *New York Press* as drama critic, reviewing individual plays and writing weekly articles for the Sunday editions. He remained with the *New York Press* until June 1914.

Van Vechten, Mabel Dodge, and Hutchins Hapgood had discussed among themselves the possibility of printing one of Stein's plays (either *What Happened, A Five Act Play* or *White Wines*) as part of the Sunday supplement of the *New York Press*. Dodge, who had written about Stein at the time of the Armory Show earlier in the year ("Speculation, or Post-Impressionism in Prose," *Arts and Decoration* [1913], 3:172–74), would write an introduction to the play. When the idea was presented to Florence Bradley, possibly in a letter by Hutchins Hapgood, Bradley objected. In a letter she wrote to Stein on 12 October 1913 (YCAL) she included a copy of her letter to Dodge setting out her reasons:

> In answer to Hutchins [Hapgood] letter—I understand that I have the option of giving these plays—I shall not know for a month—at least—when—whether it is practical now or later to produce them—of course the moment the plays are published they *lose practical value*—this they stand in need of already. The novelty is what I'm banking on to get the nonthinking and over thinking public—it must not have time to make up its mind beforehand. However if Miss Stein and you think otherwise all well and good.
>
> Why not work up for a production in New York and *after* publish with your introduction. That would be complimentary to all. . . .
>
> P. S. You can easily understand that Miss Stein writer of *portraits* makes Miss Stein writer of *plays*—plays which have not *yet been published* a practical interest that can not be ignored by the producer quite apart from any personal enthusiasm he might have.

Stein herself also wrote to Dodge about the plays (undated letter, 1913, YCAL): "No decidedly not, I do *not* want the plays published. They are to be kept to be *played*. Florence Bradley understands about that perfectly." Bradley was not able to produce the plays in New York. They were eventually published in Stein's *Geography and Plays* (1922).

2. "George Moore, British Playwright, Tells How He Will Finish New Play, 'The Apostle,' " *New York Press*, 28 September 1913, Pt. 6, pp. 1, 7. When Van Vechten left for Paris, Mabel Dodge had given him several letters of introduction. One of these was to the painter Jacques Emile Blanche, at whose home Van Vechten met George Moore (Van Vechten to Marinoff, postmarks 30 May 1913 and 2 June 1913, NYPL-MD).

3. Van Vechten was not the only person who had trouble spelling Toklas' name. Other correspondents spelled it "Toklus," "Tocklass," or "Taclos." I have retained Van Vechten's misspelling. Henry McBride summed up the question at the close of a 1913 letter to Stein, "[A]nd kindest regards to your charming friend whose name I can't spell" (Gallup, *The Flowers of Friendship*, p. 83).

4. Stein and Toklas had first heard about Fania Marinoff from Alice and Eugene Paul Ullman. It cannot be determined which photographs Van Vechten sent Toklas. They would have been of Marinoff in various theatrical roles.

5. E. H. Sothern and Julia Marlowe presented *Hamlet* as part of a repertoire season at the Manhattan Opera House from 22 September to 25 October 1913. Sir Johnston Forbes-Robertson and Gertrude Elliot performed in *Hamlet*, as part of a season of revivals to mark Forbes-Robertson's farewell American tour, at the newly opened Shubert Theatre from 29 September to 29 December 1913. Van Vechten reviewed Forbes-Robertson's *Hamlet* in the *New York Press*, "New Shubert Theatre Opens," on 3 October 1913.

6. Robert ("Robin") de la Condamine was an Englishman who lived part of the year in Florence, where he first met Mabel Dodge. Under the name of Robert Farquharson he had appeared on the London stage.

To Carl Van Vechten
[Postcard: Valencia—Baile al estilo del pais]

[postmark: 18 November 1913]   [27 rue de Fleurus
                                                 Paris]

My dear Van Vechten,

Thanks for the clippings a little didactic but hopeful and so good luck,[1]

Yours
Gertrude Stein

1. The clippings are the *Press* articles mentioned in notes 2 and 5 of Van Vechten to Stein [? October 1913].

Note by Carl Van Vechten, 18 January 1914
Typed on a 3 × 5 inch index card

In the summer of 1914 I was again in Paris and this first letter is probably a reply to my request to see GS. I left Paris on the last train to carry passengers (circa August 1) to join Mabel [Dodge] again at the Villa Curonia. Neith Boyce was with her and we left at once for the Albergo Paradiso in Vallombrosa. Mabel has never visited the villa again until now, at least.

To Gertrude Stein

4 July 1914[1]   American Express Co.
                                                 11 rue Scribe, Paris

Dear Miss Stein,

I'm in Paris for a few days with the latest gossip about Tender Buttons,[2] Mabel [Dodge], Hutch[ins Hapgood],[3] and everybody. —I hope I can

see you—and I should like to bring over a little Russian called Fania.[4]—I'm
stopping at the Hotel Fribourg, 46 Rue de Trévise.

Sincerely
Carl Van Vechten

If you are in town and will set an hour I shall come at once.

1. Van Vechten and Fania Marinoff sailed from New York to England on the R.M.S. *Mauretania* on 13 June. After a few days in London they arrived in Paris on 2 July.

2. At the suggestion of Van Vechten and Mabel Dodge, Donald Evans (1885–1921), a poet and at that time a copyreader on the *New York Times*, wrote to Stein asking permission to publish a volume of her plays (Gallup, *The Flowers of Friendship*, pp. 95–96). Evans had founded the publishing firm of Claire Marie, named after the actress Claire Marie Burke, who had recently played the leading role in *The Good Little Devil*. Although it was named for her, she had nothing to do with the firm.

None of Stein's letters to Evans have survived, but it can be assumed that Stein, still hoping that Florence Bradley would arrange a production of the plays, replied to Evans in much the same language she used to Mabel Dodge (see Van Vechten to Stein [? October 1913], note 1). Stein did, however, offer Evans three manuscripts—"Food," "Objects," and "Rooms"—which Evans agreed to publish, and Stein signed the contract on 18 March. By the time Evans wrote to Stein again on 15 April 1914 (YCAL), she had already cabled him to use the collective title *Tender Buttons* for the three manuscripts.

Tender Buttons was published in June 1914, in an edition of one thousand copies with yellow covers and a circular label printed in two shades of green. The book received little serious critical attention, but it proved to be a *succès de scandale* (see Sherwood Anderson, "The Work of Gertrude Stein," in her *Geography and Plays*, pp. 5–8, and Van Vechten to Marinoff, postmark 5 June 1914, NYPL-MD).

3. Hutchins Hapgood (1869–1944) was an author, journalist, and social critic. In the late fall of 1895 Leo Stein and his cousin Fred Stein were on the first leg of a world tour, going from the West Coast to Japan, when they met Hapgood. Later, Hapgood and his wife the writer Neith Boyce, whom he married in 1899, saw Leo and Gertrude Stein frequently in Paris and in Florence in the pre-World War I years. It was through Mabel Dodge, in 1913, that Van Vechten met the Hapgoods.

For several summers the Hapgoods had lived in Provincetown, Massachusetts. Among their neighbors were George Cram Cook and Susan Glaspell. It was the Hapgoods, Cook, Glaspell, and Eugene O'Neill who, in 1915, founded the amateur theatrical group that eventually became the Provincetown Players. The first plays of the group were given on the veranda of the Hapgoods' cottage, with Cape Cod Bay as the backdrop.

In June 1914, before sailing for Europe, Van Vechten spent several days in Provincetown. Mabel Dodge had rented a cottage there to be near the Hapgoods. Also at Provincetown were John Reed; Maurice Sterne, the painter whom Dodge would later marry; Mary Foote, a portrait painter whom Stein knew from Florence; and Robert Edmond Jones, the scenic designer.

4. Fania Marinoff (1887–1971) was born in Odessa, Russia, the thirteenth child (the seventh girl) of Russian-Jewish parents. After the death of her mother, while Fania was still a baby, her father remarried. The family immigrated to the United States when Marinoff was five or six years old. They settled first in Boston and later in Denver. It was there, at the age of eight, that

she made her stage debut playing the little boy in the bake shop scene in *Cyrano de Bergerac* at the Elitch Gardens. At twelve she toured with Camilla Nartinson St. George's stock company playing soubrette roles. Later she came to the attention of Blanche Walsh and played supporting roles opposite her. After arriving in New York in 1903 she appeared in a number of plays including *A Japanese Nightingale*; *The Serio-Comic Governess*; with Mrs. Patrick Campbell in *The Sorceress*; and as Dolly in George Bernard Shaw's *You Never Can Tell*.

Marinoff was already well known in theatrical circles when, on 15 July 1912, at Claridge's, she first met Van Vechten. Marinoff was with Paul Thompson, a friend of Van Vechten's who only a few weeks earlier had helped Van Vechten in his divorce arrangements.

To Carl Van Vechten
[Rose motto][1]

[postmark: 4 July 1914]

27 rue de Fleurus
[Paris]

My dear Van Vechten

I am awfully glad to hear you are here. We are leaving town Monday[2] so come to lunch Sunday with your friend.[3] Lunch at one.

Sincerely yours
Gertrude Stein

Sunday is to-morrow

1. The motto reads, "Rose is a rose is a rose is a rose," a line that first appeared in Stein's work in a 1913 poem, "Sacred Emily" (printed in Stein's *Geography and Plays*, the line appears on page 187). It was Toklas who selected the line as a motto to appear on Stein's stationery. Toklas also embroidered it on place mats, napkins, and handkerchiefs. The motto appears in a circular design, both with and without a rose in the center, and different colors—silver, blue, and red—were used in printing the motto. I have not indicated these variations when citing the motto.

2. In an effort to interest English publishers in her work Stein had gone to London in January 1913. She was returning to London to sign a contract with John Lane for an edition of *Three Lives* and to interview other publishers (see Gallup, *The Flowers of Friendship*, pp. 97–98).

3. Note by Van Vechten, 18 January 1941: "Received I think, after my return to Paris after my trip to Florence. The 'friend' would probably be Pitts Sanborn as I was stopping with him." Van Vechten was in error; the friend was Fania Marinoff, and the letter was received before he left to join Mabel Dodge in Florence.

To Gertrude Stein

14 July [1914]¹   Venice [Italy]

Mabel [Dodge] says in her last letter—"We have decided not to go to Vallambrosa and we haven't a single notion of what we're going to do—so find out from Gertrude S[tein]. if you see her what *she* thinks we'd better do—that is can *she* join you and Neith [Hapgood] & me somewhere?"[2]

And there you are! Mabel arrives on the 27th. I am in Venice now but expect to be back in Paris this week. Mabel says she is coming directly up there.—The American Express Co. 11 Rue Scribe will reach me.

Fania was fascinated by you—and we both had such a good time. Please shake hands with Miss Taklos for me.[3]

Ever,
Carl Van Vechten

1. The first page of this letter is missing or lost.

2. Van Vechten quotes from a letter of Dodge to him (postmark 3 July 1914, YCAL). Dodge and her son, John Evans, and Neith Hapgood and two of her children, Beatrix and Boyce, sailed on 15 July on the *Stamphalia* and arrived in Genoa on 27 July.

In 1913 and again in 1914 Dodge had tried to persuade Stein to spend part of the summer with her in Florence. Both times Stein refused, saying she had made other plans. It is clear that the friendship between Stein and Dodge had cooled after the summer of 1912, the summer when Stein wrote *Portrait of Mabel Dodge at the Villa Curonia*. Dodge claims that the change in their relationship resulted from sexual jealousy on the part of Toklas, who resented what she perceived to be Stein and Dodge flirting with each other (Dodge, *European Experiences*, pp. 332–33). It is possible, however, that Stein grew bored with the gushing recounting of Dodge's sexual adventures, her marital problems, and her possible divorce from Edwin Ddoge. It is also possible that Stein resented the proprietary manner in which Dodge had cabled her about not publishing with Donald Evans: "WOULD COUNSEL HESITATION BEFORE PUBLISHING WITH EVANS IS GETTING NAME OF SECOND RATE AND DECADENT CO[a]DY SEEMS BETTER PROPOSITION FOR PRESTIGE EVANS WILL PROCEED IMMEDIATELY UNLESS YOU CABLE" (Dodge to Stein, 15 March 1914, YCAL).

Dodge reiterated her objections to Evans in a letter she wrote a few days later (Gallup, *The Flowers of Friendship*, pp. 96–97). Despite Dodge's objections, Stein did not withdraw her manuscript from Evans.

3. Van Vechten returned to Paris to see Marinoff off on the boat train to Cherbourg. She sailed on 25 July for New York, and on 30 July Van Vechten returned to Italy to join Dodge and Neith Hapgood.

Carl Van Vechten and Fania Marinoff, Venice, Italy, July 1914.
COURTESY OF BRUCE KELLNER.

Mabel Dodge at the Villa Curonia, circa 1912.
PHOTOGRAPH BY JACQUES-EMILE BLANCHE.

To Carl Van Vechten

[postmark: 21 July 1914]   The Knightsbridge Hotel
                                            Knightsbridge, London, S.W.

My dear Van Vechten,

We are staying over here a little longer than we intended.[1] We will get back about the tenth of August. Do have a good time whatever your plans turn out to be. I have just heard from Mabel [Dodge]. I will write to her at the villa.[2]

Always sincerely yours
Gertrude Stein

1. Stein had originally planned to conclude her business with John Lane early in July. But Lane was delayed in Paris and did not return to London until the third week in July. (Lane to Stein, 1 July 1914 and 21 July 1914, both YCAL). The actual agreement for publication of *Three Lives* was not signed until September 1914.

2. Dodge had written Stein (? June 1914, YCAL) from Provincetown that she and Neith Hapgood would sail for Europe on 15 July. She proposed that if Stein did not want to come to Italy they would gladly meet her anywhere she chose. Stein's reply to Dodge (? July 1914, YCAL) informed her that they intended to stay in England, where they were visiting friends in the country.

To Carl Van Vechten
[Postcard]

[postmark: 10 September 1914]   [Wiltshire Cottage
                                           Sarsen Land, Lockeridge
                                           near Marlborough, England]

My dear Van,

Where are you and how are you. We were caught by the war in England and have been with friends in the country.[1] Address Knightsbridge Hotel, Knightsbridge, London. Expect to be back in Paris 15 Oct.

Gertrude Stein.

1. Because of the delay in signing the contract with John Lane, Stein was free to accept an invitation to spend several days at Cambridge. The offer had come from the mother of Hope Mirlees, a young woman Stein and Toklas had met in Paris. Stein spent ten days in Cambridge, and while there, at a luncheon given at Newnham College by the classical scholar Jane Harrison, Stein met Alfred North Whitehead and his wife, Evelyn.

When they returned to London, Stein and Toklas met the Whiteheads again and were invited to spend a weekend at the Whiteheads' country home in Lockeridge, near Salisbury Plain (Whitehead to Stein, 29 July 1914, YCAL). During their stay with the Whiteheads, England entered World War I. Except for a brief trip to London to arrange their luggage and to draw on their letters of credit, Stein and Toklas remained with the Whiteheads for eleven weeks.

To Gertrude Stein

6 October [1914][1]

210 West Forty-fourth Street
[New York]

Perhaps you haven't read *How to read Gertrude Stein* so I am sending it to you.[2] Your postcard came back to me from Paris a day or so ago saying that you are in London. Donald Evans thinks you are still there—I am just back from Italy on an immigrant steamer[3] and, for the present, I am fooling with The *Trend* magazine—sort of editor.[4] I wish you could let me have one of your Spanish dancers for the December Number.[5] Where is Marsden Hartley? It's *such* an English name for Berlin.[6] And how are you and Miss Taklos? Do write to me. I may go to jail—for *not* being a suffragette or something—[7]

love,
Carlo V. V.

1. The first part of this letter is missing or lost.

2. Carl Van Vechten, "How to Read Gertrude Stein," *The Trend* (August 1914), 8:553–57.

3. Van Vechten, Neith Hapgood and her children, Boyce and Beatrix, and Mabel Dodge's son, John Evans, sailed from Naples on 22 August aboard the *San Guglielmo*. Dodge waited in Naples for the arrival of John Reed, who was coming to Europe to report on the war. Van Vechten's graphic account of his return to the United States, "Once Aboard the Lugger San Guglielmo; an Account of a Flight from Italy in War Time," was published in *The Trend* (October 1914), 8:13–24.

4. At the instigation of Pitts Sanborn, then serving as secretary-treasurer of *The Trend*, Van Vechten assumed editorial responsibilty for the magazine with the October 1914 issue. He announced his editorial policy in "The Editor's Workbench," signed with the pseudonym "Atlas," in *The Trend* (October 1914), 8:100–1. Van Vechten edited the October, November, and December issues. He resigned before he could publish any of Stein's work.

5. Stein's poem "Preciosilla" was inspired by a singer in Madrid who used Preciosilla as a stage name. Her poem "Susie Asado" was inspired by the flamenco dancer, La Argentina (Antonia Marcé, born in 1890 in Buenos Aires, she died in 1936).

6. Marsden Hartley (1877–1943), the American painter, had come to Paris in April 1912, shortly after the completion of his second one-man show of paintings at Alfred Stieglitz's Little Gallery of the Photo-Secession in New York. It was at this time that Mabel Dodge and Van Vechten met Hartley.

Hartley was introduced to Stein by the painter Carlock, who introduced him as a friend of the painter Lee Simonson, who knew the Steins (see Donald Gallup, "The Weaving of a Pattern: Marsden Hartley and Gertrude Stein," *Magazine of Art* (November 1948), 41:256–61).

From 12 January to 12 February 1914 Hartley had his third one-man show at Stieglitz's gallery. This exhibition included paintings executed in Paris, 1912–13, and his first Berlin paintings, 1913. The brochure for the exhibition had texts by Hartley, Mabel Dodge, and Stein. Stein's text was four excerpts from "IIIIIIIIII" (in Stein's *Geography and Plays*, pp. 189–98). In February 1914 Dodge, Hartley, and the painter Andrew Dasburg went to Buffalo with a selection of the pictures from this exhibition. The pictures were shown in the home of Nina Bull. In March the same works were shown in the Chicago home of Florence Bradley (Hartley to Stein, late February 1914 and 12 March 1914, both YCAL).

Hartley left for Germany in March 1914 via London and Paris and had arrived in Berlin by 30 April. He remained in Germany until 11 December 1915, when he sailed for New York.

7. Van Vechten was divorced from his first wife, Anna Snyder Van Vechten, on 2 August 1912 and was ordered to pay alimony of eighteen dollars per week. He continued to make payments until 26 March 1914, when, because of his meager income, he found himself unable to continue. Anna Van Vechten was threatening litigation for nonpayment of alimony.

To Carl Van Vechten

[postmark: 19 October 1914]   27 rue de Fleurus
                                                           [Paris]

My dear Van,

We are back in Paris, just got here a couple of days ago.[1] Everybody is pleasant and determined otherwise Paris is very quiet. What kind of a magazine is the Trend and what do you pay for a Spanish dancer.[2] Send me a copy of the Trend. I have been doing a good deal of work this summer, one long play, a half of a long thing and a number of short ones all influenced by London under the war.[3] Do tell [Donald] Evans that Tender Buttons copies have come alright. How has it sold. I don't know anything about [Marsden] Hartley, nobody here knows anything about him. As far as I know he didn't come to London. Doesn't Bobby Jones know anything about him. Mabel [Dodge] thought he might. If [Alfred] Stieglitz does do let me know,

Always sincerely yours
Gertrude Stein.

1. Stein and Toklas returned to Paris on the evening of 17 October. They had traveled from London with Mrs. Alfred North Whitehead, who had received permission to visit her son, North, who was then stationed in France.

2. *The Trend* was a monthly review founded in 1911. It printed poetry, fiction, reviews and articles on the arts, and articles dealing with political and social issues. It ceased publication in February 1915.

3. It is unclear which works Stein is referring to. A chronology of Stein's works can be found in Robert Bartlett Haas and Donald Clifford Gallup, compilers, A *Catalogue of the Published and Unpublished Writings of Gertrude Stein* (New Haven: Yale University Library, 1941), pp. 44–55. This catalogue lists works through 1940. Richard Bridgman, *Gertrude Stein in Pieces* (New York: Oxford University Press, 1970), pp. 365–85, slightly revises the Haas and Gallup *Catalogue* and continues the listing until 1946. These chronologies give an approximate order of the composition of Stein's works. Among the works listed for 1914 there are no plays. It is possible that *Not Slightly, A Play* (printed in Stein's *Geography and Plays*, pp. 290–301), which is listed in both chronologies as 1915, may have been begun in England in 1914 but not completed until 1915.

To Carl Van Vechten

[postmark: 25 October 1914]   27 rue de Fleurus
                                               [Paris]

My dear Van

I am very pleased with the Trend and I am very well pleased with your article about me. I am sending you four things. They are
Sacred Emily
England

Gallerie Lafayette
Preciosilla

You can have the collection for the Trend for $150 or $50 apiece for England and Sacred Emily and $25 apiece for Preciosilla and G. Lafayette. I am wanting money these days as all the artists over here are having and are about to have a very hard time.[1] Do you know anything of Marsden Hartley. Do let me know about him,[2]

Gertrude Stein

1. Van Vechten left *The Trend* before he could publish any of these pieces (see Van Vechten to Stein, 26 November 1914).

2. Hartley was in Berlin, but Stein had had no news from him since a postcard (postmark 12 March 1914, YCAL) in which he told her about the exhibition of his works in Florence Bradley's home in Chicago.

To Gertrude Stein

26 November 1914 210 West Forty-fourth Street
[New York]

Dear Gertrude Stein,

I have left The Trend. It was amusing but there was no money behind it. So I took your articles with me. Some other way to dispose of them may come up, or I will return them to you if you like. Tell me what to do.[1]

In a curious way, not through Mabel [Dodge], of course, I have met Mrs. Knoblauch and she has given me The History of a Family to read, at least the first volume.[2] And I have achieved a phrase to describe you: "Gertrude Stein," I say, sententiously, "uses words for their detonation and their connotation."

Did I tell you that Fan and I are married?[3]

And I don't know where Marsden Hartley is.

I am writing an article about letters and I am putting one of yours in, I think. Do write me another one![4]

Regards to Miss Taklos.

Always,
Carlo Van Vechten

[32]

1. Van Vechten left *The Trend* on 7 November (Van Vechten to Marinoff, postmark 5 November 1914, NYPL-MD). He had, however, already prepared the December issue.

2. May Attair Bookstaver (later Mrs. Charles Knoblauch) and Stein met in Baltimore. Stein was a student at the Johns Hopkins University School of Medicine; Bookstaver, a graduate of Bryn Mawr College, was part of a group of Bryn Mawr students then living in Baltimore. Stein lived through an agonizing love affair with Bookstaver, which is recounted in minute detail in Stein's novel *Q.E.D.* After the affair ended and after her marriage to Charles Knoblauch, the two remained friends. Stein sent her typescripts of her manuscripts, which Mrs. Knoblauch tried to place with publishers. It was Mrs. Knoblauch who convinced Alfred Stieglitz to publish Stein's portraits "Matisse" and "Picasso" in *Camera Work*, Special Number (August 1912), pp. 23–25, 29–30.

Writing to Mabel Dodge (? December 1912, YCAL) about people whom Dodge should meet in New York, Stein wrote:

> Then there is a Mrs. Charles Knoblauch, she is the one whose letter I quoted to you about your portrait. She is a Bryn Mawr woman and a friend of Georgiana King etc. . . . I won't write to her about you so you can let her know or not about meeting her. She has my long book *[The Making of Americans]* at present. She is awfully good about helping me to place my things. She was the one who thought of Steiglitz.

Precisely how Van Vechten met Mrs. Knoblauch is unclear. Her brother-in-law, the playwright Edward Knoblauch (Knoblock), and Van Vechten's friend Avery Hopwood, who were friends, may have been responsible for the introduction (see Van Vechten to Marinoff, postmark 13 August 1923, NYPL-MD). It is doubtful if Van Vechten knew anything about Stein's affair with Bookstaver until after Stein's death. The most informed discussion of Stein's relationship to May Bookstaver is in Leon Katz's introduction to Stein's *Fernhurst, Q.E.D., and Other Early Writings*.

3. Van Vechten and Marinoff were married in Stamford, Connecticut, by a justice of the peace on 21 October 1914.

4. There is no listing in Kellner, A *Bibliography*, for a piece on letters. In the Van Vechten Collection at the NYPL-MD there are some notes for an essay on letters. There are also notes about his 1914 visit with Stein. Some of these have been included in Bruce Kellner's, "Baby Woojums in Iowa," *Books at Iowa* (April 1977), 26:3–18.

To Carl Van Vechten

[postmark: 3 December 1914]   27 rue de Fleurus
                                                           [Paris]

My dear Van

I haven't heard from you. If you can't take those things will you send them back right away by registered post. I suppose hell is lively and the war isn't that. It's getting rather dreary. Too cold. There is no news. We all see each other a great deal. I am doing a lot of work. I am very pleased with the play I did in London.

Do you know anything about [Marsden] Hartley and does Mabel [Dodge] know anything about [Arnold] Ronnebeck.[1] I guess he is dead by now. Everybody who intends to be back is back by now. This doesn't refer to Germans.

Merry Christmas to you

Always sincerely yours
Gertrude Stein.

1. Arnold Ronnebeck (1885–1947) was a German-born sculptor whom Marsden Hartley had met in April 1912 at the Restaurant Thomas on the Boulevard Raspail, the gathering place of a German coterie in Paris. It was through Hartley that Ronnebeck met Stein and Mabel Dodge.

To Carl Van Vechten

[postmark: 9 December 1914]   27 rue de Fleurus
       [Paris]

My dear Van,

Good luck to Mr. and Mrs. Van Vechten, may you both live long and prosper. I was glad to see that she was having a very successful winter.

About my articles. I want to sell my short things to the regular magazines and I think it might be done now, I have fairly good reason for thinking so, if I can get hold of the right kind of agent. Can you tell me of some regular man or woman, who is likely to be able to handle them well.[1] As I wrote to you I want to make some money just now and as you know I have quantities of things short things and long things. After all I've got ten years' work and I want to dispose of some of it.

If you will send the names of some such persons names and addresses I will be ever so much obliged.

You need not bother about publishing this letter thank you.

Best remembrances to Fan

Sincerely yours
Gertrude Stein.

1. A reference to a proposal made by Van Vechten in his letter of 26 November 1914 to Stein.

To Gertrude Stein

21 January 1915   210 West Forty-fourth Street
                                   [New York]

Dear Gertrude Stein,

Since The Trend has gone its way I have taken your four sketches to several "literary agents" to see what can be done, but they say they can do nothing with "work so advanced." Still there is talk at present of a new revue to be called *New York Mornings* or something of the sort[1] . . . they may be appreciative of the four sketches . . . Matisse has reached the Montross galleries—in other words become old-fashioned[2]—but Picabia and Picasso are still exhibiting at [Alfred] Stieglitz's . . The Carroll Galleries are showing some strange canvases . . .[3] Marsden Hartley is still in Berlin . . [Charles] Demuth gets letters from him.[4] Hartley does not seem to know there is a war . . he speaks of working away, and plans exhibitions this spring in Vienna, Buda-Pesth, and in New York next fall . . . His friend has been wounded and sent back to Berlin.[5]

I am writing all the time—I suppose you are too. . . . If you like I'll send the four sketches back to you—or else I'll keep them until an opportunity turns up—and that may be soon. Please remember me to Miss Taklos, and Fania sends greetings to you both.

As ever,
Carlo Van Vechten.

1. One of the names being considered by Allen Norton for his new review. When it was published, in March 1915, Norton named it *Rogue*.

2. An exhibition of seventy-four works by Matisse, organized by the art critic Walter Pach, was held in the Montross Gallery, New York, from 20 January to 27 February 1915.

3. Stieglitz, in his Little Gallery of the Photo-Secession (also known as "291," its address on Fifth Avenue), New York, held an exhibition of works by Picabia from 12 to 26 January 1915. *Picasso and Braque: An Exhibition of Recent Drawings and Paintings* was held at Stieglitz's gallery from 9 December 1914 to 9 January 1915.

    The *Second Exhibition of Works by Contemporary French Artists* was held at the Carroll Galleries, New York, from early January to 13 February 1915. The exhibition included over seventy works by the following artists: Lafitte, Valtat, Vera, Moreau, Redon, Duchamp-Villon, Rouault, Chabaud, de Segonzac, de Vlaminck, Dufy, and Renoir.

4. In YCAL there is an undated fragment of a letter from Hartley to Demuth in which Hartley writes of his life in Berlin. This part of a longer letter was given to Mabel Dodge, who showed it to Van Vechten.

5. Arnold Ronnebeck, the sculptor, who was in the German army.

To Carl Van Vechten

[Postcard: An English convoy crossing a river by means of a bridge of boats]

[postmark: 26 January 1915]   27 rue de Fleurus
                                               [Paris]

My dear Van

Did you get my two letters. Will you answer right away as I may be going away early this year.

Yours sincerely
Gertrude Stein.

To Carl Van Vechten

[postmark: 3 February 1915]   27 rue de Fleurus
                                               [Paris]

My dear Van

Thanks very much. Send me the things back by registered mail will you. I would like to have them right away. Thanks so much for your trouble. Yes I am writing right along. It's a good year for working. Have you any regular job or are you doing what you can.[1] I had a letter from [Marsden]Hartley, as you say he seems to have no suspicion that there won't be picture shows in Germany and Austria this year.[2] There isn't any news. I am writing sentimental novels and I like doing them, three at a time. They are very good I think only just begun. Best remembrances to Fania

Sincerely yours
Gertrude Stein.

1. Van Vechten had left the *New York Press* in June 1914. Beginning in January 1916 he contributed essays to the *New York Globe* where his friends Pitts Sanborn and Louis Sherwin were employed. Van Vechten was never on the regular payroll of the *New York Globe*. For a detailed account of Van Vechten during this period see Kellner, *Carl Van Vechten and the Irreverent Decades*, pp. 92–97, 115–16.

2. In an undated letter to Stein (November 1914–January 1915, YCAL) Hartley wrote of Ronnebeck's difficult recovery from a battle wound and his own plans for exhibitions of his newest paintings in various European cities. Hartley also told Stein of the death, on 7 October 1914, of Karl von Freyburg. Von Freyburg was a young lieutenant in the German army and a cousin of Ronnebeck's. Hartley met von Freyburg in Paris in 1912 and immediately developed a deep affection for him. Hartley's relationship with von Freyburg and his "influence" on Hartley's paintings are discussed in Barbara Haskell, *Marsden Hartley* (New York: Whitney Museum of American Art in Association with New York University Press, 1980), pp. 26–45.

To Gertrude Stein

22 February [1915]   210 West Forty-fourth Street
                                                          [New York]

Dear Gertrude Stein—

Just before your letter came Allen Norton rolled over in bed and started a new magazine to be called *Rogue.* . . . . He wanted *Aux Galeries Lafayette* for the first issue and I gave it to him—and I will have $25 for you anon—Frank Harris also is to appear in the first issue and the idea looks very amusing—a *short* magazine twice a month. I'll send you the first number immediately when it appears. Allen may want to use other of your sketches that I have—so I am disregarding, for the moment, your request to have them back. If you are going away let me know your address.[1]

Marsden Hartley has just had an exhibit here of his *old* pictures and Matisse has had an exhibit. These painters are now considered academic—[Alfred] Stieglitz is issuing a number of Camera Work entitled "What 291 Means to Me"—Everybody tells more or less.[2] We may come to Italy this summer. I have a book almost finished which Donald [Evans] may bring out . . .[3] The Post-decadents are not very active at present.[4]

Love salutes to you and Miss Taklos—Fania sends regards. Have you heard about Florence Bradley and the cactus beans?[5]

Ever,
Carlo Van Vechten

I *do* want to see your sentimental novel. John Lane is bringing out
3 *Lives*[6]

1. The first issue of *Rogue* was dated 15 March 1915. In addition to Stein's "Aux Galeries
Lafayette" (written in 1911), this issue included *The Kiss,* a one-act play by Frank Harris. Other
writers in the first issue besides Norton and his wife Louise who wrote unsigned articles, were
Wallace Stevens, Witter Bynner, and Homer Croy.

2. *Paintings by Marsden Hartley: "The Mountain Series"* was an exhibition held at the Daniel
Gallery, New York, from early January to 9 February 1915. The exhibition included seventeen
paintings by Hartley: Dark Landscapes of 1909 and Still Lifes of 1911.

     Van Vechten is referring to the Matisse exhibition held at the Montross Gallery. See
Van Vechten to Stein, 21 January 1915, note 2.

     Issue 47 of *Camera Work,* dated July 1914 but not published until January 1915, was
titled "What Does 291 Mean." This was the last issue of *Camera Work* and included contributions by sixty-eight artists and writers.

3. This may be a reference to "Sacral Dimples: A Diary," a Van Vechten book announced by
Evans' Claire Marie Press in a publicity brochure. The title seems to be an invention of Evans'
who wanted to flesh out his catalogue. Van Vechten did attempt to put together a volume of
short pieces at this time but it was never published. Van Vechten called it "Pastiches et Pistaches." Some of the pieces from this collection eventually found their way into other works.
In December 1915, G. Schirmer published a collection of Van Vechten's essays titled *Music
after the Great War.* See also Van Vechten to Stein, 17 May 1916, note 6.

4. The term "postdecadents" echoes Mabel Dodge's attitude toward Evans' Claire Marie Press.
Dodge wrote Stein that Edwin Arlington Robinson, who knew Evans, considered the Claire
Marie Press

> . . . absolutely third rate & in bad order here, being called for the most part "decadent"
> & Broadwayish & that sort of thing. He [Robinson] wrote Evans to get out of it, to
> chuck it & stop getting linked up in the public "mind" with it. I think it would be a
> pity to publish with him *if* it will emphasize the idea in the opinion of the public, that
> there is something degenerate & effete & decadent about the whole of the cubist move-
> ment which they all connect you with. . . . (Gallup, *The Flowers of Friendship,* p. 96)

5. Bradley had had a violent reaction to some peyote that she had taken at a party at Mabel
Dodge's. In the chapter "Peyote" in her book *Movers and Shakers,* Dodge recounts the party,
although she had changed Bradley's name to "Genevieve Onslow." (I am grateful to Dr. Donald Gallup, retired curator, YCAL, for verifying this information for me. The Dodge manuscripts at YCAL are sealed. Dr. Gallup kindly reviewed them and verified that Bradley was the
woman in the incident.) Various letters in YCAL offer only oblique suggestions of an "episode"
involving Bradley early in 1914, when the incident took place. In an undated letter, early 1914
(YCAL), Dodge wrote to Stein, "Florence Bradley has been staying with me & we all understand each other now you were both right—absolutely." Djuna Barnes, the writer and painter,
who was part of the Dodge–Van Vechten circle of friends, wrote Dodge 14 February 1914
(YCAL) and asked, "Did not Mr. Van Vechten tell you about the Bradley episode?"

     For a number of years Florence Bradley was plagued by the aftereffects of the peyote
incident. She was healthy enough, however, to organize an exhibition of Marsden Hartley's
paintings in her Chicago home in March 1915. After this exhibition all contact between her
and Dodge, Stein, and Van Vechten ceased for many years.

[38]

Bradley did not communicate again with Stein until 15 October 1928 (YCAL). She was encouraged to do so after she had met Katherine Dudley and Harriet Monroe at the Chicago Lyric Opera and they had all discussed Stein.

In 1929 Bradley and her husband, Gómez del Val, went to live in Mallorca. It was from there, in 1934, that she wrote to Stein after she had read *The Autobiography of Alice B. Toklas*:

My dreams took on different forms from the dreams that were mine that day I left Paris— years ago—with your plays under my arm.

After I was knocked out at Mabel's—yes—I passed on—as it were—to other parts—for so long a time I was away—and now I am back. (5 May 1934, YCAL)

6. The first edition of Stein's *Three Lives* had been published in 1909 at her expense by the Grafton Press of New York. In 1915 John Lane issued three hundred copies of the book in a Bodley Head edition. Lane's edition is identical with the Grafton Press edition except for a different title page. The spine on Lane's edition still shows the Grafton Press as publisher.

To Carl Van Vechten
[French Telegraph Cable]

[postmark: 9 March 1915]   [Paris]

GIVE NORTON NOTHING RETURN FOUR IMMEDIATELY

GERTRUDE STEIN

To Carl Van Vechten

[postmark: 10 March 1915]   27 rue de Fleurus
                                                    [Paris]

My dear Van,

You will have got my telegram and sent me the things back. Frankly I am not keen on [Allen] Norton's publishing ideas.[1] My address this summer will be as usual 27 rue [de] Fleurus, although we are going to Spain. What has [Donald] Evans been doing. I wrote to him asking him for the account of Tender Buttons but haven't gotten an answer. I'd like to have it. What is your book about. No I haven't heard anything about Florence Bradley. There is nothing new here, everything is cheerful and the war goes on.

Regards to Fania and yourself.

Sincerely yours
Gertrude Stein.

1. Norton wrote Stein (5 November 1914?, YCAL) asking for permission to publish Stein's "Spanish dancers." He also expressed interest in *The Making of Americans*, which he had probably heard of through Van Vechten. Stein's reply to Norton does not exist, but some notes that Stein drafted on the top of Norton's letter to her indicate that she had sent him details of a contract for *The Making of Americans*. At the end of Stein's "Aux Galeries Lafayette," which appeared in the first number of *Rogue*, Norton wrote, "*Rogue* threatens to publish Miss Gertrude Stein's History of a Family [i.e., *The Making of Americans*] which is in nine volumes of five hundred pages each" (*Rogue* [15 March 1915], 1(1):14).

In a telephone interview (2 December 1981) Norton's first wife, now Mrs. Louise Varese, remembered that Van Vechten thought Stein was upset because Norton had not replied to her offer that he publish *The Making of Americans*. Mrs. Varese also remembered that Van Vechten advised Norton not to write to Stein again until after she had seen the first issue of *Rogue*.

⁂

To Gertrude Stein

11 March [1915]   210 West Forty-fourth Street
                                                   [New York]

Dear Gertrude Stein—

Your cablegram arrived too late as *Rogue* is already published and it includes *Aux Galeries Lafayette*. I am sending it to you with your other three manuscripts by registered post—and in this letter I am enclosing a cheque for *Aux Galeries Lafayette*. . . . I am sorry that I have given something to [Allen] Norton—if you didn't want me to—but you wrote me to get you an agent and an agent, of course, would sell it to anyone he could sell to— even a newspaper. Naturally I thought this would be all right. If you think it is—after you have seen it—you might send him some more things—He said he would be glad to have something else later from you. His address is

Allen Norton—205 West 56th Street—New York. . . . Everyone admires *Aux Galeries* tremendously. I read it aloud with great effect! and I am frequently asked to do so.[1]

I am excited and interested about the tales you are writing and about your departure from Paris. Where are you going? We may go to Italy or Spain this summer. Fan at present is in Florida acting in a lurid moving picture drama in which the principal scene seems to be a jaunt in a boat with a *crazy* sailor[2]—I do nothing but write and go to masked balls as Heliogabalus.[3] All salutations to you and Miss Taklos, and so does Avery Hopwood![4]

Always
Carlo V. V.

1. The only other work by Stein to appear in *Rogue* was the portrait "Mrs. Th----y, *Rogue* (December 1916), 2[i.e., 3] (3):16.

2. Marinoff played the role of Dorinda Ladue in the film *The Lure of Mammon*, directed by Kenean Buel, Kalem Production Company, 1915.

3. Roman Emperor notable for his profligacy. He was slain by his troops.

4. Avery Hopwood (1882–1928), the playwright, and Van Vechten met shortly after Van Vechten arrived in New York in 1906. Van Vechten introduced him to Mabel Dodge, who arranged a letter of introduction to Stein (undated letter, 1914–15, YCAL). Presumably Hopwood met Stein during this period. His close friendship with Stein began in 1923 and lasted until his death.

To Gertrude Stein

24 March [1915]   210 West Forty-fourth Street
                                             [New York]

Dear Gertrude Stein,

You will have received your manuscripts, a copy of *Rogue* . . and a cheque by now. I am sending you a clipping from last Sunday's *Sun* which may amuse you.[1] You ask about Donald [Evans]—He has been very ill for the past few months. He has given up his position on the Times and neglected his business generally. Some time ago he left town—and is somewhere in the country. His New York address is—534 Fifth Avenue—possibly the letters you have sent him miscarried. That is his *personal* address.

All regards,
Carlo V. V.

1. An article in the *New York Sun* (21 March 1915, Sec. 3, p. 2), titled "What Is Happening in the World of Art," discussed the first issue of *Rogue* and mentioned Stein's "Aux Galeries Lafayette."

To Carl Van Vechten

[postmark: 27 March 1915]   27 rue de Fleurus
                                             [Paris]

My dear Van,[1]

I forgive you. It's hard not to forgive when one sees oneself printed and has a check beside. [Allen] Norton has a certain quality but it doesn't come off and that annoys me. We are not leaving Paris xcept for the summer. We are rather full up with war and xpect to stay some weeks in Palma where they haven't got it. The Zeppelins didn't make much noise and what there was was rather barrel like and soft but the alarm does. Later we will be in Madrid and then in the north of Spain. Continue to address here.

Always sincerely yours
Gertrude Stein.

Will you please get an accounting out of [Donald] Evans. I haven't managed to. Perhaps you can. Thanks so much.[2]

G.S.

1. This letter was forwarded to Van Vechten at 70 Ludlow Street, where he was in jail. See Van Vechten to Stein, 30 April 1915, note 1.

2. Note by Van Vechten, 18 January 1941.
   It was through me that Donald Evans published *Tender Buttons*. The Claire-Marie Press was his, named for a young actress Claire-Marie Burke whom we knew at the time.

However, he wrote directly to her [i.e., Stein], at my suggestion, & made all the arrangements. After it was published, of course, it didn't sell & so far as I know G. S. never got a penny from him. I doubt if Donald, who was a character himself, ever answered any of her letters demanding an accounting.

To Gertrude Stein

30 April 1915   210 West Forty-fourth Street
                                                             [New York]

Dear Gertrude Stein—

You will be amused, perhaps, to learn that I am again at large—We have at last arrived at an agreement which will make it impossible for Ann to incarcerate me again . . . on the other hand I am to give her no more money![1]

Walter Arensberg—is starting a new magazine—mostly of verse—in June.[2] He would like to publish something by you . . . I'll send you the first copy when it comes out and you can see what you think. . . . Of course I could sell something else to *Rogue* if you cared to.

I don't know anything about Donald [Evans] these days except that he has become manager for Lady Duff Gordon—(Lucile Ltd.) at 160 Fifth Avenue. You might write him there. . . .[3]

The war still goes on. . . .

Fania is doing many moving pictures and also playing Louka in Bernard Shaw's *Arms and the Man*. . . .[4]

She wishes me to blow her salutations to you and Miss Taklos—

Sempre.
Carlo V. V.

1. On 5 April Van Vechten was found guilty of contempt of court for his failure to comply with the divorce agreement of 2 August 1912 between him and Anna Snyder Van Vechten and was sentenced to jail until he paid the back alimony or another arrangement was made. Van Vechten had been ordered to pay alimony of $18 per week, which he did until 26 May 1914. When his ex-wife started litigation on 9 March 1915, Van Vechten owed her $738.

When on 28 April 1915 Van Vechten signed an agreement with her, he was released from the Ludlow Street jail. In consideration of the sum of $2,250, she agreed to release him from all alimony claims.

2. Walter Conrad Arensberg, writer and art collector, provided the initial financing for the new magazine *Others*. *Others* was edited by the poet Alfred Kreymborg, who had been a member of the Imagist group. *Others*, which was published between July 1915 and July 1919, never printed any work by Stein.

3. Lady Duff-Gordon (Lucy Christiana Sutherland) had started a dress business in her London home at the time of her first marriage, to James Wallace. When she moved the business from her home to 24 Old Burlington Street, she dropped the name Mrs. James Wallace and called the shop the Maison Lucile. She was married to Sir Cosmo Duff-Gordon in 1900. In 1910 she opened a Maison Lucile shop in New York.

4. In addition to *The Lure of Mammon*, Marinoff made a number of films in 1915, including *The Unsuspected Isles*, *The Galloper*, *Nedra*, *The Money Master*, and *The Battle*.

To Carl Van Vechten

[postmark: 4 May 1915] Grand Hôtel, Palma de Mallorca
Îles Baléares
[Spain]

My dear Van,

Oh dear I am so sorry because that kind of thing is amusing for a bit and then it gets monotonous. As your alimony must have been so very little alimony they ought only to keep you in a little while. Do get out soon. We are peacefully on an island.[1] The cigarettes are xcellent and contraband. The natives piratical but roundfaced, and the sunshine all we can ask.

I was awfully sorry to hear that [Donald] Evans has been ill. I like him very much. I also liked your description of him in Rogue.[2]

I guess we will be staying on here several months. I did a little thing about the islands one page and I am doing a longish peaceful one.

Regards to Fania and do get out comfortably,

Always sincerely yours
Gertrude Stein.

1. In early March Stein and Toklas became alarmed by German zeppelin raids on Paris. In late April they took a train for Barcelona. They remained there for several days and then took a boat for Mallorca.

2. Van Vechten's "How Donald Dedicated His Poem," *Rogue* (1 April 1915), 1:8–10.

❧

To Carl Van Vechten

[postmark: 26 May 1915]   Grand Hôtel, Palma de Mallorca
                                           Îles Baléares
                                           [Spain]

My dear Van,

I am glad you are out of jail. I don't like jail even when it's alimony.
I suppose it's only a prejudice but that's the way I feel about it. We are staying on here another two months I imagine. It's very pleasant and I am working fairly well, on a longish thing. About Rogue I would be willing to sell
them Preciosilla for $50 if they want it, if they do you can armed with this
letter get it from Mrs. Knoblauch who has it.[1] I got a letter from [Donald]
Evans saying he was sending me the account but as it hasn't come we will
assume it went down in the Lusitania and I will write to him about it again.[2]
If Rogue takes the Preciosilla send me the check here if it is sent within the
month which it will be if they are to have it. Thanks so much.

Best to you both
Gertrude Stein.

1. Note by Van Vechten, 18 January 1941: "Mrs. Charles Knoblauch who had many of Gertrude's mss. including The Making of Americans at this period."

2. Evans to Stein (26 March 1915, YCAL): "For some unaccountable reason your letter of
several months ago relative to Tender Buttons only reached Claire Marie yesterday. I have ordered a statement prepared and it will be forwarded to you with a check in a day or two. I am
very sorry for the delay." No statement or check was received by Stein.

❧

To Gertrude Stein

12 July 1915   Fairfax Arms
                                           151 East 19th Street
                                           New York

Dear Gertrude Stein,

You are splendidly in Spain while we are moving—(You will note
that we have a new address.) We have been West—and now I am settled

down to write, while Fan is becoming a celebrated moving picture star.—
New York is cool this summer and I don't mind it for a change, especially
as the new apartment is very high in the air and there are many breezes.[1]
But it would be nice to be in Spain. In fact I think we'll be there before the
winter is over. Does the war make a difference there?—You must like it or
you wouldn't go so often.

I find myself writing about nothing but music now—and people like
the articles well enough to buy them. I suppose one should write about the
war. Will it never be over!

Rogue is pausing for a few weeks. It is an impertinent pause—just as
his movements were impertinent.

Regards to Miss Taklos and yourself from both of us.

Carlo Van Vechten

1. Before their marriage both Van Vechten and Marinoff had lived on the west side of Man-
hattan, he on West Forty-fourth Street and she in the St. Margaret, an apartment hotel on
West Forty-seventh Street. This apartment, on the top floor of an apartment house on East
Nineteenth Street, was their first joint apartment.

❧

To Carl Van Vechten

[postmark: 10 August 1915]   45 Calle del dos de Mayo
                                                       Terreno
                                                       Palma de Mallorca
                                                       Îles Baléures
                                                       Spain

My dear Van,

Yours is a very red address.[1] I think ours is very pretty. Anyway we
have taken this little house for a few months and have imported our french
servant who remains critical of the blue of the Mediterranean.[2] It isn't water
color she says. We don't know how long we are going to stay. A few months
anyway. We have just been to Valencia for a week and saw all that there is
to see of bull-fighting, Gallo, Gallito, and Belmonte. Those names don't say
anything to you but we saw five of the best fights. It's the only thing that
can make you forget the war that is it's the only thing that's made me forget

[46]

the war. I hope Rogue isn't dead for keeps. I kind of looked forward to their doing some of my longer short things like my sentimental novels etc. You can continue to address to Paris or here as you like. Best to Fania and yourself.

Gertrude Stein.

1. Van Vechten's stationery reflected his new address: the Fairfax coat of arms printed in red.

2. Jeanne Poule, Stein's Breton servant, had come from Paris.

To Carl Van Vechten
[Postcard]

[postmark: 23 August 1915]

[45 Calle del dos de Mayo
Terreno
Palma de Mallorca
Îles Baléares
Spain]

My dear Van,

It's getting a little damp here now that the sun isn't hot so we will probably be going to Paris for a bit and then somewhere in Spain. So address Paris for the present. Best to you both

Gertrude Stein.

To Gertrude Stein

24 October 1915

Fairfax Arms
151 East 19th Street
New York

Dear Gertrude Stein—

Rogue sort of bobs up and down like an apple in a tub of water—and I don't know when it will come again.[1] I envy you the bull-fights—they must make everything else seem less brutal—but we are to see them soon. We expect to go to Spain in April if we can get away. But now Fania is so occupied doing moving pictures that we can find no time for anything else. We are just returned from the Bahama Islands—Nassau—a city of 10,000 niggers, beautiful fish—and cocoa nut trees—where Fan was the heroine of a marvelous film[2]—Stephen Haweis is down there doing colored fish in cubes and circles—pretty things.[3] Maurice Sterne has twelve—almost nudes of Mabel [Dodge] in the Montross Galleries—she takes several attitudes. In one she is reading a book with her feet on the chandelier.[4]

I am writing a great deal—are you?

We saw a negro religious revival in Nassau that in some ways must be said to excel a bull-fight. The creatures went into such violently hysterical conditions that they had to be held and tied—it was very diverting and made me forget God.

Do stay in Spain until we get there. I am told that we must go to Granada in May. . . . I suppose Spain is cold in the winter.

Remember us to Miss Taklos

Carlo V. V.

1. Financial difficulties caused Norton to abandon plans to publish *Rogue* twice monthly.

2. Marinoff and Van Vechten sailed from New York on 22 September 1915 on the S. S. *Havana* for Nassau in the Bahamas. Marinoff was engaged to play the role of Lady Hungerford in *Nedra*, a film by George Barr McCutcheon. Van Vechten appeared briefly in the film in the role of a warship captain.

   Van Vechten utilized his experiences from this trip in two essays: "The Holy Jumpers," in his *In the Garret*, pp. 131–45; and "On Visiting Fashionable Places out of Season," in his *Excavations*, pp. 1–26.

3. Stephen Haweis (Hugh Oscar William Haweis) was an English-born painter and husband of the poet and painter Mina Loy (1882–1966). The Haweises were married on 31 December 1903. They first met Leo and Gertrude Stein in 1905 and became frequent visitors to the Stein's Saturday night salon. The Haweises moved to Florence in 1906 and did not see the Steins again until 1909, when the Steins were staying in Fiesole. It was in Florence that the Haweises met Mabel Dodge, and through her, in July 1913, they met Van Vechten. Haweis had left Italy in 1913 and had traveled to the Fiji Islands, Tahiti, and Australia. He returned to New York and was planning on sailing to the Bahamas. The Haweises were divorced in October 1917.

4. Sterne exhibited twelve color drawings (tempera), studies of Mabel Dodge, in a group exhibition at the Montross Gallery, New York, 2–23 October 1915.

To Carl Van Vechten
[Postcard: Palma de Mallorca—Interior de la Catedral]

[postmark: 22 December 1915]

[45 Calle del dos de Mayo
Terreno
Palma de Mallorca
Îles Baléares
Spain]

Best wishes of the season to you and Fania. I guess we will be going back to Paris in the Spring but if you come over we will meet there or somewhere. I am glad everything is going so well with you. We are very peaceful. I am making plays quite a number of them. Conversations are easy but backgrounds are difficult but they come and stay.[1]

Happy new year to you both

Gertrude Stein.

1. Classifying Stein's work according to a strict interpretation of particular genres is often difficult. Strictly speaking, only two works from 1915 can be considered plays: *Not Slightly, A Play* and *He Said It. A Monologue.* The Haas-Gallup *A Catalogue of the Published and Unpublished Writings of Gertrude Stein* lists many more plays in 1916. It is possible that Stein worked on pieces over a long period of time and that works begun in 1915 were completed in 1916. Except in a very few cases there is little internal evidence to help determine a closer date of composition. See Haas-Gallup, *A Catalogue,* pp. 46–47, for works composed in 1915 and 1916.

To Gertrude Stein

[late March 1916]

Fairfax Arms
151 East 19th Street
New York

Dear Gertrude Stein,

I am sending you my book, which—in spots may amuse you. I hope so anyway.[1] It has gone into a second edition in two months. . . . I am hard at work on another.[2] Do tell me something about Spanish dancing or music. I am doing an article on the subject surrounded by difficulty. Are you still in Spain, I wonder? We are coming over sometime but just now we're afraid of submarines.

Your name pops up in current journalism with great frequency. You are as famous in America as any historical character—and if you came over I think you might have as great a reception as say Jenny Lind.[3] But if you are in Spain I can understand why you won't ever come over!

Please say, How do you do, to Miss Taklos for us.

Greetings,
Carlo Van Vechten

I've seen Leo [Stein] once or twice but he never sees me.[4] The Russian ballet *scenery* is here but none of the dancers.[5]

Marsden [Hartley] is here giving exhibitions[6] and Lou Tellegen is married to Geraldine Farrar.[7]

1. Van Vechten's *Music after the Great War and Other Studies*. The book, consisting of seven articles by Van Vechten, had been published in December 1915. Van Vechten means a second printing; there was no second edition of the book until circa 1920 (see Kellner, A *Bibliography*, p. 6).

2. Van Vechten was preparing his book of essays *Music and Bad Manners*. It included his essay "Spain and Music," pp. 57–132.

3. Jenny Lind (1820–87), Swedish soprano. Under the management of P. T. Barnum she toured (1850–52) the United States with great success.

4. Gertrude Stein and her brother, Leo (1872–1947), had shared the studio at 27 rue de Fleurus since 1903. Beginning in 1911, there was a growing tension in the household caused by disagreements over Picasso's work and Leo's attitude toward the direction in which Gertrude's writing was developing. They separated definitively in early 1913, and Leo went to live in Settignano, near Florence. He returned to the United States in 1915 and had met Van Vechten through Mabel Dodge. For the break between Leo and Gertrude see Leo Stein, *Journey into the Self*, pp. 51–55, and Leon Katz, "Weininger and *The Making of Americans*," *Twentieth Century Literature* (Spring 1978), 24:21–22.

5. Diaghilev's Ballet Russe had performed in New York in January 1916 at the Century Theatre to less than enthusiastic reviews. It then made a tour of the United States and returned to New York to present a second season at the Metropolitan Opera House. Because of the war, the ballet's two leading dancers were prevented from coming to New York. Karsavina could not leave Russia, and Nijinsky had been detained for more than a year in Budapest and then in Vienna. Through the efforts of Otto Kahn, chairman of the board of the Metropolitan Opera Company, and the American ambassador in Vienna, Nijinsky and his wife were granted travel permits. Nijinsky arrived in New York on 5 April and made his debut on the afternoon of 12 April.

6. Nine works by Hartley were included in an exhibition, *The Forum Exhibition of Modern American Painters*, held at the Anderson Galleries, New York, from 13 to 25 March 1916.

7. Lou Tellegen (Von Dommelen) was a Dutch-born actor who had come to America as a member of Sarah Bernhardt's company in 1910. He married the opera singer Geraldine Farrar on 8 February 1916. It is possible that Stein had seen Tellegen act with Bernhardt in Paris or knew him as the model for Rodin's sculpture *Eternal Spring*. Tellegen and Farrar were divorced in 1923.

To Carl Van Vechten

[postmark: 10 April 1916]

[45 Calle del dos de Mayo
Terreno
Palma de Mallorca
Îles Baléares
Spain]

My dear Van,

Thanks so much for the book. I have been reading it and find you have a charming enthusiasm and know so much and are so conscientious xcept when you say there were three of us in that box instead of four. Now the great question is which one did you leave out. Anyway I am very pleased.[1] So I am sure is Fania. What are you to do this summer. We are leaving our island with some sorrow.[2] It has been an xtremely nice island and we have gotten so that we really know its gossip. What between our neighbours our landlord casual acquaintances and our servant we know a lot. When Jeanne [Poule] comes in with an especially complicated story and we ask her how she understood it she says it's easy as all the real words in the language resemble the french. Crime is not rampant. The worst offense is selling false contraband tobacco. Everybody sells contraband but a woman was taken up the other day for selling false contraband. Such is Mallorca. We are leaving now in a few weeks and we will go to Madrid etc and get back to Paris sometime in June. One wants plenty of daylight in Paris these days. I am awfully sorry I did not keep a beautiful article that came out in our local paper telling about Spain's peaceful revenge for the Spanish war. How music dress painting and everything in Yankhilandia, as they poetically call Us is dominated by Spain. They were very pleased with it and now comes the Sussex but in the best Mallorcan manner they are chiefly worried about what has become of the money he had on his person.[3]

I have been working very prettily. I have done several plays and some funny things quite a number of funny things.

Once more thanks and best to you and Fania.

Address me 27 rue de Fleurus that will reach me.

Always sincerely yours
Gertrude Stein

1. Note by Van Vechten, 18 January 1941: "This refers to my famous description of the first performance of Sacre du Printemps in Paris in Music After the Great War." See Appendix A, "The First Meeting of Gertrude Stein and Carl Van Vechten."

2. Encouraged by the Battle of Verdun, Stein and Toklas made plans to leave Mallorca for Paris. They arrived back in Paris on 20 June.

3. On 24 March the channel steammer *Sussex* was torpedoed by a German submarine off the coast of Mallorca.

To Carl Van Vechten

[postmark: 18 April 1916]

[45 Calle del dos de Mayo
Terreno
Palma de Mallorca
Îles Baléares
Spain]

My dear Van,

Your letter has just turned up and I was pleased with it.[1] I am awfully glad your book is selling so well. I am sorry that I can't help you with Spanish dancing but all we know of it is seeing it at the little dance hall theatres in Madrid. The best is the classical dance done by the Argentina.[2] This winter we haven't seen any as the Catalans being progressive go in for Munich school and Isadora [Duncan] school and any mixed school and the island is just a weak Catalan just as Catalan but not so progressive.[3] Then we have seen the peasant dancing of Valencia which is pretty but dull. Occasional men dance well but it hasn't much variety, it's a little too Moorish and not wild enough for the kind it is. That's all I know about Spanish dancing. We will be in Madrid and I hope we will see some more but that won't help you any will it not unless they do a companion volume of Spanish dances and Mallorcan scenes. Alas about every three months I get sad. I make so much absorbing literature with such attractive titles and even if I could be as popular as Jenny Lind where oh where is the man to publish me in series. Perhaps some day you will meet him. He can do me as cheaply and as simply as he likes but I would so like to be done. Alas. Anyhow it's been a delightful winter here and really one does get to amuse oneself endlessly with Mallorcans. Just now we and our local paper are so xcited because our local boats have just rescued real sailors who have been sunk by submarines.[4] I don't blame your not liking to be a drunken sailor.[5] By the way is John Reed being a hero in Mexico or is he letting [Francisco "Pancho"] Villa do it all by himself this time.[6] Best to you both address Paris where we'll get to by and by.

Always yours
Gertrude Stein.

1. Van Vechten's letter to Stein [late March 1916].

2. Stein's poem "Susie Asado" is a portrait of La Argentina, a noted Spanish dancer.

3. "Munich School" may be a reference to the dancer Loie Fuller, who performed to great success there, or it might be a reference to Isadora Duncan (1880–1927). Duncan was an important innovator and pioneer in expressionism in dance. The Steins and Duncans had known each other in California.

4. See Stein to Van Vechten [10 April 1916], note 3.

5. See Van Vechten to Stein [late March 1916].

6. On 9 March 1916 some of Francisco "Pancho" Villa's men raided Columbus, New Mexico, killing thirteen American citizens. Although it is not certain whether Villa participated in the raid, he was held responsible. President Woodrow Wilson ordered an expedition into Mexico under General John J. Pershing to capture Villa dead or alive. General Pershing pursued Villa from March 1916 until February 1917 but failed to capture him.

John Reed (1887–1920), who had been in Mexico from December 1913 until April 1914 reporting on Villa and the Mexican revolution, did not return to Mexico.

To Gertrude Stein

17 May 1916   Fairfax Arms
                                                   151 East 19th Street
                                                   New York

Dear Gertrude Stein,

It's so amusing of you to notice that I wrote there were *Three* in the box. As a matter of fact I left out more than that—a German and his wife—for instance, entirely. Four seemed *too* many somehow. No-one would ever believe so many sat in a box and I think I decided to leave out Florence Bradley's sister . . . and it wasn't the *first* night of *Sacre* either, it was the second night. But one must only be accurate about such details in a work of fiction. The real point is that in my own consciousness I am not a bit muddled about the *facts.*[1] I think you will like my new book better—but I am afraid I shall not get over soon my "pleasing enthusiasm." We are always apparently on the way to Spain and then it never happens. Just now, Fan has made a very big hit playing Ariel in Shakespeare's "The Tempest," she is unbelievably lovely in it. I do wish you could see her, one never thought the part could be played before.[2]

You ask about John Reed. He has just published a book about the Balkans, and is writing stories mostly about Broadway *grues.*

He's just the same, leading the Washington Square life with an Irish girl, who is interested in the Irish Republic.[3]

I never see Mabel [Dodge] any more—but I meet ton frère, Leo, every now [and] again scowling in galleries at manifestations of modern artists, and *talking* but never to me. He seems to be quite certain that he doesn't like me. Why, I don't know.[4]

Muriel Draper is here. She is divorcing Paul and working in an interior decoration shop and running about with Nijinsky, who is more marvelous than ever.[5] The ballet sailed for Spain without him.

I am also unpublished—in regard to a book *not* on music—which has been ready ever so long. When it appears I have dedicated one thing to you which you said once you liked—[6]

Marsden [Hartley] gave an exhibition[7] of very *pro*-German pictures—and Lee Simonson has done some very good stagy decorations.[8] All hail to you and Miss Taklos. Fania said love—

                                                   ever—
                                                   Carlo Van Vechten.

1. See Appendix A.

2. The production was presented by the Drama Society at the Century Theatre and opened on 24 April 1916. Louis Calvert played Prospero and Walter Hampden played Caliban.

3. Reed made two trips to Europe after the declaration of war in August 1914. On the first, from August 1914 to January 1915, he visited France, England, Germany, and Belgium. On the second, from May to September 1915, he visited eastern Europe. Reed's reports to the *Metropolitan* from this second trip were published in his *The War in Eastern Europe* (New York: Scribner's, 1916).

Between November 1915 and May 1916 Reed published five short stories which were realistic slices of life in much the same style as his journalism: "The Rights of Small Nations," *New Republic* (November 27, 1915), 5:94–96; "The World Well Lost," *Masses* (February 1916), 8:5–6; "The Capitalist," *Masses* (April 1916), 8:5–6; "Broadway Night," *Masses* (May 1916), 8:19–20; and "The Head of the Family," *Metropolitan* (May 1916), vol. 46.

In December 1915 Reed returned to visit his family in Portland, Oregon. A few days after his arrival he met Louise Bryant (1885–1936) and they fell in love. When Reed returned to New York in January 1916, Bryant left her husband and followed Reed. They lived at 43 Washington Square South.

4. Van Vechten and Dodge became estranged in August 1914. Dodge could not understand why Van Vechten wanted to return to the United States after the outbreak of war. Van Vechten wanted to return to ask Fania Marinoff to marry him. Marinoff had returned earlier than Van Vechten because she had to start rehersals for a new play. It was after she had sailed that he realized he wanted to marry her.

Although they saw each other and corresponded from time to time, Van Vechten and Dodge were not reconciled until January 1927 when he visited her in Taos. This meeting did not go well and he did not see her again until he visited her in Taos in 1933. Dodge fell out with Van Vechten in 1935 because of his negative response to her *Movers and Shakers*. They were not reconciled again until 1950, when Van Vechten, who was on his way to Los Angeles, met Dodge while he was staying at the La Fonda Hotel in Santa Fe, New Mexico.

> [A] large woman plunged toward me on the sidewalk before La Fonda in Santa Fe. She embraced me heartily with the salutation, "You old fool, you!" repeated several times with considerable force, led me to her car to speak to Tony, her Indian husband, and that was the conclusion of our longest feud. (Van Vechten, *Fragments*, II, 37)

I am grateful to Bruce Kellner for his assistance in clarifying details of the relationship of Van Vechten and Mabel Dodge.

5. Shortly after their marriage in 1909, Muriel Draper (1887–1952) and her husband, the singer Paul Draper (1886–1925), settled in Florence, Italy, and met Mabel Dodge. It was Dodge who introduced the Drapers to Stein in 1911. The Drapers first met Van Vechten in the summer of 1913 when they were all guests of Dodge at her Villa Curonia. The Drapers were divorced in 1916.

6. After the publication of his book *Music after the Great War and Other Studies* (1915), Van Vechten tried to interest different publishers in a projected book of thirteen "sketches, half-story, half-essay, in the semi-fictional vein that has been worked by George Moore." The book, "Pastiches et Pistaches," was rejected by thirteen publishers. Eleven of the pieces in the book were published separately. In her letter of 4 May 1915 to Van Vechten Stein had praised one of his pieces which had appeared in *Rogue*, "How Donald Dedicated His Poem." Van Vechten intended to dedicate that to Stein. See Kellner, *A Bibliography*, p. 111, for details on "Pastiches et Pistaches."

7. There was a Hartley exhibition at Stieglitz's Little Gallery of the Photo-Secession from 4 to 22 April 1916. The pictures were all from Hartley's German military series, 1914–15.

8. Lee Simonson (1888–1967), scenic designer, painter, and art critic. Stein had met Simonson soon after he arrived to study in Paris in 1910. It was through Mabel Dodge that Van Vechten had met Simonson. Simonson designed several of the plays in the Washington Square Players season (4 October 1915 to 20 May 1916) of one-act plays presented at the Bandbox Theatre, New York. Simonson designed *The Red Cloak*, by Josephine A. Meyer and Lawrence Langner; *The Magical City*, by Zoe Akins; and *Pierre Patelin*, adapted and translated from the French by Maurice Relonde. Van Vechten may also have seen Simonson's designs for the Washington Square Players production of *The Seagull*, which was presented from 20 to 31 May 1916.

To Carl Van Vechten
[Greeting Card: 1916–1917]

[postmark: 29 December 1916]

[27 rue de Fleurus
Paris]

My dear Van,

Best wishes to you both. Haven't heard from you for years. How are you and when are you coming over.

Always yours
Gertrude Stein.

To Gertrude Stein

31 January [1917]

151 E. 19 St.
[New York]

Dear Gertrude Stein,

A very *flowery* Christmas card from you indicates that you haven't received the hundred letters I sent you. I hope you got my new book, mailed to you registered, last month. Certain parts of it may amuse you.[1]

Allen Norton has left us for Europe. Why? I don't know as I didn't see him before he sailed—but if he gets as far as Paris doubtless you'll see him. . . . There was to have been a divorce but, I believe, that was called off—when he departed.[2]

There is to be a Salon des Independentes and I am going to exhibit.[3]

Do you know Paulet Thenevaz? he paints and dances—He is here now—[4]

I'm at work on a few more books.

I'd like to see you. Fania sends her love to you and Miss Taklos.

Carlo V. V.

You know that Mr. Haweis is here?[5]

1. Van Vechten's *Music and Bad Manners* had been published on 14 November 1916.

2. Stein did not meet Norton. Norton and his wife were eventually divorced.

3. The Society of Independent Artists organized an exhibition from 10 April to 16 May 1917 at the Grand Central Palace (Lexington Avenue and Forty-sixth street), New York. Van Vechten was not a participant.

4. Paulet Thévenaz was an artist who did many decorative portraits. Thévenaz was also a member of the New York School of Dalcroze Eurhythmics.

5. See Van Vechten to Stein, 24 October 1915, note 3.

❧

To Carl Van Vechten
MS. New York Public Library, Manuscripts Division
[Rose motto]

[postmark: 23 February 1917]   27 rue de Fleurus
                                                [Paris]

My dear Van,

Thanks so much for the book, I really did enjoy it. Did you really like the Argentina. I always like what you say about me.[1] I haven't very much news. I am at present engaged in good works which includes running a little Ford into the country for the American relief committee and am enjoying it.[2] Otherwise I am working. I have done a number of plays and short things

[57]

and a long one with a title that I know would please you. Some day I want to do a volume of Spanish things, if [Robert] Coady gets publishing really I suppose he will do it.³ If you know anybody who wants to why don't hesitate to let me know. Paris is nice, looking for coal is xciting and now we have it. Do write to me and tell me all about yourself. Are you going to be a soldier.

Always yours,
Gertrude Stein.

1. In the essay "Spain and Music," Van Vechten discussed the dancer La Argentina. He also compared Stein's writing to the rhythmic qualities of Spanish dancing.

> Gertrude Stein, who has spent the last two years in Spain, has noted the rhythm of several of these dances by the mingling of her original use of words with the ingratiating medium of *vers libre*. She has succeeded, I think, better than some musicians in suggesting the intricacies of the rhythm. I should like to transcribe one of these attempts here, but I have not the right to do so as I have only seen them in manuscript, they have not yet appeared in print. These pieces are in a sense the thing itself—I shall have to fall back on description of the thing. (*Music and Bad Manners*, pp. 88–89)

2. After their return to Paris Stein and Toklas wanted to do something for the war effort and offered their services to the American Fund for French Wounded. The A.F.F.W. needed vehicles to deliver medical supplies. Stein appealed to her American relatives for aid. Eventually a Ford van was purchased and sent to Stein in Paris. Stein christened it "Auntie," after her aunt Pauline, Mrs. Solomon Stein.

3. Robert J. Coady and Michael Brenner owned the Washington Square Gallery, New York. They admired Stein's work and through Mrs. Knoblauch had secured copies of *Three Lives* to sell in their gallery (Coady to Stein, 27 April 1914, YCAL). They proposed to Stein a deluxe edition (in imitation of the Editions Galerie Kahnweiler) of her "Letters and Parcels and Wool." This idea fell through when they had difficulty securing a copyright for the work (Coady to Stein, 11 May 1916, 29 May 1916, and 30 May 1916, all YCAL). Coady and Brenner did print Stein's portrait "Mrs. Th----y," in *Soil* (December 1916), 1(1):16.

To Gertrude Stein

[5 April 1917]   151 East 19 Street
April—of a Thursday   [New York]

Dear Gertrude Stein

Almost everything is happening here . . besides our going to war.¹ Sarah Bernhardt has been operated on at the age of seventy-three and had several kidneys [i.e., kidney stones] removed . . A day or two after she sits up in bed and eats spinach, a vegetable which had been denied her for two years previously. She plans to begin another farewell tour of America in August, and is really intending to put on the whole of *L'Aiglon*[2] . . . The Romanoffs, I gather, are lucky if they get spinach. We are hoping that the Hohenzollerns will soon be in a similar predicament.

Isadora Duncan is dancing the Marseillaise and Tschaikowsky's Marche Slav, with a symbolic reference to the Russian revolution, to packed houses. People—this includes me—get on the chairs and yell . . Then Isadora comes out slightly covered by an American flag of filmy silk and awakens still more enthusiasm . . It is very exciting to see American patriotism thoroughly awakened—I tell you she drives'em mad; the recruiting stations are full of her converts—by someone who previously has not been very much interested in awaking it.[3]

Then there is the Salon des Independentes (so to speak—at least), which has already had two scandals. The first concerned the rejection by the board (which is not supposed to have the power to reject anything) of an object labelled "Fountain" and signed R. J. Mutts. This porcelain tribute was bought cold in some plumber shop (where it awaited the call to join some bath room trinity) and sent in . . When it was rejected Marcel Duchamp at once resigned from the board.[4] [Alfred] Stieglitz is exhibiting the object at "291" and he has made some wonderful photographs of it. The photographs make it look like anything from a Madonna to a Buddha. The exhibition itself is pretty tiresome but there is one picture, The Claire Twins, which you may hear of again. It will probably be bought by the Prado. It belongs in Spain.[5]

Fania has been appearing in [Frank] Wedekind's "The Awakening of Spring." At least she appeared in it once. Then the police stepped in and now all concerned are awaiting a decision from the bench of the Supreme Court.[6]

I am writing. My new book is finished, but it will not appear until fall.[7] We do want to see Paris again soon. I have a feeling that the war will last a very long time; everybody is so anxious that it should stop, but it won't. I should like to see you run a FORD. Perhaps I will yet.

all felicitations and salutations to you both from us,

Carlo V. V.

Oh yes, Valentine de Saint Point is here too . . She gave an exhibition of métachorie (gratis) at the Metropolitan Opera House, about which people are still talking. She has two boys and a monkey with her . . .[8]

Did you ever know Paulet Thevenaz? He is here too.

Ever so many are here . . . but few are chosen!

I never see Mabel [Dodge]. Does she write to you?

Mina Loy (Mrs. Haweis) has a wonderful primitive (sort of Cimabue) in the exhibition.[9]

Do write me soon . . and vibrantly!

1. The United States severed diplomatic relations with Germany on 3 February 1917. President Wilson called for a declaration of war against Germany on the evening of 2 April 1917. The Senate approved 82 to 6, the House of Representatives 373 to 50, and President Wilson signed the war resolution on 6 April.

2. Bernhardt's American tour began with a two-week engagement at the Knickerbocker Theatre on 1 September 1917. The program consisted of monologues and scenes from plays long associated with her. The final piece on the program was the sixth act of Edmond Rostand's epic verse drama, *L'Aiglon*.

3. Duncan had given a solo performance at the Metropolitan Opera House on the evening of 6 March 1917. On the afternoon of 28 March she and pupils from her school performed at the Metropolitan Opera House.

4. "Fountain" was in fact an inverted urinal, the auteur of which was Duchamp himself. It became a celebrated exemplar of the Dada movement.

5. See Van Vechten to Stein, 31 January [1917], note 4. *The Claire Twins* is a painting by Dorothy Rice.

6. On 30 March 1917 the Commissioner of Licenses, James C. Bell, saw a morning rehearsal of Frank Wedekind's play *The Awakening of Spring*. He immediately obtained a court order prohibiting performances of the play on the grounds that it would offend public decency.

The play, in a translation by Geoffrey C. Stein, was being presented under the auspices of the *Medical Review of Reviews* at the Thirty-ninth Street Theatre. Marinoff played the role of Wendla.

When Frederick H. Robinson, chairman of the producing committee, learned that Bell had obtained an order blocking performances, he and his lawyers rushed to a second judge, Justice Guy. After a brief argument in his chambers Justice Guy issued an injunction allowing one performance to take place, remarking that the performances should not have been stopped on such short notice.

On 11 April the courts decided that performances of the play would offend public decency and have "no proper place on the stage of a public theatre" and did "infinitely more harm than good." (*New York Sun*, 31 March 1917, 8 April 1917; *New York Globe*, 2 April 1917; *New York Morning Telegraph*, 12 April 1917. These clippings are in Marinoff's scrapbooks, NYPL-Lincoln Center)

7. Van Vechten's *Interpreters and Interpretations* was published in October 1917.

8. Valentine de Saint Point gave a dance recital in the Metropolitan Opera House, New York, on 3 April 1917. The performance, *Festival of Metachorie* consisted of readings by Wallace Cox of poems Valentine de Saint Point had written herself. After the reading Valentine de Saint Point danced the ideas expressed by the poem.

9. Mina Loy exhibited a painting, *Making Lampshades*.

To Gertrude Stein

[May–June 1917]

151 E. 19 Street
New York City

Chère Madame Stein,

The enclosed clipping may amuse you.[1]
You are in my new book too which I will send you in the fall.[2]
Fania has been on a short tournée and I accompanied her—[3]
and we salaam you both!

Carlo V. V.

1. The clipping cannot be identified.

2. The half-title page of each essay in Van Vechten's *Interpreters and Interpretations* contained a quotation. For his essay "Mary Garden," Van Vechten used a line from Stein's poem "Sacred Emily": "Rose is a rose is a rose is a rose." This was the first time that this line appeared in print.

3. Marinoff appeared in the role of Marie in Eugene Walter's play *The Assassin*. The play toured Poughkeepsie, New York, and New Haven and New London, Conneticut, from late May to early June 1917. Van Vechten attended the 30 May performance in Poughkeepsie (Van Vechten to Marinoff, postmark 28 May 1917, NYPL-MD).

To Carl Van Vechten
[Postcard: Birthplace of Marechal Joffre at Rivesaltes, April 1917][1]

[postmark: 18 August 1917]

[Perpignan, France][2]

My dear Van

This is a nice photo, perhaps I will send you some others by and by.

Always sincerely yours
Gtrde Stein.

[61]

1. Stein had postcards made from a photograph of herself and Toklas standing by their Ford van outside the house of Marechal Joffre. Joffre had been one of the architects of the French victory at the Battle of the Marne.

2. On 18 March 1917 Stein and Toklas had driven their supply van from Paris to Perpignan. They then returned to Paris and later opened a distribution center for the American Fund for French Wounded in Nîmes.

The most detailed account of Stein and Toklas' activities for the next two years can be found in the *Weekly Bulletin*, published by the A.F.F.W. Toklas wrote weekly reports to the Paris office, and many of these were used in the one-sheet (two-sided) *Weekly Bulletin*.

To Carl Van Vechten
MS. New York Public Library, Manuscripts Division

[postmark: 24 March 1918]   Hotel du Luxembourg
                                         Paris, France[1]

My dear Van,

You have been neglected but not forgotten neither am I. Thanks so much for the book.[2] I liked it a whole lot. I like the book and then I always like me in it. I always want to know at once, Am I in it. And very nicely I am always in it. We saw a picture of Fania in Vogue. She looked very nice.[3] Are you coming over this summer. It would be nice to see you both again. We are most active these days and in between I make little poems. I make very nice little poems perhaps I will make you one for your next book. Mabel Dodge is or is not Mrs. Sterne not that it very much matters.[4] What is the news.

Always yours
Gertrude Stein.

1. Stein wrote the return address "Hotel du Luxembourg, Paris" on the letter paper. She should have written Nîmes instead of Paris.

2. Van Vechten's *Interpreters and Interpretations*. See Van Vechten to Stein [May–June 1917], note 2.

3. *Vogue*, 15 February 1918, p. 52, published a photograph of Marinoff by Charlotte Fairchild. The photograph showed Marinoff in the role of Karen Borneman from *Karen*, a play by

the Danish writer Hjalmar Bergström, which opened at the Greenwich Village Theatre on 8 January 1918.

4. Mabel Dodge married Maurice Sterne on 18 August 1917.

To Carl Van Vechten
[Postcard: HANSI.—Saverne. (D'après l'estampe) Lt von Forstner back from schopping (after the drawing)]

[postmark: 4 March 1919]   [Mulhouse, France][1]

My dear Van,

How goes it. Am looking forward to seeing you again one of these days. We are enjoying Alsace. It's almost too story-book to write about and besides we're busy but will write just the same

Gtrde Stein

1. In November 1918, shortly after the armistice was declared, Stein and Toklas returned to Paris from Nîmes. In late February or early March 1919 they left Paris to open an A.F.F.W. station from which to supply the devastated country in the Vosges district of France. They opened their depot in Mulhouse and remained in that area until late May 1919, when they returned to Paris.

To Gertrude Stein

7 April 1919   151 East 19 Street
                                                        New York City

Dear Gertrude Stein,

You do pop around so—the latest card seems to come from Alsace—and one before that came from Spain, I think—or was it Norway? Will 27 Rue de Fleurus still reach you? You do not say and I am sending this to find out . . . you are just like a page or two in one of my new books, and you shall have one as soon as I discover where you can be surely reached.

Many very interesting things have happened. I do hope we can all meet again for a *Conference* . . Nothing like the one now going on in Paris,[1] of course—we want—we hope—to go to Spain. I have a feeling that I'll never go anywhere else after.

Fania sends her love to both of you—and so do I.

Carlo V. V.

1. The Versailles Peace Conference had begun on 7 January 1919.

To Gertrude Stein

12 September 1921[1]   151 East Nineteenth Street
                                                  New York City

Dear Gertrude Stein,

May I introduce you to the picturesque & amusing Lochers (Monsieur et Madame), who can, and *will*, tell you everything about everybody? Look forward to a delightful afternoon with them—I think they are almost sailing for Paris for the pleasure of meeting *you*.[2]

Sincerely,
Carl Van Vechten

1. There is no explanation for the break in correspondence between Van Vechten's letter to Stein of 7 April 1919 and this letter. Nor can I find an explanation for the break between this letter and the next letter from Stein of 2 June 1922. Stein had returned to Paris in May 1919. In a letter to Harry Phelan Gibb (postmark 23 December 1921, YCAL) Stein would write that "I was laid up more or less for a month." There is no further explanation of this illness. It may be that Stein was ill although there are no other references to an illness. It is also possible that a number of letters from this period have been lost.

2. Robert and Beatrice Locher. Robert Locher (1889–1956) was a well-known stage-set and costume designer and interior decorator. His illustrations appeared in *Rogue*, *Vanity Fair*, and

V*ogue,* among other magazines. An illustration by Locher was used on the dust jacket and as a frontispiece for Van Vechten's *The Blind Bow-Boy.*

To Carl Van Vechten
MS. New York Public Library, Manuscripts Divison
[Rose motto]

[postmark: 2 June 1922]   27 rue de Fleurus
                                                                  [Paris]

My dear Van,

"Am I in it" there is one certainly one could never be more pleasantly more faithfully nor more gently in it than when one is put in it by you.[1] I am awfully pleased with your book. You are indeed the most modern the least sentimental and the most gently persistent of romantics. I like the romantic and so does every one else to whom I have loaned your book. I have been hearing a lot of you from the Lochers, Baron de Meyer etc.[2] Mabel Dodge was funny. She was afraid I would miss the book so she sent me a copy. Anyway we all like it. Do write once in a while if you won't come over. Best to Fania

Always
Gertrude Stein.

1. Van Vechten's novel *Peter Whiffle: His Life and Works* included two mentions of Stein. Van Vechten, who is a character in his own novel, mentions "I met the Steins" (p. 59) after a list of things Americans do when they go to Paris. In describing Edith Dale's villa near Florence (Dale is a character based in part on Mabel Dodge), the story of Stein's composition of the *Portrait of Mabel Dodge at the Villa Curonia* is recounted (pp. 121–22).

2. Baron Adolphe de Meyer (1868–1949), a photographer who worked for *Vogue* and *Harper's Bazaar.*

❦

To Gertrude Stein
[3" × 5" blue index card]

23 June [1922]
151 E 19 St.
N.Y.C.

Loved your piece in *Broom!*[1]
Thanks for your letter—
Peter in *fourth* edition—out two months—[2]

Carlo V. V.

1. *Broom* printed Stein's "If You Had Three Husbands" in three parts: (January 1922), 1(3):211–15; (April 1922), 2(1):74–77; and (June 1922), 2(3):242–46.

2. Van Vechten means a fourth printing, which was issued in late June 1922.

❦

To Gertrude Stein

22 February 1923
The Colonial Inn
Fairhope, Alabama[1]

Dear Gertrude,

The book is lovely, and I thank you. I adored the *Nations & Marcel* & one or two of the plays are too divine. *Me* especially I like, but I had seen that before. How nice, nevertheless, to be in a big book by Gertrude Stein.[2] But I *always* put you in my books. You are in the next one, The Blind Bow-Boy, which comes out next August when I shall send you a copy.[3] Mabel [Dodge] will not like this book. She is not in it. What has become of *The Family?* I want to show the mss. to my publisher. It has occurred to me that the time is getting ripe for its publication now that you are a classic & have Imitators & DISCIPLES! Please do something about this![4]

You probably have seen Avery [Hopwood] and I am sending you one or two others later. Have you read Ronald Firbank? You should. His last one, The Flower beneath the Foot published by Grant Richards in London

[66]

will do. I am sending him your book to Bordighera. He will love it.[5]

I am sending you a (bad) photograph of Florine Stettheimer's new portrait of me. Perhaps you can tell something even without the colour. She has also done Marcel [Duchamp]. Get him to get you a photograph of it.[6] I wish we could see you again. Fania & I send all salutations to you & Miss Taklos.

By the time this letter reaches you I will be back in New York again.

> *Tout coeur,*
> *Carl Van Vechten*
> *151 E. 19 St., N.Y.C.*

1. Van Vechten was in Alabama visiting his father. "I find my aged father installed in a single-tax—Theosophist—socialist community, where I fit very nicely. You know I always did like serious thinkers" (Van Vechten to Arthur Davison Ficke, 22 February 1923, YCAL).

2. Stein's *Geography and Plays*. This collection of Stein's work contained fifty-three selections and included works written between circa 1908–9 and 1921. The reference to "Nations" may be to either "Land of Nations. [Subtitle: And Ask Asia]" (pp. 407–8) or "The Psychology of Nations or What Are You Looking At" (pp. 416–19). "Marcel" is "Next. Life and Letters of Marcel Duchamp" (pp. 405–6). The book also included Stein's "One Carl Van Vechten" (pp. 199–200).

3. Van Vechten put a reference to Stein in the novel on page 211: "Campaspe made an attempt to define her impression of the work of Gertrude Stein. She uses words, thought Campaspe, for their detonations and their connotations." Van Vechten is quoting the phrase he himself had written and had quoted to Stein in his letter of 26 November 1914.

4. As early as 1909 (the final draft of the novel was not completed until October 1911), Stein had sent sections of *The Making of Americans* (known then as "The History of a Family") to friends in America. In 1912 she had arranged for all parts of the novel that were in the United States to be sent to her friend Mrs. Knoblauch, who was trying to interest a publisher in the novel. After several unsuccessful attempts Mrs. Knoblauch returned the volumes of typescript, minus one volume which had been mislaid, to Stein. The war and its aftermath put an end to any plans to publish the novel. For the history of the publication of *The Making of Americans* see Donald Gallup, "The Making of *The Making of Americans*," in Stein's *Fernhurst, Q.E.D, and Other Early Writings*, pp. 173–214.

5. Van Vechten had first heard of Ronald Firbank (1886–1926), the English novelist, in early 1922. After reading his work Van Vechten became an enthusiastic admirer of Firbank. Although Van Vechten made several attempts to have Firbank and Stein meet, there is no record that they ever did. At this time Firbank was staying in Bordighera, a resort on the Italian Riviera.

6. Van Vechten had met Florine Stettheimer in 1916. He was introduced to her and her sisters Carrie and Ettie by Avery Hopwood, who had met them in Germany a few years before the war. Stettheimer's *Portrait of Carl Van Vechten*, 1922, oil on canvas, 28 × 26 inches, is now in YCAL. Stettheimer's *Portrait of Marcel Duchamp*, 1923, oil on canvas, 30 × 26 inches, is now in the collection of Virgil Thomson.

❧

To Gertrude Stein
[Postcard: "The Bay thru the Pines"—Fairhope, Alabama]

23 February [1923]   [The Colonial Inn
                                       Fairhope, Alabama]

Counting her Dresses is *Kolossal!* I am going to produce it as soon as I get back to New York.[1]

Who is Polybe?[2]

C. V. V.

1. *Counting Her Dresses, A Play,* in Stein's *Geography and Plays,* pp. 275–85.

2. See Stein to Van Vechten [20 March 1923] and [31 May 1923]. Polybe appears in a number of pieces published in Stein's *Geography and Plays,* including "A Collection, My Dear Miss Carey: A Story" (pp. 23–26), *Turkey and Bones and Eating and We Liked It, A Play* (pp. 239–53), "Every Afternoon, A Dialogue" (pp. 254–59), and *Captain Walter Arnold, A Play* (pp. 260–61). See also Stein's letter to Van Vechten, postmark 31 May 1923, where she explains about Polybe: a dog she had while living in Mallorca.

❧

To Carl Van Vechten

[postmark: 15 March 1923]   27 rue de Fleurus
                                              [Paris]

My dear Van

I was awfully pleased and touched by your pleasure in my book. It is very nice liking each other and liking each other's books. And the idea of getting the Family published that delights me more than I can say. It's a long book 2428 pages of typewriting 19 lines to the page. There is none of it in America now xcept loose sheets. I could send you what you liked to see of it, but as it is the only copy I have xcept the ms. I think I would like to send it a piece at a time to you. What do you think, should I send you the beginning and you show that and if they want more send the rest. Tell me just what you want me to do about sending it to you.

[68]

We have been seeing a good deal of Avery [Hopwood], I like him very much, there was a time in between when he seemed to have lost some of his charm but this time it has come back mellowed and increased.

It's nice being back in Paris. I do wish we could see you and Fania over here one of these days. Do you ever see Mabel [Dodge] any more or is she completely mired in D. [H.] Lawrence, who it seems does not want to put her in a book, Totems not being really interesting.[1] There really isn't much news over here xcept that the weather is rotten. I am working a lot, some more plays and some religions that are very good and now for elucidation.[2] Thanks and thanks again for all your kind thoughts and may they as always bear fruit.

Love to you both
Gertrude.

1. After reading D. H. Lawrence's (1885–1930) *Sea and Sardinia* in 1921, Mabel Dodge wrote to Lawrence and asked him to come to Taos, New Mexico. Dodge hoped that Lawrence's descriptive powers would be employed on the Taos country and the Indians. After a great deal of hesitation Lawrence and his wife, Frieda, arrived in Taos on 11 September 1922. Almost at once Lawrence proposed that he and Dodge collaborate on a novel about her life. He went so far as to propose an outline of the work (see Moore, *The Collected Letters of D. H. Lawrence*, II, 724). The idea of a collaboration was blocked by Frieda Lawrence when she realized that Dodge was seducing Lawrence. In December 1922 Lawrence left the adobe house that Dodge had lent him and went to live on a ranch about twenty miles from Taos. In March 1923 the Lawrences left to visit Mexico. Lawrence spent a little more than half of the years from September 1922 to September 1925 living in Taos.

2. The "religions" referred to is Stein's "Lend A Hand. Four Religions." The word elucidation refers to Stein's "An Elucidation," first printed in *transition* (April 1927), 1:64–78.

To Carl Van Vechten
[Rose motto]

[postmark: 20 March 1923]   27 rue de Fleurus
                                                          [Paris]

My dear Van,

I am sending you the first volume of the family and a little later I will send the second and the third and after that I won't send any more until

I hear from you. There are eight in all but they aren't all as long as the first and the second.

Thanks for the photo of the portrait, how big is it, I mean the portrait. I liked it but I liked the still lives particularly the curtains almost better than I liked you, the curtains are very feeling full.[1] Do you look like that now Van. You see I made you larger in size didn't I, I kind of think of you larger as to size.

Do you really think you will produce me. That would be nice as Mohammed said about street cars in Tangiers. You will be amused to know that I did a play my version of one of Avery [Hopwood]'s which he loaned me, he was I think puzzled and intrigued, he has gone off with his mother to Monte Carlo. I am looking forward to seeing him again.[2]

They I don't mean Avery and his mother took us to see Raquel Meller, she displayed herself beautifully in the first song, really standing so straight she might have fallen backwards, but after that alas she became too xpository although she has a delicately trained voice and is not xciting.[3]

What else is there, lots of pink hyacinths they do smell good.

Love to yourself and Fania
Gertrude

Oh Polybe was a Mallorcan hound who went crazy in the moonlight and I had to whisper in his ear and spell his name to him.

G.

1. Stettheimer's *Portrait of Carl Van Vechten*, 28 × 26 inches. In the "upper left are allusions to the sitters interests and affections: a café in Paris, the marquee of a theatre with the name of his wife, Fania Marinoff. Above, a figure in white represents Carl Van Vechten as a cook, with the *cordon-bleu*. A piano indicates his activity as a music critic. Upper right: the actress' dressing table with a Japanese print and a No mask of Fania Marinoff" (McBride, *Florine Stettheimer*, p. 28). In the portrait Van Vechten is seated, and behind him are four black curtains.

2. See Van Vechten to Stein, 16 April 1923, note 1.

3. Raquel Meller was a Spanish-born singer who won international acclaim with the songs "La Violetera" and "El Relicario."

❧

To Gertrude Stein

30 March 1923   151 East Nineteenth Street
                                 New York City

Dear Gertrude Stein,

There is an eruption in Taos but no one seems quite sure *what* has happened.[1] You write that Mabel [Dodge] is angry because [D. H.] Lawrence won't put her in a book. She wrote to Leo [Stein] that Mrs. Lawrence was angry because they started to write a book together. Bobby Jones says that Mabel has written a Portrait Intime of Lawrence,[2] and Mabel herself writes me: "The village doctor came in the other day and told me that they are mooching about the Plaza that Lawrence has written a terrible book about me and Taos—that he ricochetted off me up to the mountain and sat down and wrote it with memory fresh. And that an old timer here—a painter named Phillips said to Bill Hawk, Lawrence's landlord,[3] that he was to take a message up to him—that if he had written a wicked book about an American woman whose hospitality he had accepted and taken advantage of that a selected bunch from Taos would proceed up the mountain and horsewhip him! The doctor says that's why Lawrence is going to Mexico on Monday. Well! Selzer has the book! Do you know him? If so do find out about it! I may say I am petrified for D.H. is absolutely a 'mal hombre' as they say here and would do the worst. Completely unreliable and unprincipled. He has tried to destroy every friend he ever had—in his books. That is his aim. I remember his saying in a rage one day, 'Mabel, I will destroy you too!' I didn't think much about it since but probably that's what he has spent his winter on! Ora pro nobis!!!"

There is a long paper about *you* by Kenneth Burke in the April Dial.[4] About the Family I would suggest that you send me registered enough to make the first volume and tell me how many more volumes there would be. I can't promise anything except that Knopf shall see it recommended. He may be afraid of so long a book. I don't know. I only know that I want to show it to him. Hope, therefore, nothing for the present.

The Blind Bow-Boy comes out in August and I have started a new one. Peter Whiffle has just appeared in London and is getting marvellous notices.[5]

[71]

I'm glad you like Avery [Hopwood]. I'm very fond of him. And I'm going to send you more soon. All and sundry ask me for letters to you, but I try only to send the amusing ones.

Love to you both,
Carlo Van Vechten

Did you get my picture?

1. The Lawrences had left for Mexico. Van Vechten quotes from Dodge's letter to him, 16 March [1923], YCAL.

2. Dodge's account of her relationship with D. H. Lawrence is in her *Lorenzo in Taos* (New York: Alfred A. Knopf, 1932).

3. Phillips cannot be identified. William Hawk owned the Del Monte ranch at Questa, New Mexico, which Lawrence had rented when he left Taos. Thomas Seltzer (1873–1943) was Lawrence's principal American publisher in the 1920s.

4. Burke's review of Stein's *Geography and Plays*, "Engineering with Words," *Dial* (April 1923), 74:408–12.

5. *The Blind Bow-Boy* was published by Knopf on 15 August 1923. Van Vechten's *Peter Whiffle: His Life and Works* (London: Grant Richards, Ltd., 1923).

To Carl Van Vechten

[postmark: 8 April 1923]   27 rue de Fleurus
                                                      [Paris]

My dear Van,

I do like mooching around the Plaza. It seems to be a case of "Yes" said Bill or words to that effect. Anyhow [D.H.] Lawrence seems to have left, do you think he will find Mexico calmer or just safer. It will be awful if Mabel [Dodge] has gotten back a taste for white man.

I was awfully pleased about Peter Whiffle's success in England. It deserves [it] alright, it's a mighty nice book. I have sent you the first three volumes of the Family, each one separately, do let me know if they get there, perhaps he might like the third volume first and perhaps he mightn't. Perhaps he might like the first volume first. Anyway I won't xpect but just hope.

[72]

Send along any one you like. You always send nice ones, Avery [Hopwood]
& the Lochers. By the way what has become of the Lochers. I had a charming card from them at Christmas without an address,

> *Lots of love to you both*
> *Gertrude*

To Gertrude Stein

16 April 1923   151 East Nineteenth Street
                                                     New York City

Dear Gertrude,

Three volumes have arrived. Please don't send any more until you
hear from me. When Mary Knoblauch had the set I read a little in the first
volume but now I have read it *through* and my feeling is that you have done
a very big thing, probably as big as, perhaps bigger than James Joyce, Marcel
Proust, or Dorothy Richardson. [Alfred] Knopf won't be back until the middle of May. I don't know what he'll make of it. You see the thing is so long
that it will be hellishly expensive to publish, and can one expect much of a
sale? I mean, to the average reader, the book will probably be *work*. I think
even the average reader will enjoy it, however, once he begins to get the
rhythm, that is so important. To me, now, it is a little like the Book of Gen-
esis. There is something Biblical about you, Gertrude. Certainly there is
something Biblical about you . . I liked the passages about fat people, and
washing, and religion, and old man Hersland certainly emerges complete
from this first volume.

There is another thing, the type is so dim in this copy, and there are
so many errors in spelling, etc. that it is much harder reading than it would
be in print. I shall explain these things to Knopf. I wonder what he will
make of it? Hope for nothing until we find out. I am sure, however, that, if
not now, sooner or later this book will be published.

The portrait is not very big . . . and I am thinner now. The colour
is important. The picture is more about me than of me. You are right about
the curtains; they are a stroke of genius in the picture.

I am also interested in what you say of Raquel Meller. I have heard so much about her, and she is coming to America in a year or so. So many people come to America after they have tired Europe of themselves, but you and I *started* in America. And that is more important for America than Raquel Meller and the Russian Ballet are important for America.

Which of Avery [Hopwood]'s plays did you rearrange? Was it the Gold-Diggers or The Demi-Virgin? I am crazy to see it![1]

Marinoff and I send our love to you and
Miss Taklos,

Carlo Van Vechten

1. Stein had read Hopwood's *Our Little Wife,* a play first produced in New York at the Harris Theatre on 18 November 1916.

❧

To Gertrude Stein

3 May 1923   151 East 19 St.
New York City

Dear Gertrude—

I think I wrote you that all three volumes are here. I asked Edna Kenton to read them & she is as enthusiastic as I am—well, we'll see about what [Alfred] Knopf says.[1] He arrives next week. Edmund Wilson, Jr. of Vanity Fair came down the other night to inspect my Stein collection. He is writing a paper about you for Vanity Fair.[2] I told you about Kenneth Burke's review in The Dial for April. Then I am writing one about you for the Tribune. That I will send you later . . By the way, if you are sending that play after Avery [Hopwood]'s—Vanity Fair may want it. Can I let them have it?— Please don't be annoyed by the list I have put you in for the International Book Review—they couldn't all be *Three Lives!*[3] I sent you one clipping about Mabel [Dodge] & here's another! She hasn't written me a word about the new situation—if it can be regarded as new.

All salutations,
Carlo Van Vechten.

[74]

1. Van Vechten first met Kenton (1876–1954) while he was a student at the University of Chicago. Kenton was a novelist, short story writer, and journalist. She was also a leading figure in the feminist movement.

2. Van Vechten's review of Stein's *Geography and Plays*, "Medals for Miss Stein," appeared in the *New York Tribune*, 13 May 1923, Pt. 9, p. 20. Edmund Wilson (1895–1972) reviewed Stein's *Geography and Plays* in *Vanity Fair* (June 1923), 20(4):18. On the verso of Wilson's letter to Stein, 6 June 1923 (see Stein to Van Vechten [6 July 1923], note 3) Stein drafted a reply thanking Wilson for his review. See Stein to Wilson, postmark 2 July 1923 (YCAL) for the letter she sent.

3. In the *Literary Digest International Book Review*, (May 1923), 1(6): [7], Van Vechten, along with nine other writers, listed the ten most important books published since 1900. Van Vechten's list contained Stein's *Three Lives* as well as Proust's *À la Recherche du Temps Perdu*, George Moore's *Hail and Farewell*, Arthur Machen's *The Hill of Dreams*, Henry Handel Richardson's *Maurice Guest*, Max Beerbohm's *Seven Men*, Joseph Hergesheimer's *San Christobal de la Habana*, James Branch Cabell's *The Cream of the Jest*, Hugh Walpole's *The Cathedral*, and Sinclair Lewis' *Babbitt*. Van Vechten indicated that Arnold Bennett's *The Old Wives' Tale*, Henry James's *The Golden Bowl*, and Samuel Butler's *The Way of All Flesh* would certainly appear on another list. He also regretted that he did not have room to include Ronald Firbank's *Valmouth*.

To Gertrude Stein

3 May 1923   [151 East 19th Street
                                                           New York]

Dear Gertrude Stein,

    This note will introduce you to the extremely agreeable Madeleine Boyd, who will doubtless amuse you with some account of life on East 19 Street.[1]

Ever,
Carl Van Vechten

1. The French-born wife of the writer and editor Ernest Boyd. The Boyds were the Van Vechtens' neighbors in 151 East Nineteenth Street. Mrs. Boyd did translations of books into French.

To Carl Van Vechten

[postmark: ? May 1923]   27 rue de Fleurus
                                                          [Paris]

My dear Van

What has happened to Avery [Hopwood] the last I heard was a pleasant postal from Monte Carlo the beginning of April saying that he would be back here and seeing us soon since then not a word. If he were not such a serious person one might be worried.[1] I am inclosing the thing inspired by him and I hope you will like it and I would be very glad to have Vanity Fair do it.[2] I hope Avery is alright, have you heard from him. And Van what were Mabel [Dodge]'s business reasons, Mina Loy suggested that Mabel was marrying for John [Evans]'s sake or is it to show the end of an epoch.[3] I had a tender postal from Mabel just before the event but the event was not mentioned, I am rather xpecting to see her soon aren't you.[4]

Thanks more than thanks for making me a list, I love to be a list one does doesn't one. I am awfully glad you like the Family, it was so long ago I was almost afraid to reread it. What is Edna Kenton like. The Dial review was a very good send off although one does get a bit mixed in it.

Paris is very lively just now but mostly with balloon ascensions and fairs at San Sulpice (ancient) and the Invalides (mechanical) and 5000 Americans weekly.

The salons are mutually destructive, the independent is dying and its death is destroying the old salon. There is no more artistes francais, new ones are springing up all claiming to be unique but nobody believes them. The logic of the french triumphs. If you can't epater the bourgeois you can't rebel and if you can't rebel you can't have tradition and so it tumbles together. Perhaps America well yes perhaps America. That's us

Lots of love
Gertrude.

1. Hopwood to Stein, undated postcard, YCAL.

2. Stein's play *A List* was inspired by Hopwood's play *Our Little Wife*.

3. Dodge married Antonio Lujan (later changed to Luhan), a full-blooded Pueblo Indian, after he divorced his Indian wife. The marriage ceremony took place 16 April 1923 and was performed privately by an Episcopal minister at Taos.

John Evans was Dodge's son by her first marriage, to Karl Evans. John Evans was at this time twenty-one years old. In December 1922 he had married Alice Corbin, the daughter of the poet Alice Corbin.

4. Dodge to Stein, postcard 10 March [1923], YCAL.

To Gertrude Stein

14 May 1923

151 East 19 Street
New York City

Dear Gertrude,

Enclosed two more clippings—which may interest you.[1] Not a word yet from Mabel [Dodge]—It seems, however, that it is the Indian custom to take the wife's name. He is now Antonio Sterne. [Alfred] Knopf is back & has the first three volumes of The Making of Americans, warmly recommended. I'll let you know when I hear any news.

love,
Carl Van Vechten

1. Van Vechten sent Stein a number of articles that had appeared after the marriage of Dodge to Antonio Luhan. Among the articles he sent her were ones that had appeared in the *New York World*, 28 April 1923, p. 1; the *New York World*, 29 April 1923, p. 3; and the *New York Sunday News*, 6 May 1923, p. 4.

To Carl Van Vechten
[Rose motto]

[postmark: 31 May 1923]

27 rue de Fleurus
[Paris]

My dear Van,

It would take an awful lot more than the perfect letter writer to tell you how much I liked your thing on me. It did just what I have always wanted to be done that it should be said that they all would like it if they just would like it, and you did tell them.[1] I have just received a letter from Madeleine Boyd inclosing one from you. I will be seeing her soon. Jane Heap turned up distracted but sensible, very sensible and gave us news of you, and I liked hearing all about you and how you are.[2] Lots of funny things happen in Paris. She also said that [Andrew] Dasburg[3] said that Antonio [Luhan] deserted Mabel [Dodge] two days after the wedding, that might account for one's not hearing from her but it does not sound very likely does it. Business reasons are business reasons.[4] Oh I always forget to tell you who Polybe was. Polybe was a Spanish hound the kind you have especially in Mallorca a red and brown stripe, whom I named after Salomon Reinach who signed himself Polybe in the Figaro. It was a good name wasn't it, and Polybe was a good Mallorcan, bon accueil à tout le monde et fidéle à personne, Mallorca was a nice place though we dream of going there again some day, but alas the xchange, it's just as easy to go to America. I mean just as cheap. In the meanwhile we are staying here and will be for some time yet. It would be nice to see you.

> *Lots of love and to Fania*
> *Gertrude.*

1. A reference to Van Vechten's review of Stein's *Geography and Plays*. See Van Vechten to Stein, 3 May 1923, note 2.

2. Jane Heap and Margaret Anderson had founded *The Little Review* in Chicago, Illinois, in 1914. They moved it to New York and finally to Paris.

3. Andrew Dasburg was born in Paris in 1887. He came to the United States as a small child. He studied painting at the Art Student's League under Kenyon Cox. His first exhibition in New York was in 1911. Dasburg was a close friend of Dodge's and had gone to live in Taos.

4. In one of the articles Van Vechten had sent Stein about Dodge's marriage, Dodge was quoted as saying that "business considerations" had partly determined her act, although she said she was very much in love with Luhan (*New York World*, 28 April 1923, p. 1). Dodge never explained what she meant by "business considerations."

❦

To Gertrude Stein

5 June 1923   151 East Nineteenth Street
                                               New York City

Dear Gertrude,

[Edmund] Wilson, the young man on Vanity Fair says A List is too long and wants to cut it. He seeks my permission but I have written him that I have no power of attorney and that he must communicate with you. He adores the whole thing, but says that the mechanics of V. F. prohibit publishing manuscripts of that length.

There is no news as yet about your Americans, and no further news from Mabel [Dodge], unless I might confide to you that it was the United States government, no less, that drove her to this step. But marriage, with Mabel, is but a springboard to the higher life.

I'll be sending you my new book in about a month. I have just finished the first draught of a new one, to be published next year.[1]

I do not know what has happened to Avery [Hopwood], except that he wrote me that now that Mabel had married an Indian he saw no reason for returning to New York before June.

On your note, I conclude: "Perhaps America, well yes, perhaps America! That's *us!*"

love to you and Miss Taklos,

Carlo V. V.

1. Van Vechten's *The Blind Bow-Boy* was published 15 August 1923. The "new one" was *The Tattooed Countess*, published by Knopf on 15 August 1924.

❧

To Carl Van Vechten

[postmark: 6 July 1923]   27 rue de Fleurus
                                                            [Paris]

My dear Van,

Thanks for the clippings of Mabel [Dodge]. [Henry] McBride[1] has just turned up and xplained some more and now some American unknown has feverishly written to ask me if they can buy Mabel's villa in Florence. I have solemnly replied that it is Edwin [Dodge]'s not Mabel's, it is isn't it at least it was. Do tell me more. It was nice hearing about you from McBride he seems very well and happy and says you are the same, you ought to be you are a mixture of best seller and matinée hero, the American blushes and trembles when it asks Alice if I know you.

What's the news beside the heat wave, it has struck us at last. How about [Alfred] Knopf I have lots of things to ask if he won't, but mightn't he do a volume at a time, it would be so much better than a volume of Portraits and Prayers but I have such a volume even including the background of a detective story.[2]

I wrote [Edmund] Wilson that I was sorry but I didn't want the List cut, he did a very nice little review in V[anity]. F[air]. didn't he quite charming and intelligent you filled him up nicely.[3]

We have just been having a great time with the fete at Versailles, for the benefit of the Palace, Juan Gris did the decor and the Russian ballet the rest, it was a typical french fete Juan Gris the Spaniard did the decor, de Diaghileff a Russian the ballet and [Gabriel] Astruc an Austrian Jew organised it, and the audience was mostly American as it ran to a 1000 francs per, we saw it unofficially that is the decor and it was charming it was funny seeing Louis XIV bedroom filled with Russian ballet arms and legs, [name?] said she never never xpected to undress in Louis XIV bedroom, but she did. It made the palace quite nice, they even put in electricity,[4]

Always yours
Gertrude.

1. Henry McBride (1867–1962) was an art critic who had met Stein in 1913. The Stein-McBride correspondence is in YCAL.

[80]

2. Stein here refers to her habit of making lists of titles for projected volumes. She made numerous different lists for a volume to be entitled "Portraits and Prayers." When *Portraits and Prayers* was published by Random House in 1934, the piece of which Stein speaks here, "Subject-cases: The Background of a Detective Story," was not included. It was published posthumously in Stein's *As Fine As Melanctha*.

3. Wilson wrote to Stein (6 June 1923, YCAL) that he had received from Van Vechten "your Avery Hopwood thing." Wilson wanted to publish it in *Vanity Fair*, but he found it too long and asked Stein if she would be willing to have it cut. Stein replied to Wilson on 20 June 1923, (YCAL): "I am awfully sorry not to be able to consent to your cutting 'The List' [i.e., *A List*], but the quality of it is in the way it fills itself out and so I must say no. The play Avery Hopwood gave me to read, and that I played with was 'Our Little Wife.' I tried to translate its liveliness into this liveliness that is the connection."

There are many conceivable parallels between the Stein and Hopwood plays. Stein, who in her compositions often played with the moving around of partners and identities, may have responded to Hopwood's farce with its wife-swapping as part of the plot. Hopwood's play also employs the use of baby-talk names for characters. Baby-talk names were also part of the intimate life of Stein and Toklas.

4. A "Fête Merveilleuse" was organized by Gabriel Astruc and Serge Diaghilev on 30 June 1923 at the Palace of Versailles. The fête was to raise funds and draw attention to the need for the restoration of the palace. Diaghilev employed Juan Gris to build a stage in the Salle des Glaces and to design some of the costumes. The evening included performances by the Comédie Française and members of Diaghilev's Russian ballet.

To Gertrude Stein

23 July 1923   151 East Nineteenth Street
                                                        New York City

Dear Gertrude,

I am returning A List, which I found very hearty and pleasant.[1] You will have heard from [Edmund] Wilson. He couldn't, it seems, publish it without cuts, and you were quite right not to want it cut. About The Making of Americans I have not heard a word . . and I am not asking questions. Knopf is doubtless still considering it. But I think it would be impossible (considering its form) to do one volume at a time. Edna Kenton agrees with me about this.

Who is Kate Buss? A mss. in which your name frequently recurs by her is going around town, seeking a publisher.[2]

About August first, two weeks before the publication date, I will send

you my new book. The first edition was oversold a week ago, and the second
is on the press. It is about America.[3]

Not a word from Mabel [Dodge] . . . but some one told me that her
estates in New Mexico are offered for lease.

bien à vous,
Carl Van Vechten

1. Wilson had returned *A List* to Van Vechten (Wilson to Van Vechten, 6 July 1923, YCAL).

2. Buss (d. 1943) was an American journalist and writer who had met Stein in 1921 through
Elmer Harden, an American living in France. It was Buss who arranged for the publication of
Geography and Plays and who tried to place other Stein manuscripts. In a letter to Van
Vechten (22 December [1923], NYPL-MD) Buss wrote: "I am writing a book of people in Paris—
I quote from you in it." In her correspondence to Stein (YCAL) Buss mentions that she is
writing a book about Stein. This may be the same book mentioned to Van Vechten or it may
be a different book. Neither book was published and the manuscripts, if they have survived,
cannot be located. Buss did write a number of articles about Stein and her works.

3. Van Vechten's second novel was orginally titled "Daniel Matthews' Tutor." In the second
draft the title was changed to *The Blind Bow-Boy*, a reference to a masked statue of Eros in the
heroine's garden. Word about Van Vechten's "modern *Satyricon*" had been circulating in New
York, and the original trade edition of 3,500 copies was sold out even before the book was
released on August 15. The book went through five printings by October 1923.

To Carl Van Vechten
[Rose motto]

[postmark: 5 August 1923]   27 rue de Fleurus
                                                                [Paris]

My dear Van,

Bully for the boy, I am awfully pleased in your success. It's just the
age it should come. I am looking forward to seeing it. I'll have to do another
portrait of you, the twenty years after effect.[1] We are still in Paris which
really is very pleasant just now and won't be leaving until the end of the
month. You'll be seeing Henry McBride perhaps, he had a very good time
here with us all, surely you and Fania will be coming along, perhaps next
winter while we are still in the South, that would be nice but just at present

[82]

Stein to Van Vechten, postmark 5 August 1923.

27 RUE DE FLEURUS

Buss is from Medford, Mass.
She is the one who arranged
for Geography & Plays for
me, she is a newspaper
woman, writing at that
time for the Transcript
and Philadelphia Ledger.
I knew her though Harden
who also comes from Medford
and who is a friend of the
Lockes. Both Harden
and Kate Buss are
rather strange products
of New England xcepting
that New England inevitably
produces strange products
Not without interest. We

I am not impatient about
Knopf, I do want the
Log book done and I'd
rather have Knopf than
anybody do it. I like
the way he gets up
his books. When he
doesn't make up his
mind does he make up
his mind. Anyway accidentally
one can wear something
inside out and that's always
good luck. Not a word
from Mabel at all. For
the poor Indian.

Lots of love and good wishes
Gertrude.

Knopf was considering the
publication of the works of
Americans. But eventually
decided against it.
CVV. Jan 18. '41

you are not thinking of the future. Oh Kate Buss is from Medford, Mass. She is the one who arranged for Geography & Plays for me, she is a newspaper woman, writing at that time for the Transcript and Philadelphia Ledger. I knew her through [Elmer] Harden who also comes from Medford and who is a friend of the Lochers.[2] Both Harden and Kate Buss are rather strange products of New England xcepting that New England inevitably produces strange products. Not without interest. No I am not impatient about [Alfred] Knopf, I do want the Long book done and I'd rather have Knopf than anybody do it. I like the way he gets up his books. When he doesn't make up his mind does he make up his mind.[3] Anyway accidentally one can wear something inside out and that's always good luck. Not a word from Mabel [Dodge] at all. Lo, the poor Indian.

    Lots of love and good wishes

Gertrude.

1. For a detailed discussion of Stein's unpublished and published "second" portrait of Van Vechten see appendix B.

2. Harden was an American who had fought with the French army in World War I. After the war he continued to live in France. Harden's letters to his family, written during the war, were published in his *American Poilu* (Boston: Little, Brown, and Co., 1919).

3. Note by Van Vechten, 18 January 1941: "Knopf was considering the publication of The Making of Americans, but eventually decided against it."

❧

To Carl Van Vechten
MS. New York Public Library, Manuscripts Division

[late August 1923]   27 rue de Fleurus
                                             [Paris]

My dear Van,

    I spent the afternoon of the fête of the Assumption of the Virgin reading the Bow boy and it went very very well. You have invented your own brightness and Fanny is one of the best things that have been done in a long time. Laura and Amy. It's all the background and the background, as yet American life is the background. Others have tried to make background foreground, but you have made foreground background, and our foreground is our background. To follow one before the other. Now to follow one before the other, and that's it. Fania likes it and Campaspe is as moral as a sister and Fanny. Fanny is the name. Actually can sunder as to the same, actually can sunder and as to the same and actually can sunder and as to the same, the sundered sisters and as to the same. And as to the sundered sisters and as to the same. Fanny as a name. I like melodrama and background, melodrama is background and so is the rest. Anyway it is clear. What you have done is very clear and I like it.[1]

Hunter Stagg turned up with a friend, a charming fellow is Stagg, with an intensive Va. enthusiasm and an appreciation of you. We like him as well. I gave him something for the Reviewer called An Indian boy.[2]

Love and best wishes Van
Always
Gertrude.

1. In Van Vechten's novel Fannie is Campaspe Lorillard's mother. Amy is Paul Moody's ex-wife (parts of these characters are drawn from Van Vechten's experiences. Van Vechten, like Paul Moody in the novel, spent time in the Ludlow Street Jail for failure to pay alimony. Anna Snynder Van Vechten, like Amy, developed a relationship with a woman named Paula, Paula Jacoby). Laura is a friend of Campaspe's. Many of the phrases used in this letter are also used in the unpublished portrait of Van Vechten that Stein wrote at this time. See Appendix B.

2. Stagg with Emily Clark and Mary Dallas Street was one of the editors of *The Reviewer*, a journal published in the 1920s in Richmond, Virginia. Stagg, who was traveling with his friend Montgomery Evans, had gone to see Stein at the suggestion of Van Vechten. *The Reviewer* printed Stein's "An Indian Boy" (January 1924), 4(2):[104]–6. *The Reviewer* also printed Stein's second portrait of Van Vechten, "Van or Twenty Years After" (April 1924), 4(3):[176]–77.

To Gertrude Stein

3 September 1923 [151 East 19th Street
New York]

Dear Gertrude,

What a wonderful letter to write me about my little Bow-Boy. I'm glad you liked him. He was fun to do. I'm glad you liked [Hunter] Stagg.

He is a charming fellow and has talent. Edmund Wilson, Jr. has over a page about you in the September Vanity Fair. You will see this in Paris.[1] Not a word yet about your book. Your promise to do another portrait of me "twenty years after" naturally delights me. I like your portraits. I like your work. I like you. Not a word from Mabel [Dodge]; this either means that Tony [Luhan] is interesting or uninteresting. D. H. Lawrence has been in New York, but I have not seen him.[2]

> *love,*
> *Carlo Van Vechten*[3]

1. Wilson's "A Guide to Gertrude Stein," in *Vanity Fair* (September 1923), 20(7):60, 80. Stein wrote Wilson about this article in a letter to him on 3 October 1923 (YCAL). The letter was important to Stein and she made two drafts for it. One draft is written in a manuscript notebook that contains her "Van or Twenty Years After," "As A Wife Has A Cow A Love Story," and her "Co[a]dy and Brenner." The second draft is on torn sheets that have been clipped into the manuscript cahier. In her letter Stein wrote Wilson:

> You are right, there do exist portraits and stories but although imitation may be the highest from [i.e., form] of flattery it isn't continuation, and so as the world completes itself stories are not to be chosen they are to be refused likewise portraits, when you realise that to take the commonest example the bible lives not by its stories but by its texts you see how inevitably one wants neither harmony, pictures stories nor portraits. You have to do something else to continue. Do you see what I mean, to continue you have to be persistent and stories don't persist they repeat and they vary, in a way a modern public knows this and so Van really succeeds because he doesn't tell a story. References you see are association, one refers to one's associates but not to oneself, and all literature is to me me, that isn't as bad as it sounds. Some one complained that I always stopped while I was driving to read the sign posts even when I knew the road and all I could explain was that I am fond of reading, well I am, I like people and politics and painting but I am really fond of reading, there that's all.

2. Lawrence had been in New York in August when *Studies in Classic American Literature* was published by Thomas Seltzer.

3. Stein used the verso of Van Vechten's letter to draft a review of Ernest Hemingway's *Three Stories and Ten Poems* (Paris: Contact Publishing Co., 1923). She also drafted a letter to W. Dawson Johnston, literary editor of *Ex Libris*, a monthly review published by the American Library in Paris. *Ex Libris* did not publish the review; it did, however, publish Stein's "He and They, Hemingway: A Portrait," *Ex Libris* (December 1923), 1(6):192. Stein was in Nice, where she had gone to visit Picasso.

> Dear Dr. Johnson,
>
> Am sending you a little review of Hemingway's book for the x Libris. That and the portrait will I think do nicely together. We are resting happily on the shore. Haven't begun to write yet but I will, this isn't a threat but a promise. It's very nice here, best regards to ~~yourself~~ Johnson and Mrs. Johnson and yourself
>
> > *Sincerely*
> > *Gtde Stein*

Stein's review of Hemingway's book appeared in the column "Recent Publications," *Chicago Tribune*, Paris ed., 27 November 1923, p. 4. Except for an error in the title of the book, which was corrected in the printed version, this draft is what was printed in the *Tribune*.

Ten stories and three poems is very pleasantly said. So far so good, further than that, and as far as that, I may say of Ernest Hemingway that as he sticks to poetry and intelligence it is both poetry and intelligent. Rosevelt is genuinely felt as young as Hemingway and as old as Rosevelt. I should say that Hemingway should stick to poetry and intelligence and eschew the hotter emotions and the more turgid vision. Intelligence and a great deal of it is a good thing to use when you have it it's all for the best.

Gertrude Stein

The misspelling of the poem "Roosevelt" is in both the manuscript and the printed version. The draft of the letter is the only manuscript of this work. There is no typescript in YCAL.

To Carl Van Vechten

[postmark: 26 September 1923]   Hôtel Suisse, Nice

My dear Van,

We are here for a few weeks but continue to address 27 rue de Fleurus because that follows. I am glad you like my letter, I am inclosing the second portrait[1] I wonder if you will like it, I think it piles up rather well, if you do like it and Vanity Fair would like to print it, I would be very pleased. I saw an advertisement of Mabel [Dodge]'s Taos home in the New Republic, July, (some one sent it to me) a very modest and unpretentious statement, as an advertisement perhaps too much so.[2] Lots of love. I hope you'll like the portrait

Always yours
Gertrude.

1. Note by Van Vechten, January 1941: "This must have been Van or 20 Years After." From Van Vechten's reply to Stein of 22 October 1923 it would seem that it was this portrait and not the hitherto unpublished portrait that Stein sent to Van Vechten. The portrait, "Van or Twenty Years After; A Second Portrait of Carl Van Vechten" was first printed in *The Reviewer* (April 1924), 4(3):[176]–77.

2. On the back cover of *The New Republic* of 4 July 1923 there was an advertisement: "For Rent: From August first attractive five room furnished adobe house near Taos Pueblo. Communicate Mabel Sterne Luhan, Taos, New Mexico.

🕸

To Gertrude Stein

22 October 1923
         151 East Nineteenth Street
         New York City

Dear Gertrude,

Mabel [Dodge]'s letter about The Bow-Boy almost knocks me flat.[1] She identifies herself with Campaspe, which, of course, she *isn't*: says it's the most perfect character in fiction: "showing the perfect equilibrium which results from a soul in utter conflict." Not a word about the chief! and to this day I don't know how to spell her FIFTH name.

The new portrait I liked very much, although as yet it is little but meter and rhythm to me. More will come later. It is a little difficult for me to *ask* Vanity Fair to publish it as it is about *me* but I thought, as occasion offers, I might show it to an editor or two and perhaps one of them might ask me for it. Would you mind if it were published elsewhere than Vanity Fair?

There is news about the History of a Family at last. [Alfred] Knopf thinks the best thing to do is to issue a circular, which he plans to do a little later, telling something about the book and inviting subscriptions. If he gets enough he will go ahead. I think this is an excellent plan. If he does the book he wants to do it *beautifully* and that will cost money: three or four volumes of large type, with possibly portraits of you by [Jo] Davidson, Picasso etc. as frontispieces. And signed by you. This will all cost money and it will probably be necessary to charge $25 for the set! Therefore, before plunging, it seems advisable to see how many copies he can sell in advance by subscription. The whole idea of publishing a novel of this length all at once is so novel, the book itself is so original, that I should not be surprised to find collectors leaping for it. Let him, however, take his time; if he does it he will do it better than anyone else. In the meantime I may inform you that another publisher has *asked* to see the book, and if Knopf decides against it in the end, which I hope he won't, I'll pass it on to him. Please have the other volumes ready to ship if they are demanded, but keep them until I ask for them. The first volume has so many misspelled words and is written in such dim ink that it is very difficult to read; this is unfortunate.[2]

with much love,
Carl Van Vechten

1. Dodge to Van Vechten, 28 September [1923], NYPL-MD.

2. Although Van Vechten tried valiantly to convince the Knopfs to publish Stein's *The Making of Americans* his efforts failed. Even after the book was printed by Robert McAlmon in association with William Bird in the fall of 1925, Stein never gave up hope that a commerical publisher would issue the book. See Stein to Van Vechten [22 February 1925, note 1].

To Carl Van Vechten

[postmark: 5 November 1923]   Hôtel Suisse, Nice

My dear Van

I am as pleased as can be with the news of the Family. I too think Knopf's plan an xcellent one and I certainly would like him to do it. It is too bad about the first volume being in such bad shape but the good volume of it got lost once and never found and this was the old and original copy when type-writing was with us in its infancy. I can't tell you what I feel about all you are doing for me. Well anyhow there it is. About your portrait no I don't want it especially for Vanity Fair in fact I would be very pleased to have some one else use it. I have just read it over, it isn't quite as full as I would like it to be but it does some of it pretty well.

No Mabel [Dodge] isn't Campaspe, she Mabel is alright but perfect equilibrium isn't as one might say it.[1] Do tell me what people are saying about the Bow boy, I would so much like to know.

We are leading a peaceful life here and in between we go to see Juan Gris directing the scene painting of his schemes of decoration for the Russian ballet at Monte Carlo. It is mostly done by an Englishwoman who does it as if she were a lady gardener. He seems pleased, we are going back to Paris shortly.[2]

Always
Gertrude.

1. Note by Van Vechten, 18 January 1941: "One of the characters in the Blind Bow-Boy."

2. In the summer of 1923 Diaghilev had commissioned Juan Gris (1887–1927, born José Victoriano Gonzalez), to do the decor for *La Colombe*, an opera by Charles Gounod. In October Gris and his wife Josette arrived in Monte Carlo, where he supervised the excecution of his decor.

In a letter to Daniel-Henry Kahnweiler, 20 October 1923, Gris wrote of meeting Stein: "Yesterday I was in Nice with Gertrude who kept us for dinner. I went to see Matisse to whom I had written in advance. He was very cold and could only spare us about half an hour on the pretext that he was working hard, etc. He won't do anything for Diaghilev because he says he loses money when he's not painting pictures. Altogether we didn't get on well. He wouldn't come and dine with Gertrude and myself when I invited him on Gertrude's behalf" (see *Letters of Juan Gris [1913–1927]*, collected by Daniel-Henry Kahnweiler, translated and edited by Douglas Cooper, letter CLXXXII, pp. 154–55 [incorrectly printed as 1932], London: Privately Printed, 1956).

To Carl Van Vechten
[Postcard: Le Thor (Vaucluse)—Le château]

[postmark: 21 December 1923]

[27 rue de Fleurus
Paris]

Back in Paris and Greetings to you both

Always
G. S.

To Carl Van Vechten

[postmark: 4 February 1924]

27 rue de Fleurus
[Paris]

My dear Van,

How goes it and what is the news. Nothing very xciting over here, I am amusing myself with a Gertrude Stein birthday book, Picasso is going to make illustrations to go with it and that will be nice it's going to be the kind you write your name in,[1] and how is [Alfred] Knopf, any news and does he not want the other volumes they are all ready. And what are you doing, and did you get laurel leaves from Mill Valley and Mabel [Dodge] too.[2]

Always
Gertrude.

1. Stein's "A Birthday Book" was published posthumously in her *Alphabets & Birthdays*. Stein wrote this book for Picasso's son, Paulo, born 4 February 1921 (Stein's birthday was 3 February). The book was originally planned to be part of the Editions Galerie Simon, published by Daniel-Henry Kahnweiler. Although Stein repeatedly writes of Picasso's working on the illustrations, there is no indication that he did so. In the introduction to Stein's *Painted Lace* Kahnweiler writes:

> Picasso's "passive resistance"—a term which seems to me more apt than Gertrude's "period of unreliability," resistance which shows itself in him, perhaps unconsciously, when he is faced by any commission, any work not spontaneously born of his own spirit but brought to him from outside—caused the failure of our project. In 1926 it was necessary to face the facts and give up plans for a book of which I should have been proud. (p. xiv)

2. Dodge had taken a house in Mill Valley, California, for the winter of 1923–24.

To Gertrude Stein

5 March 1924   151 East Nineteenth Street
                                                [New York]

Dear Gertrude,

I've not written you for such a long time because I've been so busy & I've had nothing to write you about *your* business—nor have I yet. [Alfred] Knopf has not spoken again. You see he has been moving—& getting out his *new* magazine, The American Mercury—and what not.[1] Presently, I will speak to him again. If he doesn't do The History of a Family somebody some day will: I feel sure of that. Don't send the other volumes until I ask for them,—as for your wonderful portrait of me—[Frank] Crowninshield[2] who has had it ever since you gave it to me at last decided that Vanity Fair had been publishing a good deal of your work & so he would lay off awhile—a stupid decision—But I have sent it elsewhere—& it will be published, I am sure. The Indian garçons in The Reviewer have created a sensation.[3] I am sending one to Mabel [Dodge].

My new book, The Tattooed Countess, is all done & the proofs read. It will appear in August. Now, I am getting together a book of musical papers—& I have two introductions to write to other people's books.[4]

Of course I must have the Gertrude Stein birthday book as soon as it is out—I like Jo Davidson's thing about you[5] & so does most everybody else. It is, however, lacking in humour & I think of that as a very essential part of you but nobody else who writes about you seems to get this. Anyway you are a grand & noble person & I salute you!

Carl Van Vechten

1. The *American Mercury* was a monthly magazine founded in 1924. H. L. Mencken and George Jean Nathan were its editors.

2. Frank Crowninshield (1872–1947) was the editor of *Vanity Fair* from 1914 to 1935.

3. *The Reviewer* had printed Stein's "An Indian Boy" (January 1924), 4(2):[104]-6. The piece generated a great deal of reader response—including a few subscription cancellations. The editors commented on this response in the column "Things in General," in *The Reviewer* (April 1924), 4(3):233, and (October 1924), 4(5):[410]–11.

4. Van Vechten's *Red: Papers on Musical Subjects* was published by Knopf on 9 January 1925. Van Vechten wrote an introduction, "An Icing for a Chocolate Eclair," for Ronald Firbank's *Prancing Nigger* (New York: Brentano's Publishers, 1924). It was Van Vechten who suggested that Firbank's "Drama in Sunlight" might better be titled *Prancing Nigger*. Firbank was delighted and wrote Van Vechten that "It never occurred to me, & any success the novel has will be due to you." (See Miriam G. Benkovitz, *Ronald Firbank: A Biography* [London: Weidenfeld and Nicolson, 1970], pp. 250–52).

Van Vechten also wrote an introduction, "A Prolegomenon to be read, if ever, only after you have read The Lord of the Sea," in M. P. Shiel's *The Lord of the Sea* (New York: Alfred A. Knopf, 1924).

5. This may be a reference to *Vanity Fair* (February 1923), 19(6):48, 90, which published Stein's "A Portrait of Jo Davidson." The unsigned article, "An American Revolutionary of Prose Sets Down Her Impressions of an American Scupltor," was illustrated by three photographs: Davidson working on his sculpture of Stein, the Jacques Lipschitz bust of Stein, and the Picasso *Portrait of Gertrude Stein*. It is possible that Davidson's sculpture was being shown in New York in 1924.

To Carl Van Vechten

[postmark: 17 March 1924]   27 rue de Fleurus
[Paris]

My dear Carl,

I think you will be pleased that the History of the Family is starting as a serial in the Transatlantic.[1] It begins in the April number, beginning with 15 pages and the May number will have 20 odd pages and so on. Hueffer or Ford you know Ford Madox Hueffer the editor is moved he says it is magnificent and is terribly impressed with it having been done some odd 18 years ago, and as he is more or less the old guard it's very good, and would it be too much trouble to ask [Alfred] Knopf to send back the III volume. I thought I had it all here in duplicate but that volume seems to be missing and I'll have it copied and if he wants it again will send it back. You are pleased with its appearing aren't you. The Transatlantic will have to go on for a long time to do it all which may be a comfort to them and they are paying me nicely which is also a comfort.

I am pleased with the Tattooed Countess going to be a story of Iowa. I have a weakness for Iowa. Iowa is entirely different from the others. It always is, it even was when it was a dough-boy, I have always felt that way about Iowa, even though I did not think of it as having an uplifting effect on American youth.

Oh and I met Mrs. Acton at a lunch yesterday do you remember the Actons of Florence and she was funny about Mabel [Dodge], she remembered all the times Mabel told her not to bother and she also said that in Florence Mabel is supposed to have done it again with a Mr. Wu. I imagine however that is only the aftermath of Mabel's interview about the yellow races since you don't seem to have heard it. Mrs. Acton did make Florence sound wonderfully just the same.[2]

The birthday book is all done and Picasso is at the illustrations and when the Simon Gallery gets it done I'll send it to you I think it is going to be pretty. And Van it is alright about Knopf, I am looking forward to his doing it the history of the Family, and anyway some day. I am glad you like your portrait. I want to get out a volume of Portraits and Prayers I am getting it ready, not a bad title and it will be both.

Lots of love always
Gertrude.

1. It was Ernest Hemingway who convinced Ford Madox Ford, editor of *the transatlantic review*, to serialize part of Stein's *The Making of Americans*. Stein was paid at the rate of thirty francs per printed page (see Gallup, *The Flowers of Friendship*, pp. 159, 163–67).

   The Making of Americans appeared monthly in *the transatlantic review* from April through December 1924 (1, nos. 4–6; 2, nos. 1–6).

2. The Actons lived in the villa La Pietra just outside Florence.

To Gertrude Stein

13 April 1924
151 East 19th Street
[New York]

Dear Gertrude,

I am delighted to hear the news about The Family. I think this will be an excellent way to get some public reaction to this work and also will furnish it with a lot of splendid publicity. I hope it will enable [Alfred] Knopf to make up his mind about it. I have asked him to return Volume III to you; if it doesn't arrive within a reasonable period let me know.

I have given my portrait, Van After Twenty Years, to The Reviewer. There were about fourteen editorials about The Indian Boy and they were overjoyed to have the new one. When I was recently in Richmond I was asked more questions about you than about any one else.[1]

A bookseller friend of mine wishes to know if copies of the birthday book are to be on sale, and, if so, from what publisher or dealer in Paris they can be ordered. Will you let me know about this.

Mrs. Acton is all wrong about Mr. Wu, but almost everything else has happened. D. H. Lawrence has returned to Taos, and according to a recent letter, beer and jazz records can only be brought out after he has retired. His scorn, it seems, is feared.[2]

I think you will like Prancing Nigger by Ronald Firbank. It is published by Brentano's in this country and you can probably get it at Brentano's in Paris.

saluti,
Carl Van Vechten

1. Stein's "Van Vechten or Twenty Years After; a Second Portrait of Carl Van Vechten," in *The Reviewer* (April 1924), 4(3):[176]–77. Van Vechten is exaggerating about the number of editorials. See Van Vechten to Stein, 5 March 1924, note 3. He may have meant the number of letters to the editor.

2. Van Vechten's information comes from a letter sent to him by Willard ("Spud") Johnson, editor of the magazine *Laughing Horse*. Johnson, who lived in Santa Fe, was visiting Dodge in Taos. Johnson wrote Van Vechten:

> Each night about midnight we have decided to play jazz records on the vic and to drink near-beer (two things we have not dared to do before D. H. Lawrence has retired—for

fear of his scorn). And each night we have rehashed Lawrence's conversation of the early evening, discussed Dorothy Richardson—and have asked questions about you. [Johnson to Van Vechten, postmark 2 April 1924, NYPL-MD]

To Carl Van Vechten
[Radiogram]

16 April 1924   Paris

PLEASE GET THREE VOLUMES FROM KNOPF AT ONCE AND HOLD THEM

GERTRUDE

To Carl Van Vechten
[Radiogram]

17 April 1924   Paris

LIVERIGHT WILL CALL FOR THREE VOLUMES AND PLEASE LEND HIM THREE LIVES

GERTRUDE

To Carl Van Vechten
[Radiogram]

18 April 1924   Paris

PLEASE TAKE THREE VOLUMES AND THREE LIVES TO LIVE-RIGHT IMMEDIATELY

GERTRUDE

To Carl Van Vechten

[postmark: 20 April 1924]   27 rue de Fleurus
                                             [Paris]

My dear Van

That was an eruption of cablegrams wasn't it. It was this way, the beginning of the Long book in the Transatlantic seems to have started Liveright's representative over here[1] and he made me a very good proposition subject to Liveright's approval and he wanted Liveright to see the beginning of the Long book, and also Three Lives as the idea is to do both of them, and he also hoped that you would see Liveright in the course of the giving of the books which he was sure would have an xcellent effect, I more than thought so hence all those cables. There is also some idea of your doing an introduction to the long book, which also would please everybody.

We are seeing the Lochers again Tuesday having met unexpectedly in our usual meeting place the bank, in fact we met them at two banks, the less money we all have the more we seem to meet in banks but that again is on strictly classic lines. I wish we were meeting you at the bank too but they all say you won't come over and I don't seem to go over but we have each other just the same.

Always
Gertrude

1. Harold Stearns (1891–1943), an American writer, was acting as an agent for Horace Liveright in Paris.

To Gertrude Stein

22 April 1924   151 East Nineteenth Street
                                 [New York]

Dear Gertrude,

Following your cabled instructions I secured the first two volumes of The Making of Americans from Knopf and passed them on to Liveright.

[98]

The third volume had already been sent to you, following your letter with a request to that effect.

I am reading proofs[1] and in the mood that that occupation creates. I am dying to see your birthday book.

always, your friend,
Carl Van Vechten

1. Van Vechten was reading proofs for his novel *The Tattooed Countess.*

To Gertrude Stein

6 May 1924   151 East Nineteenth Street
                                                              [New York]

Dear Gertrude,

This is just a short note to tell you that I am moving this week. Please address me hereafter at 150 West Fifty-fifth Street. I have been very busy moving and getting ready to move. We have lived on East Nineteenth Street for nine years and it seems like the Old Homestead and so I don't know what Liveright is doing, but when he sent for the books he called me up for my opinion and I told him . . . but you know that already. I hope it will be possible for me to do the introduction.

I'll write you more later.

with every good hope,
Carl Van Vechten

To Gertrude Stein

13 June 1924   150 West Fifty-fifth Street
                                                              New York City

Dear Gertrude,

I'm sorry about Liveright—and sorrier still that it was taken away from [Alfred] Knopf so abruptly—because sooner or later I am sure I could have persuaded him to do it, and now that [Horce] Liveright has refused it, I can't very easily bring the subject up with him again. As for the books, if you will write Liveright to send them to me I'll be glad to take care of them—but I can't ask for them as he hasn't mentioned the subject to me, it would look as if I were getting them back for Knopf.

As for Mabel [Dodge] the situation is this. D. H. Lawrence & his big german wife Frieda, are living in a cottage on Mabel's estates. Mabel and The Indian are living at the big *house*. Every morning at 7—Mabel hurries up the hill, gets breakfast for D. H. & *Frieda*, washes pots & pans etc.

Mabel has written a long poem called "The Ballad of a bad girl" which relates how she jumped on her grandfather's walking stick & rode up to heaven where she tried to talk with god—until out of god's heart jumped a man with blue eyes & a fiery crest who kicked her back to earth with curses. The poem ends:

> Something made me sorry for what had taken place,
> I took my father's silver cane & put it in the hall
> Then I lay down in the pansy bed & whispered:
>   'Mother! Mother me,
> and teach me how to mother and that's all, all.'[1]

Mabel writes me about the poem: "It is an indictment against all Feminism and an earnest appeal to women to leave off trying to steal the world away from men—and to return to their original function—motherhood. . . . If men want mothers they should have them. There's enough power in that for any woman. Let them leave off stealing the masculine secrets of the will to power, magic & all the other occult-wills. They have reached to the godhead in their rummaging around in the man's region—trying to emulate his ultimate divinity. Well there destruction awaits them. Let them turn & climb down in time—lest they be kicked down like the Bad Girl—for, of course, not many women can endure *Her* fall & survive it. Only the geniuses can Come Back—& woman genius is scarce." Aren't you happy to see Mabel functioning so nobly.

I'm dying to see the new Picasso book. Did you receive The Reviewer with your new portrait of me? I asked them to send you several. You also will receive a copy of The Tattooed Countess in about six weeks. Let me know all details of the Birthday Book as soon as possible.

Constellations to you[2]
Carl Van Vechten

1. Dodge sent Van Vechten a copy of her poem, "The Ballad of a Bad Girl," which Willard Johnson had printed in *Laughing Horse*, May 1924. The poem was illustrated with a drawing by D. H. Lawrence. In December 1927 Johnson issued the poem as a pamphlet. Dodge reprinted it in her *Lorenzo in Taos* (New York: Alfred A. Knopf, 1932), pp. 95–97.

2. This is an early instance of Van Vechten's elaborate closings that form a part of his correspondence with all of his close friends. See, for example, Van Vechten to Stein, 15 July 1924, 8 September 1924, and 10 December 1926.

To Carl Van Vechten
[Rose motto]

[postmark: 23 June 1924]
27 rue de Fleurus
[Paris]

My dear Van

I am awfully sorry that it did happen so and am most disappointed. I have just written to Liveright to return the volumes to you. You see there is a man here Harold Stearns who was apparently Liveright's agent had bought things for him and according to him he bought the History of the Family and Three Lives of me. The terms were all arranged, you see I have the Three Lives plates and everything and it seemed an absolute certainty. What all happened I don't yet know xcept that Liveright cabled a refusal to him. It is a shame because there seems no doubt of its market because everybody likes it in the Transatlantique even its worst enemies say it is like Dostoievsky which is none so dirty from an enemy. You see I don't understand yet why they hesitate. I see that a copy of Three Lives with my signature is selling to-day for $13 why then Knopf should hesitate so long, well it's not for me to understand. You know how more than grateful I am and I am awfully sorry I balled things up but it did look like a sure thing. About the birthday book it will be out definitely this fall, a limited edition of about 100 with etchings by Picasso zodiacs and things. I'll send you prospectuses when I have them and a copy for you I have reserved already, so no mistake about that. And have you seen the Lochers and didn't you like my fantasy on three careers or haven't you seen it yet. I was quite pleased with it.[1] And do tell that villain Hunter Stagg to send me copies of the Reviewer with my things in it. I have written to him in that sense but not a squeak. I love him just the same though.[2] Mabel [Dodge] sent me the girl in the pansy bed,[3] dear old Mabel I suppose if one did not dish wash in one's youth it is always pleasant to do it in one's old age. So it never was a boarding house, well that was just Florence. Florence would have those ideas. We will be in Paris for another month or so and then I think Nice for the autumn again but continue to address here. Did you see [Ford Madox] Ford in New York he is over there gathering in moneys for the Transatlantic. A nice man. The long book does read well in print, I am awfully pleased and will be more pleased well twenty years isn't so long and lots of love

> *Always*
> *Gertrude.*

1. Stein had given the Lochers a typescript of "And so. To change so. (A Fantasy on Three Careers) Muriel Draper Yvonne Davidson Beatrice Locher." The piece is printed in Stein's *Portraits and Prayers*.

2. The letter is printed in "Hunter Stagg: 'Over There in Paris With Gertrude Stein,' " in the *Ellen Glasgow Newsletter* (October 1981), 15:3.

3. Dodge's poem, *The Ballad of a Bad Girl*.

To Carl Van Vechten
[Rose motto]

[postmark: 25 June 1924]   27 rue de Fleurus
                                            [Paris]

My dear Carl,[1]

There have been alarums and xcursions which leave us pretty much where we were, at any rate Liveright is off, and now there is a new proposition from an English firm,[2] anyway I am awfully grateful to you and will you get the volumes back from Liveright and keep them until the next time. It's a nuisance but then it is a long book which will make it all the pleasanter when it comes. I can't tell you well you know that, anyway you are all that.

We had several nice parties with the Lochers and I have done a fantasy on three careers I'll send it to you pretty soon it is finished now it's about Muriel Draper Beatrice Locher and Yvonne Davidson, Muriel Beatrice and Yvonne and I am sure it will please you a lot.[3] The birthday book is coming out this fall, Picasso is to do etchings for it and it will be limited I imagine to 150 copies, will send you prospectuses when there are any, and I guess that's all about me and enough. The Hapgoods you know Hutch and his wife turned up but they only had ancient stories of Mabel [Dodge] they were not at all up to date and as they had just come from Florence Mrs. Acton must have made it up. All they did add was that the house in Taos is now a boarding house and that Mabel had written to both [Maurice] Sterne and Edwin [Dodge] asking them if they didn't want to go out there with their wives.[4] This seems to have come direct from Sterne. Why do you move.[5] Some people do. I am glad you don't. Have not seen [Ronald] Firbank's book but will soon.[6] And what is happening to you now, do write soon

> *Love to Fania*
> *Yours*
> *Gertrude.*

1. Note by Van Vechten, 18 January 1941: "First time for this address, I think." Van Vechten is incorrect. Stein first used "Carl" instead of "Van" in her letter to him postmarked 17 March 1924.

2. The English publishers Jonathan Cape had learned of the book through Robert McAlmon, the writer and editor. See Cape to Stein, 16 May 1924 and 30 May 1924, YCAL. Cape did not publish the book.

3. See Stein to Van Vechten [23 June 1924], note 1.

4. Note by Van Vechten, 18 January 1941: "Maurice Sterne & Edwin Dodge earlier husbands of Mabel Luhan."

5. Note by Van Vechten, 18 January 1941: "I had just moved to 150 W. 55 from 151 E. 19, NYC."

6. Firbank's *Prancing Nigger*, which Van Vechten had sent to Stein.

To Carl Van Vechten
[Postcard: Plant basket decorated with ribbons and flags]

[postmark: 30 June 1924]   [27 rue de Fleurus
                                             Paris]

Just received some clippings with xtracts of your portrait,[1] it sounds very nice, do tell that faithless Hunter Stagg to send me copies of the Reviewer that have my things in it, I wrote him but no answer, I like to see them printed. No new news. Looking forward to your next,

Always
Gertrude.

1. The clippings, which would have mentioned Stein's "Van or Twenty Years After; a Second Portrait of Carl Van Vechten," cannot be identified.

❧

To Gertrude Stein

15 July 1924   150 West Fifty-fifth Street
[New York]

Dear Gertrude,

Liveright sent me back the two volumes of The Making of Americans. So there is an end of that chapter. I shall hold them until you instruct me to deliver them to some one else. I haven't seen Liveright—but I doubt if he says anything to me if I do & I can't say anything to him. I have written [Hunter] Stagg to send you the magazines. I had written him before, too. But you know *Southerners*. It takes them some time to do anything simple. I am dying to see the Birthday Book. Please send me some circulars— if there are any—& maybe I can get you some orders. I haven't seen the Lochers, nor your Three Careers. Who has this? Mabel [Dodge] writes that she is coming back to Croton this fall, Indian and all.[1] Neith Boyce came in the other day & we talked about you—& yes, I did meet [Ford Madox] Ford. I liked him but it was a party & I was too occupied & he was too occupied for us to meet again.

Just opposite our new home they are building a mosque of pink marble with a facade of effulgent tiles, cupolas, balconies, turrets, grated windows, a vast dome, surmounted by a scimitar & crescent, & everything else delightful. Soon funny fat men in fezzes will run in & out.[2] Down the street is a Venetian palazzo with a painted façade. This is my environment.

I shall be sending you my Countess in another week.

Poppies & cornflowers to you!

Carl Van Vechten

[104]

1. Stein's "And So. To Change So. (A Fantasy on Three Careers) Muriel Draper Yvonne Davidson Beatrice Locher." Dodge's letter to Van Vechten is not in YCAL or NYPL-MD.

2. The Shriners' Temple, now the New York City Center.

To Carl Van Vechten
[Rose motto]

[postmark: 23 July 1924]   27 rue de Fleurus
                                                       [Paris]

My dear Van,

Have just read Prancing Nigger and am delighted with it. It is sweet and funny, do tell [Ronald] Firbank how much I like it. I would like very much to meet him, I imagine he comes to Paris from time to time. We are leaving for a couple of months but do continue to address here it is the best way to reach me,

Love
Gertrude.

To Carl Van Vechten
MS. New York Public Library, Manuscripts Division

[postmark: 25 August 1924]   Hotel Pernollet
                                                      Belley, Ain

My dear Van

The Tattooed Countess has just followed me down here. I like it. After having been tender to everyone else you are now tender to yourself. It's nice to be tender to oneself. I imagine it will have a very lasting success, it ought to. What is so good is that you can be gentle to Iowa. Iowa is gentle. And Miss Colman and the boy quite complete and just right makes one a youth again he says it just right. The descriptions I liked immensely, well I like it all, the best of good luck always to you.

We are here on our way to Nice but it is so nice we may not get to Nice, otherwise there is no news, at least nothing very new. I have been giving myself a vacation but now I xpect to go on with Birth and Marriage, and so on.[1] Once more my best thanks and likeing

Always
Gertrude.

1. Stein's "Birth and Marriage," in her *Alphabets & Birthdays*.

To Gertrude Stein

8 September [1924]   150 West Fifty-fifth Street
                                      [New York]

Dear Gertrude,

Thanks for your nice letter. I'm glad you found my Iowa gentle. In Iowa they seem to take the book that way but in the east they seem to regard it as a vicious attack. I have written [Ronald] Firbank that you want to see him & I hope he will call on you someday but he is described by those who have seen him as excessively shy.

Mabel [Dodge] dropped into New York unexpectedly the other day & came up to see me. Avery Hopwood happened to be here a little drunk. He was amusing. The next day Mabel wrote me a letter saying she couldn't come to my house again, that she didn't like to see people in that condition. "You know," she wrote, "that one of the modern conventions that I can't conform to is the continual public catharsis" etc. etc. etc. O, such a long letter! "I like *you* very much" etc. etc. I was very much amused.[1] I cannot keep Avery sober—and I don't want to keep him out of the house when he wants to come. And some people like to see him just as much as they like

[106]

to see an Indian chauffeur, drunk or sober—so I just haven't answered Mabel's letter—I can't think of anything to say.

Mignonette & pansies to you and Miss Taklos.

Carl Van Vechten

1. Dodge to Van Vechten, postmark 6 September 1924, YCAL.

To Carl Van Vechten

[postmark: 11 October 1924] Hotel Pernollet[1]
Belley (Ain)

My dear Van,

I was delighted to see that Brentanos is listing the Tattooed Countess as one of the five best sellers, that's awfully nice, good luck and more good luck to you, I liked it a lot and I am glad to see that it has had the same effect on others. What is coming next. I was awfully amused about Mabel [Dodge], but what did happen to Avery [Hopwood]. We always used to see him when he came to Paris, he used to come and see us and we always used to have a couple of evenings together and the last couple of times he has been in Paris he has given no sign. I am very fond of him and very sorry not to see him. He was announced in the Herald as being engaged to be married and since then we haven't seen him and he seems to be dead, what was it a disappointment in love or did he get married. It's kind of a storybook thing to happen to him at his time of life. Do tell me about it.[2] Thanks for forwarding my message to [Ronald] Firbank. I hear he was shy the man who came with the faithless Hunter Stagg he never has sent me any copy of the Reviewer I mean Stagg, well Evans[3] I think his name was turned up again and he said he would bring Firbank sometime he knew him in London so I am hoping to meet him sometime. Did I tell you that Jane Heap is going to be a sort of agent for me in New York and hopes to sell me to the American public, well among other things there is the Making of Amer-

[107]

icans and I told her to go to you if she wanted the volumes or any information. That's alright isn't it. Its appearance in the Transatlantic seems to be arousing a certain amount of what you might call middle class interest which is all to the good. You also will be amused to know that there is a small but steady sale of Geography & Plays into Japan, it seems to continue, as a Californian and an American should I be pleased or not, I should I guess is the answer. We are leaving for Paris tomorrow it has been most pleasant here Belley is its name and Belley is its nature.

Do write soon best to Fania

Gertrude.

1. Note by Van Vechten, 18 January 1941: "This seems to be the first letter from Belley where Gertrude Stein & Alice spent subsequent summers at the Pernollet until they began to live in their villa in Bilignin near by." Van Vechten is in error. Stein's first letter to him from Belley was postmarked 25 August 1924. Stein had, however, first been to the Hôtel Pernollet in Belley for a few days in September 1923 on her way to Nice to visit with Picasso (Stein to Henry McBride, postmark 8 September 1923, YCAL).

2. Note by Van Vechten, 18 January 1941: "Avery Hopwood's 'engagement' was a gag."

3. Montgomery Evans

To Gertrude Stein

15 November [1924]   150 West Fifty-fifth Street
                                                     [New York]

Dear Gertrude,

I think it is an excellent plan to put your affairs in the hands of Jane Heap and I shall be ready to turn over The Making of Americans to her whenever she asks for it. As for myself I have finished another novel, to be called Firecrackers, and to be published next August, and I have visited the home of my fathers in Iowa, and I am interested in Negro poets and Jazz pianists. There is always something in New York, and this winter it is decidedly Negro poets and Jazz pianists. Have you heard George Gershwin's Rhapsody in Blue? The best piece of music ever done by an American. There is a phonograph record.[1] Mabel Luhan has taken the Finney Farm in Croton for the winter, and I have had lunch with her once in town. Tony [Luhan] has not yet arrived, but he and the D. H. Lawrences will come on in relays.

magnolias and camelias to you and Miss Taklos!

Carl Van Vechten

1. Gershwin's *Rhapsody in Blue* was first performed by Paul Whiteman and his Palais Royal Orchestra, with Gershwin as piano soloist, in a concert, "An Experiment in Modern Music," at Aeolian Hall, New York, on 12 February 1924. Gershwin recorded the work with Whiteman and his Concert Orchestra on 10 June 1924. The recording was released on the Victor label, number 5525-A.

To Carl Van Vechten
[Radiogram]

[Received] 20 January 1925   Paris

PLEASE SEND TWO VOLUMES MAKING AMERICANS IMMEDIATELY PUBLICATION ARRANGED HERE

GERTRUDE

To Carl Van Vechten
[Rose motto]

[postmark: 22 February 1925]   27 rue de Fleurus
[Paris]

My dear Van,

Thanks so much for sending me the volumes so promptly,[1] as you see by the inclosed the arrangements for publication have now definitely been made and they start printing at once, I know you will like its being done almost as much as I do you have always been so wonderful about it and kept up everybody's interest in it and everything. They are doing an edition of 500 and they xpect to sell it at $6, at first we thought of doing several volumes but now it has been decided, one volume of about 750 pages, it would have been nice if it could have been otherwise but this will be very nice I hope.[2] I am sending you several prospectuses and will give one to a man named [Burton] Rascoe connected with the Times or something, he came to see me and was much interested and does syndicated book-reviews but I have no idea what his address is but he said he was a friend of yours.[3] The birthday book is getting on Picasso is working on the plates now and Gris is doing another one, a book rather amusing which ends up with 'As a wife has a cow' a love story.[4] I think you will like it, this to be illustrated by Juan Gris in color and Picasso is doing the birthday book in etchings, one for each month and two beside, but I'll send you the prospectus of those and the books when they are ready, that and the fact that England seems to be discovering me is the present history of my life. That and a chimney on fire[5] and bumping my little Ford against a woman who claimed 100 francs damages for deterioration of her earrings is all our excitement, and Mabel [Dodge] and Avery [Hopwood], and why don't we ever see him any more. We did like him. The Lochers wander to and fro. We always like to have them do so. And I guess that's all and best love

Gertrude.

1. Robert McAlmon (1895–1956), publisher of the Contact Editions, agreed, in association with William Bird and the Three Mountains Press, to publish Stein's *The Making of Americans*. (See Gallup, "The Making of *The Making of Americans*," in Stein's *Fernhurst, Q.E.D., and Other Early Writings*, pp. 194–214, for a detailed account of the agreement to publish with McAlmon and the ensuing problems.)

2. Stein presumably sent Van Vechten a preliminary announcement of the publication of the book. This announcement is not with the letter.

3. Burton Rascoe (1892–1957) was an editor and author. From 1924 to 1928 he wrote a syndicated column, "The Daybook of a New Yorker."

4. Stein's *A Book Concluding With As A Wife Has A Cow A Love Story* was published by the Editions de la Galerie Simon (Daniel-Henry Kahnweiler) in mid-December 1926. The book contained four lithographs by Gris, one of which was in two colors.

5. The story of the chimney fire is recounted by Kahnweiler in his introduction to Stein's *Painted Lace and Other Pieces*, pp. x–xi.

To Carl Van Vechten

[March–April 1925]   27 rue de Fleurus
                                      [Paris]

My dear Carl,

Here are the definite announcements of Making of Americans, I think it is pretty well done.[1] I am sending you a big bunch of them to put about wherever they will do the most good. I am working on the proofs now and will send you a copy as soon as it is printed. I have very much the feeling that it is you that have kept the interest of the public in it all these years and so well I am very fond of you anyway

Always
Gertrude.

1. Stein sent Van Vechten a number of subscription announcements for *The Making of Americans*. This announcement corrected the early one. It stated that the book would be printed "in ONE quarto volume of about 1,000 pages." The verso of the subscription blank included "some extracts from critiques" by Van Vechten, Edmund Wilson, Sherwood Anderson, and Edith Sitwell.

To Gertrude Stein

18 April 1925   150 West Fifty-fifth Street
                                 [New York]

Dear Gertrude,

The announcements of The Making of Americans arrived and I was thrilled; I am scattering them about where I think they will do the most good. And I am waiting with tremors of excitement for the book. And, of course, I am awaiting the volumes illustrated by Juan Gris and Picasso with enormous interest too. It seems to me that with the dawning of another year all the world will know of your glory!

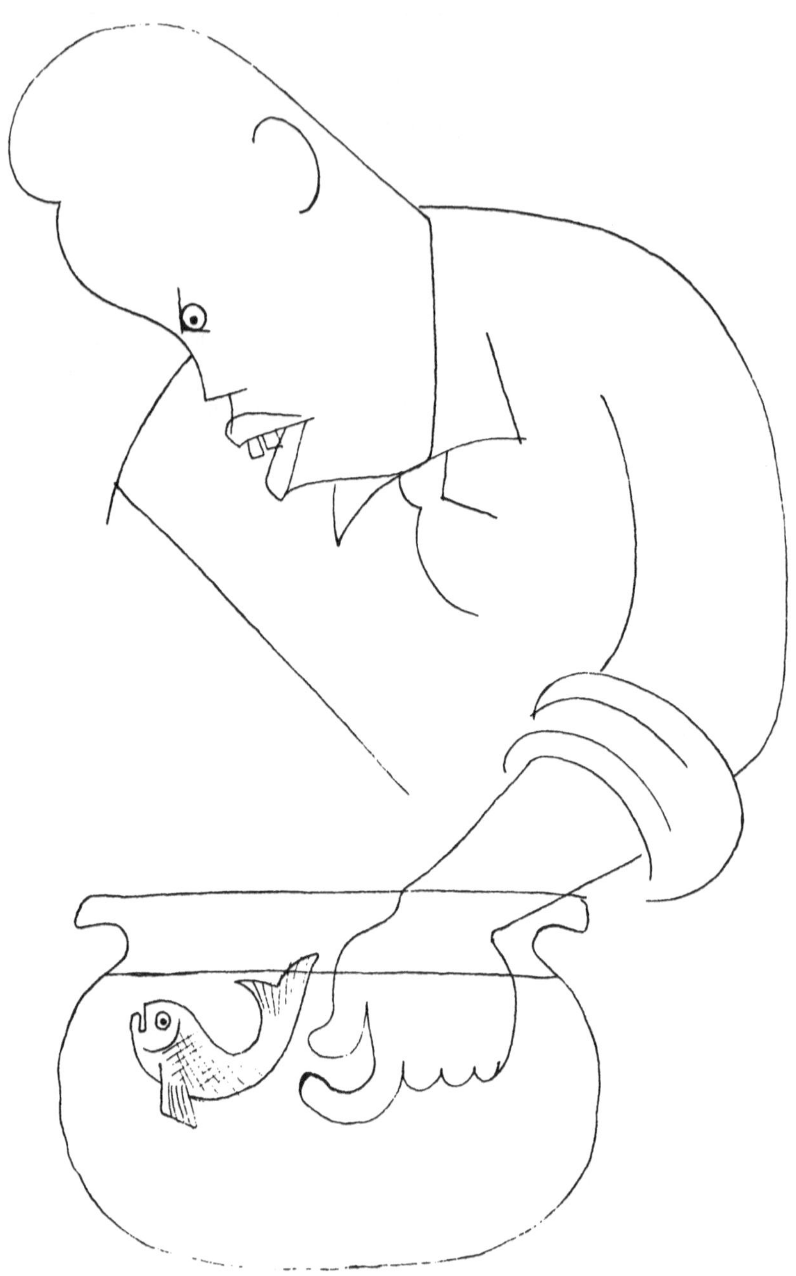

Carl Van Vechten by Miguel Covarrubias. Inscribed, "As Mr. Van Vechten gooses a gold fish. Miguel."
PHOTOGRAPH COURTESY OF BRUCE KELLNER.

You didn't say if you had received RED, which I sent you. Presently I'll be sending you Firecrackers, my new novel, and I have been arranging a book of essays called Excavations which is to come out next January. Also I am doing prefaces to books of drawings by Alastair and Miguel Covarrubias, the young Mexican, whose work you may have observed in Vanity Fair.[1] In the meantime I'm sending you Fania, who sails on April 29 on the Aquitania and will be in Paris towards the end of May. If you are moving about write her (Care the American Express—London, until May 15, and after that Paris) and tell her where you'll be, as she wants to see you. Also Alfred and Blanche Knopf are going over and I'm giving him a letter to you. We may get The Making of Americans done over here yet!

> *don't forget me,*
> *Carlo*

Avery [Hopwood] is over there now. You can get him at the Farmer's Loan and Trust Co. 3 Rue d'Antin, Paris.

1. Van Vechten wrote an introduction to Alastair's *Fifty Drawings by Alastair* (New York: Alfred A. Knopf, 1925), pp. [7–8]. Van Vechten also wrote a preface to Miguel Covarrubias' *The Prince of Wales and Other Famous Americans* (New York: Alfred A. Knopf, 1925), pp. [5–8].

To Carl Van Vechten
[Rose motto]

[postmark: 4 May 1925]

27 rue de Fleurus
[Paris]

My dear Carl,

Delighted with Tony [Luhan]'s thrills,[1] and with your photograph. We will have left Paris I am afraid before Fania gets here, but as we will be where we were last year at Belley near Aix les Bains not quite inaccessible perhaps she will come to see us, I will write to her in London all about it, I do want to see her ever so much. I do hope too to connect with the Knopfs, they ought to be my publishers it's awful foolish of them not to be, Portraits and Prayers and Making of Americans is their manifest destiny,[2] well I am very cheerful these days and your sympathy means a lot to me almost more when I am hopeful than when I am despairful, and happily hopefulness does succeed despair, nicely. I am doing a thing that amuses very much called Natural Phenomena, there are a lot of them so it may be long.[3] What's Firecrackers about, are they strings of them the way we used to set them off or single big ones under a can. Anyway good luck to it, and didn't I thank you for Red of course I did, well anyway I do.

Lots of love to you and I will write to Fania

Always
Gertrude.

1. Van Vechten had sent Stein a section from Bernardine Szold's "About Town" column in the *New York News*, 22 March 1925, Sec. 2, p. 46. It told of Van Vechten's party in a Harlem nightclub for Antonio Luhan, the husband of Mabel Dodge. "Tony was thrilled," Szold wrote, "and that is a great achievement for nothing has ever been known to disturb his passiveness."

2. Even though she had signed to publish *The Making of Americans* with Robert McAlmon, Stein still hoped for a commercial edition by an American publisher.

3. "Natural Phenomena," in Stein's *Painted Lace and Other Pieces*, pp. 167–233.

To Fania Marinoff
[Rose motto]

[postmark: 10 May 1925]   27 rue de Fleurus
                                           [Paris]

My dear Fania[1]

Carl has just written of your plans and we do want to see you. We are leaving Sunday the seventeenth and we want you for dinner Saturday evening seven o'clock the sixteenth, Carl says you will be here on the fifteenth and will you and will you dine on Saturday we do want to see you

Always
Gtrde Stein

1. Addressed to Marinoff at the American Express Office in London.

❦

To Gertrude Stein

[12 May 1925]
Tuesday

Grand Hotel
London
W. C. 2

Gertrude Stein dear,

Carl was wrong It's the twenty second that I arrive, not the sixteenth. But I expect to be in Paris for three weeks, so I do hope you will have returned some time before I leave. I, too, want to see you both, very much. Do drop me a line here or to The American Express, Paris that it will be possible,

love
address Fania Marinoff

❦

To Carl Van Vechten

[postmark: 9 June 1925]

Hotel Pernollet
Belley (Ain)

My dear Carl,

We did have a delightful visit from Avery [Hopwood] and Gertrude Atherton just the day before we left,[1] but no Fania, we are hoping that perhaps as France isn't so large we may manage it yet. Avery is as nice as ever if not nicer you do always send nice ones. I am sorry about the Knopfs but perhaps they may want to cool off at Aix les Bains and then we could meet. I am hard at the Long Book,[2] one quarter of it is already to print, they don't make plates so you get a whole piece ready at a time and then they finish it, and now we commence the second quarter. It is long but it ain't bad. Nothing else xciting xcept my little Novel[3] and my long Natural Phenomena at which I am working and lots of love to you

Always
Gertrude.

1. Hopwood and Atherton visited Stein on Sunday 17 May 1925 (Hopwood to Stein, two pneumatics, 16 May 1925, YCAL).

2. Stein's *The Making of Americans.*

3. Stein often worked on a number of compositions simultaneously. The references in the next few letters to "my little novel" are difficult to associate with a particular work. Van Vechten himself, in his introduction to the final volume of the Yale Edition of the Unpublished Writings of Gertrude Stein, thought that Stein was referring to *A Novel of Thank You,* a work which occupied Stein from the spring of 1925 until December 1926. The novel might have begun as a short work but eventually it grew in length (in the Yale series it is 240 pages).

To Gertrude Stein

30 June 1925

150 West Fifty-fifth Street
[New York]

Dear Gertrude,

I'm sorry that you and Fania could not connect. She is passing through Paris again along the middle of July. Perhaps something will happen then. She had at least one evening with Avery [Hopwood] in Paris . . . . The Knopfs, it seems, are not going to Paris at all. Their route embraces London, San Sebastian, and Poland: God's truth! Nobody has ever made this tour before; It has something to do with AUTHORS!

I am so excited about *all* your new books and hope they will soon be coming along. I shall soon send you Firecrackers. At least two pages of it are sure to amuse you. I am reading proofs on Excavations, which is to come out in January, and when I have finished reading proofs, I shall start on my Negro novel.[1] I have passed practically my whole winter in company with Negroes and have succeeded in getting into most of the important *sets.* This will not be a novel about Negroes in the South or white contacts or lynchings. It will be about NEGROES, as they live now in the new city of Harlem (which is part of New York). About 400,000 of them live there now, rich and poor, fast and slow, intellectual and ignorant. I hope it will be a good book. One of my best friends, Paul Robeson, goes to London in September to play The Emperor Jones.[2] He is a great actor and when he sings spirituals he is as great as Chaliapin. I want you to meet him. If you are going to London in the fall let me arrange it. I can send you a letter or give him a letter or you can just collide.

with much love,
Carlo

Mabel is back in Taos, though she plans to return to Croton in the fall. All the magazines are bursting with her work, now signed Mabel Dodge Luhan.[3] She is sending me nice cowboy records. Have you a phonograph and would you like some nice *Negro* records? If you see Vanity Fair do read my paper on the Blues[4] in the August number.[5]

1. Van Vechten's *Nigger Heaven*.

2. Robeson played the role of Brutus Jones in Eugene O'Neill's *The Emperor Jones* in London in September–October 1925.

3. Among the articles published by Dodge in 1925 were "Native Air," *The New Republic*, 4 March 1925, pp. 40–42, and "The Santos of New Mexico," *The Arts* (March 1925), 7(3):127–30.

4. Van Vechten's "The Black Blues. Negro Songs of Disappointment in Love: Their Pathos Hardened with Laughter," *Vanity Fair* (August 1925), 24:57, 86, 92.

5. In Stein's hand on the verso of the letter:
212 three S
Page 274, 276, 277, 344, 347
279, 284, 303, 351, 356, 361
305, 311 314 363 367
321 322 325
327 332 338
339 341 342

These numbers may refer either to pages in the typescript or to page proofs of *The Making of Americans*.

To Carl Van Vechten

[postmark: 9 July 1925]   Hotel Pernollet
Belley (Ain)

My dear Carl

Avery [Hopwood] said you were getting thin if not thinner and it does look like it, we all do and well don't we. We are down here well not per-

[117]

manently but until the best part of the book has been printed, we are all through with a third of it now it is even printed and we go on and on. You know it is rather funny and youthful there are moments when I think I should prune it but then after all it was done as much done as it could be and after all these years I guess it will do. It is quite xciting, I don't know why it should be but it is that and its large thoughts I was not so young then but it does seem young are what hit me most. I am so sorry about not seeing Fania, it is too bad, but Paris this summer and besides there is here and the book, better luck next time and I do hope there will be a next time soon. A friend has just come along with some samples of Mabel [Dodge] in the Mags,[1] she is trustingly Buffalo in it, it is funny and in a way sweet but then Mabel always was sweet, it was an elderly damsel who told me all about Tony [Luhan] and his cracking of nuts. You don't tell about his cracking of nuts. So the Knopfs are not to be in Paris, I would like to see them. Something might happen and I have always rather hoped it would. I have an idea that when I finish my little novel well it isn't a little novel but then you know how it is, it is a novel, well when I finish that and the Phenomena of Nature together they would make a volume of 100 pages or a little more 150 perhaps it would be rather nice A Novel and Natural Phenomena. Perhaps he might be induced to venture on such a little venture, anyway tell me if you think it at all worth my while writing to him about it some time later. At present I am very full and happy and so are you, and so that's all.[2]

Always
Gertrude.

1. See Van Vechten to Stein, 30 June 1925, note 3.
2. See Stein to Van Vechten [9 June 1925], note 3.

To Carl Van Vechten
[Postcard: Roma—Esposizione Etnografica]

[postmark: 10 July 1925]   [Hôtel Pernollet
                                             Belley, Ain]

I forgot to say do tell [Paul] Robeson to come to see us if he gets to Paris. I would a lot like to know them now, and hear them anyhow, and I am much intrigued to know what your plot is to be for the Negro story of Harlem, Good luck to it.

Always
Gertrude.

To Carl Van Vechten
MS. *New York Public Library, Manuscripts Division*

[postmark: 21 July 1925]   Hotel Pernollet
                                                  Belley (Ain)

My dear Carl,

Your Fireworks[1] came and I have just read it, you know it is rather strange but for the first time there is you around through and behind it, I mean a book, hitherto you have always been completely impersonal. I don't mean anything you say or anything you conceive in it that of course is you but in this case the you has come in differently in a way it seems to have gotten out of your control you I mean and gotten into the book, it intrigues and puzzles me and I am wondering if it will continue in the other new ones and if it does what it will do. It's what interested me most that and the party I like your parties and I like your parties because they always are parties and one does like parties I like parties, this one is a very nice party, I wish we could have a party, we would so have liked to give Fania a party and both of you a party, all the party that would have been a party were disappointed with Fania when there was no party. I am looking forward enormously to the nigger book but that won't be for a year yet, I'll be kind of sorry if you in this new way aren't in the next book, it bothers and kind of pleases me, lots of love to you always

Gertrude.

---

1. Stein means Van Vechten's novel *Firecrackers*.

[119]

❧

To Gertrude Stein

1 August 1925   150 West Fifty-fifth Street
[New York]

Dear Gertrude,

I'm glad you found some strange new quality in my book and hope it is really there. I feel, however, that it is a logical successor to the other. I am very anxious to get to work on my new one[1] and now that Fania is back to order my meals I may be able to; she was desolée not to have seen you. But I saw Dorothy Harvey who said she had seen you and I flushed with pleasure when she told me what you had said about me.[2] And now I bow. And I am impatient to receive The Making of Americans and The Birthday Book and EVERYTHING Else. And I am sending Paul Robeson to you, that is if he goes to Paris, and if he doesn't, if you go to London, look him up because I will give him a letter. You see he is to play The Emperor Jones and if it is a success he will play it till December 15 when he has to come back here for his concert tour. He is a lamb of God; I like him better than almost anyone I ever met and I think you will too and he will love you and you will like his wife just as much. I'm glad you decided against pruning the History. I want it all. I've only seen three of the manuscript volumes, you know. I have never heard the story of Tony and the cracking of nuts. If you are kind in heart you will write it to me. It is very hot and I may possibly come over in October. Anyway I will send all the *nice ones* to you.

hortensias, caviar, and moonstones to you!

Carlo

My *real* parties are even nicer than the parties in my books. Get Paul & Essie to tell you.

1. Van Vechten's *Nigger Heaven*.

2. Dorothy Harvey was a writer and journalist. It was her sister Caroline Dudley who brought the Revue Nègre to Paris. Under her maiden name, Dorothy Dudley, she wrote *Forgotten Frontiers: Dreiser and The Land of the Free* (New York: Harrison Smith and Robert Haas, 1932). This book contained a brief discussion of Stein (pp. 277–78).

❧

To Gertrude Stein

1 August 1925[1]   150 West Fifty-Fifth Street
                                                     [New York]

Dear Gertrude,

This letter preludes the approach of two of the nicest people left in the world: Essie and Paul Robeson. But you know already what I think about *that!*

> *My affection to you*
> *Carlo*

1. This letter, written on 1 August 1925, was not sent to Stein until sometime in Ocotber 1925. It was enclosed in a letter of Eslanda Robeson to Stein ([? October 1925], YCAL). Eslanda Robeson wrote Stein that she and Paul planned to be in Paris about the first week of November.

❧

To Carl Van Vechten

[postmark: 22 August 1925]   Hotel Pernollet
                                                     Belley (Ain)

My dear Carl,

That is a nice even if it is only a perhaps, the prospect of seeing you, I mean that it is nice that there is at least a perhaps of seeing you, but you will come over, it's been a long time, and everything would be nice, I am inclosing a print of the title page and cover it is to be,[1] looks rather well we are almost all done now and it makes me feel well I don't know xactly what it does make me feel but there he is the eldest son, Three Lives being the eldest but a daughter, and ainé as I call him has been a bother, we will hope now that his travaux and all is nicely done that he will make the future easy for his parents, anyway there we are and you are his god father so you're responsible at least for his religion and morals, poor dear ainé. Otherwise no news, we will be going back to Paris now in about two weeks, we have enjoyed it here and I've done a lot of work I like my novel and my P[henomena]. o[f] N[ature]. and will tell you all about all when we get back and do let me know soon that the perhaps is sure, and best to Fania and once more lots of regrets, will she come back too,

Anyway always
Gertrude.

1. For *The Making of Americans*.

❧

To Gertrude Stein

9 September 1925   150 West Fifty-fifth Street
                                     [New York]

Dear Gertrude,

A charming young man, hight Donald Angus, is leaving for Paris on the Berengaria next Wednesday and I am giving him a letter to you. You will, I think, find him amusing. Among other things, he was present on the occasion when Antonio Luhan visited the Harlem cabarets. Donald is going to Paris as secretary-treasurer-manager of the Hotsy-Totsy Co., an all Negro revue which opens at the Champs Elysées on October 2.[1]

Yesterday I sent you [Miguel] Covarrubias' new book of caricatures. I am the subject of one of these, and also I contributed a preface to the volume.[2]

I saw Jo Davidson the other evening and he told me that you say nice things about me; all the world knows that I have been saying nice things about you for ten years. So: each one of us is one and we say nice things about two!

I can scarcely control my impatience in regard to The Making of Americans. You didn't send me the Contact book but, of course, I got it.[3] Please don't let me miss anything.

My love to you!

Carlo

I may come over in October. Pourquoi pas?

1. This was the Revue Nègre, which starred, among others, Josephine Baker.

2. See Van Vechten to Stein, 18 April 1925, note 1.

3. Stein's "Two Women" had been published in *Contact Collection of Contemporary Writers* (Paris: The Contact Press, 1925), pp. [303]–25. "Two Women" is a portrait of Dr. Claribel Cone ("Bertha" in the portrait) and her sister Etta ("Ada" in the portrait).

❧

To Carl Van Vechten
[Rose motto]

[postmark: 9 November 1925]   27 rue de Fleurus
                                           [Paris]

There is no doubt about it Carl that you have awfully good taste in friends and it's a great pleasure to me that I am one of the oldest and best of them because I feel it to be a proof of how charming and gentle I am it's true alright and we have had a good time with them. [Paul] Robeson is a dear and he sang for us and I had a long talk with him and everybody liked him[1] and [Donald] Angus[2] is a nice boy and they all together made a nice party and everybody I think was pleased. It doesn't sound much as if you were coming over to see us and that is a pity because it would be nice but I love [you] just the same. I hope you like the looks of your god-child Making of Americans, I am on the whole very pleased with it but a little anxious naturally he is so very large well anyway always best to you both and

Always all yours
Gertrude.

1. Stein had invited the Robesons to tea on Friday 6 November (Eslanda Robeson to Stein, undated letter, YCAL).

2. Note by Van Vechten, 18 January 1941: "Donald Angus who went to Paris to help Caroline Dudley with the Revue Nègre."

&

To Gertrude Stein

13 December 1925   150 West Fifty-fifth Street
                                    [New York]

Dear Gertrude,

The Making of Americans arrived and I was excited for two days. It is even bigger and more imposing than it was in all those typewritten volumes. And I knew all along that it would be published someday and so I am gladder that the day has come. I have reread parts of it with delight and I shall go through it more carefully when I have finished my book which is called "Nigger Heaven." Do you like the title? I am working day and night on that. I knew you would like Paul Robeson. He is a lamb of God. And, of course, everybody *loves you.* Donald Angus writes that he has never before met anyone so beautiful, so witty, and so nice.[1] I saw Jo Davidson the day before he sailed. I think he can tell you some amusing things. Mabel [Dodge] is here and he has seen her. I am sending you my new book for Christmas,[2] but you haven't told me whether you received [Miguel] Covarrubias's book, "The Prince of Wales and other famous Americans" which I sent you over a month ago.

Love to you always,
Carlo

1. Angus to Van Vechten, postmark 12 November 1925, YCAL.
2. Van Vechten's *Excavations: A Book of Advocacies.*

&

To Carl Van Vechten
MS. New York Public Library, Manuscripts Division
[Rose motto]

[postmark: 28 December 1925]   27 rue de Fleurus
                                                [Paris]

My dear Carl,

Happy new year and I am sure I thanked you for the book Excavations which I enjoyed immensely and which were wildly like and here you say I didn't and perhaps I didn't but I am sure I did but anyway Carl I love your new book and I like it a lot, I like it about dedications, I do miss though to the Influences what I have made me what I am but and I like all the other parts. I am waiting impatiently for nigger heaven and who is in nigger heaven all of them, they are and they are. What's the news, just the same I am hoping you will like my big book more and more and I am still at my novel and my Natural Phenomena and I am still liking to look at my big book, and Jo [Davidson] came back and told us all about everything, this is the first time he has liked America better than France. I think he does just now any how lots and lots of love and good wishes.

Always
Gtde.

To Gertrude Stein

18 January [1926]   150 West Fifty-fifth Street
                                                  [New York]

Dear Gertrude,

You *were* kind to me in that Paris Herald Interview, as if I . . . well, you were kind to me.[1] I've just been to Iowa for my father's funeral . . . he was 86 . . . and funerals are very hard to bear and I am very tired and I *must* finish Nigger Heaven by March; so I can't do anything else until I have finished it. But I am sending you Langston Hughes's poems and when Langston goes to Paris again I will send you Langston and you will like him.[2] Mabel [Dodge], after a quick trip Indianward, is back and has taken her house at Croton again, but I have not seen her yet.[3] [Paul] Robeson's first concerts have been very successful.[4] I think, perhaps, when you read Nigger Heaven you will want to come to New York. When I get through my work I shall examine The Making of Americans more carefully.

with my love,
Carlo

1. An interview with Stein, written by Sadie Hope Sternberg, appeared in the *New York Herald* (Paris edition), Sunday, 27 December 1925, p. 9. In the interview Stein spoke about *The Making of Americans* and about her career.

[125]

Van Vechten was then unknown. We have become very good friends since. He, perhaps, did more than any other to keep me before the public, though Sherwood Anderson was very decent when he was at his height and people were only making fun of me.
Henry McBride completes the trio who have been my most persistent friends and champions in America.

2. Langston Hughes's *The Weary Blues* (New York: Alfred A. Knopf, 1926) contained Van
Vechten's "Introducing Langston Hughes to the Reader" (pp. 9–13). Van Vechten had met
Hughes (1902–1967) at an NAACP cabaret party at Happy Rhone's Club, New York. Van
Vechten had been brought there by the writers Walter White and James Weldon Johnson.

3. Some years earlier, Dodge had found a house in Croton-on-Hudson to serve as a school for
Elizabeth Duncan and acquired a house for herself on the same site.

4. Robeson had begun a series of concerts with one at Town Hall, New York, on 5 January
1926.

❧

To Carl Van Vechten

[postmark: 3 February 1926]   27 rue de Fleurus
                                                       Paris

My dear Carl,

I am awfully sorry you are tired but I am looking forward to Nigger
Heaven and thanks for the preview. I think you will be pleased with my
news. The literary society of Cambridge England, the Cam asked me some
time ago to give them an address on myself, and I said no at first but now I
have said yes, and it looks as if I will also be going to give it at Oxford and
London University, more than that I have written it and it is a pretty good
address really clarifies I believe.[1] Katherine Dudley[2] Mrs. Harvey's sister will
tell you how much anyway perhaps with that recognition, Knopf may see
his way to publishing me how about Portraits and Prayers with an introduction by you, do try it on, anyway I am a little nervous never having spoken
before, it's coming off in May, lots of love

Gertrude.

1. It was Edith Sitwell who had first tried to get Stein to lecture at Cambridge University. At
first Stein refused, then later reconsidered and agreed to lecture. In March 1926 she was invited
by Harold Acton, eldest son of Arthur Acton, whom she had known in Florence, to lecture at

[126]

Oxford University (see Gallup, *The Flowers of Friendship*, pp. [184]–86). Stein delivered her lecture, "Composition as Explanation," at Trinity College, Cambridge University, on Friday 4 June 1926 at 8:30 P.M. The same lecture was delivered at Christ Church, Oxford University, on 7 June 1926.

2. Note by Van Vechten, 21 January 1941: "Katherine Dudley who took the Revue Nègre to Paris and married Joseph Delteil the French writer. Mrs. Harvey is Dorothy Dudley who wrote 'Forgotten Frontiers.' "

To Gertrude Stein

4 March 1926   150 West Fifty-fifth Street
                                               [New York]

Dear Gertrude,

Every once in a while somebody tells me about a lovely piece you wrote about Negroes: was it about Josephine Baker?[1] Anyway I have never seen it and will you send me a copy? NIGGER HEAVEN is finished at last—all but the proofs and in about three months I shall be sending you a copy. I have quoted a long passage from Melanctha in it. I hope you will like this book which you will find somewhat different from the ordinary volume about Negroes.[2] By the way, the race is getting more popular every day. Lenore Ulric is a sensation in Lulu Belle—there are over a hundred Negroes in the cast—and three Negro plays are announced for next fall. Paul [Robeson] is to star in one.[3] His concerts are a huge success. I am excited about your address at Cambridge. Could I have a copy of that, too? Mabel [Dodge] and her Tony [Luhan] have gone in intensively for Gurdjieff and I haven't seen much of her.[4]

easter lilies and magnolias to you!

Carlo

1. Stein's "Among Negroes" was published in her *Useful Knowledge*, pp. 60–62. The piece begins, "A story of the Three of you Josephine Baker Maud de Forrest and Ida Lewelyn." The three women were stars of the Revue Nègre whom Stein had met. The piece also mentions Paul and Eslanda Robeson. It is possible that one of these people or Donald Angus had written to Van Vechten about the Stein composition.

2. In Van Vechten's novel *Nigger Heaven*, Mary Love, who works in a library in Harlem, is reminded of Stein's "Melanctha" when she comes home at two in the morning after an evening of dancing. She recalls from memory a conversation between Dr. Jeff Campbell and Melanctha. Van Vechten quotes at length from this conversation. See *Nigger Heaven*, pp. 57–58.

3. Lenore Ulric played the roll of Lulu Belle, a black "harlot of Harlem," in *Lulu Belle*, a play by Edward Sheldon and Charles MacArthur. The play was produced by David Belasco and opened at the Belasco Theatre on 9 February 1926. There were fifty-eight performers in the cast and the play ran for 461 performances.

The plays Van Vechten refers to were *Black Boy*, by Jim Tully and Frank Dazey, starring Paul Robeson, which opened on 6 October 1926 at the Comedy Theatre, New York, and ran for thirty-seven performances; a revival of Eugene O'Neill's *The Emperor Jones*, starring Charles Gilpin as Brutus Jones, which opened at the Mayfair Theatre, New York, 10 November 1926; and *In Abraham's Bosom*, by Paul Green, which opened at the Provincetown Theatre, New York, on 30 December 1926, and ran for 116 performances. *In Abraham's Bosom* received the Pulitzer Prize in May 1927.

4. Georgi Ivanovitch Gurdjieff, a Russian mystic who arrived in Paris in the early 1920s and attracted a large number of followers with his philosophical teachings. Groups based on his teachings are still active today.

⅋

To Carl Van Vechten

[postmark: 25 May 1926] 27 rue de Fleurus
Paris

My dear Carl,

No Nigger Heaven, yet, what has happened to it, Avery [Hopwood] and I both xpected it and neither of us had it, but we had Avery, and now he has gone, the hotel says he has gone,[1] he is a dear though, and we are xpecting him again before long. As for me I leave for England on Sunday, a little nervous, never having been in that kind of thing before, but I manage not to think of it so there we are, I am all dressed anyway so that is always that, I will send you the lecture and the negroes when we get back. And how are you, Max Ewing says you are alright,[2] but then you would be

Lots of love always
Gertrude.

1. Hopwood arrived in Paris on 4 May 1926 and stayed at the Carlton Hotel (Hopwood to Stein, postmark 5 May 1926, 11 May 1926, and undated letter, May 1926, all YCAL).

[128]

2. Max Ewing (1903–1934) was a writer, painter, composer, and musician. His "Chocolate Thunder," a recitative and air for piano and tenor from his oratorio "Sacred Emily" (based on Stein's poem of the same name) was sung by the tenor William S. Rainey as part of *An Intimate Review* presented by Joseph Mullen at the Cherry Lane Playhouse, New York, on 22 November 1925. Ewing was introduced to Stein by Van Vechten.

Note by Van Vechten, 21 January 1941: "A young American boy who was to commit suicide ten years later."

To Gertrude Stein

7 June 1926

150 West Fifty-fifth Street
[New York]

Dear Gertrude,

This will introduce you to Blanche Knopf.[1] If you like each other as much as I like each of you, it will mean a lot!

love,
Carlo Van Vechten

1. Wife of the publisher Alfred A. Knopf.

To Carl Van Vechten
[Rose motto]

[postmark: 27 June 1926]

27 rue de Fleurus
[Paris]

My dear Carl,

I have been meaning to write to you but I have been so xcited by my adventures that it has taken me some time.[1] It was a nice adventure one of the very nicest I ever had, real sympathy understanding and enthusiasm and so many admiring young men and my thing is good it is to appear in the Hogarth Essay series press[2] and is to be called Composition as Explanation and in the discussion I was very bright and I am really very happy about it all, I am hoping it will lead to many things. No book of yours yet,[3] when will it come and anyway lots and lots of love

Always
Gertrude.

1. A reference to her lectures at Cambridge University and Oxford University. See Stein to Van Vechten [3 February 1926], note 1.

2. The Hogarth Press volume *Composition as Explanation* printed Stein's lecture "Composition as Explanation" and the pieces she had read as examples of her work at the end of her lecture: "Preciosilla," "A Saint in Seven," "Sitwell Edith Sitwell," and "Jean Cocteau."

3. Stein had not yet received Van Vechten's novel *Nigger Heaven*.

To Gertrude Stein

15 July 1926   150 West Fifty-fifth Street
[New York]

Dear Gertrude,

This will introduce you to Mrs. Edwin Swift Balch of Philadelphia, who as Emily Clark was responsible for the Reviewer in Richmond.

love,
Carlo V. V.

To Gertrude Stein

24 July 1926   150 West Fifty-fifth Street
[New York]

Dear Gertrude,

I am so excited about your adventures in England, but you promised to send me the lecture and you didn't. I am sending you Nigger Heaven

[130]

today, and I am sending you several people, all of whom matter more or less, but the most is Nora Ray, who is slightly mulatto, terribly amusing, adorable, rich, chic, et autres choses aussi. Get her to sing for you if you can.[1]

much love,
Carlo

1. Nora Ray (1885–1974) was known professionally as Nora Holt. Holt had a career as a singer and as a professional music critic. From 1917 to 1921 she wrote for the *Chicago Defender*, and from 1943 until shortly before her death she was music critic for the *Amsterdam News*. In 1919 Holt founded the National Association of Negro Musicians. In a note attached to her letters to him that are part of Yale-JWJ, Van Vechten wrote:

> At first she was Nora Ray: this husband was head of the commissary at the Bethlehem Steel Works. Nora was a friend of Charley Schwab: but when she broke with Ray she took the name of her former husband, Holt, who was a liquor merchant in Chicago. Her original name was Douglas. She was the prototype of Lasca Sartoris in *Nigger Heaven*.

To Carl Van Vechten
MS. New York Public Library, Manuscripts Division

[postmark: 9 August 1926]   Hotel Pernollet
                                                Belley (Ain)

My dear Carl,

I am delighted delighted, Nigger Heaven came and I have just read it, it is awfully good and made up of light and delicate work and I am pleased and proud to be in it. You have never done anything better it is rather perfectly done and that is one of the things I like about it most, a thing like the best niggers the Sumners that is actually perfection neither too delicate nor too anything and yourself in it, it is really in a big and delicate way and the Sill man who comes forward and back from being nigger to being white really Carl the way you have kept it delicate and real it is the most perfect workmanship and the first party, the party at Adora's is one of your best parties and you know what I think of your parties, the rest of it is all good and the interest as the critics say never stops, I am awfully pleased that it is so good more pleased than I can say and so much love to you and Fania she must be awfully pleased at the book being so good. I am sending you by this mail a type written copy of Composition as Explanation which is my address, the Dial is printing it in November and I have just corrected the proof of it with the things I read to illustrate for the Grafton Press which brings it out in the fall.[1] I will send you As a wife has a cow, a love story in September, [Juan] Gris has done the illustrations and they are good, well lots of love again and I can't tell you how pleased I am with Nigger Heaven, it is a nice heaven.

Always
Gertrude.

I hope we will be back in time to see Nora Ray and the others, will be in Paris end of September.

G.S.

1. Stein means the Hogarth Press. The Grafton Press had been the first publisher of her *Three Lives* in 1909. The Hogarth Press volume, *Composition as Explanation*, in addition to the lecture "Composition as Explanation," printed Stein's "Preciosilla," "A Saint in Seven," "Sitwell Edith Sitwell," and "Jean Cocteau."
    The Dial printed "Composition as Explanation" (October 1926), 131(4):[327]–36.

To Gertrude Stein

5 September 1926   150 West Fifty-fifth Street
                                                         [New York]

Dear Gertrude,

Your marvelous letter came and also Composition as Explanation. I only wish I had been at Oxford and Cambridge, and when will you do this in America? I hope to hear you at Harvard and Howard and Lincoln. Well, it is a splendid piece and as I read it I listen to you speak and it clarifies and illuminates but it does not explain, and that is what I hoped it didn't, for the sense of an artist is the sense that an intuitive reader puts into a reading of his work and not what the artist announces . . . . But you know all this and that is why . .

I was delighted that you liked Nigger Heaven. Everybody likes it, which surprises me. Even in the South . . where it is hailed as an "important social document," "a serious work of the first importance to all who would know the workings of the Negro mind," etc. and all of my Negro *friends* like it, but, naturally, not all Negroes. You will like Nora Ray and she will adore you. I suppose she has looked you up while you have been out of town but I think she will still be there in September.

I am waiting anxiously for your new books. You never sent me, by the way, your piece about Josephine Baker and Maude de Forest[x] and I have heard so much about *that*. May I have that piece?[1]

I may come over to swim the English channel. Until then, my affection,

Carlo Van Vechten

[x]or maybe two or three others

1. See Van Vechten to Stein, 4 March 1926, note 1.

To Carl Van Vechten
MS. New York Public Library, Manuscripts Division

[postmark: 19 September 1926] Hotel Pernollet
Belley (Ain)

My dear Carl,

I am most awfully pleased that Nigger Heaven is being so successful, it is true that there is nobody whose success gives me as much pleasure as yours does, I don't know why but it does. I was awfully sorry not to see Blanche Knopf it would have been very much what I would like but she wrote me and said that she xpected to be in Paris later this year and so we will meet before the winter is over, it would mean a lot to me if something happened but on the whole I can't complain. The As a wife has a cow, will be out in a few weeks' time and I will send you a copy at once also the Hogarth Press of Composition as Explanation. I am glad that you think it just right. It pleased me to do it and it still seems to be xciting them over there over there being these days across the channel for me, and others. You will be interested that one of the dons at Oxford said to me at the end, what he liked was that it was not an xplanation but a creation, well he said more but he said that. I can eat it with a spoon or a soup ladle or anything and I like it, but you always come first to me and that you know, you meant it first and said it first. Just had a letter from Avery [Hopwood],[1] he likes Nigger Heaven too, we are very fond of Avery, I do hope that I will see Nora Ray, if you write her tell her to let me know where she is and I will write as soon as I get back. We are staying here a little longer, because this year we left for the country so late on account of England and the weather is still of the best. Alice is typing Josephine Baker for you.[2] Lots of love and best to Fania

Always
Gertrude.

1. Hopwood to Stein, 9 September [1926], YCAL.
2. See Van Vechten to Stein, 4 March 1926, note 1.

To Gertrude Stein

30 September 1926							150 West Fifty-fifth Street
										[New York]

Dear Gertrude,

You can reach (Mrs.) Nora Ray through the American Express Company. Do write her when you get back to Paris. A letter just received from her tells me that she is going to sing in a cabaret just off the Champs-Elysées, beginning October 15, the same cabaret in which Yvonne George appears.[1] She is an excellent musician and has even done orchestration, but I think this is her first professional engagement, although before she married she sometimes entertained at parties in Chicago. At the piano she is fascinating.

Nigger Heaven is in its fourth printing and my biggest success. I'm glad you like it. I have not yet received your Josephine Baker. Paul Robeson opens in a play about a Negro prize-fighter next week. It is called Black Boy. [Edward] Steichen has taken some amazing photographs of him, one of which will appear in an early number of Vanity Fair.

Hearts and flowers to you!

Carl Van Vechten

DON'T MISS NORA RAY ! ! ! ! ! !

1. Holt appeared in the nightclub Les Nuits du Prado from 14 to 28 October 1926 (see Holt to Van Vechten, 18 September 1926, Yale-JWJ; Gallup, *The Flowers of Friendship*, p. 197).

To Gertrude Stein

6 October 1926

150 West Fifty-fifth Street
[New York]

Dear Gertrude,

May I introduce to you my sister, Mrs. Shaffer, and her daughter, Elizabeth?

always,
Carlo V. V.

To Carl Van Vechten
[Rose motto]

[postmark: 31 October 1926]

27 rue de Fleurus
[Paris]

My dear Carl,

Just back and settling in and have seen your sister whom we like very much and your niece whom we like too although she is a little ponti[fi]cal

[135]

but your sister is awfully nice and she told me a lot about you and I liked hearing about you the way she told about you, I always like hearing about you but her way of telling about you is particularly pleasant.[1] And the book is booming, I am awfully glad. Have not seen Nora Ray yet but will very soon now, now that the preliminaries of settling in are finished. I worked a lot in the country and I am doing a new thing here, a kind of a something, well anyway there is an announcement of [Juan] Gris' book, it is very pretty,[2]

Lots of love
Gertrude.

1. Stein had seen them for dinner on 28 October 1926 (Emma Van Vechten Shaffer to Stein, 26 October [1926], YCAL).

2. From 1909 to 1939 Daniel-Henry Kahnweiler issued a subscription bulletin which announced the publication of each book printed by the Galerie Kahnweiler and then later by the Editions de la Galerie Simon. The bulletin that appeared for Stein's *A Book Concluding With As A Wife Has A Cow A Love Story* printed an extract from "Composition as Explanation."

To Carl Van Vechten

[postmark: 4 December 1926]

27 rue de Fleurus
Paris

My dear Carl

I have just given Robert Coates a letter to you, he is a young fellow who has written the Eater of Darkness, I like what he is doing he does not do much because he is still in the stage where he has to earn his living by regular work but it is good. I do hope you will like him, we like all yours so much I hope mine is the same.[1] I just had a charming postal from Nora Ray,[2] from Monte Carlo, she was only here once but she left a very complete flavor of intermingling in a way that makes most words which would describe her be either too weak or too strong, and she is just that. Some day when she comes back [Pavel] Tchelitcheff wants to do a portrait of her he met her here and he would do it very interestingly perhaps well anyway we

will see her again.[3] I am sending you As a wife has a cow next week. I know
you will like both what [Juan] Gris and I have done in it, and I guess that's
all. I am working a lot on examples. I have just finished a longish novel, I
rather like it.[4]

Lots of love
Gertrude.

1. Robert Coates (1897–1973) had first met Stein in 1922 (Coates to Stein, postmark 26 July
1922, YCAL). His novel *The Eater of Darkness* was first published in Paris by the Contact Press
in 1926.

2. Holt to Stein, 22 November 1926, YCAL.

3. Stein had met Tchelitchew (1898–1957), the Russian-born painter, through Jane Heap in
the spring of 1926.

4. Stein's *A Novel of Thank You.*

To Carl Van Vechten

[4 December 1926]   27 rue de Fleurus
                                                     [Paris]

My dear Carl,

I want you to know Robert Coates whose work I have liked for the
last three years and as he is young that will do.[1]

Always
Gertrude.

1. Note by Van Vechten, 21 January 1941: "He came to see me, but apparently we didn't get
on too well, as I don't recall I ever saw him again. All I remember about his visit now is his
brilliant red hair!"

Coates wrote Stein on 11 October 1927 (YCAL) that he had met Van Vechten and that
her photograph, presumably one by Man Ray, was very prominent in his apartment.

To Gertrude Stein

10 December 1926   150 West Fifty-fifth Street
                                    [New York]

Dear Gertrude,

Nora Holt writes "I went to tea at Gertrude Stein's and adored her. She is a great person," but I've heard nothing from you about her.[1] She is now singing at Monte Carlo. I like the Hogarth Press edition of Composition as Explanation and have taken an especial fancy to the one about Jean Cocteau. Did you ever know Germaine Tailleferre, by the way? She has just married my friend Ralph Barton, three weeks after they met.[2] Useful Knowledge (among Negroes) is simply stupendous and would help with white people too. And I learn that the Bonis are to do Three Lives. Hurray for our side! . . . I have a bad cold and don't feel that I can ever write again . . . and I haven't written a line since March 1, and do you think I'd like Antibes? Mrs. Regan is trying to put on another Révue Nègre, here, this time, and she wants Nora Holt among others. New York has gone almost completely native and soon we'll be all mixed up, but those that are born already can never be any darker or lighter. Nora wrote me that you had written her: "You write Holt and Carl writes Ray." "Well," added Nora, "Rose is a rose is a rose!"[3] Mabel [Dodge] is still in New Mexico, or should I say *yet.* .

hortensias and mimosa to you!
Carlo V. V.

1. Holt to Van Vechten, postmark 14 November 1926, Yale-JWJ.

2. Ralph Barton (d. 1931) was an artist who did illustrations for Van Vechten's *Peter Whiffle: His Life and Works* and *The Tattooed Countess*. Van Vechten dedicated his book *Red: Papers on Musical Subjects* to Barton.

3. Holt to Van Vechten, postmark 27 October 1926, Yale-JWJ.

To Carl Van Vechten
[Rose motto]

[postmark: 26 December 1926]   27 rue de Fleurus
                                                                 [Paris]

My dearest Carl,

Of course you will like Antibes and we will like [to] see you in Paris because you would have to be in Paris en route and there are lots of nice things in Antibes and in Paris, we were just talking about you the other day, you could so wonderfully do some of the American women in Europe the other version [of] the tattooed countess, Rene Crevel has tried to do one of them in his la Mort difficile, but he does not understand[1] and you so wonderfully would well anyway, you have by this time gotten a long letter I wrote you about Nora [Holt] and everything, I like Nora a lot she is tender and I like her postal cards. I guess she is having a good time alright but then it is easy anybody would like her, I don't know it's quite tender. What other news is there I like you taking the Jean Cocteau and what is funny about it is that the people who don't know English get something out of it when it is read to them that is rather nice.[2] Then we [have] several things on the tapis a new magazine in which I am to be featured etc.[3] but more of all that later when it is more and other things and anyway I do adore that those that are born already can never be any darker or lighter, it has all our native everything in it, that, go on writing Carl, I think you are most wonderfully in the vein and come to us and happy New Year and best to Fania and always yours

Gertrude.

1. René Crevel (1900–1935), the French writer, had met Stein through Pavel Tchelitchew (see Gallup, *The Flowers of Friendship*, pp. 197–98). Stein is referring to the character of Mme. Dumon-Dufour in Crevel's novel *La morte difficile* (1926; rpt. Paris: Jean-Jacques Pauvert, 1974).

2. Note by Van Vechten, 21 January 1941: "The motto 'a little too much is just enough for me' which I used on my stationery for some time." The line comes from an anecdote in Cocteau's essay "Visites A Maurice Barrès" in his *Le Rappel A L'Ordre* (Paris: Librairie Stock, 1926, p. 173):

Un chef des Peaux-Rouges fut récemment l'invité de la Maison-Blanche. A la table du président Wilson, ses intimes lui laissant entendre qu'il mangeait et buvait peut-être un

peu trop: 'A *little too much is just enough for me*', répondit-il. (Un peu trop, c'est juste assez pour moi.)
Si je devais prendre une devise, je choisirais cette réponse magnifique.

Van Vechten's first use in this correspondence of stationery with this motto does not occur until a letter to Stein and Toklas postmarked 17 December 1934. The stationery is used with frequency throughout the middle 1930s. In annotating this letter Van Vechten did not have the advantage of having his letters to Stein before him. He may have assumed that when Stein wrote "I like you taking the Jean Cocteau," she was referring to the motto. Stein is certainly echoing Van Vechten's letter to her of 10 December 1926 when he wrote: "I like the Hogarth Press edition of Composition as Explanation and have taken an especial fancy to the one [i.e., Stein's word portrait 'Jean Cocteau' which is printed in the volume] about Cocteau."

3. Stein is referring to *larus the celestial visitor*, a review edited by Sherry Mangan, which printed her "Water Pipe" (February 1927), 1(1):6–9, and her "Elie Nadelman" (July 1927), 1(4):19–20.

❧

To Gertrude Stein

16 February 1927

150 West Fifty-fifth Street
[New York]

Dear Gertrude,

I return to New York to find your very beautiful book awaiting me: and I have read about the lady who has a cow three times and each time with more fervor. This book seems more gay than the others and it is typographically the most beautiful.[1] I am very happy to have it . . . . In Hollywood I talked about you a great deal. Wherever I go there is curiosity about you.[2] The Scott Fitzgeralds were there and they both love you.[3] Hollywood is a fabulous place and I shall soon write about it. I also took the trouble to motor into Mexico to see five thousand Americans drunk at once: that's a good title. And before that was Mabel [Dodge] and the Indians. She is just the same (and I think she should be a little different by now) and she is writing the story of her same life, but she is nice sometimes . . . and so am I. Robert Coates never came, but I met Robert McAlmon in Taos and think he has too much starch. I'm glad you like Nora [Holt], but who could help it? . . Nigger Heaven is going very well in London and it is running in German in the Frankfurter Zeitung and is soon to appear in Swedish and perhaps in French: le Ciel de Nègres—what a title![4] I really may come over in April. I hope to.

my love to you!!!
Carlo

1. For the text of Stein's *A Book Concluding With As A Wife Has A Cow A Love Story* the publisher, Daniel-Henry Kahnweiler and the Galerie Simon, had used the printer Leibovitz, 64 rue de Maubeuge. The four lithographs by Juan Gris were printed by Pitault, 5 rue de la Banque.

2. Van Vechten had left New York early in January 1927 on a cross-country trip. He stopped in Chicago, several cities in New Mexico, and several cities in California. While in New Mexico he also made a short trip into Mexico. In an interview in the *Los Angeles Evening Herald* (20 January 1927, p. 1) Van Vechten told his interviewer, "[S]ay that I am one author who came to Los Angeles not to make money or to write for the movies, or to get color for a story." In fact, Van Vechten saw a number of people in the movie industry who were interested in turning his novels into films. In a letter to Marinoff he wrote: "Last night I met Paul Bern in charge of all productions at Metro-Goldwyn & today King Vidor & both want to do *Nigger Heaven*. Well of course they won't" (Van Vechten to Marinoff, 23 January 1927, NYPL-MD). Many of Van Vechten's experiences in Hollwood were used in his novel *Spider Boy*.

3. It was Ernest Hemingway who first introduced F. Scott Fitzgerald (1896–1940) and his wife Zelda to Stein (see Fitzgerald to Edmund Wilson [Spring 1925], in Turnbull, ed., *The Letters of F. Scott Fitzgerald*, pp. 341–42). This meeting probably took place in May 1925. Either at that meeting or at a subsequent meeting Fitzgerald gave Stein a copy of his novel *The Great Gatsby*. Stein wrote Fitzgerald, probably from Bilignin on 22 May [1925], about the novel. See Bruccoli, *Correspondence of F. Scott Fitzgerald*, p. 164. Van Vechten had met the Fitzgeralds sometime in the early 1920s.

4. For a complete list of the translations of *Nigger Heaven* see Kellner, *A Bibliography*, pp. 40–45. In French the novel was translated as *Les Paradis des Nègres*.

To Carl Van Vechten
[Rose motto]

[postmark: 7 March 1927]   27 rue de Fleurus
                                                   [Paris]

My dear Carl,

I like your looks immensely,[1] it is a long time since I have seen them and looks are hard to remember but yours are more than satisfactory and it

[141]

will be nice to really see you you are really coming, a new magazine crowd
here were talking of the translation of your book into french and I was awfully pleased the french do make niggers into a heaven not a nigger heaven.
I did too hear some rumor about it in Russian, good luck to us all.[2] Avery
[Hopwood] is in town but I imagine non-seeable for the moment he was so
xtremely good for so long and then he is no more, I am very very fond of
him with or without well you might say his mother.[3] I am awfully pleased
that you have done the jacket of the new edition of Three Lives have not
had it yet but am looking forward to it,[4] and there is a possibility of a novel
that I finished this year being printed here soon, I think you will like it, it
describes itself but everything when we meet.[5] [Robert] McAlmon is pretty
bad. [F. Scott] Fitzgerald and [E. E.] Cummings are the best of the crowd,
the rest are fairly weak in the head, but more of more of it when we meet
and we will,

Lots of love
Gertrude.

1. Van Vechten had sent Stein a photograph of himself.

2. The translation of *Nigger Heaven* was published as *Les paradis des Nègres*, trans. J. Sabour-
ant, pref. Paul Morand (Paris: "Es Documentaries," Simon Kra, 1927). There has been no
Russian translation of the book. An Estonian translation appeared in 1931.

3. Stein is referring to her last meeting with Hopwood in May 1926 and to his excessive drinking, which had caused a scene. On that occasion Hopwood had invited Stein and Toklas to
dinner with himself and the English writer Beverly Nichols at the Hôtel Ritz. At the dinner
Hopwood became so drunk that he broke glasses and splashed wine on Stein. He later apologized to Stein (see Hopwood to Stein, undated letter [May 1926?], YCAL). The incident is also
recounted in Nichols' *All I Could Never Be: Some Recollections by Beverly Nichols* (London:
Jonathan Cape, 1949), pp. 191–93. For another reaction to Hopwood's drinking see Mabel
Dodge to Van Vechten, 6 September 1924, YCAL. See also Van Vechten to Stein, 8 September [1924].

4. Van Vechten had written an advertising blurb for the dust jacket of John Lane's 1927 edition of Stein's *Three Lives*.

5. Edward W. Titus, the Polish-born husband of Helena Rubinstein, had opened a bookshop,
At the Sign of the Black Manikin, in the rue Delambre, Paris, in 1924. In 1926, under the
imprint of the Black Manikin Press, Titus began publishing books. He suggested printing a
work by Stein and went so far as to issue a prospectus for *A Novel of Thank You*. Before the
book could be printed Stein and Titus quarreled and the publication was canceled.

🐍

To Gertrude Stein

3 April [1927]
150 West Fifty-fifth Street
[New York]

Dear Gertrude,

Just a line to tell you that Fania is arriving on the President Harding and that her Paris address is the Banque de Paris et des Pays Bas, 3 Rue d'Antin. She will undoubtedly write you. We have very much enjoyed Paul and Madame Morand who have been here for ten days and also NORA HOLT!!![1] Fania will tell you about her. And about anything else you want to know. Isn't it nice that Three Lives is available once more. I have to buy so many copies to send about to people I want to read it.

gold and silver orchids and white peacocks to you!

Carlo

1. Paul Morand (1888–1976), French diplomat and author. Morand had written the preface for Van Vechten's *Les paradis des Nègres*.

🐍

To Gertrude Stein

10 April [1927]
[Hôtel Littré
9 rue Littré
Paris]

My dear Gertrude Stein

I hope you are in Paris and I hope I may see you. I expect to be here for three weeks, and my visit would be incomplete without at least a glimpse of you. I am at the Hotel Littré 9 rue Littré Phone Fleurus 67–71 and will be happy to see you and hear from you.

Fania Marinoff

❧

To Gertrude Stein

[postmark: 11 April 1927]
Monday

[Hôtel Littré
9 rue Littré
Paris]

Dear Gertrude Stein

I would love to lunch Friday, will be chez vous at 12.30.

Fania

❧

To Gertrude Stein

[postmark: 24 April 1927]
Sunday

[Garches, France]

Dear Gertrude Stein

I've written Marcel [Duchamp] a note saying that you have asked us on Tuesday evening for dinner, so we will be there and Rose Rolonda, too.[1] I had such a nice time the other evening, you've both been so charming to me, and I adore you both for it. I'm writing from Garches—it's grand but cold—

*Affectionately
Fania*

1. Stein had known Marcel Duchamp (1887–1968) since before World War I. The Van Vechtens had met him at the home of Louise and Walter Arensberg during his first visit to New York in June 1915.

Rose Rolanda (Rosemonde Cowan) was a dancer. In 1930 she married Miguel Covarrubias (d. 1957), the Mexican-born caricaturist.

✼

To Gertrude Stein

[25 April 1927]   [Hôtel de Crillon, Paris]
Monday

Dearest Gertrude Stein

Please may I bring Marcel [Duchamp] and Rose [Rolanda] Wednesday evening instead of to-morrow night? A friend of mine is sailing Wednesday morning and to-morrow night will be my only chance to see her. I've written Marcel and in case he can't come Wednesday evening, I'll send you *another* petit bleu and please don't think I'm a nuisance, I hate breaking engagements but this was unforeseen so forgive me.

Love to you both
Fania

✼

To Fania Marinoff
[Rose motto]

[postmark: 29 April 1927]   27 rue de Fleurus
                                                                   [Paris]

My dear Fania,

Here is Bernardine Szold breaking loose I did not think we had the pleasure of each other's acquaintance but we seem to have anyway I am sending it to you as it may be an opening for you to play, well place in me, or in me, of course I am not in it presumably because I don't and can't do those things. We have liked having known you, really and every time it was nicer at least it felt like it.

And so bon voyage and best of luck

Gtrde.

To Carl Van Vechten

[postmark: 5 May 1927]

27 rue de Fleurus
Paris

My dear Carl,

Fania has been here and gone and we liked her being here immensely.[1] It made you all kind of real you have always been real but this was a different real and a very nice real but then that is as it is. And now she has gone but I am hoping that we will see her again later as we are staying on in Paris a little later than usual this spring and a beautiful spring it is. Hyacinths turn into wisteria alright. Are you ever to see yourself in France won't you come and otherwise. Working a lot as usual some very funny little narratives and quite a lot of them. At the same time a very great grief as my very very dear friend Juan Gris is dying.[2] Anyway lots and lots of love and how is Nora [Holt] enjoying herself best to her too and always

Yours
Gertrude.

1. Marinoff had left for England on 2 May.

2. Gris had been in ill health since 1925. His illness was diagnosed as uremia in January 1927. He died on 11 May and on 13 May was buried in the cemetery at Boulogne-sur-Seine, France.

To Gertrude Stein

28 May [1927]

150 West Fifty-fifth Street
[New York]

Dear Gertrude

Thanks thousands of times for An Elucidation which to me is very fine.[1] And I am so glad that Three Lives is again available for now I can again advise people to read Melanctha. Nella Imes,[2] one of the most intelligent people I know (you will see her in Paris next winter) says it is the best Negro story she has ever read (she is Negro herself) . . . I know you will like Rose Wheeler[3] & Taylor Gordon.[4] Your home in fact is becoming a mecca—an excuse for travel. Americans now go abroad to meet Gertrude Stein. . Fania raves about your beauty & your charm. She writes me how adorable you were to her. And I must have Man Ray's photograph.[5] The Picasso portrait goes into the new illustrated edition of Peter Whiffle which I shall send you when it is ready.[6] Nora [Holt] has been a sensation in New York. Everybody loves her, but now she has gone to Chicago. Lead her to a piano & ask her to sing for you when she comes back.

My love to you!
Carlo

1. Stein's "An Elucidation" was printed in *transition*, (April 1927), 1:64–78. In setting this issue, the printers garbled the text, and at Stein's insistence *transition* reprinted the article as a separate pamphlet.

2. Nella Larsen, Mrs. Elmer Imes (1893–1963), was a black writer, author of the novels *Quicksand* (1928) and *Passing* (1929).

3. The Van Vechtens had met Rose Wheeler, wife of the stockbroker Arthur Wheeler, at the home of Donald Angus.

4. Taylor Gordon (1893–1971) was a member of the only black family in White Sulphur Springs, Montana. He worked as a car attendant for John Ringling and traveled widely with him. He studied singing for a short time and appeared in a vaudeville act, "The Inimitable Five," organized by J. Rosamond Johnson. In 1925 he began a series of concerts of Negro spirituals with Johnson. In 1927 Johnson and Gordon traveled to France and England to give concerts. The decline in Gordon's career is traced in Robert Hemenway's introduction to Gordon's autobiography, *Born to Be* (1929; rpt., Seattle and London: University of Washington Press, 1975). Van Vechten's enthusiastic foreword to the original edition is reprinted in the 1975 reprint (as is Muriel Draper's introduction). A later appraisal by Van Vechten of Gordon should also be consulted. See *The Yale University Library Gazette*, (October 1980), 55(2):85.

5. Van Vechten is alluding to references in a letter from Marinoff to him (postmark 29 April 1927, MYPL-MD). Marinoff wrote:

> Gertrude Stein has been perfectly wonderful to me. I've dined there several times. . . . Today after lunch Marcel [Duchamp] and Rose [Rolanda] and I went over to Man Ray's studio. I like his things enormously, even his photographs. . . . He had a marvelous photo of Gertrude Stein taken recently. Of course she no more looks like the same person she was in 1914 . . . she's beautiful now and her head is extraordinary.

The photograph is Man Ray's 1927 portrait of Stein taken after she had cut her hair to a close-cropped style.

6. An illustrated edition of Van Vechten's 1922 novel, *Peter Whiffle: His Life and Works*, was published in New York and London by Alfred A. Knopf in September 1927.

※

To Gertrude Stein and Alice Toklas

[16 June 1927]
Thursday

[Hôtel Littré
9 rue Littré
Paris]

My dears,

Here I am once more, but only because I'm sailing from France June 25th. I would so love to see you both again before I depart and Miguel Covarrubias wants very much to meet you. When can you be seen I'm at the same Hotel Littré and will come to see you any time you suggest but tomorrow and I hope it may be soon.

Fania

※

To Gertrude Stein

[postmark: 19 June 27]
Sunday

[Hôtel Littré
9 rue Littré
Paris]

Dearest Darlingest lady Stein

Look, oh look what I drew yesterday I hope the gentleman who drew mine did as well cause I got an invitation to tea.[1] But really when may I drop in to see you both make it soon, Please

Fania

1. Whatever Marinoff drew cannot be located.

To Gertrude Stein

[postmark: 20 June 1927]
Lundi

[Hôtel Littré
9 rue Littré
Paris]

Alright lady dear

[Miguel] Covarrubias and I will be chez vous demain à cinq heures and I for one will be very glad to see you both again

Fania

To Fania Marinoff
[Rose motto]

[22 June 1927]

27 rue de Fleurus
[Paris]

My dear Fania

Here is the address of the Moroccan dinner, and we are planning to say how do you do in case you are there but in case you are not there we are xpecting you for dinner Friday at 7.30 and hoping you are enjoying yourself and all,

always
Gtrde Stein

To Fania Marinoff
[Rose motto]

[22 June 1927]

27 rue de Fleurus
[Paris]

My dear Fania,

I just remembered this and here it is and all to you and Carl.[1] I am writing to him very soon and we did enjoy having you it kind of brings us closer not that we were not awfully close but it has kind of bridged the physical years and you know how much I love Carl and you. Best of happy times. I like your Miguel [Covarrubias] a lot.

Always
Gtde

1. Stein sent Marinoff a print of Man Ray's photograph of Stein that she had admired in the artist's studio. See Van Vechten to Stein, 28 May [1927], note 5.

To Gertrude Stein and Alice Toklas

23 June [1927]   [Hôtel Littré
                                            9 rue Littré
                                            Paris]

Darlings

Really you have quite spoiled me, besides making me feel fearfully important this last attention was the comble as they say so classically. You are both such darlings, Carl has missed a great, great deal by not having been here. But he'll be delighted with the photograph which to him will be a new Gertrude Stein, yet the same, and the earrings, Alice chère are quite lovely, and becoming. I know you robbed yourself in giving them to you [i.e., me]. But that's why you did it, of course. I think you're both too wonderful and I send you heaps of love and showers of great blessings

Fania

To Gertrude Stein

[6? July 1927]   Newlands Corner Hotel
Wednesday morning   near Guildford
                                           Surrey [England]

Dearest Gertrude Stein

First you and Miss Toklas must know that the customs official in London refused to permit me to even open my trunk and after reading the list of dutiable articles I had *nothing* of that sort but the average amount of perfume which every female carries about with her. No mention of clothes or things of that sort whatsoever. Mr. Church is quite mad I think, and I'm indebted to him for a great amount of worry, an unnecessary deposit on a passage back to the U.S.A. and several bad night's sleep and I came very nearly being silly enough to leave many of the things I had in Paris to pick up on my way back to the states.[1] So that's that Darling, your note with Bernadine's[2] letter came while I was packing your note was very hard to read, I couldn't quite make it out, something about doing one of your plays for the benefit, instead of you speaking, was that it? Your letter is in my trunk. It's not lost But I won't unpack till I return to London on Monday, then I'll get in touch with Bernadine, etc etc.

I came out here last night. It's delightful and was recommended to me by Carl's sister who had stopped off here while motoring. It's only a half hour from London. It's really quite a place marvelous service and food reasonable prices and comfortable accommodations, I felt I had to have a few days good air and quiet to get rid of this darn cold of mine. In London after much searching and trouble through a friend a [i.e., I] found a room at the Park Lane Hotel Piccadilly, only open three months and looks wonderful.

I saw Avery [Hopwood] Monday night But we were with other people, so I haven't talked with me [i.e., him] at all. He looks spendid and is rehearsing his new play, The Garden of Eden.[3] You were both such darlings to me. It's my happiest and most charming remembrance of Paris and I love you both. My address in London will be American Express Co *Haymarket not the Bank*.

Fania

1. Ralph Withington Church and his mother had met Stein and Toklas through Sherwood Anderson. Church was, at this time, working on his doctorate in philosophy at Oxford University.

2. Bernadine Szold was a journalist who wrote about the Van Vechtens in her column "About Town" in the *New York Sunday News*, 11 May 1924, p. 14.

3. Hopwood's play *The Garden of Eden* opened at the Lyric Theatre London on 30 May 1927. The play starred Tallulah Bankhead (1902–1968) in the role of Toni Lebrun. *The Garden of Eden* opened in New York on 27 September 1927 at the Selwyn Theatre and ran for twenty-three performances.

❧

To Gertrude Stein and Alice Toklas
[Postcard: Greek Head of an Athlete—Fifth Century B.C. *The Metropolitan Museum of Art]*

[postmark: 20 July 1927]   [150 West Fifty-fifth Street
                                             New York]

Darlings,

Loving greetings and embraces for you both. I'm glad to be back, and Carl has never been so nice. Your photo is our delight and every one else's. We both love you both very much—

Fania

❧

To Carl Van Vechten

[postmark: 11 August 1927]   Hotel Pernollet
                                               Belley (Ain)

My dear Carl,

I am pleased to hear that Fania got home safe and New York is alright. I do wish you would come over and see us do come we are putting up a bust for Brillat Savarin on the 15 of September you could just make it, it is a nice little town Belley almost as nice as New York and quite as peaceful.[1] We are here until the end of September and I am working a lot. I have gotten awfully interested in narrative and I am telling the pleasant events in the life of Lucy Church. You know I just did an opera about St. Therese and Loyola.[2] I do want you to see it one of these days. I am very pleased with it but then we are often pleased happily for us. They also are sending you something which is a magazine called Close Up. I hope you will like Three sitting here.[3] What are you doing, I know why you like niggers so much [Paul] Robeson and I had a long talk about it[4] it is not because they are primitive but because they have a narrow but a very long civilisation behind them. They have alright, their sophistication is complete and so beautifully finished and it is the only one that can resist the United States of America. Of course Mabel [Dodge] and her Indian business is wrong because they were an undeveloped people and the Indians learn but the niggers don't which is their problem. I am sorry we did not meet the last one but we will this fall, I guess.[5] I like Miguel [Covarrubias] enormously, he did give me a charming bit of Mexico and he himself is like all your friends intelligent and delicate. It is a wonderful way that you can make them so different and yet all having these two qualities. It is kind of funny, Anyway I'd like to hear from you and I would like to see you.

> *Lots of love*
> *Gertrude.*

1. A monument to Jean Anthelme Brillat-Savarin, who was born in Belley in 1755 and died in Paris in 1826, was inaugurated on Sunday 11 September 1927. Brillat-Savarin was a lawyer, deputy to the National Assembly, and a high functionary in several departments of the French government. He is best known for his *La Physiologie du goût* (1825), a volume of meditations on gastronomy.

2. Stein is referring to her novel *Lucy Church Amiably* and to her opera *Four Saints in Three Acts*.

3. Stein's "Three Sitting Here" was published in two issues of *Close Up* (September 1927), 3:17–28, and (October 1927), 4:17–25. *Close Up* was edited and published by Kenneth Macpherson and his wife Bryher.

4. Stein is here referring to a conversation with Paul Robeson when she first met him. See Stein to Van Vechten [9 November 1925].

5. A reference to Nella Imes (Larsen), the black writer. See Van Vechten to Stein, 28 May [1927]. Stein did not actually meet her until two years later.

To Carl Van Vechten

[postmark: 6 September 1927]   Hotel Pernollet
                                                Belley (Ain)

My dear Carl,

I am delighted with the photo you are a good looking chap and your head does come out awfully well nice in front and nice behind and well distributed in the middle.[1] We are still in Belley but leave next week for Paris. I am meeting Blanche Knopf there on the sixteenth and I hope something will come of it, I would like to be along with you, anyway it is getting nearer. Avery [Hopwood] is with you now he is delightfully literal and I am so sorry I did not see him before he left but he will be back soon and you,

Lots of love to you always and to Fania and to Avery, and thanks again for the photo,

Always
Gertrude

1. Precisely which photograph Van Vechten sent Stein cannot be determined.

To Carl Van Vechten
MS. New York Public Library, Manuscripts Division

[postmark: 20 September 1927]

27 rue de Fleurus
Paris

My dear Carl,

Thanks so much for the new Peter Whiffle, we are all enjoying it enjoying it and enjoying the memories of it. I knew it was good I remembered it as good but it is even a whole lot better than that.[1] It has an astonishing freshness, I think that is what is its very great quality, how to make a work keep alive and you do. I am most awfully pleased. Alice says thanks for having put in Lina Cavalieri, Janet [Scudder?] says thanks for Mabel [Dodge] only it is sweeter than she was but then she was sweet and I say thanks for having kept it all so fresh.[2]

Blanche Knopf turned up, I liked her and I think she liked me and we got along, something may come of it and that will be a great pleasure to me and thanks to you. And what is this about your not writing, do write anyone who can have things keep as fresh as this will make some,

Lots of lots of love
Gertrude.

[154]

1. See Van Vechten to Stein, 28 May [1927], note 6.

2. Lina Cavalieri (1874–1944) was a celebrated Italian soprano. She was at one time married to Van Vechten's friend Bob Chanler. Cavalieri is mentioned on page 54 of *Peter Whiffle: His Life and Works* (New York: Alfred A. Knopf, 1922). Stein had received the 1927 printing of the book (Knopf) that contained illustrations.

Janet Scudder (d. 1940) was an American-born sculptor who lived for many years in Paris. She had met Stein through Stein's friend Mildred Aldrich.

The character of Edith Dale in Van Vechten's novel is partly based on Mabel Dodge.

To Gertrude Stein

10 October 1927

150 West Fifty-fifth Street
[New York]

Dear Gertrude,

Blanche Knopf is back and *raving* about you. She talks of nothing but your beauty and personality, thus lining up with everybody that's met you. I hope some publication can be arranged. Paul [Robeson] is sailing Friday for a year's concert tour, beginning in Spain. You will see him when he reaches Paris. I am trying to write a book. I am also trying to get an old farmhouse in Massachusetts where I can revert to type. Perhaps you can be persuaded to come to see me there. I am awfully interested in Tony Church[1] and Marinoff and I send our love to you!

Carlo

1. Van Vechten misread the title Lucy Church in Stein's letter to him postmarked 11 August 1927.

To Carl Van Vechten
[Rose motto]

[postmark: 26 October 1927]

27 rue de Fleurus
[Paris]

My dear Carl,

[Paul] Robeson came in to see us and we had a long and delightful talk about you all.[1] He is really a perfectly ideal companion, the last time I saw him it was only once and it was in a crowd of people. I liked him then but now after a quiet time alone with him we are really very good friends. I am sorry that I will not hear his first concert but I have had a bad cold and am a little afraid of the inside of a Paris theatre but we will hear his second. He is lunching with us next week to tell us all about it. And he did give charming pictures of you Carl, he does that awfully well makes the people he is talking about very really in front of you and it was nice having that done with you. Thanks for him. And I am delighted about the Mass. farm. We are trying for one in the Ain and hope to be having it in a year or so it would be nice to xchange visits to each other's country.[2] We are now getting there alright that is to the country stage. I am sending Blanche Knopf Lucy Church Amiably. I think it dances along nicely. Do have her show it to you and if you like it I am sure she will and that would be nice,

  Lots and lots of love to each of you

Gertrude.

1. Robeson was in Paris for a series of concerts with Lawrence Brown. The first concert, at the Salle Gaveau, was on 29 October, the second on 2 November. Robeson also refers to seeing Stein when he was in the midst of a crowd of people in an undated letter to her from the Hôtel Paris-New York, 148 rue de Vaugirard, Paris (YCAL).

2. Van Vechten never acquired a country house. Stein and Toklas had first stopped in Belley in 1923 while they were on their way to visit Picasso in Nice. They returned to the Hôtel Pernollet in Belley each summer until 1929, when they acquired a lease on a house in Bilignin, a hamlet a few kilometers from Belley.

To Gertrude Stein

8 January [1928]   150 West Fifty-fifth Street
                   [New York]

Dear Gertrude,

  I've had a rotten fall: two teeth out and then a succession of terrifying colds: in bed half the time: days in terrible hotels in Atlantic City, trying to get well, etc. I saw Paul [Robeson] for a few minutes the other day and he told me how nice to him you were: he adores you. The baby, by the way, is his miniature image.[1] Marinoff is in Baltimore, trying to discover, via a stock company, whether she wants to (or can) act any more.[2] In odd moments I am trying to write a book.[3] Did you ever receive The Autobiography of an Ex-Colored Man which I sent you?[4] Paul Morand was here the other day but he is about the only foreigner I've seen except Beverly Nichols who is very young.

a great deal of love to you, dear Gertrude!

Carlo.

1. Robeson's son, Paul Robeson, Jr., was born 2 November 1927.

2. Marinoff had acted on the stage in New York and on tours regularly since 1913. Her last appearance in New York had been in *Tarnish*, by Gilbert Emery, a play that opened in New York on 2 October 1923. Marinoff had gone to Baltimore to act in Edwin Knopf's company, which presented a season of plays at the Auditorium Theatre, Baltimore, beginning 26 December 1927. Marinoff appeared in the plays *He Who Gets Slapped, Spring Cleaning, In the Next Room,* and *Captain Applejack.* Marinoff did not play again in New York until 1931.

3. Van Vechten was working on the third draft of his novel *Spider Boy.* See Kellner, *A Bibliography,* p. 49.

4. Van Vechten had written the introduction to James Weldon Johnson's *The Autobiography of An Ex-Colored Man* (New York: Alfred A. Knopf, 1927). Johnson (1871–1938) was one of Van Vechten's closest friends. After Johnson's death Van Vechten initiated the founding of the James Weldon Johnson Memorial Collection of Negro Arts and Letters at Yale University Library.

To Carl Van Vechten
[Rose motto]

[postmark: 13 January 1928]   27 rue de Fleurus
                                                             [Paris]

My dear Carl,

I am so sorry that you are not well but I hope it is all over and you are all better now do be comfortable it is so much peacefuller and I hear you are finishing a book, what is it about. I liked the Colored Man, particularly the first part but surely in all those letters I wrote you I had already thanked you for that and much else. Here we are as usual. I am working very much these days, I have a new problem in construction, it is Finally George but it promises to be long, little things happen on the road.[1] Oth-

Gertrude Stein and Virgil Thomson in the studio at 27 rue de Fleurus looking at
the score of *Four Saints in Three Acts*, circa 1928–29.

erwise there is no news, a great many people are young and others [have?] half of it, and beside I have written an opera and a rather amusing young American is making it put on the stageable well anyway lots and lots of love and do be all well.[2]

Always
Gertrude

1. "Finally George A Vocabulary of Thinking" in Stein's *How to Write*, pp. [271]–382.

2. Virgil Thomson (b. 1896), composer and critic, first read Stein when his friend at Harvard University S. Foster Damon, composer, poet, and Blake scholar, gave him a copy of Stein's *Tender Buttons*.

Although Thomson traveled with the Harvard Glee Club on a European tour in 1921 and remained in Paris for a year to study with Nadia Boulanger, the celebrated teacher of composition and counterpoint, he did not meet Stein until 1926.

Thomson had returned to Paris in the fall of 1925. Early in 1926 the composer George Antheil received an invitation to visit Stein's home. Antheil invited Thomson to accompany him. Stein and Thomson quickly became friends. In April 1927 Thomson composed a work for four men's solo voices and piano using as a text Stein's "Capital, Capitals." The work was performed at a *Grande Semaine* costume fête held at the home of Stein's friend the Duchesse de Clermont-Tonnerre. The success of this work encouraged Thomson to suggest that he and Stein collaborate on an opera. After some discussion of the subject matter for the work, they settled on the lives of saints, particularly Theresa of Avila and Ignatius Loyola. Stein sent Thomson a typescript of *Four Saints in Three Acts* in mid-June 1927. Thomson began work on the score in November, and by mid-December the vocal score for the first act was completed. Act Two was finished in February 1928 and the remainder of the work in midsummer 1928.

Stein had told Thomson to use his judgment in making the opera work on a stage, but Thomson cut nothing, setting even the stage directions to music. Later he did make some cuts, divided the role of Saint Theresa into two parts, and introduced two narrators, Commère and Compère.

In 1929 Maurice Grosser, an American painter and close friend of Thomson's, wrote, with Stein's approval, a working scenario for the opera. It is this scenario which has been used for all performances of the opera.

To Gertrude Stein

17 January [1928]
150 West Fifty-fifth Street
[New York]

Dear Gertrude:

I loved the "turn out" picture you sent on & it will be lovely in our Victorian room which is rather sweet anyway and it would make us so happy if you & Alice might sit there in the sun with us. And Fania is *insane* about her earrings. But she will write Alice about them. *She wears them in her sleep!*[1]

But I am dashing this off (while some one is waiting for me) mainly to tell you that I sent Marie Doro "Three Lives" & she sent me the enclosed letter which I thought you would like to see. Please send it back to me.— And now I have sent Marie Geography & Plays[2]

And I send you & Alice 17 purple dachshunds with silver legs! & lots of love!

Carlo

1. See Marinoff to Stein and Toklas, 23 June [1927].

2. Marie Doro, a friend of the Van Vechtens'. This letter is not in YCAL.

To Gertrude Stein

31 March [1928]   150 West Fifty-fifth Street
                                                       [New York]

Dear Gertrude,

You should have heard from me long ago but I have been to the coast again where I met Aimee Semple Mcpherson[1] [i.e., McPherson] and Jack Dempsey,[2] to say the least. Also saw Mabel [Dodge] on her way to Santa Barbara to wheedle a new motor out of her mother. Tony [Luhan] is staying with her mother at Santa Barbara. Mabel has written the New York part of her book and wanted me to read it, but I couldn't get to Taos, although I stopped at Santa Fe. Maurice Sterne has been asked to paint himself *and wife* for the Ufizzi or is it Uffizi (well, anyway somewhere in Florence.) Think what Mabel missed.[3] I have written a book about Hollywood which will be out in August.[4] And I have been reading proofs on it ever since I got back. I may go to the country this summer and I may come abroad. It would be *nice* to see you again. Paul [Robeson] may go to London with Show Boat.[5]

Love and purple parrots to you!

Carlo

Marinoff is playing in Baltimore

[160]

1. Aimee Semple McPherson (1890–1944), the American evangelist. McPherson opened her Los Angeles Temple in 1923. Van Vechten wrote Marinoff a detailed letter describing his meeting McPherson in a restaurant and then his visit to her temple (see Van Vechten to Marinoff, 2 March [1928], NYPL-MD).

2. Jack Dempsey, the American heavyweight fighter.

3. Maurice Sterne (1878–1957). Sterne was born in Libau, Latvia, and came to New York in 1889. While studying painting in Paris in 1904, Sterne met Leo and Gertrude Stein. (It was Leo Stein who introduced him to the paintings of Cézanne and the impressionists and post-impressionists that were shown in the gallery of Ambroise Vollard.) Sterne was an important figure in the notebooks that Gertrude Stein kept while she was writing *The Making of Americans* (these notebooks are at YCAL).

Sterne married Mabel Dodge in 1917 but in the fall of 1918 left her in New Mexico, where she had fallen in love with the landscape around Taos and with an Indian, Antonio Luhan. Stern was married to his second wife, Vera Segal, in Vienna in 1923. Segal was at that time studying dance with Elizabeth Duncan in Salzburg.

In 1925 Sterne had been invited to paint a self-portrait for the Uffizi Gallery, Florence, which has a collection of self-portraits.

4. Van Vechten's *Spider Boy*.

5. Robeson opened in Oscar Hammerstein and Jerome Kern's musical *Show Boat* in London 3 May 1928.

To Carl Van Vechten
[Rose motto]

[postmark: 26 April 1928]   27 rue de Fleurus
                                                           [Paris]

My dear Carl

It is nice getting a letter and a photo from you that sounds and looks like you I was not at all likeing it that you were not really enjoying yourself, and now you are. I will like seeing your book, I too am correcting proofs, Payson and Clarke are bringing out a book of collected things, Useful Knowledge or Americana, all my or at least some of my American things collected, your portrait among them, there is one on Woodrow [Wilson] and A Hundred prominent men that I think you will like.[1] Then Gallerie Simon is doing another little thing with very nice illustrations so you see I am for me quite cheerful.[2] I do wish too you could hear my opera Four Saints in Three Acts but if you come over you will and will you come over. Absolutely, as dear Paul [Robeson] says, by the way the little nigger thing is in Useful Knowledge.[3] Poor dear Mabel [Dodge] and Edwin [Dodge] has been with us, it is hard to know whether Edwin is or was Mabel and Mabel seems rather to lose it. Anyway I am more pleased than I can say that you are alright again and lots of love and good luck to Fania

Always
Gertrude.

1. Stein's *Useful Knowledge*. In addition to "Advertisement" and "Introducing," this volume collected twenty-one works by Stein, including "Van or Twenty Years After. A Second Portrait of Carl Van Vechten," "Woodrow Wilson," and "An Instant Answer or A Hundred Prominent Men."

2. The success of Stein's collaboration with Juan Gris, *A Book Concluding With As A Wife Has A Cow A Love Story*, encouraged Daniel-Henry Kahnweiler, the picture dealer and publisher, to request another manuscript from Stein. Stein sent him *A Village. Are You Ready Yet Not Yet. A Play in Four Acts*, which Kahnweiler published with illustrations by Elie Lascaux. See Gallup, *The Flowers of Friendship*, p. 213.

3. Stein's "Among Negroes" was included in *Useful Knowledge*.

To Gertrude Stein

19 May 1928 150 West Fifty-fifth Street
[New York]

Dear Gertrude,

Just a line, in haste, to tell you that Marinoff is sailing on Friday, May 25, on the France directly for Paris. Her address will be Banque de Paris et de Pays Bas . . . . I suppose you have noted Paul [Robeson]'s enormous success in Show Boat at Drury Lane, and Nora [Holt] will sail in a week or two.

love,
Carlo

I am sending you a picture.

[162]

To Gertrude Stein and Alice Toklas

[4 June 1928]
Monday Morning

[Hôtel Littré
9 rue Littré
Paris]

My dear dears,

The small bad penny has turned up once more, and is to remain here for several week[s] at the Hotel Littré. Do not let me interfere with your weent[s]iest plan. But when you wish, and can spare a few minutes I should like to run in, that is hoping you are both in Paris.

Affectionately always—
Fania Marinoff

To Fania Marinoff

[postmark: 4 June 1928]

27 rue de Fleurus
[Paris]

My dear Fania

I am so sorry we are just leaving Paris we leave to-morrow morning and we won't see you and we are not at all pleased, but better luck next time. Avery [Hopwood] will tell you all about us, we have been enjoying him and are you to be here for long not long enough for us I am afraid as we are away until September. Do tell us all about yourself this address always reaches us. I wish you had come a few days earlier, you would have liked the concert where they sang my thing, it really was interesting,[1] lots of love to you and lots of regrets,

Always
Gertrude.

1. A concert of Virgil Thomson's music was presented on 30 May 1928 at the Nouvelle Salle d'Orgue du Conservatoire. The program included *Capital, Capitals* (text by Stein), sung by

Parker Steward, Victor Prahl, O. S. Walker, and Emory Foster, with Edmond Pendleton as
the pianist. Also included was *Le Berceau de Gertrude Stein (8 poèmes of Georges Hugnet to
which have been added a Musical Composition by Virgil Thomson entitled Lady Godiva's Waltzes)*,
sung by Madame Marthe-Marthine, with Victor Prahl, pianist.

To Gertrude Stein and Alice Toklas

[postmark: 8 June 1928]

[Hôtel Littré
9 rue Littré
Paris]

My dears,

I'm really very sorry I'm not going to see you I looked forward to it
so much. You were both so adorable to me last year, I shall never forget it.
Oh, Why won't you come to New York once, Carl and I would try to show
you how much we think of you. The concert must have been a wow! as we
say in the U.S.A.

Blessings on you and have a very happy summer,

love always
Fania

Avery [Hopwood] went to Antibes to-day, so I missed him too. I never
did have no luck.

To Carl Van Vechten

[Postcard: Environs de Belley—Vieu—Gentilhommière de Brillat-Savarin]

[postmark: 16 June 1928]

Hotel Pernollet
Belley, Ain

My dear Carl

So sorry we missed Fania it would have been a pleasure seeing her,
we did see a bit of Avery [Hopwood] and he is sweeter and more delightful

than ever. And you, no doubt about you but there you are well anyway lots of love

Gertrude.

To Carl Van Vechten

[postmark: 22 June 1928]   Hotel Pernollet
                                                 Belley (Ain)

My dear Carl,

Here is a picture of me in my last of the Fords, it is one of my sorrows that Henry [Ford] won't make any but I do what I can to prove that America is the mother of modern civilization. It's nice here in a Ford car and eating pleasantly. Henry McBride is coming to see us soon but alas not you, well anyway lots of love

Gertrude.

To Carl Van Vechten

[postmark: 6 July 1928]   Hotel Pernollet
                                                 Belley (Ain)

My dear Carl,

I have just seen the news in the paper of the death of dear old Avery [Hopwood] by drowning. I was awfully fond of him and we did have a charming time together this spring and I just had a note from him saying how happy he was at Juan les Pins and was looking forward to our seeing each other in September. He was a very wonderful creature and I was always awfully pleased that you had made us friends. Will you give me the address of his mother? I do want to write to her and tell her how much he meant

[165]

to us.[1] I hope everything is all cheerful with you. I am still doing the same writing and sitting and walking and sometimes talking, Love to you

Always
Gtrde.

1. The last letter from Hopwood to Stein had been sent from the Hôtel Provençal, Juan-les-Pins, France (26 June [1928], YCAL). The details of Hopwood's death were at first confused. Van Vechten, who had read of his death in the New York newspapers, wrote Marinoff a letter in which he reported the version he had read (Van Vechten to Marinoff, 5 July [1928], NYPL-MD):

> I know only what details I have read in the papers. After dinner Sunday July 1, Avery went swimming at Juan-les-Pins about 8 o'clock. He was out beyond the reach of the other bathers and sank almost immediately with heart disease or cramps. It was daylight and the beach was crowded. His body was immediately recovered.

In a subsequent letter Van Vechten corrected the details of Hopwood's death (Van Vechten to Marinoff, 20 July [1928], NYPL-MD):

> But the facts of his death are reassuring. He died of heart disease instantly in front of Otis Skinner's house in two feet of water. The Skinners saw the whole thing and he was fished out immediately. There was not a drop of water in his lungs. This might have happened anywhere.

To Gertrude Stein

14 July [1928]   150 West Fifty-fifth Street
                                                   [New York]

My Gertrude,

Avery [Hopwood]'s death nearly knocked me flat. I don't think anything before has ever affected me so much. On your last card to me you had written "We did see a bit of Avery and he is sweeter and more delightful than ever," and I passed this on to him in a letter which he never received. I love your picture in the Ford and I shall see you in it soon, for I am really coming over in September. And in a week or two now I shall send you my funny book called Spider Boy.

Love,
Carlo

🐿

To Gertrude Stein

18 July [1928]   150 West Fifty-fifth Street
                                         [New York]

Dear Gertrude,

Mrs. James Hopwood's address is 5902 Clinton Avenue, Cleveland, Ohio. I saw her off the boat last night, poor dear. AND I am sailing on the Mauretania, September 5, I shall be in Paris for a few days after the 10th, and probably again later. I am not quite sure about my address but you can reach me through Fania at the Banque de Paris et des Pays Bas, 3 Rue d'Antin. I think I wrote you that my cable address is Carlvecht New York.

love always,
Carlo

🐿

To Carl Van Vechten

[postmark: 25 July 1928]   Hotel Pernollet
                                                 Belley (Ain)

My dear Carl,

It will be nice seeing you and if you did come over early in September it would be nice if you came down here for a day or so and we could have quiet talks, I know how awfully cut up you must have been about Avery [Hopwood], when we saw him he was at his sweetest, the last couple of times he was in Paris he was all upset and we almost did not see him but this time he was so dear, he came and spent several afternoons and I introduced him to some of the younger frenchmen and it all amused him and then the last night he begged us to come and do Montmartre with him, he said he knew we did not do that sort of thing but it would give him so much pleasure, so we dined with a lot of them and stayed with them until for us the unholy hour of two in the morning and he was wonderful, he told me at one time

when we were together going from one place to another a good deal about
his complications, and he was very wonderful and then he broke down and
he said some day you must know all about me but I never want you to know
anything of me xcept from Carl, always know anything about me from Carl,
I want him always to tell you anything about me, the whole thing moved
me very deeply then afterwards he was very delightful and then at the end
he thanked us so prettily for having been his guests, and he said in his own
dear flattering way, everybody asks me do I know Gertrude Stein, and I always say yes I know her but she is something I keep for myself, and he said
it in the lamb like way he always said those things. I am telling you all this
but you will know why, I had after that a postal from him saying how happy
he was at Juan les Pins which I answered but I don't think it reached him.
My dear Carl lots and lots of love and it will be nice seeing you,[1]

Always
Gtrde.

1. See Stein to Van Vechten, postmark 7 March 1927, note 3.

To Gertrude Stein

9 August [1928]

150 West Fifty-fifth Street
[New York]

Dear Gertrude,

Thanks a lot for your second lovely letter about Avery [Hopwood]. I
read it to his mother last night . . If I miss you in September . . . and I do
not think I shall be able to visit Belley then . . . I shall see you in October
and November on return from the grand tour which Marinoff and I are
making.

love always,
Carlo

To Carl Van Vechten

[postmark: 3 September 1928]   Hotel Pernollet
                                                Belley (Ain)

My dear Carl,

Welcome to Paris, I do wish I were there to say it in person but we do not get back for a month yet and I am hoping awfully hoping that in the course of the grand tour you will come by us, Aix les Bains you know is more or less on the road to anywhere and we are just there, do try to make it on the way but if not then it will be in October and November, it will be in October and November anyhow but I would like it awfully if we did see you here all by yourself and Fania and then later again in Paris. Thanks for the Spider Boy, I liked lots of it even though I really can't realise that my California has turned into that but then after all it is not my California because even in those far off days we always despised Los Angeles and we were right.[1] Anyhow it's good fun and did they do all that to you. Do try to come to see us here but anyway we are [nearer?] seeing each other than we have been for an awfully long time and that is something

    Lots and lots of love and happiness

Always
Gertrude.

1. Stein was born in Allegheny, Pennsylvania, 3 February 1874. From the spring of 1875 until 1879 the family lived in Europe (Austria and France). The Steins returned to the United States in 1879 and lived in Baltimore, Maryland, until 1880, when they moved to Oakland, California. They lived in Oakland in a succession of houses until 1891, when, after the death of Stein's father (her mother had died in 1888), her eldest brother, Michael, as head of the family, moved the Stein children (Simon, Bertha, Leo, and Gertrude) to San Francisco. In 1892 Stein and her sister Bertha went to live with their mother's sister Fannie Bachrach in Baltimore. Except for summer visits to Michael Stein and his wife Sarah in 1897 and 1899, Stein did not return to California until she lectured there in 1935.

❧

To Carl Van Vechten

[postmark: 14 September 1928]   Hotel Pernollet
                                                 Belley (Ain)

My dear Carl,

It was a pleasure to see us together in the Herald this morning but it will be a realler pleasure when we are really together, I am awfully pleased you are here and here's to our meeting very soon,[1]

Lots of love
Gertrude.

1. In an unsigned article, "America Has Literature, Says Tourist Van Vechten," in the *New York Herald*, Paris ed., 12 September 1928, p. 11, Van Vechten lauded Stein:

> "She is like yeast—" he said, "the yeast that makes the bread. Only time can disclose just how important her own work is, but the fact remains that at present she is one of the greatest influences of our age. According to his own admission she has greatly affected the writings of Sherwood Anderson. She has also been important in the literary development of James Joyce, Dorothy Richardson and others. . . "
>
> Mr. Van Vechten, with a humorous lift to his eyebrows, declared that he fully expected to find Miss Stein's fall salon filled with "new Algerian poets and new Spanish painters."
>
> "They all get a broadening technique from her—and that is the important thing. One perhaps might say that her poetic medium is the forerunner of a changed language, but if so—what of it? Why shouldn't there be changes of language. Look at the difference between Chaucer's and ours?"

❧

To Gertrude Stein

14 September [1928]   Café Anglais
                                       Restaurant
                                       119 avenue des Champs-Élysées
                                       Paris

Dear Gertrude,

So glad to get your letter. We are off for Strasbourg and the grand tournée on Sunday, but we shall be back in Paris towards the end of Octo-

[170]

ber. Paris is wonderful. I haven't been here in 14 years but she does not seem to have changed at all.

The Banque de Paris etc. etc. will always reach us, but when we return we shall stop at the Carlton and I shall write you at once.

love always,
Carlo

❧

To Gertrude Stein
[Postcard: München—Schloss Nymphenburg—Pagodenberg Speisesall]

[postmark: 20 September 1928]   [Munich Germany]

Dear Gertrude,

We are going on to Kar[l]sbad tomorrow & then to Prague—Buda-Pesth—Vienna—& a lot of other places. I don't think will strike Paris again till the middle of November.

Love
Carlo.

❧

To Carl Van Vechten
[Postcard: Une Pensée de Meximieux]

[postmark: 7 October 1928]   Hotel Pernollet
                      Belley, Ain

My dear Carl,

Is the grande tour continuing happily and in order, we are still down here and will be still for a couple of weeks but then it will be Paris and the pleasure really of seeing you

Love
Gertrude.

[171]

❧

To Gertrude Stein
[Postcard: Roma—Carro da vino (Costumi Romani)]

26 October [1928]   [Rome]

Dear Gertrude—

We arrive in Paris on Monday—Oct 29. I hope we shall see you & Miss Taklos almost immediately. We shall be at the Carlton.

C. V. V.

❧

To Gertrude Stein

29 October [1928]   Carlton Hôtel
Monday   Champs Elysées
                                                               Paris

Dear Gertrude,

Are you returned? And can you and Miss Taklos dine with us to-night? We are so anxious to see you. If you can dine with us please send me a pneumatique before two & we shall call for you at 7.30!

Love always,
Carlo V. V.

❧

To Carl Van Vechten

[postmark: 29 October 1928]   27 rue de Fleurus
                                                         [Paris]

My dear Carl

We are just back and as pleased as pleased as can be that we will be seeing you soon, got your pneu[matique] just five minutes after the postal

[172]

and then I tried to telephone but you were not in and the telephonist promised to tell you how pleased we will be to go with you this evening but somehow she did not inspire confidence so here it is sure.

At 7.30 to-night and lots of love to you both

Gertrude.

To Gertrude Stein

[30 October–2 November 1928]
9 A.M.

Carlton Hôtel
Champs Elysées
Paris

Darling,

Carl was ill all night with chills and fever. The doctor [said] that perhaps it is Malaria. He's coming in a few minutes again. We're heartbroken about to-night, but of course it will be impossible to do anything—I expect to be here all day, if you should call up later or to-morrow morning—or any time

love—
Fania

To Carl Van Vechten

[3 November 1928]
Saturday

27 rue de Fleurus
[Paris]

My dear Carl,

It was awfully nice seeing you. I liked it while it was happening and I like it now that it has happened and I will like it to go on happening. I am sending you this catalogue, I think it would amuse you to go and see the things. They are by that South American[1] you remember that we spoke about in connection with [Ronald] Firbank's Prancing Nigger.[2] I am asking him to meet us with some others at the Colonial ball,

Lots of love and we'll be seeing you
as ever
Gertrude

1. In 1927, through Edith Sitwell, Stein had met the Chilean-born painter Alvaro Guevara and his wife Meraud (see Gallup, *The Flowers of Friendship*, p. 205). Stein sent Van Vechten a catalogue of an exhibition of Guevara's paintings at a gallery on the rue de Seine, Paris. The catalogue is not in YCAL.

2. Van Vechten was active in promoting the novels of Ronald Firbank in the United States.

To Gertrude Stein

[4 November 1928]

Carlton Hôtel
Champs Elysées
Paris

Dear Gertrude,

Your splendid note received while I was lying flat—as usual—much bandaged. But I am better today & shall try to go chez [Tristan] Tzara.[1] Can't you & Alice dine with us tonight? I *must* stay in & that would make such a *beautiful* staying in—& we would dine in our rooms. I shan't go out until a quarter of four—but if you don't receive this in time to reply before a quarter of four—why telephone hotel anyway & leave word if you are coming—& *please* come—say at 7. Bring [Alvaro] Guevara—if you can. I like him.

Every single kind of rose to you!

Carlo.

It *has* been marvellous, and it will be more. I think I shall come back in the spring & be *well*.[2]

1. Tristan Tzara (1896–1963) was a Romanian-born poet, essayist, and editor. Tzara is generally credited with having used the word "Dada" for the first time on 8 February 1916 at Meieres

Cafe in Zurich and founded the review *Dada* there in 1917. Tzara came to live in Paris in 1919.

2. The French doctors diagnosed Van Vechten's illness as phlebitis.

To Gertrude Stein

[5 November 1928]
Monday

Carlton Hôtel
Champs Elysées
Paris

Dear Gertrude,

You did me so much good yesterday! Then I ate a dinner—went to sleep & slept. Got up this morning feeling any amount better—took a bath—my formula arrived (it's mostly aluminum) and now I am sitting up before a fire quite cheered up. I think in a day or so I'll be quite ready to fly. If you are up & about today I'd love to see you—but that is probably expecting too much. And bring someone if you like.

best love,
Carlo V. V.

To Gertrude Stein

[9 November 1928]
Friday night

Carlton Hôtel
Champs Elysées
Paris

Dear Gertrude,

After coming home from your delightful party I found my ankle quite swollen again & Marinoff was kept very busy with poultices all night. Save for an hour at Natalie Barney's I have been in bed all day.[1] So we are not going to London Monday—if ever. Salomon Reinach[2] at Miss Barney's was

much perturbed & said I had a very dangerous disease & Madame Clermont-Tonnerre[3] insisted that I put my foot on the couch & recline. I felt
like Thaïs or a grand courtisane quelconque. Anyway I loved your party &
you & Alice are my favorite characters in history & I don't think I want to
go to London. I hope to see you both soon.

Yellow roses to you!
Carlo

1. Natalie (or Nathalie) Clifford Barney (1876–1972) was an American, born in Dayton, Ohio.
She settled in France in 1899 and maintained a salon frequented by many of the leading writers, artists, and intellectuals in French society. Barney's own writings, primarily in French,
include poems, drama, fiction, and essays. She was the *Amazone* to whom the French writer
Remy de Gourmont addressed his *Lettres à l'Amazone* (Paris: La Centaine, 1926).

2. Salomon Reinach (1858–1932) was a classical scholar, archaeologist, and director of the
Musée de Saint-Germaine. Under the signature "Polybe" he wrote articles for *Le Figaro* (see
Stein to Van Vechten, [31 May 1923]).

3. Elisabeth de Gramont, Duchesse de Clermont-Tonnerre (1875–1954). It was through Natalie Barney that Stein had met Elisabeth de Gramont, who as a young girl had met Proust and
had served as a model for his Duchesse de Guermantes. Under the name Elisabeth de Gramont
she wrote a number of books dealing with nineteenth-century French life, memoirs of her family, autobiographical works, travel books, and two works on Proust: *Robert de Montesquiou et
Marcel Proust* (Paris: Flammarion, 1925) and *Marcel Proust* (Paris: Flammarion, 1948).

❧

To Carl Van Vechten

[postmark: 10 November 1928]   27 rue de Fleurus
                                                [Paris]

My dear Carlo

I did wake up with a bit of a cold this morning so I stayed at home
and sat with it or rather slept for it the whole afternoon and so we did not
see you which is a pity because I do want to see you both again. Everybody
was so awfully pleased with you, they went on quite at length about your
charms after you left, but after all I like your charms best, and I can tell you
how completely and entirely I have enjoyed being with you. We loved each
other very much by correspondence but there is even more of it face to face.

[176]

When can we say good-by to you both, and au revoir with very much intention

> *Love always*
> *Gertrude.*

To Carl Van Vechten

[postmark: 12 November 1928]　　　　　　　　　　27 rue de Fleurus
　　　　　　　　　　　　　　　　　　　　　　　　[Paris]

My dear Carl,

We were certain that it was the defile that had come between us but
it was rather wonderful with the true Paris color all about it, triste but not
sad, but now when do we meet because we do most awfully want to hear all
your adventures, I like your having seen Nathalie Barney's at its best between Salomon Reinach and the Duchesse [de Clermont-Tonnerre], we will
be around your way to-morrow afternoon, not any time precisely and do not
bother about us we will only be dropping in but if we do not connect we
will connect, it takes a whole procession really to get us apart even for a day,
lots and lots of love, I must show you a poem of [Georges] Hugnet's to me
that is being printed by Burton Rascoë as he writes it, like Edgar Poë, Rascoe would be pleased in his Almanach, but anyway lots when we meet and
once more to you both,[1]

> *Always*
> *Gertrude.*

1. Stein wrote to Hugnet [postmark 23 June 1928, Texas], telling him that Burton Rascoe had
asked her about young French writers. She suggested that Hugnet send Rascoe his poem "Le
Berceau de Gertrude Stein, ou le Mystère de la rue de Fleurus." This series of eight poems
was set to music by Virgil Thomson under the title *Le Berceau de Gertrude Stein (8 Poèmes de
Georges Hugnet to which have been added a Musical Composition by Virgil Thomson entitled
Lady Godiva's Waltzes)*. Rascoe did not publish Hugnet's poem.

　　Burton Rascoe was the editor of *Morrow's Almanac* for 1928 (New York: William Morrow & Company, 1927), which published Stein's "Van or Twenty Years After A Second Portrait of Carl Van Vechten," pp. 81–83. The book, *Morrow's Almanac* was published 18 October 1927.

###

To Gertrude Stein
[Calling Card: Carl Van Vechten]

[12? November 1928]   [Paris, France]

Dear Gertrude—

We were across the street & couldn't get back on account of the parade & the moment we did get back we came right over here—and you are
out & I am crying. I am returning J' adore which you were an angel to
leave—because I already had bought a copy—and I see that your copy is
autographed.[1] *When* can we meet? I wish you were here now—& Je suis
desolé.

Carlo.

4 o'clock.

1. Jean Desbordes's *J'Adore* (Paris: Bernard Grasset, 1928). In 1926, Jean Cocteau met Jean
Desbordes who was serving in the Navy as courier for the *Ministère de la Marine* in Paris. With
Cocteau's help *J'Adore* was published. The book, a collection of short pieces lyrically extolling
love and sensual cravings, also contained several essays, fervent appreciations of Cocteau. Cocteau wrote a preface for the book and for the publicity slogan conceived *"jeune homme, ne vous
tuez pas avant d'avoir lu 'j'adore!'"* Desbordes, a member of the resistance, died during World
War II after being captured and tortured by the Germans.

###

To Gertrude Stein

[12 November 1928]   Carlton Hôtel
Monday   Champs Elysées
                                                  Paris

Dear Gertrude,

Everything is *all* messed up because we are leaving *tomorrow*—I'm
so afraid we'll miss you this afternoon—and that would be dreadful. So can't
you come to dinner? & watch Fania pack—she is sure to be doing that at
the last minute. I am forehanded & all packed.

If you can't come to dinner—please do—both of you—we are likely to be here between three & four—but quite surely, I should think, after dinner.

We must see you. Dinner, say, at 7!

all sorts of fancy roses to you both—and a ripe pomegranate!

Carlo.

To Carl Van Vechten

[12 November 1928]   Carlton Hôtel
                                                          Champs Elysées
                                                          Paris

My dear Carl

Alas and alas here we are but here you are not and we do so want to see you and we cannot come to dinner and see Fania pack because we have to be back right after dinner to see some one who I told I would be at home and you are leaving so unexpectedly, we do want to see you we will be at home all this evening but so will you but perhaps you can just come over to say good-by, this sounds like a wail but really we have so much enjoyed seeing you and we do want to see you again and wish you good-luck for London & Cambridge

Lots & lots of love to you & Fania

Gertrude.

To Gertrude Stein

[13 November 1928]   Carlton Hotel
Tuesday   London, S. W. 1.

Dear Gertrude,

In the last night's excitement—and nothing to me is more exciting than mutual appreciation—I forgot to tell you that apparently we always stop at the Carlton, anyway here we are again!—and we sail on the Ile de France on Nov 29 from Plymouth—she leaves Havre on Nov. 28. You and Alice are two very good reasons why I shall not remain away from France so long again, but travelling terrifies me & we have 14 pieces of baggage—aside from 3 we left at the hotel to be shipped to the boat. Quelle vie!

Tell Monsieur [Kristians] Tonny to signe the sketches he sends—and even to *name* them, names are very important in America—& perhaps *everywhere*.[1]

Yellow, red, and blue roses to you & Alice & very much love!

Carlo.

How does George Lynes spell his name?[2]

1. Kristans Tonny, born in Paris of Dutch parents, was one of a number of young artists Stein took an interest in in the 1920s. Through Stein Van Vechten met Tonny and agreed to take a number of his drawings back to America to try to sell.

2. George Platt Lynes (1907–1955), the photographer, first met Stein in November-December 1925, when he was eighteen years old. Lynes was brought to meet Stein by Walter B. Hardy and his wife Katharine. The Hardys, who lived in Paris, had known Stein since 1916. They were active in setting up the Mildred Aldrich Endowment Fund which provided an income for Stein's friend Mildred Aldrich during the last years of her life. Lynes acquired a copy of Stein's *The Making of Americans*, which had just been published, and brought it to her to inscribe. See Lynes to Stein, 6 December 1925, YCAL. When he returned to America, he continued his studies at Yale University. Lynes began issuing a series of small pamphlets published by his own As Stable Press. One of these was Stein's *Descriptions of Literature*. On 15 October 1927 Lynes had opened the Park Place Bookshop in Englewood, New Jersey.

To Gertrude Stein

[14 November 1928]   Carlton Hotel
Wednesday   London, S.W. 1.

Dear Gertrude:—

Well, here I discovered a doctor who discovered what was the matter with me—and it is not phlebitis at all, but something serious & oriental—caused by a fungus, and he put me right to bed. So I am having a nice time reading the English & Tallulah Bankhead while he is curing me.[1] So we

[180]

have had to postpone our sailing to December 10 on the Paris and we shall be in London till then, partly in bed, partly, no doubt, out.

I'll send you more comments later. In the meantime please write me to my bed—not of pain—but of boredom—and write me all the news. Tell Virgil Thomson that I'll be in New York about the 17th & if he leaves before then to leave [Kristians] Tonny's drawings for me at 150 W. 55 Street, New York.

Love to you both,
Carlo V. V.

1. Tallulah Bankhead was in London appearing with Leslie Howard in *Her Cardboard Lover*, at the Lyric Theatre. The play, by Jacques Deval, had been adapted from the French by P. G. Wodehouse and Valerie Wyngate. Bankhead played the role of Simone.

To Carl Van Vechten
[Rose motto]

[postmark: 17 November 1928]
27 rue de Fleurus
[Paris]

My dear Carlo,

I do hope everything is just as well and happy with you as it can possibly be, just as well and happy, everybody is here xcept that we are all xhausted with Virgil Thomson's concert which fortunately was largely attended and seems to have been a success at least they all stayed to the end and they were all interested.[1] I hope everything goes well with him in New York. I do want you to hear the opera I would be awfully pleased if you liked it but then you will anyway we are sleepy and loving and George Lynes is his name and this morning [Kristians] Tonny brought his drawings, we have selected 8 and he is to give you a list of titles and prices. It is awfully good of you to take on my young men but they are pretty good I think, anyway you fill them with hope and that is always pleasant and they like you and that is always pleasant too but then we love you and that is even

[181]

more pleasant isn't it. You know I did like your being here a lot, it kind of
made up to me for Avery [Hopwood], and then yourself,

Love to Fania
Gertrude.

1. Thomson, Georges Hugnet, and Henri Cliquet-Pleyel had organized a "Concert d'oeuvres
musicales et poetiques" in the ornate ballroom of the Hotel Majestic, Paris, on 14 November
1928. Thomson wrote of this concert:

> The program included piano music by Cliquet-Pleyel and by myself played by our-
> selves, poems by Georges Hugnet set to music by Cliquet and myself and sung by Marthe-
> Marthine and two extended poems by Hugnet read by the actor Marcel Herrand. There
> were in addition six of my portraits for solo violin, played by Lucien Schwartz, and *The
> Death of Socrates*, from Satie, which I played for Marthe to sing. Among the other
> vocal pieces were my *Commentaire sur Saint Jerome* and *Les Soirees bagnolaises*, to poems
> of Hugnet. [Virgil Thomson, *Virgil Thomson*, pp. 124–25]

❧

To Carl Van Vechten
[Rose motto]

[postmark: 23 November 1928]   27 rue de Fleurus
                                                 [Paris]

My dearest Carl,

It is xciting having a really truly Oriental mushroom, and do see to
it that the doctors don't get so busy with King George that they give up the
chase, dear Carl what between watering places and beauty cures in France
and oriental mushrooms in London, Europe will cure you yet, anyway Europe has enjoyed it.[1] As Virgil [Thomson] is only in New York in passage
until he comes back from his visit home and you won't be on the boat how
about sending them, the drawings,[2] to you in London, they will be under a
hundred dollars, seven of them and so we only have to have a consular declaration particularly as they are being taken by you for an exhibition, therefore no duty, and you could have them with you in the Carlton to amuse
you, if this suits let me know by return post and we will go ahead and do
so, otherwise the usual Paris xcitements that come and go which would be

[182]

fun telling you but too complicated to write, anyway I won't forget the most amusing for next time,

Lots of love to you and Fania,

Gertrude.

1. Note by Van Vechten, 21 January 1941: "A reference to my leg."

2. Note by Van Vechten, 21 January 1941: "I took Tonny's drawings to New York & sold them all."

To Gertrude Stein

24 November [1928]   Carlton Hotel
                                            London, S.W.1.

Dear Gertrude—

It is *much* too complicated having the drawings in London—we just haven't room for a rice wafer in our luggage. So have [Virgil] Thomson take them to New York & drop them at 150 W. 55 Street. *Please*. They will keep them for me—or he can bring them to me there after Dec. 17.

Dear Gertrude, I was so glad to get your letter & I am still in bed—and I couldn't go to Cambridge. I hope to get up for the party Paul [Robeson] is giving for me on Monday—but oriental mushrooms are very persistent & my doctor *makes* me stay in bed—However, everybody comes to see me including Cambridge.

Love to you both,
Carlo.

To Carl Van Vechten

[postmark: 25 November 1928]   27 rue de Fleurus
                                            [Paris]

My dear Carl,

I am sorry that although you are enjoying yourself you are still in bed, it is damp weather to get the best of fungi let us hope a cold spell will improve matters but anyway I am glad that you are amusing yourself, young Cambridge is sweet isn't it and you will get there later surely. I am not sending the drawings to New York by Virgil [Thomson] because it would appear that there can be in this affair only the sender and the receiver which would have been alright if you had been on the boat but as it is he would be an intermedière and as such he can have no xistence and so we will wait till you are in New York and then you will let me know and we will send them to you direct, that will be the easiest, and do as soon as it has been tell us about Paul [Robeson]'s party, I would love to know about Paul's party only ought you to go to a party, lots of love and have a good time and get well and love to Fania

Yrs
Gertrude.

To Gertrude Stein

27 November [1928]   Carlton Hotel
Tuesday   London, S.W.1.

Dearest Gertrude—

Well, the doctor permitted me to go to Paul [Robeson]'s party if I promised not to drink & directly after went to bed for the week. So I promised & this is the next day & I am in bed . . . Paul & Essie, & Mrs. Goode, Essie's very distinguished mother & the baby have taken a large, late-Victorian house in St. John's Wood—there are cockney servants & in the dining room large oil paintings of *turks*. Elsewhere whatnots, porcelain, glass & various knick-knacks. The party was lovely. There was a great deal of food & much champagne. All the distinguished Negroes in London were there: Layton and Johnston, who sang, Leslie Hutchinson, and some very socially distinguished . . . Also Mrs. Patrick Campbell, Lady Ravensdale (Lord Curzon's daughter), Lord Beaverbrook, Lady Laski, Hugh Walpole—most of the stars of the English stage: Fred & Adele Astaire, Cathleen Nesbit, Jeanne de Cassilis, *Delysia*—who sang. Nicholas Hassan, Constance Collins, Athenée Scyles, etc. Paul sang & was a lamb. It was their first party &

a great success. I think you should come to London to go to a party at Paul's. And I'm sure he would give one for you.

I don't understand why it's so difficult about the [Kristians] Tonny drawings. Why couldn't [Virgil] Thomson just slip them between his shirts? Anyway I'll get them later—but don't make me sign papers & things. Couldn't they just be handed to me simply? You don't know the bother that I'll have to go through if I have to get them out of customs. So have *somebody* smuggle them in. Because I *quote* 6 ms & I don't want any bad feelings transferred to the pictures.

I am having such a nice time in bed. I wish you & Alice would come to London. Marinoff is combing her hair & I am awaiting a luncheon guest . . . *Don't* forget me!

Carlo.

The channel seems to be rough.

To Carl Van Vechten
[Rose motto]

[postmark: 2 December 1928]   27 rue de Fleurus
                                               [Paris]

My dear Carl,

Voici a new fountain pen I have not had one since you were last in Europe and I am very pleased with the same it was almost time wasn't it. And are you being unfaithful to Paris you almost sound seduced by London, Fania combing her hair and you enjoying your doctor it is suspicious.[1] I delighted in Paul [Robeson]'s party and what are your plans London seems to be full of oriental funguses but they are fortunately not too dangerous to Americans more so I gather to the British, but Dolly Wilde has just barely escaped from the fangs of one and returned to us in Paris.[2] Otherwise no news, we are all now that Virgil [Thomson][3] has left who was to do it translating Making of Americans only 60 pages but oh my. Our little George Hugnet 20 years old hair is turning white with the struggle but it really does

[185]

not sound so bad but it is a funny language not mine of course but the french, lots of love to you both and be faithful to us[4]

Gertrude.

1. Note by Van Vechten, 21 January 1941: "I was confined to my rooms in the Carlton for a month with a bad leg. Every morning I got out of bed to visit Sir Aldo Castelfani in Harley Street and I did manage to go to a party at Paul Robeson's who was living in St. John's Wood."

2. Dorothy ("Dolly") Ierne Wilde (d. 1941) was the daughter of Oscar Wilde's brother William. Dolly Wilde was one of Natalie Barney's lovers. A decade after her death Barney edited a volume of souvenirs of Dolly Wilde contributed by various friends, *In Memory of Dorothy Ierne Wilde* (Dijon, France: Darantière [1951]).

3. Thomson had returned to the United States.

4. The translation by Hugnet was *Morceaux choisis de La Fabrication des américains* (Paris: Editions de la Montagne [1929]).

To Gertrude Stein

6 December [1928]   Carlton Hotel
                                            London, S.W.1.

Dear Gertrude,

London has been splendid, in and out of bed, but it has not effaced memories of YOU and ALICE and Paris and we did love it and we shall come back soon and be much better next time. I am awfully well now, but I don't drink or eat fish or sweets, but otherwise I eat everything and how! What am I going to do with these stamps, and so I send them to you,

with lots of love,
Carlo

We sail on the Paris from Plymouth early Monday morning.

To Carl Van Vechten
[Rose motto]

[postmark: 8 December 1928]   27 rue de Fleurus
                                               [Paris]

My dear Carl,

Thanks for the stamps although they have induced violent unsuccessful mental arithmetic but anyway here it is hoping for many happy returns of the same. Have a good trip a good Christmas and a good new year and come back to us full of food and health, if not there is always Bagnolles [de l'Orme][1] but there will be. I did not send [Kristians] Tonny's drawings by Virgil [Thomson] because as he was traveling steerage and arriving with not very much in his pocketbook he might have had a bother but if you are still interested couldn't I send them to you by Mr. Dudensing or perhaps you would rather wait and see for yourself when you come back.[2] Anything you decide I will do and most of all is my love for you and do be happy both of you well and happy

Always
Gertrude.

1. Note by Van Vechten: "Where Yvette Guilbert was advising me to go for my leg."
2. Valentine Dudensing was a New York art dealer.

To Gertrude Stein

12 December 1928   Bord S.S. "Paris"

Dear Gertrude,

Three days out and at last I am able to sit up a little. Your grand letter came to the boat and made things pleasanter: they were very unpleasant for awhile what with Father Neptune knocking up the waves and all.

But now it is better and so am I. Do send the [Kristians] Tonny drawings by some one. I think I can sell some of them and it would be too bad if he had to wait till I came back for that.

We had great fun at the Caledonian market in London. It is like the Marché aux puces, except everything is stolen. And with Emilie Grigsby, and Hugh Walpole, and ever so many others.[1] Paul [Robeson] is divine and you must go to London to see him. Their house is 76 Carlton Hill. But nothing is like you and Alice or ever will be, worlds without end.

with our love and please remember me to any one who likes me!

en voyage

Carlo

I'm sorry I didn't see [Alvaro] Guevara again. I hope he paints you. If he does, send me a photograph.

Original works of art, I hear come in to America, duty free. Can this be true?

1. Emilie Grigsby and Hugh Walpole (1884–1941), the English writer, were friends of Van Vechten's.

⁋

To Carl Van Vechten

[postmark: 27 December 1928] 27 rue de Fleurus
[Paris]

My dear Carl,

We were awfully pleased to have your cable[1] and know you were all well and happy, may you have always more and more and more of the same, and we are sending on the [Kristians] Tonny drawings by a Colonel and Mrs. [Emmet] Addis[2] old friends of ours who are sailing on the 18 of January they are on their way to Boston but they will connect with you in New York and deliver them to you somehow, I'll send you along the list of names and prices very soon, I am glad you continue interested in Tonny I think he is pretty good and getting better which is very nice when one is as young as that, an amusing kid, just send me a nice Christmas card of phantoms[3] and let me know if you ever received [Georges] Hugnet's book of poems with

Max Jacob drawings, he sent them to you in June,[4] otherwise we are enjoying ourselves as usual, I am almost getting a new Ford car, Virgil Thomson writes that he has arranged for Capitals to be sung at the Little Theatre in the end of February, I think you will like it,[5] I rather like myself in song, and always more than lots of love from us, to you and Fania,

Yours
Gertrude.

1. Probably a Christmas telegram from the Van Vechtens which has not survived.

2. Louise Hayden Addis (later Taylor) (d. 1977) had first met Toklas in the 1880s when they were both living in Seattle, Washington, and shared an interest in music. While visiting California in 1899 Louise Hayden met Gertrude Stein through mutual friends. Her acquaintanceship with Stein was renewed in 1905–6 in Paris where Hayden had become assistant to Isidor Philipp (a famous piano teacher), and in September 1907 she renewed her friendship with Toklas, who had just arrived in Paris. The three remained close friends for the rest of their lives.

In 1922 Hayden married an American army officer, Colonel Emmet Addis, and she returned to the United States, where her husband was stationed. They did, however, manage frequent trips to Paris. After the death of Colonel Addis in 1932, Mrs. Addis lived exclusively in a house she had acquired some years earlier in Deya, Majorca. In 1939 she married an English army officer, Colonel Redvers Taylor. Mrs. Taylor moved to England, where she lived until her death (Personal interviews, 1974, 1975).

3. This card cannot be identified.

4. Georges Hugnet, 40 *Poèsies de Stanislas Boutemer*, illustrated by Max Jacob (Paris: Ed. Th. Briant, 1928).

5. See Van Vechten to Stein [February? 1929], note 1.

To Carl Van Vechten

[postmark: 19 January 1929]

27 rue de Fleurus
[Paris]

My dear Carl,

We have at last got [Kristians] Tonny's drawings off to you and here is the list, I do hope you like them, I am also sending you the notice of the translation of Making of Americans, it has been very amusing all of it, and given me quite a lot of pleasure, I will also be sending you in a few days a catalogue of a show that Tonny is giving and which has some very good things in it, otherwise all is peaceful xcept that I am getting a new Godiva[1] having given my old one to my editor, we had a touching farewell, [Georges] Hugnet, [Georges] Maratier[2] and I on Godiva when we left her in his garage au borde de la Marne, it was most historic, and what is [Miguel] Covarrubias's address, he sent me from Mexico a perfectly delightful angel it has given me a lot of pleasure and I want to write to him about it. It is very very lovely and it was very sweet of him, and I guess that is all just at present and what is your news, how are you and have you a pleasant memory of us all, we all have of you they were all touched that you wanted to be remembered to all of them who had found you gentle and they all agreed that they had very much so,

   Always lots of love to you and to Fania

Gertrude.

1. "Godiva" was Stein's name for her Ford automobile.

2. Maratier was involved in the Editions de la Montagne and later opened the Galerie de Beaune, Paris.

To Gertrude Stein
[Telegram]

[postmark: 12 February 1929]   New York

   VIRGIL [Thomson] PLAYED FOUR SAINTS LAST NIGHT EVERY-BODY LOVED IT WHERE ARE [Kristians] TONNY DRAWINGS

        CARLO

To Gertrude Stein

[13? February 1929]   150 West Fifty-fifth Street
            [New York]

Dear Gertrude,

   Virgil Thomson came & played "Four Saints in Three Acts" to a select crowd which included Mabel Luhan, Muriel Draper, Les Stettheimers, Alma Wertheim, Witter Bynner etc. & everybody liked it so much that yesterday I cabled you. I liked it so much that I wanted to hear it all over again right away. Mabel liked it so much that she said it should be done & it would finish opera just as Picasso had finished old painting—Well I cabled you but everybody loved it & I think your words are so right & inevitable in music. "Capital-Capitals" is being done next week.

I *did* receive [Georges] Hugnet's poems & I did write him, but *where* are [Kristians] Tonny's drawings. You wrote that they were arriving by a Col. [Emmet] Addis who was sailing on Jan. 18 & I waited to get them before writing you & I am still waiting. *Where* are they?

I am terribly thrilled—naturally—about the "morceaux choisis" from "La fabrication des Americains"—& I see that it is due in February.

Nobody knows exactly where [Miguel] Covarrubias is but Vanity Fair. So write care of that. They send him cheques so he always lets them know. He is somewhere in New Orleans, I think.

Max Ewing's exhibition is astounding. I think you have had a catalogue.[1] & I am *very* well again, but am having all my teeth taken out. Some of us took Virgil to Harlem after the concert, & he behaved very well, but in spite of that I think he was a little astonished.

Love to you both from us,

Carlo.

We might come over any minute; so I hope the Tonny drawings come before we go after them.

1. An exhibition, *Max Ewing: Collection of Extraordinary Portraits*, was held in Ewing's apartment, Apartment Quatre Vingt Quartre, 19 West 31 Street, New York, beginning Christmas 1928. The collage portraits, which were scattered throughout the apartment, included several of Van Vechten, Marinoff, and Stein.

To Carl Van Vechten
[Rose motto]

18 February [1929]   27 rue de Fleurus
                                                           [Paris]

My dear Carl,

The people bringing you the [Kristians Tonny] drawings are Mrs. [Emmet] Addis 104 Revere Street Boston, you should have had them 10 days ago if you have not had them by this time, communicate, I have just sent them an urgent summons, I am awfully pleased you like the Four Saints, I liked it a lot myself, I hope the Capitals go off well, I am interested in me and in Virgil [Thomson], and a lot of hope in us both, just also had a charming letter from Nella Imes, it touched me a lot, I am waiting to write her till I get her book she promised me[1] and don't forget [Miguel] Covarrubias's address, I want to write to him his angel continues to please me, I like in short all your friends but I love you best, we have gotten our summer house at last we are almost certain at Belley and we do want to see you and Fania in it,[2] lots and lots of love to you

Always
Gertrude.

1. Imes wrote to Stein how impressed she had been with Stein's story "Melanctha." She offered to send Stein a copy of her first novel, *Quicksand* (New York: Alfred A. Knopf, 1928). Imes's letter to Stein is in Gallup, *The Flowers of Friendship*, p. 216. The date on the letter should be 1929.

2. Stein and Toklas had taken a lease on a house in Bilignin, a hamlet just outside of Belley.

To Gertrude Stein

[February? 1929]   150 West Fifty-fifth Street
                                                        [New York]

Dear Gertrude,

The [Kristians] Tonny pictures came at last. The Addises mailed them down apparently after they had heard from you. I have sold two of them & hope to sell some more, but they are very *late* & I have missed some people who are now gone away for some time. However . . .

We saw Henry McBride the other evening & he told us all about Belley & now you write you have a house! I do hope we shall see Belley this summer, but our plans are not settled yet at all. We may sail any day, but New York is pretty good just now. They sing Capital, Capitals at concerts and people *love it*.[1] I hope some one will do the opera.

[192]

Well, anyway, here's lots of love to you both, & I'll try to sell some more pictures for Tonny.[x]

Carlo

[x]They are swell pictures!

1. The Thomson-Stein work, *Capital, Capitals*, was performed on Sunday, 24 February 1929. It was part of the second in a series of three Copland-Sessions concerts at The Little Theatre, New York. Thomson accompanied the singers, the Ionian Quartet: Harold Dearborn, Frank Hart, Baldwin Allan-Allen, and Hildreth Martin. The other composers on the program were Roy Harris, Alexander Lipsky, and Vladimir Dukelsky.

To Carl Van Vechten
[Rose motto]

[postmark: 15 April 1929]   27 rue de Fleurus
                                         [Paris]

My dear Carl

Virgil [Thomson] is back[1] and he has been telling all about how sweet you are and that we know and what a good time you gave him and everything and it all sounds very pleasant, and what are your plans, Nathalie Barney asked most tenderly about your phlebitis yesterday but I told her it wasn't and she seemed much relieved. We are leaving for our Belley house in a couple of weeks, we bought ourselves a white caniche [poodle] of two months which we call Basket to go with it and with us and I am working making sentences about the sentence and there we are.[2] And if you have any money for [Kristians] Tonny, will you send it to him, he is at St. Tropez and languishing for it because he wants to stay longer, his address 5 rue de la Mairie, Puteau Paris I think you have,

Lots of love to you and to Fania

Gertrude.

Tonny's address is
Kristians Tonny
5 rue de la Mairie
Puteau
Seine

1. Thomson had returned to Paris from New York in March 1929.

2. Stein's "Saving the Sentence" was published in her *How to Write*, pp. [11]–21.

❧

To Gertrude Stein

22 April 1929   150 West Fifty-fifth Street
                                                 [New York]

Dear Gertrude,

I have sold *four* of [Kristians] Tonny's drawings ("Deux Clous" à $20; "Les oiseaux apprivoisés" à $16; "l'Esprit s'envole" à $10; "Acrobatie equestre" à $5.) and I am sending you two cheques for these, according to the advice of Virgil [Thomson] who told me the easiest things to get cashed in Paris were cheques on N.Y. banks. I hope he is right. I am sending this on in case Tonny needs the money—I still have three sketches which I hope to dispose of.

We are sailing on the Majestie on May 10—first for London, but I do hope we shall get to Paris before you & Alice leave for the country. When will that be? We shall probably be at the Carlton in London, but the Guaranty Trust, 50 Pall Mall will surely reach us. My N.Y. cable address is "Carlvecht New York" & our permanent European address is Banque de Paris et des Pays Bas, 3 Rue d'Antin. There!! Now we can all draw a long breath. We hope to be seeing you very soon.

> *our love to you both always!*
> *Carlo.*

Virgil is a *lamb!*[1]

1. At the bottom of the first page of Van Vechten's letter Stein wrote the word "Bilignin." At the end of the second page she wrote a list of names: "Jean Cocteau Jean [Aman?] E. Renan Robert Graves Picasso."

❦

To Gertrude Stein
[Postcard: The King Taking the Salute of the Guards]

25 May [1929]   [Carlton Hotel, London]

Dearest Gertrude,

We have no plans as yet. We shall be at the Carlton in London at least till June 3—and then we are coming to Paris & I shall probably go to Berlin. But we'll try to get to Aix [les Bains] later. We must see you both.

Love
Carlo.

❦

To Carl Van Vechten

[postmark: 2 June 1929]   Bilignin par Belley
                                                           Ain

My very dear Carl,

Here we are and there you are, alas Paris and London seem about as far away as New York not to mention Berlin but anyway we must be on your way, it's a nice way your way and our way and it ought to be all the same way. Virgil [Thomson] writes for your news,[1] he is having a bit of a piece of a concert on the eight[h] or ninth of June I think[2] and he is looking forward to you being there, his address is 17 Quai Voltaire, I can't tell you how sorry we are to be missing you but I can't say I am not awfully pleased to be here because we are, it is nice and I am looking forward to your seeing it. It is a case of In the greenest of our valleys by good angels tenanted,[3] and so will you love to you and Fania always and always

Gertrude.

How is the leg.

1. Thomson to Stein, 13 May [1929], YCAL.

2. *Concert d'Oeuvres de Jeunes Compositeurs Américains* was given on 17 June 1929 at the Salle Chopin, 8 rue Daru, Paris. The composers represented were Aaron Copland, Israel Cit-

kovitz, Carlos Chávez, Roy Harris, and Virgil Thomson. The works by Thomson, all for soprano and piano, were *La Valse Grégorienne* (text by Georges Hugnet), *La Seine* (text by the Duchesse de Rohan), *Le Berceau de Gertrude Stein (Huit Poemes by Georges Hugnet to which have been added a Musical Composition by Virgil Thomson entitled Lady Godiva's Waltzes)*, *Susie Asado* (text by Stein), and *Preciosilla* (text by Stein). The works were sung by the soprano Madame Marthe-Marthine, with Thomson accompanying.

3. The first two lines of "The Haunted Palace," a poem by Edgar Allan Poe in his story "The Fall of the House of Usher."

❧

To Gertrude Stein
[Postcard: Elizabeth of York, Queen Consort of Henry VII. 1465–1503]

4 June [1929]   [Carlton Hotel, London]

The leg is all right, dear Gertrude, & this time I am making whoopee in London. We must try to get to Aix [les Bains]. I think we shall manage Paris next week. Love to you both.

Carlo.

Banque de Paris et
des Pays Bas
3 rue d'Antin, Paris.

❧

To Carl Van Vechten

[postmark: 11 June 1929]   Bilignin par Belley
                                                        Ain

My dearest Carl,

Alas and yet it is nice to be here we are not to be in Paris when you get there but then you are going to be here when we are here because you

[196]

are going to take a cure at Aix les Bains and so we will be together because it will be most awfully nice seeing you, and what are your plans where are you going to be we have the home we wanted and it is very satisfactory and we are very pleased with it and we have a dog named Basket and he is asleep and all we need now is seeing you and Fania and that will be soon, Virgil [Thomson] came home very happy about you, write to me right away and tell me just when we fit in to your plans because we must fit in very soon,

Lots and lots of love
Gertrude.

To Carl Van Vechten

[postmark: 20 June 1929]   Bilignin par Belley
Ain

My dearest Carl,

Where are you and how are you and are you in Paris and Ain is on the way surely it is and even if it isn't we are on the way sure we are, it's at first a nice and quiet way and that will do you a heap of good in between and there will have to be a lot of in between, do let us know and we do love you and lots of love to you and to Fania

Gertrude.

To Gertrude Stein
[Postcard]

[postmark: 21 June 1929]   [Hôtel Bristol, Paris]

Dear Gertrude,

We are now in Paris at the Hotel Bristol—112 Faubourg St. Honoré playing around. I am extremely well this time. I think we shall stay here two or three weeks more & then go motoring. Why not to Aix [les Bains] to see Gertrude & Alice? J'espere que oui.

Love,
Carlo

🐿

To Gertrude Stein
[Postcard: Photograph of Jack Taylor]

[postmark: 27 June 1929]   [Hôtel Bristol, Paris]

Dear Gertrude—

A thousand thanks for the morceaux choisis which arrived at exactly the same moment as Georges Hugnet, so he wrote in it too.[1] More about these matters & others later, but I think I gave the boys a good time one night.[2]

Love,
Carlo.

1. Van Vechten's copy of Stein's *Morceaux choisis de la fabrication des américains* (Paris: Editions de la Montagne, [1929]) is in YCAL. His copy bears two inscriptions, Stein's and Hugnet's. Stein wrote, "Always with love for Carl to Carl Gtrde," and Hugnet wrote, "A Carl Van Vechten En m'excusant de no pas savoir l'anglais avec toute mon amitié Georges Hugnet 1929."

2. A reference to Hugnet and Maratier, both of whom were part of the Editions de la Montagne. Stein gave her car to Maratier.

🐿

To Carl Van Vechten

[postmark: 17 July 1929]   Bilignin par Belley
                                                             Ain

My dear Carl,

Ci inclus Mabel [Dodge], and when are you and Fania going to eat our peas and beans which I am so actively cultivating and Alice is so actively

[198]

picking and then so actively cooking, when, and were you with Hart Crane[1] when he was overcome, if you see him speak to him[2] for me I am very fond of him he is so sweet he might almost come from Iowa, well anyway let us know what you are doing and how you are, and lots of love to you both and à trés bientôt

Gertrude

1. Laura Riding and Robert Graves had written to Stein about the young American poet Hart Crane (1899–1932). When he arrived in Paris, Crane wrote to Stein asking to meet her (Gallup, *The Flowers of Friendship*, p. 227). He had been drinking heavily for nearly a week, and on 10 July he became involved in a brawl at the Café Select and was arrested. Stein had probably read about this incident in the New York *Herald* (Paris edition). For details on Crane in Paris see John Unterecker, *Voyager: A Life of Hart Crane* (New York: Farrar, Straus and Giroux, 1969), pp. 595–99.

2. Note by Van Vechten, 21 January 1941: "So far as I know I never met Hart Crane, the American poet."

To Gertrude Stein
[Postcard: Photograph of a bullfighter]

[July-August 1929][1]   [Spain]

Dear Gertrude,

I don't know exactly how it happened but somehow we got cold & came down here to get warm & we *did*. However, it is lovely & we are enjoying it & will stay down here two or three weeks.

Love,
Carlo.

I adored the *Saints* in Transition.[2]

1. The stamp and postmark have been removed from this card.

2. Stein's *Four Saints in Three Acts. An Opera To Be Sung* was published in *transition* (June 1929), 16/17:39–72.

To Gertrude Stein
[Postcard: Marinus—The Usurers]

[postmark: 2 August 1929]   [Hotêl Bristol, Paris]

Dear Gertrude,

Am afraid we are not going to see you this time after all, altho we still may run down to Aix [les Bains] for a day or two. Anyway we are sailing on the Ile de France Aug. 13. Much love to you both

Carlo.

We are back at the Bristol.

To Carl Van Vechten

[postmark: 3 August 1929]   Bilignin par Belley
                                             Ain

My dearest Carl,

No it would not be pretty of you to see everything in Europe excepting us now would it, we do want to see you and Fania and we do want you to lunch and dine with us or why have we been growing all these vegetables all by ourselves if it isn't to have you eat them and when will you and how did you like Spain,

And love to you both
Gertrude

To Carl Van Vechten
[Telegram]

[12 August 1929]   Belley

DID SO HOPE TO SEE YOU BUT DO BE BACK SOON ENDLESS LOVE TO YOU BOTH

GERTRUDE

[200]

❧

To Gertrude Stein

16 Aout [1929]   S.S. Ile de France

Dear Gertrude,

I think I was *afraid* of Aix [les Bains], I am always terribly afraid of fashionable places in season. At the last minute Virgil [Thomson] told me he thought we could stay in the little hotel where you used to stay. Anyway it would be *horrible* if we hadn't seen you in the winter. I think we shall be back before long. I really don't know why we are going to New York—except that my laundry is running low. You know it is one of my idiosyncrasies that I won't have my clothes washed in Paris. We *adored* Spain.

Milles embraces to you both.

Carlo.

❧

To Carl Van Vechten

[postmark: 21 September 1929]   Bilignin par Belley
                                                 Ain

My dearest Carl,

I wonder have you gotten the postal card we all sent you from Aix [les Bains] it was addressed simply to New York but that ought to do,[1] anyway we all told you how much we liked you, George Hugnet and Virgil [Thomson] have been here with us and it was all very gay and it would have been nice if you and Fania had been here too, you will be pleased that there is a fair chance of the opera being done in Darmstadt, they are much taken with the libretto their only condition being that it should be done into German but to that since they think they can make a good translation I see no objection, and now if they like the music as well they will put it on the beginning of the spring, it would be nice if we were all at the first night well anyhow that's a dream, and dreams are pleasant, give me news of you and lots of love[2]

Always
Gertrude.

1. Stein's postal card was not delivered.

2. Carl Ebert, director of the Hessisches Landestheatre in Darmstadt, Germany, and Karl Bohm, general music director of the theatre, had expressed an interest in *Four Saints in Three Acts*. Thomson sent them a piano-vocal score, and there was some discussion about a premiere. Heavy financial losses, caused by productions of modern works, resulted in the resignation of several members of the theatre, and the Thomson-Stein project was abandoned.

To Gertrude Stein
[Postcard: Intreurer Freundschaft: Herzl, Grüsse & Gluckwünsche über Land & Meer]

[postmark: 4 October 1929]
[150 West Fifty-fifth Street
New York]

Dear Gertrude,

I am thrilled at the possibility of Darmstadt. We have never been there & we must all go there officially & fill all the hotels. But I wish they would do it in English.—However, I think Geo[rges] Hugnet has done something remarkable in his translaion & his preface. Perhaps a German can be found.

(a book went to you last week)

Much love to you both.
[Carl Van Vechten]

To Carl Van Vechten
MS. New York Public Library, Manuscripts Division

[postmark: 5 October 1929]
Bilignin par Belley
Ain

My dearest Carl,

Thanks a thousand times for the Born to be of Taylor Gordon,[1] I have enjoyed it immensely and the illustrations of [Miguel] Covarrubias, I am enormously taken with Gordon, already I have been impressed with [Paul] Robeson who made me realize middle class America as no one else had made me see it, the middle class America of to-day and now Gordon makes clear the kind of America I knew as a kid as it is to-day, I don't know they have a way of seeing it from the inside and the outside that makes it clear, the way a white can't do it, it is not realism it is reality and that's what interests me most in the world, do give Gordon my love and tell him if he should ever come to Paris to come to me sure with a letter from you, and the picture of the three of you by Covarrubias is a wonder and Fania is a wonderfully real angel, I have never known anything realler, do tell Covarrubias from me that I am sure some day he will do a new religious picture that will be all any of us could want. Thanks a thousand times for everything Carl and best of all for yourself and always yours

Gertrude.

1. See Van Vechten to Stein, 28 May [1927], note 4.

❧

To Gertrude Stein
[Postcard: View of the Skyline, New York City]

[postmark: 20 October 1929]

[150 West Fifty-fifth Street
New York]

Dear Gertrude,

Loved getting your swell letter about Taylor Gordon, and I am thrilled about Darmstadt. Don't forget me.

Love,
Carlo.

To Carl Van Vechten
[Rose motto]

[December 1929–January 1930]   27 rue de Fleurus
                                                [Paris]

My dear Carl,

Merry Christmas and happy New Year to you and Fania and the best of everything and plenty of it including new and old, life has been xciting and tranquil since our return, [Kristians] Tonny now completely interested in Anita [Thompson][1] is an older and a sadder man, we have been doing our bit if you can do anything in the way of selling anything let me know, otherwise the little company is happy it enlarges somewhat and they all speak tenderly of you, I will send you soon a little thing that was printed of mine in the original french of which I am inordinately proud,[2] and more than that I love you very much

Always
Gertrude

Everybody likes born to be. I liked the serious essays in the anthology, thanks a lot[3]

G.

1. Note by Van Vechten, 21 January 1941: "Anita Thompson, a negro girl to whom I introduced Kristians Tonny, with whom he became infatuated."

2. Stein's "Film: deux soeurs qui ne sont pas soeurs," in *Revue Européenne* (mai/juin/julliet 1930), 5/6/7: [600]–1. A note indicates that this is "Le premier texte écrit et publié en français par Miss Stein."

3. Stein may be referring to Van Vechten's foreword and Muriel Draper's introduction to Taylor Gordon's *Born to Be* (New York: Covici, Friede Inc., 1929).

࿋

To Carl Van Vechten
[Postcard: Birthplace of Marechal Joffre at Rivesaltes—April 1917]

[postmark: 29 January 1930]   [27 rue de Fleurus
                                               Paris]

My dearest Carl,

We all lunched with the Duchess [de Clermont-Tonnerre][1] and talked tenderly of you, the opera is now all copied and being sent to Darmstadt if they said yes it would be nice but anyway things are quite nice all the little band are having their ups and their downs their boils and their results,[2] figuratively and litteraly, but anyway we all love you

Gtrde.

1. By "we" Stein is probably referring to herself, Toklas, and Virgil Thomson.

2. By the late 1920s Stein had become friendly with a number of young artists. The group included Virgil Thomson, Pavel Tchelitchew, Georges Hugnet, Georges Maratier, Christian Bérard, Kristians Tonny, Bravig Imbs, René Crevel, Eugene Berman, and Leonide Berman. For a variety of reasons Stein quarreled with almost everyone in this group. She eventually became reconciled with Thomson and Maratier.

࿋

To Gertrude Stein
[Telegram]

2 March 1930   New York

IF NOT TOO EXPENSIVE WE WANT PICASSO TO ILLUSTRATE NIGGER HEAVEN COULD YOU HELP PERSUADE HIM LOVE

CARLO

❧

To Carl Van Vechten

[postmark: 3 March 1930]   27 rue de Fleurus
                                            Paris

My dear Carl,

I am writing instead of cabling because it is too long to xplain. The trouble with asking Picasso is that he is just as liable to say yes as no but having said yes he is more than likely not to do anything, and the thing would drag on and there would always be a possibility and probably nothing would happen and the effort to have anything happen would be disagreeable to everybody concerned and at the end probably nothing would happen, that is the way it is. On the other hand it might be entirely different but it is most likely to be that way. It sounds as if it is going to be a beautiful edition and lots of love to you always and all

Gertrude.[1]

1. Note by Van Vechten, 21 January 1941: "This letter refers to a proposal I made to Gertrude to try and persuade Picasso to make illustrations for the deluxe Nigger Heaven. The illustrations were eventually made by E. McKnight Kauffer and are at present in my possession, but the book was never published because Kauffer was so late in getting them done that the depression of 1929 was upon us." Van Vechten gave these illustrations to the Museum of Modern Art, New York, in 1942.

❧

To Gertrude Stein
[Postcard: Portrait of Kee San holding flower]

[postmark: 25 May 1930]   [150 West Fifty-fifth Street
                                            New York]

Dear Gertrude:

We are sailing June 11 on the Mauretania & will be in London for a week or two & then come to Paris early in July & I hope to motor to Aix [les Bains] to see you. Banque de Paris et des Pays Bas, 3 rue d'Antin, Paris will be our address as usual. They will provide mail to London.

Love,
Carlo.

☙

To Carl Van Vechten and Fania Marinoff

[postmark: 7 June 1930] Bilignin par Belley
Ain

My very dear Carl & Fania

Will we be glad to see you well I guess yes, and we will be glad to show you us and Belley and Bilignin and Basket. It will be nice let us know just when and how you could spend a couple of days at the Hotel Pernollet at Belley you know and not be too uncomfortable and then be with us all day well anyway we will see you that is the important thing, we [are] very busy farming, we like farming, and we are busy being published we like being published[1] here is the cover of Lucy Church and we will go and see her she is in the neighborhood and I think you will like her,[2] anyway, you will like the portraits they are almost ready, and we like each other and à trés bientôt

Lots of love
Gertrude.

1. Through Ford Madox Ford, Stein had met William Aspenwall Bradley (1878–1938), an American writer and editor, who had started a literary agency in Paris with his wife Jenny. Bradley agreed to serve as Stein's agent and sent out manuscripts to a number of publishers, including Little Brown; Macaulay; Viking; and Harper's. All of the publishers rejected the manuscripts. Disappointed by these results, and by negotiations with Lee Furman, president of Macaulay Company, to publish the cut version of *The Making of Americans*, Stein and Toklas decided to start their own publishing company, to be called the Plain Edition. To finance this project, Stein sold to Marie Harriman, a New York art dealer, the Picasso Blue Period picture *Woman with a Fan* (1905).

The plain Edition published five books by Stein: *Lucy Church Amiably* (1930); *Before the Flowers of Friendship Faded Friendship Faded* (1931); *How to Write* (1931); *Operas and Plays* (1932); and *Matisse Picasso and Gertrude Stein, With Two Shorter Stories* (1933).

2. Lucy Church refers to a church in Lucey, a small village not far from Belley.

To Carl Van Vechten

[postmark: 7 June 1930]
Bilignin par Belley
Ain

My dearest Carl,

Nous voilà here in our country home and seeing to the peas and beans and barley grows all thanks for the book,[1] I don't think I am going to like it as well as Born to be but then I liked that better than I do most books and so did everyone I showed it to. I am inclosing an announcement of the new book of mine that Georges [Hugnet] is doing, if anybody wants it tell them to send for it this of course does not include you bien entendu.[2] You see Carl the reflections of the underworld the professional thieves etc. always make me think so sadly of Hutch[ins] Hapgood who used to tell me so much that bored me about professional thieves, they are always full of wisdom but I do now it's never very wise now the Born to be man's and yours and [Miguel] Covarrubias's and mine that is all wisdom that is wise but I do know I guess if I have to have it Dickens but then I never liked the professional thieves in Dickens I guess it is too professional, all this of course before I have read the book and just read his maxims, anyway I have a prejudice against professional thieves not because of their thieving but because of their professionalism they are a little like school teachers or school teachers' scholars I don't know which, but you do know what I mean. And what are your plans and how do you like them, and what's the news and how's the book and love to Fania and to you[3]

Always and always
Gertrude.

1. Van Vechten had probably sent Stein a copy of Tuft's *The Autobiography of a Criminal: Henry Tufts*, ed. Edmund Pearson (1804; rpt. New York: Duffield & Co., 1930). Hutchins Hapgood had written *The Autobiography of a Thief* (New York: Fox, Duffield & Co., 1908).

2. Enclosed with the letter was a *Bulletin de souscription* for Stein's *Dix Portraits*. This volume contained ten of Stein's portraits in English and in a French translation by Georges Hugnet and Virgil Thomson. The book contained a preface by Pierre de Massot and was illustrated by Picasso, Pavel Tchelitchew, Christian Bérard, Kristians Tonny, and Eugene Berman. The portraits were "If I Told Him: A Completed Portrait of Picasso," "Guillaume Apollinaire," "Erik

[208]

Satie," "Pavlik Tchelitchef or Adrian Arthur," "Virgil Thomson," "Christian Bérard," "Bernard Faÿ," "Kristians Tonny," "George Hugnet," and "More Grammar Genia Berman."

3. Van Vechten's new novel, *Parties*, was published by Knopf in August 1930.

To Gertrude Stein
[Postcard: The Old Houses, Holburn, London]

[postmark: 30 June 1930]   [London]

Dear Gertrude:

So happy to get your letters. We are going to Paris Tuesday—July 1—and shortly after *probably* will motor South. In any case we are surely coming to see you!

Love
Carlo.

address Banque de Paris et des Pays Bas 3 rue d'Antin.

To Carl Van Vechten

[postmark: 4 July 1930]   Bilignin par Belley
                                                               Ain

My dear Carl,

Welcome to France and I do hope that we will be seeing you and Fania soon, the Hotel Pernollet Belley really is a very nice hotel and in a week is to have its six rooms new with bath installed, and I think you would like it there and be with us and see the country, and you could be very comfortable and anyway it would [be] nice but only you must be sure to give a few days' notice particularly if it is anywhere near the 14 of July, we are xpecting to hear from you and see you very very soon,

Always
Gertrude.

To Gertrude Stein
[Postcard: Wallace Collection: Reynolds. The Strawberry Girl]

[postmark: 7 July 1930]   [Hôtel Bristol, Paris]

Dear Gertrude—

Thank you a thousand times for Dix Portraits. I have already read about Kristians Tonny with excitement & appreciation. You shall hear our plans as soon as we make them. The weather is *bad*.

Love—
Carlo.

To Gertrude Stein
[Postcard: Les Petits Tableaux de Paris—"Le Lapin Agile" cabaret
artistique de Montmartre; le "Père Frédé"]

[postmark: 14 July 1930]   [Hôtel Bristol, Paris]

Dear Gertrude—

We start on our motor trip Wed. July 16 & eventually will get to the Hotel Pernollet. We are going down by Tours & [2 words?] Biarritz—[coming back?] by Macon—Aix-les-Bains etc. Paris address will always reach me—

[210]

but write me Comp. Nationale d'Escompte de Paris—Toulon—we shall reach there next Sunday or Monday. Dying to see you.

Love
Carlo.

⁂

To Carl Van Vechten
[Postcard: La Maison de Jeanne d'Arc à Domrémy]

[postmark: 17 July 1930]   [Bilignin par Belley
                                                       Ain]

My dearest Carl,

It is nice that you are really coming, we come on the road from Macon before Aix [les Bains], and you will be comfortable at the Pernollet and happy with us and I know you will like seeing a little of rural France, in a typical provincial town and let us know just when and you will have nice weather and everything and lots of love

Gertrude.

I liked the postal of Frederic.

⁂

To Gertrude Stein
[Postcard: Carcassonne (Aude)—La Cité L'Entrée du Château—Porte
Narbonnaise]

22 July [1930]   [Carcassonne, France]

Dear Gertrude:

We are here now, but slowly coming your way, by way of Barcelona, & Toulon, perhaps late next week or early the week after. I'll telegraph you to reserve a chambre at the Pernollet. We are sure to come, because our chauffeur did his military service at Belley & can hardly wait!

> *Love,*
> *Carlo,*

To Gertrude Stein
[Postcard: Tarascon—La Tarasque]

25 July [1930]   [Arles, France]

Dear Gertrude,

We could not get the proper visas soon enough & so did not go to Barcelona. We are going to Toulon today & should be with you by the end of next week. I will let you know.

> *Love,*
> *Carlo*

you could reach me for a few days Comp. Nat'l d'Escompte de Paris at Toulon.

To Gertrude Stein
[Postcard: Souvenir de Monte Carlo. Salle de Roulette l'Heureux Gagnant]

29 July [1930]   [Cannes, France]

Dear Gertrude—

These are the dernier chic enjoying themselves. We are at Cannes in the *sun* & love it.—I think we'll stay here until Saturday or Sunday & then start for Belley—

> *Love,*
> *Carlo.*

Comp. Nat. d'Escompte de Paris—Cannes.

❧

To Gertrude Stein
[Postcard: Young Black Boy and Black Girl]

31 Aug [i.e., July 1930]   [Cannes, France]

Dear Gertrude,

I have instructed my banque at Paris to forward my mail to the Hotel Pernollet—so you see we are on our way. Please ask them to guard it carefully, and in a day or so I'll telegraph or write you the exact day. We go back to Toulon tomorrow & then up, but Virgil [Thomson] wants me to see Le Puy & perhaps we shall stop 2 or 3 other places.

Love
Carlo

❧

To Carl Van Vechten
[Postcard: Route de Belley à Yenne—Port Pierre-Châtel]

[postmark: 1 August 1930]   Bilignin par Belley
                                                             Ain

We can't offer you sun or chic but I think you will like it all the same any way you will like us, and it will be nice, and on your way eat at Mme Bourgeois' at Priay it's worth while[1]

Love and very soon
Gertrude.

1. The restaurant of Madame Bourgeois was one that Stein and Toklas were particularly fond of. The town of Priay is not in the Bugey (the region around Belley) proper.

❧

To Gertrude Stein
[Postcard: Jeux Provençaux—Arènes d'Arles]

[2 August 1930]   [Avignon, France]

Dear Gertrude:

We are now in Avignon & it is raining which may delay us—otherwise we go tomorrow to Orange & Valence Monday to Le Puy—Tuesday or Wednesday—Belley. Why don't you tell the hotel that they will get a telegram from me the day before & to reserve chambre à deux lits—très tranquille & as much running water as possible—

Love—
Carlo

I will also telegraph you, of course.

❧

To Gertrude Stein
[Telegram]

[postmark: 4 August 1930]   Valence [France]

Arrivant demain avant diner s'il vous plait reserver chambre a pernollet mille pensees

Carlo

❧

To Carl Van Vechten

[6 August 1930][1]   [Bilignin par Belley
                                                       Ain]

My dearest Carl,

Welcome to our little city, and we are expecting you to dinner now this evening you and Fania and the chauffeur too and we will be there at

[214]

seven o'clock at Bilignin and anxiously waiting for you and it will make us all very happy, lots of love to you and Fania

Gertrude[2]

1. This letter was left for Van Vechten at the Hôtel Pernollet in Belley.

2. Note by Van Vechten, 21 January 1941: "This summer Fania and I were motoring through Spain & we stopped off at Belley for a night at the Hotel Pernollet & spent parts of two days with Gertrude and Alice at Bilignin."

To Alice Toklas
[Postcard: Valence: Le Musée—Portrait de Comte de Montalivet, par Couder]

[postmark: 7 August 1930]   [Hôtel Pernollet, Belley]

Dear Alice,

When you asked me about being recognized in restaurants last night I forgot to tell you that I am frequently mistaken for Harry Thaw![1]—We had a fabulous day with you & Gertrude yesterday. The most perfect I can remember. I am leaving in tears & hope to see you both very soon again. The Hotel Bristol—Paris will reach us until we sail Sept. 11.

Love to you both
Carlo.

1. Harry K. Thaw, the man who murdered the architect Stanford White on 25 June 1906.

***

To Carl Van Vechten and Fania Marinoff
[Postcard: Environs de Belley—Entrée du Château de Lucey]

[postmark: 8 August 1930]   [Bilignin par Belley
                                             Ain]

My dears,

We did have a nice visit and I am wearing the brooch and it was a very pleasant occasion in every way and we are hoping for more of the same and how was everything going home to Paris, and we are glad you liked our country and our home and us and lots of love

Gertrude

***

To Alice Toklas
[Postcard: Young Black Boy and Black Girl]

[postmark: 9 August 1930]   [Beaune, France]

Dear Alice,

Before we leave Beaune there must be a special word of thanks for the honey cakes of Aix-les-Bains which are delicious. It is 8 A.M. and in a short time we are off for Paris where we shall arrive tonight. Much love to you both,

Carlo

I liked the [oeuf?] of Bourg[1]

---

1. *Oeufs à la Coque* are a speciality at Bourg-en-Bresse, where Toklas had advised Van Vechten to stop for lunch.

To Carl Van Vechten and Fania Marinoff
[Postcard: Brillat-Savarin, Gravure par Bertall]

[postmark: 9 August 1930]   [Bilignin par Belley
                                             Ain]

My dears,

I forgot to give you Mike [Stein]'s address and telephone number, it is Chemin de la Plaine Vaucresson, and his telephone no. is Garches 392, I have just written to him that you will ring him up.[1] I'll be sending you Lucy Church soon, we are still talking about you.

Yours with lots of love
Gtrde.

1. Stein's eldest brother, Michael, together with his wife Sarah and their son Allan, lived in the Villa Stein (Les Terrasses), erected in 1927 at Garches on the outskirts of Paris by Le Corbusier.

To Gertrude Stein

[12 August 1930]   Le Bristol
                                    Hotel et Restaurant
                                    112 Faubourg St Honoré
                                    Paris (VIII)

Dear Gertrude,

Fania discovered that Guerlain had no tuberose, and so she sent Alice Champs-Elysées. . Floris has a tuberose. I wonder would she like to try that? I sent Alice two cards. I hope she received them. And something strange is going to happen about *you* very soon . . . . I have ordered the illustrated Dix Portraits.

Dear Gertrude:[1]

this letter is about the plates. Do you think your pottery could make something like the enclosed?[2] These are cards that a man writes for us in

Montmartre each year we come over . . . I don't mean exactly, of course, but *with a dove with a missive in its beak and a horseshoe and two transfig-ured hearts and Carlo et Fania pour la vie* somewhere or anyhow, whatever colors he fancies, and I should say 12 plates of salad size, but if he prefers to make dinner plates I leave it to him. . And I will send the money right away if you will tell me how much. And if he can get the plates done in time (we sail Sept 11) he can send them to the Bristol in Paris (perhaps with one of the Rose is a rose ones!) and if he can't they can be shipped to New York. Whatever you think and whatever you like. I hope it won't be too much bother for you. We had such a happy time with you and Alice and do hope we can have lots of them here there and everywhere and intense love to you both,

Carlo

We went to see Mistinguett[e] last night. I shall never get over think-ing she is a great artist.

The weather is better, but Louis has given me a very queer feeling about automobiles. I never used to be afraid before.[3] Now I tremble and quake and get all tense.

Your card came about your brother's house. Thank you.

1. This second salutation may simply be an indication that Van Vechten had begun the letter and was interrupted.

2. To illustrate the design, Van Vechten enclosed the small card.

3. Louis was the French chauffeur whom the Van Vechtens had hired for their tour of France.

To Alice Toklas
[Postcard: Marseille—Le Square de la Bourse]

[postmark: 12 August 1930]   [Hôtel Bristol, Paris]

Alice darling

Guerlain is sending you to-day some perfume called Champs Ely-sées, I hope you will like it. It's one of my favorites. It rains here nearly all the time otherwise we love it. It was grand seeing you two marvelous gals whom we adore—

Fania

☙

To Carl Van Vechten
[Postcard: Aix-les-Bains—Lac du Bourget La Route au bord de l'Eau]

[postmark: 15 August 1930]   [Bilignin par Belley
                                               Ain]

Yesterday afternoon we had a long palaver with the potter—alas they won't undertake to reproduce any of the symbols on your charming card— nothing but the lettering—so I've not given them that order and won't un- less you say so. I'm so sorry to be so ineffective. Do try me out on something else.

Your p[ost]. c[ard]s are lovely—it proves how fundamentally honest the french really are—our postman was enamored of them—but delivered them—however reluctantly. Fondest remembrances to you both always—

A. B. T.

☙

To Gertrude Stein
[Postcard: Paris La Nuit—La Madeleine]

15 August [1930]   [Hôtel Bristol, Paris]

Dear Gertrude:

Today or tomorrow a very *big* & very beautiful shell box will be dis- patched to you. I telegraphed to Toulon for it, but had it sent here first to be sure it was quite all right. *It is!*—I hope it gets to you unbroken. It came here in *beautiful* shape. *Basket* is inside.

Love always,
Carlo.

[219]

To Alice Toklas
[Postcard: Cours de Taureaux—Avant l'Estacade]

18 August [1930]   [Hôtel Bristol, Paris]

Dear Alice:

I am sorry about the plates, but we will play with the idea some other time. I hope he will make Rose is a Rose is a rose. We went to Le Touquet yesterday & expect to leave for Germany soon but Banque de Paris et des Pays Bas—3 rue d'Antin will always reach us. Forgive me for sending Gertrude the box, but she wanted it so *badly* & it is beautiful!

Love
Carlo

To Carl Van Vechten and Fania Marinoff
[Postcard: Environs de Belley—Vieux Pont de Bognens]

[postmark: 18 August 1930]   [Bilignin par Belley
                                                     Ain]

My dears

I am all xcited about the B. B's the box and Basket, and I will have them any day now, and the weather is lovely and it would be nice seeing you again, and it may be just the french rear seat that makes you worry, try a Buick, with Louis[1] and anyway come to see us and lots of love

Gertrude

and go to see George Biddle[2]

---

1. Van Vechten's chauffeur in France.

2. George Biddle, an American artist then living in Paris. Biddle had met Van Vechten in New York through Bob Chanler and had met Stein in the spring of 1923 when he came to Paris. See George Biddle, *An American Artist's Story* (Boston: Little, Brown & Co., 1939), pp. 204–5, 210–11.

❧

To Alice Toklas
[Postcard: Young Black Boy and Black Girl]

22 August [1930]   [Berlin]

So glad you liked the perfume—your note was charming. We're in
Berlin for a few days—Carl has never been here. It's grand but I'm tired and
will be glad to get home. Traveling is a hard job—oodles of love to you and
Gertrude

Fania

❧

To Gertrude Stein
[Postcard: Pudelwohl! (A poodle lying on a bearskin rug)]

[postmark: 23 August 1930]   [Berlin]

Dear Gertrude:

Here is another view of Basket for you. I think this is why we came
to Berlin. Back in Paris next week. Did the shells arrive?

Love
Carlo.

❧

To Carl Van Vechten and Fania Marinoff

[postmark: 26 August 1930]   Bilignin par Belley
                                                    Ain

My dearest dears,

It's come and it's beautiful beautiful more beautiful than even I
dreamed and so beautiful that even Alice says yes it is beautiful, I will have

to tell Carl that it is beautiful and Fania is forgiven and I am so happy with it and it mounts up wonderfully it really is beautiful, et sans blague and the last adventure of it was funny. We got the announcement from the gare and went down to get it, Alice went in and came out with a fair sized bundle well wrapped up and said here it is and I said isn't it any bigger than that and Alice said that is big enough it is the size of a nice glass box but said I a little sadly Carl said it was a big box with a great big shell on top I don't see quite how it could have a very big shell on top, and Carl did say it was a big shell on a big box and Alice said well Carl xaggerated a little and we brought it home and we opened it and out came three tins of some kind of electric autogene, and I said I knew it couldn't be as little as that and it was a mistake and it was not our package so it was too late and we could not get it any more last evening so all night I worried about some one opening up my package and spoiling my box so bright and early this morning we went down to the station at Belley and took back the package and Alice came out this time with a big case and I said yes I told you Carl said it was big and then we got home and we opened it and it is beautiful and Alice said it was beautiful and it is beautiful and everybody came in and said it is beautiful and it is even more beautiful and I have locked it with its key and Basket is jealous of the little basket which is darling but my box is lovely and Fania is forgiven and I don't know whether it was not almost better to wait for it and get it like this it makes [it] all the more xciting, and I kiss you both and lots of love always and always

Gertrude.[1]

1. Note by Van Vechten, 21 January 1941: "This is about a big seashell box I saw in Toulon. Fania said no Gertrude won't like it and Gertrude when she heard about it almost wept. So I asked Willie Seabrook who was living in Toulon to get it for her and he did."

To Gertrude Stein
[Postcard: Grevy—Zebras aus Abessinien]

28 August [1930]   [Berlin]

Dear Gertrude,

I loved your letter! it is a work of art, and how could anybody help saying that the box was *beautiful*. Alice could not help it & Fania now thinks it is beautiful & wants one herself! It is beautiful—in a complete way, like a city of shells or the room we saw today at Potsdam. Did you know that Frederick the Great had a whole room made of shells? Anyway I loved your letter. And we'll be back in Paris towards Saturday.

> *Love to you both,*
> *Carlo.*

To Carl Van Vechten
[Postcard: Photograph of a street in Belley]

[postmark: 30 August 1930]   [Bilignin par Belley
                                                    Ain]

My dearest Carl,

We are all very nicely enjoying ourselves, and it would be nice if you were here too, I am sending you by Virgil [Thomson] Lucy Church Amiably all about the nice country where I was given shells and brooches and also I am sending a paper weight, which I found at the [bien a la main?] and it is large anyway and I am sending lots and lots of love always and all[1]

> *Gertrude.*

---

1. There were several *brocanteurs*, second-hand dealers, in Belley, but none was named "bien à la main." It is possible that this was Stein's private name for one of the shops.

❧

To Gertrude Stein
[Postcard: Amenophis Der Vierte Aus El-Amarna, Um 1370 V. Chr.
Berlin, Altes Museum]

30 August [1930]   [Hôtel Bristol, Paris]

Dear Gertrude,

We are now back in Paris till we sail Sept. 11 on the *Paris*. Next to our stop in Belley—I like Berlin best of anything this summer.
Our love to you both.

C.

❧

To Gertrude Stein
[Postcard: Vendôme—Porte d'entrée de l'Eglise de la Trinité]

1 September [1930]   [Hôtel Bristol, Paris]

Dear Gertrude:

Very much excited about Virgil and Lucy Church & the paper-weight. Will be waiting. Did you receive Basket rolling on rug rather obscenely from Berlin?

Love to you both.
Carlo

❧

To Gertrude Stein
[Postcard: Child with Helmet and with Butterfly Wings]

1 September [1930]   [Hôtel Bristol, Paris]

Dear Gertrude:

I always forgot to ask you: please write me a letter & tell me what does "Adrian Arthur" mean?—I now have the illustrated Dix Portraits.[1] Some day I'd like to do a book in Paris with this firm or another, something special,

Love,
Carlo.

1. One of the portraits in Stein's *Dix Portraits* was "Pavlik Tchelitchef or Adrian Arthur." Stein never explained the reason for "Adrian Arthur."

To Carl Van Vechten
[Postcard: Alphonse de Lamartine]

[postmark: 3 September 1930]   [Bilignin par Belley Ain]

My dearest Carl,

It is lovely weather and we are loving you a lot, the weather is lovely Virgil [Thomson] has been darling, he has put the film to music with a portrait of Basket but he will be telling you all about us and everything very soon[1]

Gertrude.

1. Thomson had set Stein's "Film: Deux soeurs qui sont pas soeurs" to music for soprano and piano. The piece is one of the few that Stein wrote directly in French. Stein's dog, Basket, appears in the work.

To Gertrude Stein
[Postcard: Photograph of Josephine Baker by Walery, Paris]

5 September [1930]   [Hôtel Bristol, Paris]

Dear Gertrude:—

Thanks so much for the beautiful paper-weight. You *did* think of something nice & Lucy Church Amiably which I shall go into more later.

[225]

—You make me very happy, just to know you. People are writing frightful things about *Parties*. But anyway we are sailing on the 11—on the Paris[1]

Love to you both

Carlo

1. Van Vechten's novel *Parties* had received a number of very negative reviews. The reaction to *Parties* is summarized in Kellner, *Carl Van Vechten and the Irreverent Decades*, pp. 244–46.

To Gertrude Stein
[Postcard: Saule Pleureur, Expiatory Chapel, Square Louis XVI, Paris]

[postmark: 6 September 1930]   [Hôtel Bristol, Paris]

Dear Gertrude:

I have *not* a photograph of [Kristians] Tonny's portrait of you, may I have one![1] Also there is a translation of a [Georges] Hugnet poem in mss. Please send this to me if it is published. I hear it is magnifique.[2]

Love,
Carlo.

1. Tonny had done a pen and ink portrait of Stein. The portrait is in the collection of the heirs of Gertrude Stein. See Burns, ed., *Staying on Alone: Letters of Alice B. Toklas*, p. 313.

2. Stein's sequence of poems begun as a translation of Georges Hugnet's *Enfances* evolved into a reflection on Hugnet's poems. The two works were printed, on facing pages, in *Pagany* (Winter 1931), 2(1): 11–37. As published in *Pagany* the poem was titled "Poem Pritten on Pfances of Georges Hugnet." The quarrel between Stein and Hugnet developed at the time that book publication of the two works was planned. The poems were to be published with both the French and English texts by Galerie Jeanne Bucher, Paris, with illustrations by Picasso, Pavel Tchelitchew, Léon Marcoussis, and Kristians Tonny. Stein objected to the composition of the title page, particularly the line "Suivi par la traduction de Gertrude Stein." Stein felt that "traduction" would give a false impression of what she had done. For a while it appeared that an agreement could be worked out, but by Christmas 1930, they were still at an impasse. Virgil Thomson, a friend of both Stein's and Hugnet's, attempted to mediate the dispute. Thomson suggested a typographic solution that would place both names on the title page in the same size type and would not mention Stein's work as a translation. Hugnet agreed to this proposal, but Toklas, and therefore Stein, rejected it. The result was the break with Hugnet, a quarrel with

Bravig Imbs, an American writer living in France, whom Stein accused of siding with Hugnet, and a short-lived break with Thomson.

Stein's poems on Hugnet's *Enfances* were published as *Before the Flowers of Friendship Faded Friendship Faded.* Hugnet's *Enfances* was published by Editions Cahiers d'Art in 1933 and was illustrated by Joan Miro.

To Carl Van Vechten
MS. New York Public Library, Manuscripts Division

[postmark: 8 September 1930] Bilignin par Belley
  Ain

My poor dear Carl,

I am awfully sorry I kind of feel it was my fault liking Parties so much just would make the critics say frightful things but anyway I do like it so much, and I am right, and you are nice and we are nice and we will all live happily ever after. Have a good trip and think of us sweetly but then you will do that. I am glad that you will help with Mary Garden[1] and perhaps the opera it would give me a great deal of pleasure and would lead perhaps to our seeing a nut store and other nice things give our love to all of it and all of it to you and Fania[2]

Gertrude.

1. It had been suggested by Van Vechten that Mary Garden (1874–1946), the opera singer and an old friend of Van Vechten's might be interested in singing the role of Saint Theresa in the Thomson-Stein opera *Four Saints in Three Acts.* Stein went so far as to write to Garden, who was then in Paris (see Stein to Thomson, postmark 4 October 1930, YCAL). Before she received a reply, however, Stein read that Garden had announced that she would no longer sing in public.

2. Van Vechten had told Stein about the Chock Full O'Nuts stores in New York that advertised "every kind of nut available."

To Gertrude Stein
[Postcard: Musée du Louvre: Chat Bronze]

[postmark: 10 September 1930]   [Hôtel Bristol, Paris]

Dear Gertrude:

Your letter came & the photograph of [Kristians] Tonny's picture which I think is very interesting. Why have I never heard of it before? Did you pose for it or did Tonny just paint it. Last night in bed I read a little in Lucy Church with great pleasure. It is like Virgil's Bucolics & still it isn't! We sail at dawn tomorrow—but you can think of us as living in nut stores.

Much love to both!
Carlo.

Please send me Tonny's new address. I seem to have lost it.

To Carl Van Vechten
[Postcard: Man and woman dancing in a cave]

[postmark: 23 September 1930]   [Bilignin par Belley
                                                  Ain]

Do you like this collection that Georges [Hugnet] and I formed for you at Champagne where Brillat-Savarin ate.[1]

Gertrude

1. Hugnet had come to see Stein in Bilignin to work out the details of Stein's "translation" of his poem *Enfances* (see Van Vechten to Stein [6 September 1930], note 2). While he was there they visited Champagne-en-Valromey, a small town about thirty kilometers from Belley. Hugnet sent Van Vechten messages written on three postcards. The postcards are in YCAL.

❧

To Gertrude Stein
[Postcard: Greeting from New York, Standard Oil Building,
Bowling Green]

14 October [1930]   [150 West Fifty-fifth Street
                                     New York]

Dear Gertrude:

I always think of you when I go into a nut store, lots of other times
besides. You will be back in Paris now. New York is wilder & more terrifying than ever.

Our love for you both.

Carlo.

I have a whole shelf of your books!

❧

To Carl Van Vechten

[postmark: 15 October 1930]   Bilignin par Belley
                                               Ain

My dearest Carl

Here we still are and will be till the middle of October, and it is
rather nice autumn weather, the translation of [Georges] Hugnet's poem is
to be printed in the winter number of Pagany, they all seem nuts about it,
and I guess it is because I have in it for the first time kind of solved the
problem of modern poetry which torments them all, I kind of have invented
a new music which is that and difficult well you'll see.[1] Also here is a prospectus of another of the Edition de la Montagne books,[2] perhaps you would
like to buy one if so it would give pleasure to all concerned one must en-
courage the young, as to my portrait you bet your life I posed and so did
Basket, so much so that all his hair was worn off with the struggle, and
[Kristians] Tonny's address is 1 rue Jacques Mawas, Paris, he also did a very

interesting portrait after he did mine of Ralph Church, and since then one of Bernard Faÿ.[3] Let's see what else well lots else but then it kind [of] does seem as if we would see you to tell you, they did do some plates for you not at all what we wanted but there they are and perhaps you will like them even so, and anyway we love you both very much always[4]

Gertrude.

1. See Van Vechten to Stein [6 September 1930], note 2.

2. Stein may have sent Van Vechten the prospectus for Hugnet's *Le Droit de Varech* (Paris: Editions de la Montagne, 1930).

3. Van Vechten had asked Stein if she posed for her portrait by Tonny. See Van Vechten to Stein [10 September 1930].

4. Notes by Van Vechten, 21 January 1941: "Envelope partly addressed by Georges Hugnet, the French poet," and "The plates were eventually brought to me by Aaron Copland and others." These plates are now in YCAL.

To Alice Toklas

13 November 1930 [150 West Fifty-fifth Street New York]

Dearest Alice

Virginia Hammond, one of my best friends and one of the most charming women in the world will come to you for those much thot [i.e., thought] of much desired and much dreamed of earrings which you said were to be mine.[1] She will send you a note and make an arrangement to see you when it will be convenient. She is an actress, and a lady in it's real sense, and she will love meeting you, earrings or no earrings—Carl and I both send you and Gertrude our warmest love (we have many varieties) and hope all is well with you—Blessings on you both and a big hug and kiss for *them*—the earrings—I'm sure I'll be crazy about, I'll probably have my picture taken in them just to show you.

Fania

1. Virginia Hammond, the American actress.

[230]

To Carl Van Vechten
[Postcard: S. A. R. Monseigneur le Duc de Guise]

[postmark: 29 November 1930]   [27 rue de Fleurus
Yesterday was Thanksgiving   Paris]

My dearest Carl

Here we are in Paris and if there is not a flood or even if there is we are glad to be here, lots of pleasant xcitement, and many hopes and everybody has well anybody has, I won't tell you but you will hear all about it, and anyway perhaps you will never but first where is Fania's actress for the earrings and a little keepsake for Carl and how is the building and we like the nut stores more than ever we eat so many nuts, and lots of love[1]

Gertrude.

1. Note by Van Vechten, 21 January 1941: "I happened to mention to Gertrude one day that there were stores in N.Y. where they sold nothing but nuts. She never got over it!"

To Gertrude Stein
[Postcard: El Greco—Landscape—Toledo—The Metropolitan
Museum of Art]

[postmark: 14 December 1930]   [150 West Fifty-fifth Street
                                                  New York]

Dear Gertrude:

So glad to hear from you & Virgil [Thomson] and to hear that Santa Theresa may be published, introduced by me![1] Goody, Goody for our side . . . We have a lovely Victorian room which I wish you could see. There are shell pictures in it. Spent the afternoon shopping in a nut store.

Love to you both
Carlo.

1. There is no letter from Stein to Van Vechten in which she proposes that he introduce an edition of *Four Saints in Three Acts*. Stein did mention the possibility of a Van Vechten introduction in a letter to Virgil Thomson, postmark 15 December 1930, YCAL.

    Four Saints in Three Acts was first published in *transition* (June 1929), 16/17, and was first collected by Stein in her *Operas and Plays* (1932). When it was published as a separate volume by Random House in 1934, the book contained a preface by Van Vechten.

To Carl Van Vechten
[Postcard: Les Petits Tableaux de Paris—l'avenue Foch]

[postmark: 22 December 1930]

[27 rue de Fleurus
Paris]

    Happy New Year, and I just had found a very pretty Victorian print and I am sending it by Miss Harcourt [i.e., Virginia Hammond] to you with lots of love, and it would be nice to be introduced by you and be the opera and we are looking forward to it and we are in the midst of the usual Paris turmoil and we are loving you both very much. It looks quiet on the p[ost]. c[ard]. Paris does but it isn't,

*Love
Gertrude.*

To Gertrude Stein
[Postcard: Rembrandt: Flora. The Metropolitan Museum of Art]

10 January [1931]

[150 West Fifty-fifth Street
New York]

Dear Gertrude:

    I always say I am not coming back, but as the New Year turns I always get out the old atlas & have a look up new pastures to turn to . . .

We are dying to see the Victorian picture & the earrings & expect Virginia [Hammond] on every boat.

> *Love to you both.*
> *Carlo*

To Carl Van Vechten

[postmark: 17 January 1931]

Plain Edition
27 Rue de Fleurus (VI)
Paris

My dearest Carl,

Voila pourquoi j'avais [désiré?], well anyhow we have decided to publish ourselves,[1] Alice is managing director I am author, and we hope there will be purchasers, and so to be so, best to you both, and will you Carl if you can do a notice somewhere or get somebody else too of the edition and the book, perhaps that would help, anyway it's a try and I am very happy about it, We have been having a hectic one might almost say lurid winter so far, there is this and many other things and then we have quarreled beginning with Bravig Imbs going on through [Kristians] Tonny and Georges Hugnet and ending with Virgil Thomson and now we don't see any of them any more, but we seem to be seeing almost everybody else such is life in a great capital, otherwise calm.[2] Basket had distemper but he is now well, I am writing plays rather nice ones, Bernard Fay is translating me on Mme Récamier,[3] that pleases me, Henry McBride agrees with me that Parties is first rate[4] and what else, almost everything else, well anyway here are the subscriptions and here are we and there you are and we are very fond of the same and love

> *Always*
> *Gertrude.*

---

1. The decision to "publish ourselves" had been made several months before. See Stein to Van Vechten [7 June 1930], note 1.

2. Stein believed that both Imbs, a young American writer living in Paris, and Virgil Thomson had sided with Hugnet in the dispute about her "translation" of Hugnet's poem *Enfances*. See Van Vechten to Stein [6 September 1930], note 2.

3. Bernard Faÿ (1893–1978) was a professor of American history at the University of Clermont-Ferrand. In 1932 he was elected to the chair of American Civilization at the Collège de France. His appointment was revoked on 27 Jue 1945 as a result of his wartime activities. Faÿ, who was made director of the Bibliothèque Nationale on 6 August 1940, was tried after World War II as a collaborationist and sentenced to enforced hard labor for life. He escaped from a prison hospital in October 1951. After many years of teaching in Switzerland he was pardoned and allowed to return to France.

Faÿ translated a number of Stein's works. His translation of *Madame Récamier. An Operatic Drama* was never published. The piece was printed, in English, in Stein's *Operas and Plays*, pp. [355]–93.

4. A reference to the negative critical reaction to Van Vechten's novel *Parties*. See Van Vechten to Stein [5 September 1930], note 1.

To Carl Van Vechten

[postmark: 29 January 1931]

Plain Edition
27 Rue de Fleurus (VI)
Paris

My dearest Carl,

I was pleased with the 17 purple dachshunds with silver legs[1] and the letter of Marie Doro it touched me a lot,[2] and I would like her to see Making of Americans, but alas that is so unattainable sometime when the Plain Edition gets awfully prosperous it may bring out the one third abbreviation of the original which I prepared this summer but Carl they are translating the whole of the thing into Spanish unsolicited by an honest to God edition in Madrid and they just seem to have read it somehow somewhere and in the peaceful Spanish way they are doing the whole of it,[3] I probably have told you all this once but anyway I know you will be patient and will listen again because for me to be appreciated by a publisher in that way well it has been awfully important but now to go on with other matters, but I like the way Marie Doro describes the way she went on, I think her letter and the one of the one [Nella Larsen] Imes whom by the way you never did get to come to see us pleased me the most of any of the letters I have ever seen about Melanctha, do thank her for me and some day you will bring her to see me.[4]

And now the Plain Edition, we have just had our first subscription and that is most awfully nice and from somebody in Florence and that is nice too, we have lots of good plans for distribution in Europe, and I think it will work out alright there, in America will you Carl make out some lists for us of people all kinds of people Hollywood all the other places where they might subscribe, you see what I want is to really get this going, so that I can get one thing after the other printed, and it kind of looks as if it would be possible, we begin with Lucy, and then Grammar, and then Operas and Plays, I am doing some plays that will please you, it is a series of historical ones so far it has been Mme Récamier, Louis XI and George of England, I am working on the last one now,[5] and then it will be a volume of short things, and then on older things and then a couple of volumes of portraits, this would make me very happy and I am quite certain now that the time has come to reach the audience that is there, and so will you write something some where about the edition and will you send me lists of all the possible people anywhere who might subscribe. There that is all of my affairs. Otherwise we have been having a nice peaceable time having really quarreled for keeps with all our young friends and there are lots of stories that will amuse you and will pretty well occupy us several peaceful days in the country. Paris is rather wonderful and now the old Paris the before the war Paris is coming back so quickly it is more than ever wonderful, it is all so intimate again and so very lively, well anyway I am pleased that you are pleased and you are pleased that I am pleased and it's alright

Lots of love
Gertrude.

1. Note by Van Vechten, 21 January 1941: "It is my custom to subscribe myself 'with 141 orchids' or 'with 17 purple dolphins' etc."

2. The letter by Marie Doro about *Three Lives* cannot be located.

3. The plan to publish *The Making of Americans* in Spanish fell through.

4. See Stein to Van Vechten [18 February 1929], note 1.

5. The plays *Madame Récamier. An Operatic Drama, Louis XI and Madame Giraud,* and *The Five Georges, A Play* are all published in Stein's *Operas and Plays.*

To Gertrude Stein
[Postcard: Pueblo of Isleta—New Mexico]

2 February [1931]   [150 West Fifty-fifth Street
                                                      New York]

Dear Gertrude:

Your news is all very startling. How did you quarrel with so many
all at once?!!! And it is so delightful to think you are publishing too!—We
have no plans yet, but we send you both much love!

Carlo.

To Gertrude Stein

[? February 1931]   150 West Fifty-fifth Street
                                                      New York City

Dearest Gertrude,

Thrilled about Spain and the Plain Edition and here are some names
of people to send announcements to:
Holliday Bookshop
49 East 49 Street
New York City
James F. Drake
14 West 40th Street
New York City
Thomas Beer
227 Palisades Avenue
Yonkers, N.Y.
Miss Emily Clark
1634 Spruce Street
Philadelphia, Pa.

Witter Bynner
342 Buena Vista Road
Santa Fe, N.M.

Mrs. Mina Curtiss
461 East 57 Street
New York City

Mrs. Dorothy Crawford
124 East 53 Street
New York City

Muriel Draper
312 East 53 Street
New York City

Mrs. Walter Douglas
Wayzata
Minn.

Theodore Dreiser
200 West 57 Street
New York City

Max Ewing
19 West 31 Street
New York City

Miss Ettie Stettheimer
182 West 58 Street
New York City

Lilyan Tashman
718 Linden Drive
Beverly Hills, Cal.

Alma Wertheim
Hotel Montalembert
rue Montalembert
Paris VII

Lewis Galantière
Hotel Algonquin
New York City

Julia Hoyt
25 Sutton Place
New York City

Jascha Heifetz
247 Park Avenue
New York City

Edna Kenton
92 Charles Street
New York City

Lawrence Langner
14 West 11 Street
New York City

Ellery Larssen
541 East 88 Street
New York City

Colin McPhee
188 Sullivan Street
New York City

Lloyd Morris
15 West 12 Street
New York City

Georgia O'Keefe
Hotel Shelton
New York City

Aileen Pringle
722 Adelaide Place
Santa Monica, Cal.

Rita Romilly
434 East 52 Street
New York City

Burton Rascoe
40 Stuyvesant Avenue
Larchmont, N.Y.

Ben Ray Redman
230 East 50 Street
New York City

Love!
Carlo![1]

1. On the second page of this letter Toklas wrote : "C. A. Robertson Box 268 Olean New York."

米

To Gertrude Stein
[Postcard: Museum Schloss Monbijou (R24) Friedrich der Grosse König von Preussen von G. W. v. Knobelsdorff um 1745]

[postmark: 9 March 1931]   [150 West Fifty-fifth Street
                                                            New York]

Dear Gertrude:

I take it for granted that you have seen a copy of Edmund Wilson's "Axel's Castle" in which you figure so conspicuously. It has just been published by Scribners. If you haven't & can't procure a copy in Paris, let me know & I will send you one forth with.

Much love,
Carlo V. V.

米

To Carl Van Vechten
[Postcard: Comic Dogs by Pol Rab]

[postmark: 20 March 1931]   [27 rue de Fleurus
                                                            Paris]

My dear Carl,

Yes I have seen Bunnie Wilson's book, thanks so much, I was not born in Baltimore, and I am not *german*, and I do make poetry, which can be read otherwise I was pleased,[1] and Carl did you ever see Pagany with the famous two poems,[2] I'll be sending you ours one of these days and Carl will you tell them what you feel about Lucy it would please me and are you coming over. That would please us even more

Gertrude.

1. Edmund Wilson's *Axel's Castle: A Study in the Imaginative Literature of 1870–1930* (New York: Charles Scribner's Sons, 1931) includes a chapter on Stein. Stein's references in this letter are difficult to understand, since Wilson writes, "Gertrude Stein, born in Allegheny, Penn-

sylvania . . . ," and the references to "german" are to characters in Stein's *Three Lives* and the German-Jewish families in Stein's *The Making of Americans*.

2. See Van Vechten to Stein [6 September 1930], note 2.

To Carl Van Vechten

[postmark: 8 April 1931]   [27 rue de Fleurus
                                                           Paris]

My dearest Carlo,

We did enjoy Emily Clark particularly you and Fania, she did you both charmingly and really, the rest of the book was alright but not so good as so evidently it is the model that counts,[1] I am awfully pleased with it and have a nice Easter and make nice plans and love us nicely, I will be sending you the Flowers of friendship very soon, we are most awfully busy, I am working a lot and Alice is editing a lot and lots is happening besides and anyway we love you a lot

*Always
Gertrude.*[2]

1. Emily Clark (Mrs. Edwin Swift Balch) (1893–1953) was an educator and author born in Virginia. She was one of the founders of *The Reviewer* in Richmond, Virginia, in 1921. She served as coeditor from 1921 to 1925. Her memoir, *Innocence Abroad* (New York: Alfred A. Knopf, Inc., 1931) contains numerous references to the Van Vechtens.

2. Enclosed in the envelope were two blank postcards from the Société des Editions Militaires: "Chasseurs à pied—Le Drapeau" and "Ecole Polytechnique."

To Carl Van Vechten
[Postcard: Société des Editions Militaires: Infirmiers]

[postmark: 16 April 1931]   [27 rue de Fleurus
                                                      Paris]

My dearest Carl,

Am sending you by today['s] mail Flowers of friendship, it is a beautiful book, and we are proud of it, anyway it is for sale $4 so [if] anybody wants it tell them to apply early and often,

Gertrude.

Poem XIV will speak of Bilignin.

To Gertrude Stein

4 May 1931   150 West Fifty-fifth Street
                                             [New York]

Dear Gertrude,

Flowers of Friendship came and it is a beautiful book typographically and I love the paper, and I think it has a more classical air than your other books and I think everybody will love it except perhaps Georges Hugnet.[1] The canto about Belignin[2] is beautiful and I have to take an especial pleasure in cantos 29 and 30 and I enclose eight dollars and please send me two more copies. . I wrote you, perhaps, that I have been ill, but I am all right now, but we cannot decide what to do this summer, although I am sure the Colonial Exposition[3] will be amusing. . and it would be nice to see you on the terrasse at Belignin again or to tramp with you and Alice through the triste and romantic streets of Aix-les-Bains. You should be seeing Nella Imes soon and you will like that and so will she.

much love to you both!

Carlo.

Congratulations on F. of F.!!

[241]

1. Stein's *Before The Flowers of Friendship Faded Friendship Faded* had been printed for the Plain Edition by Durand, at Chartres, France. The edition consisted of 120 copies on Antique Montval paper and was published on 1 May 1931. Stein sent Van Vechten copy number III (one of eighteen made for the author—this copy is now in YCAL). It bore the inscription on the title page: "To my dearest Carl whose flowers of friendship never do and never can and never will fade, not they, Gtde." The verso has the following inscription: "To Carlo with love Gertrude."

2. Van Vechten means Bilignin.

3. The International Overseas Exhibition, also known as the Colonial Exposition, opened in the Bois de Vincennes, Paris, on 7 May 1931.

To Carl Van Vechten

[Postcard: Saint-Point—Château de Lamartine. La fille du Poète; Julia. Née à Mâcon en 1822 et morte à Beyrouth en 1832]

[postmark: 10 May 1931]

[Bilignin par Belley
Ain]

My dear Carlo,

Did you ever get the flowers. Here we are back in Bilignin and likeing it. Gardening flourishes and so does literature and editions, and you both always

Gertrude.

To Carl Van Vechten

[postmark: 18 May 1931]

Bilignin par Belley
Ain

My dearest Carl,

No I did not know you had been laid up, although I was a little bothered at not hearing from you and I sent you a postal mentioning the same. I am glad you like the Flowers. The Plain Edition is doing very well, Lucy is in considerable demand and Alice is a proud editor, and I am an equally pleased author. And perhaps you will come, we left before the Colonial [Exposition] was opened, but it ought to be pleasurable, and we hope it will keep open till we get back. And it would be nice seeing you and the terrace is most inviting, it is quite wonderful here in May, well it wouldn't be May of course, but any other month will do as well. Do come, and there [are] lots of stories to tell, and Aix [les Bains] will be as [triste?] as you like, and there is Hautecombe we didn't get to, where the music is the best in France,[1] etc, well anyway I am awfully glad you are all well, and the mixed photos of the 400 living authors is awfully funny, I happened to see an advertisement of it and we spent an hour recognizing and not recognizing, from the mixed photos, where they get the [information?] they advertise, I should think nobody could know, well it's always pleasant to be together[2] even in a long photo and once more lots of love and it will be nice being together

Gertrude

1. The Abbaye d'Hautecombe in Saint-Pierre-de-Curtille, Chindrieux, was not far from Belley. Stein visited there often and was extremely friendly with Le Père Edmond Bernardet (1903–1978), who had entered the monastery in 1926.

2. I cannot locate the specific advertisement referred to.

To Gertrude Stein
[Postcard: The Paramount Broadway Building, New York City]

[postmark: 6 June 1931]   [150 West Fifty-fifth Street
                                           New York]

Dear Gertrude:

I do not think we will be coming over for the summer.—Marinoff is rehearsing[1] & I am very happy & comfortable in a cool New York apartment—The books came & thank you, and Gaston Lachaise has done a bronze head of me.[2]

Love to you & Alice!
Carlo.

[243]

1. Lawrence Langner, one of the founders of the Theatre Guild in New York, had organized a summer stock theatre in Westport, Connecticut. Marinoff performed in three plays there: *The Streets of New York*, by Dion Boucicault; *The Bride the Sun Shines On*, by Will Cotton; and *The Pillars of Society*, by Henrik Ibsen. All three plays were later done in New York in the fall of 1931. See Van Vechten to Stein, 19 October [1931], note 1.

2. Gaston Lachaise (1882–1935), the French-born sculptor. Van Vechten gave this bronze to the Art Institute of Chicago.

≷

To Carl Van Vechten
[Postcard: Au Grand St. Bernard. Dernière nichée]

[postmark: 5 August 1931]   Bilignin par Belley
                                             Ain

My dearest Carlo,

We have been talking about you a lot, [Aaron] Copland[1] has been with us and he says you are just as nice as we say you are only we all think you are much nicer than that. He will at Christmas take you a couple of plates that we at last with much effort got the potteries to do and we will love to have you have them although they were not at all what we wanted, we have had a lovely summer and do wish you had been here

Yours
Gertrude.

1. Aaron Copland (b. 1900), American composer.

❧

To Gertrude Stein
*[Postcard: Degas—Woman with Chrysanthemums—The Metropolitan
Museum of Art]*

[postmark: 15 August 1931]   [150 West Fifty-fifth Street
                                               New York]

Dear Gertrude:

Terribly thrilled about the plates & about being nicer. I am sure you
& Alice are the same. I have stopped drinking *for ever*, to get new sensations
of sobriety. I may get a car, Fania is still at Westport.—176 lovely purple
dachsunds to you!

Carlo.

❧

To Carl Van Vechten and Fania Marinoff
[Postcard: Souvenirs de Lamartine: Julia de Lamartine]

[postmark: 18 September 1931]   [Bilignin par Belley
                                                 Ain]

My dears,

There was an American actress here who is married to a frenchman,[1]
we dined and she had seen Fania act and was quite mad about her and told
us all about it most delightfully and we were most awfully pleased and wish
we could see it too, wouldn't it be nice if she did come to Paris, they are
coming right along now, and the sobriety is it all there still and do you all
like it, anyway lots and lots of love we almost had the flood 3 days and 3
nights, But the roses are sweet and the dahlias

G. & A.[2]

1. The couple cannot be identified.
2. Both initials are in Stein's hand.

☙

To Gertrude Stein
[Postcard: U. S. Dirigible Los Angeles over Lower Manhattan]

19 October [1931]   [150 West Fifty-fifth Street
                                                     New York]

Dear Gertrude:

Here are a few pieces about Fania—and some french stamps I found.[1]
I am working a little & *flying* & loving it. From Washington in one hour is
sufficiently exciting . . . I am sending you The Negro Mother, by Langston
Hughes.[2] Langston one day bemoaned to me the fact that Negro elocution-
ists had nothing to recite like Kipling, or The Boy Stood on the Burning
Deck.[3] So he wrote these. Nobody has any money. So I guess it's all right.
Love to you both.

Carlo & Fania.

1. Van Vechten had probably sent Stein reviews with photographs of the plays that Marinoff
was acting in for Lawrence Langner's New York Repertory Company. Marinoff played the role
of Alida Bloodgood in *The Streets of New York*, by Dion Boucicault, which opened at the 48th
Street Theatre, New York, on 6 October 1931 and ran for eighty-seven performances. On 14
October Ibsen's *The Pillars of Society* entered the repertory (for only two performances) with
Marinoff in the role of Martha Bernich. The final play in the New York Repertory Company's
season opened at the Fulton Theatre, New York, on 26 December 1931. Marinoff played the
role of Mrs. Lane in Will Cotton's *The Bride the Sun Shines On*, which ran for seventy-seven
performances. The other leading players in the company were Dorothy Gish, Rollo Peters, and
Moffat Johnson. See Van Vechten to Stein [6 June 1931], note 1.

2. In 1931, with the encouragement of Mary McLeod Bethune, president of Bethune-Cook-
man College, Hughes began a series of poetry readings at black educational centers in the South
and West. To help support this project, Knopf issued a special edition of *The Weary Blues*, and
a pamphlet titled *The Negro Mother and Other Dramatic Recitations* (New York: Golden Stair
Press, 1931), containing six of Hughes's poems, was issued. It was this pamphlet that Van Vechten
sent to Stein.

3. The opening line of "Casabianca," a poem by Felicia Dorothea Hemans.

To Carl Van Vechten

[postmark: 7 November 1931]   Bilignin [par Belley
                                                                             Ain]

My dear Carl,

We were delighted with the photos of Fania and the french stamps
and the flying; are you going to Lindbergh us that would be most xciting I
have taken to love a tunnel the one they have made between us and Aix [les
Bains] and a long tunnel it is and xciting but the air well anyway perhaps
Fania will be asked to come to Paris and play They do you know and you
will come too and then we will see you fly. We have been awfully busy so
much more happens in a village than in a city and it all happens so much
more quickly whether they are or whether they are not timid. Cee inclus
our prospectus and the new book is to be very pretty and it's an awful comfort to see it all printed and the book sellers are beginning to take an interest
so go on telling them about it.[1] Basket is bothered because we are packing
and we are bothered because we are packing, we even pack our vegetables
and anyway lots of lots of love and don't fall off

                                                                    Gertrude.

1. Stein's *How To Write* was printed in Dijon, France, by the Darantière Press.

To Gertrude Stein

22 November [1931]   [150 West Fifty-fifth Street
                                                                     New York]

Dear Gertrude:

This is our Victorian room which started around my mother's piano—
and I am sending you three views of it, so you can begin to see how we are
living.[1] You have never known how we are living, but now that I have car-

ried my postcard craze to its legitimate & *personal* conclusion, you will see how we are living & even how *you are* because I now have postcards of [Kristians] Tonny's & Picasso's portraits of you & if you can get me a photograph of it, I would have postcards of Jo Davidson's statue too![2] I want to have this very much!—I hope you will notice the white *poodle* in this picture. It is of kid on a blue velvet cushion. Also notice the swan cushion in the chais. This is raised bead work. Mabel [Dodge] got me both of them in Mexico City. Fania is still playing in The Streets of New York & I am about to read proofs of my "Sacred & Profane Memories" which will come out on April 15.[3] You, of course, will have a copy at once (when it is published). I hope you are sending me How to Write when it comes out. I think I have the best collection of Gertrude Stein any one has. I'll send you pictures of my library next time. I am dying to see the tunnel to Aix[-les-Bains]. But we're dying to fly from Paris to Constantinople. You can do it from dawn to dinner!—And you can fly over South America in 17 days! Low enough to see the parrots & the temples!—much love to you & Alice from us both.

Carlo

Mabel's about D. H. Lawrence (Lorenzo in Taos) is going to be published!!![4]

Please send me a photograph of the Davidson.

1. This letter was written on the back of three photographs that Van Vechten had taken of the "Victorian room" in his New York apartment.

2. In 1923 Jo Davidson had done an almost-life-size bronze portrait of Stein in a sitting position.

3. Van Vechten's *Sacred and Profane Memories.* This collection contained twelve previously published essays by Van Vechten.

4. Mabel Dodge Luhan's *Lorenzo in Taos* (New York: Alfred A. Knopf, 1932).

To Carl Van Vechten
[Rose motto]

[postmark: 9 December 1931]   27 rue de Fleurus
                                               [Paris]

My dearest Carlo,

Awfully pleased with the postal cards, Alice is particularly nuts about the curtains and the two things next to them and my favorite is the little girl with the dog,[1] we are also awfully pleased with all your and Fania's good news. [Aaron] Copland is taking three plates to you, and that was all they succeeded in doing, anyway you will like the intention, everything is progressing cheerfully, for those who are not too poor, the crise is not unpleasant, even in Paris, am sending you the only photo I have of Jo [Davidson]'s statue, do you know George Lynes but I know you do he did some very nice photos of Bilignin do look at them at Julien Levy's Gallery, it will make you come back the sooner, I think it would be rather nice if you went over the Col du Chat[2] while we went under, anyway lots of love and Christmas and New Year and all to you both from all of us, and send the memoirs soon, hope you will like How to Write,

Love lots,
Gertrude.

1. One of the photographs Van Vechten had sent Stein, 22 November [1931], contained an octagonal plate attached to the wall on each side of the window. Another photograph showed a needlepoint of a young girl and a white dog. This needlepoint was given by Fania Marinoff to Bruce and Margaret Kellner.

2. *Col du Chat* is a pass between mountains in the French alps. The pass begins in Chambery, about twenty kilometers from Belley, and has a superb view of the Lac de Bourget.

To Gertrude Stein and Alice Toklas
[Telegram]

[? December 1931]   New York

XMAS ROSES TO YOU BOTH

FANIE CARL

To Gertrude Stein

31 December [1931]   150 West Fifty-fifth Street
New York City

Dear Gertrude:

Aaron Copland brought the For Carlo plates and they are lovely and the next minute the postman came with How to Write and it is such a pretty book and the inscription is breaking-down-making.[1] I have been reading the chapter In Narrative tonight with much pleasure and I like to read the page about Harold Acton aloud.[2] Of course, you know that you are a cult. A young man named Ben Wesson stood on his hind legs and began to scream about you the other night. Why isn't Gertrude Stein in the Modern Library? Well, the editors were there, and I was eloquent too. Then Edna Kenton meets Lindley Hubbell in the Public Library and he begins to talk about you and she invites him to her apartment to see her collection and he shows her *his*. Isn't it all lovely? . . . Fania is now in The Bride the Sun Shines On. I talk intermittently of flying all over South America. In the meantime I read proofs and get everything photographed. I think these pictures will amuse you and Alice, these pictures of the apartment, of Fania in her plays, of Fania in my mother's flowered taffeta wedding dress, of Gaston Lachaise's head of me.[3] I hope all these things will amuse you and Alice.[x] The Jo Davidson photograph has not yet arrived, but it will come: I am sure. I am

[250]

enclosing my cheque for 3.50 for which please send a copy of How to Write
to

> Miss Edna Kenton
> 92 Charles Street
> New York City
> U.S.A.

Lots of love and New Year's greetings to you both from us both!

Carlo

^xIf these pictures amuse you and Alice, tell me and I'll send you some
more!

1. Stein inscribed Van Vechten's copy of *How To Write*, "To Carl who in the sky or near by is always faithful and delighted with endless love from Gtde."

2. *How To Write* collected eight pieces by Stein that had been written between 1927 and 1931. "Regular Regularly In Narrative," the sixth piece in the book, was written in 1927. Stein mentions Harold Acton on pages 232–38. Acton was the son of Arthur and Hortense Acton, whom Stein had known in Florence in the years 1902–1912 when she regularly spent summers there. Harold Acton was responsible for inviting Stein to lecture at Oxford University in 1926 (Gallup, *The Flowers of Friendship*, p. 186).

3. Enclosed with this letter were eighteen photographs printed as postal cards. Included in the group were photographs of various rooms in the Van Vechten's apartment, Marinoff in Ada Van Vechten's (Carl's mother's) wedding dress, Marinoff in two theatrical roles, Gaston Lachaise's bronze of Van Vechten, and Florine Stettheimer's portrait of Avery Hopwood.

To Carl Van Vechten
[Rose motto]

[postmark: 15 February 1932]

27 rue de Fleurus
[Paris]

My dear Carl

We have been so busy I don't know why or how but there it is, since
the *crise* social life seems to have increased enormously, I suppose nobody

having any outside interests they want to see somebody greatly and they have taken to seeing me I rather like it and have taken equally to going out to see them, I am also working a lot on plays our next volume is Operas and Plays,[1] well anyway do send a lot more picture postals Alice and I enjoy them immensely and so does everybody else, we have some more For Carlo plates but I did not want to burden [Aaron] Copland unduly, but alas they are only the one pattern they bucked at any variety, which was sad perhaps now after the crise they will be more amenable, and the Memoirs when are they coming out,[2] Mabel [Dodge] sent her book, the financial struggles were really the most amusing part of the book, ending up with Florence, and the villa.[3] Write soon and come soon

Love
Gertrude.

1. Stein's *Operas and Plays* was published in August 1932.

2. Van Vechten's *Sacred and Profane Memories* was published in August 1932.

3. Mabel Dodge Luhan's *Lorenzo in Taos* (New York: Alfred A. Knopf, 1932) deals with her relationship with D. H. Lawrence. Details of her early life in Buffalo, New York, and her life in Florence, Italy, are only briefly touched upon in this book. Dodge was to expand this material into four volumes of memoirs collectively titled *Intimate Memories* (New York: Harcourt, Brace and Co., 1933–37).

To Gertrude Stein
[Postcard] Victorian Cushion—Photograph by Carl Van Vechten

[postmark: 28 February 1932]   [150 West Fifty-fifth Street
                                                New York]

Dear Gertrude:

I wonder if I sent you this one? The poodle is white kid on blue velvet. It is lovely. . . . I do nothing but take photographs now—hundreds and hundreds of photographs. You will soon see. [Alfred]Stieglitz has promised me an exhibition.[1] I am glad there are more Carlo plates. Please send them

by the next safe person. Sacred & Profane Memories will go to you soon &
I impatiently wait your new plays.

Love always to you both!

Carlo.

You didn't yet send me a photograph of the Jo Davidson statue. *Please.*

1. Stieglitz never gave Van Vechten an exhibition at his gallery, An American Place.

❊

To Carl Van Vechten
[Postcard: Le Drapeau de l'Ecole Polytechnique—1914]

[postmark: 30? March 1932]

[27 rue de Fleurus
Paris]

My dearest Carl

We delight in your postal cards may they increase and multiply, I
have asked Jo D[avidson]. to send you a copy of the bust and he has promised to do so, I only had the one I sent you we are very busy, Maurice Darantière is to do our next book himself that is Operas and Plays, and I imagine it will be pretty and are you flying to us it seems you can by S. America.
Do

*Love
Gtrde.*

To Carl Van Vechten
MS. New York Public Library, Manuscripts Division
[Rose motto]

[postmark: 12 April 1932]   27 rue de Fleurus
                                                            [Paris]

My dearest Carl

Thanks for S[acred]. & P[rofane]. M[emories]. I liked lots of it but what I liked the most were the Folksongs in Iowa it's a wonderfully fine piece of America it's very real and very living,[1] I don't know but that I would like you to do more like that, please, of course some of the descriptions of Mabel [Dodge] are awfully good and awfully funny, Bernard Faÿ has just given his first College de France lecture,[2] it and we were awfully distinguished and awfully xciting also we have [been] having the first show of my real discovery Francis Rose inclosing his card,[3] Paris has been nice and quiet and xciting, but most awfully xciting, just like the so long ago, and are we seeing you that would be nice lots and lots of love

Gertrude

1. "The Folksongs of Iowa" is one of the essays in Van Vechten's *Sacred and Profane Memories*. In the essay "July–August 1914" (originally published in *The Trend* [October 1914], 8:13–24, and called "Once Aboard the Lugger, San Guglielmo; an Account of a Flight from Italy in War Time") Van Vechten writes of how his visit to Dodge at her Villa Curonia was interrupted by the outbreak of World War I and of the hardships he endured in returning to the United States.

2. Faÿ had been nominated to the chair in American Civilization at the Collège de France on 15 February 1932. That year he gave two courses: "Les Traditions Américaines et le rôle de Washington" and "Problèmes et Méthodes de l'histoire des Etats-Unis." His first lecture, for the first course, was given on Monday, 11 April 1932.

3. Sir Francis Cyril Rose (1909–1979), English painter. Stein enclosed a card in the latter which announced the first exposition of Francis Rose from 12 to 25 April 1932 at the Galerie Vignon, 17 rue Vignon, Paris.

Stein had seen some of Rose's pictures at the gallery of Jean Bonjean, Paris, in late 1929 / early 1930. She bought a picture and then returned and bought another. At that time she expressed no interest in meeting the artist. She continued to admire his work and asked her friend Georges Maratier, an art dealer, to acquire others for her. Stein was introduced to Rose at a tea at the home of the Chilean painter Alvaro Guevara and his wife Méraud in late 1930 / early 1931. That afternoon Stein took Rose to the rue de Fleurus to show him his paintings hanging in her home. Stein and Toklas became extremely fond of Rose, and although his difficult personality often exasperated them and tried their patience, they remained completely devoted to him. It was Rose who designed Stein's (and, eventually, Toklas') tombstone in Père Lachaise Cemetery in Paris.

To Gertrude Stein
[Postcard] Gertrude Stein by Jo Davidson—

26 April [1932]   [150 West Fifty-fifth Street
                                                   New York]

Dear Gertrude:

Jo sent me 2 photographs: so I am all right now. Here is one of them—I wish you were here so I could take some of my own.[1] I do nothing but take photographs now—every hour. So I don't think I'll be coming to Europe, but Marinoff may come—very likely will. I suppose you are going to delightful Bilignin soon. When will I get the rest of my lovely Carlo plates? I eat off these so often muttering pleasurably: Rose is a rose is a rose.

And you and Alice are Woojums![2]

Lots of love,
Carlo

1. The postcard is made from a photograph Van Vechten took of the photograph Davidson had sent him.

2. This is the first use of the term "woojums" in these letters. Van Vechten never explained the term's origin or meaning when used in reference to people. In his novel *Parties* a "Woojums" is a cocktail: "five parts gin, one part bacardi, a dash of bitters, a dash of absinthe, a teaspoonful of lemon juice, and a little grenadine" (p. 252).

"Woojums" was a term of endearment that Van Vechten often used in addressing his close friends. At the time of Stein's American lecture tour (1934–35) the term came to be used almost exclusively among Stein, Van Vechten, and Toklas. It was around "woojums" that the three of them created a family unit. Gertrude was Baby Woojums, Carl was Papa Woojums, and Alice was Mama Woojums. Fania Marinoff was rarely included in the "Woojums" family, but when she was, she was referred to as the Empress or Madame Woojums.

To Gertrude Stein and Alice Toklas

4 July [1932]
Address *Fania Marinoff*

On Board the Cunard
R. M. S. "Aquitania"

Darlings,

Am arriving sans Carlo (I haven't left him) in London July 6th where I will remain for about two or three weeks—Grosvenor House Park Lane will reach me, then I'm coming on to Paris. For how long, I know not. Have made no plans. Where are you both. Do please drop me un petit mot I would so adore seeing you. Banque de Paris et des Pays Bas 3 rue D'antin will reach me in Paris. But like dears let me hear where you are and what [is] doing in London

> *Bless you both*
> *Fania*

To Fania Marinoff
[Postcard: Environs de Belley—Lac de Saint-Champs]

[postmark: 22 July 1932]

[Bilignin par Belley
Ain]

My dear Fania,

Where and how are you you did not answer and tell me and now you must be in Paris and now you will answer and tell if and when we are to see you and everything and how you like it and lots of love

> *Gertrude.*

To Gertrude Stein and Alice Toklas

6 August [1932]   Le Bristol
Saturday   Hotel et Restaurant
                                                   112 Faubourg St. Honoré
                                                   Paris (VIII)

Dearest Gertrude and dearest Alice,

Judging from your little card you answered my boat note, which I did not receive, alas, and I kept wondering why I didn't hear from you. Well, anyway here I am in Paris est toute seule, and How I miss Carl—who has been with me these last times here, and I'll miss not seeing you. I only arrived here a couple of days ago, and expect to remain here another week, then I shall go somewhere for *Sun* for a week and complete relaxation I've been socializing in London and travelling in Belgium and Holland and I'm exhausted. Then I expect to go back either the 24th Aug—or 31st, et Voila— I hope you are both well and comfortable, I can't imagine anyone being "Happy" and are enjoying your summer—Carl would so adore having his plates He's mad about the ones you sent. Is there any way I could take the others back without causing you a great deal of trouble? We would both appreciate it ever so much. Honest. What a pity I can't see you while I'm here. But I send you warm and my permanent love,

Fania

To Fania Marinoff
*[Postcard: Environs de Belley—Béon et le Pic de
Bellecombe (Massif du Grand Colombier)]*

[postmark: 9 August 1932]   [Bilignin par Belley
                                                   Ain]

My dear Fania

Am sending the plates to your hotel to-day I hope they get there alright, they are all the people would do but I like them and am glad they give Carl pleasure, so sorry we are not seeing you, I am sending Carlo my new book, Operas and Plays, I am very pleased with the same sorry you don't like our summer it is a nice summer a nice quiet summer and makes you appreciate everything including sunshine well lots of love and lots of love

Gtrde

❧

To Gertrude Stein
[Postcard: Paris—La Rue de la Paix]

[postmark: 11 August 1932]   [Hôtel Bristol, Paris]

The plates this morn—[just?] arrived. How pleased Carl will be and what a darling you are. Now, please, my lady. How does one pay for them and how much? I insist on doing that, and Carl will be angry with me, if it isn't done. So be nice and let me know all about it. It's hotter than seven Hells here. But the sun is shining so I like it.

Heaps of love to you both—

Fania

❧

To Gertrude Stein

15 August [1932]   Le Bristol
Monday   Hotel et Restaurant
                                    112 Faubourg St. Honoré
                                    Paris (VIII)

Gertrude, darling

The Hotel paid 67 francs something or other when the plates arrived which they had (how unFrench[)] forgotten to tell me. But they seem rather vague about *why* they paid that amount they showed me the receipt—with no amount on it. It's all a little phony—so perhaps, if you don't mind, you can tell me what it was for. Was it for the amount of the plates and the express?—or the express alone, or what? It's only a tiny matter. But I would like to know—They *do* such queer things in hotels as you know. I didn't go to Le Touquet after all, I couldn't give up my lovely room here and pack and unpack and pack again it was too much, so here I am and liking it. I think it's a crime to come all the way over here and miss seeing you and Alice—We'll (Carl and I) have better luck next time I hope—always love to you both

Fania

To Fania Marinoff

[16 August 1932]   Bilignin par Belley
                                                   Ain.

My dearest Fania

No there was nothing to pay and the hotel paid nothing the transport was paid to domicile that is to the hotel and the hotel had nothing to do but receive it and the plates were of course a gift to Carl with my love, I am so sorry you have been bothered, it is good and hot weather is it not, we are liking it too as there has been none for three years. I am sending Carl my new book Operas and Plays which I know he will like

Lots of love always
Gtrde.

To Gertrude Stein
[Postcard: Les Petits Tableaux de Paris—La Place de la
Concorde—Vue prise de la Chambre des Députés]

[postmark: 18 August 1932]   [Hôtel Bristol, Paris]

Yes, they had made a mistake? Thanks so much for your letter you are a darling. Carl will simply adore the plates—we use the other ones all the time. I do hope you are keeping cool. The heat here is killing.

Love to Alice—love to you

Fania

To Gertrude Stein

13 December 1932[1]   150 West Fifty-fifth Street
Tuesday   [New York]

Dear Gertrude:

This is one of the books you have sent me I like best: Operas and Play[s]. It is printed so well.[2] It is so homogeneous, and anywhere you open it, there is a play—a play like Four Saints that I know, or a play like A List—which I should exceedingly like to see performed. And those French historical plays! Somehow this book reminds me of Aix-les-Bains. Anyway I was happy with it all. I did not receive any announcement of this book & I was surprised. . . . . I do nothing but take photographs now, but I take wonderful photographs & oh ! how I long to take you and Alice. I took 64 photographs of Mary Garden last night: We are both well & I wish you would come over and see us and then you . . . you have never seen the Nut stores— or Harlem . . or Roxy's . . or even our apartment. Do come over and be photographed.

Love,
Carlo.

1. This appears to be the first letter from Van Vechten to Stein since his postcard to her of 26 April [1932]. (Between 4 July and 18 August 1932 it was Marinoff and Stein who were in contact while Marinoff was in Europe.) The fact that there is no correspondence from either Van Vechten or Stein during this period does not necessarily indicate a break between them. This period was for Stein one of enormous creative energy. She was working on a long sequence of poems that was to be titled *Stanzas in Meditation*. At the same time she had begun writing *The Autobiography of Alice B. Toklas*.

There are indications in the Stein manuscripts (YCAL) that she had entertained the idea of writing an autobiography sometime before she actually wrote *The Autobiography of Alice B. Toklas*. Precisely what prompted Stein to write this book cannot be determined. It is clear, however, that Toklas was pushing her to write a book that would make Stein a popular success and earn a great deal of money. In *Everybody's Autobiography* Stein reduces what were clearly complicated motivations to "If there had not been a beautiful and unusually dry October at Bilignin in France in nineteen thirty-two followed by an unusually dry and beautiful first two weeks of November would The Autobiography of Alice B. Toklas have been written. Possibly but probably not then. And still one does not, no one does not in one's heart believe in mute inglorious Miltons" (p. 1).

When *The Autobiography of Alice B. Toklas* was finished and typed, Stein sent it to her literary agent in Paris, William A. Bradley. Bradley was enthusiastic, and without any difficulty he placed the manuscript with Harcourt, Brace and Company (see Bradley to Stein in Gallup, *The Flowers of Friendship*, p. 259).

During this period of silence between Stein and Van Vechten, Van Vechten was preoccupied with his photographic work. He and Marinoff were in good health (both had given up drinking in January 1932).

2. Stein's *Operas and Plays* had been printed in an edition of five hundred unnumbered copies by Maurice Darantière. The cover consisted of tan paper wrappers and the book fit into a tan slip case. *Operas and Plays* collected twenty-two works by Stein written from 1913 to 1931. Van Vechten's copy of the book, with the inscription "Always to Carl from Gtde.," is in YCAL.

To Carl Van Vechten
[Postcard: Photograph of Stein's house at Bilignin]

[postmark: 27 December 1932]   [27 rue de Fleurus
                                                          Paris]

A happy new year to you and to photography. This is a nice photo of Bilignin isn't it. Did the plates reach you alright and were you pleased. I am glad you like Operas and Plays and A List strangely enough was suggested by something in Avery [Hopwood],[1] anyway lots of love

Gtrde.

[261]

1. Stein's play *A List* was inspired by Avery Hopwood's play *Our Little Wife*. See Stein to Van Vechten [6 July 1923], note 3.

🙊

To Carl Van Vechten
[Rose motto]

[postmark: 1 January 1933]   27 rue de Fleurus
                                              [Paris]

My dear Carl,

Happy happy New Year I have already written it and now I wrote it on New Years day it seems more real that way even if you get it later and lots and lots of love to you and Fania and may you live long and prosper

Always
Gertrude.

🙊

To Gertrude Stein
[Postcard] Carl Van Vechten [and] Fania Marinoff
[Photograph by] Harrison, 1915

[postmark: 9 January 1933]   [150 West Fifty-fifth Street
                                              New York]

But, dear Gertrude, you write to ask me how do I like the plates and I wrote to thank you for them ages ago and told you I loved them. Somebody must steal my postcards 'cause they are very pretty. But now I do *nothing* but take pictures. Would you & Alice were here to be taken! Maybe you will be when the opera is produced—as I understand it is going to be—many violets, gardenias, and a whole hibiscus tree to you![1]

Our love!
C.

Loved the pictures of Bilignin![2]

1. Thomson had finished the score of *Four Saints in Three Acts* in mid-summer 1928 (see Stein to Van Vechten [13 January 1928], note 2). From that time on, whenever the opportunity presented itself, Thomson would entertain his friends with a solo performance of the opera (see Van Vechten to Stein, 12 February 1928 and [13? February 1929]). No support for a full-scale production developed until 1933, when Kirk and Constance Askew undertook to ensure a production of the opera. One of the friends they invited to hear Thomson perform parts of the opera was A. E. "Chick" Austin, the director of the Wadsworth Athenaeum in Hartford, Connecticut. Austin had formed, in 1928, a nonprofit society, the Friends and Enemies of Modern Music. It was this organization that produced the first performance of *Four Saints in Three Acts*, in the Avery Memorial Auditorium of the Wadsworth Athenaeum on 8 February 1934.

2. Van Vechten may be referring to the photograph of Stein's house at Bilignin that was used as a postcard by Stein for the letter of [27 December 1932]. There are three small photographs in YCAL that may have been sent at this time to Van Vechten. One is a photograph of Toklas and the dog Pepe inscribed on the verso by Stein: "Alice and the Mexican dog Pepe my photo G." The next two are of Stein seated on the terrace at Bilignin. In each photograph she is seated at a small *guéridon* that has two levels. One photograph is inscribed: "Basket Pepe and me and we love you well all three, at least I do and the two others would if they could. Gtde." On the verso of another photograph, at the same *guéridon* but in a slightly different pose and with only one dog, Stein has inscribed the verso: "To Carlo Gertrude and Peppe [sic], and this was where I sat when I wrote the autobiography and it was Indian summer and lots of love Gtde." This statement, about writing *The Autobiography of Alice B. Toklas* at this writing table may be an example of one of Stein's smooth, concealing maneuvers that she employed in recounting the history behind the composition of this book. The table (now in a private collection in Germany) would appear to be too small and unsteady to have been used as a work table.

To Gertrude Stein
*[Postcard: Nora Holt, Prentiss Taylor, and Gladys Bentley.
Photograph by Carl Van Vechten]*[1]

[postmark: 16 April 1933][2]　　　　　　　　　　[150 West Fifty-fifth Street
Easter Sunday　　　　　　　　　　　　　　　New York]

Dear Gertrude:

Thank you for the copies of the Francis Rose pictures.[3] I like 'em . . . . The whole town, nay, the world, is excited by your Atlantic Monthly debut[4]—we are waiting in line for April 20 when the first number appears . . Have you seen Vol I of Mabel [Dodge]'s memoirs?[5] . . and did you know

that Fania left her appendix in a hospital?   Our Edith[6] prefers the Carlo plates to all others. If we tried[x] we could not keep 'em off the tables.
743 rosy flamingos to you both!

C.

[x]we don't try!

1. Holt and Bentley were both singer-pianists. Taylor was an artist who had designed Van Vechten's bookplate and the dust jacket for Van Vechten's *Sacred and Profane Memories*.

2. There is no correspondence between Van Vechten and Stein from the time of his postcard of [9 January 1933] and this postcard. There is no explanation for this interruption.

3. Stein may be referring to photographs of two paintings by Sir Francis Rose. One was a photograph of a portrait of Toklas in the garden at Bilignin. On the verso Stein wrote: "Alice by Francis Rose and are you going to like my autobiography of Alice B. Toklas, I think so because it is good, Love Gtde." On the verso of the second photograph, a portrait of Stein by Rose, Stein wrote: "Me by Francis Rose and you won't Carl be like Max Jacob who says he is going to love it all xcept about himself but I know you won't be like that. Love Gtde." Both photographs are in YCAL, the portrait of Toklas is also in YCAL. See Van Vechten to Stein, 1 May 1933, note 3.

4. *The Atlantic Monthly* printed four excerpts from Stein's *The Autobiography of Alice B. Toklas*: "Autobiography of Alice B. Toklas—I" (May 1933), 151(5): [513]-27; "When We Were Very Young" (June 1933), 151(6): 677–88; "The War and Gertrude Stein" (July 1933), 152(1): 56–69; and "Ernest Hemingway and the Post-War Decade" (August 1933), 152(2): 197–208. The titles for these excerpts were supplied by the editors of *The Atlantic Monthly*, not by Stein.

5. Mabel Dodge Luhan's *Background* (New York: Harcourt, Brace and Co., 1933).

6. The Van Vechten's cook.

To Gertrude Stein
[Telegram]

20 April 1933   New York

AUTOBIOGRAPHY DIVINE MUCH LOVE[1]

CARLO

1. Van Vechten had just read the first installment of *The Autobiography of Alice B. Toklas* in *The Atlantic Monthly* (May 1933), 151(5): [513]–27.

❧

To Carl Van Vechten

[postmark: 27 April 1933]   [27 rue de Fleurus
                                             Paris]

My dear Carl

We are not in Bilignin yet we are leaving to-morrow but we just had this letter paper made and am baptising it on you.[1] I was so touched by your telegram I can't tell you and to-day comes your postal card,[2] I am most pleased with everything, I love being rich, not as yet so awful rich but with prospects, it makes me all cheery inside I don't know why it should but it does, you always are so sweet Carlo and I love you very very much and love to Fania

Gertrude.

1. Stein had had stationery printed at the shop of J. Beauvais on the rue du Bac in Paris. The imprint was:

   Bilignin par Belley
   Ain

2. Van Vechten to Stein [16 April 1933].

❧

To Gertrude Stein

1 May 1933   150 West Fifty-fifth Street
                                        [New York]

Dear Gertrude,

Wherever one goes—and I have just gone to Baltimore—one hears about your paper in the Atlantic. Everybody loves it. Even Harry Hansen who made some asinine remarks about it really loves it. Anyway, it seems the whole town rose to write and correct him.[1] We are all dying for the 20 of May when the June number comes out and when I think I have to wait till July 20 to get at the whole I some times think I can't bear it and other times I am happy because I have so much pleasure ahead of me![2] You are a woojums and Alice is a woojums and I foresee now that you *must*, soon or late, come to America, and then I will photograph you. . I do nothing but make photographs now and they *are* good. . I like your Francis Rose portraits.[3] . Edith brings in food on the Carlo plates more often than not, but it does not need that to remind us of you. . Fania had her appendix out and is much better than she has been in years. I didn't have mine out, but I am better too! In this crazy world it is nice to remember that there are two people we love called Gertrude Stein and Alice B. Toklas.

a great many shell boxes and four orchids to you!

Carlo[4]

1. Harry Hansen was a syndicated newspaper columnist. I have been unable to locate the remarks made by Hansen about *The Autobiography of Alice B. Toklas.*

2. See Van Vechten to Stein [16 April 1933], note 3.

3. Stein had sent Van Vechten a photograph of a portrait done of her by Sir Francis Rose, 1930–33, oil on canvas, 31½ x 25¼ inches (sight), which is now in the collection of the heirs of Gertrude Stein. She also sent him a photograph of Rose's *Portrait of Alice B. Toklas*, 1932, oil on canvas, 29⅞ x 19 inches, now in YCAL. See Van Vechten to Stein [16 April 1933], note 3.

4. The recto of this letter contains the following in Stein's hand:

> Made by with full
> [~~laid~~ ?]
> acceptance by author

The verso of the letter contains the following in Toklas' hand:

> following [to? f.? for?] author or [in?] [b.?] take out
> ~~That~~ Neither composer or author are
> privileged to use their part
> of the opera with anyone
> elses work: that is the
> author may not ~~give~~ use the
> libretto ~~to~~ with any other composer
> ~~the~~ music—the composer
> may not use the music of
> the opera with any other
> libretto
> 6 ~~eliminate~~ elimination "said contract to
> be duly accepted and signed
> by both parties"
> "royalties"—

These notes are a draft of part of the contract between Stein and Virgil Thomson for their opera, *Four Saints in Three Acts.*

To Gertrude Stein

*[Postcard: Photograph by Carl Van Vechten] Jacket Design
for the Tattooed Countess by Ralph Barton. Collection
of Carl Van Vechten*

22 May [1933]   [150 West Fifty-fifth Street
                                                New York]

Dear Gertrude—

And now Bennet Cerf tells me that Three Lives is to go into the
Modern Library and has asked me to write a preface.[1] I am *thrilled!!* It is
your year. You'd better come over & be photographed. I know very little
about the opera, but here arrangements are being made for its production.
I photographed Matisse on Saturday.[2]—The second number of the Autobiography is *grand*—I loved the story of M[ildred]. Aldrich & the canaries!
I can't wait till I see the whole thing![3]

                                        Much love to you both,
                                        C.

1. Bennett Cerf (1898–1971), the publisher and one of the founders of Random House, had
written Stein asking for permission to republish her *Three Lives*. The plates for the book were
in New York with the publishers Albert and Charles Boni, who had brought out an edition of
the book in 1927. See Cerf to Stein, 16 May 1933, YCAL.

2. Van Vechten had photographed Henri Matisse (1869–1954), the French painter, on 20 May
1933.

3. See Van Vechten to Stein [16 April 1933], note 3.

To Carl Van Vechten

[postmark: 27? May 1933]   Bilignin Par Belley
                                                  Ain

My dear Carl,

I am so pleased so very very pleased that you are doing the introduction for Three Lives for the Modern Library, do you remember how touched

I was when you first became famous and they asked you for a list of the ten important books of the world and you put in Three Lives and it was the first time I had ever appeared in a real list and I was pleased, my dear we are very fond of each other and I am very pleased.[1] Are you coming over or do I have to come over there, well anyway lots and lots of love

Gertrude.

1. See Van Vechten to Stein, May 1923.

＊

To Carl Van Vechten
[Postcard: Photograph of Gertrude Stein in the garden at Bilignin]

[postmark: 11 June 1933]   [Bilignin par Belley
                                                            Ain]

My dear Carl,

I am delighted and do tell [Stephen] Haweis he mustn't worry he will have his tea.[1] I am glad Fania is so much better, have you heard about the opera, they seem to be sincerely thinking of doing it in Hartford, tell me what you think of the idea and what do you do in Baltimore.[2] You know they are only doing a little over half in the Atlantic as soon as I get an advance copy of the whole I will send it to you. I am very happy

Gtrde.

1. Haweis, the painter, was the ex-husband of Mina Loy. In this correspondence there is no earlier reference to Haweis to account for mention of him. Either a letter was lost or else Van Vechten and Stein had both seen someone who talked about Haweis.

2. Van Vechten had been visiting friends in Baltimore. See Van Vechten to Stein, 1 May 1933.

[268]

🐛

To Gertrude Stein

10 July [1933] 150 West Fifty-fifth Street
New York City

Dear Gertrude,

Here is the preface. I hope you will like it.[1] I wish I might have talked it over with you. However, if you dislike it very much there might still be time to change something. I have written about you so often and never succeed in writing quite what I want to, but *I will some day. And when you come over this winter* I will photograph you!

Love to you and the lady of the autobiography!

Carlo

1. Van Vechten's preface to the Modern Library edition of Stein's *Three Lives*.

🐛

To Carl Van Vechten
*[Postcard: Photograph of Picabia drawing of
Gertrude Stein]*

[? July 1933] [Bilignin par Belley
Ain]

My dear Carl,

It is all signed and settled about the Modern Library and Three Lives and I am awfully pleased and have just written to [Bennett] Cerf to tell him how pleased I am that you are introducing it.[1] Picabia has been staying with us and we talked of you and perhaps you will like this, he also did an amusing one of Alice, if anybody comes along who can photo it, I will send it.[2]

Lots of love
Gtrde.

It has rained.

1. Cerf had cabled Stein on 5 June 1933 (copy of cable, Columbia-Random House) requesting a reply to his letter of 16 May (YCAL) about republishing *Three Lives*. Stein's signed contracts must have crossed with Cerf's cable, and on 13 July (YCAL) Cerf wrote to Stein that the plates for *Three Lives* had been received and that he had sent an advance of $400 to her agent, William A. Bradley.

2. Francis Picabia (1879–1953), the French painter. The drawings of Stein and Toklas are now in a private collection in New York. Picabia had visited Stein in Bilignin on 5 June 1933.

To Carl Van Vechten
[Postcard: Photograph of Gertrude Stein and Picabia holding portrait of Gertrude Stein by Picabia]

[? July 1933][1]

[Bilignin par Belley
Ain]

My dear Carl,

This is a portrait Picabia just made of me out of his head, I hope you like it,[2] but not as much as I like the introduction, I am awfully happy about it all, I can't tell you how happy it makes me, everything you said pleased me and I felt it was just right that is the way I feel you feel about it and that is the way I liked and like it,

Thanks a thousand times

Gtrde.

1. Both this letter and the previous one were mailed in envelopes that have not survived. It is possible that they were mailed on the same day.

2. Picabia had painted the portrait of Gertrude Stein that he is holding in these photographs in Golfe-Juan, France. He had brought it to Stein on his way back to Paris in June 1933. This portrait of Stein, oil on linen, 45⅝ x 34¼ inches, is now in YCAL.

☙

To Gertrude Stein
[Postcard: Photograph of an oriental soldier]

22 July [1933]   [San Francisco]

Dear Gertrude:—

In El Monte I discovered a lion tamer from Aix-les-Bains—which reminded me of the only time I've been there & the wonderful day we had.[1]— Now in San Francisco for the first time & flying back to N.Y. tomorrow.

Love to you both
Carlo.

1. Van Vechten and Marinoff had visited Stein in Bilignin for two days in August 1930. One of the excursions they made was to the nearby city of Aix-les-Bains, France.

☙

To Gertrude Stein and Alice Toklas
[Postcard: Palermo—Carro Siciliano]

[postmark: 29 July 1933]   [Turkey]

My dears,

I'll be in Paris Aug 5th for a week. Am cruising in Greece. I suppose you are in Beligin [i.e., Bilignin] as always. But I'll feel a little nearer to you in Paris. I'll be at the Hotel Bristol comme toujours. I would love a word from you

Love
Fania

❦

To Fania Marinoff

[postmark: 29 July 1933]   Bilignin par Belley
                                                           Ain

My dear Fania

Welcome to Europe, I am so sorry that we are still 500 kilometers apart but anyway we use the same postage stamp and that is always a comfort, and I am so happy about Carl's introduction to Three Lives and everything, it would be nice to see you even nicer than just being in the same country, perhaps you will manage and that will be nice, anyway enjoy yourself and lots of love

Gtrde.

❦

To Gertrude Stein
[Postcard: Victorian Cushion—Van Vechten apartment.
Photograph by Carl Van Vechten]

10 August [1933]   [150 West Fifty-fifth Street
                                                   New York]

Dear Gertrude,

Did I ever send you this (almost) portrait of Basket? It is cut out of kid, stuffed & implanted on a blue velvet cushion in the Victorian Room.— I'm so glad you liked the preface. I like *all* the Picabia portraits. Please remember me to him. F[ania]. M[arinoff]. is in France or England on her way home after Greece but you will be in the country & so can't see her. . I have just returned from *flying* to San Francisco. Saw Mabel [Dodge] at Taos. . Three Lives will be out in a minute. Also the Autobiography!

Love to you both.
Carlo.

[272]

To Gertrude Stein
*[Postcard: Daring Jump by a Forest Ranger, Near Bright
Angel Cove, Grand Canyon National Park, Arizona]*

22 August [1933]   [150 West Fifty-fifth Street
                                                    New York]

Dear Gertrude—

Soon after my return from the West—Américains d'Amérique arrived. It is a grand idea—this abridgement—why couldn't it appear in English like this? I shall read it later together with [Bernard] Faÿ's introduction.[1] At present I am locked in my darkroom trying to get the pictures finished
I did in the west. The proofs of Three Lives arrived & that will be out soon.

*Love
Carlo.*

1. An abridged version of *The Making of Americans* had been prepared by Stein and Faÿ. It
was published as *Américains d'Amérique*, translated by the Baroness J. Seillière and Bernard
Faÿ (Paris: Libraire Stock, 1933). An English equivalent of this abridgment, together with Faÿ's
preface, was published by Harcourt, Brace and Co. in February 1934.

To Carl Van Vechten

[postmark: 3 September 1933]   Bilignin par Belley
                                                    Ain

My dear Carl

We have been talking about you, The Seabrooks were so taken with
the autobiography, so moved by it that they came and made what they called
a pilgrimage here to see me, and I was awfully touched and pleased. We
saw them for several days and naturally we talked a lot about you, and how
much we all liked you, and we do.[1]

I am glad you like Américains d'Amérique, it is I think an xtraordinary translation. Of course I want it done like that in America, and I hope somebody soon will want to do it. You will see when you read it that I did it very well, the abridgment at least I think so. Have you had the Autobiography yet, I asked Harcourt to send you a copy direct to save time, I hope you will like it all, do tell me that you do, and that you were pleased with everything. Write soon and lots of love, I liked the postal, are there more like that, lots and lots of love

Gertrude.

1. The American writers William Seabrook (1886–1945) and his wife Marjorie Worthington (1900–1976). The Seabrooks, whom Stein had met through Van Vechten, were then living in Toulon, France.

To Gertrude Stein

8 September 1933   150 West Fifty-fifth Street
                                    [New York]

Dear Gertrude:

I have been rereading The Autobiography in book form and have nothing but words of praise for it. It seems to me, indeed, that I have talked about nothing else since the first part appeared in the Atlantic. What a delightful book it is! I am showering copies on my happy friends. . . I find we are alike in two important ways: our passion for breakable things and for pigs—this passion might be united in a painted Mexican porcelain pig! Have you ever seen one? They are banks, pottery banks, and you put pennies in them. Have you a passion for banks too? I have and I am sure you have. . Anyway, I loved every minute of the book and the second reading made it seem even fresher. . I've also been reading Américains d'Amérique with [Bernard] Faÿ's preface which I liked very much. I was pleased that he spoke of your laugh. And this book is very convincing in French and in this abridgement. Why couldn't it be issued in English in this shorter form? Well, you are certainly a woojums and I think you had better come to America where you can properly smell your triumphs and listen to your opera and be

[274]

photographed (both of you) by the Maestro luimême. . . There is little news otherwise. I flew to San Francisco and thought of both of you there: though I dare say neither of you would recognize the place now. I constantly was afraid the taxicabs would slide down hill backwards and I caught cold in one of the fogs. Nevertheless I loved the place. . . I also had sciatica for a coupla days, but that was later. .

Anyway it is a joy to know you and to shake your hand across the sea and I think you'd better come over and take the tribute due you and be photographed.

178 pink-lipped poodles to you both!

Carlo.

Fania, just back from Greece, adds her greetings.
In a few days we'll have 3 Lives with the new preface!

To Gertrude Stein
[Postcard: Photograph of Carl Van Vechten and his mother
November 7, 1883]

9 September [1933]   [150 West Fifty-fifth Street
                                       New York]

Dear Gertrude—

I forgot to tell you that Muriel Draper went out to Taos to visit Mabel [Dodge] last week so we can expect *more* memories!

Love,
Carlo.

❧

To Gertrude Stein
[Postcard: Jacob Epstein—Head of Paul Robeson. Photograph
by Carl Van Vechten]

14 September [1933]   [150 West Fifty-fifth Street
                                       New York]

Dear Gertrude—

Harcourt did *not* send me a copy of The Autobiography. I let you know this—not that I needed one, because I bought several copies—because he may have failed you with some other people you wished to receive copies.— You say "I liked the post card—are there more like that" & I don't know which one it is. You tell me & I'll tell you! This one is a photograph I took of Epstein's bust of Paul Robeson. Did you know that "Lorenzo in Taos" seems to be called "Ma vie avec Lawrence" in French translation! Mabel [Dodge] is justifiably furious.[1] How nice for you & the nice Seabrooks to get together. But I expect to see you & Alice in America soon—entering the city triumphantly on elephants & visiting the Nut stores & yr admiring

Carlo.

1. The translation of Mabel Dodge Luhan's book *Lorenzo in Taos* was published as *Ma Vie avec D. H. Lawrence au Nouveau Mexique,* translated by Jacques Emile Blanche and Armand Pierhal (Paris: Editions Bernard Grasset [1933]).

❧

To Gertrude Stein
[Postcard: Detail—Hall of Science. Chicago World's
Fair, 1933]

19 September [1933]   [150 West Fifty-fifth Street
                                       New York]

Dear Gertrude:

Today—September 19—a copy of The Autobiography arrived with a card announcing "with the compliments of Harcourt Brace"—So they did send it—if belatedly. Little do they know that I have already owned 10 copies. I had a very extraordinary time at the Barnes foundation at Merion, Pa. last Sunday. He now has 195 Renoirs & God knows how many Matisses & Picassos & Cezannes—[1]

Love.
Carlo.

1. Dr. Albert C. Barnes (d. 1951), who made a fortune with patent medicine, had set up a private foundation to house his art collection in Merion, Pennsylvania. Admission to the foundation was strictly by an invitation from Dr. Barnes.

Stein first met Dr. Barnes in 1912 when he was brought to the rue de Fleurus by his friend the painter William Glackens. A number of pictures once in the collections of Leo and Gertrude as well as Michael and Sarah Stein were eventually acquired by Dr. Barnes.

To Gertrude Stein
[Postcard: Jacob Epstein—Head of Paul Robeson.
Photograph by Carl Van Vechten]

21 September [1933]   [150 West Fifty-fifth Street
                                        New York]

Dear Gertrude:—

The first copies of OUR Three Lives came in today & I am sending out 20 at once![1] I am so excited! You are on every tongue like Greta Garbo![2]

Love,
Carlo

I seem to write you every day!

1. Stein's *Three Lives* with an introduction by Van Vechten.

2. The Swedish-born actress.

To Carl Van Vechten

[postmark: 27 September 1933]   Bilignin par Belley
                                                          Ain

My dear Carl

The post card I meant was the one of you and your mother, I liked
that immensely and you have hardly changed at all really and truly not, it
is all there my dear, very dear friend.[1] I am glad you liked Américains
d'Amérique I think it very beautifully done myself and I do so very very much
want it to appear in America like that and I think it ought to be soon. There
is some pourparler at present with Harcourt about it, if you know any of
them or see any of them throw in your weight, please and see if it can be
pulled off, it would give me a lot of contentment, it was through you the
Modern Library happened and I do so much want this to happen. We are
still in the country and the rain is quietly dripping but we rather like that as
well as other things, we have lots of people here, Bernard Faÿ and Charles
Henry Ford[2] are still with us so I have not worked much but I am beginning
to want to, and I am also beginning to wonder if perhaps I may not get to
America, and be photographed and be taken to nut stores what do you think

Lots of love
Gertrude.

I'd love a Mexican pig, I have a mexican calvaire that I am devoted
to and a Mexican dog so I would love a mexican pig.

Always
G.

1. See Van Vechten to Stein, 9 September [1933].

2. Charles Henri (or Henry) Ford (b. 1910), the writer and artist. Ford had first written to Stein
requesting a contribution from her for the expatriate number of *Blues: A Revue of Modern Literature*, which he had helped to found. (See Gallup, *The Flowers of Friendship*, p. 230.) Stein
contributed a piece, "Evidence," *Blues* (Spring 1930), 8:508.

To Carl Van Vechten

[postmark: 11 October 1933]   Bilignin [par Belley
                                               Ain]

My dear Carl,

Three Lives has just come and it is a darling little blue book and a
darling not at all blue introduction but a sweet one and a rosy one and I am
as happy as can be, happier than I can tell you.[1] I first solemnly read the
introduction and then I solemnly read the good Anna, one was young and
sweet and solemn, powerfully solemn in those days, we are just as sweet
now only not quite so solemn, just as powerful as you so sweetly say but not
as solemn, anyway I am as happy as I can be about it all, and I like our
being together as we always have been and always will be my very dear Carlo.
Perhaps who knows perhaps we will come over to be photographed, but anyway I am always and always yours

Gertrude.

[on back of envelope] Do send me a Mexican mountain pig.

1. The Modern Library edition of *Three Lives* had a flexible cloth cover which was variously
printed in (one of four) colors: sage green, cocoa brown, brick red, or blue.

To Carl Van Vechten

[postmark: 15 October 1933]   [Bilignin par Belley
                                               Ain]

My dearest Carl,

I have just had a charming letter from Hunter Stagg but he does not
give me his address and so I don't know where to send him the inclosed so
will you see that he gets it, he said he wanted to have me sign a portrait of
me that you had given him but that he was too modest to send it, I hope

this will please him.[1] I have not sent you one, it was taken by a very temperamental valet de chambre who inspired me to write my first detective story, Blood on the dining room floor, it is a short story but a very nice one, what shall I do with it, would you like to see it.[2] I have not sent you the photo because I don't know whether it is good form to send a photograph to a photographer, anyway you are my favorite photographer and I like them all even including the Washington, I am doing a long book all about 4 eminent Americans and the first one is Grant it is beginning well,[3] I am at last getting used to my fame and am beginning to work, it would be nice to see you Carl we do love each other

> *Always*
> *Gertrude.*

1. Stagg's undated letter to Stein (YCAL) is printed in an article by Edgar E. MacDonald, "Hunter Stagg: 'Over There in Paris With Gertrude Stein,' " *The Ellen Glasgow Newsletter* (October 1981), 15:4–5. Van Vechten sent Stagg the photograph Stein had inscribed (Van Vechten to Stagg, 23 October 1933, quoted in MacDonald, p. 5).

2. The valet de chambre worked in the Hotel Pernollet in Belley. Stein's *Blood on the Dining-Room Floor* was not published until 1948.

3. Stein's *Four in America* includes sections on U. S. Grant, Wilbur Wright, Henry James, and George Washington.

To Carl Van Vechten
[Postcard: Les Charmettes—La chambre à coucher de Mme de Warens]

[postmark: 21 October 1933]   [Bilignin par Belley
                                                Ain]

My dear dearest Carl,

I am so pleased, Harcourt's bringing out the Makings this spring and I just feel more than ever like being photographed.[1]

> *Lots and lots of love,*
> *Gertrude.*

1. The abridged version of Stein's *The Making of Americans*, with a preface by Bernard Faÿ, was published by Harcourt, Brace and Co. on 8 February 1934, to coincide with the first performance of Stein's opera *Four Saints in Three Acts*.

To Gertrude Stein

23 October [1933]   150 West Fifty-fifth Street
                                                       [New York]

Dear Gertrude:

I was thrilled to receive the English edition of the Autobiography and more thrilled to read the inscription.[1] You are certainly a WOOJUMS. There seem to be some illustrations in the English that are not in the American . . . About that Painted Pig, of course you shall have one. These are the difficulties: they are very breakable and probably will get smashed in transit and you might have duty to pay. (2) all the dealers who carry Mexican goods in N.Y. are out of pigs . . . I have written to Santa Fe to a shop I know there to send me a pig. If you come over, well and good, I'll hand the pig over to you. If you don't, perhaps you could suggest somebody who would take it back to you. Maybe Marjorie Worthington would take it back to you . . . But you must come over. I Must photograph you both. I think you will. James Weldon Johnson (whose Along This Way is very fine) writes me: "You have introduced me to Gertrude Stein. Of course, I have long known about her but a prejudice has kept me from knowing her, I think. Your introduction to Three Lives intrigued me and I immediately read 'The Good Anna'. It is amazing. I can't understand why such work has not had a wider audience—but I can see why it has had a strong influence on writers. I still have 'Melanchtha' and 'The Gentle Lena' to read, and it is probable that by the time I finish them I shall be a Gertrude Stein fan. I am sure now that I must read her Autobiography. I thank you for sending me the copy of 'Three Lives'." And in a later letter he writes: "I think 'Melanctha' is marvellous. What surprises me is that in it Gertrude Stein is the first (I believe I'm right) white writer to write a story of love between a Negro man and woman and deal with them as normal members of the human family. Her style, which on the surface seems so naïve—some might say childish, is really consummate artistry."[2]

I sent the picture off to Hunter Stagg, but I felt a tinge of jealousy. Please send me one at once. You've seen very few pictures taken by me. When you do, I think you'll be a little surprised. How I am aching to take you! I'd love to see Blood on the Dining Room Floor. And I'm glad you've gone back to work and are doing GRANT.

Of course, it is grand that you like the introduction. You couldn't, as you say, write this book now, because it is true that you *are* less solemn and enjoy life more, and any book you would write now would be bound to have some of your own delightful humor in it . . . Anyway, I send you a lot of love and so does Fania, and we send a lot of love to Alice too!

Carlo!

Charles Ford sent me The Young and Evil and said you told him to. I'll read it.[3]

A lot of reviewers thought Fania was the unhappy wife of CVV in The Autobiography! Ann, by the way, died last summer in a cancer hospital in Germany.[4]

Mable [Dodge] and Muriel [Draper] are getting along like two happy puppies in Taos.[5]

1. The inscription in the presentation copy, now YCAL, reads: "To my own dear and very dearest Carl from Gtde."

The placement of the illustrations is different in the American and in the English editions. The English edition contains three illustrations that are not in the American edition: "Marie Laurencin" (seated looking into a mirror—the American edition has a photograph of Laurencin on a staircase), "The [Stein] Family Having Come to California," and "Mildred Aldrich and Gertrude Stein at the Hill Top on the Marne." One illustration included in the American edition is not in the English edition: "Gertrude Stein at Johns Hopkins Medical School."

2. Johnson's *Along This Way: The Autobiography of James Weldon Johnson* (New York: The Viking Press, 1933).

Johnson, then teaching at Fisk University, had written Van Vechten about Stein's *Three Lives* on 8 October [1933] and then again on 15 October [1933] (both letters Yale-JWJ). Except for two changes in punctuation, Van Vechten transcribed the letters accurately.

3. Charles Heni Ford and Parker Tyler's novel *The Young and the Evil* (Paris: Obelisk Press, 1933).

4. In *The Autobiography of Alice B. Toklas* Stein told how she had met Van Vechten's wife before she met Van Vechten and how Mrs. Van Vechten confided in Stein the difficulties of her married life. The reviewers had confused Fania Marinoff with Van Vechten's first wife,

Anna Snyder Van Vechten. Anna Snyder Van Vechten had died on 9 May 1933 in Frankfort-on-Main, Germany. See Stein, *The Autobiography of Alice B. Toklas*, pp. 166–68.

5. This letter is the first instance in which a drawing by Van Vechten appears after the close of the letter. The drawing appears to be the rear end of a cat. Future instances of this device will not be individually noted.

To Gertrude Stein

2 November [1933]   150 West Fifty-fifth Street
                                                         [New York]

Dear Gertrude,

I ordered a pig from New Mexico for you and they sent me such a little one. I sent it right on to you registered, without opening the package. I hope it will be all right. I am now enclosing the bill for the customs. Isn't it amusing that the things you desire are so cheap? And I have ordered a great big mamma pig for you which will arrive in due time, but this may have to be sent to you by hand. At [Serge] Lifar's exhibition yesterday we saw some lovely drawings by Sir Francis Rose, and Virgil [Thomson] was there.[1] He plunges into preparations for the Opera. And at dinner last night were Willie Seabrook and Marjorie Worthington. We spoke of you and Alice at least 5467897654 times!

Four crocus buds and a yellow canary to you from your loving

Carlo!

1. *Twenty-five Years of the Russian Ballet*, an exhibition to benefit the Architect's Emergency Committee, was held at the Julien Levy Gallery, New York, 2 to 18 November 1933. The exhibition included works from the collection of the dancer Serge Lifar. Among the artists represented were Leon Bakst, Alexandre Benois, Matisse, Picasso, Braque, de Chirico, Jean Cocteau, André Derain, Rouault, Marie Laurencin, Léger, Miró, Christian Bérard, Max Ernst, Jose-Maria Sert, and Sir Francis Rose.

To Carl Van Vechten and Fania Marinoff

[postmark: 4 November 1933]   [Bilignin par Belley
                                                          Ain]

My dears

I gathered that Fania was protesting about the autobiography from some clippings I saw, but how could anyone who knew Fania think Fania could be like that, now I ask you, they just did not know Fania. Here are two photos instead of me, and I hope you like them both, Carl, [Bennett] Cerf has just written to me that Three Lives is selling like hot cakes, I am as pleased as pleased can be, you and me.[1] I should be working instead of writing so many letters, but what of it, glory comes belated but glorious and one must like it and I do. Cerf also wrote that he wanted to do the Makings but Harcourt has already made a contract for that. Now I am proposing to him to do a volume of reprints, all the things mentioned in the Auto[biography]. The Tender Buttons, the things in Rogue, Flowers of friendship, the portrait [of] Mabel Dodge, Four Saints Mildred's Thoughts, and enough more to make a nice fat volume, what do you think about it and will you talk to him about it, I think it not a bad idea, tell me what you think.[2] It's cold but nice, it ought to [be] St. Martin's summer but it is pretty wintry but we like it,

Gertrude.

1. Cerf wrote to Stein and reported that Macy & Co. had bought 1,300 copies of *Three Lives* since its publication. Total sales of the book already exceeded 4,500 copies. Cerf to Stein, 23 October 1933, YCAL.

2. Stein's proposal was made in a letter to Cerf [? November 1933], Columbia-Random House.

To Gertrude Stein
[Postcard] Carl Van Vechten December 17—1881 photograph by Kilborn,
Cedar Rapids.

10 November 1933   [150 West Fifty-fifth Street
                                                        New York]

Dear Gertrude:

I have now for you a large pig—too big I'm afraid to send on to you. I'm afraid it will get broken. It's in a package 14 x 10 x 15 inches, and is well packed. I will not undo the wrappings. So if you know anybody[x] who is going to Paris why please tell them to call me up & bring it along with them.

love
Carlo

[x]I mean someone you can ask to carry it to you, & *depend on.*

To Carl Van Vechten

[postmark: 15 November 1933]   [Bilignin par Belley
                                                      Ain]

My dearest Carl,

I am eagerly awaiting my little pig and then I will be eagerly waiting my big one. By all means give it to [William] Seabrook and Marjorie Worthington, because then they will be sure to come back via Paris and see us and we like them both immensely and as they are conscientious they will then have to come. We did like them a lot and we will like seeing them again. I had a rather amusing time to-day, we were lunching with some people in the little town of Yenne, he is a retired army general and it would appear that he had in his division at the front two American Negro regiments, he was very interesting about them and more than that he reads all the books that he can get hold [of] translated from the American about anything to do with Negroes. He has all of Seabrook's[1] and was very xcited about hearing about your Paradis de Negres[2] and I am sending it to him as soon as we get to Paris, he hopes to meet you both and I promised him that if you should ever get here again he would. This is his card,[3] I am glad you liked Francis Rose's paintings, I care for him a lot, both works and man and some day but you are arriving back again some day why not with the Seabrooks, you might even come over some day to take us home who knows, well anyway lots and lots of love

Gertrude.

1. Stein is probably referring to two of Seabrook's books: *The Magic Island*, translated by Gabriel de Hons as *L'Ile magique* (Paris: Firmin-Didot, 1929), which deals with Haiti and voodooism; *Jungle Ways*, translated by Suzanne Flour as *Secrets de la jungle* (Paris: J. Haumont, 1933), which deals with social life, witchcraft, and travel in French West Africa.

2. The translation of Van Vechten's *Nigger Heaven*

3. Stein enclosed the card:

> Génèral De Division M. Goybet
> Commandant en 1918 la 157ᵉ Division dont
> faisaient partir des 371 et 372 R. I. U. S.

To Carl Van Vechten
[Postcard: The Black Watch: Piper, Full Dress]

[postmark: 18 November 1933]   [Bilignin par Belley
                                                 Ain]

My dear Carl

I had a charming letter from your niece but she did not give me any address, will you thank her for me, I liked her letter[1]

Gertrude.

1. Elizabeth Van Vechten Shaffer wrote to Stein expressing her pleasure in *The Autobiography of Alice B. Toklas* (2 November [1933], YCAL).

❧

To Carl Van Vechten
[Postcard: Photograph of the Villa Stein (Les Terrasses)] [1]

[postmark: 21 November 1933]   27 rue de Fleurus
                                            Paris

My dearest Carl,

The dear dear pig has come he came just like that perfectly intact and looking at me so sweetly while I write, but he isn't a tiny pig he is a very very substantial pig, a very portly pig indeed, now is he the mother pig or is he the baby pig, he seems what you may call a normal pig, but whatever he is he is a lovely lovely pig, and I look into his black eyes and at his admirable tail and am filled with [word?] So much love to you now and always And what is the most wonderful is that it is glass it is almost unbelievable.

Gertrude.

My eldest brother's house at St. Cloud.

1. Designed by Le Corbusier (Edouard Jeanneret) and erected in 1927, this was the home of Stein's brother Michael and his wife Sarah. The villa is in the town of Garches, a few kilometers outside of Paris.

❧

To Gertrude Stein
[Postcard] Carl Van Vechten 1906

13 December 1933   [150 West Fifty-fifth Street
                                            New York]

Dear Gertrude—

I'm glad you liked the pig—I think I'll have to send the big one on as nobody is going over now. The Seabrooks won't go back. Do you know anybody who is leaving?—It is a very big pig, & is not afraid of the Big Bad

Wolf. I *love* the photographs with the dogs you sent. Soon I'll send you a lot of pictures of *myself* I take *myself*. (All alone) I like your idea for a book for [Bennett] Cerf. But I like all your ideas. [Louis] Bromfield has been here & we talked about you & Sherwood Anderson & we talked about you. Lots of love to you both!—[1]

Carlo.

1. Louis Bromfield (1896–1956), the American writer, and his wife Mary, had lived in Senlis, France, for many years. Stein and Toklas often went for Sunday lunch at the Bromfields.

    Sherwood Anderson (1876–1941), the American writer. Anderson first met Stein in 1921 through Sylvia Beach, the owner of Shakespeare and Company, an American and English bookshop in Paris (see Gallup, *The Flowers of Friendship*, pp. 138–39).

    Anderson wrote "The Work of Gertrude Stein" as a foreword to Stein's *Geography and Plays*. Throughout her life Stein remained fiercely loyal to Anderson. One reason given by Stein for her break with Ernest Hemingway was the satire of Anderson's style in Hemingway's novel *The Torrents of Spring* (New York: Charles Scribner's Sons, 1926). The Anderson-Stein correspondence was published in *Sherwood Anderson/Gertrude Stein: Correspondence and Personal Essays*, edited by Ray Lewis White (Chapel Hill, North Carolina: University of North Carolina Press, 1972).

To Gertrude Stein

2 January 1934

150 West Fifty-fifth Street
[New York]

Dear Gertrude,

I guess nobody but me would have the nerve to turn a duchess into an errand boy, but I have done just that. The Duchesse de Clermont-Tonnerre is sailing Friday (probably on the boat which will take you this letter!) and she is accompanied by the BIG Painted Pig! She was extremely sweet about the whole thing and acted as if she considered it a favor to be permitted to be the go-between for two such charming people! It is to the duchess too that you must turn for the latest news about the Opera. She was in Florine Stettheimer's studio the day I first saw the divine décors and costumes and she will tell you all about them. Also I believe she has attended rehearsals. As for me I am staying away from rehearsals so that I may get an entirely fresh impression. I have booked seats for the two opening nights and will go to Hartford on a sort of pilgrimage. You will get a full report from me then. But I don't want to say too much until then. However, there is the kind of excitement in the air that always indicates the arrival of something important and I think something is really going to happen this time! Besides, isn't it your year?

The Skinner paper in the Atlantic doesn't seem to me to make sense, but isn't that the way they always write about the Men and Women who have arrived?[1]

I sent you about a ton of my photographs a couple of weeks ago and the Duchess will tell you something about my photographs too, as I photographed *her*. She is an altogether charming person and I was delighted to see her again. Besides she is taking the PIG to Beloved Gertrude!

Alice is right. The pig is *not* glass. It is a kind of mud pottery.

Isn't life exciting? I am sloughing off pounds and expect soon to appear in a norfolk jacket, but the thinner I am the more I shall love Gertrude and Alice!

156 red roses and four orchids to you! & Fania sends five blue hyacinths!

Carlo!

1. B. F. Skinner, "Has Gertrude Stein a Secret?" *The Atlantic Monthly* (January 1934), 153:50–57. Skinner, then a junior fellow at Harvard University, had read Stein's two early contributions to Harvard University's *The Psychological Review*. Skinner theorized that Stein's "eccentric" writing style, particularly in *Tender Buttons*, was simply a continuation of her experiment in automatic writing. The first article, "Normal Motor Automatism," *The Psychological Review* (September 1896), 3(5):492–512, while listing the authors as Leon M. Solomons and Gertrude Stein, was entirely written by Solomons. Stein's name was added to recognize her participation in the experiments on which the article was based. "Cultivated Motor Automatism. A Study of Character in Its Relation to Attention," *The Psychological Review* (May 1898), 5(3):295–306, was actually Stein's first published piece. This article deals with an experiment in automatic writing that Stein had done under the tutelage of William James at Harvard University.

❧

To Carl Van Vechten

[postmark: 6 January 1934]   27 rue de Fleurus
                                              [Paris]

My dearest Carl,

Did I tell you how delighted I am with your photos, I look at them a good deal and they do look very tender and true, and that undoubtedly is you. But they do, they really do, the one all light is rather wonderful, and I think what you do with the ears is very curious, ears are curious, but what you do with them makes them even more so. It will be nice being photographed by you. I can't wish you happy new year too often, because I do hope it will be a nice one, it is always nice when it is. I have just had a charming letter from a colored boy all about the opera, his feelings were hurt because it would appear they said in the newspapers they chose the Negroes as singers because they would not giggle and he said that of course they would not because why should they giggle since of course they would understand. Very sweet of him,[1] it begins to sound most xciting and I am almost sorry we are not there, but you will tell us all about it and in a way I suppose it would kind of be too xciting to be there, but from Virgil [Thomson]'s letters it does sound rather good.[2] Well anyway, lots and lots of love. It is rather nice weather and I am working a lot, and I am likeing it, and the autobiography is translated and coming out in reviews,[3] I will send them as soon as they come out, and lots and lots of love, always

Gertrude.

1. At the time he wrote Stein, Ulysses G. Lee, Jr. (1912–1969) was a student at Howard University, Washington, D.C. (A.B., 1935, M.A. 1936; he later earned a doctorate from the University of Chicago). Stein was deeply impressed with Lee's letters to her and she had Toklas make typescripts of them for her agent, William A. Bradley, to bring with him to New York. See Lee to Stein, 28 December 1933, YCAL.

2. Stein and Thomson had not written to each other since the winter of 1930–31 when Stein fought with Georges Hugnet over the title page of her translation of his poem *Enfances*. See Van Vechten to Stein [6 September 1930], note 2. Thomson again wrote to Stein on 30 May 1933 to discuss details for the planned production of *Four Saints in Three Acts*. He corresponded with her again on 3 June [1933], 22 June [1933], and 3 July [1933]. These letters deal with contract arrangements, changes being made in the text of the opera, and general information about the progress of the production. On 6 December [1933] Thomson wrote to Stein

that the cast had been hired and that rehearsals had already begun. The Thomson-Stein correspondence is in YCAL.

3. *The Autobiography of Alice B. Toklas* was translated by Bernard Faÿ, *Autobiographie d'Alice B. Toklas* (Paris: NRF, Gallimard, 1934). Prior to its publication on 13 October 1934, two excerpts were printed: "L'Atelier de Gertrude Stein," *Gazette des Beaux-Arts* (April 1934), 6(11):[232]–43, and "Souvenirs de Gertrude Stein: Vollard et le Premier Salon d'Automne," *Nouvelle Revue Française* (September 1934), 22:[358]–72.

To Carl Van Vechten

[postmark: 18 January 1934]

27 rue de Fleurus
Paris

My dear dear Carl

What a pig what a wonderful wonderful pig, the first pig the little pig is a flower and we love it but this is a marvel, it is better than all the douaniers Rousseau's souvenirs de Mexico.[1] Mme Clermont-Tonnerre was an angel,[2] she put her hats in her trunk and the pig box into her hat box could anyone be more sweet and charming nobody but he who sent the pig. But really and truly Carl never have I seen an object more wonderful, the nose the eyes all golden all pig, it's a marvel, thanks and thanks a thousand times. You do know what I like but this is better than anything. We had a nice lunch to-day at Nathalie [Barney]'s and Mme Clermont Tonnerre told us all about the opera and all about your flat and all about everything and it was very delightful, and I am as pleased as can be and very xcited, and the pig is between the two Picassos in the corner on the Spanish meuble and I can't stop looking at him. Thanks oh more than thanks, he is a wonder. Alice adores him for his embroidery but I adore him for his shape, love and lots and lots of it

Gertrude.

1. Henri Rousseau, called "le Douanier" (1844–1910), was a French amateur, or "Sunday," painter. As a young man he enrolled in the Army and was assigned to the 52nd Infantry Regimental Band, in which he played saxophone. In later life he claimed that the inspiration for his elaborate, fanciful, and exotic pictures derived from his service in the Mexican campaign of 1861–67. There is no evidence, however, that this is true. After leaving the Army he worked for the French customs service. In 1880 he began painting, and beginning in 1886 he showed his works.

2. Note by Van Vechten, 21 January 1941: "Elisabeth Gramont, Duchesse de Clermont-Tonnerre who carried this Mexican pottery pig all painted with flowers back to Gertrude."

To Gertrude Stein
[Postcard: Briarcliff Lodge as seen from an aeroplane]

19 January [1934]   [Briarcliff Lodge
                                      Briarcliff Manor, New York]

Dear Gertrude:

I'm glad the pictures amused you I am dying to get at you and Alice.—What is the name of the colored boy who wrote to protest? I may know him. Do you know anything about Dr. Hay? This is now his sanitarium & I am on a diet there, getting very healthy for the opera for which I have seats for the opening night & the dress rehearsal. Everyone asks me will I take them. So I guess everybody wants to go. I am staying away from the entrepreneurs as I want it all to be *fresh*. I hope the Duchess [de Clermont-Tonnerre] has walked in with that nice painted pig intact. Think of travelling by Duchess-express. Quel chic!

Love to you both
Carlo,

I go back to N.Y. in two days.

To Gertrude Stein
[Postcard: Rockefeller Center, New York]

27 January [1934]   [150 West Fifty-fifth Street
                                      New York]

Dear Gertrude:

I knew the little pig was not enough. I knew the big pig would not be an anti climax—but what a lamb of a duchess to carry pigs to G. Stein!

. . . Next week I am going up to Hartford to see the opera & hear it. Henry McBride is going up too. I shall cable you & write you. It is already announced it is coming to N.Y. for a run on February 19 & I am sure it is going to be grand. "Grand" grand opera at last. You'd better come over later & hear it & have your photographs taken by the old Maestro.

164 red carnations to you!

Carlo.

To Gertrude Stein

[Postcard: View from Carl Van Vechten's window. Photograph by Carl Van Vechten]

1 February 1934

[150 West Fifty-fifth Street
New York]

Yesterday, Bennett Cerf called me up to say goodbye & he was going to Nassau, and I said, "Aren't you going to publish the book of the opera," and today he telephoned me that he had cabled you & you had consented & he asked me to write a preface &, as you know, I am not writing now but I could not refuse to do this. So we are appearing together again & it will be out in 2 weeks!!! So again I must write something you will not see until it is published. Will you please like it? Lots of love & I'll communicate with you directly after the opera is produced.[1]

Carlo

1. Cerf cabled Stein on 1 February 1934 (YCAL) offering to publish *Four Saints in Three Acts* under the Random House imprint. A second cable, also 1 February (YCAL), asked Stein whether she wanted to use the text Thomson had established for the performance or whether she preferred her original text. To establish an American copyright, the text used by Random House, and published on 20 February 1934, was slightly abridged from that used in *transition* (June 1929), 16/17: 39–72, and in Stein's *Operas and Plays.*

To Carl Van Vechten

[postmark: 5 February 1934]   27 rue de Fleurus
                                               Paris

My dear Carl,

The first night is drawing near and I am getting very xcited, I kind of feel that I am feeling and seeing it through you and that is very contenting. The big pig is so much admired we are giving a party for it next week. Bernard Faÿ fills the little one up with pennies but he says he has not had as yet in these days coinage to commence filling the big one but he xpects to commence very soon. I met the Duchesse [de Clermont-Tonnerre] at dinner the other day and I told her how you called it the Duchesse Xpress and she was delighted.[1] She is immensely looking forward to her photographs they ought to be very amusing. Everything is moving along sweetly and we love you very much oh so very much, Pépé is being taught to love you, Basket does so already, and best to you always[2]

Gertrude

1. Note by Van Vechten, 21 January 1941: "When I sent the Mexican painted pig to G. S. by the Duchesse de Clermont-Tonnerre I wrote Gertrude I was sending it by 'Duchess Express.' "

2. A dog Stein had acquired in 1932 shortly after the death of Byron, her Mexican chihuahua. Pépé was named after the painter Francis Picabia, who had given Stein the dog.

To Gertrude Stein
[Telegram]

7 February 1934   Hartford, Connecticut

OPERA BEAUTIFUL TRIUMPH[1]

CARLO

1. Van Vechten attended both the invitational preview on 7 February and the official opening the following night.

To Gertrude Stein

8 February 1934

The Heublein Hotel
Hartford, Connecticut

Dear Gertrude,

Four Saints, in our vivid theatrical parlance, is a knockout and a wow. I cabled you when I got home from the invited dress rehearsal last night (I mean you were invited to buy seats). It was a most smart performance in this beautiful little theatre. People not only wore evening clothes, they wore sables and tiaras. Henry McBride sat just in front of me.[x] I haven't seen a crowd more excited since Sacre du Printemps. The difference was that they were pleasurably excited. The Negroes are divine, like El Grecos, more Spanish, more Saints, more opera singers in their dignity and *simplicity* and extraordinary plastic line than *any* white singers could ever be. And they enunciated the text so clearly you could understand every word. Frederick Ashton's rhythmic staging was inspired and so were Florine [Stettheimer]'s costumes and sets. Imagine a crinkled sky-blue cellophane background, set in white lace borders, like a valentine against which were placed the rich and royal costumes of the saints in red velvets, etc. and the dark Spanish skins. The wedding funeral in the third act was like an El Greco. The manager who is taking it to New York expects it to be a success and I am sure it will be *something*. I'll ask Virgil [Thomson] today if he is sending you programs etc. and if he isn't I'll send you some of this kind of thing when I get back to New York. I suppose your clipping bureau will attend to the rest. But I enclose a couple of samples and the coupons from our two seats. Now, please let me write this preface.[2] I really think you should see, hear, and feel Four Saints. Maybe you and Alice can be persuaded to try it out. Dollars go farther here too now than they do there and perhaps you would escape the revolution.[3]

love always,
Carlo

[x]& was really wild with delight.
[2]I have to send it in *today!*
[3]& be photographed *officially.*

Edward Matthews as St. Ignatius in *Four Saints in Three Acts*.
PHOTOGRAPH BY CARL VAN VECHTEN (1934). COURTESY OF BRUCE KELLNER.

Four Saints in Three Acts, Act Two with Beatrice Robinson Wayne, Bruce Howard, and Edward Matthews.
PHOTOGRAPH BY WHITE STUDIOS.

Four Saints in Three Acts, Act I, Cathedral of Avila.
PHOTOGRAPH BY WHITE STUDIOS.

To Carl Van Vechten

[postmark: 10 February 1934]

[27 rue de Fleurus
Paris]

My dearest Carl,

Thanks and thanks again for the good cable, it made us most awfully happy and I knew you would but when you said triumph I knew it was alright, really alright, since then others have come but yours brought us the good news and I keep it as a book mark and to be a mascot. What theatre is doing it in New York Virgil [Thomson] in his xcitement has told us everything but that.[1] And I am so pleased by [Bennett] Cerf and the libretto and your doing the introduction for me, I like owing you a lot and I never stop and that, that is an enormous pleasure. Dear dearest Carl, you know or really you do not know how much your unfailing sympathy and thoughtfulness and understanding means to me and it means even more than that, lots of love now and always

Gertrude.

1. After the performances in Hartford, Connecticut, *Four Saints in Three Acts* opened in New York on 20 February 1934 at the Forty-fourth Street Theatre. This production was presented by Harry Moses by special arrangement with the Friends and Enemies of Modern Music.

To Gertrude Stein

18 February 1934
Sunday

150 West Fifty-fifth Street
New York

Dear Gertrude:

The opera with a preface by C. V. V. is not yet out, but this letter from me in the Times this morning will appear in the souvenir program under the title: How I listen to Four Saints in Three Acts![1] All New York is

Agog & waiting for the opening on Wednesday (completely sold out). I am told the entire USA is awake to this unique work of ART. Of course, you must have a clipping bureau & will KNOW! But what do you think of this story about St. Theresa of Avila in the Times this morning? Is this coincidence or the HAND OF GOD?[2]

LOVE!
Carlo.

1. Van Vechten's letter, "On Words and Music: A Letter About Gertrude Stein's *Four Saints*," appeared in the *New York Times*, 18 February 1934, Sec. 10, p. 2. This is the same article that appeared in the souvenir program of *Four Saints in Three Acts*, pp. 2–3. This article is not the same as the preface Van Vechten wrote for the Random House Edition of the opera.

2. An article in the *New York Times*, 18 February 1934, Sec. 1, p. 2, "A Religious Image Carved on Wood," spoke of a statue of the Virgin Mary in the Church of Saint Theresa of Avila at 187the Street and Broadway, New York. The article spoke of the numerous visitors to the church but did not mention the Stein-Thomson opera.

To Carl Van Vechten
[Rose motto]

[postmark: 18 February 1934]   27 rue de Fleurus
                                                [Paris]

My dear Carl,

Yours was the first letter and pleased I was to have it, it does sound beautiful as well as [meaningful ?] and I am very very happy. And Carl will you tell Florine Stettheimer[1] how much I appreciate all she has done and how beautiful it sounds, and how happy it has made me, and Carl please inscribe a copy of the Saints for me before they send it to me, I will like having it. The party for the pig was a great success, among others [Ambroise] Vollard[2] was here and he was quite mad about the pig, as for us we love him better and better all the time, we sometimes dispute as to whether we prefer his tail to his head, I his head and Alice his tail but we love him all. Once more Carl so often once more all my love and all my thanks

Gertrude

[299]

1. Note by Van Vechten, 22 January 1941: "Florine designed the costumes and the sets for Four Saints."

2. Ambroise Vollard (1865–1939), the French art dealer who first opened a gallery in Paris in 1893. Vollard organized the first great Cézanne exhibition in his gallery in December 1895, Stein had met Vollard in 1904, when she and her brothers Leo and Michael began buying art from him.

To Gertrude Stein
[the program of 4 Saints in 3 Acts—Forty-Fourth Street Theatre]* [1]

21 February 1934   [New York]
Wednesday

Dear Gertrude:

Here is the historic program. It was a *wonderful* night. *Your* name in electric lights over the theatre. Cecil Beaton in tears, Jo Davidson saying, "this is the best thing I have ever seen in N.Y." Cheers. Everything you can imagine. Oh, I do wish you might have seen this!

You should have the book by now, & the souvenir programs with my article. And you always have my love!

Carlo.

It is the greatest night I have ever seen in the theatre since Sacre du Printemps. And this was all *for*—not *against!*

1. Written on page 1 of the program.

To Carl Van Vechten

[postmark: 8 March 1934]   [27 rue de Fleurus
                                                              Paris]

My dearest Carl,

Our book has just come and it's lovely, and your introduction is lovely writing and says lovely things, just the lovely things I wanted to hear, it really is lovely.[1] I am very happy about it all and I want to see you more and more. The Duchess [de Clermont-Tonnerre] was here the other day and we talked about you, she is a little sad the Duchess I think in a funny kind of way she misses America, and she is very sweet. But Carl is that a true story about the school teacher, and Toasted Susie, I like it so much because it is a line I have always liked very much, and I like it all, and mostly I like you and everything you do.[2] [William Aspenwall] Bradley my agent is going over to America in about two weeks, he has a number of projects for me and he wants to talk everything over with you and I know you will because don't you do everything for me, I love you very much and all the time

Gertrude

Bradley's address will be Columbia University Club, but he will let you know when he gets there.

G.

1. Stein's *Four Saints in Three Acts* with a preface by Van Vechten was published on 20 February 1934.

2. In his introduction to *Four Saints in Three Acts*, p. 9, Van Vechten wrote:
   A friend of mine who teaches school has told me that he had been asked by one of his pupils to write some sentiment in her autograph album. He chose to comply by inscribing his name under a familiar Steinian phrase: "Toasted Susie is my ice cream!" During the recess-hour he fancied the children were shouting louder than usual and he caught a more intense note of pleasure in their voices. Venturing into the courtyard he heard the cry taken up antiphonally: Toasted Susie is my ice cream! Toasted Susie is my ice cream!

"Toasted susie is my ice-cream" is the final line of Stein's poem-portrait "Preciosilla."
   Note by Van Vechten, 22 January 1941: "Quite true."

To Gertrude Stein
[Postcard: Pigeons feeding. Photograph by Carl Van Vechten]

12 March 1934   [150 West Fifty-fifth Street
                                                  New York]

Dear Gertrude:

"If they were not pigeons on the grass alas what were they?—" with this I am sending you *registered*—photographs I made especially for you of

the electric signs over the 44th Street Theatre. I must have made the photograph on this card especially for you too! Did you see Stark Young's review
of 4 Saints in the New Republic?[1]

Love,
Carlo.

1. Stark Young, in his review, "One Moment Alit," wrote, "In my opinion the production of
this opera is the most important event of the theatre season: it is the first free, pure theatre that
I have seen so far," *The New Republic*, 7 March 1934, p. 105.

✣

To Gertrude Stein
[Postcard: Self-portrait with walking stick. Photograph by
Carl Van Vechten]

21 March [1934]   [150 West Fifty-fifth Street
                                                   New York]

Dear Gertrude:—

Yes, the story about "Toasted Susie" is quite true. Hunter Stagg told
it to me. It happened to one of his friends[1] . . Did you get the souvenir
program I sent you with my piece in it?—different from the piece in the
book. This was also published in the N. Y. Times & I sent you the clipping
. . . Bennett Cerf (one of your publishers) & Harold Guinzberg (of the
Viking Press) are presently to be in Paris for *one night* on their way to Cairo,
Palestine, Athens, Moscow, Stockholm & London . . They are hoping they
can spend this one evening with you![2]

Love to you both,
C.

1. See Stein to Van Vechten [8 March 1934], note 2.

2. Cerf wrote to Stein, 15 March 1934 (YCAL), that he was sailing on the *Ile de France* on
14 April and would be in Paris, at the Hôtel Crillon, on 20 April. Cerf invited Stein to have
dinner with him and Guinzberg that evening.

[302]

&

To Carl Van Vechten

[postmark: 21 March 1934]   [27 rue de Fleurus
                                             Paris]

My dear Carl,

The Duchess [de Clermont-Tonnerre] is doing a whole series of articles about America in the Comodia and they are very good and I'll collect them all and send them on to you, I have not seen her since but she is awfully pleased with herself and she has reason to be.[1] And Carl I have just had a fan *cable* from an unknown in New York and addressed to Gertrude Stein Paris and it got here. I am most undoubtedly proud. The Negro whom I told you about is Ulysses G. Lee and he has written another admirable letter about Melanchtha.[2] [William Aspenwall] Bradley who has just left for America has a copy of it with him, please ask him to show it to you, I am asking you to get in touch with him, his address is Columbia University Club, because he wants to consult with you about several things, also Thomas Whittemore[3] just turned up and brought the first viva voce of the opera and it was thrilling, I am so busy I don't know quite with what but I am so busy, and I love you so much my dear Carl always

Gertrude.

1. Elisabeth Gramont, the Duchesse de Clermont-Tonnerre, had arrived in the United States in November 1933. William A. Bradley had arranged a series of lectures on French culture and history that took her primarily to the Midwest and to Massachusetts. See Bradley to Stein, 11 October 1933, YCAL.

2. Lee to Stein, 11 February 1934 (YCAL). Lee wrote that he couldn't make up his mind about Stein's story "Melanctha." Lee expressed surprise at "how any young white woman could have known enough about Negroes to draw such different people as Rose, Jane, and the Herberts. To me, 'Melanctha' is one of the most inviting studies I have read. I can't help thinking that she and T. S. Stribling's Gracie Vaiden are about the truest Negro pictures in our literature." See Stein to Van Vechten [6 January 1934], note 1.

3. Thomas Whittemore (1871–1950) and Stein had known each other since their student days at Harvard-Radcliffe. Whittemore had worked for the Byzantine Institute of Boston and was responsible for the discovery of the mosaics of Hagia Sophia in Istanbul. In 1933 he became keeper of Byzantine coins at Harvard University.

❧

To Carl Van Vechten

[postmark: 22 March 1934] [27 rue de Fleurus
Paris]

My dearest Carl

Nobody would have done anything sweeter or to please me more than to give me the photos of my name in electricity and nobody but you does these darling things that give me so much joy. They came this morning and Alice and I have been looking at them all day and they look just like real pictures of New York and it is very wonderful. The pig has had a triumphant day; the Mexican pig, the Duchess [de Clermont-Tonnerre] wrote a little article about me in the Comodia and she spoke so sweetly of the pig,[1] I am sending you the whole lot of her articles they are awfully nice and the Gazette de Beaux Arts took a photo of the room to put in their magazine and the pig is there, perhaps a little indistinct xcept for those who love him but all there every bit there, oh Carl I am very happy and I feel it all with you and lots and lots of love[2]

Gertrude

1. This article became part of the chapter "Ecrivains étrangers que j'ai connus," in Elisabeth Gramont, Duchesse de Clermont-Tonnerre, *La Treizième Heure* (Paris: Bernard Grasset, 1935), tome 4 of *Mémoires*, 226–35.

2. The *Gazette de Beaux Arts*, April 1934, pp. 232–43, printed "L'Atelier de Gertrude Stein," an excerpt from Bernard Faÿ's translation of *The Autobiography of Alice B. Toklas*. The excerpt was illustrated with eight photographs of the walls of the studio at 27 rue de Fleurus as well as with photographs of individual objects in the studio.

❧

To Gertrude Stein
[Postcard] Fania Marinoff Frank Fay's Fables 1922

29 March [1934]   [150 West Fifty-fifth Street
                                        New York]

Dear Gertrude—

I am sending you today my photographs of 3 of the Saints—the costumes are still Florine Stettheimer's. but the décor in these photographs of the lilies, peonies etc. are by C. V. V. many happy easters to you & much love

Carlo.

❧

To Gertrude Stein
[Postcard: The Broadway Limited]

9 April [1934]   [150 West Fifty-fifth Street
                                        New York]

Dear Gertrude:—

Has any one told you about the table clothes designed by Marguerita Morgantima & displayed at the Industrial Arts Exhibition at Rockefeller Center & sold at Gimbels is inspired by Gertrude Stein's much heralded opera; "Four Saints in Three Acts" one is called "Instead of" and another "once in awhile."—This reminds me of the old Trilby days![1]—Four Saints with a remounted 4th act is even better at the Empire Theatre.[2]

Love,
Carlo.

1. In *Trilby*, a novel by George Du Maurier, published in 1894, Trilby O'Ferrall is an artists' model in Paris with whom various young English art students fall in love. She becomes a famous singer under the mesmeric influence of Svengali, a Hungarian musician. Trilby loses her

voice when he dies and herself languishes and soon dies. This popular novel inspired a line of Trilby dresses, black dresses with black stockings.

2. After it closed at the Forty-fourth Street Theatre, *Four Saints in Three Acts* reopened at the Empire Theatre, New York, for a limited run.

&

To Carl Van Vechten

[postmark: 11 April 1934]

[27 rue de Fleurus
Paris]

My dear dearest Carl,

The photographs are wonderful I have never seen such photographs, and the background what wonderful stuffs and paper and flowers, and the black one of Saint Ignatius, it has completely upset everybody, everybody wants to see them, I do honestly think they are the finest photographs I have ever seen.[1] [Winifred] Bryher and Kenneth Macpherson were here a few days ago, he likes you a lot and we talked about you, it is the first time I ever saw him and he seems very nice. They too were immensely taken with the photographs.[2] You know they are the first time that photographs are rich things instead of poor things, I am so happy to have them and please do some more. I am sending you the Gazette de Beaux Arts and in the photo of the room there is the pig but I love you so much Carl and I love and like everything you do.

Gertrude.

1. Saint Ignatius was sung by Edward Matthews.

2. Bryher (Annie Winifred Ellerman) (1894–1983), the English historical novelist. Because she had spent some of her happiest childhood moments on the island of Bryher, off the coast of Cornwall, England, she legally changed her name in the 1920s to Mrs. Winifred Bryher, later dropping her first name for literary purposes. She was married to the Scottish-born novelist and editor Kenneth Macpherson (1903?–1971) in 1927. From 1927 to 1933 they edited *Close Up*, a magazine devoted to films. Their marriage was dissolved in 1947.

🐿

To Gertrude Stein
[Postcard] Avery Hopwood. Painting by Florine Stettheimer

20 April [1934]   [150 West Fifty-fifth Street
                                                      New York]

Dear Gertrude—

On my way to the theatre the other evening the car passed Gimbels & I was amazed to see the sign over *all* their windows: "4 Suits in 2 *Acts!*" So yesterday I went out to photograph this new phenomenon for you and there was your lovely letter commending my photographs on the doormat. This made me very happy, because if *you* like my photographs I *know* they are good. I'll send you the new ones in a few weeks (not important as photographs, but records of the signs!)

Much love to you both
C.

🐿

To Carl Van Vechten

[postmark: 29 April 1934]   27 rue de Fleurus
                                                      [Paris]

My dearest Carl

They want to reproduce some of your photos of St Theresa and St Ignatius in two things here, the Figaro Illustré and a Catholic weekly called Sept, and I have said yes and I hope that is alright, and if they don't give them back to me although they solemnly promise they will you will send me others because I love to look at them.[1] You have no idea how much they have been admired. Everybody thinks they are the most wonderful photographs speaking photographically that they have ever seen. I hope it is alright my having given permission. We are awfully busy because we leave for Bilignin in two or three days how I wish you and Fania were going to be

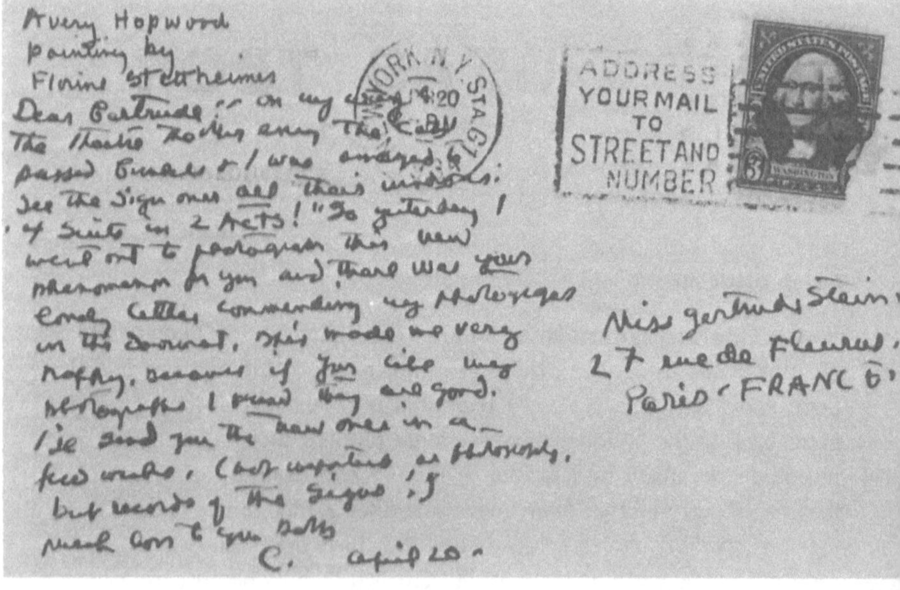

Photograph by Carl Van Vechten of Florine Stettheimer's *Portrait of Avery Hopwood.*
Photograph used as a postcard for Carl Van Vechten to Gertrude Stein, 20 April [1934].
COURTESY OF THE YALE COLLECTION OF AMERICAN LITERATURE,
BEINECKE RARE BOOK AND MANUSCRIPT LIBRARY, YALE UNIVERSITY.

there with the [word ?] and the sad streets of Aix [les-Bains]. It was nice lots and lots of love,

Gertrude.

1. I have only been able to locate an article, "Quatre saints en trois actes," by Arthur K. Griggs, in *Sept*, 9 June 1934 (YCAL). Two photographs one of St. Theresa / Beatrice Robinson-Wayne and one of St. Ignatius / Edward Matthews—illustrated the article.

❧

To Gertrude Stein

[Postcard] Carl Van Vechten painting by Florine Stettheimer. Collection of
Carl Van Vechten

[postmark: 11 May 1934]   [150 West Fifty-fifth Street
New York]

Dear Gertrude:—

I am usually awfully fussy about my photographs being reproduced & usually charge a big fat fee . . . so that any one who pays the fee wants the *exclusive* rights; but I haven't yet sold any of the Saints, & besides pretty nearly anything you would want to do is all right. So please send me copies of the magazines in which they appear and if you don't get your pictures back, let me know!—Besides, when you get this I shall be in London! and with me are some even more fabulous photographs of Saints for Saint Gertrude, but they are too big to mail. So you must tell me where I can leave them for you in Paris. I do hope to see you, but Belley is almost impossible because I will be in Europe such a short time. Guaranty Trust—20 Pall Mall, London, will reach me till about the 24 May & then Morgan Paris,

LOVE
C.

[309]

❧

To Gertrude Stein
[Postcard: Garret Hostel Lane Bridge, Cambridge, England]

[postmark: 25 May 1934]   [London]

Dear Gertrude:

Fania isn't here—she is in Hollywood, but there is a man with me, and I think we could arrange to come down for a day—I think you & Alice should be photographed by the MAESTRO.[1] Flying to Rome on Tuesday but will be in Paris a week or so later.—Write me c/o Morgan & Co. 14 Place Vendome Paris & tell me if we could come some time between June 14 & 22.

Love,
Carlo.

1. Van Vechten made the trip with Mark Lutz (1901–1968). Lutz was born in Richmond, Virginia, and it was there that he met many of the people associated with *The Reviewer*. Hunter Stagg arranged for Lutz to meet Van Vechten in New York in July 1931. The friendship between Lutz and Van Vechten ripened immediately, and Lutz became the model for some of Van Vechten's earliest photographic experiments. Their friendship lasted until Van Vechten's death. In accordance with Lutz's wishes the correspondence they exchanged during that period, estimated at nearly ten thousand letters, was destroyed. Lutz gave his collection of Van Vechten's photographs to the Philadelphia Museum of Art. See Bruce Kellner, *Friends and Mentors: Richmond's Carl Van Vechten and Mark Lutz; An Address given by Bruce Kellner on the Occasion of the Spring Meeting of the Friends of the Boatwright Memorial Library at Windsor, May 29, 1979* (n. p.: privately printed, 1979).

❧

To Carl Van Vechten

[postmark: 27 May 1934][1]   Bilignin par Belley
                                                    Ain

My dearest Carl,

It is nice that we are going to meet I would have been quite brokenhearted if we had not, and we do want to be photographed by the *maestro*.

You can come any time and between the 14 and 22 suits perfectly and we hope the roses and the nightingales will be doing as well as they ever can in your honor. And as I told you we can put you up for as long as you will stay you and the man and I imagine you can fly very near to us and we will meet you and call for you and it will be wonderful seeing you come out of flying and do let us know when as soon as you know and lots of love and did you hear from [Arthur] Griggs and is it alright and again lots of love[2]

Gertrude.

1. This letter was addressed to Van Vechten in Paris and was forwarded to his bank in Rome.

2. Arthur K. Griggs (1891–1934) was an American writer and critic who lived for many years in Paris. He offered to help Stein in trying to promote the idea of mounting *Four Saints in Three Acts* in Paris. See Griggs to Van Vechten, 23 May [1934], YCAL, and Stein to Van Vechten [29 April 1934], note 1.

To Carl Van Vechten

[postmark: 2 June 1934]   Bilignin par Belley
                                                              Ain

My dear dearest Carl

It would be most sad and disappointing if you and Fania were over here and we were not seeing you.[1] Could you not come. We can put you up now, we have a bath-room and you would be not too uncomfortable and I have a four seated respectable 8V Ford so that we could come and call for you at the train and it is not such a long trip, you leave Paris at eight in the morning and you get here at four and we would so love to see you, there is so much to tell and hear and please do. And about the reproductions of the photos. I imagine nothing definite has been done yet. It is Arthur Griggs who had the idea and he was thinking of making propaganda for the possible future of the opera in Paris and for the translation of the autobiography which is to be out on Oct 15 chez Gallimard, and his idea was to have the photos reproduced in as many places in Paris as possible, Paris always seems to do that, each paper reproduces for its audience as most people do not seem to read more than one and as for paying I am afraid in Paris they don't pay, but at any rate I am writing to him to write to you and here is his address Arthur Griggs 90 rue d'Assas, and he has a telephone, it is in the telephone book. I did so love the photos and everybody else did so love them that I wanted everybody to see them, and I did think it would help having the opera in Paris and I am afraid that is all I did think about. I would so like to talk so many things over with you. About lecturing in America this fall about that because I don't quite know what I want or what I ought or what I will do and anything you say would so help me but mostly we want you for ourselves alone and if we could have you we would be delighted but anyway always and lots of love to you and Fania

Always
Gertrude.

And I do so much want to see the new photos and I am still hoping you will bring them yourselves but they can be sent by Chemin de fer, and they get here alright, and once more it is nice to be on the same side of the water but it will be nicer being together.

1. Stein had apparently forgotten Van Vechten's postcard of [25 May 1934] in which he told her that Marinoff was in Hollywood, California, and would not be traveling with him.

To Carl Van Vechten

[postmark: 8 June 1934]   Bilignin par Belley
                                                           Ain

My dearest Carl,

Where are you, you have not flown too far away, anyway we are waiting for you, and we do so want to see you, where are you with all love

Gertrude

❧

To Gertrude Stein

8 June 1934   [Hotel] Excelsior
                                               Rome

Dear Gertrude:

Think of it! I'll be seeing you both soon. We are leaving here for Amalfi tomorrow & returning Monday (June 11) in time to take the sleeper (9.50 P.M. for Turin, at 8.30 A.M. we embark on a day train from Turin & arrive at Chambéry at 12.57 P.M. Tuesday June 12. So please will you meet us at this train. We wanted to fly but there seems to be no direct way of getting there—without going first to Paris. So, the train, *now*. I suggest that we have lunch somewhere in Chambéry. There must be a suitable place & visit the house where John Paul Dunbar & Madame Walker carried on! and then proceed in grand style to Bilignin![1] In case you are making plans, we shall stay about a day! and so you won't be disappointed I must tell you that the grand photographs of 4 Saints are in *London* in a trunk which is to meet me in Paris as I thought I should be coming that way to you. You shall receive them later. There doesn't seem to be any way of finding out if all this is convenient for you & it is even two days ahead of schedule. But if I step off the train & you are not there I shall know it is impossible & proceed to Paris! But I think you will be there.

Love!!
Carlo.

Till Tuesday at 12.57

1. Presumably Van Vechten is referring to A'Lelia Walker (1885–1931). A'Lelia Walker was born the daughter of a poor washerwoman, Sarah Breedlove (Madame C. J.) Walker (1867–1919), who perfected a process for the straightening of kinky hair and developed various beauty preparations. With the money she received from her mother, A'Lelia became one of the most picturesque figures of the Harlem Renaissance. She lived in a mansion in Irvington-on-Hudson and in a town house in New York where she entertained a steady stream of black artists, writers, and musicians. See Kellner, *"Keep A-Inchin' Along,"* for Van Vechten's "A'Lelia Walker," pp. 152–54.

[313]

To Carl Van Vechten

[postmark: 14 June 1934]   [Bilignin par Belley
                                                           Ain]

My dear Carl

When Trac did up the little package this morning he forgot to enclose this—which I so carefully gave him.[1] And since then he hasn't remembered that Gertrude doesn't eat Queen Anne cherries nor that the dessert this evening needs candied cherries—otherwise we're all quiet but missing you. You will come back every year won't you. A good crossing and best of luck—

Always
Alice

Remembrances to Mark Lutz
[Enclosed with letter]
For Carl, with all the love of Bilignin and we enjoyed every minute of the visit.
Don't tell any one because perhaps they didn't belong to us.

[Gertrude Stein]

1. Note by Van Vechten, 22 January 1941: "Trac, the Indo-Chinese cook. In the package were two swan tie backs, from the villa at Bilignin. At present these hold back the blue satin curtains in the Victorian room at 101 Central Park West."

Gertrude Stein with her dogs Pepe and Basket I
on the terrace at Bilignin, 13 June 1934.
PHOTOGRAPH BY CARL VAN VECHTEN. PRIVATE COLLECTION.

❧

To Gertrude Stein

[14 June 1934]
Thursday

Le Bristol
Hotel et Restaurant
112 Faubourg St. Honoré
Paris (VIII)

Dear Gertrude!!

It was too divine—that all too short 24 hours chez vous—and Marco[1] has it down (he wants me to thank you & Alice) as among the Alpine moments of his life!. The last picture on the platform of Le Grande Veriule was one of the best and pleasantest to recall.[2] But it was all *SWELL!*

Bernard Faÿ did *not* telephone this morning.
Paris is *hot* and very expensive.
Much love to you both!

Carlo!

The photographs in my trunk have arrived!

1. Mark Lutz.
2. Virieu le Grand, the train station nearest to Belley.

❧

To Alice Toklas

15 June [1934]

[Hôtel Bristol] Paris

Dear Alice:

Trac not only forgot the message, he forgot the package! We have searched everything carefully & il n'y en a pas! *Please* find it & send it up before sailing! What could he have done with it? Bernard Faÿ telephoned this morning & I am going there tomorrow. I am taking him the Grand photographs!—What a nice letter! I was as happy about the visit as happy can be!

love to you both
Carlo

To Gertrude Stein

[16 June 1934]

Le Bristol
Hotel et Restaurant
112 Faubourg St. Honoré
Paris (VIII)

Dear Gertrude!!

The beautiful tie-backs arrived only this afternoon—Alice addressed them to the "Place Vendôme" but they found me anyway. They made me very happy. I saw Bernard Faÿ this morning & he and I seem to be agreed on your career. He also was of the opinion that the Hotel Algonquin could be the place for you. Write to the manager Frank Case, & see what he can do for you when you are ready to come & be sure to mention my name! I gave Faÿ *ten* big pictures to take to you: 9 of 4 Saints and 1 of Saint Carlo. . Also I visited the Boul[evard]. Rasp[ail]. today & took a picture of the NUN,[1] and Rue de Fleurus & took a picture of 27! So you see this has been a Stein Day.

Love to you both.

Carlo!

1. Van Vechten visited a shop at 131 Boulevard Raspail, Paris. Stein had told him that the photographs of nuns in the shop window had had a direct influence on the writing of *Four Saints in Three Acts*.

❧

To Carl Van Vechten
[Postcard: Photograph of Stein's house at Bilignin]

[postmark: 26 June 1934]   [Bilignin par Belley
                                                            Ain]

My dear Carl,

I wish you could see the easter lilies all in bloom and I wish you were here to take our pictures in front of them, and that at present seems to be all I do wish. Are you liking Paris are you photographing Paris but you did like us best. Trac went to the circus last night and is more prayerful than ever, well anyway one way or another we will see each other soon, we all love you best to Marc [i.e., Mark Lutz]

Gtrde.

❧

To Carl Van Vechten

[postmark: 2 July 1934]   Bilignin par Belley
                                                            Ain

My dearest Carl,

It is nice that you liked Europe this time because you will be coming back early and often and that will be nice. Europe liked you a lot and it likes it that you liked it, we are quite breathlessly awaiting our photos. I do wish our band of lilies had been out for you to do with us, but you and they will be here again. Picabia has just been with us and we were talking of the old times of Mabel [Dodge] and you all in New York when he was there, do you remember him, you will have to photograph him too some day for the portraits.[1] I have asked [William Aspenwall] Bradley to leave the Four in America and the Birthday book ms, with you, and we are not writing to [Bennett] Cerf or anything until you tell us to. There is a young fellow named

[318]

Jones whom Cerf knows who has some ideas about the Birthday book he may even at present have the ms.[2] I do not know whether Bradley left it with him, but as I say Cerf knows him. I have written three of the lectures already and I think you will like them I think if I may say so that they are rather sweet, well anyway, you are, and we are, and we love each other very much. Kind remembrances to Mark [Lutz], and best to Fania

and always
Gertrude.

1. Picabia had come to New York to visit the Armory Show of February 1913. At that time he met Dodge and Van Vechten. In a note of 22 January 1941, Van Vechten wrote, "Picabia, the Cuban abstract painter." Van Vechten is in error. Picabia was born and died in Paris; his father was Cuban and his mother was French.

2. For Richard Jones, see Stein to Van Vechten [16 August 1934].

To Gertrude Stein

3 July 1934

150 West Fifty-fifth Street
[New York]

Dear Gertrude,

[William Aspenwall] Bradley was here yesterday (he sails today) and he seemed to think it essential for you to have a lecture bureau, if you want to make enough money to pay expenses in a short time. He says everything else will be sprawling and unsatisfactory. From his point of view, he is completely right, and from yours enough so, so that I think you should listen to him carefully. My objection to lecture bureaux is that they usually exploit their clients frightfully, that they send them out to odd spots at odd times, and generally behave without discretion or tact. But Bradley says he has discovered an angel-lamb lecture bureau who promises only to send you to Colleges, and to arrange dates so that they will have some sequence and rapidity, to get you quite a lot of money, in other words to work for *you*, rather than have you work for *him*. Well, Bradley will tell you all about it, but I think you had better listen to him sympathetically unless you have objections I haven't heard of.[1] Perhaps, however, by the time you arrive, Bernard Faÿ's friend may have lined up all the dates you want.[2]

Bradley also left a couple of your manuscripts with me which I am holding for your instructions. He says [Bennett] Cerf has not sailed yet and will see you again abroad: so you may talk to him before I do.

Well, whatever happens and however it is done, Four Saints must go marching on, you must continue to be published, and you must visit America to talk to her citizens the way you do!

I found Fania here when I arrived, *very hot*. It is, in fact much too hot to develop or print pictures, but the pictures will all be coming along later and swell they will be too. I am sure we will all love them.

In any case you and Alice are often in my thoughts and always in my heart and you are woojums of the first order.

love,
Carlo!!

Bradley says some one has dramatized Melanctha!

F. M. is mad about the tiebacks and so is Carlo.

I didn't see the Duchess [de Clermont-Tonnerre] or Natalie [Barney] in Paris. Do ask the Duchess if she got a Rivera book I sent her.[3] Max Ewing drowned himself two weeks ago.[4]

I photographed Max Jacob.[5]

1. Bradley and Van Vechten discussed the Leigh Lecture Bureau.

2. Marvin Chauncey Ross (d. 1977), an American art historian. Stein had met Ross through Bernard Faÿ in Paris. Ross, who was then working for the Brooklyn Museum, agreed to help arrange Stein's lecture tour. (See Ross to Stein, 8 July 1934, YCAL.)

3. Diego Rivera, *Portrait of America*, with an explanatory text by Bertram D. Wolfe (New York: Covicci, Friede, 1934). The book reproduces various murals made by Rivera in the United States.

4. Max Ewing (1903–1934) was a writer, composer, and artist born in Pioneer, Ohio. In 1923, while an undergraduate at the University of Michigan, he wrote a front-page piece about Van Vechten's novel *Peter Whiffle* for the campus newspaper ("Carl Van Vechten," *Michigan Daily, Sunday Magazine* (Ann Arbor), 14 January 1923. The piece was reprinted in the *Detroit Free Press*, Literary Section, 4 February 1923. Van Vechten, who saw the article, was delighted with it and began corresponding with Ewing.

Ewing arrived in New York in September 1923 with the intention of studying music. His "Extraordinary Portraits," a series of collages, included portraits of Stein, Van Vechten, and Marinoff. "The Recitative and Air for Piano and Tenor," from Ewing's oratorio based on

Stein's poem "Sacred Emily," was sung by William S. Rainey as part of *An Intimate Revue* presented at the Cherry Lane Theatre, New York, in November 1925. Ewing met Stein in April 1926 when he visited Paris. Through Van Vechten's efforts the papers of Max Ewing were deposited in YCAL.

5. Van Vechten had photographed Max Jacob (1876–1944), the French writer, on 21 June 1934.

To Carl Van Vechten

[postmark: 13 July 1934]   Bilignin par Belley
                                                                Ain

My dearest Carl,

Yes I know [William Aspenwall] Bradley['s] angel lamb lecturing bureau, I have been fighting him on that subject for a year and a half, I met the representative then and he struck me as being the kind of angel lamb who is red riding hood's grandmother after she changed, and I have had no reason since to have any other impression, no if I go over and it looks as if I will go over as a private person who will give some lectures just as we decided was right.[1] The wife of one of the regents of Chicago University and the head of the Arts Club there has just been here and she does not seem to think there is any doubt that half of our xpences of the whole trip will get payed by Chicago,[2] I guess New York and New England will do the other half, anyway that is I think the right way for me to act and I know you think so too. Part of the plan is that we are to be in Chicago for the premiere of the opera there, it would be wonderful if you were to be there too, it is to be sometime in the middle of November. I go on writing my lectures, I have four written now and I do think they are pretty good. Poor Max Ewing, with his little mouth and pretty ways, remember you sent me those early little poems of his, I don't know why but he and Donald Evans always come together in my mind, I suppose on account of their early poetry, which was in both cases such very good early poetry. Oh dear.[3] Thanks for taking care of the ms. What are they, the Birthday book and Four in America. I do not imagine there is any liklihood of my seeing [Bennett] Cerf down here, and anyway it is you that have the right ideas and I am waiting for them and they come, we have lost our one china boy and now we have two, they replace each other so sweetly that we have no responsibility and hardly have to learn their names,[4] but anyhow I wish you were here and Fania too

Always
Gertrude.

1. Note by Van Vechten, 22 January 1941:

Bradley, when I saw him was determined that G. S. should appear in America under the auspices of a regular lecture bureau. I was opposed to this idea—and so was G. S. but I thought it fair to put the pros & cons to her again. The ensuing tour had perhaps the most haphazard management & arrangement of any lecture [tour] ever undertaken, but it was a complete success & G. S. left America for France several thousand dollars the richer.

2. Elizabeth Fuller Goodspeed (later Chapman) (1893–1980) was known to her friends as Bobsy (or Bobsie). Mrs. Goodspeed was president from 1931 to 1941 of the Arts Club of Chicago, the innovative group that mounted many exhibitions of contemporary artists. Through her activities at the Arts Club, she became close friends with artists, writers, and composers. She was responsible for organizing the exhibition of modern sculpture and drawing for the Century of Progress exhibition at the 1933 Chicago World's Fair. Her second husband was Gilbert W. Chapman.

3. Ewing's *Sonnets from the Paranomasian* (New York: Blue Faun Bookshop, 1924). The title page announced that it was "Conceived with a bow to Mrs. Browning and Salaams to Donald Evans." Ewing had probably read, through Van Vechten's encouragement, Donald Evans' *Sonnets from the Patagonian: The Street of Little Hotels* (New York: Claire Marie, 1912).

4. The succession of Indo-Chinese cooks is recounted by Toklas in *The Alice B. Toklas Cook Book* (New York: Harper & Bros., 1954), pp. 186–93.

To Gertrude Stein
[Postcard: Blake—Satan Smiting Job]

17 July 1934   [150 West Fifty-fifth Street
                                                 New York]

Dear St Gertrude:

I thought this would please you. You did see that frontispiece of Vanity Fair in which Picasso & I hovered in your background, didn't you?[1] The pictures, I think, are going to be grand! However they are not printed yet—

only developed & even not all developed. But I think they'll get printed &
sent to you before August is over. . Did you get the pictures—including the
one of moi même—from Bernard Faÿ? I hope so. . People are complaining
that Marvin Ross isn't answering letters promptly, but maybe he isn't even
working for you yet.

176 sticks of angelique to you both!

Carlo

1. Van Vechten enclosed a caricature of Stein, *The Apotheosis of Miss Stein*, 1934, by William
Cotton, from *Vanity Fair*, May 1934, p. 20.

To Carl Van Vechten

[postmark: 21 July 1934]   Bilignin par Belley
                                                           Ain

My dear Carl,

Well I guess it's alright, Marvin Ross arrangement holds and the lectures go on.[1] I'm writing the fifth now, and hoping I can go on not thinking
about what comes next. On the other hand [William Aspenwall] Bradley
and I have agreed to part,[2] he got a little too insistent on the commercial
side, of course it's nice earning money but there are some things that a girl
can't do, so he is not acting as my agent any more, which I imagine from
the standpoint of [Bennett] Cerf is all the better, it will be nicer if we do our
business together. Sometime when you have time will you tell me if you
like the birthday book, I mean will you read it and the Four in America.
Golly it has been hot, poor little Pepe is very sad, and also Francis Rose is
going to have a big show in Chicago, I am lending 13 of mine, he is awfully
happy about it,[3] otherwise there is no news, but America and Carl in it has
never been so near, but the Carl in it is the comfort,

Always
Gertrude.

[323]

1. Note by Van Vechten, 22 January 1941:

   Marvin Ross was a young American friend of Bernard Faÿ's who was supposed to arrange the lecture tour. He succeeded in balling everything up *completely* by neglecting to answer queries from colleges etc. When G. S. and Alice arrived in this country they found affairs in such a tangle that Alice took over—and, altho[ugh] she had never done anything like this before and made many many serious mistakes; somehow it worked anyway. Once she lost her address book with all her dates for lectures.

   Marvin Ross subsequently became curator for some department of the Walters Art Gallery in Baltimore, a post for which, I hope, he had more aptitude.

2. Note by Van Vechten, 22 January 1941: "Bradley & Gertrude quarrelled irrevocably at this time." Stein and Bradley were eventually reconciled, and after Bradley's death his wife, Jenny, acted as literary agent for Stein. She continued to advise Toklas about Stein's literary affairs after Stein's death.

3. An exhibition of paintings by Sir Francis Rose was held at the Arts Club of Chicago, 9 to 30 November 1934. Fourteen paintings, including a portrait of Alice B. Toklas (now YCAL) and a portrait of Stein, were lent by Stein. The catalogue contained a foreword by Stein.

To Gertrude Stein

27 July 1934   150 West Fifty-fifth Street
                                                New York City

Dear Gertrude,

I think you are quite right in this matter and I have always thought you were right. Myself, I do not go for lecture bureaux. BUT, you told me to see [William Aspenwall] Bradley and as he has had experience in such matters and is your agent and seemed perturbed and anxious for you to have a Lecture Bureau, I considered it only fair to present to you his side of the case. I did not want, in any event, you to believe I was arguing against him, had you any disposition to take his advice. . . I'm glad you are coming over as a private citizen! I wrote you, I think, that Marvin Ross didn't answer letters. It seems Mark [Lutz], who is trying to arrange something at the University of Virginia, wrote him and didn't get a reply immediately. But he did get one later and Ross explained that he had been waiting until he heard that he *was* definitely your accredited agent.[1] So that is all right. . And I've seen [Bennett] Cerf and we had a talk and I told him about your lectures and your Confessions and what not, and he is writing you and I think everything should be all right. His idea is to publish the lectures this fall. He also says he will handle the Plain Edition for you without commission. In other words any copies he sells you will get the price on. I told him why I was against remaindering them, and he agreed with me. Well, I never know how any one is going to act *tomorrow*, but he acted all right *yesterday* and I hope what he writes to you will be all right. And if it isn't you just tell Uncle Carlo and he will see what he can do. In any case, you can talk (at length) to Cerf (or whomever) when you visit our shores this fall.

I hope [Bernard] Faÿ has brought you the pictures by now. I think the pictures I took this summer are going to be KNOCKOUTS, but they are not printed yet—only developed. To think, there is no longer a Trac! Anyway I took his picture.

Fania is going into a play, and I suppose there is going to be a new war.[2] Will you drive a Ford in this one? Maybe I'd like to come too.

> *Much love to you both!*
> *Carlo*

Edith still show[s] a marked preference for the "Carlo—Rose is a Rose" plates.[3]

1. Ross answered Lutz on 18 July 1934 (YCAL). Ross explained that he had not answered Lutz's letter because he was waiting for further information from Stein. Ross also emphasized that Stein preferred direct contact with the students and so Lutz's idea of lecturing before student organizations sounded very promising.

2. Marinoff played the role of Madame Crevelli in Elmer Rice's play *Judgment Day*. The play opened at the Belasco Theatre, New York, on 12 September 1934 and ran for ninety-three performances.

3. Edith Ramsey was the Van Vechtens' cook.

To Carl Van Vechten

28 July 1934   Bilignin par Belley
                                                    Ain

My dear Carl,

Bernard [Faÿ] has not come yet he is not coming until next week and then we will have the photos, and we are very xcited about that and also about the new ones, we can't wait to have them, it's all right now I guess about [Marvin] Ross, he was confused by the confusion and beside had gotten a job in Baltimore,[1] but now it is all straightened out and I guess everything will go well.[2] I am slowly but steadily getting pleased about getting over there and so is Alice, we begin to talk about it quite now as if we were going and even beginning to feel comfortable about it. When it is all really decided we will write to the Algonquin, and we will write to you all the time which is very necessary.[3] Yes I liked the Vanity Fair frontispiece, I thought it was very good, and I like everything just now but mostly we all love you, but then that is an established and happy habit,

> *Lots of love*
> *Gertrude.*

1. Ross had signed a contract in June 1934 to begin work as a curator for the Walters Art Gallery in Baltimore, in September 1934 (see Ross to Stein, 8 July 1934, YCAL).

2. Note by Van Vechten, 22 January 1941: "It didn't."

3. Note by Van Vechten, 22 January 1941: "I suggested to them that they go to this hotel and they did and loved it."

To Carl Van Vechten

3 August 1934   Bilignin par Belley
                                             Ain

My dearest Carl,

Bernard Faÿ has just come and brought the photos and they are standing all about in Bilignin, there was one of St Ignatius that we had not had the one of the back of his head and I don't know which I think is the finest. There is one of St Theresa that is much more stunning this size than the other size although when we got the other size we thought it was as fine as could be. I am terribly xcited about all the photos and Trac is very likely coming back so there would be one for him, he dreamed about it. Bernard says you took some xtraordinary ones of Max Jacob, although he did not entirely do what you wanted him to do. Anyway we are just waiting for them.

I had a letter from [Bennett] Cerf saying just what you said he would say,[1] but I don't think the lectures should be printed until they have all been delivered, which would be in the early spring, and I do think that a book should be out when I get there, and one of the lectures I have just written is called Portraits and Repetition and I think it will be one of the most popular so I still think that he ought to do about 168 page volume of all my best portraits, and Harcourt would probably give me permission to reprint the second portrait of you and the first from Geography and Plays and Sherwood [Anderson], and Mabel [Dodge]'s which has never been printed in a book, and Matisse and Picasso likewise never printed in books, and this volume could be announced by [Marvin] Ross along with the lectures, and it seems to me a very good idea, then the lectures could be done in the early spring, what do you think, there is a good one portrait of Muriel Draper, of Hemingway and then there would be for the 168 pages about 50 portraits, Jean Cocteau, Fay, Virgil [Thomson] etc. Mme Clermont-Tonnerre which is very good and Max Jacob, and then the Gallery Lafayette that was printed in Rogue, I think you could do it very well, tell me what you think, I will just mention it in the letter I write to Cerf leaving you to really bring it about if that is what you think should be done.[2] Everything is progressing nicely, Pepe and Basket are happy, and life is peaceful, and we look at your photo and it has just your eyes, and it is very nice and we love you and we would love it if it really turned into you one day, but it is very lovely in itself.

 Lots and lots of love

Always
Gertrude.

1. Cerf to Stein, 26 July 1934 (YCAL), confirms the information in Van Vechten to Stein, 27 July 1934.

2. Stein to Cerf [postmark: 5 August 1934, Columbia-Random House], proposes the idea of a book of portraits. Cerf cabled Stein on 22 August 1934 (YCAL) accepting the idea and asked for the manuscript by 25 September. Stein cabled her acceptance on 24 August 1934 (Columbia-Random House).

𝕬

To Gertrude Stein

5 August 1934   150 West Fifty-fifth Street
Sunday night   [New York]

Dear Gertrude,

[William Aspenwall] Bradley left me a package, saying, here are some books by Gertrude which she asked me to leave with you, but I didn't open them until you told me to. I was waiting for instructions! There is *no* birthday book. One is called A Novel, toutsimple, just like that.[1] I am reading in that and have found some pretty delicious bits. But the other, Four in America, I think must be one of your major works. I've just gone through it with the greatest interest and delight and will go through it again soon. My first preference is for the James chapter, with its discussion of subjective and objective writing, but there are parts of the Grant chapter I like equally well. There is *no* birthday book.

So you have left Bradley!

Has [Bennett] Cerf written you? One never knows. He agreed to send me a copy of the letter he was sending you. This he has not done: so I don't know and, of course, I can't ask *him*. So you tell me, please . . In the meantime, Harcourt Brace have announced they are printing your lectures! . .[2]

Have you got those BIG photographs from [Bernard] Faÿ yet. You have not mentioned them or him and yet he was to go to you early in July.

The photographs of Max Jacob are magnifique!

I embrace you both and Fania sends love,

Carlo

(I have just heard that if you eat an oyster on August 5 you get your wish, whatever it is. It seems a good way to commit suicide—very painful, too!)

1. Probably a reference to Stein's A *Novel of Thank You.*

2. To mark Stein's arrival in America, Harcourt Brace and Company published the condensed version of Stein's *The Making of Americans* and Random House published her *Portraits and Prayers.* It was not until March 1935 that Random House published Stein's *Lectures In America.*

[328]

To Carl Van Vechten

[postmark: 16 August 1934]   Bilignin par Belley
                                              Ain

My dearest Carl,

   I cannot tell you how happy you have made me by liking the Four in America. I do think it is one of my major works,[1] and now I want to tell you all about it. That is xtraordinary that [Alfred] Harcourt has announced my lectures because I refused his contract, and split with [William Aspenwall] Bradley about all that. You see I insist that I will not give my lectures to anybody who will not print the Four in America and then later a portrait book and I broke with Bradley and I refused Harcourt on that issue and I do think I am right. Now [Bennett] Cerf is trying it on but I think if I hold out and with your aid that I will find somebody who will be enthusiastic about doing the three. I think the Four in America should be done this fall then the lectures and then the portraits at proper intervals. Harcourt said he would do lectures and another biography and I said another biography did not interest me and that I would not give him the lectures without the two other things and returned him the contracts unsigned, do find out and tell me what they are up to and where did Harcourt announce the lectures. My dearest Carl you do so much for me that I just hoggishly go on asking for more but then I always did like pigs, and you have so encouraged me in that. The Birthday book is in the hands of one Richard Jones who was much interested in doing designs for it, his address is 115 E. 26 Street, if you could see him it would be nice for me, he has interested Remington of the John Day publishing Co in it, is that alright, anyway I am so happy that you like the Four In America.[2] I kind of felt I had done something in that, show it to anyone you want in any way you want, you know I and mine are all yours. I hope you like the envelope all this goes in it was brought us by the butcher boy,[3] but yours and the stamp which was not brought by the butcher boy is very lovely, the photos are not alone our joy but the joy of the whole neighborhood, Mme Recamier's descendants are all delighted with them and well they may be, we are breathlessly awaiting ours,

> *Lots of love*
> *Always*
> *Gertrude.*

1. Stein's *Four In America* was posthumously published by the Yale University Press in 1947.

2. Jones had the idea to print Stein's "A Birthday Book" with decorations for each letter and the text to be in Stein's hand. See Jones to Stein, 8 April and 16 April 1934, YCAL. Nothing came of this project.

3. The envelope is light green in color and is not unique.

To Gertrude Stein
[Postcard: Lord Byron—Drawing by C. H. Harlow]

19 August [1934]   [150 West Fifty-fifth Street
                                               New York]

Dear Gertrude:—

Your pictures are divine & so are Alice's & so are Pepe's and Basket's. I am printing them now. If I ask you to wait a little longer for them you will understand why later . . . . I think you are right about the lectures. You spoke about the Portraits in Bilignin—but in talking to [Bennett] Cerf I forgot this. However, I think it is an excellent idea & if he calls me I will tell him so. I cannot call him—you can see that—without its appearing I am trying to manipulate him.

Love offers & bowls of emeralds to both of you!

Carlo.

To Carl Van Vechten
[Cablegram]

24 August 1934   Belley

SO HAPPY MAY I DEDICATE PORTRAIT BOOK TO YOU LOVE[1]

GERTRUDE.

1. See Stein to Van Vechten, 3 August 1934, note 2.

To Gertrude Stein
[Telegram]

[postmark: 25 August 1934]   New York

Deeply honored by dedication am very happy too love

Carlo

To Gertrude Stein

25 August 1934   150 West Fifty-fifth Street
                                                     [New York]

Dear Gertrude:

Your cablegram made me very happy, happy that you and [Bennett] Cerf have got together and especially happy that the Portraits are to be dedicated to ME! I cabled you at once. By the way if you have occasion to cable me again: Carlvecht New York is the cable address. If I have not given you this it is perhaps because you have never cabled before! So this is quite an historical occasion. . . And this morning your letter is here. I think now that it is arranged (this is what you suggested in your letter to him) that Cerf do the Portraits this fall and the Lectures in the Spring, it would be an error in technique to get anything else out at present and I think by far the better book coincident with your arrival would be the Portraits, which you have already agreed upon. I also think it would be a breach in publishing etiquet to take the Four in America anywhere else. When you arrive you can talk this over with Cerf and come to some agreement about it. At any rate it would be *crazy* to plan to publish anything else this year and now that things are rolling along so nicely I hope you will leave all future plans in abeyance till you come to New York and sit in Bennett's pleasant office and converse with him viva voce. In the meantime, please hurry up with the portraits, because I can't wait till I see this with my name all across the dedication page!

[331]

About Harcourt, I don't know them at all and so can't find out much there. I seem to have lost the clipping in which it was announced they would do the lectures.[x] It appeared so far as I know in only one paper and so may not have been officially inspired. Maybe somebody just guessed they would because they have been publishing you lately.

It will be at least two weeks before I can send the pictures. They are being prepared for their long journey very carefully. When you see them, you will understand and forgive the delay.

You are a woojums and Alice is a woojums and I embrace you both!

Carlo!!

[x]I cut it out to send to you & it may turn up yet.

⁂

To Carl Van Vechten

[postmark: 25 August 1934]   Bilignin par Belley
                                                             Ain

My dearest Carl,

You are a wiz and you have made me as happy as happy can be, and do you like this as a dedication.

To Carl
Who knows what a portrait is
because he makes and is them.

and do you like Portraits and Prayers as a title that was the original title I had for the book and I think it is a pretty good one, I am so pleased and we are so busy, that I have no time to worry about how it will be to lecture.[1] I finished writing them yesterday, I am awfully anxious to have you see them, most likely I will send over a copy to [Marvin] Ross who is to decide which is to be given to which and he will have strict orders to show them to nobody but you, but you I do want to see them, Alice and I are having our clothes made for this event and anyway it is getting very near, but happily it is going to be near you, and so we will be all safe, I am so pleased and we are waiting for the photos and everything and lots of love and to Fania,

Always
Gertrude

[332]

1. The title "Portraits and Prayers" appears very early in Stein's copy books where she made lists of works to include in volumes of her work. See Stein to Van Vechten [6 July 1923], note 2.

***

To Gertrude Stein

27 August 1934   150 West Fifty-fifth Street
[New York]

Dear Gertrude,

The first character of the first Revue of the year is named Gertrude Stein and they started right off with a scene about you! This may be a good omen.[1] The photographs are marching along.

> *much love,*
> *Carlo!!!*

1. In *Keep Moving*, a revue featuring Tom Howard and directed by John Murray Anderson, there was a scene, "Murder in a Fishbowl," that burlesqued Stein's *Four Saints in Three Acts*. *Keep Moving* opened at the Forest Theatre, New York, on 23 August 1934.

***

To Gertrude Stein
[Postcard] Fania Marinoff [and] Henry Hull in the Bride the Sun Shines
On 1932

27 August [1934]   [150 West Fifty-fifth Street
New York]

Dear Gertrude:

Will you tell the conscripts of Belley to get their pictures from
Antoine Berthat—Boucherie Lambert—Belley or
Joseph Décroze, Biens par Belley—

I sent off two packages registered today.
You will get yours in due course.[1]

Love
Carlo

1. Photographs Van Vechten had made in Belley. See Stein to Van Vechten [1 October 1934], note 2.

❧

To Carl Van Vechten

[postmark: 1 September 1934]   Bilignin par Belley
                                                Ain

My dear Carl,

The portrait book is all in shape and Alice is busy typing it and I am busy correcting it, and I think and I am happy about it that it is going to be worthy of the dedicatee, which is you, I hoped you liked the dedication, it rather pleased me but then we do please each other Carl and nothing can be nicer than that. My heart is very full of happiness. [Bennett] Cerf has done everything he has done very charmingly and I am most awfully grateful to be in his hands. I entirely agree with you that the Four in America should not come out until a considerable time after the lectures have been out, on the other hand the portraits are so entirely right as that will be what I am reading from mostly. About the pictures don't worry I perfectly understand and nobody will have one of them in their possession xcept us. You see what happened was that I was completely knocked in a heap by them, they are pretty wonderful and all the french people who saw them and we were seeing a lot of french people then were so taken aback by them, they were so different from anything they knew that I lost my head and wanted to show them to everybody in France, and that was how it happened. They are pretty wonderful, and you do understand. Had a nice letter, Alice did from Cerf about the Plain Editions.[1] About the Birthday book, if I hear from the John Day people, from whom I have not heard I will do as you and Cerf think will be best for our books in general. Of course that was all begun

[334]

before there was any hope of the portrait book, and the portrait book is the thing, in that I think everything comes together. And now I am going on correcting and the book will be already the end of next week so it will get to Cerf in plenty of time and lots and lots and lots of love.

Gertrude

We stay here until the 28 of September, but you have to allow for two days more for a registered package to get here than to Paris, we are wanting to see them and Trac is to be with us in Paris, and we will tell the cafe [man], I am sorry about Virieu there will be another Virieu avec nous[2]

love
Gertrude

1. Cerf wrote to Toklas (22 August 1934, YCAL) and asked for five copies of each volume in the Plain Edition series.

Note by Van Vechten, 22 January 1941: "Bennett Cerf agreed to have copies of the Plain Edition in his office for sale, if anybody queried for them."

2. See Van Vechten to Stein [14 June 1934].

❧

To Gertrude Stein
[Postcard: Amstel House, Built 1730—New Castle, Del.]

5 September 1934 [150 West Fifty-fifth Street
New York]

Dear Gertrude:

The dedication seems perfect. —I can't wait. The photographs should get off on Saturday, I think—this is Wednesday—There will be a couple extra ones for Trac if you know where he is. If you don't, it doesn't matter. The lectures & the portraits were announced in the papers today & it all looked quite thrilling. . . . Everything seems to point to this being your year. But so is any year! Portraits & Prayers is an inspiration as a title! —By all means tell [Marvin] Ross to show me the lectures. —I haven't met him yet but expect to next week.

Love & Love!!
[Carl Van Vechten]

❧

To Carl Van Vechten
[Postcard: Saint-Paul de Varax—Le Portail de l'Eglise]

[postmark: 8 September 1934]   [Bilingnin par Belley Ain]

My dearest Carl,

The ms. of the Portraits went off yesterday and I am so happy. We saw the cafe man at Belley and he will give them all their photos, and he is very xcited about it, and so are we, and most certainly wanting and lots of love

Gertrude.

❧

To Carl Van Vechten

[postmark: 21 September 1934]   Bilignin par Belley Ain

My dearest Carl,

We sail on the Champlain Oct 17, and get to New York supposedly the 24 but it will probably be later as the french line is I believe always late. It never has been so near, so far no photographs have come but we xpect them every day, and Carl I do want to bring to you a really nice present, a present you will like, the only thing so far I could think of was my portrait by [Kristians] Tonny which I think you do like, tell me Carl honestly would that please you, it is fairly large of course and might only be a nuisance but I do want to give you something that you would really and truly like, tell me truly to 27 rue de Fleurus, and if you say yes we will bring it, if not there will be something else but I love you so very much I want to bring you something you will really truly like, you can imagine we are xcited, we have written to the Algonquin, and xpect an answer soon,[1]

Lots of love
Gertrude.

1. Stein bound the manuscript of *Four Saints in Three Acts* and brought this as a gift for Van Vechten. Van Vechten presented this to YCAL in 1941.

To Carl Van Vechten

23 September 1934   Bilignin par Belley
(Ain)

My dear dearest Carl

The photographs have come and I wish I wish I wish you could have heard the literal screams of delight with which we looked at them and at last Alice said with a sigh, it is fantastic that they are so beautiful. You are a magician Carl that is all there is to it. It is the first time that photographs have been made by light being inside as well as outside, I never saw anything like the wonder of the way the lights from the hair in Alice's head come to be inside and through. It's marvellous. And perhaps the one the really one that I think is the best photograph that ever is or will be done is the one of me sitting with Basket very small on the wall and the little house and the landscape all big, I think now that I would almost rather have that as a frontispiece of the Portraits and Prayers, it is so beautiful, Alice says, but we will always travel with them. And the two of Basket on the chair and Pepe everywhere. And then the two of us at les Chaumettes each one against the foliage and such each one of us and such foliage, and the roses, it's really not believable. And then one that is perhaps another most favorite is the back of my head against the pillar of box, but all of them against the pillar

[337]

are marvellous, and also Lucy Church, Lucy Church is beautiful and one of me at the cross is very fine, and they have just come and we have only looked them through twice yet; and they are so beautifully put up but we really even Alice could not pay much attention to that with those photographs. You are really leading the way to something Carl, it's another thing, I don't know what it is but it is another thing, and we are so happy about them it is the very first time that we have really loved any photographs of the other one, the very first time. Trac will have his, then our first China boy is so jealous he quite dropped tears, and I am going in to Belley and I will ask and see if the Cafe have had theirs, and we leave here day after tomorrow, they just came in time to make a lovely end to a lovely summer, and we sail on the 17 on the Champlain and we will see you soon and we will always travel with them, I can't believe them

> *Always and always*
> *Gertrude.*

※

To Carl Van Vechten

[postmark: 1 October 1934]   27 rue de Fleurus
                                               Paris

My dearest Carl,

Here we are and the beautiful book traveled with us, and it is beautiful,[1] it is wonderful having the photographs of the photographs of St. Thérèse, and now every day brings us nearer to you, and being nearer to you is nice. We are most awfully busy, but that is a good thing,

> *lots and lots of love*
> *Gertrude*

Oh and I asked at the café du Marché, Place des Ternaux if they had ever gotten the photographs of the conscripts and they said no they had not. That was on the 27 of September, that they had not yet received them.[2]

1. It may have been an advance copy of *Portraits and Prayers*, which was published on 7 November 1934.

2. Note by Van Vechten, 22 January 1941: "Photographs I made of conscripts in the Square of Belley and that I promised to send them."

To Gertrude Stein
[Postcard: Cherry Blossoms, Hains Point, Washington, D.C.]

[postmark: 3 October 1934] [150 West Fifty-fifth Street
New York]

Dear Gertrude:

You are a woojums & Alice is a woojums to appreciate the photographs. You will be delighted with Portraits & Prayers. I have seen a "dummy" of it & it is beautiful . . . . I don't know what to write you about [Kristians] Tonny's portrait. I admire this, but I have no place to hang it now[x] & also I am very much embarrassed by your bringing me a present. It is so much if you bring *yourself*. But anything you do will be all right. The portraits[x] to me give almost a complete picture of you & Alice . . . . at least I can easily fill in what is lacking. I love 'em! I will be seeing you soon! Hurrah! Love to you both.

Carlo.

[x]and it is so big for you to carry!
[x]I mean my photographs!

To Carl Van Vechten

[postmark: 4 October 1934] 27 rue de Fleurus
Paris

My dearest Carl,

We have just had an awfully nice letter from Mr. [Frank] Case of the Algonquin, and making very nice arrangements for us,[1] and it all sounds pleasanter and pleasanter, we are just kind of going ahead and before we know it there we will be, it is the Champlain which sails the 17, and Trac is back with us and so happy about the photos, he looked as if he did not think it was possible that he could have been so beautiful. I am xpecting to hear from you before we leave which is still ten days, and then we will be there. Lots and lots of love and thanks so much for the nice Algonquin arrangements

Always
Gertrude.

1. Case to Toklas, 22 September 1934, YCAL. Case thanked Toklas for her letter of 13 September and gave her the rates for the room Toklas had requested: a double room with two beds and bath not higher than the sixth floor. Case offered Toklas a suite with the same arrangements plus a sitting room. The rate was $5 per day or $30 per week.

To Gertrude Stein
[Radiotélégramme]

[23 October 1934] New York

Will you dine with us tomorrow night

love
Carlo

To Carl Van Vechten
[Radiogram]

23 Oct[ober] 1934 SS Champlain

OF COURSE JOYFULLY LOVE[1]

GERTRUDE

1. Note by Van Vechten, 22 January 1941: "I had radioed the boat to ask Gertrude and Alice to dine with us the night they arrived."

❧

To Fania Marinoff

[2 November 1934]

Hotel Algonquin
59 to 65 West Forty-fourth Street
New York

My dearest Fania

You are and were an angel, before the lecture I just ate oysters and your fruit,[1] and I will be doing that each day till I get used to it and how I ask you how could I have eaten so much lovely fruit if you had not sent it to me, but there you had, and Alice and I regaled ourselves and we are going on and blessing you all the time. Carl told you all I said about your acting and it is true, it is dramatic and natural you are just our natural Fania and yet you are something else,[2] Carl also told you of my dreams that some day they will do a play of mine and you will be in it but anyway we all love each other a lot which is most awfully awfully nice

Always and always
Gtrde

1. Stein delivered her lecture, "Painting," at the Colony Club, New York, on 2 November.

2. Van Vechten had taken Stein and Toklas to see Fania Marinoff who was performing the role of Madame Cevelli in Elmer Rice's play *Judgment Day*.

To Gertrude Stein

[10 November 1934]   150 West Fifty-fifth Street
Saturday   [New York]

Dear Gertrude,

I am in town for only a minute and flitting away, but I thought perhaps you had missed this sensible [Heywood] Broun article. . Gilbert Seldes writes he had one too, which he is sending.[1] You will see: the worms will turn, but the early birds caught 'em long before they turned!

The party for 9 P.M. November 18 is shaping magnificently. I hope you will have it happily with a spoon. . It has occurred to me that the blessed St. Therese No. 1 will be back and I am going to ask HER.[2]

We flew back in four and a half hours (a half hour early!) without a jolt. . and flying at night is very wonderful.

I shall be back early Monday. Please call me up when you get up to say hello. I want to go to the Cosmopolitan Club on Tuesday if it is a different magpie: You must tell me. Whenever you want to go to Florine [Stettheimer]'s, let me know. Whenever you want to do anything, let me know.

I am going to make you both Ladies of the Royal Order of Woojums, and you will go out with medals after this instead of orchids and gardenias.

567 white hyacinths in jade pots to you both!

Carlo

May I give one of your pictures to Mrs. Goodspeed?

1. Heywood Broun, in his column "It Seems to Me" in the *New York World Telegram*, 7 November 1934 (YCAL), wrote that while he was no expert in Stein's work, "I am moved to the support of Gertrude Stein because I bridle at the popular habit of making some member of a minority group a joke on no better basis than the lack of willingness to conform."

Gilbert Seldes wrote about *Four Saints in Three Acts* in "Delight in the Theatre," *Modern Music* (March/April 1934), 11:138–41.

2. Beatrice Robinson-Wayne.

To Carl Van Vechten
[Postcard]

[postmark: 15 November 1934]

The Deanery
Bryn Mawr, Pennsylvania

Gertrude is very peaceful in her mind about Chicago and knows you are always right—there is so continually proof of it. The least of the Woo- jums to the Chief—greetings and dearest love to Fania and to you from

Alice

To Carl Van Vechten
[Postcard]

[postmark: 15 November 1934]

The Deanery
Bryn Mawr, Pennsylvania

My dearest Carl

Here we are on our travels and enjoying it, so much happens and so pleasantly but we like New York best and New York is you, and that is that, the Woojums will be coming home Friday morning,

Lots of love
Gertrude

To Gertrude Stein

[15 November 1934]   150 West Fifty-fifth Street
Thursday   New York]

Dear Gertrude,

You gave me these to read on the plane and I seem to have carried them away. .[1]

I will call you tomorrow[x] night at a quarter of eight to take you to Columbia. I think it would be good if you and Alice would arrive at 150, fifteen minutes before nine on Sunday: so we may smirk and say how-de-do before the black and white carnival begins!

Much love to you both: Royal WOOJUMS BOTH!

Carlo!

[x]Friday

1. The reading material cannot be identified.

To Carl Van Vechten
[Postcard: United Airlines—Science Makes
Night Flying Routine]

[postmark: 24 November 1934]   [The Drake Hotel
                                                Chicago, Illinois]

–1–

The Woojums lonesomely on their way[.] I'm thinking perhaps you may have created Chicago too. Am sending schedule.

[Alice Toklas]

[344]

⁂

To Carl Van Vechten
*[Postcard: United Airlines "3-Mile-A-Minute" Multi-
Motored Boeing]*

[postmark: 24 November 1934]
The Drake Hotel
Chicago, Illinois

–II–

last lecture Dec. 4th probably. Dec. 8th—St. Paul's Woman's Club.
Why not meet us somewhere. Do you think the Woojums don't miss you.
Dearest love to F[ania]. & to you.

[Alice Toklas]

⁂

To Carl Van Vechten

[postmark: 26 November 1934]
Twenty four thirty Lake
View Avenue
[Chicago, Illinois]

My dearest Carl,

Here we are fetishes and all,[1] we got in so smoothly and just on the
minute when we were due, and we are devoted to it and to you but all to
you because you are it too or rather it is you too, everything is you. Carl
what a good time we had in your New York, what a good time, there never
was or has been such a good time as you gave us, never ever in the whole
wide world it was marvelous every moment, and I really cannot believe [it]
only it was all true. We are very comfortable here and resting pleasantly[2]
and Wednesday we will go to the Drake Hotel and by that time Alice will
have worked out our itinerary and we will meet somewhere which will be
nicest of all and Bobsy Goodspeed showed us your photograph the slim young
Carl on the Auditorium stage, my dearest dearest Carl we did have such a
happy time I cannot tell it to you often enough and lots of love and all of

Van Vechten, Stein, Toklas, and the flight crew of the United Airlines flight that took them to Chicago on 7 November 1934.
COURTESY OF BRUCE KELLNER.

our love and always all and our love, and love to Fania and remembrances to Edith and always all our love

Gertrude

and remember us to Pearl too.[3]

1. Note by Van Vechten, 21 January 1941: "Beaded representations of men & women made over rabbits feet by Hopi Indians. I had given them these for their first flight."

2. When they first arrived in Chicago, Stein and Toklas were staying with Mrs. Charles B. Goodspeed.

3. Edith Ramsey and Pearl Showers were the Van Vechtens' cook and housekeeper.

To Carl Van Vechten

[27 November 1934]   Twenty four thirty Lakeview Avenue
Tuesday Morning   [Chicago, Illinois]

Chicago which is nice but which is not N[ew]. Y[ork].

Dearest Carl—

A hasty line—Gertrude is beautifully rested. Bobsie Goodspeed has been so very kind—considerate and sweet. The first lecture at the Arts Club went off very well. G[ertrude]. had a fine time—a hard boiled audience with several university profs who came anti and went away convinced. G. likes Thornton Wilder.[1] The tangle in the lectures here is working out alright— though it was a mess. By keeping one of our last conversations (you remember about correctitude bringing its reward) I got rid of the one at Evanston by their not being able to accept (!!!) and by giving their fee to the agency I was able to deal directly with the club presidents. So that's that.

Now about dates: the sixth is not free as I wrote from the plane (The trip was so easy I forgot to mention it. We arrived on the *minute*). Two lectures at the Univ. of Wisconsin to the students *very* satisfactory. G. will like them I know. Saint Paul is the next. G. lectures 11.30 morning of the 8th at Women's Club. Why not go with us. Then the Univ. of Iowa evening of the 10th. Will continue to send schedule but don't we see [you]

[347]

before. Say yes. I don't feel as if I'd hold out if not. I need the recomfortant morale. I'm sorry but that is the way it is. The Woojums miss you terribly— no Chicago is not N. Y. and that's because you are not here and didn't create Chicago.

I've just to fly and only time to send my dearest love to Fania and to you

Ever yours
Alice

1. Stein and Toklas had met Thornton Wilder (1897–1975), the American writer, then teaching at the University of Chicago, through Mrs. Charles B. Goodspeed.

To Carl Van Vechten

[postmark: 29 November 1934]   The Drake [Hotel]
                                                Chicago [Illinois]

My dearest Carl,

The happiest of thanksgivings for us all only we would like to be with you, but we are full of thanks just the same and there is no doubt about that, we are having a good time but we are lonesome for you most lonesome, and did you not get the first letter I wrote you the day we got here, you did not say so, but perhaps it was late in getting mailed, I never do believe that when you drop a letter way up high that it ever gets there but I guess it does, listen Carl we have been having funny times, the lectures are going off well, last night at the University went very well, at least they seemed very interested it was Grammar and Poetry and that was the third in Chicago, and last that is night before last they took Alice and me around in a squad car, no murders but lots of fun, we and the police liked each other a lot, and we heard all about baby face[1] as we went but they took us to some most amusing places and one of them was the place where they walk a marathon, a most xtraordinary thing, they are like shades modern shades out of Dante and they move so strangely and they lead each other about one asleep completely and the other almost, it is the most unearthly and most beautiful movement I have ever seen it makes the dance like nothing at all, I have never imagined [anything] like it, and the manager of the place came up and said to our head policeman that is the lady who wrote the opera, and the policeman said how did you know that, said the policeman, oh I know he said and then later as we were leaving he said wouldn't you like to be photographed with some of the kids but it seemed better not, but if we are ever together in Chicago we will see it together and be photographed together, it is a wonderful America and I am enjoying every minute of it, and now we are lunching with Mrs. Goodspeed and dining at the P.E.N. club, and I had a nice letter from [F. Scott] Fitzgerald,[2] and Alice is getting everything straightened out and a charming letter from Mark [Lutz][3] and lots oh so much love and thanksgiving for you and lots of love for Fania and always us for you

Gertrude.

1. When "Pretty Boy" Floyd was killed on 22 October, George "Baby Face" Nelson became Public Enemy Number One.

2. Fitzgerald wrote to Stein, 23 November 1934, asking to see her when she visited Baltimore. See Turnbull, *The Letters of F. Scott Fitzgerald* (London: The Bodley Head, 1964), pp. 517–18.

3. Lutz to Stein, 30 October 1934, YCAL. Lutz, writing from Richmond, Virginia, reported that everyone was talking about her visit to the United States and looking forward to her lectures in Richmond.

To Carl Van Vechten

[postmark: 29 November 1934]　　　　　　　　　　The Drake [Hotel]
　　　　　　　　　　　　　　　　　　　　　　　　Chicago [Illinois]

My dear Carl,

Thanks for all these interviews, St. Therese is a darling[1] and a very beautiful darling and please tell her so for me, I like the one that says my manager subscribes to a clipping bureau, and how she does not, only you know that, Muriel [Draper] was very sweet have you any address that will reach her.[2] Thornton Wilder has just been with Mabel [Dodge], he is awfully nice, and told nice stories about her,[3] it's still thanksgiving and we have been having a nice time, I do like America but my heart is true to New York and to you Carl, Lots of love and lots of love from the Woojums, who want their Carl,

Gertrude.

1. The role in the opera sung by Beatrice Robinson-Wayne.

2. Muriel Draper (1887–1952), the political activist and writer. Stein had met her and her husband Paul Draper in Florence in 1911 through Mabel Dodge. Muriel Draper (in imitation of Stein's style) cabled Stein from Moscow on 24 November 1934 (YCAL): "Being here is not being here to not be there where you are and I am not being where at the same time always where you are I am being love and more so."

3. Without knowing him, Mabel Dodge had written Thornton Wilder on 6 April [1929] (YCAL): "I read The Bridge [*The Bridge of San Luis Rey*] & Cabala [*The Cabala*] today and what I want to say without preambles or arrangements is won't you come out here to Taos and do something about these people?" Wilder did not immediately visit Dodge. In subsequent years he did visit her when he was staying in Santa Fe. Dodge had written to D. H. Lawrence in much the same way that she had written to Wilder. In her letter she wrote Wilder, "I wrote in the same way to Lawrence before I ever knew him, because he is so sensitive to animals & flowers & things & he came . . ."

To Carl Van Vechten

[postmark: 1 December 1934]
The Drake [Hotel]
Chicago [Illinois]

My dearest Carl,

Everything is going beautifully and what will interest and please you the most is the story of the University, suddenly everthing has changed, it's a long story, but it has ended up in the president's personally asking me to consider coming back in March to give a two weeks course at the University and to be very well payed for it too, and to do anything I want, I think it might be very interesting to do, and I am about accepting it, but I would like to know what you think, it all came about from a meeting with the President and [Mortimer] Adler,[1] a violent discussion and next day my lecture, Grammar and Poetry which seems to have made a really deep impression, it makes me awfully happy because it is just what I wanted to do, please let me know just what you think. We like it here immensely everybody is most awfully nice but we miss you a lot more really than I can tell you, it was always such a comfort to know that you were just there, you are still there but there is just a little farther away, do tell us that we will be seeing you on the road somewhere, it is xactly what we need and what we want, everthing is comfortable and peaceful, all complications do get simple over here and it is most restful, I do love it all but we love you best Carl so do come to us

Always
Gertrude

1. Robert Maynard Hutchins was the president of the University of Chicago from 1929 to 1945. Mortimer Adler was professor of the philosophy of law at the University of Chicago.

❧

To Gertrude Stein

[1 December 1934]   150 West Fifty-fifth Street
Saturday   [New York]

Dearest Gertrude,

Your letters about the Dance Marathon and the Squad Car are pretty cute and Thornton Wilder has got me down with jealousy. Don't go and like him BETTER, PLEASE! . . . What I mean by schedule is, how long can I write you at the Drake, and where do I write you after that? So please ask Alice to let me know. *All* your letters are here, including one from Alice addressed to 150 West *50th* street, so the heart of the postoffice is in the right place. . Did Alice write Mrs. Walter Douglas, Wayzata, Minnesota? PLEASE DO NOT MISS THIS.[1] . Address Muriel Draper, care of the American Embassy, Moscow and it will reach her (in time for Christmas). Marie Harriman sent me a telegram (which I am looking for this minute and cannot find) asking me to ask you to be the guest of honor at the opening of the Rose Show (Sir Francis and not the "is a" kind) on Friday.[2] I telephoned her and told her you wouldn't be back till after the holidays. . Beau Broadway in the N[ew] Y[ork] Telegraph says spies have discovered you call each other Lovey and Pussy. No one he says has yet reported on what you and Alice call C. V. V. (so Woojums is still inviolate![3] Don't you go calling T[horton] W[ilder] a woojums! I will bite him!). Tell Alice I never got her letter from the Plane, so where was this sent? (Oh yes, I remember I did get two serial cards!) Did you get Arthur Griggs obituary?[4]

I spend all my time in the darkroom crying for my beautiful pair of Woojumses who are TRAVELLING in the WEST.

LOVE, LOVE, to you BOTH!

Fania and Pearl and EDITH send LOVE![5]

Carlo

1. Mrs. Douglas had known Van Vechten when he was a boy of eight in Cedar Rapids, Iowa. She and her husband were aboard the *Titanic* when it went down. Her husband was killed in the sinking. Mrs. Douglas inherited the Quaker Oats Company of Cedar Rapids. She left Cedar Rapids and eventually settled in Minnesota.

2. An exhibition of paintings by Sir Francis Rose, similar to that shown at the Arts Club of Chicago, 9 to 30 November 1934, was shown at the Marie Harriman Gallery, New York, from 7 to 29 December 1934. The catalogue for this exhibition, a large folded sheet of paper, contained a statement by Stein on Rose.

3. In the column, "The Town in Review," signed "Beau Broadway," *New York Telegraph*, 21 November 1934, p. 1:

> A man who has been haunting Gertrude Stein, attending all her lectures, luncheon, and other public appearances, reports that he is able to tell the world that Miss Stein calls her secretary, Alice B. Toklas, and what Miss Toklas calls Miss Stein. It seems that Miss Toklas calls Miss Stein "Lovey," and Miss Stein calls Miss Toklas "Pussy."
>
> No report yet on what both of them call Carl Van Vechten.

4. An obituary for Griggs appeared in the *New York Times*, 27 November 1943, p. 21.

5. Pear Showers and Edith Ramsey, the Van Vechtens' household staff.

To Gertrude Stein

[3 December 1934]   150 West Fifty-fifth Street
Monday   [New York]

Dear Gertrude,

All the morning courrier that is not *from* you (I had two delightful, *serial* cards from Woojum Alice) seems to be for you. I opened Muriel

[Draper]'s cablegram because it was so folded, it seemed to be addressed to me. Think of her getting wind of your American triumphs in far-off Moscow. Please return the other communications to me. . All the pictures you asked me to send have gone off[x]. . [Alexander] Woollcott's,[1] of course, is waiting for you to come back and sign it. . I am not sure I know which one you mean, as there seems to be no number 20, but we will go into this later. . We miss you both frightfully and tell Alice that I did *not* make Chicago and never would or could or wanted to or would want to. Oh, NO, Pu-leese!

as for you Rose is a rose is a rose and how!

Carlo!

[x]including several to the Duchesse Expresse

1. Through Van Vechten Stein had met Alexander Woollcott (1887–1943), the critic, actor, and author. Woollcott was the drama critic for the *New York Times* from 1914 to 1922. In 1929 he began broadcasting on American and British radio networks.

To Gertrude Stein

[3 December 1934][1]   150 West Fifty-fifth Street
                                        [New York]

Dear Gertrude,

Of course you must stay on to deliver a course at Chicago. I am so proud of you and I always feel a little personal about the University because it is my Alma Mater. . HAVE YOU WRITTEN MAHALA [Douglas] YET? I must know that you are all getting together in St. Paul and environs. . . And maybe I will join you soon somewhere. James Weldon Johnson writes to ask where he may send a copy of his God's Trombones[2] to you and I am writing him to leave it with me. . The weather is divine here and Fania's play closed Saturday and she is thinking of sailing to Bermuda, but I won't be going there.[3]

1,89,067,453,872 beautiful big hugs for the two queenly woojums!

Carlo!

1. Van Vechten had apparently written and mailed the previous letter before Stein's letter, postmarked 1 December 1934, had arrived.

2. James Weldon Johnson, *God's Trombones: Seven Negro Sermons in Verse* (New York: The Viking Press, 1927).

3. Marinoff was playing the role of Madame Cevelli in Elmer Rice's play *Judgment Day*.

To Carl Van Vechten

[postmark: 3 December 1934]   The Drake [Hotel]
                                                                  Chicago [Illinois]

My dearest Carl,

We were so pleased with the Rose joke, it was the prettiest little line I ever read,[1] and I have telephoned it already to all Chicago, and herein inclosed, two things that will amuse you, the poem slipped to Alice by the uninspired one,[2] we have been having a good time but don't you worry, there is all the difference in the world between a Woojum and a not Woojum no matter what the not Woojum is and the Woojums is the Woojums and they do not inlcude anything but Woojums, I signed at Marshall and Fields yesterday and it was lots of fun, crowds solemnly solemnly looking until I finally told them perhaps they had better go home and then they all giggled and went home but we had the consolation there of having you in photograph behind me while I signed and Carl I would like to be there with you in [a] photograph and I know Mrs. Hahner of the book department would, could we be there together in photograph, Wednesday evening I am going to the class, [Robert] Hutchins and [Mortimer] Adler teach Aristophanes to teach along with them, but this is a dead secret nobody knows that I am going to do it but they and we, (and anybody else anybody else tells), but anyway I am only telling you, I have my last lecture to-night and then two days of a little society and a little farewell and then we go off on our travels, and Alice has written to Mrs. [Mahala] Douglas and I wish oh how much I wish you were with us. We are giving a dinner party Wednesday evening to everybody who has been nice to us here I wish you would just drop in from the air and take the head of the table that would be nice, I will write to

Muriel [Draper], and I guess I love you very much Carl and I guess we love you very much Carl, I guess we most certainly do, and love to all, from all,

Always
Gertrude

1. See Van Vechten to Stein [1 December 1934].

2. The two enclosures are lost or missing.

***

To Carl Van Vechten
[Telegram]

[4 December 1934]   [The Drake Hotel, Chicago]

MRS [Mahala] DOUGLAS INVITED US IN CHARMING NOTE JUST RECEIVED FOR WEEK END STOP WE WOULD LIKE TO ACCEPT STOP WONT YOU COME TOO STOP WE FLY FROM MADISON WISCONSIN FRIDAY MORNING TEN OCLOCK STOP DO SAY WE WILL FIND YOU ON PLANE FRIDAY MORNING AT MADISON STOP ENDLESS LOVE[1]

GERTRUDE ALICE

1. Douglas to Stein, 30 November [1934], UCAL.

***

To Gertrude Stein and Alice Toklas

[4 December 1934]   150 West Fifty-fifth Street
Tuesday   [New York]

Dear Woojums, BOTH!

How sweet of you to telegraph me to join at Mahala [Douglas]'s: nothing would give me greater pleasure, but it is absolutely impossible this coming weekend. BUT YOU MUST GO. YOU WILL LOVE IT: YOU ARE SURE TO. BESIDES YOU MUST SEE SOMETHING OF RICH AMERICAN COUNTRY LIFE. I'll be seeing you soon somewhere. How much longer is the Drake your address?

LOVE,
Carlo!

Bennett [Cerf] and Donald [Klopfer] got their pictures yesterday. This means everybody you told me about except [Alexander] Woollcott whose picture is ready for you to sign and give him.[x]

Do you know who in N[ew] Y[ork] sells that Pigeon wallpaper?[1]

[x]I want to take some more when you get back.

1. Stein and Toklas had seen a wallpaper, white pigeons on a blue background, at the shop of Nancy McClelland, a decorator, at 15 East Fifty-seventh Street, New York. They later ordered this paper and used it in the bedroom of their apartment at 5 rue Christine. See McClelland to Stein, 3 May 1938, YCAL.

To Gertrude Stein
[Telegram]

5 December [1934]   New York

HAVE IT HAPPILY WITH A SPOON TONIGHT AND REMEMBER THAT YOU ARE BOTH ROYAL WOOJUMS

CARLO

To Carl Van Vechten

[postmark: 5 December 1934]   The Drake [Hotel]
Chicago [Illinois]

My dearest Carl,

I am glad you are going to be somewhere with us because we do want you and we do need you and we do like to have you and it's wonderful

[356]

to do so. I enjoyed myself immensely last night. President [Robert] Hutchins and [Mortimer] Adler asked me to take their conversational class with them last night, a course in which they teach by talking with the students and I took it on and I had a wonderful time just enjoyed every minute of it, and we are to come back in March for 2 weeks and a half for a regular course. I xpect to enjoy it a lot, they are interesting students and they say good things to you and they catch you up and it goes hammer and tongs pretty well and I liked it I liked it a lot, it lasted amost two hours and I guess a good time was enjoyed by all. They are an interesting lot of Chicago students and why not nice it is your college,[1] but really truly I am awfully happy about all this because it is xactly what I wanted and it has so beautifully come about and just in the right way without anybody pushing but just naturally, just the Carl way, well here we are our last day in Chicago and now into the great prairie wilderness, and soon we will see you, and I will report from every town, you also will be pleased that the plane did not stop at Iowa City and we had to get to Iowa City and we could not get there by the train because it would take too long so the postmaster general is stopping the plane for us in Iowa City, is not that Woojumesque and it should and would and does happen in Iowa after all Carl's Iowa so you see well that is the way it is, dear Carl I can't tell you how much we love you and how we grab for the red envelopes, and lots of love and so much love and Fania and I hope it all ended well and that it will all begin again soon, but it will as she has the light and the life of the Play,[2]

lots of love,
Gtde.

Oh Carl and could [Alexander] Smallens who directed the Four Saints orchestra have a photograph with my name and yours by the way I dedicated Mrs. Goodspeed's which is being framed from you and from me, and she wants one of Alice, you see we are shameless but to know to know to love them so, four Saints prepare for Saints and there we are there we all are, I wish you were here

Gertrude[3]

1. Van Vechten graduated from the University of Chicago in the spring of 1903.

2. See Van Vechten to Stein [3 December 1934], note 3.

3. Included with the letter were two cartoons by McCutcheon that had appeared in the Sunday *Chicago Tribune*, 2 December 1934 (YCAL). At the top of one cartoon Stein wrote, "A pleas-

ant winter landscape as the orthodox painter would represent it." Below the second cartoon she wrote, "As the ultra-modernist painter would claim he saw it." On the page with the cartoons Stein also wrote, "Proof of the McCutcheon cartoon to come out next Sunday."

To Carl Van Vechten

6 December [19]34

The Wisconsin Union
University of Wisconsin
[Madison, Wisconsin]

Dearest Carl—

Here we are in Wisconsin and no you and no you tomorrow nor the day after tomorrow. Well I ask you when then may we hope you'll come flying to us? The lectures here went beautifully—students and faculty afternoon and eve. Then G[ertrude]. met about 30 afterwards and we've just come up. They've made us very comfy with excellent food and kindness. Chicago is marvelous—the university—I mean G's being asked there for March. It was so exciting G. didn't sleep and I dreamed all night a locomotive ran over me—each time freshly. It was all accomplished by being correct as you said we should be.

 Tomorrow to St. Paul—we will be staying at some stage of our stay.
 The eve. of the 10th c/o University of Iowa—Iowa City
  " " " " 11th " Book - Cadillac Hotel—Detroit
 Probably until " 15th " "   "   "   "
 And I'll continue to send itinerary.
 Very sleepely—very fondly

Alice

When does Fania go to Bermuda? She's not too tired I hope and my dearest love and we want to see her in something new in Jan[uary].

To Carl Van Vechten

[postmark: 8 December 1934]   Hotel Lowry
                                               Fourth and Wabasha Sts.
                                               St. Paul, Minnesota

My dearest Carl,

Here we are. We have seen Mahala [Douglas] and she was very sweet brought us beautiful flowers but we are not there because she was afraid lest the blizzard that was predicted would keep us from coming in in the evening to lecture which would have been awkward so we are lunching with her on Sunday.[1] I do so wish you might be there. We had a wonderful time flying from Madison here, we went in a little moth plane just the two of us and the pilot, no stewardess no nothing and we flew low over the snow covered country and I never saw or felt anything like it, I am still all filled up with emotion about it, oh Carl bless you for everything but bless you most perhaps most for making us fly, it is wonderful, wonderful wonderful, the lectures in Madison went off very well both of them given in the University, very intelligent students and one youn[g] professor in the history of language who was one of the very best people I have met yet, it was the English literature one that I gave them, then there is a bedside radio the first hotel that has had one, and that too is sweetly funny because it seems to be all local radio, well we are enjoying ourselves the Woojums are and they only wish Mr. Woojums would Woojum with them here or somewhere dear dear Carl we love you so

> *Always*
> *Gertrude*

Oh and Carl do please ask Frank Case if he got the letter of thanks I wrote him the first day in Chicago, these letters seem to have gotten themselves not mailed and I would not like him to think me ungrateful.

---

1. Note by Van Vechten, 22 January 1941: "Mrs. Walter Douglas of Minneapolis. I wrote her to look after them."

To Gertrude Stein

[10 December 1934]
Monday

150 West Fifty-fifth Street
New York City

Dearest Gertrude,

I have had such wonderful letters from you but until this morning when I heard from Woojums Alice I didn't know where to write. So here I am sending you back your poem and your telegram.[1] Mrs. Hahner and [Alexander] Smallens will get pictures of you and Bobsie Goodspeed will get a picture of Alice but don't you think I should wait till you can sign them all, please! So I will wait till you can sign them and then we will send with our blessing. I am very excited about your March lectures and about their stopping planes wherever you want them to stop. . . The weather here is very cold, like Whittier's SnowBound, without the snow. Or like a Currier and Ives print without the sleighs, but the bustles and tippets and muffs and all that are here,[x] and I think you would love it. Everybody misses you, but the great public thinks you are still here because your name is in every story that is printed in the papers including accounts of the Six Day Bicycle Race. I hope you get this letter and I send you lots of love and did you go to Mahala [Douglas] and did you like her?

78(789)65 yellow pumpkins to you both!

Carlo!

EDith and PEarl send love and F[ania] M[arinoff] has gone to Bermuda where she is resting in the HEAT at the Hotel Langton in Hamilton.[2]

Just as I am sealing this your letter from St. Paul arrived. Frank Case *did* get the letter of thanks. He spoke of it the other day and was very proud and happy and wants you back QUICK as do we all.

[x]again.

---

1. See Stein to Van Vechten [3 December 1934].

2. Edith Ramsey and Pearl Showers, the Van Vechtens' household staff.

♨

To Carl Van Vechten

[postmark: 12 December 1934]   Hotel Book-Cadillac
                                                Detroit [Michigan]

My dearest Carl,

Here we are and we were met so sweetly by your letter, we came on a Douglas plane that had only been flying a week and it was enormous and silent and commodious and Carl, don't you think it would be nice to buy a second hand plane of the Hanford Line and we all three pilot it together here and there, don't you think the three Woojums would be lovely woojum pilots up above the sky so high, all by themselves, we spent the day with Mahala [Douglas] and enjoyed it, I think we all liked each other a lot and made up our minds to meet again, in Pasadena, she was charming to us, and we delighted in hearing all about Carl as a very young man, and they told us such nice stories and how everybody sat around and said and what is he doing now and now what is he doing, and at first they were so shocked and then they were so proud. Her brother was there and he drove us back to St Paul and he talked charmingly about you and we had a very pleasant time. Then we had our first air affair, we left St. Paul for Chicago to change for Iowa City as per front man and programme, and the plane did not want to leave the ground, finally after a great deal of coaxing it did and we were on our way, then they suddenly announced after being very considerably later that they were stopping in Milwaukee, Alice protested, and the second assistant pilot who was also a steward said Lady wouldn't you rather be even in Milwaukee than in your coffin, well Milwaukee it was and there they put us in a tram-car for Chicago where apparently was raging quite locally the worst blizzard they had had for some years, the Goodspeeds tried to get to the air-port to get us as they were worried their car got on fire, we did not turn up and finally we all got home that is Chicago and got to bed, but it was xciting. And now here we are, and next is Ann Arbor then Indianapolis, Toledo, Columbus and then Baltimore, and always dearest dearest Carl all our love

Gertrude.

To Carl Van Vechten
[Telegram]

13 December 1934   Detroit, Mich[igan]

JOSEPH BREWER TAKES US TODAY TO SPEND THE NIGHT AT OLIVET AND TOMORROW TO ANNARBOR STOP HOTEL CLAYPOOL INDIANAPOLIS FOR THE FIFTEENTH STOP THE WOOJUMS WELL AND HAPPY BUT LONESOME FOR THEIR CHIEF SEND ENDLESS LOVE[1]

GERTRUDE AND ALICE.

1. Joseph Brewer had been with the firm of Payson & Clarke when they published Stein's *Useful Knowledge* in 1928. Brewer was president of Olivet College, Olivet, Michigan, from 1934 to 1944.

To Carl Van Vechten

14 December [19]34   Olivet College
                                                           Olivet, Michigan

Dearest Chief Woojem,[1]

As you know we are here, and a blessing it is and all due to the Van Vechten grandmamma of Joseph Brewer, who came over night before last with part of his faculty, his administrators and his students in numerous cars to rescue us from Detroit, which we did not "get" but which did not get us, as we thought it might. Perhaps it was a Chevrolet convention, perhaps it [was] too much darkness, perhaps it was a hotel that was full of adventure, one or all was commencing to overwhelm us when PRESIDENT Brewer took us away. In any case it was not the lecture which G[ertrude]. really liked, the audience very sympathetic.

Well here we are and it really is too nice. The students all hovering about G. and [Joseph] Brewer doing the honours quite darlingly. We have

[362]

twenty-four hours and after lunch the cavalcade advances to Ann Arbor where G. lectures and where we spend the night. On Saturday, which turns out to be to-morrow on to Indianapolis, Hotel Claypool. On Monday to Colu[m]bus, Ohio, c/o of Miss Jean Reeder, Chi Delta Phi, University of Ohio (know [i.e., no] one seems to be able to advise a hotel) to Toledo, Commodore Perry Hotel. Dec. 18th to 20th and then Cleveland until the morning of the 23rd when we fly to Washington to be picked up for Baltimore. At Baltimore until morning of 29th when Emily Chadbourne comes for us to take us to Washington[2] where we stay with Mrs. Ann Archibald, 8905 Reservoir (neither St. nor Ave. mentioned) then we go back to Baltimore. G. lectures Washington 29th Phillips Memorial[3] and 30th Univeristy Women.

Now for Mrs. [Mahala] Douglass, she was quite wonderful in her home, brilliant and brittle and fin de siecle, when she came into the room she did what no once since Lady Windermere's Fan has done to me, not even The Crust of Society. She is quite quite perfect and I did love it, she and her home. I think our hotel room appalled and smothered her.

And where are you meeting us perhaps (I'm only quoting you—you know. This room is invaded and so all my love

Woojems Alice

1. This is the first letter to use the term "Woojums" (misspelled by Toklas as Woojem) in the salutation. See Van Vechten to Stein, 26 April [1932], note 2.

2. Emily Crane Chadbourne and her friend Ellen La Motte had been introduced to Stein and Toklas by Dr. Claribel Cone in 1913.

3. For an account of Stein's visit with the Phillips' and her lecture see Marjorie Phillips, *Duncan Phillips and His Collection* (New York: W. W. Norton & Co., 1970), pp. 184–87.

To Carl Van Vechten

[postmark: 17 December 1934] Claypool Hotel
Indianapolis, Indiana

My dearest Carl,

Here we are in Indiana, and alas we did not get to Iowa, but we will, we certainly will, if not now then later because we must see the state which gave you to us but we are not seeing Allegheny [Pennsylvania][1] either just now so I think we are determined to pilgrimage to our birthplaces together later in our moth plane. I think it would be a wonderful thing to do to pilot each other to remember [where] we each were born, it was nice to be born and to have it be us, then we would go out to San Francisco and have Alice born and so the Woojums would be complete, sometimes I get tempted by the idea of a car but I really am faithful to the moth plane. [Joseph] Brewer came to Detroit and kidnapped us, he said we should have that xperience and why should it not be he, and so in two cars and five men strong they carried us away to Olivet, and we had a good time there, I never had known that he was a cousin of yours and that makes him just that much nicer. Then they brought us back to Ann Arbor, and there I had a long talk with the man who is administering Avery [Hopwood]'s fund, he has just instituted a library room, a room that is to contain only contemporary literature, and he wants in it a painting of Avery, I told him that I knew only of the one done by Florine Stettheimer but that he should write to you as you may know of something else, I think of course the Stettheimer one would be wonderful to have there but could that be, we also had several other ideas about things that he was rather interested in and that I would like to talk over with you, they might really do something rather important there about it all, and he says [he is] very ready to do anything you or I suggest,[2] but all that when we see each other and when do we see each other, we are so disappointed that it has not been anywhere yet, I want it to be somewhere yet. We go on from here to Columbus and then Toledo and then Cleveland Wade Park Manor Hotel, will reach us there and we would be really disappointed if there were no red envelope there when we got there. I am sorry Fania did not get warm but one never does in the South at this time, never, oh Carl we love you so much and we always tell you so

Gertrude.

1. Stein's birthplace.

2. Note by Van Vechten, 22 January 1941:

    Avery Hopwood left the bulk of his fortune to his Alma Mater, the University of Michigan, where the interest is used yearly as prizes for writing. I suggested to Florine she give the portrait of Avery to this room at the University of Michigan and at first she favored the idea but later was never able to make up her mind what to do.

    In reply to an inquiry about the Stettheimer portrait, Jane G. Flener, Associate Director for Public Services, Department of Rare Books and Special Collections, University Library, The University of Michigan, Ann Arbor, wrote that Professor Roy William Cowden (1883-

1961), assistant director and later, in 1934, director of the Hopwood Awards, had been seeking a photograph of Hopwood from which a painting could be made.

> In a letter to Carl Van Vechten on December 19, 1934, [Cowden] reports that Gertrude Stein had lectured here on December 14, and in his discussion of his plans with her, she had mentioned the one "made by a friend of his whom you know." Carl Van Vechten replied on December 25, 1934, that he had already heard from Miss Stein and had then talked to Florine Stettheimer. It was first proposed that the portrait be loaned with further arrangements to be made later, but it lacked its frame and Miss Stettheimer wished to delay until her return from a trip to California. A letter from Florine Stettheimer to Professor Cowden on January 13, 1935, promised to send it in the spring. She did not send the portrait, however, perhaps because of the frame. Then on July 3, 1944, Carl Van Vechten wrote that Florine Stettheimer had died very recently and that Ettie Stettheimer offered to give the portrait to the University of Michigan provided it should hang in the room devoted to the Hopwood Awards. A letter from Ettie Stettheimer on July 14, 1944, states that the portrait is a gift. . . . The portrait shows Hopwood standing before a *Fair and Warmer* poster; and Ettie Stettheimer on February 26, 1945, surmised that it was probably painted shortly after or during the run of *Fair and Warmer*. (*Fair and Warmer* was first produced at the Eltinge Theatre in New York on November 6, 1915.) Carl Van Vechten, on March 22, 1945, guessed it would have been painted between 1915 and 1918, but probably 1917. (Letter received from Jane G. Flener, 19 March 1981.)

To Gertrude Stein and Alice Toklas
["A Little Too Much" motto][1]

[17 December 1934]   [150 West Fifty-fifth Street
Monday   New York]

Dear dear DEAR Woojumses! (pronounced Woo-Jums-Ez, pelase!)

You seem to be having all the excitements what with blizzards and squad cars and marathons. Have you ever seen a wrestling match? It is the only thing I can think of to compete with your excitements. If you haven't I'll see that you do when you return. Such a tour! No one except Sarah Bernhardt and William Jennings Bryan has ever seen so much of our country. You will have fabulous stories to tell for years and when some one mentions Blue Bell City, Maine, or Sight Unseen, Idaho, you will pipe up and say I spent several weeks there during the Great Freeze of 1934. It's too wonderful. The only thing I don't know is whether you are getting any of my letters, because you don't tell me that. Anyway you'll soon be East again and that will be nice for the East and Carlo. I can't wait until I photograph the Woojumses, after their Marcopoloesque journey. They will surely have new glints in their eyes, new smiles around their dimples. I'd like to see you both this minute! But please tell me if you are getting my letters.

178,968 yellow ir[i]ses, singing Hallelujah to you!

Carlo!!!

1. For the source of this motto see Stein to Van Vechten [26 December 1926], note 2.

❧

To Gertrude Stein

[20 December 1934]   150 West Fifty-fifth Street
Thursday   [New York]

Dearest Gertrude,

When you talk about getting a plane, I think it would be wonderful and then we could ride right on through the blizzard and *not* have to get out in Milwaukee. Did you get to Iowa City at all? I am wondering. My nephew expected to walk in on you there. You would know him because he looks rather like me, so maybe you didn't get in. . I went to [Pavel] Tchel-icheff's show yesterday[1] and there were THREE portraits of Charles Ford and Alan [i.e., Allen] Tanner was wandering about looking very gloomy be-cause there were not pictures of him. .[2] Pavel's new pictures are mostly spanish and bull-fighting and full of color and very pleasant indeed. . And I saw the Sir Francis Rose show and what a pretty picture of Bilignin! And I like the one of Alice in the Garden.[3] You are all over the catalogue, all over the show. Maybe you painted these pictures. . And you are in the new [Alfred] Stieglitz[4] book and Sherwood Anderson has written a book called No Swank and he has such a pretty paper about you,[5] and did you get my letter in Detroit, you didn't say. . Sugar statues, sugar babies, airplanes, flamingos, poinsettas, and all other creature comforts to you both, DIVINE Woojums!

Carlo

Fania telegraphs that Bermuda is BLEAK—all rains & colds—and she is coming back tomorrow!

You are both being very "correct" & I am so proud of you!

[366]

1. An exhibition of drawings and paintings by Tchelitchew was held at the Julien Levy Gallery, New York, from 12 to 21 December 1934.

2. Charles Henri Ford, the writer, and Allen Tanner, the composer, were both friends of Tchelitchew's.

3. This picture is now in YCAL.

4. Stein's portrait "Stieglitz," in *America and Alfred Stieglitz: A Collective Portrait*, ed. Waldo Frank, Lewis Mumford, Dorothy Norman, Paul Rosenfeld, and Harold Rugg (Garden City, N.Y.: Doubleday, Doran & Co., 1934), p. 280.

5. Sherwood Anderson's *No Swank* (Philadelphia: The Centaur Press, 1934), pp. 81–85, discusses Stein.

To Carl Van Vechten

[postmark: 20 December 1934]　　　　　　The Commodore Perry [Hotel]
　　　　　　　　　　　　　　　　　　　　Toledo, Ohio

My dearest Carl,

What do you mean by saying that I don't tell you about your letters why we are being most dreadfully spoiled the most spoiled Woojumses in history but the thing that spoils us the most and the sweetest is the finding a letter from Carl whenever we get here if we did not have that we will be lost in this large sized America but we do have that we always do and that makes us all not lost, we passed Marion Ohio, yesterday and were so xcited the home of [Warren G.] Harding and the home of the mother of Harding's child and the home of Mrs. Harding and the home of the sister of Harding who was the school-teacher the high school teacher of the mother of Harding's child, could anything be more historical[1] and then we were right near Dayton Ohio, where Wilbur Wright was[2] and now we are in Toledo where poor dear Max Ewing was,[3] Europe nothing in Europe was ever anything to this,

We have just been taken out to drive up the river where Tecumseh fought and bled,[4] and on the way in a magnificent house I heard lived the man and his wife who gave the Champion spark plugs to the world, and to us, to our little Fords we drove so long, so I said I must see them so the procession stopped and we were taken in to see them and they were so nice and they are sending me glass souvenir champion spark plugs, it's a wonderful world, lots of nice stories, and we are remembering them, in the back parts of Columbus two perfectly nice citizens stopped me and said solemnly we just wanted to say that if there was anything that we needed to be done that was not being done for us they would be most glad to do it, anything connected with the police or anything as they were old Columbus families and here were their names, and a reporter girl, told me and she swears she did not make it up here in Toledo that she went to the station to meet us on a train we did not come on and she asked the gate man if we had come through and he looked blank and a shabby citizen leaning on the wall said no she did not come through and the ticket man said who and the shabby man said sure I know her I never saw her but she would not get by here without my knowing her and then he said to the porter, you know her the one who said a rose is a rose is a rose is a rose you know her.

Do you believe that can be true.

Now we go to Cleveland and then all aboard the airplane to Baltimore, and when and where and how do we see you, we are in Washington the 29-30-31, I wish we would be seeing you somewhere your dear envelopes and letters are a comfort but your darling large sizedness would be more even more of a comfort because the Woojums love you with all their hearts and they always tell you so every way

Always
Gertrude

1. Warren Gamaliel Harding (1865–1923) was the twenty-ninth President of the United States (1920–23). Nan Britton became Harding's mistress in 1917, when she was twenty years old. She claimed that the child she bore him was conceived in the Senate Office Building. See Francis Russell, "A Naughty President," *The New York Review of Books*, 24 June 1982, pp. 30–34, for a summary of Harding's sexual adventures.

2. Wilbur Wright (1867–1912) and his brother Orville (1871–1948) were pioneers in avaition. Wilbur was born in Millville, Indiana, and Orville was born in Dayton, Ohio. It was in Dayton that the brothers formed the Wright Cycle Company in 1892. Stein was fascinated by Wilbur Wright, and in the "Wilbur Wright" section of her *Four in America*, she speculated on what would have happened had Wilbur become a painter.

3. See Van Vechten to Stein, 3 July 1934, note 4.

4. Tecumseh (1768?-1813), American Indian chief of the Shawnee tribe. He was killed in action at the battle of the Thames on 5 October 1813.

꩜

To Gertrude Stein and Alice Toklas

22 December 1934   150 West Fifty-fifth Street
                                             [New York]

Dearest Woojumses!

Merry Christmas or whatever else you want from Fania and me. You are a little dim about your address but I guess this is the right one. . I have such a gadget for you as will knock crystal spark plugs out of your mind, but I won't send it to you. Wait till I walk in with it. You will EXPIRE. . Florine [Stettheimer] is going to send her picture to Anna Arbor (that is a missprint but I shall always call it Anna Arbor after this). She was much touched when I told her you had suggested it and wondered how you had heard of the picture. I told her you knew everything and much more than that. . Did you see how Henry [McBride] wrote about the shows of Sir Francis Rose and [Pavel] Tchelicheff, who one knew you and the other used to know you, and how hard it was to paint unless one knew you? Well, the town is buzzing about this and poor Pavel is in despair. .[1] Mahala [Douglas] wrote that you had called me the Patriarch. Well, it makes me feel like Moses or Abraham, but I guess I did lead you into the Promised Land (Les Belles Woojumses, if I ever did see any!). Mahala is still thrilled and loves you both. Yes, you must go back to Iowa. My nephew had put Clean Sheets on the Beds. . Bill Bullitt is here from Russia;[2] so there will be news of Muriel [Draper], and Bobsy Goodspeed has done the cutest Christmas trick anybody has thought of FOR YEARS.[3] And really it all sounds as if you had written it to be done that way, like a really and truly rosier book. Well, I just love it. And [Miguel] Covarrubias in Vanity Fair is pretty cute too although the text underneath has nothing of your delicate and peculiar savor.[4] Hundreds and Holiday Hugs from Fania and me, and please come back intact save for the places Love of the Country has bitten into you!

178 pots of jam and 189 (best buttered) water spaniels, who can cry Mama and Papa, to you!

Carlo!

1. McBride's review, "Two More Parisian Painters," in the *New York Sun*, 15 December 1934, p. 15.

2. William C. Bullitt, the American diplomat, was ambassador to the Soviet Union from 1933 to 1936.

3. Mrs. Goodspeed published as a Christmas card in 1934 a limited number of copies of a pamphlet, *Chicago Inscriptions*. The text consisted of the inscriptions written by Stein in the copies of her books that she gave to Mrs. Goodspeed. On the cover of the pamphlet was a sketch of Stein done by Mrs. Goodspeed.

4. *Vanity Fair*, January 1935, p. 25, had a portrit of Stein by Covarrubias. In the portrait Stein is seated at a writing table, her right hand in an oath-taking position, and has finished the line "Toasted Susie is my ice cream." The illustration is captioned, "Impossible interview: Gracie Allen vs. Gertrude Stein."

To Gertrude Stein
[Telegram]

24 December 1934   New York

FANIA AND I SEND LOVE AND LOVE AND ROSES AND ROSES TO BOTH LES BELLES WOOJUMSES ON CHRISTMAS DAY AND ALWAYS[1]

CARLO.

1. Stein was staying with her cousins Mr. and Mrs. Julian Stein at Rose Hill, near Pikesville, Maryland.

To Carl Van Vechten and Fania Marinoff

[1 January] 1935   Westover, Virginia
New Year's Morning

The very happiest of New Year's to Fania and to Carl the dearest of dearests and many many more happier and happier new years.

You'll have had Mark [Lutz]'s wire so that you know we are here—where I am sure you too have been. It was all quite unexpected we came down from Wash[ington]. yesterday and go back as soon as G[ertrude]. wakes & is ready.[1]

That they should have known Mark was of course natural but that we should see him here was a lovely surpirse. Mark is sweeter and gentler and nicer even than I remembered. He made my hideous incorrectitude so easy but that is caused from his nature and his feeling for you and G. At any rate it is understood that we—G. & you and I come to Richmond etcetera the first week in Feb[ruary]. and G. & I are so happy about it. G. adores the landscape in Vir[ginia]. Tonight we stay with Mrs. A[nn Archibald]. in Washington—[2] tomorrow we lunch with Prin[cess]. Cantacuzene to see her [U. S.] Grant souvenirs and then early take the train for N. Y. and at once teleph[one]. you.[3] If you are not home I ring you up at 9 a.m. Thurs. And oh then the Woojums will meet—that will be better than the trip which has been perfect. All my love to both of you, you dearest dears—

Alice

1. Stein had been visiting her cousins Mr. and Mrs. Julian Stein in Maryland during the Christmas holidays. For New Year's Eve she and Toklas accepted the invitation of Emily Chadbourne and Ellen LaMotte to join them in visiting Chadbourne's brother, Richard Crane, of Westover, Virginia. By coincidence Mark Lutz, who knew the Cranes, had also been invited.

2. Stein's Washington, D.C., lecture in December 1934 had been organized by Ann Archibald, a friend of Ellen LaMotte's. Mrs. Archibald had arranged for Stein to lecture before the Women's University Club and had sent Mrs. Eleanor Roosevelt an invitation to the lecture. Although she could not attend, Mrs. Roosevelt invited Stein and Toklas to tea at the White House on 30 December 1934 (see LaMotte to Stein, 20 December 1934, YCAL).

3. Julia Grant Cantacuzene (1876-1975) was the granddaughter of President Ulysses S. Grant. She had married, in 1898, the Russian Prince Michael Cantacuzene. At their lunch, on 2 January 1935, the Princess Cantacuzene gave Stein an inscribed copy of her autobiography, *My Life Here and There* (New York: Charles Scribner's Sons, 1930). The inscription reads: "To a Lion from a Mouse! Souvenir of a visit to my home with appreciation. 1935 Jan. 2nd. Julia Cantacuzene Grant" (YCAL).

❦

To Gertrude Stein and Alice Toklas
[Postcard] Carl Van Vechten—Bronze by Gaston Lachaise— 1931.
Collection of Carl Van Vechten

[postmark: 5 January 1935]   [150 West Fifty-fifth Street
Saturday Night   New York]

Dear les Belles Woojums!

The name of the place I want you to see in Boston, please, is Lewisburg Square, and I am wondering if Alice got her hat with the pigeons, but I don't dare telephone because I'm afraid we would talk for HOURS!

Love
Carlo

❦

To Gertrude Stein

[8 January 1935]   150 West Fifty-fifth Street
Tuesday   [New York]

Dear Baby Woojums,

My idea for the Jaegers is something like the enclosed,[x1] plus a tub of champagne and perhaps underneath: We do what we do which is a pleasure! . . . . Most of the photographs are going off today, but I don't seem to have cardboard enough to pack them all. This lack will be remedied by tomorrow. Tell Mama Woojums to wear her rubbers and believe me always

Papa Woojums,
and how!

[x]without a mask!

1. Van Vechten and Stein had discussed a crest for the Woojums family. The crest would contain, among other elements, a pair of jaegers, or undergarments. Two postcards in YCAL, one enclosed with this letter and the other with Van Vechten's letter to Stein of [9 January

[372]

1935], illustrated Van Vechten's idea for the crest. One card, with a printed marking, "Y. R. 51," is a photograph of a seated black-masked woman who is wearing gloves, a black corset (known as a merry widow), black stockings, and black high-heeled shoes. The second card, marked "Y. R. 103," shows the same woman in the same outfit, although in this card she is standing.

To Gertrude Stein

[9 January 1935]　　　　　　　　　　　150 West Fifty-fifth Street
Wednesday　　　　　　　　　　　　　New York City

Dear Baby Woojums,

Maybe you would like something like this? . . . (I mean when we take the Jaegers). No letters from you yet. I wonder if you are sending 'em to Detroit? . . . All the photographs have gone now and your friends will be happy. . . . They asked about you in the bank yesterday. The cashier said, "How's Miss Stein? I haven't seen her lately." . . . And what about wrestling? I asked you this before. Did you ever see a wrestling [match]? If you haven't, you *must*. They happen in N[ew] Y[ork] on Monday nights and we must arrange it when you come back if you haven't. . I hope Mama Woojums is wearing her rubbers and both Woojumses are carrying their rabbits. . That Michigan man wrote to Florine [Stettheimer]: so that's all right.[1]

Love to you both,
Carlo! (Papa Woojums)

1. See Stein to Van Vechten [17 December 1934], note 2.

❧

To Carl Van Vechten

[postmark: 11 January 1935]   Ellen Emerson House
                                Smith College
                                Northampton, Massachusetts

My dearest papa Woojums

Yes I like the stand up Jaegers much better and beside she has such a slim waist, and here we are, and having a very good time, Amherst was awfully nice, the next morning the students went around collecting faculty opinions and the football coach said yes I'd like to have Gertrude for the tackles but I don't know whether she would be good to call the signals and then reflectively but I guess Alice B. would do that, and another one said, I was dead against her and I just went to see what she looked like and then she took the door of my mind right off its hinges and now it is wide open. I had awfully good talks with a lot of them and it was really awfully nice, and now we are at Smith and at the president's there was the youngest Morrow girl and Alice said why how interesting she looks just like Lindbergh,[1] so you see Mama Woojums is in the best of form, and everything is so sweet but the only really truly sweet is our own dear papa Woojums, the rubbers have been neglected but the rabbits are always there, right in our laps and in our pockets,[2]

Lots and lots and lots and more lots of love

Your
B. W.

* * * * * *

These are hugs and kisses.

1. Stein lectured at Smith College on Thursday, 10 January 1935. At a reception given by William Allan Neilson, president of Smith College, Stein met Constance Morrow (Smith, class of 1935), the sister of Anne Morrow Lindbergh (Smith, class of 1928).

2. Note by Van Vechten, 22 January 1941: "I always said when she went out 'Don't forget your rubbers!' A reference to the Hopi Indian fetishes.

[374]

To Carl Van Vechten

[postmark: 12 January 1935]

Hotel Kimball
Springfield, Massachusetts

My dearest Carl,

Really and truly I think your letter carrier is a collector of auto-
graphs, there surely is something mysterious about it, it is going to turn into
another Lindbergh story sure as anything it is not the Woojums they kidnap
but the Woojums' letters, I am going to disguise my handwritting on the
envelope here and see if it improves,[1] so many things to write but I won't
until I know this comes safely, I have had an answer from Chicago for the
same post I sent off your post, so here is my disguised handwriting and if it
works then I will write all about everything because we do want papa Woojums to get our letters so that he may know everything about his family perhaps it is a deep plot to find out that we are the Woojums.

B. W.

1. In an attempt to disguise her handwriting, Stein had printed Van Vechten's name and address on this envelope.

To Carl Van Vechten

[? January 1935]

Hotel Kimball
Springfield, Massachusetts

My dearest papa W.

Here is something that came this morning and I thought might amuse
you[1] we are going sleigh riding to-morrow, we come home to you next
Thursday or Friday and we love you more every minute and everybody wants
me with the American flag[2] I think even the flag does and lots of love from
a most obedient B. and M. W.

Gertrude.

1. Enclosure is a clipping from an ad in the *Toledo* (Ohio) *Times*, which reproduces a clipping from the *Toledo Sunday Times*, "Over Teacups With Babette." The ad is an anecdote concerning Stein and Tiedtke's department store in Toledo, Ohio.

> Mrs. Flora Ward Hineline was taking Gerty on a sight-seeing tour. They finally went in Tiedtke's store and Gerty purchased some winesap apples. Then Mrs. Hineline couldn't get her out. Gerty was fascinated, she wandered around and peered at everything. Later she told Mrs. Hineline that the things that impressed her most in Toledo were Tiedtke's store and the Maumee river.

2. Van Vechten had photographed Stein with an American flag in the background.

❦

To Gertrude Stein

[14 January 1935] 150 West Fifty-fifth Street
Monday [New York]

Dear Gertrude,

The letter addressed as per Bruno Hauptmann arrived.[1] They didn't want *his* autograph. . and one other. Have you sent any more. None from Alice (alias Mama Woojums) and I don't know anything about Virginia yet. So please write some more and disguise your hand all you want to, but don't disguise your heart! . . . Will you PLEASE answer me about wrestling. You don't seem to think I mean this. I began asking you at the Drake hotel in Chicago. I asked you in Detroit and Baltimore. I ask you in Springfield: have you ever seen professional wrestling? If not we must go when you get back.

768 banners of triumph to you both

Papa Woojums!

I saw Kit [Katharine] Cornell last night and she begged me to bring Baby and Mama Woojums to Romeo and Juliet and come up for supper later. Would you like to do this when you return?[2]

One of your flag pictures is the TOP. They are not all printed yet!

1. See Stein to Van Vechten [12 January 1935], note 1.

2. Katharine Cornell was appearing as Juliet in a production of Shakespeare's *Romeo and Juliet*. Also in the cast were Basil Rathbone as Romeo and Dame Edith Evans as the nurse; others included Brian Aherne and Orson Welles.

To Carl Van Vechten

17 January [19]35

Hotel Kimball
Springfield, Massachusetts

My dearest Papa Woojums,

It is quite too dreadful all these years we have been separated, it is more than I can bear this not having you to ask how and why and when and where I should do or not do it. I've not been in hot water, no not at all, it is just the dread of it and no Sweet Papa Woojums to smile and say at the end, I think it will come out all right. The only consolation is that we will be back within the week. For these are our plans,

We leave here very probably Fri., the 25th for N.Y.

Feb. 4th, Univ. of Vir., Charlottesville

   "   6   " " Richmond, Richmond

   "   8   Mary and William [i.e., William and Mary], Williamsburg (Not concluded but more than probable)

   "   10   Sweet Briar College, Sweet Briar

It is of course Mark [Lutz] that has secured William and Mary. There was a sweet letter from him upon our return from Emily C[lark].'s by way of Wesleyan where G[ertrude]. lectured. He asks if he may make reservations for us in Richmond. I have answered him that we wait until we see you, which we do. There are several things about that that the Woojums in holy and happy conclave will settle.[1]

We had a nice time at Sally *Tock's.* Something there that I will tell you when we put Baby W. at Choate. I hope you will agree with me about Choate, they won't suppress Baby's lovely little personality a bit, they will help him to develop his literary aspirations, he will charm them and be the joy of the headmaster, but—will he really be happy at any school. It would be best for him. And how will we ever bear it? Ah me. This too we will have to talk over seriously.[2]

Now to go back to plans, Miss [Josephine] Pinckney has not answered yet.[3] I have only four days for Charleston and Chapel Hill, North Carolina and as yet no reliable air guide. The 18th Tulane University, New Orleans. I am looking for another lecture for New Orleans so that we may stay a bit to enjoy N[ew]. O[rleans]. Then Saint Louis, nothing definite yet and the 27th or better the 26th at Chicago.

Gertrude Stein, Carl Van Vechten, and Alice Toklas, New York, 4 January 1935.
PHOTOGRAPH BY CARL VAN VECHTEN. PRIVATE COLLECTION.

We go to Texas about the 17th March, Arizona and Cal[ifornia]. for the first two weeks of April, then N.Y. and then alas alas alas back to France or what may then be what France was. Of course when we get to France 27 [rue de Fleurus] and Bilignin had better be there. It would be a million times worse to go back without them.

Dear papa Woojums I'm not dispirited about the end of this magical visit which came out of the bottle you made and held upon our arrival but I'm just not courageous any more for two soux. We won't talk about it.

Do send a word to say that Fania really found a smashing good play and will play it and soon and tell her what a supremely lovely and intelligent darling she is on the stage. All my love to her and to you.

Mama Woojums

1. This letter to Toklas is not in YCAL. Stein and Toklas' letters to Lutz are in NYPL-Berg.

2. Stein had delivered the lecture, "How Writing is Written," at the Choate School, Wallingford, Connecticut, on 12 January 1935. The lecture was published in *The Choate Literary Magazine* (February 1935), 21(2):5–14. Stein is often referred to by the masculine pronoun—or by the neuter pronoun.

3. Josephine Pinckney (1895–1957), the writer, was helping to arrange Stein's lectures in her native South Carolina.

To Alice Toklas

[19 January 1935] Saturday

150 West Fifty-fifth Street
[New York]

Dear Alice,

Your letter is here with all kinds of sweet information and your prospective tours sound bewildering! Your pictures are ready. I sent you a little one which you don't mention, so maybe you don't like it. And I can't get a word out of GS (Baby Woojums) about a WRESTLING or Miss [Katharine] Cornell in R[omeo] and J[uliet]. Grand news that you are coming back Friday! I guess I'm going south with you, though I may let you drop me off in Richmond. However maybe I'll stay and hold your hand all the way to the coast! You'll hear from J[osephine] Pinckney if she is alive. Doubtless she is collecting her data. I forwarded a letter from California[x] and Mrs. [Gertrude] Atherton again writes plaintively she hasn't heard from GS.[1] Has Baby Woojums written her yet? F[ania] M[arinoff] is tottering on the edge of two jobs, but will probably take a third. The pictures are Marvels, I am sure you will say, especially the Flags, and you (dear Mama Woojums) with the Tree! Think of your having been at Sally TOCK'S! I had a letter from GS's niece or cousin or whatever in Baltimore and she says she mailed that letter. It hasn't turned up.

Sweet calla, easter and water-lilies to you both!

Papa Woojums!

[x]to G. S.

1. Gertrude Atherton (1857–1948), the writer. Van Vechten had met Atherton through Avery Hopwood probably in 1915. At that time she was living in an apartment at the Madison Square Hotel, New York. It was Hopwood, too, who introduced Atherton to Stein (see Hopwood to Stein, postmark 16 May 1925, YCAL).

Atherton had written Stein, 31 October 1934 (YCAL), inviting her to a dinner in her honor to be given by the San Francisco P. E. N. at the end of November 1934. Because of lecture commitments, Stein declined but said that she might be in California in January 1935 (Atherton to Stein, 14 November 1934, YCAL). That plan, too, had to be canceled.

Atherton sought in vain to interest various clubs and universities in sponsoring a lecture by Stein. She did succeed, however, in interesting Alice Seckles, a well-known San Francisco literary figure, in Stein's California plans, and it was Seckles who finally arranged for several university lectures.

To Carl Van Vechten

20 January [19]35   Hotel Kimball
                                                       Springfield, Massachusetts

Dearest Carl,

Well it was most awfully nice for one Woojum to hear its chief's voice. Mama W. felt she had gotten the better of Baby W. who was that surprised at the ways of the grown up Ws. He always is surprised, so freshly surprised and so frequently surprised.

This is only to ask hurriedly, at what hotel do we stop at Richmond? Mark [Lutz] asks and suggests the Jefferson as probably the one you prefer. Is it necessary to make reservations long in advance? To be sure we don't know when we start, will it be the second or the third? The first lecture is on the evening of the fourth. And then here I am find out nothing about flying, they say the schedules are being changed.

I had a letter from Miss [Josephine] Pinckney, who charmingly asks information to give to the Poetry Society.[1] (I had in haste confusion and featherheadedness put Virginia instead of N[orth]. C[arolina]. Don't let us ever speak of that before either Papa W. or Baby W. Mama W. would lose prestige.) I have given her Feb. 14th as the date; Feb. 12th Chapel Hill.

Heaps of love, in a towering hurry,

Mama W.

1. This letter does not appear to be in YCAL.

To Carl Van Vechten

[postmark: 20 January 1935] Hotel Kimball
Springfield, Massachusetts

My dearest papa W.

I have a suspicion amounting almost to a certainty that all my lost letters have been sent to 55 W. 150 Street instead of where they should go, do you suppose one could tell the sad story to the Dead Letter office and they could get them back, do you think so. We had a sleigh ride yesterday, in a real sleigh with a black horse but we did not go very fast because they take the snow off the roads and when they don't there are ruts but we liked it so much love from the family to Papa W. and we are to see him soon,

xxxxxxxxxxxxx B. W.

[381]

❧

To Gertrude Stein
[Telegram]

21 January 1935   New York

GUESTS OF KIT [Katharine] CORNELL AT ROMEO AND JULIET AND SUPPER MONDAY JANUARY TWENTY EIGHTH DINNER WITH PAPA WOOJUMS BEFORE IS THIS ALL RIGHT LOVE TO BABY AND MAMA WOOJUMS

CARLO.

❧

To Gertrude Stein and Alice Toklas
["A Little Too Much" motto]

21 January 1935   [150 West Fifty-fifth Street
                                                    New York]

Dear Mama Woojums and Baby Woojums!

You will see from the enclosed one of the reasons why I don't get all my letters. This has happened before. Sometimes, I suppose, the postoffice is not sufficiently ingenious! . . . . I have written Kit [Katharine] Cornell that we will accept her invitation but have not heard from her about the date yet. I'll let you know at once, of course . . . BUT on Thursday January 31th,[1] the [Louis] Bromfields are coming here to dinner *for you and Alice*, that is if you will come (at 7 o'clock). Will you? . . Dying to see you both and to go into everything with you!

love,
Papa Woojums (and how!)

Two more letters have just arrived. You are correct, Baby Woojums, you *do* address your letters wrong, and now Alice says she addresses letters to Virginia instead of NC! Why don't you write to the Post Office and ask them to collect ALL letters addressed ANYWHERE to Papa Woojums and send them to him! . . It's the Jefferson Hotel in Richmond, of course. It's the older hotel and the one where the haute Monde are most comfortable. Certainly we'll let Mark [Lutz] make the reservations. Time enough to do this when you get back here. Also I think it would be a good plan to write (for me to write) Miss Ellen Glasgow. I want *her* to entertain for us if possible. A party at the Academy, ANYTHING, could be arranged, but Miss Ellen would be best.[2] I'll talk to you about this. If the lecture at Charlottesville is Monday night, we could go down Monday easily, I think, flying to Washington, if the weather is good. If not, taking a train. We'd go on to Richmond Tuesday or Wednesday. If you don't want to RUSH, it might be better to go to Charlottesville on Sunday. . I think this might be better.

We'll talk about everything. Call up at once when you arrive.

1. 30 was changed to 31, but the "th" remained.

2. Van Vechten had met Ellen Glasgow (1874–1945), the writer, in the mid-1920s during one of his frequent visits to Richmond, Virginia. When Stein visited Richmond, Glasgow gave a dinner in her honor.

To Carl Van Vechten
[Telegram]

22 January 1935   Springfield, Massachusetts

LOOKING FORWARD GREATEST PLEASURE THEATRE AND SUPPER WITH YOU AT KITTY [Katharine] CORNELLS ALSO DINNER AT PAPA WOOJUMS TO MEET [Louis] BROMFIELDS STOP HAVING LOVELY TIME BUT LONG FOR YOU AND NEW YORK STOP RETURN FRIDAY AFTERNOON STOP DEAREST LOVE

M AND B WOOJUMS.[1]

1. Note by Van Vechten, 22 January 1941: "Katharine Cornell asked us to a performance of *Romeo and Juliet* and to her house after."

𝕬

To Gertrude Stein

[February? 1935]   [150 West Fifty-fifth Street
                                                    New York]

Dear Baby Woojums!

[Thomas] Whittemore never wrote me: so I couldn't do anything about that.[1] Les Belles Woojumses never wrote me either. I haven't had a peep since you left God's country. I wonder if you are sending my letters to Ain?

mille pensées, a tub of hydrangeas, five candy hearts, 167 flawless emeralds, and much love to you and Mama Woojums from

PAPA WOOJUMS!

1. Whittemore had probably asked Stein for a copy of one of Van Vechten's photographs of her.

𝕬

To Gertrude Stein
["*A Little Too Much*" *motto*]

[4? February 1935]   150 West 55 Street
Monday   New York City

Dear Baby Woojums,

This card will show you what *may* happen to baby woojumses,[1] so please don't let it! . . I saw Louis Bromfield and he grinned for three minutes as he reflected on your American triumphs. I hear that all American authors, except your loving friends, have gone to bed as a result! . . Well it seems incredible you've gone away again, even for a minute, and very sadmaking. So let me know about Virginia and give my love to Mama Woojums and yourself, woojie, woojie, woojie (very fast),

Papa Woojums!!

1. This letter is written on a 7 x 5-inch card with Van Vechten's motto engraved in the upper left-hand corner. Van Vechten, when sending a card, usually used a picture postcard or one of his photographs used as a card.

To Gertrude Stein
[Postcard: Houdon's Statue of Washington in the Capitol Building, Richmond, Virginia]

[10–13? February 1935]   [150 West Fifty-fifth Street
                                          New York]

Dear G. S!

I have always liked the South, but the last line in this review of Mark Lutz's—probably you have seen it already in the *bundles* of reviews sent you— makes me reel with enthusiasm.[1] Of course, we must look forward to the Autobiography of Gertrude Stein!—

Love.
Carlo

1. Articles about Stein by Lutz appeared in the *Richmond News-Leader* on 7, 8, and 9 February 1935. It is impossible to determine which article is being referred to.

To Carl Van Vechten
[Postcard: Sweet Briar House, Sweet Briar, Va.]

[postmark: 12 February 1935]   [Chapel Hill, North Carolina]

Dearest P. W.

They were all so sorry that you were not with us and the sorriest were we, it is a lovely place and mighty pretty everything is inside and out, and now here we are in Chapel Hill and I took out my speedometer [i.e., pedometer] for xcercise and it and I wanted to come back and tell you about it but no Papa W. no Papa W. our only consolation is that Fania has you, best and best love to you and best love to Fania

B. W. and M. W. and very very lonesome very xxxxx.

[Gertrude Stein]

To Carl Van Vechten
[Telegram]

14 February 1935   Charleston, South Carolina

CHARLESTON LOVELY BUT HIDEOUSLY LONESOME WITHOUT PAPA WOOJUMS LOVING FELICITATIONS FANIAS SUCCESS[1]

THE WOOJUMS

1. Marinoff was rehearsing the role of Susanne Pentland in the play *Times Have Changed*, by the French writer Edouard Bourdet. The play was adapted by Louis Bromfield. It opened at the National Theatre, New York, on 25 February 1935 and ran for thirty-two performances.

To Carl Van Vechten

14 February [19]35   Villa Margherita
                                                        Charleston, S. C.

Dearest Papa Woojums,

It is a lovely Charleston but very lonesome, all your friends have been so sweet to us considering that they almost feel we didn't bring you, they don't see that *we* are the ones who suffer the most. Miss [Josephine] Pinckney was charming and intriguing and a little mysterious, the Dubose Heywards even more charming, so little mysterious that one felt that one had known them always and so loved them at once,[1] and the unknown Mr. Ben Kittredge Jr. sat next [to] me at lunch at Oxford in '25 or '26 and he has a beautiful car but a marvellous garden, the famous cypress garden and we rode on boats on the swamp for hours this afternoon.[2] This I tell you so that you may know what you are missing. Do come to New Orleans next Sunday evening, Roosevelt Hotel. Yes? Yes.

And now why Marvin Chauncy Ross made an engagement one night at Charlottesville and the next night at Amherst. Two miles from Sweetbriar and about twenty from Charlottesville there is an Amherst, not the Amherst but an Amherst just the same. On the whole Sweetbriar was not quite as much so at home in Sweetbriar as in the train, there were half a dozen who were fairly faisandée, the others not half so good looking as Vassar.

Dearest Carl, come to New Orleans, do or we won't know what to do.

Do say a thousand things to Fania about how lovely she will be in the new role and how thrilling we will find it when we get back in April.[3] A Mrs. Clem Little, who wrote Dust in my shoes, says Fania was perfect the only time she saw her and she lives to see her again.

All my love and à bientot,

Mama Woojums

1. DuBose Heyward (1885–1940), the writer, and his wife, Dorothy (1890–1961).

2. Benjamin Kittredge, Jr. (1900–1981), and his wife Carola de Peyster Kip, lived on a former plantation, Cypress Gardens.

3. See Stein to Van Vechten, 14 February 1935, note 1.

To Carl Van Vechten

[postmark: 14 February 1935]   Villa Margherita
                                                           Charleston, S.C.

My dearest Carl

Everybody says where [is] Carl and we have to say with a tear in the eye no Carl, it is a sweet Carl but we do not no we do not like to have to say there is no Carl here no we do not. The lectures in Charleston went off well, and Chapel Hill is lovely I wish you had been at Chapel Hill and so do they all, it is one of the nicest places and the pig eater was sweet and Spanish and careful and we liked him but he did not replace Papa,[1] nothing replaces Papa say the Woojums ladies with a tear in each eye. Love to Fania and everything is beautiful that she is acting that we are sure of

Gertrude

Address Hotel Roosevelt, New Orleans.

1. This letter and Toklas' of 14 February were mailed together. The "pig eater" of this letter and the "Salvation Figeater" of Van Vechten to Stein and Toklas [February? 1935], are the same, but which spelling is correct is impossible to determine. The reference is to someone Van Vechten had spoken about whom Stein would probably meet while in Charleston, South Carolina.

❦

To Gertrude Stein and Alice Toklas

[February? 1935]   [150 West Fifty-fifth Street
Tuesday   New York]

Dear Ladies Woojums, Mama and Baby!

I have been worried about you ever since you went off with Salvation Figeater: you must tell me all about him. I'm sure he was fascinating and made you swerve (slightly) from your allegiance to Papa Woojums![1] Anyway, here I am back in NY anxiously awaiting news of the dear ladies. And how was Sweet Briar and did the filles strike any more Alma Tadema attitudes? Well, please write me right away![2]

Love to both and Fania and Edith send love too!

Carlo!!

Rehearsals are going *badly*: but they always do.
I am forwarding a letter from Mabel [Dodge].[3]
If you are not sending a copy of Lectures in America to Miss Ellen Glasgow, 1 West Main Street, Richmond, Virginia, please let me know. But I believe you are!

1. See Stein to Van Vechten [14 February 1935], note 1.

2. Sir Lawrence Alma Tadema (1836–1912), an English painter known primarily for his paintings of Greek and Roman set pieces.

3. Dodge had written Stein, beginning 9 October [1934], urging her to come to Taos, New Mexico, where Dodge lived. Subsequent letters of Dodge to Stein in 1934–35 urged Stein to meet her in either Taos or Carmel, California. Stein steadfastly refused to meet Dodge during her American tour.

❧

To Gertrude Stein and Alice Toklas

[16 February 1935]   150 West Fifty-fifth Street
Saturday   New York City

Dear Mes! dames Woojums (Baby and Mama)

Your New Orleans address for tomorrow couldn't possibly reach you (I just got it today) and so I am sending this to the Algonquin. . Ed Wynn, a comic, who performs on the radio had it the other night that his aunt's phonograph got stuck on a record of a song and it went on repeating "a rose is a rose is a rose." She was enraptured, thinking it was Gertrude Stein. . I have entreated Mark [Lutz] to send you a poem a bright (?) Richmond boy wrote to one of the papers there on this subject.[1] He says that like Lee you will always be remembered in those parts and frequently spoken of. . I am not so sorry about Sweet Briar after your report, but think of [Marvin] Ross being right about Amherst! Maybe we have been harsh with this Baltimore beauty. . Charleston and its dismal swamps sounds most appealing, and I am sure New Orleans will be all fanlights, magnolias, and soft-stepping, sweet-voiced blacks. DO MEET HUEY LONG! . .[2] Be kind to Republicans everywhere, but I think if you would run on the ticket (Baby Woojums for President) it would pull through. Mabel [Dodge] writes she is getting out another book of Memoirs,[3] and Baby Paul Robeson (age 8) came to see me with his distinguished grandmother yesterday. F[ania] M[arinoff] has gone to Philadelphia and opens Monday at the Garrick there.[4] She will be all right. I have another niece here who asks questions about you and so does the superb actress Judith Anderson, who is also dying to meet you. I think I shall give a garden party for you (in some apple orchard) in April. So get out your organdies. New York will be hot as hot in that sweet month. You have forgotten how hot! . I don't need to remind you, dear Mama, to wear your rubbers any more. This sweet tour is drawing to a close. I shall cry for days when you sail!

love, love, love!
Carlo (Papa Woojums!)

the Virginia pictures are mostly developed but not printed. You will like 'em.

1. The poem was quoted in the *Richmond News-Leader*, 1 January 1935, p. 1.

2. Huey Long (1893–1935), lawyer and politician, was governor of Louisiana from 1928 to 1931 and United States senator from Louisiana from 1931 to 1935. Stein never met Long, although an article in the *New York Sun*, 22 February 1935, (YCAL) has the headline "Gertrude Stein for Huey Long," which indicates that she had read about him.

3. Dodge to Van Vechten, 9 February [1935], YCAL.

4. See Stein to Van Vechten, 14 February 1935, note 1.

To Carl Van Vechten

17 February [19]35   Tutwiler Hotel
                                            Birmingham, Ala.

Dearest Papa Woojums,

Why, oh why didn't you come to Birmingham. It's a S C R E A M! I M P A Y A B L E ! U N B E L I E V A B L E ! Why didn't you come, how can I laugh tears without you? And it can't ever quite be told and when W H E N I A S K Y O U A R E W E G O I N G T O S E E Y O U ? And if we don't soon what is the use of, well anything.

Duncan is one story, there are ten Duncans and we saw all of them most all the time yesterday and we are here until this afternoon when we fly to New Orleans where you may be (and would be if you weren't busy with other Woojumses, you're not taking them on permanently, just until I can get at them, it's hateful to think of the possibilities)

Yes Birmingham is unique, and we wouldn't have missed it for anything but we don't want to come back. The intelligence of the Birmans (that's what they called themselves in their newspaper yesterday) descends through their women and the men are weirdly bashful and gauche. And it's a feministe who is telling you this.

Will you please write us at once Hotel Roosevelt, New Orleans to tell us everything, but especially about Fania's play. Heaps of love to you both and millions of good wishes.

Your
Mama Woojums

&

To Gertrude Stein

[17 February 1935]   150 West Fifty-fifth Street
Sunday   [New York]

Dear Gertrude,

I heard from you yesterday, thank heaven, and you are having a sweet time as usual. Besides sweet Miss [Ellen] LaMotte wrote me about your photograph[1] and the Cosmopolitan came out and I love your article.[2] But the editor got very fresh and asks his readers to judge whether you are "genius or charlatan." Does he mean all his authors are one or the other? He should be flipped on the nose for this! I am soon going into the darkroom to print your pictures. Shall I send a little one of the Three Woojums? I think I will. . Fania is back from Atlantic City and it is very cold. New England is the place to be on cold nights. Have they still got feather beds? You will not answer my questions about a Wrestling. Have you ever seen a wrestling? We must see a wrestling. A girl who has just married a man who believes in the devil and is going to raise goats (for milk) wants very much to meet you. Who doesn't? The Bromfields are melodious in their appreciation of your triumphs. They fancy you will find Paris very meagre after all this.[x]

my love to Baby and Mama Woojums!

Carlo (Papa Woojums)

[x]as no doubt you will.
XXX right back at you!

[391]

1. LaMotte wrote to Van Vechten [10 January 1935] (YCAL), thanking him for the pictures of Stein and Toklas he had sent her.

2. Stein's article, "I Came and Here I Am," *Hearst's International Combined with Cosmopolitan* (February 1935), 98(2):[18]–19.

To Alice Toklas

[18 February 1935] 　　　　　　　　150 West Fifty-fifth Street
Monday 　　　　　　　　　　　　　New York City

Dear Alice,

What can I do, sweet Mama Woojums, but pass on Miss [Frances] Steloff's letter to you?[1] Do what you think best about it. . It is cold one day and warm the next but the apple blossoms will be out for your organdie party in April. Shall I ask Walter Winchell?

567 bright red dolphins with pretty ribbons in their
mouths to you both!

Papa Woojums!

1. Van Vechten enclosed a letter he had received from Frances Steloff, 16 February 1935 (YCAL). Steloff, owner of the Gotham Book Mart, New York, was disappointed that Stein, who had signed books at Brentano's while she was in New York, had not arranged to do the same at the Gotham, where Steloff had been a longtime supporter of her writings. Steloff also wrote Van Vechten trying to clear up a misunderstanding about the prices being charged for copies of the Plain Edition volumes.

To Carl Van Vechten

21 February [19]35 　　　　　　　The Roosevelt [Hotel]
　　　　　　　　　　　　　　　　　New Orleans, Louisiana

Dearest Papa Woojums,

It was my hope and intention to write you a pretty letter to-day but instead I'm writing you a business letter. Baby W. however is writing you one full of love from herself and from her lesser parent.

Well, here goes for Miss F[rances]. Steloff. She used to order books of the Plain Edition and eventually payed for some of them. Any one who ordered books of P. E. had my eternal gratitude and I didn't forget The Gotham Book Shop. So when we got to N. Y. I trotted our precious baby to the Gotham Book Shop, presented Miss Steloff and Baby W. took a violent and instant dislike to the nice lady and kicked and screamed and said it would go right back to the hotel. (I must say that the figures she quotes are correct, they were the price when she *ordered* them, naturally Random House had other arrangements) Which was accomplished. Later I hoped to go to see Gotham Book Shop and just say this, that is all but Baby W.'s reasonable enough prejudice. Now I am writing it to her and asking her, is [i.e., if] I can without saying it, why she behaves thusly when and where and how she shouldn't in writing to our Papa W. who says one should be correct always, but smiles when Mama W. isn't.

Now about Mrs. [Gertrude] Atherton, I've frankly not known what to do about the subject of the announcement that G[ertrude]. was visiting her. But her letter to you shows so sweetly that she considered it to be merely extraneous and unconnected. What she says about Alice Seckels confirms my final judgement of my namesake, she is honest but untruthful, perhaps not too dishonest, but honest enough. But she doesn't know what is true and false and therefore to be watched. She has finally arranged as we wish four lectures, two in S[an]. F[rancisco]., one at Mills College and one at Stanford.

We will stay in S. F. more than four days, we certainly will be there for the ninth. That is half the reason of going west, to go to the P. E. N. dinner. It certainly was your and Mrs. Atherton's arrangement that is giving us the trip west. BUT it was understood that Papa Woojums was to be there, now you didn't come to Charleston (so Baby says it caught a cold there because it felt too lonesome), you didn't come to New Orleans (so Baby said it couldn't lose its cold but it was so furiously lonesome) SO YOU WILL COME TO S.F. PLEASE SAY YOU ARE THINKING ABOUT IT AND WILL TELL US THAT YOU WILL LET US KNOW SOON THAT YOU ARE DEFINITELY COMING. PLEASE SAY YES.

It was about the radio that I found Miss Seckels untruthful. She wrote me that she had said it could be arranged to the man who asked for it, because the Chronicle had had word that Miss Stein's publisher said she would accept. It is all stupid and tiresome. But I answered Miss S[eckels]. that G[ertrude]. would arrange such matters herself if it suited her to do them.[1]

Now that leaves me only time to hope that we have news before leaving to-morrow morning by air (7.45 from the hotel a. m. and G. not pleased) for Saint-Louis, Hotel Park Plaza until Sunday at 2.30 P.M., that Fania had no cold, that she liked her role when it was given to an audience, and that they thought the role and play not too unworthy of Fania's delicious, delicate, penetrating, poignant, interesting, intelligent gift God-given. Please lend us clippings my [i.e., by] registered post c/o Thornton Wilder Esquire, 6020 Drexel Avenue, Chicago where we will be Sunday evening.

There is something I am always about to write you and never quite do, something that comes over me to say to you but is a poor way of saying how dear you are to be dear to me.

Alice Mama Woojums

1. See Van Vechten to Toklas [19 January 1935], note 1. Alice Seckles had a gathering in the Fairmont Hotel, San Francisco, one Thursday morning each month. A commentator would speak on current events and books. Seckles also arranged lecture tours for certain authors. Atherton had written Van Vechten, 16 February [1935] (YCAL), confirming Seckles' arrangements for Stein's visit. Atherton also detailed her plans for entertaining Stein. Seckles' letters to Toklas are not in YCAL.

To Carl Van Vechten

[postmark: 24 February 1935]   The Roosevelt [Hotel]
                                                New Orleans, Louisiana

My dearest papa Woojums

Here we are still in New Orleans, hot and delicious and the only thing missing is you, and you would make it hotter and deliciouser which would have been so nice, and we do like it, and have seen the levies and ferried across the Mississippi and have been given bulbs of a Mexican lily given to the first governor of New Orleans and the social register of the bawdy houses a charming little blue book with the simple advertisements of the ladies by themselves and we have eaten oyster a la Rockefeller and innumerable shrimps made in every way and all delicious and we were taken to visit the last of the Creoles in her original house unchanged for a hundred years and you would have enjoyed it, and all the time papa Woojums hundreds of miles away and he did say papa Woojums did say that he would not be hundreds of miles away and the moral of that is put no faith in papa Woojums, no not any. It is wonderful unblameable weather and the clouds go up and down, and it is all very lovely and very lively, oh and we have seen the most wonderfully large camellia trees growing with camellias, they were transplanted from old plantations a hundred years old and still cheerful, and we are coming back and buy a Ford and just run around, we have met up with Sherwood [Anderson] and now to-morrow we must leave all these joys behind us. We are so happy about Fania not that she is nervous but that [it] will be and has been alright and lots of love always and always

B. W. to her pa

To Carl Van Vechten
[Postcard: The Park Plaza Hotel, St. Louis, Mo.]

[postmark: 24 February 1935]   The Park Plaza Hotel
                                                Kingshighway and
                                                Maryland Avenue
                                                St. Louis   [Missouri]

Just two words to say, that we are here and will be in Chicago, c/o Thornton Wilder, 6020 Drexel Ave., this afternoon if the plane is kinder than the one from N[ew]. Orleans Friday which because of a storm, left us at Memphis to take a train here, 10 hours and Baby W. in a temper!
Heaps and heaps of love from

B. & M. Woojums

To Carl Van Vechten

[February 1935]   [New Orleans, Louisiana]

Dearest love to Papa Woojums from lonesome—lonesome Baby and Mama Woojums[1]

1. Note by Van Vechten, 22 January 1941: "This card from Alice probably came with some stuffed dates."

❧

To Gertrude Stein and Alice Toklas

[25 February 1935]   101 Central Park West
Monday   New York

Dear Baby and Mama Woojums,

Whatever you two dear relatives do to the Gotham Book Mart is okay by me. I sent you the letter because I thought it might amuse you to see how they go on. . And I'm glad San Francisco is okay. Enfin. You will see, mama, that it is you who goes in for misaddressing now. The end of Mama Woojums' letter was quite affecting and made me cry a little. . F[ania] M[arinoff] still has a cold and is rehearsing madly. She opens tonight. I'll let you know about this later. . Georgia O'Keefe was here being photographed Friday and moaned because she had not met you. I invited her to the garden party in April (get out your organdies) but she may not be in town. . The wonderful candy came from New Orleans with the sweet card and a lovely letter also arrived from the Baby. Virgil [Thomson] telephoned this morning for your address, as some publisher wants to print Pigeons on the Grass. This will lead eventually to the opera being printed, I should think![1]

Lots of everything to you, including eighteen yellow sapphires and enough poodles to please you!

Carlo Papa Woojums

Please remember that *you* were sending Miss [Ellen] Glasgow, 1 West Main Street, Richmond, a copy of Lectures in America. If for some reason you are not, let me know and I will. Let's all go visit that bibulous Mrs. McCrea at Carter's Grove![2]
[collage on letter] STEIN DEMANDS
ANDHOW!
Please send Thornton Wilder to be photographed! I loved his new book[3]

1. "Pigeons on the Grass Alas," an aria from *Four Saints in Three Acts*, was published by J. Fisher & Brothers, New York, in 1935. One hundred copies were published 8 May 1935 for the Berkshire School Musicale Association.

2. While in Richmond, Virginia, Stein had driven through Williamsburg with Mr. and Mrs. Archibald McCrea of Carter's Grove, Virginia.

3. Wilder's *Heaven's My Destination* (New York: Harper & Bros., 1935).

To Gertrude Stein and Alice Toklas

[25 February 1935]   150 West Fifty-fifth Street
Monday   [New York]

Dear Ladies Woojums!

Here is a letter from Mrs. [Gertrude] Atherton which apparently offers you the keys of the city but still implicates Alice Seckles. I don't know what to write to her. So I am forwarding this letter to you. Will you please return it to me. Certainly Gertrude A is working for the Cause and if she can't get the Key to the Ravens she might at least have a feather from a pigeon on the Grass. This is all the news there is just now. Fania just called up. She is very nervous and has a cold and opens tonight.

157 varieties of orchid and bright green emeralds to you both!

Carlo! (P. Woojums, Esq.)

To Carl Van Vechten

25 February [19]35   6020 Drexel Avenue
                                                    Chicago, Illinois

Dearest Papa Woojums,

We finally flew from Saint Louis yesterday afternoon and broke a record, 4 minutes less than ever before. Perhaps the pilot knew that very shortly that is half an hour afterwards snow would have made landing impossible. It was a marvelous trip quite as if on greased rails. Thornton [Wilder] was here to greet us and took us to dine at Mr. ? house where after dinner seven students from an honour fraternity met seven faculty members and Baby W., Mama W. chaperoning or nursing The Baby. It was a good dinner and a nice time after, Mr. [Robert Morss] Lovett presiding.[1] Mr. Lovett said charming things about Papa W. Thornton wants to be photographed and meet you and have a photograph of Gertrude Stein in front of the American flag! And he would like to read Four In America and so Baby W. says would you please send it to her here at this address.

All to-day has been taken up with arranging the hours of the lectures, the hours of the classes, the subjects of the lectures and the subjects of the classes, writing the first lecture and arranging the reading for the students of the classes in preparation. There are to be four new lectures.[2] I will be typing them au fur et mesure for Baby W. and then for you to read. You know that at Tulane at New Orleans it wasn't read but just discarded and hotly said. And perhaps what you wanted will happen, don't you think you had better come on?

Mrs. [Gertrude] Atherton has written to say about the dinner of the P. E. N. Club and asking when we arrive and will we dine, lunch or tea with her and her daughter.[3] Of course you come, I say of COURSE, OF COURSE

And don't you ever want us to hear from you again, and won't you tell us about Fania's play,[4] I don't believe you really know how long it is since we have had one word from you. Dearest Papa the two Pompadour ladies in woolen suits (one in Jaegers) aren't as happy as they should be. And please please write to say you and Fania are all all well. We love you so

Mama W.

---

1. Robert Morss Lovett (1870–1956) was a member of the English Department of the University of Chicago from 1893 to 1936. He was also one of the editors of the *New Republic*.

2. Stein's four lectures, given during her second visit to the University of Chicago, were published as *Narration*. The volume contained an introduction by Thornton Wilder.

3. Atherton to Stein, 20 February 1935, YCAL.

4. See Stein to Van Vechten, 14 February 1935, note 1.

To Gertrude Stein

[26 February 1935]   150 West Fifty-fifth Street
Tuesday   New York City

Dear Daring Young Woojums on the Flying Trapeze!

Fania opened last night and as you request I am sending you a couple of notices.[1] Will you please return these. The play, I'm afraid, is not too hot, but her interpretation has the authenticity, the fervor, the real underneath feeling, that she gives everything she touches in the theatre. . . . I am quite excited over Miss [Fanny] Butcher's NOCES. Was this fellow in the box with us at Four Saints? I think so. Please congratulate Miss Butcher's young man for me. She forgot to send an address with her wedding cards, or maybe she isn't ever going to be "At Home."[2] Louis [Bromfield] is sailing after his De Luxe, next Tuesday.[3] . The Choate School Magazine has just arrived. With a classy article by G[ertrude] S[tein].[4] . Did you know there were crossword puzzles in the newspapers called Gertrude Stein? Did you know that? I send you four sticks of chewing gum and all the icebox cake you like!

Carlo (Papa W!)

Your account of your record-breaking just received. I am not surprised about what happened at Tulane. You know I looked over the lecture Baby W was to give at William and Mary, and she said a great many things that weren't written down. I am delighted San Francisco is all arranged. You *must* meet Noël Sul[l]ivan in S[an] F[rancisco]. I'll arrange this later. But tell G[ertrude] A[therton], if there is any slipup, to produce N[oël] S[ullivan]![5] Four in America goes to you today registered. And of course Thornton Wilder will get a flag photograph when you come back to inscribe it and I am delighted he will come to be photographed. When, please?

1. Marinoff opened in the play *Times Have Changed.* See Stein to Van Vechten, 14 February 1935, note 1.

2. Fanny Butcher was the literary critic of the *Chicago Tribune.* She was also a pioneer in the "Little Theatre" movement and the founder of Fanny Butcher Books, a bookstore in Chicago. She married Richard Drummond Bokum. Butcher's souvenirs of Stein are in her book *Many Lives—One Love* (New York: Harper & Row, 1972), pp. 411–26.

3. In addition to his *Times Have Changed*, Bromfield was preparing another play for a Broadway opening. *Deluxe*, by Bromfield and John Gearon, opened at the Booth Theatre, New York, on 5 March 1935.

4. See Toklas to Van Vechten, 17 January [19]35, note 2.

5. Noel Sullivan (1890–1956) was a patron of the arts. He was a friend of both Atherton's and Van Vechten's. His home, in Carmel, California, was a well-known gathering place for writers and musicians.

To Gertrude Stein

[28 February 1935]   [150 West Fifty-fifth Street
Thursday   New York]

Dear Baby Woojums,

Since getting the Choate Literary Magazine I am more and more interested in Choate. Please tell me all about Choate. Did you meet Robert T. Vanderbilt, Jr. ? . . . . Here is a piece about the actors in Times Have Changed in last night's Post. I have never known before 10 actors in a cast of 14 to be praised universally but this has happened this time.[1] F[ania] M[arinoff] is already getting fan mail, but the most excited member of the family is Madame Pearl Showers who has been promoted to the role of theatre maid. . Madame Showers and Madame Bottoms send their respectful greetings to Baby and Mama, by the way![2]

And I guess this paper will send you, eh, baby?[3]

love to you both from
Papa W!

1. In an article in the *New York Post*, 26 Feb. 1935, p. 9, John Mason Brown wrote, "If Mr. Bromfield's *Times Have Changed* reaches The National as a disappointment, it is not any of the people who have contributed to the New York production who can be blamed."

2. Madame Bottoms is a reference to Marinoff.

3. At the top of the stationery there is a picture of a female mouse standing on a stool talking into a telephone.

To Carl Van Vechten

[postmark: 28 February 1935]

The Midway Drexel
6020 Drexel Avenue
Chicago, Illinois

My dearest pap[a] W.

Here we are here we really are and pretty soon I will be sending you the mimeographed[?] copy of what I am doing, golly, but first thanks for the clippings and I am sorry the play is not better but one thing sure Fania got over and I do wish we could see her, well perhaps even so the play may last out until we get there and if not she will have another, I am awfully interested in Fania's acting she really has the technique of the old and the spirit of the new, she really has, and it all is so xciting, had a letter from Mary Bromfield they seem to have good hopes of [De]Luxe do let us know how it comes off,[1] we have not seen Fanny Butcher yet she just got back from the voyage de Noce last night and telephoned us this morning and we see her this afternoon, she speaks quite cosily of her young man as my husband so I guess everything is very well, to be sure he had toothache on the honeymoon and the car went to pieces but anyway they seem happy, we saw [Robert Morss] Lovett the other evening he was conducting an honors's evening about propaganda and literature and we were invited to attend, they gave us a cold buffet first which as eats were only second to Carl and Charleston, I still am sad that you did not eat shrimps in Charleston at the Kittredges I still am sad about that such shrimps such very sweet shrimps in a pale pink sauce, such lovely shrimps, we have had shrimps lots of shrimps in New Orleans but the Charleston shrimps are a thing apart and a whole xistence, we did not see Hughy [Huey Long] but I was photographed by the Associated press photographer who for eight years has been photographing him and who got black jacked by mistake by his body guard, and he told me a lot about him. I still am interested in him and when we get back I'll tell you all I heard. I am terribly frightfully busy because I have 4 lectures to write about narrative, I have just finished 2 in three days and now I have to do two more, I have found some interesting things to say so Thornton [Wilder] and Alice and I think well anyway and then I have 10 conferences with small bodies of students and then two hours consultations a time with anybody

[401]

who wants to talk to me, well I guess, I ought pretty soon to be talked about [i.e., out] but there always does seem to be more where the last came from. I guess that is all our news, we flew not all the way to St Louis they let us down at Memphis where they said there was a storm but we did not believe them anyway we trained from Memphis to St. Louis and then we had a record making breaking flight from St Louis to Chicago, 10 minutes quicker than it was ever done before, so here we are and loving papa Woojums so but think he ought to come and be here with mamma and me, yes we do, we are dining with Lovett Saturday, lots of love and a hug for Fania and tell her how pleased we are and always and always and always

x x x x x x x x x x x x x x x Baby W.

Thornton says that he won't be in New York before mid-summer but he certainly will be on our doorstep when he gets there.

1. Mary Bromfield, 22 February [1935] (YCAL), had reported to Stein on the Boston opening (19 February) of the Bromfield and Gearon play *Deluxe*.

To Gertrude Stein

[3 March 1935]
Sunday

[150 West Fifty-fifth Street
New York]

Dear Baby Woojums:

The Virginia photographs will be ready in a few days and I think I'll send them to you, so you and Mama Woojums will have something to remember me by. Maybe Fania's play will last till you get back. Anyway maybe she'll do another before that, and you can come and wear your organdies. The garden party will be in the apple orchard of a friend. You will be SHOWERED with blossoms and there will be pie à la mode. . I am enclosing the program of the VERY American Ballet. It is almost as American as the steppes and chalets of Rome. But it is quite d[e]lightful and you would like William Dollar who would make a success, of course, if he wasn't good with a name like that! . . Please acknowledge receipt of *Four in America*, because I worry about such matters. 689 carnations to you both![1]

Papa Woojums!

1. The American Ballet, which became Ballet Caravan and later the New York City Ballet, gave a series of performances, 1 to 5 March, at the Adelphi Theatre, New York. The program for the first three nights, which Van Vechten had seen, included four ballets by George Balanchine: *Errante*, *Alma Mater*, *Serenade*, and *Reminiscence*. These were the first performances of the company that had been founded by Lincoln Kirsten, Balanchine, and Edward Warburg in 1934. William Dollar was a young dancer in the company.

To Carl Van Vechten

3 March [19]35   6020 Drexel Ave.
[Chicago, Illinois]

Dearest Papa W.

It is Sunday morning, our car awaits below (Baby W. has got a drive yourself and with a map we will soon start to drive about Chicago and its environs), and now I will tell you all about it as Baby W. used to say in its lectures.

Well, we are delighted with the newspapers on Fania because they do a little understand what it is all about, and even before the organdie garden party we will see her in this new role. I would like to write to her and say how really pleased I am, but does she read fan mail, I just seem to see her letting it pile up. Perhaps mine might pile up but eventually tell her how very very happy she makes me just to think of her. Please, Y[our]. R[oyal]. H[ighness]. Chief Woojums, give her all my love.[1]

Our news is brief but sweet, lecture and conference very happy and enjoyed; dinner last night with the [Robert Morss] Lovetts at Hull House, Baby said she liked him like you do and knows why you do, Miss Jane Addams in Arizona;[2] Bobsy G[oodspeed]. returns Fri. in time for a dinner and Massine ballet;[3] Fanny Butcher Bokum very shy and happy, her young man wasn't in the box but should have been, he's as nice as possible and adores Fanny, they ought to be happy in the old fashioned way;[4] we have a kitchenette and an electrical refrigerator and I am at it often and cooked a dinner for Thornton [Wilder] which he politely said was good, why don't you come on and try me out as a cook; I say why don't you, unless you are afraid of the cooking, why don't you; we are here until the 17th when we go to Dallas, the P. E. N. in S[an]. F[rancisco]. is on the 9th, have you sent them your acceptance; we haven't forgotten about Miss [Ellen] Glasgow's L[ectures]. in A[merica]., and you were a darling to send the clippings; and have you seen [Eugene] Jolas' pamphlet about the Autobiography, it's a scream, the press came up in hordes yesterday to know what Baby W. was doing about it, it said that for 25 yrs. it has been attacked and not answered and wouldn't now, but it would say that it was to be noticed that they mostly concerned themselves with saying that Picasso did not invent cubism which seemed strange as it had always noticed that the great figure did create the thing and that certainly it couldn't be denied that P[icasso]. was the great painter of his period, Baby W. was dignified and discreet as is its best habit;[5] it will meet the Mr. [Lloyd] Lewis who wrote the Life of Sherman and go to Pinafore with him,[6] also A[lexander]. Woollcott; and this is all the news.

Dearest Carl come to Chicago, please come to Chicago soon.

Mama Woojums

1. See Van Vechten to Stein [28 February 1935], note 1.

2. Jane Addams (1860–1935) was a social settlement worker and peace advocate. With Ellen Gates Starr she opened Hull-House in Chicago in 1889; she remained at its head until her death. Jane Addams was the first president of the Women's International League for Peace and Freedom. In 1931 she shared the Nobel Peace Prize with Nicholas Murray Butler.

3. *Le Bal*, a ballet with music by Vittorio Rieti, a new libretto and choreography by Léonide Massine, and décor by Giorgio de Chirico, was presented by the Ballets Russes de Monte Carlo (de Basil company) at the Auditorium Theatre, Chicago. The ballet had been originally presented by the Diaghilev Ballets Russes de Monte Carlo on 7 May 1929, with a libretto by Boris Kochno, choreography by George Balanchine, music by Rieti, and the curtain, décor and costumes by de Chirico.

4. Fanny Butcher's husband, Richard Drummond Bokum.

5. *Testimony Against Gertrude Stein* (The Hague, Netherlands: Sevire Press, 1935). This pamphlet (16 pages) was issued as a supplement to *transition* number 23 (the pamphlet was not for sale separately). It contained numerous excerpts from *The Autobiography of Alice B. Toklas*, with refutations of these passages by various individuals, including Georges Braque, Eugene Jolas, Maria Jolas, Henri Matisse, André Salmon, and Tristan Tzara.

6. It was through Sherwood Anderson that Stein met the author and journalist Lloyd Lewis (1891–1949). Lewis, who worked on the *Chicago Daily News*, had already written *Sherman, Fighting Prophet* (New York: Harcourt Brace & Co., 1932). With Lewis, Stein shared a pas-

sionate interest in Ulysses S. Grant. Stein lent Lewis the typescript of the then unpublished *Four in America* (George Washington, Ulysses S. Grant, Henry James, and Wilbur Wright). In a review of *Hamilton Fish* by Allen Nevins, Lewis wrote, "I am reminded that it was religion that was in Gertrude Stein's mind when she wrote about Grant in her 'Four in America' a work as yet unpublished. More than any other of those who have written about Grant, did she catch the essence of the man" (*Chicago Daily News*, 18 November 1936, YCAL). In 1937 Stein wrote to Lewis suggesting that they collaborate on a book about Grant (see Lewis to Stein in Gallup, *The Flowers of Friendship*, pp. 321–22). Because of the war the collaboration never materialized. Lewis died in 1949, his *Captain Sam Grant* appeared in 1950 (Boston: Little Brown).

❧

To Alice Toklas
[Postcard: Zurburan—A Lady as S. Margaret. London,
The National Gallery]

[postmark: 5 March 1935]   [150 West Fifty-fifth Street
Tuesday   New York]

Dear Alice (M W):

Fania and I went to the Metropolitan yesterday & saw *your* Zurburan which is divine & which we had *never* seen before. So we thank you for discovering this picture of pictures.[1] So here is another Zurburan for you! And love from

P. W.

1. In 1935 the Metropolitan Museum of Art, New York, owned two paintings by the Spanish artist Francisco de Zurburan (1598–1664): the large *Battle of Christians and Moors at El Sotillo*, which had been purchased in 1920, and the much smaller *Young Virgin Reading*, purchased in 1927, which shows the Virgin as a child in the Temple seated on the ground with a piece of embroidered linen on a cushion on her lap. Sir John Pope-Hennessy, director of the Department of European Paintings, at the Metropolitan Museum of Art, wrote, "I think that there can be little doubt that Alice Toklas's reference is to the second of these paintings (letter received from Pope-Hennessey, 17 March 1981).

To Alice Toklas
[Postcard: Renoir—Madame Charpentier and Her Children. The Metropolitan Museum of Art]

[postmark: 6 March 1935]   [150 West Fifty-fifth Street
Wednesday   New York]

Dear Alice:—

Thank you for your delightful letters, but *please* tell *me*: Did "Four in America" arrive? You haven't said *yet*. . . . On Saturday or Monday I'll be sending you the photographs of the Uncle Tom tournée, with Eliza crossing the ice and Baby Woojums meeting the Ravens![1] You will see!—. I am getting my wardrobe ready in case I can go to California, but I'm afraid I can't. Don't leave me addressless, please!

Love always—So say Edith [Ramsey][2] and Fania

Papa W!

1. A reference to a number of photographs taken by Van Vechten of Stein while she was in Richmond, Virginia. Several of the photographs show Stein beside the Poe Fountain, which is covered with ice.

2. The Van Vechtens' cook.

To Carl Van Vechten

[postmark: 7 March 1935]   The Midway Drexel
                                                          6020 Drexel Avenue
                                                          Chicago [Illinois]

My dearest papa W.

Being a really truly college professor is hard work, particularly when you have never been one before, I have had to write four lectures I think you will like them, they are a going on of the other ones and I got not very many but a few real ideas into them,[1] then two hours of class every day and then two hours of meeting individual students and looking at their ms. and telling them how not to go on doing the same, that part is easy, and anyway although I really do not like work I am enjoying it a lot and finding it very interesting, it's a nice University Chicago's and yours and there are some pretty interesting fellows among the lot of them and Thornton [Wilder] is a darling, and helpful in every way, so now we are going shopping, I wish that is we wish that is she wishes, Alice wishes that she might cook you a meal on in Thornton's kitchenette, and it would be nice oh so nice to see you, but you deserted us once and I guess you will desert us always and be one of those disappearing fathers that the friends of my youth had, the father was not divorced dead or in jail he had just disappeared, and is not that what Papa W. did out of the South, he just disappeared, and now New York has got him. Oh the Four in America arrived alright and we will be sending it back to you before we leave here and so you will keep it for me, Alice wrote you all about the manifesto and I suppose you have seen it, what I enjoyed was [André] Salmon's statement that he was drunk only in appearance to impress the American ladies and so he ought to be happy that he fooled them instead of complaining that they were fooled, apparently Paris is amusing itself greatly about it all it seems to have made them forget politics for a brief moment and my french publishers are naturally very pleased,[2] did we tell you that we had hired ourselves a drive yourself Chev[rolet] and that I career around the streets of Chicago just like nothing at all that is like anybody and we are planning spending the rest of our days just riding over all the roads there are in these United States, somewhere you will join us, won't you oh yes you will and lots of love, and love to Fania and we miss you both so and lots and lots and more lots of love

Gertrude B. W.

1. See Toklas to Van Vechten, 25 February [19]35, note 2.
2. See Toklas to Van Vechten, 3 March [19]35, note 5.

❧

To Carl Van Vechten

9 March [19]35

The Midway Drexel
6020 Drexel Avenue
Chicago [Illinois]

Dearest Papa Woojums,

Four in America came as safely and as promptly as only a Papa Woojums package could come. And if Baby doesn't tell you so it's because he is working on his last lecture and they are pretty cute, surely that is what you'll say to our prodigy's efforts. I've commenced typing them for you and they will be ready within a few days I hope to send.

We have a busy life, over here, not in Chicago, as B. W. says. Emily [Chadbourne] and Ellen [LaMotte] have come out to see us. Bobsie G[oodspeed]. has returned from Arizona, we went to Massine's ballet, go to see the [Giorgio de] Chirico decor, please, but avoid seeing the dancing, it's incredibly bad, B. W. went to Pinafore with L[l]oyd Lewis,[1] who remarked casually apropos of the Midshipman, you know[,] Miss S[tein,] [Admiral David] Farragut commanded a boat at twelve years of age.[2] There is a marvellous museum here, the Chicago Historical, full of the most astounding souvenirs imaginable, and so unostentatiously shown. And the food is very good, even such as I prepare myself. It probably has something to do with the way the lake churns up the water. At any rate that is what they claimed at Palma de Mallorca for their unique dough.

What is your advice about the enclosed, Baby has no feelings, I'd say yes if you could tell me if the gentlemen are not perhaps the Dutch Treat Club gone a little high-brow or glorified.[3] Would you please, Papa Woojums say the word that will make an answer possible, is it yes is it no?

The U[niversity]. of Cal[ifornia]. has come around and probably is being arranged, Mrs. [Gertrude] Atherton is going to give G[ertrude]. a cocktail party, though the Baby W. never takes cocktails, it says. And a lunch party and is going to take us to the Dominican convent in San Rafael. You had better come and don't bother about a wardrobe or anything, just come, come Maud; did I ever tell you the thing the incomparable "Nellie" once said of a friend. He said to Maud, Come into the garden Maud, and she did and you see with what consequences. When I protested Nellie said, you know very well Maud was always rough and ready.[4]

[408]

We have no address yet in Dallas, however will I ever find one.

Heaps of love to Fania and to you and I love the Zurburan portrait.

M. W.

1. See Toklas to Van Vechten, 3 March [19]35, notes 3 and 6.

2. David Farragut (1801–1870) was an American naval officer and hero of the Civil War battles of New Orleans (1862) and Mobile Bay (1864). At the age of twelve, during the War of 1812, he was made a prize master of the captured British ship *Alexander Barclay* and was repsonsible for bringing it to the port of Valparaiso.

3. The enclosure is not with the letter. It was probably an invitation for Stein to lecture before the American Arbitration Association. See Van Vechten to Stein and Toklas [12 March 1935].

4. One of Toklas' childhood friends, Nellie Jacot.

To Gertrude Stein

[March? 1935]

150 West Fifty-fifth Street
New York City

Dear Baby Woojums,

No, this is no disappearing Papa: here I am right here working hard for Mama and Baby. I've just finished printing your pictures and they go off to you today (the Uncle Tom tour) by the hundred. Enclosed[x] you will find a *registered* letter which arrived yesterday via the Balearic Islands.[1] Fania's play is still going on, but I think will quit next week. We saw Louis [Bromfield]'s other play on Thursday and enjoyed its old-fashioned bitterness.[2] I am getting lovely letters from Charlottesville and William and Mary about the photographs and Robert Nelson Jr says the Ravens are panting for the Pigeons. .[3] Random House sent back Donald Sutherland's mss and he brought it by yesterday.[4] . I don't seem to be able to get that Transition pamphlet. Have you actually seen a copy or have the contents been reported to you? If you plan to ride over all the roads in the USA it will take for ever because they build so many new ones every year, using up the unemployed. But of course I plan to go with you, managing adroitly and neatly to step my way between your lace flounces and fans! . But first, what Ho! for the garden party in the Apple (Delicious) Orchard. Get your organdies out of mothballs! . . [Walter] Winchell says your publisher is in the Bahamas with S[ylvia] S[idney] and what could be better?[5] . . By the time you get back from the coast Huey Long may be cracking the whip! HG Wells says he is a great man. .

6578 white orchids dabbled with yellow butterflies to my two pretty woojums!

Papa Woojums.[2]

Among the photographs, please regard the Baby as Martin Luther!
ˣwith the photographs.
[2]It has occurred to me that Woojums, Paris would be an excellent registered cable address. Think this over, please. No one could *ever* forget it.

1. This letter cannot be identified.

2. Marinoff was playing in Bromfield's play *Times Have Changed*. Bromfield and John Gearon's play *Deluxe* had opened on 5 March 1935.

3. Poe enthusiasts whom Stein had met in Richmond, Virginia.

4. Donald Sutherland (d. 1978) was a classicist who met Stein when she lectured at Princeton University, where he was a student. Stein took an immediate interest in Sutherland and had asked Van Vechten to try to help publish Sutherland's novel, *Child with a Knife*. Van Vechten was unsuccessful. The novel was published by the Courier Printing Company, Littleton, New Hampshire, in 1937.

5. Bennett Cerf was briefly married to the actress Sylvia Sidney in 1935. See Cerf, *At Random: The Reminiscences of Bennett Cerf* (New York: Random House, 1977), pp. 151–52.

To Carl Van Vechten

[postmark: 12 March 1935]

The Midway Drexel
6020 Drexel Avenue
Chicago [Illinois]

Oh papa papa papa W.

You did outdo yourself, the most beautiful photographs, that is all there is about it the most beautiful photographs, we don't know whether we like [the ones] on the [campus?] best, we just don't know, it is all so beautiful, and pieces of the University, and pieces of us, and the head of the house, and some of the iron work, and some of the sweetest pictures you ever took of me and papa papa papa W. if you can do that in Richmond what couldn't you wouldn't you do in Charleston and New Orleans and California and added and California California can be done or meet us in Texas oh Carl they are beautiful photographs, you know we want to come back right away we have not gone yet but we want to come back right away to these United States and bring us a car and go all over the land and you photograph and we all photograph and go and go and photograph and it would be all of it too heavenly just too heavenly yes it would papa W. it just would, and we will and there are wonderful things to photograph everywhere and we will make a pictorial history of these United States and I will write one and we will all be so happy yes we will, and lots and lots of love

x x x x x x x x x x x x x

Baby Woojums

these are xcited kisses[1]

B. W. for P. W.

1. Note by Van Vechten, 22 January 1941: "This letter is about the photographs I made of the ladies in Virginia."

To Gertrude Stein and Alice Toklas

[12 March 1935]   150 West Fifty-fifth Street
Tuesday night.   New York City

Dear Les Belles Woojumses:

I enjoyed Capitals Capitals and so when you are in California ask for Sacramento! Anyway, this was syndicated no end. Reports roll in from coast to coast.[1] I wait impatiently for the erudite lectures at Chicago. . When and where are the phonograph records? I don't seem to have these at hand.[2] Did you actually see that Transition pamphlet? No one here seems to have a copy. . I think Baby Woojums might deign to appear before the American Arbitration Society. Personally I know nothing about it, but the name is so amusing. Tell them it has to be some other day than the day in the Golden Delicious Apple Orchard (in organdies). . You will especially enjoy the Dominican Convent. Mrs. [Gertrude] Atherton has a granddaughter there. You must save up all the gossip for the Mother Superior who has a lust for same.[3] . If I come certainly I won't bother about a wardrobe, but you spring "Nellie" on me for the first time. Can this be an ex-president of the Republic or do you perhaps mean Bly? .[4] . I guess this is about as late as I can reach you in Chicago and will send further reports to the [Hotel] Algonquin unless you send me some kind of schedule. When, for instance, do you want to be in Los Angeles, when in San Francisco? Please let me know. . Remember little George Kennedy[5] will look you up in SA [i.e., Los Angeles], and probably Aileen Pringle.[6] She is pretty cute. Arthur Richman and Lillian May Ehrman[7] you met chez nous. They want to ring bells for you. Fania is still playing but probably won't be soon. She now thinks she will visit the [Eugene] O'Neills in Georgia.[8] . I hope you got the pictures all right.

Mimosa, long drooping branches of yellow mimosa, to you both and a lot of love.

Fania, Mrs. Showers and Miss Ramsay join in messages!

Carlo!

A letter from Dudley Fitts says that Yale *must* & *will* have the BW in April. You will hear from him.[9]

---

1. Stein's article, "The Capital and Capitals of the United States of America," *New York Herald Tribune*, 9 March 1935, p. 11.

2. Three 12-inch (78 rpm) records were recorded by Stein for Columbia University in 1935. On the records Stein read excerpts from her writings: on record one, "Matisse" and "If I Told Him: A Completed Portrait of Picasso"; on record two, "Madame Recamier" and "A Valentine to Sherwood Anderson"; on record three, exerpts from *The Making of Americans*. These recordings were reissued in 1951 by Dorian Records on a 12-inch (33 1/3 rpm) record; the were again reissued under the Caedmon record label in 1956.

3. Atherton's granddaughter was a nun, Sister Dominga, in the Dominican Convent in San Rafael, California. Stein visited her there and met Mother Raymond, the mother superior.

4. See Toklas to Van Vechten, 9 March [19]35, note 4.

5. The actor George Kennedy.

6. Aileen Pringle, a film actress who made her debut in silent films. Pringle was already a friend of Joseph Hergesheimer's, the Knopfs', and H. L. Mencken's when she met Van Vechten in 1925.

7. Lillian May Ehrman was a widely traveled socialite with an interest in the arts. When Stein visited California, Mrs. Ehrman gave a dinner for her in her Beverly Hills home. See Stein to Van Vechten, [2 April 1935].

8. Van Vechten had met Eugene O'Neill briefly in 1914. Marinoff and O'Neill's wife, Carlotta, were close friends. In May 1935 the Van Vechtens and Lawrence Langner and Armina Marshall visited the O'Neills at their home in Sea Island Beach, Georgia.

9. Fitts to Van Vechten, 12 March 1935, YCAL.

To Carl Van Vechten

[postmark: 14 March 1935]

The Midway Drexel
6020 Drexel Avenue
Chicago [Illinois]

My dearest dearest Papa Woojums,

The photographs are starting a furor I almost forgot to spell that word and Emily Chadbourne and Ellen LaMotte want them all, Emily Chadbourne you know is the one who took us to Westover and it would appear that her brother gave the statue that is on the campus of the U[niversity]. [of] V[irginia]. to the U. V. they also that is her uncle gave all the statues of Indians that are in Chicago to Chicago he having been married to a squaw and all the Grecos to Chicago although not having been married to a Greek, anyway they pine for photos and are writing to you for some we are staying with Mrs. Chadbourne's sister in Pasadena, you eat very well and are very comfortable wherever they ask you to stay like Mrs. Archibald in Washington, and our address in Dallas Texas 17–20 is care of Miss Hockaday, Hockaday School Dallas Texas and to-day is the last day of teaching and I really have had a wonderful time, [Robert] Hutchins the president who has been away came home and presented me with beautiful red roses and a call of felicitation and so we are much stuck up, and yesterday's last lecture, I guess there were nearer 8 than 500 so you see the lonely Woojums are all swelling and there will be a little delay about your having the copy of the lectures because don't say anything about it nothing is quite yet decided but the University Press wants to print them the four delivered here and the copy Alice just made for you has to go to them but you will have yours soon, I wish you were here to eat the lunch Alice is just cooking along with Thornton [Wilder] we do we do we do wish that you would, and you will have all the addresses of our future very shortly from Alice but this is the first one, Mama Woojums is telephoning desperately for sweet butter no butter can be sweet enough for Mama Woojums and Papa if he were only here where is our wandering Papa W. to-night, is what we sing every night to the accompaniment of Thornton's piano. Lots and lots and lots and so many lots of love to you and love to Fania and always

B. W.

The Transition article so the A. P. who showed it to me told me is only sold with a number of transition, and that is the reason why.

❧

To Gertrude Stein

<table>
<tr><td>18 March [1935]
Monday</td><td style="text-align: right">150 West Fifty-fifth Street
New York City</td></tr>
</table>

Dear Baby Woojums,

Lectures in America is here and grand! I haven't read it over yet but will. The picture might have had a better reproduction but looks pretty good anyway.[1] Also your writings continue in the [New York Herald] Tribune[2] and now you tell me you will have a book at the University of Chicago Press.[3] It is all pretty marvellous! Willy Seabrook says he'll come down for the Garden Party (organdies, please, with the sweet-pea design) although it be held in China, which perhaps it will be. Now that Germany is ARMING you'd better come live in South Carolina where it will be SAFER. . Those ladies will undoubtedly get some photographs of the Confederacy if they write for them. . Your Texas address only came to me this morning (March 18), for no later than the 20. So I'm sending this c/o the Algonquin. Speaking of Miss [Ela] Hockaday. Up in the wilds of Massachusetts where Bill Bullit[t] lives there is an ORGANIST named Cockaday. Mrs. [Muriel] Draper was much interested in him and his house. . I hope you got your sweet butter.

De Luxe has closed but Times have Changed is still running on and may be here even when the garden party is the rage, though I doubt it.[4] . Well, I can't wait till we drive through America in a FORD and take photographs and talk with the peasants! How wonderful that will be! Hurry back, dear Baby and Mama Woojums. . It is almost spring now and intrepid crocuses will be stepped on by me today. But you are on your way to eternal sunshine and those FOGS. . I have written Aileen Pringle and George Kennedy to look you up in Hollywood. You are sure to like them both. Your publisher is back and I wish you were!

Fania and Pearl and Edith[5] and Carlo send love to Mama and Baby Woojums!

Papa W.

x x x x x right back at you!

1. Stein's *Lectures In America* was published by Random House on 14 March 1935. The frontispiece was a photograph Van Vechten had made of Stein in front of an American flag in New York on 4 January 1935.

2. In 1935, Stein wrote several articles for the *New York Herald Tribune*: "American Newspapers," 3 March, Sec. 4, p. 10; "The Capital and Capitals of the United States," 9 March, p. 11; "American Education and Colleges," 16 March, p. 15; "American Newspapers" (continued), 23 March, p. 15; "American Crimes and How They Matter," 30 March, p. 13; "American States and Cities and How They Differ from Each Other," 6 April, p. 13; "American Food and American Houses," 13 April, p. 13.

3. Stein's *Narration*, with an introduction by Thornton Wilder, was published by the University of Chicago Press in December 1935.

4. See Van Vechten to Stein [26 February 1935], note 3.

5. The Van Vechtens' household staff.

To Carl Van Vechten

[postmark: 19 March 1935]　　　　The Miss Hockaday School for Girls
　　　　　　　　　　　　　　　　　Dallas, Texas

Papa Papa,

Here we are in a most elegant school being most elegantly fed, and earning large sums of money, it would appear so Mama W. says that I got into the habit in Chicago of talking two hours at a time and so I did it here, and Mama W. says I mustn't and so I mustn't, even though one kind lady said let her do what she likes to do in Texas, you have no idea how good the food is in Texas papa W. it really is delicious and Gertrude Atherton says Carl must let me know that he is coming and I hope Carl is letting her know that he is coming. We had a beautiful ride down over Missouri Oklahoma and Texas, it was wonderful from the air, Missouri was Miro and Oklahoma was enormous, and the bad lands and everything in Texas was most graceful, we now go on to Austin and Houston and now they want us in Oklahoma, and we will see oil, and then we fly happily by day to California, we love you so much Papa W, for everything and we love you for having taught us to fly we do love you oh yes we do love you papa W. yes yes we do

Baby Woojums.

To Carl Van Vechten

[postmark: 20 March 1935]   The Miss Hockaday School
                                             Dallas, Texas

> Where oh where is wandering papa,
> Not a word has he to say,
> To his two little two little Woojums
> Two little Woojums so far away,
> Not a word has wandering papa
> Not a word has he to say.
> If this sad lament does not touch the heart of Papa
> Woojums what will touch it.

Oh please come to California, Mrs. [Gertrude] Atherton is getting so xcited about the cocktail party, she air-mails about it and the last is that Mrs. [Robinson] Jeffers wants to reconcile me and Mabel [Dodge],[1] and do we want to be reconciled me not Mabel and is there anything to reconcile, I have said that I am reconciled to meeting Mabel which is not what you call reconciliation but an arriving, well anyway it sounds all most Gilbert and Sullivanish, and she says not Mabel but Mrs. Atherton that you must come to S[an]. F[rancisco]. and let her know right away, will you Papa Papa Woojums will you won't you join the dance, and wander with your Woojumses instead of wandering all alone, Texas is nice and warm, warm in every way but we eat heartily and are very comfortable, the book has just come and the photograph is lovely and I like the looks of the book it is like a travel book, and so much love and to-morrow we move and lots of love oh so much love

Baby W.[2]

We are at Austin Texas until the 22nd c/o R. B. Johnson 199 Cliff St.
     at Huston Texas until the 24th c/o Warwick Hotel
     at Oklahoma City Oklahoma
       Huckins Hotel
       until the 26th
     at Fort Worth Texas
       c/o Mrs. Charles Scheuber
       Carnegie Public Library
       for the 27th
     and then
       Arrago Seco Hotel [i.e., Hotel Vista del Arroyo]
       Pasadena until the 1st
     Heaps of love from a busy

Mama Woojums

1. Atherton wrote Stein, 11 March 1935 (YCAL), that a friend of Mabel Dodge Luhan's had telephoned to say that Mrs. Robinson Jeffers (wife of the poet) was very anxious to bring about a reconciliation between Mabel and Gertrude.

2. The postscript is by Toklas.

To Gertrude Stein and Alice Toklas

22 March [1935]
    150 West Fifty-fifth Street
    [New York]

Dear Ladies Woojums: Mama and Baby!

Your letters delight me. It makes me very happy that your food is giving you so much pleasure and that your words are pleasing others! I lie

[417]

awake nights and cry because I do not seem to be flying West. Maybe I will yet!. . I'm glad you received the book: it is quite lovely, I think, and I have been reading parts of it which remind me of so many places I have heard these parts before.[1] I am quite confused! . Fania is still playing and they talk of going on for three weeks more. It would be funny if you could see it before the garden party! Or even AFTER. . What with conscription and all you'd better plan to live in USA where we have INFLATION and drive around in your car (with Papa W and his Leica) and occasionally take to the air for long jumps! We could fly to Honolulu, for instance, and send the car by boat. There are riots in Harlem, but everybody I know is still living.[2]

Fania and I send heaps and tons of love to you both!

Papa Woojums

X X X X X X and how!

1. Stein's *Lectures In America*.

2. Between 4 and 6 P.M. on 19 March 1935 a riot developed in Harlem. The crowd believed that a young black boy Lino Rivera, who had stolen a ten-cent knife from an S. H. Kress store on 125th Street between Seventh and Eighth avenues, had been lynched. Three thousand people stormed the store. The police shot into the mob of rioters and one man was killed. The boy was later found unharmed in his home. (See *New York Times*, 20 March 1935, p. 1; 24 March 1935, Sec. 4, p. 11; 31 March 1935, Sec. 4, p. 11.)

To Carl Van Vechten
[Postcard: "Texas—Biggest State Biggest Jack-rabbits Everything Big!"]

[postmark: 23 March 1935]

[c/o R. B. Johnson
1909 Cliff Street]
Austin, Texas

Darling W. P. W.

Not a word from him our papa dear so far away, not a word from him and here we are so heated and so far away not a word from him from papa dear so far away.

Baby W.

[418]

❧

To Carl Van Vechten

[postmark: 24 March 1935]

Worth Hotel
Forth Worth, Texas

Dear Papa Woojums,

We are glad that you are alright with never a word from you we did get worried. We have had a wonderful time in Texas, Texas has been every bit Texas and we have liked it immensely, last night they took us to hear some Negroes who have a Little Theatre of their own do Porgy,[1] it was a wonderfully good performance, it seems they have had a little theatre of their own here for a number of years, the actors all people who work and, I went down in the green room to see them make up and one who was being made up to be a white man said to me, I am sorry Miss Stein that you had so much trouble with your chops this noon, How did you know I asked him, I waited on you he said. I am inclosing the account of our visit from Sweet Briar where they wanted you so much,[2] we really are having a most amusing time, and we are glad that you are all well and happy and this is us at the Hockaday school, and to-morrow at seven o'clock we are off for Pasadena and will you be there oh will you be there so much love from

B. W.

Will you keep the clippings picture for us.

1. DuBose Heyward's novel *Porgy* (1925) had been dramatized by Heyward and his wife Dorothy in 1927. Heyward later collaborated with George and Ira Gershwin on an opera, *Porgy and Bess* (1935). What Stein saw was the play.

2. The clipping was not kept with the letter but was possibly "Gertrude Stein Gives Talk on Recent Book Before S. B. Audience," Sweet Briar *News*, 10 February 1935, pp. 2–3. The article reported on Stein's lecture "The Gradual Making of *The Making of Americans*," which she had delivered at Sweet Briar College.

🐝

To Carl Van Vechten
[Telegram]

27 March 1935   Fort Worth, Texas

HAVE NOT HEARD FROM YOU FOR TEN DAYS WIRE THAT YOU
ARE QUITE WELL WE ARE SERIOUSLY WORRIED LOVE FROM

GERTRUDE.

🐝

To Gertrude Stein and Alice Toklas

27 March [1935]   150 West Fifty-fifth Street
Wednesday   [New York]

Dear Mama and Baby Woojums,

How sweet of you to send me a telegram inquiring after me! I replied
at once. You see I never have your addresses long enough ahead. When you
sent the last batch there was just time to write to Pasadena, and now I have
no address after April 1, which is next Monday. If I sent this by ordinary
mail it would not reach you before then. . . I do want you to see Aileen
Pringle and George Kennedy Junior in Hollywood and I have told them to
look you up . . and Arthur Richman and Lillian May Ehrman, whom you
met at my house. . If you go to Carmel, SURELY Nöel Sullivan: he may
be in S[an]. F[rancisco]. Ask Mrs. [Gertrude] Atherton about him, and if
you meet him, ask about my DEAR cousin, Mary Blanchard (Mrs. Frederic
Mason Blanchard). She also is at Carmel. As Miriam Hopkins is in NY at
present you may go to a Hotel. In that case the Château Elysée, Hollywood,
is the place for you. Fania always goes there. If you see Philip Moeller running around the lobby (he is one of the directors of the Theatre Guild and
is at present directing pictures in Hollywood) pick him up and say I told you
to! . . What a strange picture of Baby Woojums arrived this morning! What
is it? And so wonderful too! I sent Mrs. [Emily] Chadbourne (and Miss [El-
len] LaMotte) a lot of pictures yesterday. . I love to read in Lectures in

[420]

America. I still prefer the order I suggested to you: 1(4); 2(5); 3(6); 4(3); 5(2); 6(1). It is, I think, more logical, but I may be wrong.[1] . Don't ever worry about me, please, because I'm NEVER sick. . Times Have Changed closed at last Sat and Louis B[romfield] sails today on the Manhattan. Fania is going to Georgia to visit the Eugene O'Neills. . 678 sticks of butterscotch to you both! Edith just asked me, When am I going to make an apple pie for Miss Stein? When, indeed? Unpack your prettiest pink and blue organdies, with the forgetmenots[x] and pissenlits!

Love,
[Carl Van Vechten]

[x]myosotis to you!

1. The printed order of *Lectures In America* is "What is English Literature," "Pictures," "Plays," "The Gradual Making of *The Making of Americans*," "Portraits and Repetition," "Poetry and Grammar." Van Vechten had suggested the following order: "The Gradual Making of *The Making of Americans*," "Portraits and Repetition," "Poetry and Grammar," "Plays," "Pictures," "What is English Literature."

To Carl Van Vechten

[postmark: 30 March 1935]   Hotel Vista del Arroyo
                                             Pasadena, California

My dearest Carl

Isn't this [swagger?][1] and here we are and we did fly over the mountains so high and they were so high that for a moment I was scared, but it was all very fine and very safe and here we are, and thanks for giving Emily [Chadbourne] and Ellen [LaMotte] the photos they will appreciate them and we are going to ask for some for the Hockaday school, who were so good to us in Texas we did like Texas, and now we are here, and here is a letter I am sending you, will you get into communication with [George W.] Hilbitt [i.e., Hibbitt][2] you and Bennett [Cerf], and make the arrangements, Alice thinks a morning meeting might be nice but anyway Alice is suggesting to him the possible dates, we are going to take it easy here for a bit, I will get myself a drive yourself car and we will just look at fruits and flowers because

Texas was strenuous and S[an]. F[rancisco]. will be so also, had a telegram on arriving from Florine Stettheimer who is still here but leaving almost at once, but we will try and meet, one of the movie people the ones who have just done the [Max] Reinhardt show[3] also met us at the plane and asked us to lunch in the green room and look around, perhaps we will but first we are going to take it easy here, it was a wonderful trip and it is so marvelous that you taught us to fly and everything else and I wish you were to be a nice surprise and prize package in S. F. and we could then fly home to- gether and visit convents together oh it would be nice Papa Woojums it would be nice after S. F. we move back to New York and sail on the 4 May for Paris, but we do not want to go no we don't we love it so, and Papa Woo- jums the best of all, so much the best of all

Baby Woojums.

1. The reference to the stationery on which the letter was written. At the top of the paper was an engraving of the hotel as seen through an archway.

2. Hibbitt was a professor of English and comparative literature at Columbia University, New York. This particular letter from Hibbitt is not in YCAL. An earlier letter to Stein, 26 October 1934 (YCAL), had asked Stein to participate in a project of recording some of her writings for the National Council of Teachers of English organized by Columbia University. Other writers who had participated in the project were Vachel Lindsay, Aldous Huxley, T. S. Eliot, Robert Frost, John Gould Fletcher, Conrad Aiken, and Alfred Kreymborg. See Van Vecthen to Stein and Toklas [12 March 1935], note 2.

3. Max Reinhardt (1873–1943) had produced Shakespeare's *A Midsummer Night's Dream* in the Hollywood Bowl in the summer of 1934. William Dieterle suggested that he do it as a film. The film was released on 16 October 1935 and starred, among others, James Cagney, Mickey Rooney, Joe E. Brown, Olivia de Haviland, George Sanders, Dick Powell, Anita Louise, Ar- thur Treacher, and Victor Jory. Exactly whom Stein is referring to is not made clear.

To Carl Van Vechten

[postmark: 2 April 1935]   Hotel Vista del Arroyo
Pasadena, California

My dearest Carl,

Just a note as we are off to the desert and other pleasures that we have had a most amusing time and thanks to you met everybody we wanted

[422]

to meet, Mrs [Lillian May] Ehrman gave a party last night for us Charlie Chaplin, Dashiel Hammett, the highest payed directors, Anita Loos, and John Emerson and all and everything and it was most amusing,[1] and in Monterey we will meet Noel Sullivan and I have a beautiful drive yourself 8 cylinder Ford car, and we went to a mission in it yesterday and are off to the desert and then to San Francisco in it and oh dear papa Woojums would that the Woojums family could be reunited when they get there and love to Fania and everything

Always
B. W.

1. Mrs. Ehrman's party was reported in the Hollywood *Citizen's News* on 10 April 1935 (YCAL). In addition to the guests Stein mentions, the party was attended by Mrs. John Kahn (Mrs. Ehrman's mother), Ivan Kahn (Mrs. Ehrman's brother and a Hollywood agent), Dr. and Mrs. Norman Dixon (Virginia Bishop), Lillian Hellman, Paulette Goddard, Theresa Helburn, Arthur Richman, Rouben Mammoulian, William Prestema, Mario Ramirez, and John Baker Opdycke. The party is described in Stein's *Everybody's Autobiography*, pp. 4–5.

To Carl Van Vechten

7 April [19]35

Hotel Del Monte
Del Monte, California

Dearest Papa Woojums,

We are so near you if you are where I can't believe you are not, Baby W. keeps saying don't expect it, but I go on believing you are there just the same. Well to-morrow eve. we'll know. And if you aren't what will save us from finding my S[an]. F[rancisco]. not ours. But you are going to be there, we will come to the air field to meet you and this letter will be at 150 when *we* get to N. Y.

And so I don't know why I write it, except to tell you that Lillian Mai [i.e., May] Ehrman was very sweet in herself and to us and gave a lovely party and found Dashiell Hammitt [i.e., Hammett] in three hours, not having heard of him at 8.30 and receiving his acceptance at 11.30 and his address a secret, wasn't that cute and bright? And Baby W. told him a lot of things and he told her an equal number and everybody had a good time.

And then we got near to Sequoia Park and into the Yosemite Valley to our surprise and then here, all so heavenly California. And here we have gone around the 17 mild [i.e., mile] Drive and had a charming invitation from Noel Sullivan to dine with him to-morrow evening (Baby W. was fascinated with his voice) and a telephone conversation with Mabel [Dodge] who rather in the manner of Mabels wanted poor Baby W. to see Tony [Luhan] who didn't want to see her and is going away to see friends today who live down the coast, that is M. is so we will see her in S. F. and I hope her manners will have improved by then. Dear Papa W. these are my feelings, Baby W. doesn't mind anything like that. But Californians do and you can't imagine how much more Californian I am here than elsewhere. It's the sea food that does it.

Good-bye and all my love, dearest Papa W. and don't get this letter but let me tell you it in S. F.

Alice

❦

To Gertrude Stein and Alice Toklas

[8 April 1935]   [150 West Fifty-fifth Street
Monday   New York]

Dear Baby and Mama Woojums,

I have run out of addresses for you, but I guess this will reach you. So you've dined with Charley Chaplin and Phillip Moeller? I hear rumors of your Hollywood triumphs on every hand. Are you eating avocados and CRABS? Please go to Fisherman's Wharf and eat CRABS! It would be such fun to see the two Gertrudes together[1] but Papa Woojums is busy taking lots of photographs, more and more each minute. He spends all his time in the darkroom now that Baby and Mama are cruising. Fania has gone to Georgia to visit the Eugene O'Neills. . Have you seen Mabel [Dodge]'s book, Winter in Taos? She used two of the Maestro's very best photographs.[2] . I hear lots about your book and about your articles in the Tribune. . I know you must have enjoyed the flight across the rockies and the desert. It is marvellous. . And I can't bear it you are sailing on May 4, but anyway it is still too cold for your organdies. When are you getting back? You don't say. . I enclose the Sweet Briar Clippings[3] and Hibbets [i.e., George W. Hibbitt] letter.[4] I didn't do anything about this because you said Alice was writing him and I was afraid I would confuse things . . Oh yes, I photographed Natalie [Barney] and Romaine Brooks and they are superb!

189 different kinds of love to you and please tell Gertrude A[therton] how very fond I am of her and how glad I am you are all together.

Carlo (Papa W)

1. Gertrude Stein and Gertrude Atherton.

2. Two photographs by Van Vechten, A *Taos Girl*, p. 148, and *The Church Ranchos de Taos*, p. 232 were printed in Mabel Dodge Luhan's *Winter in Taos* (New York: Harcourt, Brace & Co., 1935).

3. Stein lectured at Sweet Briar College on 10 February 1935. See Stein to Van Vechten [24 March 1935], note 2.

4. See Stein to Van Vechten [30 March 1935], note 2.

To Carl Van Vechten
[Postcard: Mother and Cubs, Yosemite National Park, California]

[postmark: 8 April 1935]   [Del Monte, California]

Here we are unexpectedly and loving it, you *must* come next year with us and photograph the trees, they are worthy of your camera, really.

Grand dad's beard was harsh and coarse

That was the reason for his fifth divorce[1]

A Burmah we saw yesterday.

We're off now for Del Monte, it's heavenly and would be perfect if the wee Woojums had Papa Woojums with them. All their love.

[Alice Toklas]

1. Note by Van Vechten, 22 January 1941: "This is California advertising for a razor! This card is from Alice."

To Carl Van Vechten

[postmark: 12 April 1935]   Hotel Mark Hopkins
                                             San Francisco, California

My dearest Papa W.

We have just said good-by to Mrs [Gertrude] Atherton and Mrs. [Muriel] Russell[1] they have been perfectly charming to us and we have really all of us gotten very fond of each other, to-day they took me to see the mayor[2] and he gave me a large golden wooden key of San Francisco all dedicated to me and signed by himself and it was all very lovely and very grand and we have had a beautiful time and only one solid regret, and that is that you were not here with us, it is the last thing that Gertrude Atherton [said], Carl should have been here with us, and that is the way we all feel about it, everything has gone off well, I am giving an xtra lecture at Stanford and Friday we fly stay the night at Omaha and the next night in Chicago and then back to New York and papa Woojums, and the Woojums will once more be reunited, and how they will like being reunited And how, I have sent a copy of Lectures in America to Ellen Glasgow, but we will be telling you everything almost as soon as you get this but mostly always and entirely and completely and continuously all and all our love

Baby Woojums.

We went to a Dominican convent college with Gertrude Atherton it was delightful.

---

1. Mrs. Muriel Russell was Atherton's daughter. It was Mrs. Russell's daughter that Stein visited in the Dominican Convent in San Rafael, California. See Van Vechten to Stein and Toklas [12 March 1935], note 3.

2. Angelo J. Rossi, mayor of San Francisco (1931–1944).

To Carl Van Vechten

[postmark: 17 April 1935]   Hotel Mark Hopkins
                                                       San Francisco [California]

My dearest Carl which is Papa Woojums,

No papa here but here we are where papa was. Gertrude Atherton has been perfectly lovely to us everything is delightful, Mary Garden is here and sent us the most beautiful Easter lilies and we see her on Tuesday chez the Crockers[1] and the hills are lovely and the streets are steep and the bay and the ocean is all there and everybody went to school with me and everybody else went to school with Alice and it is all most xciting, we get back to New York end of next week and it will [be] lovely seeing you again because we have missed you so and are Natalie [Barney] and Romaine [Brooks] in New York and will they be there when we get there and that will be nice and we have been meeting Florine Stettheimer in Stanford and everybody wants your photographs and everybody is happy and we love you so and love to Fania and everybody says she is a beautiful actress, one young man was very xcited about it and soon we will be together and lots and lots of love

Baby Woojums.

1. In an undated letter (YCAL), presumably written in April 1935, Mary Garden, the celebrated soprano and a close friend of Van Vechten's, wrote thanking Stein for a book she had received inscribed with a dedication to her by Stein. Garden also informed Stein that Senator William H. Crocker and his wife would like to invite Stein to lunch or to tea.

❧

To Gertrude Stein
*[Postcard: Self-portrait in front of poster
for Socrates exhibition at the British Museum.
Photograph by Carl Van Vechten]*

8 May [1935]   [150 West Fifty-fifth Street
Wednesday morning   New York]

Dear Baby W:—

Georges [Jacques] of the Algonquin[1] just finished a broadcast in which he spoke most ecstatically (and at length) about you & your opinions of food and wine (he quoted you as saying you had found the food bad in only one hotel).

*Love to you & Mama Woojums!
Carlo. Papa W!*

1. The head waiter at the Algonquin Hotel, New York.

❧

To Carl Van Vechten

9 May[19]35   S. S. Champlain

Dearest Papa Woojums—

It had to be—es wahr zu schon es hab nicht sollen sein—but it was and is and will be beastly remembering you going down the gang plank—*this* is the part of the trip you should more than any other have taken with us. And supposing you don't come over next year and we don't then what? I ask you then what?? I'm feeling very fiercely about it—when I'm awake—but we sleep a great deal and smell your lovely your heavenly lilies—they are so like your fragrant adieux in your letters and so very consoling because they are you in blossom form—oh but really we will all four meet again and soon. Why don't you come fetch Fania at Bilignin. We will count on that. Baby Woojums talks to everybody and shows your photos. (I have them in a bag in the cabin) and it had a nice wireless from Mrs. Reid thanking for the beautiful photo[1] and we have met Miriam Hopkins' ex-husband and the writer of C. [i.e., Katharine] Cornell's play[2] and young [Richard] Halliday[3] and the widow of an American general killed in civilian life in France and M[onsieur]. [Muk] de Jari[4] who tells Baby W. how to prepare Austrian dishes so clearly Baby (who's provokingly cuter than usual[)] says it is not only clear how they look and taste when cooked but also clear how they look if not taste at each state of preparation—and M. M[uk] de Jari asks respectfully to have me send his love to you. He is travelling with an enormous electric ice cream freezer (bought at Macy's basement so he says for only $18.90 because the outside paint is scratched off—but the interior so they told him is guaranteed intact) and 1000 Havana cigars and a radio set and gramophone combined and 200 tins of condensed tins of American fruits and vegetables (crushed so he assures me as well as whole—strained some of them others only peeled) All this to pass the french customs and later the Austrian where he has greater influence in case of—

He is this moment doubtless consuming my fourth daily orange juice ordered for me by Baby G—but I see she has left her seat. Perhaps it would be best that I should follow her to see what she's doing and to tell her not to. Please—please send us quickly one kind word—sir—one kind word to say you won't find any new Woojums' now the water separates us. My mind is full of black thoughts only a nice long letter soon from Papa Woojums can dispel. Give Fania this message please—the first officer told Baby W. that the wind in Mid-Atlantic never will make planing across possible but that if the money can be found the stratosphere will unquestionably be making it soon. So we must all stratosphere—all four of the Woojums—it will be marvellous perhaps the stratospheres will be accomodating about baggage and dogs and diets and prices for families. And with this more cheerful note I end. Endless love to you two blessed Woojums who must make us glad because they made U. S. which makes us sad to leave

[Alice Toklas]

1. The wire is not in YCAL. Mrs. Reid worked for the Tribune syndicate. In a letter to Stein, 22 October 1935 (YCAL), Alfred Harcourt wrote that Mrs. Reid had spoken to him about the possibility of Stein coming back to the United States to report on the political conventions of 1936.

2. The actress Miriam Hopkins' second husband, the writer Austin Parker (d. 1938). Parker had written a play *Weekend* which was produced on Broadway in 1929. In the 1930s he became

a screenwriter in Hollywood. He wrote another play, *With All My Heart*, which may have been discussed as a vehicle for Katharine Cornell.

3. Richard Halliday (1905–1973) was a drama and film critic and later a theatrical producer. He was the professional manager for his wife, Mary Martin.

4. Van Vechten knew Muk de Jari as part of the Stettheimers' circle of friends beginning in the early 1920s. See Van Vechten to Marinoff, 28 May 1923, 24 July 1923, 24 May 1925, all NYPL-MD.

To Gertrude Stein
[Postcard: Woman in a street. Photograph by Carl Van Vechten]

[postmark: 9 May 1935] [150 West Fifty-fifth Street
New York]

Dear Baby Woojums!

I forgot to tell you the pictures aren't yet developed & so we'll *all* have to wait for these delights until July . . . The Poe Shrine is so EX-CITED. But George Kennedy's picture got *broken* in the mail. Lloyd Lewis's enthusiasm is *infectious!*[1]

*love to both
Carlo.*

Via SS Paris
sailing May 11

1. Lewis had written to Van Vechten, 2 May 1935 (YCAL), thanking him for the photographs of Stein.

To Carl Van Vechten

[postmark: Le Havre, France, 11 May 1935] S. S. Champlain

Oh papa papa Woojums,

It's awful I did not really realise that we were away until I wrote your address on the envelope and I say to Alice but I have to put U.S.A. on the envelope now and then it all came over me that we were gone away and it was awful it really was, up to this time we had just been sleeping and resting and we had not really taken it in that we were not where we belong which is where Papa Woojums is, oh oh I am all broke up about it, really and truly it just has come over me that we are on our way away, oh dear, We will come back, it won't be just the same but it will be different, it will be the Mississippi steamboat and all of the country where we will sell Harcourt Brace books while you pop the landscapes and the inhabitants thereof and oh it will be nice but anything will be nice that takes us back again to where we belong under the spreading chestnut tree which is the aegis of Papa papa Woojums. We are having a peaceful time on board, all the young gentlemen are behaving nicely, [Muk de] Jari the Serb has attached himself and taught Alice at least a dozen new dishes, he is a walking cook book, and Alice has three beside so they are occupied, I have seen Pavlik [Tchelitcheff] and his Charley [Charles Henri Ford], à travers la fenêtre, but as I saw only the backs of their heads I don't imagine they saw me but you never can tell with a Roosian,[1] otherwise there is no news, but love and more love and most love and we love you so and we did love it so and the only comfort is to tell you so and hope it will be so again, I hope Fania is all better and that all four Woojums will be soon together oh yes soon soon together

Baby Woojums not liking its french school

* * * * * * * * * *

[Gertrude Stein]

1. Note by Van Vechten, 22 January 1941: "Tchelitcheff, the Russian painter and Charles Henri Ford. Pavlick used to be great friends with G. S. but no longer."

To Carl Van Vechten

[postmark: 17 May 1935]   27 rue de Fleurus
                                                           [Paris]

My dearest Papa Woojums

Here we are and everybody thinks you are here, the newspapers all say so and now this letter[1] and no papa Woojums and the Woojumses in tears, the Woojumses like America but they do not seem to know what to do with themselves over here they are most awfully busy but they do not seem to know what to do with themselves never the less. Saw Louis Bromfield last night, he seems depressed, Mary more cheerful, Basket is here Pepe comes to-night, and Wednesday we go to Bilignin, oh dear we do so miss Papa Woojums and when they tell us he is here it makes us sadder, because he just is not, we have the photographs the baby photos of the Woojums out and it just makes us more home sick, everything makes us more home sick, do Papa Woojums do come to the Woojums and console them

> *Love all love*
> *from Baby Woojums*

xxxxxxxxxx

xxxxxxxxxx

1. Enclosed with this letter was a letter to Stein from Clara de Morinni, asking her if she thought Van Vechten would speak at the American Woman's Club, Paris, on 24 May. Clara de Morinni was under the mistaken impression that Van Vechten had accompanied Stein back to Paris.

❧

To Gertrude Stein and Alice Toklas
[Postcard: Femme Marocain en tenue de Cérémonie]

19 May [1935]   [Tangier, Morocco]
Sunday

Dearest Baby & Mama Woojums,

I seem to be going toward the heart of Africa—off for Marakesh to-day—rather than coming north. But later you might get a telegram to meet the Geneva Plane. I am dying to know what you think of Paris after your USA triumphs. So please write me c/o the Anglo-South American Bank, Madrid.

> *Love*
> *Carlo, Papa W!*

A band down by the sea under my window is playing The Stars & Stripes For Ever!

[432]

To Carl Van Vechten

[postmark: 22 May 1935][1]   [27 rue de Fleurus
                                                              Paris]

Oh papa Woojums papa Woojums papa Woojums

Oh dear oh dear everybody is awfully nice to us they give parties for us and everybody is perfectly sweet but oh dear oh dear how we do miss you it's awful and America is so far away and we loved it so and we do. Yesterday we were at Nathalie [Barney]'s and met Colette, Colette and her husband Maurice Godouchet I write it unintelligibly because I do not quite remember it are coming to America in the Normandie and will be in New York 4 days, and she wants to be photographed and he and she want to see a little something and they want to see it by means of you and not with the official French, and they are staying in the Waldorf, and will you dear papa W. not be as nice to them as you were to us but still be nice to them, he is very simple and nice and intelligent and talks English very well, they have married after 11 years of fiancee as Colette says, and he used to be a pearl merchant and now he is a writer, anyway we have just been seeing them and they are going to be seeing you and be photographed by you,[2] and Madame Ma[r]celle Chantal the opera singer is with them and she is very sweet and very pretty[3] and after seeing all our photographs is longing to be photographed and she too is to be at the Waldorf and for 4 days and they will tell you that we love you but oh we would so much rather tell you that ourselves

Always
Baby Woojums.

---

1. When she wrote this letter, Stein had not yet received Van Vechten's card of 19 May [1935]; she had no idea that he was traveling outside the United States.

2. Colette, pen name of Sidonie Gabrielle Claudine Colette (1873–1954), the French novelist. Her third husband was Maurice Goudeket.

   Note by Van Vechten, 22 January 1941: "I had sailed for Europe before Colette and her entourage arrived and so I missed them in America. But I had earlier met Colette in Paris."

3. Marcelle Chantal, the French singer and actress.

To Carl Van Vechten

[postmark: 31 May 1935]   Bilignin par Belley
                                                           Ain

My dear papa Woojums

I might have known that you had something inside of you that you had not told your faithful Woojums when you said you could have gone with us because you had your passport in your pocket, and now here we are sitting in the sun but no papa Woojums with us but he will be that we believe he will be and I'll tell you all about what we feel about France and how Paris is sad because it is xpensive, a country to be gay has to be cheap living in America is so cheap and so gay but anyway we are quite nicely established and dying to see you and we will go and weep at Geneva if we do not are not allowed to go there and get you any time and all the time and all our love

Gertrude.

To Gertrude Stein and Alice Toklas
[Postcard: Santa Teresa]

[May–June 1935]   [Madrid, Spain]

Darling Mama Woojums and Baby Woojums!

I had to send you this[1] whatever happened, and nothing much has—except it is cold as cold as cold. . . . But I guess it will get warmer soon when I move on to Sevilla, I hope so. Africa was cold too. . . The heat of New York is quite refreshing after all this. You could write me at the Anglo-South American bank in Madrid during the next two weeks!

all love to les belles Woojums!

Papa Woojums.

1. Here and in the card of 1 June 1935, Van Vechten is referring to the image of Saint Theresa of Avila on the postcard.

###

To Gertrude Stein
[Postcard: Statue: Santa Teresa de Jesús—Avila]

1 June 1935   Avila [Spain]

Dear Baby Woojums

Here she is right from her home town & love from

Carlo Papa Woojums.

###

To Gertrude Stein and Alice Toklas
[Postcard: Barcelona. Torres del Templo de la Sagrada Familia]

11 June [1935]   [Barcelona, Spain]

Dear Ladies Woojums!

Your letters to USA from the boat reached me here amidst these classic towers & were they sweet! and so now I am flying to Italy & soon will be on a paquebot for somewhere in USA, but until I sail (in two weeks) the Banca Commerciale Italiana in Florence will be my address, and please write me another sweet letter. Fancy you & Muk de Jari learning how to cook together. It's too sweet!—I've become quite friendly with Domingo Ortega, the *greatest* of living toreros & I have photographed him any way but not in jaegers. I am saving that for Baby Woojums!

love,
Carlo.

###

To Carl Van Vechten

[postmark: 15 June 1935]   Bilignin par Belley
                                                        Ain

A sweet letter to the wickedest of papa Woojums, how can I, papa Woojums who saw so much of his Woojums that he does not want to see them here. Not even to fly to Geneva to kiss them and have them kiss him, wicked wicked papa Woojums, you make us awful homesick for you and for Spain, we'd love to see you and [Domingo] Ortega, but alas we cannot even see you, we are very tranquil here and I am working a lot, I have started to describe the world as I see it under the title Geographical History of America or the relation of human nature to the human mind, it begins well and I am getting kind of wrapped up in it,[1] and Alice is having sent to you in New York an umbrella she lost in Los Angeles that a hotel keeper found and that will you keep for her or Fania [to] bring it over or she use it over when we get over well anyway we love papa Woojums even the Jaegers love papa Woojums faithless though he is to his adoring familey,[2]

Love
Gtrde.

1. Stein's *The Geographical History of America Or The Relation Of Human Nature To The Human Mind*, with an introduction by Thornton Wilder, was published by Random House on 19 October 1936.

2. Notes by Van Vechten, 22 January 1941: "Domingo Ortega, whom I photographed in Madrid." "Edward Wasserman eventually took this umbrella to Gertrude."

❧

To Gertrude Stein
[Postcard: Young Moroccan boy. Photograph by Carl Van Vechten]

7 July [1935]   [150 West Fifty-fifth Street
                                                     New York]

Dearest Mama and Baby Woojums!

Papa Woojums is back in God's Country & God's Country is very hot, and please write to Papa Woojums & console him for having left charming Italy & sunny Spain. Are you coming over for the Mississippi House boat?[1] Fania sends love & kisses & so does Carlo

The umbrella is here!

Desolé to miss Colette.

Did Natalie [Barney] get her BIG Pictures?

[Carl Van Vechten]

1. See Stein to Van Vechten [11 May 1935].

[436]

🕊

To Gertrude Stein
["A Little Too Much" motto]

27 July 1935

[150 West Fifty-fifth Street
New York]

Dear Baby Woojums,

The enclosed just arrived from Lillian May Ehrman.[1] My first reaction was, Why didn't somebody think of this before? I wrote her immediately, airmail, and suggested she get in touch with you, giving her your address. So you may be going to Hollywood to film The Good Lena! Will you please return this letter, as it goes in my Stein archives . . . We haven't heard a word from you since we got back but I guess we will soon. . Yesterday I sent you some more photographs, which I think are grand. The one of Baby and Papa together is not so hot, but the one of Baby and Fania is marvellous, and the pictures of Baby alone with her vests and scarves and ALL the pictures of Alice Mama Woojums are the Top. . I also enclosed a picture of Papa W. that you asked for. . I am living in the darkroom these days, trying to make reality out of my films of Morocco and Spain. . I'll be happier when I hear from you both. Are you coming over? Did you see Bobsie [Goodspeed]?[2]

love,
Carlo

Did you get the pictures to Natalie [Barney]?

1. Ehrman wrote to Stein through Van Vechten (27 July 1935, YCAL), asking if she might have the rights to sell for Stein the story "The Gentle Lena" to a film studio. Ehrman suggested that the matter could be handled by her brother, Ivan Kahn, a Hollywood agent.

2. Mrs. Goodspeed was traveling in Europe.

To Carl Van Vechten
[Postcard: Chillon et les Dents du Midi]

[postmark: 27 July 1935]

[Veytraux-Chillon
Switzerland]

My dearest Carl

Here we are and pretty soon I will write a wonderful long letter but now just all our love

Baby W.

We are further from you than ever but we are going to be nearer soon—or later but sometime we have a plan—on the boat a woman said I was going to have a career—it is in my hand. Heaps of love

M. W.

Dear Mr. Van Vechten:

You can imagine the wonderful talks, trips and meals we are enjoying. We accept your congratulations and look forward to the time when we may enjoy such company together. This company together in a dungeon would rob tyranny of its terror.[1]

*Sincerely
Thornton Wilder*

1. The castle of Chillon, on the Lake of Geneva, where Francois de Bonnivard was imprisoned after he and a group of patriots attempted to overthrow the yoke of the Duke of Savoy on the town of St. Victor, near Geneva. The story of this twice imprisoned patriot who fought to establish a free republic was recounted, in somewhat garbled form, by Lord Byron in his poem *The Prisoner of Chillon*.

☙

To Carl Van Vechten

[postmark: 4 August 1935]   [Bilignin par Belley
                                                              Ain]

My dearest dearest Papa Woojums,

The pictures have just come and they make us so sad and so happy, sad that you are and we are so far away and happy that we were there, we are delighted with them and we think they make us look very handsome we includes you and Fania and we also includes the vests, We have [been] having a lovely and lively summer, it has been hot and dry, the garden is burned and so are we but it agrees better with us than with the garden. I have been working a lot, the new book The relation of human nature to the human mind or the Geographical History of the U.S.A. goes on very well. Thorton Wilder has just been with us for ten days and he and a little photographer who was with him know it by heart and say it is the best thing I have done.[1] I have done about 70 typewritten pages and I guess it will be about double or a little more than that long, I do not yet quite know, when it gets done I'll send it along and then we will decide about everything, Thornton would also like to read the four in America so would you send me the copy you have here, it is the only one I have, he does not go back to America until the spring, so that is all about me, otherwise in the language of Mark Twain we get up and wash and go to bed, and as the chauffe bain has been not working very well because the sun sets on the stove pipe very often Alice does not include the washing, she was just counting that she had had only two in two weeks, Kitty Cornell's housemate Gertrude[2] something came and called the other day but we were just then in Geneva I wish we had been there calling for you Oh papa Woojums, faithless papa Woojums whom the rest of the Woojums love far far too well, love and kisses so many many kisses

Baby W.

1. Robert Davis was a philosophy student at the University of Chicago. He met Stein when she lectured there in 1934 and 1935. Davis was on his first trip abroad when he went to visit Stein in Bilignin. Davis may have taken some photographs of Stein during this visit.

2. Note by Van Vechten, 1 June 1941: "Gertrude Macy, Katharine Cornell's secretary."

To Carl Van Vechten

[postmark: 7 August 1935]
Bilignin par Belley
Ain

My dearest dearest papa W.

It all comes from you, everything comes from you and there is nothing that the Woojumses like better [than] that it always does come from their own papa. It will make us most happy to have the Gentle Lena in the films most most happy, how it will turn into what it will turn into we do not know but we are sure that it will be just so beautiful, Alice and I were quite upset in being so happy, I just wrote you a long letter, my it will be nice seeing you again and the film will help, yes we did give it to Nathalie [Barney] and I have written to her to ask and we will be seeing her soon,[1] but we all left Paris almost at once, we are so happy with ourselves and you and Fania, it will be wonderful all being together again, and lots of love

Gtrde.

Am sending you an english publication with Procession in it.[2]

1. Stein could not remember if she had given Barney the group of photographs Van Vechten had prepared for her. Stein wrote Barney on [19? July 1935]; when she received no answer, she wrote again on [5 August 1935] (Stein to Barney, MSS. 1884, 1885, Doucet, Paris). Barney wrote Stein on 7 August 1935 (YCAL) acknowledging that she had received the photographs.

2. Stein's "Procession," in *Programme* (19 June 1935), 8:[8], [11]. This review was edited at Oxford University by George Sayer and Veronica Ward. In the same issue appeared "A Note on Gertrude Stein," pp. [12–13], by Paul Treadgold. On the issue's cover Stein wrote a dedication to Van Vechten: "To Carl to Papa Woojums to our Guardian Angel with all love. The Procession is prepared to proceed. Gtde. Baby Woojums."

🐿

To Gertrude Stein
[Postcard] Carl Van Vechten. Painting by Martha S. Baker.
Collection of Carl Van Vechten

14 August [1935]   [150 West Fifty-fifth Street
                                                   New York]

Dear Gertrude:—

You gnus are good gnus and so I am sending you Four in America today for Thornton Wilder to read. Please tell me when you receive it. We may move because a garage back of us pounds & pounds & pounds, but maybe the garage will move.
Love to Mama & Baby Woojums!

Papa W!

🐿

To Gertrude Stein

19 August [1935]   150 West Fifty-fifth Street
                                                   New York City

Dearest Baby Woojums,

I had thought of almost everything, but I had never thought of putting you on an egg.[1] Will you please return this as I want it for my STEIN collection. . I hope the film all happens according to schedule, so you and Mama Woojums can come to our America again to be photographed. .[2] Please what are you going to do in the NEXT war which seems to be coming along fast? Drive a Ford? Please get back to the USA before everything busts again, although maybe it won't be so hot here either. If I were speaking of the weather I would say it was hotter than the hot rainy season in Ethiopia. But that will soon be over. . I sent you Four in America last week as you asked me to.
love to both les Belles Woojums, Baby and Mama

Papa Woojums
Who lives in a very DARK ROOM.

[441]

1. This obect is not in YCAL.

2. The proposal of Mrs. Ehrman to try to sell "The Gentle Lena" to the films. See Van Vechten to Stein, 27 July 1935, note 1.

❦

To Gertrude Stein
[Postcard: Photograph by Carl Van Vechten] Carl Van Vechten's
apartment—1931. The Victorian Room.

20 August 1935 [150 West Fifty-fifth Street
New York]

Yes, programme came, with its Royal Processions,[1] [word?] I like very much, and Treadgold's article, depending on your lectures as it does, so much better than usual. Please write some more of these lovely pieces, dear Baby Woojums! How are you both? We are better than well. . and I *live* in a proverbial DARK ROOM!

all love to you both
Carlo

1. See Stein to Van Vechten [7 August 1935], note 2.

❦

To Carl Van Vechten
[Postcard: J-E. Liotard (1702–1789) Portrait de l'Empératrice
Marie-Thérèse d'Autriche (pastel, 1762)]

[postmark: 29 August 1935] [Bilignin par Belly
Ain]

My dear Papa W.

The Four in America came alright thanks so much, and we don't want to drive a Ford car in the next war, we have 30 reservists and their machine guns in the barn, 600 in Bilignin and 2500 in Belley, and they use anything they can lay hands on and they are just like pictures of themselves and they don't remind us of war and they don't remind us of peace and more is plenty, and they leave next Tuesday, no in the next war we will be in America and tell them about it, perhaps war like dueling will go out, I think the quickest way to stop it would be to stop the salute, that is what goes to everybody's head no saluting no war, but we kiss papa Woojums with so much love, and we hope he don't bow to none

Baby. W.

The [triumph?] of the eggs or egg is fine, will they make me a nice wig do you think, I would love to see the wig, perhaps they will bring you the egg to be photographed that would be nice, and papa W. may Georges Maratier,[1] who took care of Pepe have a photo of Pepe, his address is 7 rue Rollin Paris and if he could have one of me too it would make him happy and one of me and Alice for Madame Giraud Cezarieu, Ain,[2] that would make us all happy is it asking too much dear dear papa Woojums, and I guess that's all

Baby W.

1. A French art dealer.

2. Madame André Giraud lived in the Chalet Vert, Avenue d'Alsace Lorraine, in Céyzérieu, a village in the department of the Ain, France. Céyzérieu is about ten kilometers southeast of Virieu-le-Grand, the nearest train station to Belley.

 Stein had formed several close relationships with people in the neighborhood of Belley and took her American visitors to meet them. Among those she often visited were Baronne Pierlot and her sons who lived in Béon and Madame Giraud. Madame Giraud's name appears in a number of Stein's writings during the 1930s, including the play *Louis XI and Madame Giraud* in Stein's *Operas and Plays*.

To Gertrude Stein

[Postcard: Basket of flowers—with inscription "Con mi FELICITATIÓN le envio todo mi afecto y mi mayor cariño"]

[8 September 1935]   [150 West Fifty-fifth Street
                                                      New York]

Dear Baby Woojums. . .

 Today I am sending photographs to Georges Marantier [i.e., Maratier] & to Madame Giraud, the Cezarien operation of AIN.[1] . . and I sent

[443]

you some pictures of Avila yesterday. . I think your publisher is going to marry Sylvia Sidney.[2] Huey Long is shot.[3] . and Walter Winchell says F[ania]. M[arinoff]. and I are in Mexico getting a divorce! We are just the same at 150.[4] . . and I hope you and Mama Woojums are just the same at Bilignin!

love
Papa W!

1. Van Vechten here seems to be playing with the words "Céyzérieu" and "cesarean." I have been unable to determine whether Madame Giraud had had any children by a cesarean operation.

2. Cerf wrote to Stein, 17 September 1935 (YCAL), that he was flying to Phoenix, Arizona, to marry the actress Sylvia Sidney on 10 October.

3. Long was shot on 8 September.

4. In his column in the *Daily Mirror*, 26 August 1935, p. 10, Walter Winchell wrote: "Are the Carl Van Vechtens arranging anything in Mexico? She is Fania Marinoff . . . Probably not. The same source said the Eugene O'Neills (Carlotta Monterey) were there unwinding and that isn't true, according to chums."

☙

To Gertrude Stein
[Postcard: Ivory Figure of a Gazelle—Egyptian, about 1375 B.C.
(XVIII Dyansty). The Metropolitan Museum of Art]

[postmark: 15 September 1935]   [150 West Fifty-fifth Street
                                                 New York]

Dear Baby Woojums—

You are mentioned in the talking picture Top Hat (Fred Astaire & Ginger Rogers) this will undoubtedly be seen in Paris.[1] I can't wait till I kiss your hand in person!

Love to Mama W!
Papa W.

1. In the R. K. O. Studios film *Top Hat*, written by Dwight Taylor and Allan Scott, an Italian, who miscomprehends English, reads aloud a telegram where the word "Stop" has been inserted

at the end of every sentence. As he reads the telegram aloud, the "Stops" destroy the sense of the message. The character played by Ginger Rogers says, "It sounds like something by Gertrude Stein" (final shooting script, 8 May 1935, #824, p. 43, NYPL-Lincoln Center).

To Carl Van Vechten

[postmark: 17 September 1935]   Bilignin par Belly
                                                 Aim

Oh Carl Carl what a wonderful door I never saw such a wonderful door before. I don't know how you did it but you made the portal come alive like a real one never is alive, the other two tombed us doubly[1] and Anita [Loos] did look so beautiful[2] but what is most wonderful is the door, thanks a thousand times. Autumn has come but it's still lovely weather and I am working and we will be here at least another month or so, perhaps longer. A funny thing happened, Bennett [Cerf] sent me a couple of this fall's books and on the jacket they give the list of authors Random House and Modern Library are proud to print and nowhere do they include my name. I have just written to Bennett as [Eleanora] Duse said about [Gabriele] Dannunzio [i.e., D'Annunzio] when he did La Fouca, Je sais pas si c[']etait par mechante ou mauvais gout. Of course it is not Bennett or Donald [Klopfer] but somewhere in the office, at any rate it is a mistake, and I have called their attention to it. I am sending you the dummy of the Chicago University Press' book and Life and Letters where the[y] print one of the four lectures is printed in England,[3] the University press director is very enthusiastic so I am pleased. I do love you, so much Papa Woojums we love you all

Gertrude

1. A reference to photographs Van Vechten had sent Stein.

2. Anita Loos (1893–1981), the writer, whom Stein had met when she visited California.

3. One of the lectures from Stein's *Narration*, "English and American Language in Literature," was printed in *Life and Letters Today* (September 1935), 13(1):19–27.

To Carl Van Vechten
*[Postcard: Giuseppe Bonito—Dama ignota.
R. Galleria Nazionale di Roma]*

[postmark: 23 September 1935]   [Bilignin par Belley
                                                 Ain]

Dear Papa W.

The whole country side is delighted with your Cesarian operation pictures, they all say in all these centuries that there has been a Ceyzerieu nobody has thought of it.[1] I have signed the agreement with Mrs. [Lillian May] Ehrman's brother, it would be nice if it came off, my name being mentioned like that may help.[2] We are so happy that you are safely in 150, what happened to the move, and we so want to kiss you so warmly papa dear beloved papa W.

Baby W.

1. See Stein to Van Vechten [29 August 1935], note 2, and Van Vechten to Stein [8 September 1935], note 1.

2. Ivan Kahn wrote Stein on 28 August 1935 (YCAL) expressing interest in the screen possibilities of Stein's story "The Gentle Lena." He enclosed an agreement that authorized him to act on Stein's behalf. See Van Vechten to Stein, 27 July 1935, note 1.

To Gertrude Stein
[Postcard: Self-portrait in Top Hat. Photograph by Carl Van Vechten]

23 September [1935]   [150 West Fifth-fifth Street
                                                 New York]

Dear Baby Woojums:

Has Harcourt sent you Mabel [Dodge] Luhan's European Experiences? & have you see[n] how Mabel writes (at length) about you & Alice? I think you better had. It will amuse you or something![1]

*Love from
Papa!*

1. Mabel Dodge Luhan, *European Experiences, Volume Two of Intimate Memories* (New York: Harcourt, Brace and Company, 1935). See chapter 13, "The Steins," pp. 321–33.

To Carl Van Vechten
[Postcard: Portrait of Alice B. Toklas by Sir Francis Rose][1]

[postmark: 3 October 1935] [Bilignin par Belley
Ain]

Autumn has come the time they shut puppies up in the outhouse and they cry, Mussolini I guess is awful nervous, there seems to be a [break?] of [waiting?],[2] no we have not seen Mabel [Dodge] yet but we will of course she couldn't not,[3] the Ceyzerieu family were here yesterday and they thought Papa Woojums with the tea-cup was awful chic they thought Fania most handsome and they are most pleased but not so much as we who love you so[4]

Baby W.

1. The painting is now in YCAL.

2. Tensions had been rising between Italy and Ethiopia; after a series of border clashes each nation had called up reserve troops. Benito Mussolini, the Italian dictator, refused all offers to reach an agreement with Ethiopia. On 3 October his troops invaded Ethiopia and war was declared between the two nations.

3. Mabel Dodge Luhan's *European Experiences*.

4. Stein had shown Madame Giraud and her family one of Van Vechten's photographs, a self-portrait with teacup. Note by Van Vechten: "Papa with a tea-cup is a reference to a photograph. The reference to Fania is also photographic."

To Gertrude Stein
[*Postcard: Perugino, The Resurrection.*
The Metropolitan Museum of Art, New York]

[postmark: 14 October 1935]   [150 West Fifty-fifth Street
                                                New York]

Dear Baby Woojums—

Two nice books arrived. I read the one in Life and Letters with great pleasure. But what is the one with all the blank leaves? Anyway the inscriptions are wonderful & so is Baby W & so is Mama W![1] I *can't* read half [of what] you write in your letters anymore. . Your writing gets more & more & more illegible. But it is worth working on & I do!

Perhaps you explained about that Blank book & I couldn't read it! . . . Fania is in the country & I am joining her today (Connecticut) to look again for houses. So when we live in the country Baby & Mama W. can come & stay & stay!

Love to you both!
Papa W!

Please write me when you read Mabel [Dodge]'s book! A charming letter came from your Cesarian operation friend![2]

1. Stein had sent Van Vechten a dummy, or layout, of her book *Narration*; see Stein to Van Vechten, [17 September 1935]. Stein inscribed the issue of *Life and Letters Today*: "For Carl who is the heart of all language for us. Gertrude."

2. Madame André Giraud wrote to Van Vechten thanking him for the photographs he had sent (27 September [1935], YCAL).

❧

To Carl Van Vechten

[postmark: 15 October 1935]   [Bilignin par Belley
                                               Ain]

My dearest papa Woojums,

Thanks for the clipping,[1] yes Virgil [Thomson] did do an awfully good job of the opera and I am glad they realise it, he does know how to do a whole thing, by the way what is he doing these days. We are hardly home yet, you see we have been away about a year and a half now, 7 months in America and six before and after at Bilignin and we are hoping something nice will take us to America in the spring. I have been seeing a lot of Picasso, he writes poetry, very good poetry, the sonnets of Michael Angelo, he says it takes his mind off of divorce better than painting, so he doesn't paint,[2] and Thornton Wilder is here he is quite mad about the new book of Human mind and human nature, and we have talked it over so much that we all think it would be an amusing thing if he added a running commentary of our xplicating conversations, he is leaving here soon and you will be seeing each other and he will be seeing Bennett [Cerf], and I hope you do like the idea,[3] we are lunching to-morrow with Nathalie [Barney] the Duchess [de Clermont Tonnerre] and Romaine [Brooks] and we will talk about you and we will all tell about how sweet you are because you are, have not seen Mabel [Dodge]'s book yet but we will soon, and everything is peaceful and to-day is all saints day and god bless our saint Papa Woojums

Baby W.

1. This clipping cannot be identified.

2. When in June 1935 the pregnancy of Picasso's mistress, Marie-Thérèse Walter, became known, Picasso and his wife Olga initiated divorce proceedings. The proceedings were eventually dropped because of complicated laws regarding community property. Marie-Thérèse Walter gave birth to Maria (Maia) de la Concepción (named after Picasso's sister, who died as a child) on 5 October 1935. Picasso and his wife Olga remained separated until her death in Cannes, France, on 11 February 1955.

3. Wilder contributed an introduction to Stein's *The Geographical History Of America Or The Relation Of Human Nature To The Human Mind.*

To Carl Van Vechten
[Postcard: Abbaye d'Ambronay—La Sacristie]

[postmark: 16 October 1935]   [Bilignin par Belley
                                               Ain]

Just had a letter from [Ivan] Kahn at Hol[l]ywood, he is trying the Paramount for the gentle Lena, and is to let me know, we do hope and hope so, it would be lots of fun and this time perhaps Papa Woojums would fly out with us, god bless Papa Woojums.[1]

M.W. [*i.e., B. W.*]

Madame Giraud of Ceyzerieu is looking forward to a [superb time?] with you.[2]

1. Kahn's letter is not in YCAL. In a letter to Stein, 8 January 1936 (YCAL), Kahn refers to his earlier letter: "The only time I wrote you was October 2 at Bilignin, Par Belley, Ain, in which letter I told you that I had taken 'The Gentle Lena' to the Paramount Studios. I was not able to make a deal there." Kahn's letter is confusing because he had written Stein an earlier letter on 28 August 1935 (YCAL). See Stein to Van Vechten [23 September 1935], note 2.

2. Madame Giraud was planning a visit to the United States.

To Gertrude Stein
[Postcard] Carl Van Vechten painting by Martha S. Baker.
Collection of Carl Van Vechten

[18 October 1935]   [150 West Fifty-fifth Street
                                     New York]

Dear Gertrude.

In Jubilee (Moss Hart and Cole Porter) at the Imperial Theatre. When the lions begin to roar. Mary Boland cries "That's Gertrude Stein" and the audience loves it.[1] Bennett [Cerf] writes he got a cable on the [perfect?] day

[450]

from Baby & Mama Woojums! He *was* pleased.[2] Will you send Papa Woojums a cable when he gets married to a movie star?

all love
P.W.!

1. *Jubilee!*, by Moss Hart and Cole Porter, with music and lyrics by Porter, opened on 12
October 1935 at the Imperial Theatre, New York, and ran for 169 performances. In act 2,
scene 4, which takes place in the zoo, there is an exchange between the King and Queen. The
King is locked up in a cage.

> *King:* Oh, no. There's nothing in here but me. I meant that it seemed like yesterday
> the Jubilee was next week and now it's tomorrow.
> *Queen:* There is someone in there with you and it's Gertrude Stein. Henry, the Jubi-
> lee's tomorrow.
>
> (*Jubilee!*, script #4340, NYPL-Lincoln Center)

2. Cerf had married the actress Sylvia Sidney. Cerf's letter to Van Vechten is not in YCAL.
Stein's cable to Cerf is not in Columbia-Random House.

To Gertrude Stein

20 October [1935]   150 West Fifty-fifth Street
Sunday   New York City

Angel Baby W!

Here is another pretty nice mention.[1] You see America has by no
means forgotten Baby and Mama W . . . DO READ MABEL [Dodge]'s
book and write me about it!

Sunshine, honeycakes, sugar statues, coca cola, and sweet syrups of
Asia to B an[d] M W!

Papa W!

1. An unidentified clipping.

To Carl Van Vechten

[postmark: 23 October 1935]   [27 rue de Fleurus
                                               Paris]

My dearest papa W.

We are so xcited about you turning farmers you and Fania,[1] I always did sing to Alice the sad song of the farmer, a farmer's life is a hard hard life a farmer's life for me but we are xcited and want to know all about it right away. And the idea of Baby Woojums hand-writing not being legible it always was famous for its legibility, clear as mud but anyway what it was is this, the blue book I sent you is the dummy of the book the Chicago University Press is bringing out this fall of the 4 lectures that I gave there, there is not that clear as a bell, and here we are in Paris, and beside a possible king[2] and a possible emperor vive le roi vive l'empereur, is the present cry in spite of all that and the Abyssinians[3] everybody seems more cheerful than they were. Georges Maratier[4] has just come in and says the cinema where I come in where they read a poem by me out loud while the toast burns is right around the corner Joie de famille W. C. Fields we will try to see it to-night,[5] just got your postal we'll send a cable joint because we love you you don't have to get married any more.[6] Thornton [Wilder] is coming to-morrow and we have just got here and this just to say how much we love you papa Woojums Mama and baby just love their papa W. and no mistake,

always,
Gtrde.

1. Note by Van Vechten, 23 January 1941: "Fania and I looked for an old farm house in Connecticut this summer but never very seriously."

2. King George V of England (1865–1936) was extremely ill, and newspapers were already talking about his successor, his son, the future Edward VIII, later Duke of Windsor. The King died on 20 January 1936.

3. Italy had invaded Ethiopia (Abyssinia) on 3 October 1935. In November the League of Nations declared Italy to be the aggressor. Both British and French popular opinion supported Ethiopia and its Emperor, Haile Selassie. The French Prime Minister and Minister of Foreign Affairs, Pierre Laval, and British Foreign Secretary, Sir Samuel Hoare, met in Paris on 7–8 December. They drew up a plan that would appease Italy at Ethiopia's expense. The outcry

from the British public was so great that Sir Hoare resigned on 18 December and was replaced by Anthony Eden. Laval left office in January 1936.

4. An art dealer and friend of Stein's.

5. In the W. C. Fields film *The Man on the Flying Trapeze* (Paramount, 1935), Fields (Ambrose Woolfinger) returns home after spending a night in jail on bootlegging charges to find his family finishing an elaborate breakfast. As Fields slowly chews around the edges of a piece of toast, his wife, played by Mary Brian, reads aloud a selection from a "lady writer" obviously modeled on Stein. *Joie de famille* is the French title for the film.

6. See Van Vechten to Stein [18 October 1935].

⚜

To Carl Van Vechten

[postmark: 1 November 1935]   Bilignin par Belley
                                                      Ain

Dear dear papa Woojums,

It was just about one year ago that the two Woojums mama and Baby started off across the atlantic to be received in the welcoming arms of papa Woojums and how they welcomed and how happy all the Woojums were, well here we are happy but not so happy as when the Woojums are altogether over there, anyway we are leaving soon for Paris and after that, well we don't seem to have any plans after that, but I'll tell you all about how Paris is when we get there. I have walked miles and miles this summer with the speedometer [i.e., pedometer] and it is nice to have one, everything is nice but Papa Woojums is nicest. I am sending you the ms. Relation of human nature to the human mind, it is all finished now, and I am not showing it to Bennett [Cerf] yet so don't say anything about it just read it and let me know how you like it, I am rather anxious about it.[1] The Sforzas the Italian [family] has been visiting in the neighborhood, they are a nice family, he is going to America next month and I think knows you,[2] the other [event?] is the Picasso divorce but that is going on in Paris, and Picasso has given up painting and taken to writing, but as yet he shows his ms. that is the outside of it but not the inside,[3] have not seen Mabel [Dodge]'s book yet but we will when we get back to Paris and lots of love lots of it,[4]

Always
Gtrde.

1. Stein's *The Geographical History Of America Or The Relation Of Human Nature To The Human Mind.*

2. Possibly a reference to Count Carlo Sforza (1872–1952), the Italian statesman who had opposed Mussolini and had resigned as ambassador to France in 1922. Count Sforza went into voluntary exile in 1927 and, after living in France, settled in the United States in 1940. He returned to Italy in 1943 and played a major role in Italian politics until his death.

3. See Stein to Van Vechten [15 October 1935], note 2.

4. Mabel Dodge Luhan's *European Experiences.*

To Gertrude Stein

[? November 1935]　　　　　　　　　　　　150 West Fifty-fifth Street
　　　　　　　　　　　　　　　　　　　　New York City

Dearest Baby Woojums,

I sat down for a few moments with The Geographical History of America last night and was so amused and excited and interested in the manuscript I never laid it down until it was all read. I think it is Gertrude Stein PLUS, all the best parts of you stimulated and sorted out and worked into a complete pattern: the sublimation of the SUBLIME STEIN. . I think it's more YOU than anything you've done, a great advance in clarity and definition. You have cut everything away that isn't necessary. And it's full of wit and wisdom and I can never forget "What is the use of being a little boy if you are going to grow up to be a man?" and your conjunction of TEARS and Human Nature and WRITING and Human Mind slays me, and I guess I am getting jealous of that nice Thornton Wilder because he plays such a large part in your best book, but I guess I wouldn't like to be Jo Alsop or Bennett [Cerf]'s Communist Uncle, would you? . . The airplane parts are nice. I think you got a lot out of airplanes besides the ability to get from place to place quicker than quick. . I think the idea of T[hornton] W[ilder] doing a running commentary in connection with the book is an INSPIRED one and I can't wait to see it all in PRINT. May I send the mss. to Mark [Lutz] to read? I'm sure he would love it. You ask about Virgil [Thomson]. I haven't seen him[x]; nor have I been to one or am I going to the other of these concerts (on account engagements) but here is what he is doing.[1]. I am glad you are seeing Picasso again because maybe you can get

[454]

him to let the Maestro photograph him next time Papa Woojums comes to Paris (if any). . If you don't read Mabel [Dodge]'s book soon I shall go mad. Why DIDN'T [Alfred] HARCOURT SEND IT TO YOU? Ask him, please. . Baby Woojums' handwriting is all right again, most legible. . and we are not so near being farmers as we were. We look at houses and houses and houses and they get worse. I think we might try farming in Brooklyn or in a penthouse. . Ellen Glasgow is here and we are giving her a little dinner on Friday. . The WC Fields cinema is still another one where you are mentioned: I haven't seen that. You just get more and more mentioned in EVERYTHING and by EVERYBODY and Mama Woojums and I will soon have to do something, you'll be so spoiled and won't wear your rubbers or your union suits!

I am going into a photographic show (the first in which my work has been seen) at Radio City beginning the 26th and I am sending fourteen photographs and Baby Woojums and the Flag is ONE.[2]

so lots of love to Baby and Mama W from

Papa Woojums (and how!)

x. I am pretty busy with photographs—more busy even than usual.

1. Thomson's music was the subject of a one-man concert on 8 November 1935 at the New School for Social Research, New York. This was the third in a series of five concerts devoted to different composers. Thomson played the piano for the concert; other artists included Ada MacLeish, soprano, and the Philharmonic Scholarship Quartet. The date of the concert allows placement of this letter before 8 November.

2. Van Vechten participated in the Second International Leica Exhibition of Photography. The exhibition was held on the mezzanine floor of the R. C. A. Building, Rockefeller Center, New York. Van Vechten's photographs included portraits of Stein, Theodore Dreiser, Fania Marinoff, and Lynn Fontanne.

To Carl Van Vechten

[November? 1935]   [27 rue de Fleurus
                                                     Paris]

Mama Woojums has decided because if there is a revolution it would be best that the complete works unedited of Baby W. should be in the hands of papa W. the safe hands of papa W. she is going to do them and to send them to you. Thornton [Wilder] is taking back the four in America, and soon you will have them all and then too soon we will send you a collection of the magazines that you have not got, we are having pleasant times and loving you a lot, always your loving[1]

Baby Woojums

X X X X X X X X X X X
Quite homesick for you.

[on verso, beneath child and lamb with roses, and beside rose stamped in blind] A rose is a rose and papa Woojums is close to the hearts of his Woojums two.

ever

1. France had been going through a period of political and economic unrest, and the fear of revolution was very real. Since 1931, a succession of governments, none lasting very long, had been unable to stabilize the country. The gravity of the situation brought about Léon Blum's coalition of Radical Socialists, Socialists, and Communists in the Popular Front government in 1936. Blum, however, was forced to resign the following year. Stein had sent Van Vechten typescripts of many of her writings; she now embarked on a systematic attempt to give him a copy of all published and unpublished writings. It was this collection that formed part of Van Vechten's gift to YCAL in 1941.

To Carl Van Vechten

[postmark: 21 November 1935]   [27 rue de Fleurus
                                                Paris]

My dearest Carl,

Have not heard from you for a long time it seems and when we don't we get lonesome. We are working hard getting off all the manuscripts to you of the things of mine not yet printed because although there may be no European war it does look as if there may well be a revolution and we could get out but we could not well take the ms. along, and so if the bulk is too

big why put it somewhere else but there really is not an awful lot of it because a good many things have been published in late years, however the
unpublished still does make somewhat of a pile, so if they are a nuisance do
something else with them, it is curious looking over these old things, I have
found one called Birth and Marriage, which pleased me much with its
movement, sometime look at it,[1] Alice would also like some time when you
have time if you would verify what is sent, she incloses a table of contents
with each package, she is sending off two or three to-morrow and then the
rest gradually, next week, we I've no plans, we are probably during the winter going over to England to speak at the English Club at Oxford, and staying around in some houses and I think it will be rather fun, we have a devoted Viennese servant called Othmar[2] who makes us a great deal of Viennese
cakes and we try not to grow fat, and he takes good care of us, Picasso continues making literature and reciting it to all and sundry, Nathalie [Barney]
says that if New York was populated by Carls she would live in it but as
there is only one she will only go over once in a while, Romaine [Brooks]
is telling you all about us but she can't tell you how much we love you you
did get the Human nature ms. didn't you oh so much love

Gtrde.

1. Stein's "Birth and Marriage," in her *Alphabets & Birthdays*, pp. 173–98. The first mention
of this work is in Stein to Van Vechten [25 August 1924].

2. Othmar Baumgartner.

❧

To Carl Van Vechten

[postmark: 23 November 1935]   [27 rue de Fleurus
                                                Paris]

Oh dearest papa Woojums you have made me so happy about all
you said about the ms.[1] I am never completely happy until you have said
so, and now I am, more than happy, yes do send the ms. to Mark [Lutz],
because Thornton [Wilder] has the other that is to be left with Bennett [Cerf],

and I am so happy that you are so pleased, no we have not yet got hold of Mabel [Dodge], but we have hopes to-morrow, we are lunching with Louis Bromfield,[2] and why do you not farm in Deerfield Mass. It is so beautiful and I think they are selling a home there, and Picasso is mad about the negro photos of yours, do send him the ones of St. Ignatius, he says a negro has not looked like that since the Renaissance but he won't acknowledge the receipt of it it [is] his Spanish way not to but he will love having them, and this brings me to the most xciting [thing] your show, please send us the list of those shown and what they say, Picasso thought your Virginia ones, the [Edgar Allan] Poe home beautiful but nobody thinks anything you do as beautiful as the devoted mama and baby Woojums do everything their Papa Woojums does no they don't, and we are so happy, lots and lots of love

Gtrde.

1. Stein's *The Geographical History Of America Or The Relation Of Human Nature To The Human Mind.*

2. Bromfield lived in the Presbytère-de-St. Etienne in Senlis (Oise), not far from Paris. Stein quite often went for Sunday lunch at the Bromfields'.

To Carl Van Vechten
[Rose motto]

24 October [i.e., November] 1935[1]   27 rue de Fleurus
[Paris]

Dearest Papa Woojums—

All summer I cooked and now I'm typing—please don't say you wish I weren't when the result comes in the packages to 150 W. 55th. but when I fell upon M[abel Dodge] Luhan's last published effort at the Bromfields I hugged it to my bosom—not suspecting how she dealt with us all and came back and read a good piece of it then and there. It wasn't pleasing reading—but you will know what I feel and think.

    1st. She wrote it herself—
    2nd. She shouldn't have
    3rd. I don't like how she writes

[458]

4th. I don't like why she writes

5th. I don't like what she says

6th. And most particularly I don't like what she says of Mama Woojums [i.e., Baby Woojums]. Of the rest of us she might or might not have reason to feel as she does but M. W. [i.e., B.W.] was lovely to her and she didn't wear a hat with a brown ribbon tied around no she did not. And to end la demie vierge didn't say much to me in '05 and a married one now. Oh no it's hopelessly antipathetic. So much for M. Luhan's book.

We're fine—only Pepe had une petite intervention chirurgicale on his hinder end but he's frisking about now. While he was at the vets for four days Basket first got the idea he was dead and then was sure he'd never see Pepe again. He danced about and then had to accommodate himself all over again to having a little brother.

We have a perfect Austrian cook – O O O and that and typing are a good smoke screen for Paris and its winter climate. It doesn't filter through. I always hope that I'm waking up in N. Y. and can telephone Circle 7 33399[2] and hear Papa Woojums voice or sprightly Madame Woojums. A young frenchman who met her several years ago here always asks for news and was thrilled when I could tell him how she was on the stage. Tomorrow I'm sending 2 more packages '20 inclusive. After that it will go slower and proportionately so as well—until '32.

Oh dear Carl I wish it was last year or that this year was the same. We don't seem to have many plans or rather none at all. M. W. is in very good form—the Austrian cook cooks suitably and she rather likes Paris and seems not even to mind french plumbers. The Chambers meet on the 29th and everyone except [Pierre] Laval expects the ministry to fall perhaps he's right. In which case there'll be no political news from here for a while.[3]

Now I must go and not chatter any more to my own Papa Woojums. All my love to Madame and to Papa Woojums.

from
M. Woojums

1. Although Toklas clearly dated this letter 24 October, it is an obvious error. Stein's letter to Van Vechten of [23 November 1935] speaks of hoping to see Dodge's book *European Experiences* at the Bromfields' "tomorrow." Toklas' letter was clearly written after that visit.

2. Van Vechten's phone number was Circle 7-3399. Toklas put in the extra 3 by mistake.

3. Pierre Laval was both the Prime Minister and Minister of Foreign Affairs. His government did not fall until January 1936.

❦

To Carl Van Vechten
[Postcard: Photograph of Gertrude Stein and Alice Toklas outside a War
Hospital, Hôpital Simon Violet père]

[postmark: 25 November? 1935]   [27 rue de Fleurus
                                                 Paris]

My dear Carl,

We did get Mabel [Dodge]'s book at Le Divan[1], and Alice deep in it reads me choice pieces, and they are pretty choice, but where are you in it, I hoped you would be in it it seems Muriel [Draper] is so mad she went back from Chicago although she was headed for Taos, a good time is always to be had by all[2]

lots of love
Gtrde.

1. Le Divan is a bookshop in Paris.

2. Dodge's *European Experiences* covers her life from the time of her first marriage to Karl Evans in Buffalo, New York, in 1900, until she and her second husband, Edwin Dodge, returned from an extended stay in Florence, Italy, in December 1912. Van Vechten, who did not meet Dodge until early 1913, does not, therefore, figure in this book. He figures prominently, however, in her book *Movers and Shakers: Volume Three of Intimate Memories* (New York: Harcourt, Brace and Company, 1936). Dodge discussed Muriel Draper in Chapter Ten, "Muriel," in *European Experiences*, pp. 255–73.

❦

To Carl Van Vechten

[postmark: 28 November 1935]   [27 rue de Fleurus
                                                 Paris]

My dearest Carl,

I think this may be amusing, he was a man who talked to me one windy day on Michigan Avenue, and said he had not been able to hear me because he did not belong to anything that did, we had a conversation and he had a funny looking satchel in his hand and I asked him what it was,

[460]

and he said marionettes! Then this summer he wrote me and asked would I send him a play for marionettes and I was just doing the Human nature Human mind book so I put together the plays in it and that is what he is doing, let me know what you think of it.[1] Picasso and his boy Paulo were here to-day for Thanksgiving dinner and we had a nice one but it would have been even a nicer one with you both, otherwise everything is peaceful, and very pleasant, and lots of love always and always and always to you

Gtde.

1. Donald Vestal, who manipulated marionettes and at the time was working for the Works Projects Administration, and his friend Charles Boardman, who was studying piano, met Stein on 30 November 1934 on Michigan Avenue, Chicago, Illinois. Vestal wrote Stein on 13 August 1935 (YCAL) reminding her of that meeting and asked her if she would write a play for marionettes. Stein sent him the text of "Identity" in late August or early September 1935. Vestal responded to the play by writing Stein on 9 September 1935 (YCAL), " 'I am I because my little dog knows me' is a consummated story in nine words and it sounds like delightful marionette material." On 12 November 1935 (YCAL) Vestal could report to Stein that the work on the play was progressing and that the music for it was being written by a young Chicago composer, Owen Haynes.

    Vestal presented "Identity" for some of his Chicago friends probably in early June 1936. The first official performance of the piece was in Detroit, Michigan, on 9 July 1936 at the National Puppetry Conference. The participants were Owen Haynes, piano; Rita Smith, soprano; Carl Harms, reader and manipulator; Burr Tillstrom, reader and manipulator; and Donald Vestal, who in addition to being a reader and manipulator designed and constructed the sets.

    Thornton Wilder wrote a preface for the performance, but because of the death of his father, it arrived too late to be printed. Wilder's preface, "Introduction to Miss Stein's Puppet Play," was first printed in *Twentieth Century Literature, Gertrude Stein Issue* (Spring 1978), 24(1): 94–95.

    Vestal wrote Stein about the performance in a letter, 13 July 1936 (YCAL), and later sent her photographs of the production, which are also in YCAL.

To Gertrude Stein

1 December [1935]   150 West Fifty-fifth Street
Sunday night   New York City

Dearest Baby Woojums,

    Look at Papa Woojums first photographic press notice (which you share!).[1] Isn't it pretty grand! . . . . I am awaiting the mss. and a place will be found for them (until Comes the Revolution in USA). Tell Mama Woojums I will check up on her inventory and if two words are missing I'll notify her.

l[ove] and k[isses],

Carlo Papa W!

Here I am with Norman Douglas in the Cascine in Florence.[2]

1. A review of the Second International Leica Exhibition of Photography, in which Van Vechten had participated, appeared in the *New York Sun*, 30 November 1935, p. 28.

2. Van Vechten enclosed a photograph of himself and the writer Norman Douglas taken by Mark Lutz during their visit with Douglas in 1934.

&

To Carl Van Vechten
[Postcard: Photograph of Les Terrasses—the Villa Stein][1]

[postmark: 5? December 1935]　　　　　　　[27 rue de Fleurus
　　　　　　　　　　　　　　　　　　　　Paris]

My dearest papa Woojums

You will be amused that at the Alcazar d'Ete[2] I came into a reviewer, the Duchess [de Clermont Tonnerre], and she and Nathalie [Barney], but sing your praises, heard it it was recounted in a topical song, I never did think it would happen in Paris. What is your news, we get awful lonesome for a word

Baby. W.

1. The Villa Les Terrasses was erected in Garches, on the outskirts of Paris, in 1927 for Michael and Sarah Stein by the then relatively unknown architect Le Corbusier.

2. The Alcazar d'Eté was an open-air music hall just off the Champs-Elysées in Paris.

æ

To Gertrude Stein

9 December [1935]   150 West Fifty-fifth Street
                                                     New York City

Dear Baby Woojums,

THREE PACKAGES have arrived, but I have had no time as yet to analyze them. Even Muriel Draper is holding communist meetings in her pretty room and talking like mad about Sacco and Vanzetti and the Scottsboro Boys over the telephone, so we may have a revolution here before you get one there.[1] I'll try to get the mss under cover if such is so. . . And of course Picasso may have some photographs. Does he want just St. Ignatius or would he like some assorted Negroes? Picasso can have what he wants and he needn't thank me, but some day maybe he'll let me photograph him. . Only please tell me where to send his pictures. . . Thornton Wilder hasn't been near me. I hoped he would stalk right in with all the news. . Romaine Goddard (Brooks) came to lunch. She is taking an apartment in Carnegie Hall. . I screamed over what Mama W had to say of Mrs. [Mabel Dodge] L[uhan]'s book. She was so philosophical about it, looking nonchalant and lighting a murad.[2] Mina Curtiss reviewed it in the Nation (together with the book about Harry Lehr!) under the caption (from Veblen) "Conspicuous Waste". But Time deserves an accolade. Their review was headed with one word: "TEASER.".[3] Muriel says, "She wants to die without a friend." It sounds like a song and may well be an epitaph. . Think of you with an Austrian cook. I LOVE Schnitzel Holstein. and Brabantetorte. .I think you will have fun in England. An Englishman was here this afternoon and he says all England wants to come to America now. . I love the Richelieu stamps. I won't be satisfied until USA has Stein Stamps and Mama Woojums on the Special Delivery. But wouldn't the picture with the flag make a marvelous stamp! . . Oh yes, you ask why I'm not in Mabel's book? But I didn't know her then. I'll be in the next one, never fear! O yes, I'll be in the next one. . This Donald Vestal (Could that be his name?) sounds very amusing indeed. I think I wish I could go to Chicago to see Baby Woojums' play performed by marionettes. Tell D[onald] V[estal] (IS that his name?) when you write him to call me up if he ever comes to NY. . Marco, by the way,

[463]

is quite mad about the HN and the HM.[4] I think he is writing you. He LOVED the dog parts.   And so I'll say goodnight. .

Much love, in which Fania joins me, to Baby and Mama Woojums!

Papa W!

It seems I have acquired a [Giorgio de] Chirico.[5]
F. M. is reading a play.

1. Muriel Draper was a tireless supporter of progressive political and social causes. Nicola Sacco and Bartolemeo Vanzetti were political radicals who were arrested on a charge of theft and murder in South Braintree, Massachusetts, on 15 April 1920. They were convicted of the charges on 14 July 1921. The widespread doubt of their guilt led to worldwide demonstrations and protests before they were electrocuted on 23 August 1927.

The Scottsboro Case concerned nine Negro boys who were indicted on 31 March 1931 on charges of having raped two white girls. Eight of the boys (one was only 13) were tried, convicted, and sentenced to death in early April 1931. The case against them was unproved and the verdict was the result of anti-Negro bias. The Scottsboro Case went through various appeals and retrials and became a cause célèbre among Northern liberals such as Muriel Draper.

2. See Toklas to Van Vechten, 24 October [i.e., November] 1935.

3. Curtiss reviewed Mabel Dodge Luhan's *European Experiences* and Elizabeth Drexel Lehr's *King Lehr and the Gilded Age* in *The Nation*, 27 November 1935, pp. 628–29. A review of Dodge's book appeared in *Time*, 30 September 1935, pp. 67–68.

4. Stein's *The Geographical History Of America Or The Relation Of Human Nature To The Human Mind*.

5. Van Vechten had acquired Giorgio de Chirico's painting *Self-Portrait*, oil on canvas, 1911–12, 34 3/8 x 27 1/2 inches. The painting was given in memory of Carl Van Vechten and Fania Marinoff to the Metropolitan Museum of Art, New York.

To Alice Toklas

10 December 1935

150 West Fifty-fifth Street
New York City

Dear Alice,

I have spent the better part of a day checking up on the manuscripts and everything seems to be all right, except "At" seems to be missing from No. 2 package. To make up for this there is a Volume called She and Her

Brother in the first package, and three or four papers in the third (I have received three so far) that do not seem to be catalogued at all. . You would save me a good deal of time and I think it would be just as easy for you, if you would make up your list in the order in which the papers are placed in the pile. This condition actually existed, dear Mama Woojums, in the first two bundles, but the third (which was the most difficult) seemed to be collected helter-skelter—even the subheads (not always listed at all) were not listed in order. It was as if Baby Woojums had taken the papers to play with in his crib. . I guess everything is all right and I am sure the papers arrived just as you sent them. Nothing appeared to be tampered with. Only "AT" seems to be missing. Maybe that got stuck at the back of something or is a subhead or maybe you forgot to tuck it in. . Anyway, dear Mama Woojums, you asked for a report and here it is. . I have tied all the bundles up again and will put them away as safely as possible. . But don't be surprised if we have the Revolution before you have one![1]

sugar candy and rice cakes and lemon meringue pie to you, dearest Mama Woojums!

Papa Woojums!

1. Toklas had started sending Van Vechten typescripts of all of Stein's published and unpublished writings. These were later donated by Van Vechten to YCAL. Stein's "At" (1914) is printed in her *Bee Time Vine and Other Pieces*, pp. 155–57.

To Gertrude Stein

[Postcard: Self-Portrait in front of poster for Socrates exhibition at the British Museum. Photograph by Carl Van Vechten]

[postmark: 14 December 1935]   [150 West Fifty-fifth Street
New York]

Dear Baby Woojums!

Package No. 4 is here & I have checked it off and everything is okay. Also I read Birth & Marriage, as you suggested. It is a beautiful example of

[465]

GS's middle manner.[1] Joe Louis is *pounding* Paulino Uzcudun over the radio.[2] So I will send love and kisses to you and Mama Woojums & lay off!

Papa W!

1. Stein's "Birth and Marriage" in her *Alphabets & Birthdays*, pp. 173–98.

2. Joe Louis knocked out Paulino Uzcudun in the fourth round of a scheduled fifteen-round fight at Madison Square Garden, New York, on 14 December 1935.

To Carl Van Vechten
[Postcard: Gertrude Stein and Sir Francis Rose
in the Garden at Bilignin]

[postmark: 18 December 1935]

[27 rue de Fleurus
Paris]

My dearest Carl,

Best and very best of Christmases and New Years and New Years and Christmases to you. This is F[rancis]. Rose doing the portrait of A.B.T. in the garden at Bilignin, you only see the table, but she is just behind.[1] The pig is as rosy as ever and is every inch a pig and gives us endless pleasure. Alice will not be convinced that it is glass, she says it is not possible.[2] It is lovely cold weather, makes one feel more than ever like America, and the opera begins to sound quite fabulous. I am quite moved by it, and I xpect to hear all about it from you. Paris is nice and quiet and very pleasant, do come over it is quite prewar, gentle and unworried. Lots and lots of love to you and to Fania and lots of it and more

Gtrde.

1. The Rose portrait of Toklas is now in YCAL.

2. A glass pig, a gift from Van Vechten.

To Gertrude Stein

*[Postcard: The Bandit Margato Shot, Francisco Goya,
Spanish, 1746–1828, The Art Institute of Chicago]*

20 December 1935

[150 West Fifty-fifth Street
New York]

Completely lovable Baby Woojums. Package No. V is here, is checked out, and is okay, so that's that. My, but you've written a lot, as much as Balzac or Mozart, maybe!—Anyway love and merry Christmas to Baby & Mama Woojums from

Fania & Papa Woojums

To Carl Van Vechten

[postmark: 22 December 1935]

[27 rue de Fleurus
Paris]

Dear Papa Woojums

I almost bust myself laughing in bed over your letter to Alice about the ms. you are funny papa Woojums and you delight Baby Woojums, and Othmar[1] the Austrian says he knows Brabanttorte and Holstein[er] Schnitzel so come and eat it and that would be a happy new year, we go to Oxford the 11 of February, and Carl Thornton [Wilder] is afflicted with New England shyness he calls it austerity to a formidable xtent, I am writing him again to go to see you but if you would write him it would help his address is 50 Deepwood Drive, New Haven, Conn, because I do want you to consult together, as to what to do about the new book,[2] if Bennett [Cerf] does not want to,[3] I have not heard a word from him, Harcourt might, but anyway I do want you two to talk it over. Then there is this, in going over the ms. I found a play, about Byron,[4] I think it is completely possible to do with

Virgil [Thomson], who directly and indirectly wants it, it would take a lot of stage imagination to put it on, but it does move and it is a romantic tragedy, we will send it separate, I have not mentioned its xistence to anybody, I want to know what you say, had a delightful letter from Mark [Lutz][5] about the ms. of H. N. & H. M. what a nice way of calling it, also the literary magazine of Princeton has just printed a short novel I am asking them to send you a copy,[6] and what [Giorgio de] Chirico, I met him the other day for the first time and liked him, you could photograph him, a nice head and body, and Pablo [Picasso] wants my negroes, he likes that,[7] and Picabia wants the tiny one of me he is mad about it and Pablo's address is 23 rue de la Boetie, have been seeing something of Dalli [i.e., Dali] too and his most bewitching mustache,[8] 4 of the large packages sent the last lot are all the old magazines with Baby Woojums in them and all dedicated with love and kisses each one of them inside in them to Papa Woojums, we were amused with Muriel [Draper], I have not read the [Mabel Dodge] Luhan book[9] but I have just read The Postman always knocks twice,[10] and it made me homesick oh so homesick for the good old service stations, otherwise more and more merry Christmas and more and more happy new years to Fania, and F. M. is reading a play is a lovely title,[11] and we would like to be a stamp oh yes we would

Love
Gertrude

1. Othmar Baumgartner, Stein's cook.

2. Stein wrote Wilder twice on 25 December 1935, one letter postmarked 10:45, the other 17:30. In neither letter does she mention Van Vechten.

3. Cerf did publish *The Geographical History Of America Or The Relation Of Human Nature To The Human Mind*, with an introduction by Wilder, on 19 October 1936.

4. Stein's *Byron A Play* (1933) was published in her *Last Operas and Plays*, pp. 333–86. Thomson did not set this piece to music.

5. Lutz's letter is not in YCAL.

6. Stein's "The Superstitions of Fred Anneday, Annday, Anday; a Novel of Real Life" was printed in *Nassau Literature* (December 1935), 94(2): 6–8, 24–26.

7. The various photographs of the members of the cast of *Four Saints in Three Acts* that Van Vechten had sent to Stein. Van Vechten did photograph de Chirico in 1936.

8. Francis Picabia, the French painter, and Salvador Dali, the Spanish painter.

9. Toklas had been reading Stein excerpts from Dodge's book. See Stein to Van Vechten [25 November? 1935].

[468]

10. Stein is referring to James M. Cain's novel *The Postman Always Rings Twice* (New York: Grosset & Dunlap, 1934).

11. See Van Vechten to Stein, 9 December [1935]. Which play Marinoff was reading cannot be determined.

To Carl Van Vechten
[Telegram]

25 December 1935   Paris

WOOJUNS TO WOOJUNS MERRY CHRISTMAS

[Stein-Toklas]

To Gertrude Stein and Alice Toklas
[Christmas card: Christmas greetings to you -- Bundy]

Xmas 1935   [150 West Fifty-fifth Street]
New York

And a wow of a New Year—always our love

Carl—Fania

To Carl Van Vechten
[Postcard: Photograph—Gertrude Stein Watching Sir Francis Rose Painting Lucey Church]

[postmark: 2 January 1936]   [27 rue de Fleurus
Paris]

Dear darling Papa Woojums,

Yes I do write but what else can I do like Balzac and Mozart what else can I do, and some day it will be nice if they are all printed, that is my dream, we spent New Year giving Basket his worm medicine, a long occupation, and Christmas having Christmas and to-day Madame Gay said what darlings you and Fania were and it was wonderful that Fania was not alone a clever actress but took such good care of her husband which was you and we said all of us ayes too! and we love you both and everything to you always[1]

Gertrude.

1. Undated note by Van Vechten: "Mme Gay on a visit she made, in company with the Duchesse de Clermont-Tonnerre (Elisabeth Gramont) to Carl Van Vechten's apartment at 150 West 55 Street, NYC."

To Gertrude Stein
["A Little Too Much" motto]

9 January 1936   [150 West Fifty-fifth Street
                                                  New York]

Completely Blesséd Baby Woojums,

Well packages came and arrived and were brought in, package after package: I never saw so many! I was entranced and excited and cried Noël! Noël! And Bonne Année and barked Woojums! till Fania and Edith thought I had gone crazy. Which reminds me that Edith was pleased as pleased with her card and asks me to thank you and to send both of you her love.[1]. The inscribed magazines touched me very deeply. I LOVE having these and soon or late they will be bestowed in happy slipcases and arranged against eternity.[2] I guess nobody but Baby Woojums herself ever had so much Stein material under one roof! Anyway I love having these magazines and you are more than an angel woojums to send them to me. Besides these came another package of manuscript (okay, tell Mama Woojums, quite okay), Narration, in the limited edition[3] (what a lovely book),[x] and Byron, a play itself. Also one of the sweetest letters Baby Woojums has ever written to his Pa. . Think of your having a cook named Othmar that makes Brabantetorte! I can't bear it, it's so lovely. . Think of that [Thornton] Wilder fellow NOT being afraid of Baby W. and being afraid of Pa W! I can't comprehend this. . I haven't seen Virgil [Thomson] all winter. At the moment he is busy putting on a production of Macbeth (laid in Haiti) with Negroes including Edna Thomas, whom you met at my house, as Lady Macbeth.[4] When I see him I'll tell him you've sent me Byron and I take it if he shows interest you want me to hand it to him. And presently I'll look Byron over myself. The Lit Magazine of Princeton arrived just this minute!. . I MUST photograph [Giorgio de] Chirico. Curiously I have just acquired a swell picture of his: Portrait de l'Artiste—1911 and I hope he'll sit for my camera next time I come to Paris. Once you said you wanted a picture of Lake Michigan and the Lake Shore Drive and I can't recall if I gave you one: so anyway one is going to you. This was taken that November we were together. . Picasso's Negroes went off to him in BUNCHES: Negroes in several productions and I have more, if he likes these. and I can't make out if you want me to send Picabia a tiny picture of you. You had a number of these and perhaps you have given him one. Anyway you don't send his address. I like Dali, and his Gala, and please give them our affectionate greetings.[5] So today I was out with dear Mary Garden and she has a wonderful job in the Moving Pictures and Sarah [Victor] (who presided over the cakes at the Algonquin) died and we all went to her funeral yesterday.[6] A wonderful woman, and Edith stems from her. . . You are such a woojums to send me the magazines and you are such a woojums and lots of love from Fania and me to you and Mama Woojums!

[Carl Van Vechten]

[x]I say thank you all over & over again!

If there are any Atlantic Monthlies handy around your parts, please read Juanita Harrison's My Great Wide, Beautiful World in Oct. & Nov. issues.[7]

If you would write a line to Bertha Case about Sarah I guess she would love it![8]

---

1. Edith Ramsey, the Van Vechtens' cook.

2. The magazines, in slipcases, were given by Van Vechten to YCAL.

3. Stein's *Narration* was printed in an edition of 870 copies. In addition to the trade edition, a limited edition of 120 numbered copies signed by Stein and Wilder (who had written the introduction) was published.

4. Thomson wrote the music for a production of Shakespeare's *Macbeth* that opened at the Lafayette Theatre, in Harlem, on 9 April 1936. It ran for fifty-six performances. The play was

directed by Orson Welles and was produced by the Negro Division of the Federal Theater Project, under the supervision of John Houseman. See also Stein to Van Vechten [25 May 1936], note 3.

5. The painter Salvador Dali was married to Gala (Elena Deluvina Diakanoff, 1892/93-1982).

6. Sarah Victor died on 4 January 1936.

7. Junaita Harrison was a black woman who at the age of thirty-six undertook to work her way around the world. Her adventures, between 1927 and 1935, became part of two articles, "My Great, Wide, Beautiful World," in *The Atlantic Monthly*, October 1935, pp. 434–43, and November 1935, pp. 601–12.

8. Bertha Case was the wife of Frank Case, the owner of the Algonquin Hotel, New York.

To Gertrude Stein
["*A Little Too Much*" motto]

10 January 1936   [150 West Fifty-fifth Street
                                                   New York]

Dear Gertrude and Baby Wooums:

Here is the clipping about Sarah [Victor] which didn't seem to be on hand when I wrote this morning.[1] Also, I've just returned from my first sitting with Romaine Brooks Goddard. She is painting me. She has a big studio in Carnegie Hall and if all goes well I'll be immortalized with white hair.[2] I've been painted 26 times but never with white hair. . Paul and Essie Robeson were here for lunch. They are sailing tomorrow on the Ile de France. . Hoping you and Alice are the same I wish you

> Kisses can kiss us
> Ducks and little fishes followed by wishes
> Happy little pair![3]

I have read your Princeton novel with great delight. It seems to be a complete exposition of your theory of Prose Narrative, told with some satiric intent. I wrote Mr. Severance (what names you know!) to this effect. .[4]
Please don't forget

Papa Woojums

1. Clippings about the death of Sarah Victor appeared in numerous New York newspapers on 6 January, including the *New York Daily News* and the *New York World Telegram* (Van Vechten scrapbook, NYPL-MD). Precisely which clipping he sent to Stein cannot be identified.

2. Romaine Brooks (1874–1970), the American painter. She was born Romaine Goddard, the daughter of Ella Waterman Goddard and Major Harry Goddard. In 1902 Romaine had a brief "ephemeral marriage" to a pianist and dilettante, John Ellingham Brooks. After her marriage ended she continued to use the name Brooks. In late 1935 she rented a studio in Carnegie Hall. Brooks' *Portrait of Carl Van Vechten*, 1936, oil on canvas, 40 x 32 inches, is now in YCAL. The portrait shows Van Vechten seated by a window; he is painted with white hair and wearing a white suit.

3. Van Vechten slightly misquotes the poem. It should read:

> Kisses can kiss us
> A duck a hen and fishes, followed by wishes.
> Happy little pair.

The poem, printed on a cream-colored card in black and green, was published for Van Vechten by the Banyan Press in 1947 in an edition of forty-eight—forty-six for friends and, in order to meet copyright regulations, two for sale were also sold to Van Vechten.

4. Frank Severance, Jr., was the copy editor of *Nassau Literature* (Princeton University), which had just published a short novel by Stein. See Stein to Van Vechten [22 December 1935], note 6.

To Carl Van Vechten

[postmark: 17 January 1936]   [27 rue de Fleurus
                                               Paris]

My dearest papa Woojums,

We are so happy that you are happy in everything that makes us all happy. Of course Thornton [Wilder] isn't afraid of Baby Woojums because it is Baby Woojums and is afraid of Papa Woojums because he is a papa Woojums, of course that is the way it is because if it were not that way what way would it be. Lovely stamps you sent, Othmar always begs them to make happy the Austrians he says, these he says will make Austrians happy and how can one refuse to do that. Picasso has not yet had his negroes, he says he will telephone to me as soon as they arrive so I can tell you, he is quite xcited about it, and [Giorgio de] Chirico I am sure will pose, he is very sweet, gentle and quiet a little sad but calm, not at all surrealist so he says. I like him, although I do not know him very much, with a rather beautiful head and xpression, but I know him well enough to introduce you alright, and Carl did we ever have a little photo, the one Picabia wants is the little framed one he also I think would like that same one in big it is the one you made of me when I first came over profile sitting down he is mad about it, his address is 6 Square Bois de Boulogne, Paris, you'r[e] getting a big Paris public for your photos, so everybody knows about it. We were sad about Sarah [Victor] you never had photographed her,[1] had you, she was very wonderful there, I will write to Mrs. [Bertha] Case, we had a tea-party and had Lady Troubridge and Radcliffe [i.e., Radclyffe] Hall, that would be something to photograph get Romaine [Brooks] to tell you stories of them, she knows them very well.[2] We are getting all ready for England, I am giving two lectures at Oxford one to the English Club and one to the french club, and now Cambridge writes to ask me too, so I guess we will have a good time, we go over on the ninth of February and stay about 10 days, we will tell you all about it from over there.[3] I am sending you a letter of Wendell Wilcox which will please you[4] also of Ivan Kahn there still seems a chance of Hollywood,[5] and Bennett [Cerf] has written a nice letter, he is now all his old self again and very sweet, a little sad but very sweet, he is very enthusiastic now about doing the book in the fall,[6] the thing I would like to ask you I always do ask you and you always tell me whether there should be put with it the Four in America out of which it came, or how could they be connected, of course that would make too big a book I have not said anything at all about it to Bennett I want to know what you think about it all, we will see Bennett over here so there will be plenty of time for you to tell me just what you think, good-night papa Woojums you are a very dear papa Woojums and mama and Baby Woojums don't love anybody like they do their papa Woojums and the reason why because there is nobody who ever was or is or will be anything like dear papa Woojums

Always
Baby Woojums.

[on back of envelope] Do give Mary Garden our love I will write to her soon so pleased that she is happy.

---

1. Note by Van Vechten, 22 January 1941: "Sarah Victor, the colored pastry cook of the Algonquin [Hotel], who presided over a table of cakes and pies in the dining-room died. She was a great character and had worked first for May Irwin and then for Bertha Case. I went to her funeral in a Catholic Church. Yes I had photographed her."

2. Una, Lady Troubridge, was born (1887), Margot Elena Gertrude Taylor, the daughter of Captain Henry Ashworth Taylor. From early childhood she seems to have been called Una. In 1908, she became the second wife of Admiral Sir Ernest Troubridge. In 1915 she left him and from then on lived with the writer Marguerite Radclyffe Hall (1886–1943). Their relationship is described in Hall's *The Well of Loneliness* (London: J. Cape, 1928) and in Lady Troubridge's *The Life and Death of Radclyffe Hall* (London: Hammond, Hammond and Co., 1961). Stein met Hall (who was known to friends as John) and Lady Troubridge through Romaine Brooks.

3. Stein delivered her lecture "What Are Masterpieces" at both Oxford and Cambridge Universities. At the Oxford French Club she delivered the lecture "An American and France." Both lectures are printed in her *What Are Masterpieces*.

4. Wendell Wilcox, a young writer whom Stein met in Chicago.

5. Kahn, a Hollywood agent, reported to Stein in his letter of 8 January 1936 (YCAL) that "The Gentle Lena" was being read by Frances Marion of Metro-Goldwyn-Mayer Studios. Although Kahn had hopes that something would develop from this source, no film was made of this story.

6. In his letter to Stein of 9 January 1936 (YCAL) Cerf discussed plans for Stein's *The Geographical History Of America Or The Relation Of Human Nature To The Human Mind*. The letter also gives Stein details of his marriage to Sylvia Sidney.

To Gertrude Stein

*[Postcard: Portrait of a Spanish boy at a Romería de las regiones, Madrid.
Photograph by Carl Van Vechten]*

[postmark: 24 January 1936]
       [150 West Fifty-fifth Street
New York]

Dear Gertrude:

  A wonderful letter & a package of MSS (tell Alice it is OK) from you, dear Baby Woojums! I didn't understand at first which picture you wanted Picabia to have. Of course I'll send him one. *Yours* are numbered on the back & if you tell me the number it is easier. Let me know if he gets the right one. Mary Garden adores you. I gave her your message. She is at Essex House West 59 Street New York. Roman's [i.e., Romaine Brooks] (so I have rechristened her) portrait is going to be good. I think. I'll write a letter in a day or so. LOVE to Mama & Baby W!

             Papa W.

[on front of postcard] This boy was in a Romería in Madrid.

[475]

To Gertrude Stein
["*A Little Too Much*" motto]

28 January 1936   [150 West Fifty-fifth Street
                                                   New York]

Completely angelic Baby Woojums:

We are having very cold weather, but I go on posing for Roman (so
I call her) Goddard,[1] although her studio is cold. It is in a state now where
she won't let me see it, so I can't report on it, but I'm sure it is marching. .
I am making more and more photographs, tonight a nude Negro lady, last
week Willa Cather; now the attractive Mai-Mai-Sze, daughter of the Chinese
Ambassador, later Sir Thomas Beecham! I am very happy with it all. . Think
of my making Austrians happy indirectly with my stamps. Here is another
shot at making Austrians happy! . . You weren't very clear about what Picabia wanted at first, but I guess I know now. A little one is pretty imprac-
tical but he will get a big one and if it isn't right, let me know. . Tell [Gior-
gio de] Chirico he hangs right in my room! Yes I photographed Sarah [Victor]
LOTS, quite sad and beautiful ones. Her funeral in a Catholic Church was
wonderful and the priest raved about her character. . Tell me all about England surely and if you meet any nice numbers. You are sure to have a grand
success and a good time. Tell Mama Woojums to pack you up tight in your
woollens and tell her to wear her rubbers. . Thank you for letting me see
Mr. [Wendell] Wilcox's nice letter and here it is.[2]. The films are slow but
sometimes sure. . I do not think Four in America should come out in the
same volume or at the same time as the other. The other is a Tour de Force
and quite different in feeling and movement and should make its OWN
impression.[3] Four in America is for some other time. But of course you may
think differently. . What I mean is that I think one would take the interest
away from the other and that would be unfortunate. . According to the papers Bennett [Cerf] and his Sylvia are two again, but you can take your choice!
Thousands of yellow roses with their stems in tinfoil to you and pretty Mama
Woojums and let me know what Picasso says, if any. . I had a WONDER-
FUL letter from Miro about my Barcelona pictures. . .[4]

Papa Woojums!

[476]

1. Romaine Brooks: see Van Vechten to Stein, 10 January 1936, note 2.

2. Stein had sent Van Vechten Wilcox's letter to her of [2 January 1936] (YCAL). Stein had tried to interest Harcourt in a novel by Wilcox. When Harcourt refused the novel, Stein tried to get Cerf interested in it.

3. "The other" is Stein's *The Geographical History Of America Or The Relation Of Human Nature To The Human Mind*.

4. Van Vechten had photographed the Spanish painter Joan Miró while he was in Barcelona, Spain. Miró's letter to Van Vechten is not in YCAL or NYPL-MD.

To Carl Van Vechten

[postmark: 8 February 1936]   [27 rue de Fleurus
                                               Paris]

My dearest Papa Woojums,

   We are all ready to fly to London our fetishes in our pockets and only papa Woojums behind us missing and what a miss, we wish oh how we wish that you were there to kiss us and bless us, we are staying first with Lord Berners,[1] they say he has one of the best Victorian country homes and very luxurious, then we go to Cornwall and stay with the Abdy's at Newton Ferrers very 18 century handsome,[2] in between we stay modestly at Garland's hotel in London, and then Cambridge so far nothing grand there but we hope it will come, we will be away in all ten days, Picasso was delighted with the negro photographs, he is very low in his mind and they cheered him quite a little, I asked him if he wanted any more negroes, no said he with a very pretty enthusiasm no I would like some of you he would like XIII 0:43 he and Picabia both would like beside anyone of XXIVg:2 and XXXIVG 15 XXXIII: g24, XIV g: 7 the last one with the fetishes would delight them, I get awful jealous Carl when you say you are photographing the others, you never did or will photograph any of them so often, that I know, but I get a twinge. I have not seen [Giorgio de] Chirico but I will when I get back there will be a list for you, Pablo, Picabia, Chirico, Mardrus,[3] the Egyptian men, Gaston Bergery the future Kerensky of France and his wife Bettina Jones[4] Daisy Fellowes,[5] Nadine the Belgian Chinese are all waiting in rows for Papa Woojums to photograph them, if you would send [Wendell] Wilcox a photo it would make him so happy, had such nice letters from Bennett [Cerf] he seems all himself again and very pleased to be doing my book in the fall, I am entirely of your mind about the 4 [i.e., *Four in America*], the time will come and please Carl what is the Columbia Encyclopedia where Mark [Lutz] says I am,[6] who is Ted Husing who seems to be in spite of as a negro fan said,[7] and Mrs Sherman says Charlie Chaplin seems hating G. H. Wells [i.e., H. G. Wells],[8] we are all in a stew finding out how little we can be elegant in with in England, and that is all that is all for all, Papa Woojums and us, and I was so happy to have a birthday and a wire, and love

Always
Baby Woojums

and Daisy Fellowes 19 rue St. James, Auteuil, Paris wants a photo too, she just clamored.

1. Gerald Hugh Tyrwhitt, Lord Berners (1883–1950), English composer and author. Lord Berners composed a ballet, *A Wedding Bouquet*, based on Stein's play *They Must. Be Wedded. To Their Wife.* (printed in her *Operas and Plays*, pp. 161–94, and *Last Operas and Plays*, pp. 204–38). Lord Berners' home was Farington House in Berkshire, England.

2. Stein had met Sir Robert Abdy (d. 1975) and his second wife, Lady Diana Abdy (d. 1967), in late 1931 or early 1932. The formality of Sir Robert Abdy's first extant letter to Stein, 30 March 1932 (YCAL), suggests that they had only recently met. Later the Abdys and Stein would form a very close relationship.

Abdy was a wealthy Englishman interested in antiques, furniture, china, finely printed and bound books, and eighteenth-century French painting. He was associated with the Wildenstein Gallery in Europe and later opened his own art gallery. The Abdys had homes in London and Cornwall, England, and Saint-Germain-en-Laye, just outside of Paris.

Stein wrote "A Portrait of the Abdys." published in *Janus*, May 1936, p. 15. The Abdys are referred to as Sweet William and Lillian. These characters, with their references back to the Abdys, reappear in a number of Stein's writings in the late 1930s, particularly in her play *Listen to Me*, in *Last Operas and Plays*, pp. 387–421.

3. A reference to either Dr. Joseph-Charles-Victor Mardrus or to his wife, the writer Lucie Delarue-Mardrus. Stein had met them through Natalie Barney.

4. Gaston Bergery was the publisher of the newspaper *La Flèche* and was a long-time member of the French Chambre du Députiés. Bergery began his career in politics as a member of the French Radical Party but gradually moved toward the extreme right. On 7 July 1940 he authored a resolution denouncing the Third Republic and calling for a new government based on that of Nazi Germany. Bergery served as the Vichy government's ambassador to the Soviet Union and to Turkey. His wife, Elizabeth (Bettina) Shaw Jones, was an American who had come to France with her two sisters in the early 1930s. She decided to stay in France and went to work for Elsa Schiaparelli, the fashion designer. Mrs. Bergery was a friend of Natalie Barney's, and it was probably at Barney's that she met Stein.

[478]

5. Daisy Fellowes was the daughter of the fourth Duc Decazes and the widow of Prince Jean de Broglio. In 1919 she married Reginald Fellowes, a wealthy Englishman. They lived in London and Paris. Mrs. Fellowes was a writer, an editor of *Harper's Bazaar*, and a well-known hostess.

6. *The Columbia Encyclopedia* is a one-volume encyclopedia first published by Columbia University Press, New York, in 1935.

7. Ted Husing (1901–62), a radio sports announcer. There is no correspondence at YCAL between Husing and Stein. It is possible that they met during Stein's American tour, 1934–35.

8. Charlie Chaplin, the film actor, and H. G. Wells, the English novelist.

❧

To Gertrude Stein
[Postcard: Comtesse D'Haussonville by Jean August Dominique Ingres
(1780–1867), The Frick Collection, New York]

[postmark: 17 February 1936]   [150 West Fifty-fifth Street
                                                New York]

Dearest Baby Woojums—

Another package of mss. arrived yesterday, including a copy of 4 in America. Tell Mama W everything is okay. Roman Goddard's[1] picture of me is presque terminé. I like it very much indeed & will photograph it so you can see it. .

Love to both
Papa W.

Did you know The Good Anna is in a book of short stories that Bennett [Cerf] edited?[2]

1. Romaine Brooks.

2. Stein's "The Good Anna," in *The Bedside Book of Famous American Stories*, ed. Angus Burrell and Bennett Cerf (New York: Random House, 1936), pp. 636–80.

❧

To Carl Van Vechten

[postmark: 24 February 1936]
Garlands Hotel
Suffolk Street, Pall Mall
London, S.W. 1

My dearest papa Woojums,

Yesterday it was Cambridge[1] and we did have a good time, before the lecture we went to tea in their room with all the American students in Cambridge and they were so sweet and after the lecture which was a great success they were so proud, I was awfully pleased to represent the flag to them, at the tea party there were only Americans xcept two English one admitted because he had been in America and was enthusiastic and the other I found came from South Hampton, they said they never had known before why they liked him but that was it, they said when they first came they said they would not know each other but would only know the English and they hardly spoke but as the winter got colder they drew together and now they are never apart, it did make me homesick seeing them all, they were so nice, and now we stay in London a couple of days longer, and then back to Paris, everybody has been delightful, and don't be jealous Papa Woojums but a long way after you Lord Berners is the nicest man and do not breathe it out loud because nothing will probably happen and anyway it is best that nothing is said but he kind of wants to put the play Say it with flowers, to music, and that would be nice, I also told him about the Byron, and he was interested but Say it with Flowers appealed to him a lot, you never told me what you thought about the Byron,[2] there is also a possibility of arranging an English edition of the lectures which would please me a lot,[3] and [Sir Robert] Abdy wants to de lux an edition of the Stanzas in Meditation[4] but all this of course are but happy dreams and can only be told to Papa Woojums who always has to know everything as soon as we know it, I am hoping that you will know them all sometime because they are all so nice, and to-morrow we dine with Lady Cunard[5] and the next day beside the editor perhaps we meet Havelock Ellis and anyway we love Papa Woojums all the time the best and the best [6]

Always
Baby Woojums.

[480]

1. See Stein to Van Vechten [17 January 1936], note 3.

2. Lord Berners did not set either Stein's play *Say It With Flowers* (*Operas and Plays*, pp. 331–43) or her *Byron A Play* (*Last Operas and Plays*, pp. 333–86) to music. Instead he used her play *They Must. Be Wedded. To Their Wife.* See Stein to Van Vechten [8 February 1936], note 1.

3. No English edition of either *Lectures In America* or *Narration* was published.

4. Probably in the early spring of 1932 Stein began a long meditative poem that she eventually called *Stanzas in Meditation*. This poem was written during the summer of 1932 concurrently with *The Autobiography of Alice B. Toklas*, which Stein said (*Everybody's Autobiography*, p. 9) she wrote in November 1932 but which probably was begun somewhat earlier.

Sir Robert Abdy, who had an interest in finely printed books, had proposed an edition of the stanzas to be printed by Guido Morris. Abdy went so far as to have a sample sheet made of a stanza to test the paper and type face. No copy of this sample sheet is at YCAL. A copy is known to have been given by Stein to a friend, but it cannot be located. The world economic situation was probably one of several reasons why the project was abandoned.

5. Lady Maud "Emerald" Cunard (d. 1948) was the American-born wife of Sir Bache Cunard. Lady Cunard was known as a hostess whose interests were literary, artistic, and musical. She was greatly admired by Sir Robert Abdy, who had probably introduced her to Stein.

6. Stein lunched with the editor Alan Lane and Havelock Ellis (1859–1939), the English scientist and writer who conducted research in the psychology and sociology of sex.

❦

To Carl Van Vechten
[Postcard: Delacroix. Baron Schwiter]

[postmark: 25 February 1936]

[Garlands Hotel
Suffolk Street, Pall Mall
London, S.W. 1]

Our last day in London and we have had a good time lots of funny stories and some very amusing meetings, the last a dinner with Lady Cunard, but I'll tell you all about that, everybody likes us and we are very pleased and so loving

Gtrde.

Dearest Papa Woojums,[1]

I started a letter to you but could never finish it and now I find it has mysteriously disappeared—or rather exchanged for another because here is

[481]

Baby's to you. Where did it go to or was it used as a laundry list? I only wanted to know if you had ever read "Sainte-Una Fois" and do you think it could be translated. I'm sending it to you from Paris.[2] Heaps of love to Fania and to you.

Mama W.

1. Toklas reversed the card and wrote her message between the lines of Stein's message.

2. *Sainte-Unefois* (Paris: NRF, Gallimard, 1934). This was the first book published by the French writer Louise de Vilmorin (1902–1969).

❧

To Carl Van Vechten

[postmark: London, 25 February 1936]   Newton Ferrers
Callington, Cornwall[1]

My dear Carl papa Woojums

We have had a good time and we are still having a good time, the two lectures in Oxford did go off awfully well the second one had a lot of amusing young men, the first one more high-brow, both lively, at the end of the second lecture as I went out four stalwart Americans and two Canadians lined up and one after the other said thank you for what you made them take about America thank you and solemnly shook hands, the New College wanted me to dine with them en masse but unfortunately we had to leave the next day for here, Lord Berners is charming will send you a photo of us all, I am hoping that there may be the opera in London, everybody is trying to introduce me to the right people to produce it, and I'll let you know more about it after I know, it has been nice most xtraordinarily nice, the stately homes of England are awfully comfortable now, Lord Berners I think the most amusing so far and what a cook, we were always telling about papa Woojums and how sweet he was wonderful how naturally that subject arises Alice makes me write so many polite letters that I can only once more say that Baby Woojums loves its Papa Woojums

Gtrde.

[482]

1. This letter, postmarked London, was written on the stationery of the country home of Sir Robert and Lady Abdy. It may have been written there and mailed in London or else written and mailed in London.

To Carl Van Vechten

[postmark: 25 February 1936]   [27 rue de Fleurus
                                                Paris]

My dear Carl,

Just back and have received this letter, I am inclined to accept their idea but Alice thinks perhaps just at the moment that they are trying for the other in Hollywood it might not be wise beside she thinks they would not be serious and come through with the arrangement, I hate to bother you about this but I do not like to act without your advice, I am inclosing a letter accepting which please read and send them if you think it a good thing and the letter covers it, if not tell me and I will send them a letter refusing,[1] I told you about [Lord] Berners' idea and then a man from the Xpress who interviewed me in London said why do not they put on one of your plays,[2] it is in the air but I am hoping that it will materialise and [Turner?] has had ideas about it, on the other hand I do not want to make a bad start which might spoil things so as usual it is a crie de secours to papa Woojums from his Woojumses,

Always
Baby Woojums.

1. Harry Dunham had written Stein (undated letter, YCAL) about several film projects he had worked on with the composer Paul Bowles. Dunham proposed to Stein that he film Maurice Grosser's scenario made from two of Stein's plays, *Ladies Voices* and *What Happened, A Play*. The music for the film would be written by Paul Bowles.

Stein agreed to the project in an undated letter to Dunham (probably February 1936, Collection Grosser). She wrote, "Your idea interests me as I have always felt that Maurice [Grosser] could do something with my plays, but I do want to know what form an agreement would take who is responsible and with whom is the agreement made." Stein went on to ask for a clarification of the financial terms of the agreement and Dunham's wording about Stein's words being the only ones used in the film.

Stein had not heard from Dunham by 16 March 1936, when she wrote him a postcard (Collection Grosser) asking him about the agreement, which she had not yet received. Stein signed an agreement with Dunham, witnessed by Toklas, on 12 April 1936 (Collection Grosser). Dunham wrote Stein toward the end of 1936 (undated letter, YCAL) that he hoped to have the money raised to make the film in 1937. The money was never raised and the film was not made.

Dunham, who was a student at Princeton University, had met Paul Bowles in Villefranche-sur-Mer in the summer of 1929. It was Bowles who introduced Dunham to Stein during the winter of 1930. Dunham was in Europe learning to be a photographer; later, in Berlin, he studied cinematography in the Reinmann Schule. Dunham became a news photographer for Pathe and was killed in Burma in 1943. (Information about Dunham and access to the Stein-to-Dunham letters were graciously provided during an interview with Maurice Grosser, November 1982).

2. Stein had been interviewed by the *London Daily Express* on 13 February 1936 (YCAL).

To Gertrude Stein
["*A Little Too Much*" *motto*]

25 February 1936   [150 West Fifty-fifth Street
                                                     New York]

Dearest Baby Woojums,

What a lovely time you must be having in Merrie England! . . I liked Lord Berners' book so much and I like his music too.[1] Sir Thomas Beecham has just been playing some of his nautical ballet with the Philharmonic here.[2]. I will look up those pictures of YOU, Baby Woojums, for Picabia and Picasso one day.[x] Not long ago I sent you a picture of how my pictures looked at the Leica Show and this was addressed to Baby Woojums Esq and you will be in England and maybe your Austrian cook won't understand. . When I read all the names you have lined up for photographs in Paris and realize that Baby W and Mama W are there, it does seem as if I'd have to come over right away, doesn't it? Maybe I shall. . You ask me to send [Wendell] Wilcox a photograph but I don't remember his full name and I sent his letter back to you and don't know where he lives. Maybe Wilcox is somebody else and I have this all wrong. . We haven't seen Bennett [Cerf] all winter but they've taken another firm in with them and everybody says Bennie and Sylvia are washed up.[3]. The Columbia Encyclopedia is something issued by Columbia University. It says Papa Woojums was born in 1870 which makes him very Papa Woojums indeed doesn't it?.⁴. And I'll send Daisy Fellowes something too. Roman's [Romaine Brooks] portrait of Papa W is very upstanding and handsome and I think you will like it. . Roman is enjoying NY and says she'll never live in Paris again, but it is very cold here this winter and the snow is about 50 feet deep and ice all over. Mabel [Dodge] has at last got to America and is publishing about it in two parts, the first part dedicated to John Reed, poet, and the second to Maurice Sterne, painter!⁵. . I am in a photograph show at Washington this week. . . Well, all hail and happiness to Mama and Baby W and write me all about England!

Fania joins me in love to both,

Papa W!

Brevard College, N.C. in the poor mountaineer section, has written asking me for books. So I am sending 'em some of mine . . . AND Lectures in America. . So don't be surprised if you begin getting letters from students!⁶

1009 red butterflies with blue antennae to you!

ˣI just did!

1. Stein sent Van Vechten Lord Berners' *First Childhood, An Autobiography with Plates including Portraits* (London: Constable & Co., 1934).

2. Sir Thomas Beecham gave a series of concerts in New York during the month of January 1936. The concerts with the New York Philharmonic Orchestra and the Philadelphia Orchestra.

3. In 1932 Harrison Smith and Robert Haas formed the publishing firm of Smith and Haas. At the suggestion of Bennett Cerf they merged with Random House, the firm founded by Cerf and Donald Klopfer in 1927 (Cerf and Klopfer purchased the Modern Library from Horace Liveright in 1925). Cerf wrote of the changes at Random House to Stein in a letter, 28 January 1936 (YCAL).

4. Van Vechten was born 17 June 1880.

5. Mabel Dodge Luhan's *Movers and Shakers; Volume Three of Intimate Memories* (New York: Harcourt, Brace and Co., 1936). Part One of the book is dedicated, "For Jack Reed the Poet"; Part Two is dedicated, "For Maurice Sterne the Sculptor."

6. Brevard College, in Brevard, North Carolina, wrote to Van Vechten on 15 February 1936 (YCAL) asking for contributions to their library. The college, founded in 1934 as a result of the merger of three small schools, was an independent Methodist College. In a note on this letter Van Vechten wrote: "I sent The Merry-Go-Round, Spider Boy and Gertrude's Four in America." Van Vechten's note, written in January 1941, is incorrect because Stein's *Four In*

America was not published until 1947 and Van Vechten would not have sent a typescript. Van Vechten probably sent Stein's *The Geographical History Of America Or The Relation Of Human Nature To The Human Mind*.

❧

To Gertrude Stein and Alice Toklas
[Postcard] Fania Marinoff, 1914.

27 February [1936]   [150 West Fifty-fifth Street
                                       New York]

Dear Mama & Baby Woojums!

Picabia's address turned up & the photographs have been sent. So that's that! I hope you are both having a sweet time in England. Would that I could join you. 1001 red roses & 141 yellow ones to you!

C.

❧

To Gertrude Stein
["A Little Too Much" motto]

5 March [1936]   [150 West Fifty-fifth Street
                                       New York]

Dearest Baby Woojums,

I really don't know what to say about this proposition and so I am sending this letter back to you for you to decide. You see I don't know anything about [Harry] Dunham and obviously you do because he calls you Gertrude.[1] Then, if it turned out badly I'd hate to have asked you to join. Sometimes these little things are good, sometimes bad. So follow your own hunch. . I had four letters from you in one day! Mostly from England where you seem to be having a time, as usual. I see I must meet Lord Berners. He

[486]

is a friend of Pavlik [Tchelitchew] and a friend of Cecil [Beaton]'s. . Picabia wrote me a charming letter.[2] His pictures have gone and also Picasso's. You are a bright colored Baby Woojums of the First Order and so is Mama Woojums, bless her, but I could only read two words on that postcard on which you BOTH wrote.[3]. Love and kisses,

Papa Woojums![4]

1. See Stein to Van Vechten [25 February 1936], note 1.

2. Picabia's letter is not in YCAL.

3. See postcard, Stein and Toklas to Van Vechten [25 February 1936].

4. At the bottom of this letter Stein has written: "Wendell Wilcoxs address, [Donald] Vestal Arts Club, play, photo clippings, [Harry] Dunham."

To Carl Van Vechten

[postmark: 6 March 1936]

[27 rue de Fleurus
Paris]

Dearest papa Woojums,

You said you would be getting that revolution before we did and everything papa W. says comes true, and there they are not letting you go up and down, I am glad that the windows were not your windows, but then they would not be your windows because everybody loves papa Woojums,[1] here we are back from England and kind of home-sick for England, we did have a good time a really good time, and I am awfully pleased that you like all of [Lord] Berners' work because I do too, he wrote another book called Radcliffe Hall privately printed which is very funny and I am asking him if I may send it to you, and he is doing a very funny one about a Camel, that I like immensely, he has now definitely decided to do one of my things to music and he has chosen They must. Be wedded. To their wife. and I am awfully happy about it, he thinks it will go well to music.[2] The photo of the photos came alright for Baby W. Esq. and they make a noble effect, and we are so pleased with everything,[3] I am also asking Berners to send you a photo of him and me which was quite charming, the one of the whole house party was published in the Tatler of Feb. 26., the picture world is getting quite lively, Picasso has just had a most successful show, Picabia is having one, and Max Jacob begins,[4] and they are beginning to sell and everybody likes it, but Paris itself is not as gay as London or New York, everybody is still a good deal weighted down. Yes Mabel [Dodge] has gotten to New York, [Alfred] Harcourt has just sent me some letters of mine to Mabel which Mabel wants to print, and he Harcourt says that he thinks this is the best of the books so far, it is called Makers and Shakers.[5] I am doing a play a trifle light and elegant and it is called Listen to me and I am on the third Act. Alice says the third Act has to be long. As soon as it is done I will send it on and I think you will like it,[6] I am awfully pleased and touched about Barnard College having our books together,[7] Picabia's address is 6 Square Bois de Boulogne, we are all anxiously waiting the photo of Romaine [Brooks]'s portrait of you, it sounds handsome and I guess that's all just now xcept lots and lots of love, oh Helene the original Helene is back with us, her husband died and she wanted to come back and so you will photograph her too won't you papa Woojums[8]

Always love to Fania lots of it

Baby Woojums

[on back of envelope] Wilcox is Wendell Wilcox 1120 East 55 St., Chicago, Ill.

1. Stein and Van Vechten had discussed the possibilities of revolution in Stein to Van Vechten [November? 1935]; Van Vechten to Stein, 1 December [1935]; and Van Vechten to Toklas, 10 December 1935.

Note by Van Vechten, 23 January 1941: "Referring to the elevator strike in New York, 1936." Van Vechten had probably sent Stein a clipping about the strike.

2. Note by Van Vechten, 23 January 1941: "The book was 'First Childhood.' " See Stein to Van Vechten [25 February 1936], note 1.

Lord Berners' *The Girls of Radcliff Hall*, by Adela Quebec (pseud. for Lord Berners) (n. p.: printed for the author for private circulation only [ca. 1935]).

Lord Berners, *The Camel, A Tale* (London: Constable & Co., 1936).

3. Note by Van Vechten, 23 January 1941: "Photographs of an exhibition of mine at the Leica show in New York." Van Vechten had participated in the Second International Leica Exhibition of Photography, mezzanine floor, R. C. A. Building, Rockefeller Center, New York. Van Vechten exhibited photographs of Stein, Theodore Dreiser, Fania Marinoff, and Lynn Fontanne.

4. An exhibition at the Galerie Renou et Colle, Paris, *Picasso Dessins* 14 to 28 February 1936. An exhibition, *28 oeuvres de Picasso*, had just opened (4–31 March) at the Paul Rosenberg Gallery in Paris.

Exposition Picabia was held during the month of February 1936 at the Galerie Jeanne Bucher, Paris.

Max Jacob (1876–1944), the French writer, also did drawings and water colors. Some of his works may have been exhibited in a gallery in Paris at this time.

5. Alfred Harcourt had written to Stein (21 February 1936, YCAL) to act as an intermediary between Dodge and Stein. Dodge wanted permission to include some of Stein's letters to her in her book *Movers and Shakers*. Stein gave her permission, and ten of her letters to Dodge were printed, pp. 29–36.

6. *Listen to Me*, printed in her *Last Operas and Plays*, pp. 387–421. See Stein to Van Vechten [8 February 1936], note 2.

7. Stein misread Barnard for Brevard College. See Van Vechten to Stein, 25 February 1936, note 6.

8. Hélène had probably come to work for Stein in 1905 and remained in the household until 1913/14. Hélène returned briefly in 1929/30. Principal references to Hélène are in Stein's *The Autobiography of Alice B. Toklas*, pp. 8–11, 13–14, 166, and in Toklas' *The Alice B. Toklas Cook Book*, pp. 170–71.

⁂

To Alice Toklas
[Postcard: The Morgue, Paris (etching) by Charles Meryon][1]

9 March [1936]   [150 West Fifty-fifth Street
                                                 New York]

No, Mama W dear, I have not read Sainte-Une-Fois, nor do I know anything about it nor have you sent it to me yet.[2] Happy (anyday to get a letter from Mama W to Papa W (so rare!)

Love
Papa W.

1. Another impression of this etching by Charles Meryon (1821–1868) was once owned by Leo and Gertrude Stein. See *Four Americans in Paris: The Collections of Gertrude Stein and Her Family* (New York: The Museum of Modern Art, 1970), p. 163.

2. See postcard, Stein and Toklas to Van Vechten [25 February 1936], note 2.

To Gertrude Stein

[Postcard: Photograph by Nicholas Muray] Fania Marinoff—1921

[postmark: 21 March 1936]   [150 West Fifty-fifth Street
                                             New York]

Yes, do let me see Lord Berners on Radcliffe Hall.[1] I am so pleased he is doing music for you. and please send the photograph of you & Lord B. Listen to me is a lovely name for a play & *everybody* would listen & DOES! Think of the original Hélène coming back. Why, I think she was there when I came to you in 1913!—when there was a poulet! Romaine [Brooks]'s portrait is finished all but the background. When that is done it will be photographed. I think undoubtedly it is by far the best thing she has done. It is very vital, & living.

Love to you both,
Papa Woojums

1. Lord Berners' book. See Stein to Van Vechten [6 March 1936], note 2.

To Gertrude Stein

[Postcard: View of Avila, Spain. Photograph by Carl Van Vechten]

[postmark: 24 March 1936]   [150 West Fifty-fifth Street
                                             New York]

Dearest Baby Woojums!

I dreamed last night that you & Mama Woojums arrived on a boat. Stayed an hour to visit with Papa Woojums & then sailed back!!! An idea has occurred to me. Couldn't that potter at Bilignin make some plates with BABY Woojums, MAMA Woojums, & PAPA Woojums on? Couldn't he?

Love & Kisses
C

[on front of card] AVILA

[490]

To Carl Van Vechten

[postmark: 25 March 1936]   27 rue de Fleurus (VI)
                                                         Paris

My dearest Papa Woojums

We spent all last evening having met [Edward] Wasserman[1] at [Parfaits?] telling all about dear papa Woojums, he said how wonderful you were and then we said how wonderful you were and then we all illustrated it with anecdote, and you are wonderful dear papa Woojums and we love you, and we are convinced that it was you that made America have a nice year to travel around in instead of an awful year like this year, last year. Here are some clippings [which] will amuse you and the photo. We are giving [Alexander] Woollcott a April fools party and how we wish you were to be here, we miss you every minute.[2] I am working a lot, tremendously, a book,[3] and two plays, one is done, I guess it's pretty good it is about Sweet William and his Lillian and is called Listen to me, I tried to make it like my memories of the Kirafly brothers and the Lion tamer,[4] and then I got worried lest it meant too much but mama Woojums was pleased, we did to-day almost have an awful time, we left mama W. to pick wild flowers, while the dogs and I walked all in the forests of St Germain, and then we that is the dogs and me could not find mama and the car, we all had a fit, and it was worse and worse, I pleaded with the population of the forest to find her and at last a bicycle boy reported a lady in an automobile knitting with spectacles, take us to her I said and he did and there she was, dogs' instinct is no good, all Basket had been able to find when I frantically told him to find mama Woojums was some deserted bread and cheese, I have written to Harry Dunham to go ahead and after they get started perhaps you will go and look.[5] We are all waiting for that photo of your portrait where is it,[6] and I guess that's all, Wasserman is coming to tea next Wednesday and we will talk about you some more, and I guess that's all just now xcept devoted love from Baby Woojums and all the family.

                                                                    Gtrde.

Don't bother to send clippings back.[7]

1. Edward Wasserman was a Wall Street banker and a member of the Seligman banking family. He was, however, more interested in the arts. In 1939 he founded the Soldier's Welfare Service, which provided weekly entertainment for soldiers in the American Hospital, Paris. He left France as a refugee after war was declared. He returned to Paris after the end of the war and briefly opened an art gallery.

It is difficult to establish how Van Vechten and Wasserman met; it is possible that it was through the sculptor Jo Davidson or the publisher Mitchell Kennerley as early as 1913–14. See Davidson, *Between Sittings: An Informal Autobiography of Jo Davidson* (New York: Dial Press, 1951): "Mr. Kennerley would often attend the sittings, and she [Miss Emily Grigsby] brought her friend Edward Wasserman" (p. 65).

Wasserman converted to Catholicism in 1939 (see Wasserman to Van Vechten, 28 June [1939], YCAL). This conversion would later have a profound effect on Toklas' decision to become a Catholic (see Burns, ed. *Staying on Alone: Letters of Alice B. Toklas*, p. 373).

By a court order effective 15 January 1942 Wasserman's name was changed to Waterman.

2. Woollcott had written Stein from London on 4 March [1936] (YCAL) to expect a visit from him in early April. He arrived in Paris on 29 March. The verso of Woollcott's letter to Stein of 4 March gives what is obviously a guest list for a party. These may be the names of those invited to Stein's party for Woollcott.

3. Stein had begun work on *Everybody's Autobiography*.

4. See Stein to Van Vechten [8 February 1936], note 2, and Stein to Van Vechten [6 March 1936]. The Kirafly brothers, Imre and Bolossy, were born in Budapest. They produced entertainments, lavish spectacles, that ended with elaborate processions. They were well known in Europe, having mounted a "Colossalfete" in Brussels in 1868. In 1869 P. T. Barnum brought them to the United States, where they remained for twenty-five years. They mounted such spectacles as "Nero and the Destruction of Rome" and "The Fall of Babylon." Their "Life of Columbus" ran for two years at the Chicago World's Fair. It is clear that Stein, in writing *Listen to Me*, not only used material drawn from her friends Sir Robert and Lady Abdy but was also recalling the kind of theater she had seen as a child.

In a letter to Bennett Cerf [? March 1936] (Columbia-Random House), she wrote: "I have just finished a play, I think it partly good, it is called Listen to Me. I had an idea of making an old fashioned thing like Wilson used to do in the Lion Tamer. . . ." *The Lion Tamer* was a comic opera derived from the French opera comique *Le Grand Casimir* by Jules Préval and Albert de Saint-Albin. *The Lion Tamer* starred Francis Wilson in the role of Casimir and had been adapted by J. Cheever Goodwin (words) and Richard Stahl (music). The play opened in New York at the Broadway Theatre on 23 December 1891 and ran for more than a month before moving to the Globe Theatre, Boston.

In late 1891 or early 1892 Gertrude and her sister Bertha went to live with their mother's sister, Fannie Bachrach, in Baltimore (Gertrude's mother had died in 1888 and her father had died early in 1891). Leo, who had begun college at the University of California at Berkeley, transferred in 1891/92 to Harvard University. It may have been while visiting Leo that Gertrude saw *The Lion Tamer*.

The Lion Tamer concerns the efforts of Casimir to save his circus. The first act takes place in a circus tent where Casimir (the lion tamer and owner of the circus), who is overwhelmed by debts, hatches up a scheme with his wife, Angelina, to fake suicide so that the circus can pass into her hands. In the second act Casimir is discovered in Corsica and is about to be executed. Lucia, daughter of the Count Verdegris, falls in love with Casimir and saves his life by marrying him. Just after the marriage an off-stage band is heard announcing the arrival of Angelina and the circus. There is a great procession of animals, clowns, and acrobats onto the stage. The marriage to Lucia is declared invalid and Casimir returns to Angelina.

From Stein's reference to the Kirafly brothers and *The Lion Tamer* it is clear that what she was recalling was the spectacles she had seen.

5. See Stein to Van Vechten [25 February 1936], note 1.

6. Note by Van Vechten, 23 January 1941: "Romaine Brooks made a painting of me for which I made many painful sittings—after it was done, she gave it to me, but subsequently, by a ruse, took it away and never returned it." The painting was eventually given to YCAL after Van Vechten's death.

7. Stein enclosed clippings from three English newspapers and one French newspaper: *London Star*, 25 February 1936, "Miss Stein Explains," an interview with Stein; *London Daily Mirror*, 25 February 1936 ("Yesterday I lunched at the Ivy with Miss Gertrude Stein, Alan Lane, and her friend and protector Miss Alice B. Toklas"); *London Daily Mirror*, 29 February 1936, first impressions on meeting Gertrude Stein; and the French paper *Journal des Débats*, 11 March 1936, an article by Maurice Muret about Stein which discussed questions of autobiography and biography.

To Carl Van Vechten

[postmark: 2 April 1936]   27 rue de Fleurus (VI)
                                            Paris

My dearest papa Woojums,

I have not yet sent you a copy of Listen to me because there is a chance that it is to be done in Paris and so I have had to keep here the copies in hand and mama Woojums has been so busy doing other typing that there has been no time, but let me tell it to you all. In the first place while we were in England some one proposed printing privately, the Stanzas in Meditation,[1] I rather like them and though there will not be any money in it, and oh dear we have to start in and earn money, all those beautiful $ of America are melting away, well anyway, so Alice has to do that and there are I think 180 of them, and then the Bodley Head has said that they will do an English edition of the lectures and that has to be made up for them, we are thinking of including only 4 of the lectures in America, Poetry and grammar, English Literature, Plays and Pictures, Master-pieces and America and France the two Oxford Lectures and three of the newspaper articles the one on American crime, the one on food and homes and the one on

Capitals, which will make a nice book but of course there is no money in that either because King Edward like King George takes 25% of that from you,[2] and then there is Listen to me, by the way that might be a title of the English book of Lectures, well anyway, Picabia has been approached by a man who wishes to put several millions of francs into a modern theatre and he asked him to do a decor and he refused and when he told me I told him about Listen to me, which was to be a spectacle and he could do what he liked and he is now mad about it, in the meanwhile before I knew this I had read it to Marie Louise Bousquet who and her husband have a great deal to do with the theatre and she was all xcited and said it was very theatre, so now we are once more trying to get into contact with the man who made the proposition to Picabia, but he thinks there is no doubt about it and he wants to do it in the biggest theatre in Paris and he wants 33% royalties to be divided between him and me 50-50 and all that together will perhaps keep the wolf from the door[3] and so we can like darling papa Woojums dream just go over to the shore to say how do you do to him and nothing more, so these are all our dreams and which of them dear papa Woojums will come true. What is more sure is that Mama Woojums has rashly promised in your name that you [will] send a photo of B. W. to Georgiana Ames for the Radcliffe Library, Radcliffe College Cambridge because they are to have an xhibition of my books in the Radcliffe cooperation with the Tercentary celebration at Harvard, they also said something about rare items but since you have everything will you get into correspondence with them.[4] We have had a hectic American week, we had [Alexander] Woollcott for three days and had to give him 2 parties we had to have Trac in because Hélène has permanently retired to the country to live with her dead husband's relatives and so Trac who is always ready to come to us, he just does xtra work for others, we are the ones he loves saw us through everything and he sent you all his love, si gentil says he but darling papa Woojums is gentiller than that and the portrait photo we all do want to see how beautifully she did papa W.[5]

Love
Baby W.

1. See Stein to Van Vechten [24 February 1936], note 4.

2. The Bodley Head abandoned plans to publish this volume.

3. Stein and Picabia were working on a plan to present Stein's *Listen to Me* in Paris. Picabia had interested Claude Renoir in directing Stein's play, but later Renoir's support fell through. Throughout the spring and summer of 1936 Stein and Picabia worked on this project. See

[494]

Picabia to Stein, 4 March, 27 April, 14 May, 10 June, and 1 July 1936 (YCAL). Probably because of the economic and political conditions in France this project never materialized.

Note by Van Vechten, 23 January 1941: "Marie-Louise Bousquet, who had a famous literary salon in Paris at this epoch." Marie-Louise Bousquet was, for a time, the Paris editor of *Harper's Bazaar*.

4. Georgiana Ames Hinckley, College Librarian from 1927 until 1949, organized the exhibition of publications of Radcliffe alumnae as one of Radcliffe's contributions to the Harvard Tercentenary celebration, July 20 to October 20, 1936. She wrote to Gertrude Stein along with 14 other famous authors who were given a special room in the exhibit, to ask for a bibliography, photograph and contribution of books to fill out the Library's holdings. [Letter received from Jane S. Knowles, College Archivist, Radcliffe College, 5 November 1982]

Toklas replied to Ms. Ames's letter on 26 March 1936 (Radcliffe) indicating that she had asked Van Vechten to send a photograph and was sending under separate cover a bibliography and two books. Stein sent a copy of her *Operas and Plays*, with the dedication "For Radcliffe where I acted in the only play in which I ever acted, all these plays which I have written / Gtde Stein / Paris March 27 '36 / 27 rue de Fleurus." In the copy of *Matisse Picasso and Gertrude Stein and Two Shorter Stories*, Stein wrote, "For Radcliffe Library, from Gertrude Stein who always liked and likes having been at Radcliffe / Paris March 30 '36 / 27 rue de Fleurus." The "List of Published Works of Gertrude Stein" comprises twenty-seven titles with the date of composition and the date of publication. Ms. Ames acknowledged receipt of the materials on 4 May 1936 (carbon, Radcliffe).

In the fall of 1893 Stein had entered the Harvard Annex (which in 1894 would be renamed Radcliffe College). Stein remained at Radcliffe College until the spring of 1897. She failed the Radcliffe Latin entrance examination and was not awarded her bachelor's degree. In the fall of 1897 Stein entered Johns Hopkins School of Medicine. In 1898 she passed the required Latin examination and was awarded her Harvard A. B.

5. Van Vechten had promised a photograph of Romaine Brooks's portrait of him.

To Gertrude Stein
["*A Little Too Much*" *motto*]

6 April [1936]   [150 West Fifty-fifth Street
                                                   New York]

Dear Baby Woojums,

Thank you for the picture of you and Lord Berners. Thank you for the clips. Thank you for your sweet letter. Thank Mama Woojums for The Girls of Radcliff Hall which could be funnier, indeed yes. I think The Well of Loneliness even is funnier. But I enjoyed these girls.[1]. And tell Mama

Woojums that I can't give her any advice about Sainte-Unefois because I don't understand a word of it. I read it in a kind of charming bewilderment. So I asked Fania to read it and she says she doesn't understand it too. So she is asking her French conversation teacher to read it. If she doesn't understand it, tell Mama Woojums it's sure to be a succès fou in America. . . I am pleased you are seeing [Alexander] Woollcott and [Edward] Wassermann and people beginning with W. . I am seeing Josephine Baker and Willie Seabrook and Willie Maugham.[2]. I think Listen to me is the best title I have ever heard. Here's another: Read It! . . . You know the Negroes always say during the sermon: Preach it, brother! . . Roman's [Romaine Brooks] picture is at last completely finished and I am to see it tomorrow. She had to put in the background and get a frame. So it won't be ever so much longer before it is photographed and I am sure you will like it, seeing Papa Woojums sitting up in a white suit. . John Evans has written a novel called Shadows Flying in which a Boy is in love with a Man; (2) Man's Mother is in love with Man; Man prefers sister for bedding to the other two. . I hear Mabel [Dodge] thinks the Mother is Mabel! [3]. . I was worried about Mama Woojums getting lost in the forest. . Lots of love to les belles Woojumses!

Papa Woojums![4]

I am reading the [Sidney and Beatrice] Webb book about Soviet Russia.[5]

1. See Stein to Van Vechten [6 March 1936], note 2, and Stein to Van Vechten [25 March 1936], note 7.

2. W. Somerset Maugham (1874–1965), the English writer. Van Vechten first met Maugham in the early 1920s. A letter from Maugham to Van Vechten is quoted on the back of the dust jacket of the English edition of Van Vechten's *The Tattooed Countess*. See Kellner, *Carl Van Vechten and the Irreverent Decades*, p. 156, for the text of the letter.

3. John Evans, *Shadows Flying* (New York: Alfred A. Knopf, 1936). Evans was the only son of Mabel Dodge by her first marriage.

4. The verso of this letter contains the end of a draft of a letter by Stein with an addition by Toklas.

[In Stein's hand]: hear either Pierre or myself or both if this does at all please you.

[In Toklas' hand]: of course nothing would please me more

[In Stein's hand]: Always
Gtde Stein.

In addition, held horizontally, the letter contains in Stein's hand the number "28." The letter fragment may refer to Pierre Colle who was trying to arrange for productions of both *Four Saints in Three Acts* and *Listen to Me*.

5. Sidney and Beatrice Webb, *Soviet Communism: A New Civilization?* (New York: Charles Scribner's Sons, 1936).

❦

To Gertrude Stein

13 April [1936]   150 West Fifty-fifth Street
                                   New York City

Angelic Baby Woojums,

Your letter addressed to p W. C.(!) Van Vechten reached me safely and startled me not a little . . [1] I am overjoyed and excited and pleased and delighted but NOT surprised by all your triumphs . .You will note from the enclosed[2] that Bennett [Cerf] is once more eligible.[x] There is a new book about John Reed and this ought to help Mabel [Dodge]'s sales in the fall[3]. . Think of you with two NEW English books which Papa Woojums will get (he hopes) for his superb collection.[4] Listen to Me sounds better and better. It is the title of titles and would knock Walt Disney or the Marx Brothers silly, to say nothing of Nietczhe [i.e., Nietzsche] (I don't seem to know how to spell him). . I am SURE it is going to be done in that French Theatre and will probably stop the war . . Georgiana Ames will get a photograph pronto. And Mama Woojums wasn't at all rash to promise it. She KNEW she would . . And I am very jealous of [Alexander] Woollcott because he GOT TWO PARTIES. Does Trac like him as much as he does Papa Woojums? . . Roman's [Romaine Brooks] portrait is complete and even framed but she is hanging on to it for a while and I can't photograph it until it gets over here. Then you will get a copy of this and see what you make of it.[(2)]. Jo Davidson is making electioneering busts of our beloved president at 35 a piece and [Jacob] Epstein has a lot of water colors (he beat Jo to an exhibition of these) of flowers, of all things which are all so much alike you can't tell which is the best one or the worst one,[5] but the most exciting event in years is the show Madame Cuttoli (do you know her?) is giving at the Bignou Galleries of Beauvais tapestries designed by Matisse, Picasso, Leger, Braque, and above all Rouault. They will be shown in Paris later[6] . . Macbeth is to be given in Harlem, beginning tomorrow night. The witches are to be voodoo[(3)] and the costumes are empire (like those in Christophe's time in Hayti).[7] Edna Thomas, whom you met at my house, is playing Lady Macbeth and the [William] Seabrooks are coming to town to go with us . . . I hope you are having no tornadoes or strikes or kidnappings. I sometimes think America is just one murder after another, but I must say I love it! I am reading the Webbs and getting very much excited about USSR.[8]

l[ove] and k[isses] to you both,
Papa Woojums![9]

[x]pour les noces
(2) Do you know a painter named Jean Coutaud & what do you think of him?[10]
(3) Virgil [Thomson] has arranged the music.

1. The envelope of Stein to Van Vechten [2 April 1936], was addressed by Stein, "W. P. W. C. Van Vechten" (Woojums Papa Woojums Carl Van Vechten).

2. Van Vechten had sent Stein an unidentified clipping about the divorce of Cerf and Sylvia Sidney.

3. Granville Hicks, *John Reed: The Making of a Revolutionary* (New York: Macmillan, 1936). Hicks takes issue with the portrait of Reed presented in Dodge's *Movers and Shakers*.

4. See Stein to Van Vechten [2 April 1936]

5. The exhibition, *Sculpture and Water Colors by Jacob Epstein*, contained fifty water colors of flowers by Epstein. The exhibition was at the Galerie René Gimpel, New York, 6 to 30 April 1936.

6. An exhibition, *Modern French Tapestries by Braque, Raoul Dufy, Léger, Lurcat, Henri Matisse, Picasso, Rouault*, from the collection of Madame Marie Cuttoli was held at the Bignou Gallery, Rolls Royce Building, 32 East Fifty-seventh Street, New York, in April 1936.

7. See Van Vechten to Stein, 9 January 1936, note 4. Henri Christophe (1767–1820) was the black ex-slave and cook who aided Toussaint L'Ouverture in the liberation of Haiti. He became a general and then King of Haiti (1811). Christophe began as a benevolent ruler, but the need for compulsory labor to build his citadel La Ferriere, with its palace Sans Souci, turned him into a despot. When his reign was threatened by revolt, he committed suicide.

8. See Van Vechten to Stein, 6 April [1936], note 4.

9. In Stein's hand on the verso of this letter is a list of names, possibly of persons to be written to: "Carl [Van Vechten] Bennett [Cerf] Thornton [Wilder] Picabia."

10. Van Vechten means the French painter Lucien Coutaud. Van Vechten eventually purchased a painting by Coutaud, *Stes. Maries de la Mare*. There is no indication that Stein knew Coutaud, although he did exhibit, in 1936, at La Galerie Jeanne Bucher, a gallery that Stein frequently visited.

To Carl Van Vechten

[late April 1936]   27 rue de Fleurus (VI)
                                                     Paris

My dearest papa Woojums,

We are just sending you Listen to me, I hope you will like it. I have just with my own right hand and it is xhausted in consequence translated it into french, it goes quite nicely and so we have high hopes, that the gentlemen will like it. By the way Pierre Colle is just mad crazy to put Four Saints on in Paris, he has an idea for this spring, in the month of June and then London, in English of course, he heard it 3 times in New York and he says done as it was in English with that decor and that cast and that music it would have a succes fous. I hope he does it, I am giving him Virgil [Thomson]'s address and sure you would come over for it and we would come back for it, well anyway dreams these days are very pleasant.[1] We leave next Tuesday if the sun will only shine for Bilignin, Basket has caught cold in his eye, he says it is too cold, but it's better, otherwise we are peaceful, Trac was transferred from us to the Duchess [de Clermont-Tonnerre],[2] we have replaced ourselves with a nice Russian named Yvan, I told him I knew about an Ivan the terrible, yes he said that is what they said but he did a great deal of good for Russia. Anyway he is sweet and will go to the country which is more than Trac will and Trac already has quarreled with the Duchess and left for the midi with some Americans called Strauss so although there are not as many wonders as in New York things do move, we are having the elections but it is mostly votes for women, the men are discouraged with voting, do give our love to the [William] Seabrooks and to Josephine Baker and to all the others and all our love and kisses to papa Woojums and our best love to Fania and our address is Bilignin par Belley,
    and we do love papa Woojums

                                                                    B. W.

1. When Stein was in London in February 1936, a number of people had spoken to her about a production in London and perhaps also in Paris of *Four Saints in Three Acts*. One of those who expressed interest was the producer Charles Cochran. Stein also wrote to Edward James asking for his financial support of the planned production. James replied to Stein on 23 April

1936 (YCAL) that he was ill and was not in a position to undertake such support. He did, however, suggest that Stein contact John Sutro and Cecil Beaton. The idea for the production was that it be presented in both Paris and London in the summer of 1936. Pierre Colle, an art dealer with the firm of Renou et Colle in Paris, was working with Stein's friends the d'Aiguys on plans for a Paris production. Nothing came of the production plans in either Paris or London.

2. Trac, Stein's Indo-Chinese cook who had been photographed by Van Vechten in Bilignin in 1934. Toklas writes at length about Trac in *The Alice B. Toklas Cook Book*, pp. 186–95.

To Gertrude Stein

[Postcard: Carl Van Vechten in Central Park. Photograph by Mark Lutz]

2 May [1936]   [150 West Fifty-fifth Street
                                                  New York]

Dear Gertrude:

Listen to Me is epatant and would be sensational on the stage may I play Sweet William or the brilliant epilogue? I'd love to. . . Of all your plays this seems the most spontaneous & exciting, and I'm very excited too about 4 Saints being done in Paris. . How they will love it!! I wish you were here to see Macbeth in Harlem and to see Papa Woojums who sends his love to Baby & Mama W!

[*Carl Van Vechten*]

To Gertrude Stein

[Postcard: Unidentified mask. Photograph by Carl Van Vechten]

[postmark: 10 May 1936]   [150 West Fifty-fifth Street
                                                  New York]

Dear Baby Woojums!

I sent you another photograph and a card about the EXCITING Listen to Me and what not to rue de Fleurus & I see by the very bottom of your letter which I have just reread that you have gone to Bilignin! Well I hope all reaches you safely.[1] We have signed a lease for a beautiful apartment on Central Park West from where we can see only leaves & towers. We move in September.

Love to Both.
Papa W.

Fania is going to Georgia in a day or so.[2]

1. Van Vechten's postcard, 2 May [1936], arrived before Stein had left for Bilignin.

2. Marinoff and Van Vechten were going to see Eugene and Carlotta O'Neill at Sea Island Beach, Georgia.

To Gertrude Stein

13 May 1936

150 West Fifty-fifth Street
New York City

Dear Baby Woojums,

We are at last going to move! Though not till September, there is so much to attend to that we are packing and shifting this and that already. Besides we shall be away part of the summer as usual. Tomorrow, for instance, we are off for Sea Island Beach and the Casa of Eugene O'Neill. . So I have thought it was safer and better to put your Mss. in a storage warehouse in a special room I have engaged for things of my own. . They are plainly marked as belonging to you and are ALL together. They are a little inaccessible but with some notice they can be procured, but they are almost 90% safe from vandals, fire, revolutions, strikes, and casualties due to moving. I think you will grow to like your mss. reposing in a fireproof vault.

In the fall we shall be living on Central Park West and Seventieth Street and you will hear all about it and eventually, no doubt, see pictures of it.

You are always Baby Woojums and Mama Woojums is always Mama Woojums!

[501]

I wish you might see Macbeth in Harlem!
L O V E and LET Love!

! Carlo![1]

1. The verso of this letter contains two lists in Stein's hand. The first is:
   Pay taxes
   Envelope for t. w. [i.e., Thornton Wilder]
The second list, with the paper reversed, is probably of persons to be written to.
   Carl [Van Vechten]
   Woolcott [Alexander Woollcott]
   Mike [Michael Stein]
   Hahner [?Marcella Hahner, of the book department of Marshall Field & Co., Chicago,
         Illinois]
   Johandeau [Marcel Jouhandeau, the French writer]

To Carl Van Vechten
[Postcard: Ambrenay—Le Cloître—La salle capitulaire]

[postmark: 14 May 1936]   [Bilignin par Belley
                                                 Ain]

My dearest papa Woojums,

The photo has come, decidedly one of Romaine [Brooks]'s best, I like it, the only thing is just above papa W.'s eye-brows and the point of his chin, not quite to my feeling but eyes and nose and hand, really papa woojums, and looks like rather very fine painting too, do tell R. how pleased I am and lots of love[1]

Gtrde.

1. A photograph made by Van Vechten of Romaine Brooks's portrait of him.

To Carl Van Vechten

[postmark: 25 May 1936]   [Bilignin par Belley
                                                            Ain]

My dearest papa Woojums,

Everything came and I wrote you about it and nobody will act in
Listen to me if not you, but wouldn't you like best perhaps to be the epilogue and the prologue, anyway I am so pleased that you like it, the Four
Saints is not coming off this spring they really got started with the idea too
late but the idea now is to have it next spring for the Paris Exposition[1] and
that would be a much better idea so perhaps that will be that, the Picabia
and me listen to me is still bright with hope and now [Lord] Berners writes:

> I am getting on with they must be wedded to their wife and have nearly
> finished the first act. Various people I have played it to have xpressed
> approval it is for six voices and orchestra. The voices may be doubled
> and trebled or more into a large chorus if necessary without destroying
> the balance. The voices are part of the orchestra and on the stage
> miming and dancing. There is a possibility of producing it in London
> at the Sadler Wells Theatre.[2]

So you see it may be done and you would come over for that wouldn't
you papa Woojums I think it would be lots of fun all of us in London and
P. W. photographing us all. And we were so xcited about the moving, we
don't much like your being where we have not seen you, but it is better and
just the same as Connecticut and there can't be any floods, did you do any
photos of Macbeth in Harlem, I would like to see them,[3] we are gardening
madly and are very pleased and happy and we do I do so love papa Woojums.

                                                       B. W. and M. W.

---

1. An international exposition, *Exposition of Arts and Technique in Modern Life*, scheduled to
open in Paris in May 1937.

2. An undated letter, Berners to Stein, in YCAL.

3. Note by Van Vechten, 23 January 1941: "Macbeth produced with a Negro cast at the La-
fayette Theatre. I didn't photograph this, altho' I tried to arrange it." The cast included Edna
Lewis Thomas as Lady Macbeth, Jack Carter as Macbeth (he was later replaced by Maurice
Ellis), and Canada Lee as Banquo. See also Van Vechten to Stein, 9 January 1936, note 4.

❧

To Carl Van Vechten
[Postcard: Der Volkskanzler Adolf Hitler]

[postmark: 31 May 1936]   [Bilignin par Belley
                                                          Ain]

Dear p. W.

Thanks for putting everything in the safety deposit room, it is not too much of a nuisance I hope, but papa Woojums is like that, and if you are to be away so much in the summer why not come here, the Easter Lilies will be out soon, and they would like to be photographed, and Pepe, he seeing me write came right over and said he would pose among the lilies, love and much love

B. W.

❧

To Gertrude Stein
*[Postcard: Self-portrait of hands with rings.
Photograph by Carl Van Vechten]*

9 June [1936]   [150 West Fifty-fifth Street
                                                 New York]

No, dearest Baby Woojums, I have done *no* pictures of Macbeth in Harlem. It got complicated & when things get complicated I leave em alone. . Of course if I had made any you would get some at once. We've been to Georgia at the Eugene O'Neills and we don't move till October. So maybe I'll go to Russia. So excited about your play in London. Papa W will be there with his Leica snapping Mama W. Baby W. & Lord B[erners]. . . And the mss are *safe* in a kind of Kremlin!

*Love,
Papa W.*[1]

[504]

1. In Stein's hand, written on the card in reverse under the address, is the following list of names, presumably of persons to be written to: "Carl [Van Vechten], Kiddies [Mr. and Mrs. W. G. Rogers], Thornton [Wilder], [Wendell] Wilcox[,] Janet [either Janet Flanner or Janet Scudder].

To Carl Van Vechten

[postmark: 29 June 1936] [Bilignin par Belley Ain]

My dearest Papa Woojums,

We have been having a hectic time, Bennett [Cerf] and Jo Davidson were with us for 48 hours and we moved around, but we had a good time, Bennett was very sweet and he is going to in the spring do an anthology for the modern library of all the things we like, Tender Buttons and As a wife has a cow, and 400 pages of it, The Flowers of friendship, if there is anything particularly you want in will you tell us, we will make it up in the fall when we get back, it will be about 400 pages, I am awfully happy about it, I can't tell you papa Woojums how grateful I am to you for having given us such a lovely publisher,[1] he will also do a cookbook when Alice gets it written and she is thinking of calling it Eating is her subject,[2] we are full of projects, and in between thunder showers we garden, and Papa Woojums can't you fly by us and to us on the way back from Russia, we can get you in Lyons which is central for all aeroplanes we can almost get you in Russia. And sometime if you can will you send to Pere Bernardet, Abbe d'Hautcombe par Chindrieux St. Pierre de Cuirtille Savoie a copy of St. Ignatius, he wants dreadfully to see it, and have it, the black one with him praying, against the black back ground,[3] and I have done a chapter of the new Autobiography,[4] and I guess it is perhaps going to be good, as soon as more of it is done I'll send it but don't say anything about it to anybody because it may not get written it might get stuck, but anyway we love you so dear papa Woojums we do and love to Fania and a pleasant time

Always
Gtrde.

1. This is the first mention of a project that did not see fruition until October 1946, when Random House published *Selected Writings of Gertrude Stein*, edited and with an introduction and notes by Van Vechten.

2. Toklas had from time to time discussed the idea of writing a cookbook. In 1953–54, while suffering from an attack of jaundice, she wrote *The Alice B. Toklas Cook Book*.

3. Père Edmond Bernardet (1903–1978) was born in St. Martin d'Arc (in the Savoie, France). On 19 December 1926 he entered the Abbaye d'Hautecombe and took monastic orders on 3 September 1928. He became the chief *hôtelier* of the abbaye, and it was probably in this way that he came to know Stein, who had often visited the abbaye from her home in Bilignin. Père Bernardet left the abbaye in 1958 and became a diocesian priest until shortly before his death.

In YCAL there is a letter from Père Bernardet, 9 March 1931, written to Van Vechten while he was visiting New York. Whether they actually met at this time cannot be confirmed, but it is probable that they did (see Van Vechten to Stein, 10 July 1935).

4. Stein's *Everybody's Autobiography*.

❧

To Carl Van Vechten
[Postcard: Maison de France, Famille Royale]

[postmark: 8 July 1936]   [Chambery, France]

My dear Carl p. W.

They are doing the Identity Marionette play first time in Detroit 8.30 P.M. The National Puppetry Conference, if you hear anything about it will you let me know, they say the music is very interesting, do you know anything about Owen Haynes[1] lots of love, it rains and rains every day but we don't mind and lots of love Romaine [Brooks] was here and we talked and talked about you lots of love lots of love

Gtrde.

Donald Sutherland wrote me a long letter but no address, do you know it.[2]

1. Donald Vestal had written Stein on 27 June 1936 (YCAL) to tell her the details of the first performance of the play. See Stein to Van Vechten [28 November 1935], note 1.

2. Sutherland to Stein, undated letter, YCAL.

☙

To Gertrude Stein

10 July 1936   150 West Fifty-fifth Street
                                                New York City

Dearest Gertrude,

I am more excited than I can tell you about the Anthology in the Modern Library. May I ask for a lot of things. Historically I should like Mabel Dodge at the Villa Curonia because it is the first thing I ever saw of yours. Then certainly those first portraits of Matisse and Picasso. More than anything else I crave:

> Kisses can kiss us
> A duck a hen and fishes, followed by wishes
> Happy little pair.

Might I have this, please.[1] Then something from Lucy Church Amiably, please and Susie Asado and Miss Furr and Miss Skeene [(]Pu-leese!), As a Wife has a Cow, DEAR BABY WOOJUMS, Capitals, Capitals! I could go on and on. . And I think Alice's cookbook is a marvellous idea and Mama Woojums must get to work on this immejate. . Unfortunately all my photographs are packed now and will be till I MOVE (After October 1) and so I can't send Pere Berna[r]det (Bless him) a picture of St. Ignatius till later. Anyway his address is particularly illegible: so please will you print this out again. . I'm sure the new autobiography is going to be GRAND. it should have more about the method and raison d'être of your work than the old one. . But there is Plenty to write. . I read in the paper last night that a play of yours was being given by marionettes in Detroit. . Did you read Bravig Imbs book? He doesn't write very well and he left out so many things I was dying to know and put in so many DULL places, but nevertheless the book interested me because it was mostly about Baby and Mama Woojums. . But, my gawd, Pavel [Tchelitchew] and Virgil [Thomson] simply shriek for characterization and he has done them so sloppily[2]. . . I am not going to Russia after all. The latest idea is M A I N E (in a car). . There is so much to do at home on account moving. . The new place is going to be pretty beautiful. When will you come to see it?. . Fania has just done Mrs. Frail in Congreve's Love for Love.[3]. I understood Ettie Stettheimer[4] to say

Gertrude Stein at Lucey Church, 13 June 1934.
PHOTOGRAPH BY CARL VAN VECHTEN. PRIVATE COLLECTION.

one night she had just read something by you in the Saturday Evening Post. Do you suppose I dreamed this? She now denies all memory of this and I can't find anything in the Post. Could it have been the New Republic?. .[5] Getting ready to go to Russia I read a lot of books and I got MORE and MORE bored with the idea. It must be very exciting however if you are excited about it the way Muriel Draper is. Meanwhile your precious manuscripts are buried in the Manhattan Pyramids. They should survive even an air-raid. . Love and kisses to you both!

Papa (and how!)

1. See Van Vechten to Stein, 10 January 1936, note 3.

2. Bravig Imbs, *Confessions of Another Young Man* (New York: The Henkle-Yewdale House, 1936). Imbs (1904-1946), after two years at Dartmouth College, left for Europe on a cattle boat. He worked in Paris on various newspapers including the *Chicago Tribune*. Imbs published a number of volumes of poetry, novels, and critical studies.

3. Marinoff played in a production that opened at the Westport Country Playhouse on 29 June 1936. The play starred Eva La Gallienne.

4. Ettie Stettheimer, the sister of Florine Stettheimer, who had designed the costumes and scenery for *Four Saints in Three Acts*.

5. *The Saturday Evening Post* printed five pieces by Stein: "Money" (13 June 1936), 208(50): 88; "More About Money" (11 July 1936), 209(2): 30; "Still More About Money" (25 July 1936), 209(4): 32; "All About Money" (22 August 1936), 209(8): 54; "My Last About Money" (October 1936), 209(15): 78.

To Gertrude Stein
[Postcard: Madame Gautreau Drinking a Toast, John Singer Sargent 1856–1925, The Isabella Stewart Gardner Museum, Boston, Massachusetts]

19 July 1936   [Boston, Massachusetts]

No, I don't know anything about Owen Haynes,[1] dear Baby Woojums, and the only address I have for Donald Sutherland is: Nassau Inn, Princeton, New Jersey. I am sure that will reach him. I have seen all about Paul Revere's Ride & Amy Lowell's grave, & Mrs. [Mary Baker] Eddy's grave,[2] and now I am going to Maine, but will be back in New York soon to *pack* and to *move*. Love to you both

Papa Woojums!

Did you ever see Mrs. Gardner's house?[3]

1. Owen Haynes composed the music for Donald Vestal's production of Stein's "Identity." See Stein to Van Vechten [28 November 1935], note 1.

2. Van Vechten, while in Boston, had visited the graves of Mary Baker Eddy (1821–1910), the founder of Christian Science, and Amy Lowell (1874–1925), the poet. "Paul Revere's Ride," the narrative poem by Henry Wadsworth Longfellow, describes the midnight ride of Revere from Charleston to Lexington and Concord to warn the inhabitants of the approach of British troops at the outbreak of the Revolutionary War.

3. Isabella Stewart Gardner was a wealthy Boston matron who had amassed a large collection of old master paintings. In 1898 she built a Venetian Palace (now the Isabella Stewart Gardner Museum) in the Fenway in Boston to house her collection. When the building was finished, in 1903, she began admitting a limited number of people who had applied for tickets to view her collection.

To Carl Van Vechten

[postmark: 20 July 1936]   [Bilignin par Belley Ain]

Dearest papa Woojums papa,

I [have] been writing to you over and over again about the Saturday Evening Post they have bought 4 little pieces of mine, the second one about Trac is I think very good and the fourth one I like too but I cannot tell what numbers they are in because as they pay me for them they do not send me the magazine, but they seem very pleased and they are printing them and I am doing two more and then that will be enough.[1] Why instead of Maine do you not fly to go and see Francis Rose in Indo China, it would not take long one day to S[an]. F[rancisco]. one day to Honolulu and another day to China and Indo China, I just had a twenty page letter of description from him and it sounds lovely and he has a house there and he would love to see you he lives 20 rue Ngu Vien Hué Ammam we would rather like to go our-

[510]

selves but anyway you go, I wish we could all go.[2] Lord Berners writes that [Frederick] Ashton is to do the choreography of our piece and that the music is almost done, there is a fugue a waltz a tango and a very moving adaggio on the theme Josephine will leave. He is coming here the end of August and then we will know more, and he is going to do the decor and costumes himself, it will be fun,[3] if you hear any more about the Marionettes do let us know. Yes we had decided to put P. W. out of Geography and Plays One into the Anthology, can you think of a good title for the whole of it, I am thinking, of course but nothing definite yet, what does Kisses can kiss us, come out of,[4] and we thought of including Accents in Alsace, Tender Buttons, Miss Furr and Miss Skeene, do in a leisure moment make a list, it is to be for next spring, the marionette play is out of Geographical history it is called identity, if you hear any more about it let us know, have not seen Bravig [Imbs]'s book yet, we'll keep the rest of the ms. until you move, oh Papa Woojums come over to us by way of China or some way

Baby Woojums.

1. *The Saturday Evening Post* printed five, not four, pieces by Stein about money. See Van Vechten to Stein, 10 July 1936, note 5. The piece about Trac was "Still More About Money."

2. Rose spent most of 1935–38 in China and the Far East. Rose's letter (with deletions) is printed in Gallup, *The Flowers of Friendship*, pp. 314–16.

3. Lord Berners to Stein, 18 July 1936 (YCAL). Frederick Ashton had done the choreography for *Four Saints in Three Acts*.

4. Stein's "Kisses Can" was a short poem by itself. It did not come from a larger work.

To Gertrude Stein
[Postcard: Herring River, Near the Belmont, West Harwich, Mass.]

[postmark: 30 July 1936]   [West Harwich, Massachusetts]

Dear Baby Woojums—

This is a perfectly marvellous place where I seem to be now, I have seen Plymouth Rock and the witches of Salem and Marblehead & Gloucester (all new to me) & presently am going to take in Newport . . . Your letter came to me here & is most exciting. Kisses can kiss us is in the mss. you sent me but I have a copy of it home & will send it to you when I get back. . Sir Francis Rose & Indone-Chine will have to wait a year. I love the idea of Indone-Chine & always have loved it but I guess I'd want to stay there more than a week. Pretty soon I go back to New York to get moved! Love to Both

Papa W

🎨

To Gertrude Stein
[Postcard: Degas—Nieces of the Artist]

13 August [1936]   [150 West Fifty-fifth Street
                                                    New York]

Dear Baby W:

Here is KCKU, ALL of it!

Kisses can kiss us
A DUCK a hen and fishes, followed by wishes
Happy little pair.[1]

I love it and love it and love it!
STEINIANA would be a nice title or STEIN ABRIDGED or STEIN SONGS and PROSE or GATHERINGS from GERTRUDE STEIN or REPRINTED MASTERPIECES of GERTRUDE STEIN or STEIN at a Glance. Do you want some more? Love to Baby and Mama from

Papa W!
or A STEIN POTPOURR!

1. For an accurate text of this poem see Van Vechten to Stein, 10 January 1936, note 3.

🎨

[512]

To Carl Van Vechten

[postmark: 25 August 1936]   Bilignin par Belley
                                                        Ain.

Dearest Papa Woojums

I am pretty pleased, with, Stein Songs and Prose I think that is a good title, a kind of indwelling one, send some more but I am kind of for that, and then when you get in and we get back you will help with the choices as you have the completest collection, we are full of news, Harcourt, came to the end of Alice B. Toklas and asked me if I wanted to buy back the rights, I sent the letter to Bennett [Cerf] and he has bought it and so now he has everything xcept Making of Americans and I guess it will not be long before he has that,[1] it makes me awfully happy and we owe it all to you dearest Papa Woojums cause you started it, he says that when I get my new volume ready he will make a special sale of selling them together and that will be fine. Then Lord Berners is here and he has done the music for They must be wedded and it is very fetching music and [Frederick] Ashton is to do the arrangement of the dance and Gerald Berners is to do the decor he has taken it from the rag carpet of Va. that Sherwood Anderson sent me,[2] and the Sadler Wells theatre has accepted it and it goes on in February and Pepe is going to be in it, there is a dog and they say Pepe's coloring suits better than Basket, so we did not tell Basket only told Pepe and the xcitement made him throw up a little bile but now he is so pleased, Gerald's idea was that he should be played by a little girl but Alice says the littlest girl would make too big a Pepe and she wants him just like him on wires and Gerald says no he must really dance, well anyway it's lots of fun, and we are just as happy as happy can be, and I am sleepy from having been invited to a surprise party but I could not wait to tell you how happy it makes me, dear papa Woojums all our love

Baby W. and Mama W.
and Basket and Pepe.

I can't find your stamps but look at these ads.[3]

---

1. Cerf to Stein, 13 August 1936 (YCAL), confirms that he had purchased the plates and sheet of *The Autobiography of Alice B. Toklas* from Harcourt. Alfred Harcourt wrote to Stein, 17

August 1936 (YCAL), that he had very reluctantly transferred the plates, the stock, and all the rights to Cerf.

2. In 1925, with the proceeds of his novel *Dark Laughter*, Anderson bought a farm at Troutdale, near Marion, Virginia. Except when he traveled, this remained his home until his death in 1941.

3. At this time the French government allowed advertisements to be affixed to postage stamps. The stamps on this envelope had the following messages: "Blédine pour Bébé," "Blédine La Seconde Maman," and "Contre La Chute Des Cheveux."

To Gertrude Stein

26 August [1936]   150 West Fifty-fifth Street
                                                       New York City

Dear Baby Woojums,

Here are the facts for your files and I have copies of all and every put away with my GS collection. Congratulations to the Saturday Evening Post for becoming historical and congratulations to you for your delightful prose. . I am sorry we do not agree about [Franklin] Roosevelt, but I suppose we could find nothing less controversial to disagree about![1]. . Packers have come and everything is in barrels and boxes. My room alone has forty cases of books in it! But when we will move I don't know. We have to wait for some people to get out and then decorations ensue (there is a painters' strike). Also people are moving in here on October 1. . I guess you'd better continue to write to 150 until I tell you to stop. . I am dreadfully upset about Spain and my favorite torero has been executed. .[2] Fania played Mrs. Frail in Congreve's Love for Love at Westport this summer and I made some photographs of her which I will send you prochainement. The newspapers are full of YOU and BENNETT [Cerf]! Lotz of love to both of you from fania and

Papa W!

1. Van Vechten may be referring to Stein's "More about Money," which appeared in *The Saturday Evening Post* (11 July 1936), 209(2): 30. Stein does not mention Franklin D. Roosevelt by name, but she says of the United States, "In America where, ever since George Washington, nobody really can imagine a king, who is to stop congress from spending too much money." It is possible, however, that Van Vechten is referring to Stein's "A Political Series," which opens,

"Is Franklin Roosevelt trying to make money be so that it has no existence that it ceases to be a thing that anybody can count." "A Political Series" was printed in Stein's *Painted Lace and Other Pieces*, pages 71–77.

2. In 1931 the Republic of Spain replaced the monarchy in a bloodless revolution. In February 1936 a Popular Front government was elected. General Francisco Franco, formerly Chief of Staff, who was in semi-exile in the Canary Islands, together with other generals plotted to over-throw the Republic and restore the monarchy. On 18 July 1936 military uprisings began in Seville and other towns in Andalusia, thus beginning the Spanish Civil War.

To Carl Van Vechten
[Postcard: Photograph of the garden at Bilignin][1]

[postmark: 5 September 1936]   [Bilignin par Belley
                                                Ain]

Dearest papa W.

Gerald Berners is sending you his Camel he says he was always in-terested in you and now more so and he hopes you will like his Camel,[2] and I am telling Fanny Butcher to send you my review of Oscar Wilde by [Lloyd] Lewis,[3] we are nutting I wish you were here to photo us nutting, and we are delighted with Fania and are looking forward to the photos, love and blessings on the new house wish we were there for the h[ouse]. w[arming].

Baby W.

1. The photograph shows the formal garden of Stein's house in Bilignin. Also in the photo-graph is one of the small summer houses at the edge of the terrace-garden that was used for storage.

2. Lord Berners' *The Camel. A Tale* (London: Constable & Co., 1936).

3. Stein had written a review of Lloyd Lewis and Henry Justin Smith's *Oscar Wilde Discovers America* (1882) (New York: Harcourt, Brace and Co., 1936) for the *Chicago Herald Tribune*, 8 August 1936, p. 9. See Lewis' thank-you letter to Stein in Gallup, *The Flowers of Friendship*, pp. 317–18.

Fanny Butcher was the literary critic for the *Chicago Daily Tribune*.

###

To Gertrude Stein
[Postcard: Elk Parade in Brooklyn. Photograph by Carl Van Vechten]

[postmark: 23 September 1936]   [101 Central Park West
[New York]

Dearest Baby W!

This is a lady Elk (colored) in the recent parade in Brooklyn. I wish you and Mama W could have seen it!—Yes Fanny B[utcher]. sent your review of [Lloyd] Lewis' Book on [Oscar] Wilde & I loved it. I've seen Bennett [Cerf] only once (but he was full of you!) we have been so busy moving. I am writing this at 101 Central Park West, Tel. EN. 2-8748. Come & see it soon. When is "Stein Songs and Prose" coming out? . . . I have 76 cases of books on the floor of my rooms at this moment and the rest of the house is like that! Please when I get done I'll write you a real letter & maybe send you some pictures of the beauties of 101 which is *all* stars & cocks!

Love
Carlo. (Papa W)

###

To Carl Van Vechten

[postmark: 28 September 1936]   Bilignin par Belley
Ain

My dear papa Woojums,

We are thinking a lot of you and Fania and the new house, and wishing we were there with you, this will be the last letter to the old address I guess, and you know how much happiness we wish for you in the new, outside everything seems to be xciting but inside it seems quite peaceful, the Picabias have just been with us and a great deal of country social life including surprise parties at all the neighboring chateaus, we have gotten to know so many people here that Paris will be quite solitary after it, but New York well New York would be nice, here is M. [Bourdet?] he sounds quite nice,[1] well lots of love oh so much love and so many good wishes for such a happy new apartment now and always

Gtrde Baby Woojums.

1. Stein had probably sent Van Vechten a clipping about Monsieur Edouard Bourdet (1887–1945). Bourdet was a French playwright and journalist. In 1935 Marinoff acted in *Times Have Changed*, Louis Bromfield's adaptation of his play *Les temps difficiles*. Van Vechten had met Bourdet and his wife Denise at that time.

To Gertrude Stein and Alice Toklas
[Postcard: Portrait of a Spanish boy at a Romería de las ragiones, Madrid. Photograph by Carl Van Vechten]

9 October [1936]   [101 Central Park West
                                              New York]

Here is a nice Spanish boy before he got in to a Civil War, dear Mama and Baby Woojums! Thanks for your sweet letters. We are now *installed* at 101 Central Park West, but far from settled! Do come & see us & it! Thanks for the Bourdet clipping.

love to you both.
Papa W!

To Carl Van Vechten
[Postcard: Photograph of Gertrude Stein sitting in a camp chair in a field near Bilignin]

[postmark: 9 October 1936]   [Bilignin par Belley
                                              Ain]

Love and kisses
and best of wishes

and jolly fishes and
stars and no Wars
to Carl and Fania
at West Central Dahlia
Where they are at home
I wish we could roam
And be in their home but we
love them so so we will go surely
soon moon spoon,

Baby Woojums.

To Gertrude Stein

*[Postcard] Amour dorloté par les belles femmes. Painting by Mina Loy.
Collection of Carl Van Vechten* [1]

15 October [1936]   [101 Central Park West
                                                 New York]

What a jolly little poem, like a benediction! Dear Baby Woojums!
We loved it. . Gradually we are getting into order & by July 1, 1940 we will
be spic & span. I think! I am in the new Leica show opening next week,
but it doesn't seem right not to have Baby Woojums there too! [2]

*l[ove] & K[isses] to both
Papa W.*

1. This is the only oil painting from Mina Loy's years in Florence known to have survived.
Van Vechten was with Loy when she began this work; Loy gave it to him when he returned to
Florence in July 1914.
   Van Vechten wrote about the incident that inspired the painting in "An Interrupted
Conversation," *Rogue* (1 August 1915), 1:7–9. The painting, an oil on canvas, 1913, 13 x 20
inches, was originally called *Love and the Ladies*. Loy later renamed it *L'Amour dorloté par les
belles dames*. See Mina Loy, *The Last Lunar Baedeker*, ed. and intro. Roger L. Conover
(Highlands, N. C.: The Jargon Society, 1982), p. 331, note 27.
   The painting remained in Van Vechten's collection until his death, except for a brief

period when it was "borrowed" by Loy's husband Stephen Haweis. In 1968 Fania Marinoff gave it to a friend of Van Vechten's. The painting is now in a private collection in Massachusetts.

2. Van Vechten showed twelve photographs, mostly from his 1935 trip to Spain and Italy, at the Third International Leica Exhibition of Photography, Rockefeller Center, New York, 20 October to 2 November 1936.

To Carl Van Vechten

[postmark: 26 October 1936]   Bilignin par Belley
                                                           Ain

Dear dear Papa Woojums,

I just said something and I said that is what Papa Woojums would say and here in the autumn country and a big log fire it is so far away from New York and all its lights that you can see so wonderfully from where you are but just the same we cannot help all the time thinking of you. Here is a prospectus of a book, if anyone wants to subscribe to one it would make the very charming young father so happy to have it all the way from America. We have gotten so chummy with the father Abbott and when you come next time you will take some wonderful photographs of them all.[1] And beside we have just found something we are sending you 4 recette chantee, I hope you will like them I am very attached to the Parc Espanole[?].[2] Did I tell you about my first french lecture, it was up in the mts. to about 100 students, and my it did make me remember the lectures in America, these boys were so sweet and so enthusiastic and I had to go back on the stage and go on, and I patted my hair and they photographed me and they photographed us altogether and even Basket and Pepe had to come in at the last and they all stood out in the snow and waved and waved and I knew American boys were like that but I never did think french boys were like that, and I pleased them very much and I did wish you could have been there up in the mts. and the snow, we miss you wherever we are.[3] Yesterday a little early we gave a Thanksgiving dinner to everybody before we all leave, turkey and mince pie and celery and we wished you had been there too, and I promised to show them all the photos of us and Edgar Poe, it always moves everybody that and the key of the Raven room that I always carry, we did enjoy that trip with you Papa Woojums so much so much[4]

Always
Baby W. and Mama.

1. Père Edmond Bernardet, *Un abbé d'Hautecombe, ami de Ronsard, Alphonse Delbène. Eveque d'Albi 1538–1608*, pref. Pierre Champion (Grenoble, France: Editions de la Revue "Les Alps," 1937).

2. Four short songs by the French composer Ennemond Trillat. None of the songs is in YCAL or NYPL-MD.

3. Stein delivered her lecture "An American and France," at the University of Grenoble, France.

4. Note by Van Vechten, 23 January 1941: "Reference to our visit to the University of Virginia."

To Gertrude Stein
[Postcard: Norman Douglas and Carl Van Vechten in the Cascine
Gardens, Florence. Photograph by Mark Lutz]

5 November [1936]

[101 Central Park West
New York]

Dearest Baby Woojums,

Here is the old maestro himself with Norman Douglas in the Cascine in Florence. I sent the Abbé Bernardet the picture of St. Ignatius today.[1] I hope he gets it happily & your new book is out but Bennett [Cerf] hasn't sent me one yet, not even the one I *ordered* . . . & paid for.[2] I am waiting impatiently for the sung recipes. . My dear candidate FDR was elected practically by acclamation. There is lots going on here and 101 is gradually getting settled. Oh dear, when are you coming over? Edith has left us. Long live Mildred![3]

love to Baby & Mama
Papa W.

[520]

1. Edward Matthews as Saint Ignatius in *Four Saints in Three Acts*.

2. Stein's *The Geographical History Of America Or The Relation Of Human Nature To The Human Mind*.

3. Mildred Perkins had replaced Edith Ramsey as the Van Vechtens' cook.

To Carl Van Vechten

[postmark: 9 November 1936]   Bilignin par Belley
                                                             Ain

My dearest papa Woojums,

   We are leaving here to go there but here or there we always think of you, there was a delay in sending on the music but I am sending it to-day, I hope you will like it he is an interesting man,[1] lots of small xcitements and big, the book is out, and I will send you one from Paris, do you like it, and they are doing the Choate school talk and bits of Tender Buttons for the Oxford Press American anthology [William Rose] Benet,[2] and they are getting together a little book in french of things done in the country here,[3] and the Atlantic has accepted a little story about our chinese Nuygen called Butter will melt, and Ellery Sedwick says it is delectable[4] and Alice has found millions of new recipes in everybody's cook book in the pays that is all their ms. ones and we think of you and Fania in your new home all the time

                                                             lots of love
                                                             Gtrde.

1. See Stein to Van Vechten [26 October 1936], note 2.

2. *The Oxford Anthology of American Literature*, chosen and ed. by William Rose Benét and Norman Holmes Pearson (New York: Oxford University Press, 1938), pp. 1446–51, printed Stein's "How Writing is Written." This is a slightly revised version of Stein's talk as printed in *The Choate Literary Magazine* (February 1935), 21(2):5–14. See Van Vechten to Stein, 23 December 1938.

3. This volume did not appear.

4. Stein's "Butter Will Melt," *The Atlantic Monthly* (February 1937), 159(2): 156–57.

To Gertrude Stein

22 November [1936]   101 Central Park West
                                      New York City

Dear EST Baby Woojums,

The Geographical History of America is a beautiful book inside and out, full of knowledge and gaiety and information and wit. It was sweet of you to put Basket and Pepe in so much and I am very jealous of Thornton Wilder and Joe Alsop who get mentioned and mentioned.[1] Bennett [Cerf] and his uncle . . . "What is the use of being a little boy if you are going to grow up to be a man?" is probably the most profound thought that was ever printed in a book. I'd like it for an insigne, had I not one already! It would be pretty on plates. So would the poem about "happy little pair." . . . I got a copy from Bennett. Haven't received your copy yet. Nor the music. My, but you both seem active! And you are in a book called New Directions just out here. Have you seen that?[2] Mabel [Dodge]'s new book is out and thousands of your letters are in it (I suppose Harcourt will send this to you) and I am in it briefly and pleasantly enough. The parts about [John] Reed are very much distorted and there are several actual misstatements (without digging deep). The [Maurice] Sterne part is the best. Because she wasn't in love with this one. So she wriggles and he wriggles. She emerges a pretty foolish figure, I think. No generosity; no petty kindness; no nobility; no sense of values: I mean I think she does herself an injustice. The world snickers and snickers.[3] The New Yorker review is headed Up in Mabel's Rooms (Avery [Hopwood] had a farce called Up in Mabel's Room).[4] We are gettin more settled. Virgil [Thomson] has gone back to Paris. Man Ray is here.[5] Eddie Wassermann is going around the World (while there is yet a World to go around) and on his way through Paris will drop off Mama Woojums' umbrella, tenderly preserved for some such voyage. Let me know about the Oxford Press Anthology and about the Choate School Talk. And Alice's cookbook. I am excited! Roman's [Romaine Brooks] picture is hanging in our silver and grey dining-room but Eddie will tell you how HE THINKS the house looks, although it isn't done yet. Better still, come and look at it! Love to you both from Fania AND

Papa Woojums!

1. Stein had met the journalist Joseph Alsop, Jr., during her American lecture tour, 1934–35. See Gallup, *The Flowers of Friendship*, pp. 298–99.

Alsop wrote a number of articles about Stein at this time including "Gertrude Stein Says Children Understand Her," *New York Herald Tribune*, 3 November 1934, (YCAL) and "Statement of Miss Stein's Objective," *The Art Digest* (New York, December 1934), 15: 9.

2. Stein's "A Waterfall and a Piano," in *New Directions in Prose and Poetry*, ed. James Laughlin IV (Norfolk, Conn.: New Directions, 1936), pp. [16–18].

3. See Stein to Van Vechten [6 March 1936], note 5.

4. Clifton Fadiman's review of Dodge's *Movers and Shakers*, titled "Up in Mabel's Rooms," appeared in *The New Yorker*, 21 November 1936, pp. 88–90.

5. Man Ray, the American painter and photographer, whom Stein had first met in 1922.

To Gertrude Stein

[Postcard: Portrait of Giorgio de Chirico. Photograph by Carl Van Vechten]

25 November 1936   [101 Central Park West
New York]

Dearest Baby Woojums.

The Sung recettes have arrived & I am SENT! Such a wonderful idea. The Parc l'Espagnole is something musical & edible.[1] Well Edith has gone & so we sing these recettes to Mildred now! Wish you were BOTH here for Thanksgiving dinner tomorrow and lots of love.

Carlo

A lovely card from Père Berna[r]det thanking me for St. Ignatius![2]

1. Songs by the French composer Ennemond Trillat. See Stein to Van Vechten [26 October 1936], note 2.

2. See Van Vechten to Stein, 5 November [1936], notes 1 and 3.

❧

To Carl Van Vechten

[postmark: 2 December 1936]   27 rue de Fleurus
                                               [Paris]

Dear dearest Papa Woojums,

We were getting worried not hearing from you, we knew you were well because Romaine [Brooks] had written that she and the portrait had dined in honor at the new flat and that everything was lovely[1] and we knew the harbor here was having dock strikes and ship strikes but other mail came through so we were beginning to kind of worry lest papa Woojums in all his new grandeur was forgetting mama and baby and they would not have cared about that you bet they would not, papa Woojums is theirs and they do not intend they should be anybody else's not now or any other time. We are quite peaceful and so is Paris, they had a flurry yesterday when they thought there was to be a general strike and Alice sent me out to buy some corned beef, we bought four little tins they won't keep us long but they seem safe, anyway I do like corned beef hash so as Alice says it is no waste, she is delighted at the advent of her umbrella,[2] she finds so many xciting cook-books, and then she has to cook them that the getting to the writing is another matter, she just found a first empire one, Georges Maratier's grand-grandmother used and annotated and she is very xcited. My book[3] goes on and I am now at the 135 page and your visit to Bilignin with Mark [Lutz] the summer before going to America and you are just in the act of photographing Trac, no Harcourt never sends the book, but we will get it somehow, we have read Bravig Imbs, which has some not so bad spots best about Pavlik [Pavel Tchelitchew] and Allen [Tanner], particularly Allen, but very sweet about Peter Whiffle, the Duchess [de Clermont-Tonnerre] and Nathalie [Barney] are both blooming we are seeing them to-night, all the french adore your photos of Jefferson's University and the house of Edgar Poe, also accented and I like the one of [Giorgio de] Chirico he is nice isn't he, really a very dear person, if he is there remember me to him and lots and lots of love

Gtrde.

1. The letter of Brooks to Stein is not in YCAL.

2. Note by Van Vechten: "Edward Wasserman was bringing her the umbrella she had left in the U.S."

3. Stein's *Everybody's Autobiography*.

𝕬

To Carl Van Vechten
[Postcard: Gertrude Stein and Alice Toklas at the Birthplace of Marechal Joffre at Rivesaltes, April 1917]

[postmark: 12 December 1936]   [27 rue de Fleurus
                                                Paris]

My dearest Carl,

I am so pleased with the clipping, they gave you a fine send off and I certainly am sure it was even fuller than that, if we had been only there to see that would have been a pleasure.[1] Merry Christmas to you all merry merry Christmas to all

Gtrde.

1. A review of the Third International Leica Exhibition of Photography in which Van Vechten had participated. Van Vechten probably sent the clippings from the *New York Times*, 19 October 1936, p. 23, and 29 October 1936, p. 28.

𝕬

To Gertrude Stein

23 December 1936   101 Central Park West
                                    New York City

Dearest Baby Woojums,

a very merry Christmas to you and Mama W! I received the Comtesse d'Aiguy's paper in the Belley Press and the clip about Picasso et GS sous la Coupole (very sending!)[1] and [Ennemond] Trillat's fascinating sung recipes. I turned these over right away to Eva Gauthier who is giving a series of concerts of modern music and she thinks she may sing them. So if you can tell me anything about the composer[x] (as much as possible) it will be appreciated. I laughed and laughed over your cornbeef hash diet on account the strike! You must write a story about this, dear Baby Woojums! I hope Mr. [Eddie] Wassermann returned the umbrella okay . . . I am very much excited about Mama Woojums's cookbook. We have Mildred now where Edith once was, Mildred Perkins, a little prim like her name, but very handsome . . . I can't wait for the new autobiography and predict it will be even more sensational than the old . . . Henry [McBride] is getting all scared by Surrealism and growls and growls . . I don't think he ever liked it much but he was never scared before. He usually was nonchalant and lighted a Murad. The Modern Museum Show is the show to end all this, I think.[2] Besides [Giorgio de] Chirico and [Salvador] Dali and [Joan] Miro are all having one man shows against Winslow Homer![3] There hasn't been so much art excitement in years, or at least not since Lady Baby Woojums showed the natives how to get excited.[(2)] I have been sick for a week, a return to that old leg trouble I had in France. But I'm all right now again. The house is ALMOST settled and will be completely so in a couple of minutes. I think you both will like it. It is very different from the old one. Fania sends love and Carlo sends love and Papa Woojums sends love to Baby and Mama Woojums!

[Carl Van Vechten]

A N D M E R R Y C H R I S T M A S

[x] nobody here seems to know him at all.
[2] too long ago. Come again, please!

1. The two clippings cannot be identified.

2. The Museum of Modern Art exhibition *Fantastic Art, Dada, Surrealism,* organized by Alfred H. Barr, Jr., 9 December 1936 to 17 January 1937. The exhibition provoked a great deal of controversy. See McBride's "Dali and the Surrealists," in *The Flow of Art: Essays and Criticisms* of Henry McBride, selected, with an introduction, by Daniel Catton Rich (New York: Atheneum Publishers, 1975), pp. 341–43.

3. There was an exhibition of works by de Chirico at the Julien Levy Gallery, New York, 28 October to 17 November 1936; an exhibition of works by Dali at the Julien Levy Gallery, New York, 15 December to 15 January 1937; an exhibition of works by Miró at the Pierre Matisse Gallery, New York, 30 November to 26 December 1936; an exhibition of works by Winslow Homer at the Knoedler Gallery, New York, December 1936.

❧

To Carl Van Vechten

[postmark: 28 December 1936]   [27 rue de Fleurus
                                                Paris]

My dearest papa Woojums,

Now we really do know how the new apartment looks, we cross xamined and cross xamined Ed[d]ie Wassermann, until we really had a very good idea and the only thing now is to be in it and then we will be content. He brought the umbrella, Alice almost regrets it is here, she felt it was something to go back to, but she is very grateful just the same, and I saw Zadkine on the street, he is going to America on the 6 for a show and I told him to call you up and tell him [i.e., you] it was from me and I also told him that if you liked him he would have a very good time, I said he would be sure to like you and probably you would like him but that he would have to wait to see, he is rather a sweet fellow though.[1] It's cold and we are waiting for the warm weather you are having, we have all calmed down. Mrs. Simpson had us all heated up. Everybody was knowing something new and it all was true. We have a Polish American maid and she sighed to-day and said Mrs. Simpson, I do like that name.[2] There is a new chance of The Four Saints, over here, for the promoter saw Virgil [Thomson], and we all talked it over, it may happen and if it does you will come, I would love to sit with you through a our [i.e., another?] first night somewhere, otherwise everything is peaceful xcept that Pepe has a little kidney trouble but that will be better and so much love and happy new years to you and Fania from Mama and Baby Woojums who loved their cable.

[Gertrude Stein]

1. Ossip Zadkine (1890–1967), the Russian-born sculptor. Zadkine left Russia for London in 1907 and then from 1911 on lived and worked mostly in Paris. Zadkine had an exhibition of his work at the Brummer Gallery, New York, from 25 January to 20 March 1937.

2. Mrs. Wallis Warfield Simpson, later the Duchess of Windsor. King Edward VIII insisted on his right to marry Mrs. Simpson even though her marital background made her unacceptable to the British government. When the matter could not be resolved, the King abdicated, ending a 325-day reign. On 11 December 1936 the English Parliament passed a bill of abdiction, and on 3 June 1937 Edward, Duke of Windsor, and Mrs. Simpson were married.

To Gertrude Stein
[Postcard: Portrait of Joella Levy. Photograph by Carl Van Vechten]

[late December 1936][1]   [101 Central Park West
                                           New York]

Dear Gertrude! and Baby Woojums,

I am entranced by The Stanzas in Meditation, especially "Mama loves you best because you are Spanish." But you didn't tell me you were writing this![2] Thanks also for the [Ennemond] Trillat, I have passed these on to Eva Gauthier, just what she requires, I am sure. What an amusing name! I am a little shy for writing writers, especially en francais. I saw Gertrude Macy last night & she said Kitty Cornell had had the sweetest letter from you at Xmas!

l[ove] & K[isses] & Happy New Year! This is Mina Loy's daughter, Joella Levy![3]

Carlo (Papa W)

1. The postmark is difficult to read. It is surely sometime between 20 and 29 December, the 2 being readable but the second number unclear. A Paris postmark, on the picture part of the card, indicates that it arrived in Paris on 7 January 1937.

2. Stein had sent Van Vechten a typescript of her *Stanzas in Meditation*. The line Van Vechten quotes is on page 71 of Stein's *Stanzas in Mediation*.

3. Joella Synara Haweis (b. 1907), now Mrs. Herbert Bayer, had married the art dealer Julien Levy in 1927 and was living in New York. Mrs. Bayer is one of the daughters of Mina Loy and Stephen Haweis.

To Carl Van Vechten

[postmark: 31 December 1936]   [27 rue de Fleurus
                                                Paris]

My dear Papa Woojums,

I am writing to you on the eve of the glad New Year, we are seeing it in and out with Madame Clermont-Tonnerre, I wish you were going too.

I have sent you some more things by [Ennemond] Trillat all I can tell you about him is that he lives in Lyon earning his living naturally not too well in giving music lessons. He is about 40 years old has a wife and children, I did not meet them, but I knew about them through some friends of theirs in Belley where I saw the music and was much taken with it. I have written to this friend asking Trillat to write to you and also asking for his address. He sounds a very sweet man and anything you can do to give him recognition, will be very welcome, anyway if you are over this spring or summer it will be easy to meet him. We loved your description of Henry [McBride] with the surrealist, he sounds like [Jacques Emile] Blanche with the futurists,[1] by the way they ought to have a show of [André] Masson,[2] his last lot of pictures xcept for [Giorgio de] Chirico is the best of the lot. By the way I just saw a charming Chirico of his atelier and a picture of his own photo on the wall that I think must be one of yours.[3] We lunched very sweetly at the Foyot with Ed[d]ie Wassermann again and like him more and more, he improves on acquaintance and his little book is very good, we both read it with pleasure,[4] be careful Papa Woojums about that leg, we do love you so, and we want you all well and happy, we had a good Christmas and we will all somehow have a good new year that is be together. Pepe had an attack of kidney trouble for the New Year, he used to be the roi de pipi and then there was none, and so it had to be begun, last News Years Basket had worms, otherwise the family is serene, and loving you oh so much and wishing you and Fania everything here on the eve of the New Year, Always

Baby Woojums.

1. Jacques Emile Blanche (1861–1942), the French painter. Blanche had painted a portrait of Mabel Dodge in 1911. Van Vechten had been given a letter of introduction to Blanche in 1913.

2. Stein had just seen an exhibition of seventy-four paintings, *Andre Masson: Espagne 1934–1936*, at the Galerie Simon (Daniel-Henry Kahnweiler) in Paris, 7 to 19 December 1936.

3. This picture cannot be identified.

4. Wassermann had taken Stein and Toklas to lunch at the restaurant of the Hôtel Foyot, rue Tournon, Paris. Wasserman had met the French writer Anatole France during World War I, in Tours. Wassermann later wrote a memoir of his meetings with Anatole France. It was published together with an essay by Jacques de Lacretelle as *A la recontre de France, suivi de Anatole France vu par un Américain; par Edward Wasserman*, trans. Jacques de Lacretelle (Paris: Editions M.-P. Trémois, 1930).

❦

To Gertrude Stein
[Postcard: Wooden Bird. Photograph by Carl Van Vechten]

[11 January 1937]   [101 Central Park West
                                                      New York]

Dear Baby Woojums . .

I'm afraid you'll have to ask somebody else than E[ddie] W[assermann] about the new apartment. It was not nearly settled or solidified when he left. Everything is changed! You'd better come over & look *yourselves!* I cannot make out the name in your letter. Is it Zadikies [i.e., Zadkine]? and Jos[eph] Alsop had a lovely review of your book in the Tribune,[1] and Butter will melt is announced for the February Atlantic.[2] We had a LOVELY New Year's Eve party. Henry [McBride] was here & so was Roman [Romaine Brooks]. She is ecstatic about the way her portrait is hung & so she should be. Her own apartment is very extraordinary, with enlarged pen & ink sketches all over the enormous walls!

1000 kinds of everything to you both

C.

1. See Van Vechten to Stein, 22 November [1936], note 1. Alsop's review of Stein's *The Geographical History of America Or The Relation Of Human Nature To The Human Mind,* "Gertrude Stein on Writing," in *New York Herald Tribune Books* (10 January 1937), 13:2.

2. See Stein to Van Vechten [9 November 1936], note 4.

❦

To Gertrude Stein
[Postcard: Portrait of Leonor Fini. Photograph by Carl Van Vechten]

18 January [1937]   [101 Central Park West
                                                      New York]

Dear Baby Woojums!

Tell Basket & Pepe to get well! Tell them that Papa W is quite well again & hopping around. Thanks for the notes on [Ennemond] Trillat. He sent me some piano music now. I think your cousin died in Baltimore. I am sorry.[1] Here is LEONOR FINI, whose "Game of Legs in a Key of Dreams" is one of the features of the Modern Museum Show.[2] Butter Will Melt is announced for the Feb[ruary] Atlantic.

Love to Both from Both

C.

1. Van Vechten was mistaken. Stein's Baltimore cousins were Mr. and Mrs. Julian Stein, Sr.

2. Van Vechten had photographed the painter Leonor Fini on 14 December 1936. Fini's painting *Jeux de jambes dans la clef du reve*, 1935, oil on canvas, 32 x 22 ⅜ inches, was exhibited in the Museum of Modern Art exhibition, *Fantastic Art, Dada, Surrealism*.

To Carl Van Vechten

[postmark: 19 January 1937]   [27 rue de Fleurus
                      Paris]

My dear Papa Woojums,

I loved your descriptions of Henry [McBride], that is the way Jacques [Emile] Blanche was before futurism, but tell him to cheer up, the devil is always dead, and I am sending him some photos of the nicest young crowd and they are completely not that. We have been having a very lively winter, most social for us, and there are so many people in Paris, you meet them every time you go out of the door, it did not used to be but it is so now and we like it, I'll send you some photos too of my newest painter, a long story and not an unamusing one,[1] I'll tell you when we meet, and the Atlantic Monthly sent me a check for two stories and [Ellery] Sedgwick said one called the Novel was a lesson to Proust and I hope you will like them,[2] I am supposed to be going on working, Bennett [Cerf] clamors for the autobiography but the pleasant life of Paris this year has side-tracked me, but I am going on, I am in America now and just coming, I am awfully anxious to know what you think, you have a copy of the 200 Stanzas in Meditation in among the unpublished ms. in your care, certainly you have, they were written about 3 years ago, I like the Spanish one best,[3] did you see Bryher when she was over,[4] anyway lots a[nd] lots and more than lots of love to you from us all always and always

Baby and Mama Woojums.[5]

1. The French painter Robert Toulouse. Stein lost interest in his work.

2. In 1937 *The Atlantic Monthly* printed two pieces by Stein: "Butter Will Melt" (February 1937), 159(2):156–57, and "Your United States" (excerpts from *Everybody's Autobiography*) (October 1937), 160(2):459–68. In addition, part of a letter from Stein to Ellery Sedgwick, editor of *The Atlantic Monthly*, was printed in *The Atlantic Monthly* (February 1937), 159(2), on the verso of the first leaf following page 256.

    Ellery Sedgwick accepted Stein's "Butter Will Melt" in a letter of 23 October 1936 (YCAL). In Sedwick's letter to Stein of 31 December 1936 (YCAL) he refers to Stein's "A Novel" ("What Does She See When She Shuts Her Eyes," in Stein's *Mrs. Reynolds and Five Earlier Novelettes*, pp. 375–78) as, "What a lesson to the Prousts of this World!" Sedgwick had planned to publish this novel in an early number of *The Atlantic Monthly* but decided instead to print excerpts from *Everybody's Autobiography*.

3. See Van Vechten to Stein [late December 1936], note 2.

4. The English writer Winifred Bryher.

5. Both signatures are by Stein.

To Carl Van Vechten
[Rose motto]

[postmark: 6 February 1937]　　　　　　　　　27 rue de Fleurus
　　　　　　　　　　　　　　　　　　　　　　　　[Paris]

My dear Carl,

Muriel [Draper] has just been [here] and it was so nice to have her and I don't know it kind of made us feel that you might be here too all together and that would have been and will be nice and at the same time it made us homesick for you yes it did, but she will tell you, everything is peaceful I am writing this with a camel pen that Ed[d]ie Wassermann gave me you fill it with water and it writes ink, and I am writing now in the Autobiography about America[1] and it all is so simple that I worry lest it is so simple it is nothing, well anyway it goes on and we go on loving papa Woojums and everything is cheerful and we love you

Gtrde.

1. Stein's *Everybody's Autobiography.*

To Gertrude Stein
[Postcard: Portrait of Eugene Berman. Photograph by Carl Van Vechten]

8 February 1937   [101 Central Park West
                                   New York]

Dear Baby Woojums

No, I didn't see [Winifred] Bryher, but I saw Zadkine & liked him & photographed him with his work, but there is hardly time for more. He is going away soon. Mina Loy is here and we saw her yesterday & here is Genia Berman.[1] Of course I have the mss of your Stanzas in meditation, but I have not read them all, they are treasured in VAULTS. But I did read them in the magazine & loved them.[2] Also Butter WILL melt! Marjorie Worthington has a new book[3] out & WHERE is your autobiography, and nobody says a word about Mabel [Dodge] and Love to both,

Papa W!

1. Eugene Berman, the painter.

2. Part of *Stanzas in Meditation* was published in *Life and Letters Today* (Winter 1936/1937), 15(6): 77–80.

3. Marjorie Worthington's *Manhattan Solo* (New York: Alfred A. Knopf, 1937).

🙝

To Carl Van Vechten
[Postcard: Gertrude Stein and Alice Toklas at the Birthplace of Marechal
Joffre at Rivesaltes, April 1917]

[postmark: 10 February 1937]   [27 rue de Fleurus
                                                                 Paris]

Dear papa Woojums,

Will you send a photo to a very charming fellow who is writing [a]
doctorate about me and has a complete collection that he is giving to the
University etc and could it be the profile that you made in little that I like
so much, I hate to ask so much, but he would like it so, he is Robert Bartlett
Haas, International House, Berkeley, Cal.[1] so lots of love and I just saw
Douglas from upstairs, and he told me about Mrs Douglas and everything[2]

lots of love
B. W.

1. Haas did his dissertation under Dr. Clarence Faust. The title of his dissertation was "The
Concept of the Present in the Literary Criticism of Gertrude Stein."

2. A neighbor at 27 rue de Fleurus who knew Van Vechten's friend Mrs. Mahala Douglas.

🙝

To Carl Van Vechten
[Rose motto]

[postmark: 14 February 1937]   27 rue de Fleurus
                                                                 [Paris]

Dearest Papa Woojums,

They want a picture of Pepe so as to make the mask for the ballet
and I am sending them Pepe's own idea June 13/34 xxxiif:8 and sometime
can we have another because they certainly will never give it back, the date
has not yet been settled but it will be sometime the end of March Gerald

Berners says that music copies and all is done and now he is doing the decor it is to be called A Wedding Bouquet,[1] and Madame Marie Louise Bousquet is coming to see you she is on the Paris and gets there the 24 of February, she is with the daughter of Violet Murat[2] and she is staying at the Hotel Gladstone Lexington Avenue, and she wants to lecture her husband who was Rip's partner in the old days of the revue is ill now and she has to make some money, she really did have a salon a good one and she is very charming and she has written rather a nice letter and I told her if you liked her you will tell her everything and she must do everything you tell her and she is very nervous about whether you will like her and that I said this I do not know, but I hope you will. Will you let her know. I do not know her awfully well but I like her. I have just finished writing our first month in New York, I go on but I do not know how it is, Muriel Draper was here we thought she looked awfully well and it was a pleasure to see her and we told her to tell you how much we loved you which she will, lots of love

Baby Woojums.

[on flap of envelope] speaks English charmingly.[3]

1. See Berners' letter in Gallup, *The Flowers of Friendship*, p. 321.

2. Violet Murat, Princess Lucien Murat, was a writer. Her daughter was Caroline de Gheest.

3. A reference to Marie-Louise Bousquet.

❧

To Gertrude Stein
[Postcard: Portrait of Pépé. Photograph by Carl Van Vechten]

3 March [1937]   [101 Central Park West
                                                      New York]

Dearest Baby Woojums.

I find M[arie] L[ouise] Bousquet absolutely enchanting. I met her yesterday & gave a lunch for her today at the Algonquin with the [William] Seabrooks & Caroline de Gheest, I told Georges [Jacques][1] she was a friend of *yours* & he laid himself out, and I am sending your Pepe right back to you (**XXXIIf**: 8) We also like Caroline de Gheest very much & we *love* Baby & Mama Woojums

Papa W!

1. The headwaiter at the Algonquin Hotel, New York.

To Carl Van Vechten

[postmark: 6 March 1937]

27 rue de Fleurus
[Paris]

My dearest Papa Woojums,

I know this letter will please you, and we do like your postal cards not that Meraud [Guevera] has not a more beautiful dog than that and his name is Poncho and perhaps you will photograph him when you come,[1] there are always so many new ones to photograph and will you come, I have done half of America now and Alice will be making a second copy pretty soon and send it along to you, there are only about 50 to a 100 pages more to do, I am sending pieces of it to Bennett [Cerf] I've printed several and I am doing a nice play about Daniel Webster[2] beside so you can see Baby is busy. Lots and lots of love and thanks for the photo for [Robert Bartlett] Haas.

Gtrde.

1. The English-born painter and wife of the Chilean-born painter Alvaro Guevara (d. 1951). "I am quite astonished that you ask about my dog Poncho—he was a dalmation & came from England & was a friend of Basket's—anyway they were apt to fight" (letter received from Meraud Guevara, 15 March [1983]).

2. Stein's *Daniel Webster. Eighteen in America: A Play*, in *New Directions in Prose & Poetry* (Norfolk, Conn.: New Directions, 1937), pp. [162–88]. Stein did not send a typescript of the play to Van Vechten until the following September. See Stein to Van Vechten [21 September 1937].

To Carl Van Vechten
[Rose motto]

[postmark: 18 March 1937]

27 rue de Fleurus
[Paris]

My dearest Papa Woojums,

We are so pleased that you liked Marie Louise [Bousquet], and here is the [Robert Bartlett] Haas boy who is very happy, he is one of the liveliest of the fans, just now, and have you seen the Gertrude Stein number of the Utica High School it is called the Academic Observer and is the February number, they only sent me one number but I know it would please you, they did it very well,[1] what's the news, nothing very much, Sir Robert Abdy is doing a green hand made edition of the 200 Sonnets of Meditation,[2] but as he is never satisfied with the way the printers print, and why not, it will be a long time off, Pepe is delicious, we love him on the postal card, there is a possibility of Listen to me being done in french with Picabia, we had that hope already but you think it is all dead and here it comes again, it would be funny, Daniel Webster is getting on nicely and please tell George [s Jacques] that we do not forget him and often think about how we went home to the hotel, over there

Always
Baby Woojums.

[on the flap of envelope] The premiere of the ballet is 27 April.[3]

1. The February 1937 number of *The Academic Observer*, the newspaper of the Utica Free Academy, Utica, New York, was devoted to Stein. The issue was edited by Jean Treible; the assistant editor was Margaret Lucha. The issue included a biography of Stein by Lucha, accompanied by a photograph (p. [4]); a facsimile of a letter to Lucha from Stein, "My dear Margaret" (p. [5]); and a series of unidentified quotations from Stein's works (p. [6]).

2. A reference to the proposed edition of Stein's *Stanzas in Meditation* that was to be published by Sir Robert Abdy and printed by Guido Morris. Morris had suggested printing the edition on "Barcham Green," a paper that is actually pink in color.

3. Note by Van Vechten, 24 January 1941: "The Berners Ballet at Sadler's Wells London." The ballet was the Stein-Berners *A Wedding Bouquet*.

To Gertrude Stein

24 March 1937   101 Central Park West
                                                 New York City

Dear Gertrude and Baby Woojums,

Here is [Kristians] Tonny with his wife and Zadkine. All, and you, appear in Claude McKay's A Long Way from Home, but you only be [i.e., by] inference, as it seems he never met you. .[1] The Philharmonic, under [Arthur] Rodzinski, recently gave some performances (in concert form) of Strauss's Elektra. As rehearsal time approached the lady engaged to sing the title part fell ill and Rosa Pauly of the Vienna Opera was brought over to take her place. Pauly turned out to be just about the greatest singing actress this town has ever seen or heard and we all went wild. It was like the old days come back. People always think that middle aged people are exaggerating about the triumphant performances of the past until something like this happens and then they are just bowled over. . I am glad to say that I hear Miss Pauly is Jewish (she is from Prague) and there is even a chance she has some Arabian blood.[2] If she ever sings in Paris, pawn your jewels and attend to her! . . Think of Baby W doing a play about Daniel Webster and yet what could be more natural. DYING, of course, to see the new autobiography. It will include America and the tour? . . Did you know about the man in Los Angeles who has written a 50,000 word novel without ONCE using the letter E? He tied down the E key on his typewriter . . [Marie Louise] Bousquet is a lamb and I really love her. . Bobsy Goodspeed is importing her to Chicago, I hear, for a conference. I took her to the Savoy in Harlem, along with Violette's daughter who is charming too,[3] and last Saturday night on Fania's birthday we had 35 people here to dinner (THIRTY-FIVE) so you can get some idea of the size of the new Palais de Versailles. O dear, I wish I were hearing and seeing that performance à Londres. Are you going to it? You must tell me all about it. . Anyway Fania and I send lots of love to you and Mama Woojums and I hope you are wearing your rubbers these damp days!

!Carlo!

Madame Gaston Lachaise has really turned up the most amazing painter, a Negro cleaning woman in Boston. She sells her works for 50 cents a piece and soon or late I'll be able to get an example for you. They are done in colored pencils and the background is always the same: a picture of the Virgin, a grand piano, a palm in a POT and a divan. In front of this one or two principal figures. . I thought they were grandes cocottes or maybe grues in houses of Joy. But no, says Isobel Lachaise, Mary Bell (such is her lovely name) is very religious. Rather they are saints. Saints then in ratted hair, blonde, black, and titian, and every kind of WRAPPER, in design color and lace trimmings most complicated. Sometimes a Suitor. Something like [Henri] Rousseau, but O so different. . What an artist![4]

Love and let love!

1. Claude McKay's A *Long Way from Home* (New York: L. Furman, Inc., 1937). McKay (1890–1948), the black writer, mentions Stein several times in this autobiographical work, but he does not seem to have met her. McKay mentions his reactions to meeting Van Vechten in Paris (pp. 282–83, 318–21). McKay does not refer to Tonny by name; instead he is mentioned as the boyfriend of a woman, Carmina, who is actually the black performer Anita Thompson.

2. Rodzinski conducted performances of Strauss's *Elektra* with the New York Philharmonic at Carnegie Hall, New York, on 18, 19, and 21 March 1937. The title role was sung by Rose Pauly (replacing the indisposed Gertrude Kappel). In his review in the *New York Times*, 19 March 1937, p. 26, Olin Downes called it "one of the most thrilling and dramatic performances that the writer has been privileged to hear." Rosa Pauly (1894–1975) was born Rose Pollack.

3. See Stein to Van Vechten [14 February 1937], note 2.

4. Mary Bell worked for the sculptor Gaston Lachaise and his wife. Van Vechten eventually gave ninety-seven works on paper by Mary Bell to Yale-JWJ. The works generally have titles given by the artist.

To Gertrude Stein

3 April [1937]

101 Central Park West
New York City

Dear Gertrude and Baby Woojums,

Your latest letter was (and is) almost impossible to decipher. Very very difficult penmanship! Usually I can read every word but not this time. However the message to Georges [Jacques] was clear. I gave it to him and was he delighted! He told EVERYBODY you had asked about him and his message to you is He hopes your message to him means you are coming over soon when he will devote himself practically exclusively to your pleasure and comfort. I have sent for the Utica school paper, though I could not make out the name of it. I guess THEY'LL know . . Muriel [Draper] is back with lovely news of you both. Do you ever see a friend of Aaron Copland named Victor Kraft? Paul Bowles has gone to Mexico with M et Madame [Kristians] Tonny![1] Marie Louise B[ousquet] has gone to Chicago to lecture for Bobsy [Goodspeed] and the rest. Harold Jackman, one of my Harlem boys has been helping her with her English.[2] She is SWEET. .

Angels and Ministers of Grace defend you and Mama W!

Papa Woojums!

If you could get me a couple of programs of the Ballet?!! Please!!

1. Paul Bowles, composer and author, had met Tonny and his wife, Marie Claire, in Paris through Stein. It was at that time that they planned a trip to Mexico together. Bowles and Jane Auer, who had previously met, attended a party given by the poet E. E. Cummings in his Patchin Place, New York, apartment. Auer decided to join Bowles and the Tonnys on the trip to Mexico. A year after this trip, Paul Bowles and Jane Auer were married.

2. Harold Jackman (1902–61) was a junior high school social studies teacher in New York. He was an avid collector of memorabilia on Negro Art and literature. He contributed to the Countee Cullen Memorial Collection, Atlanta University, the James Weldon Johnson Collection at Yale University, the library at Fisk University, and the Schomburg Collection, New York Public Library. Jackman's extensive correspondence with Van Vechten is at Yale-JWJ.

To Carl Van Vechten

[postmark: 6 April 1937]   27 rue de Fleurus
                                                        [Paris]

My dear papa Woojums,

We were pleased to hear from you and a little envious of Marie Louise [Bousquet] and your being so happy with her and glad that she got a job in Chicago and I hope she gets a lot more of them. The autobiography is almost getting done, I want to finish it before we go to London, I have gotten as far as Texas, it is very simple and naturally I am worried and yet have bought a brand new Ford car in the hopes the Ford car has the french and American flags on it so that should be alright, as soon as we get to the country Alice will tap it and we will send it to you, and then we will know, the xposition grows apace it might be nice are you coming, Kitty Buss sent us some Boston Negro paintings last summer, and they were Mary Bell's,[1] the premiere in London is the 27 and naturally we are xcited, Gerald [Berners] writes that it all goes on well, and I'll send you pictures of it if I can get them, we have hurried Pepe's one of the ones you sent us to the vet, who takes care of him, he is a popular character now so he got sick. Lots of love and to Fania for her birthday

Gtrde

1. Note by Van Vechten, 24 January 1941: "Mary Bell, a Negro primitive who lived in Boston and drew fabulous pictures with colored pencils on waxed tissue paper. A discovery of Mrs. Gaston Lachaise." The location of works by Bell sent to Stein by Kitty Buss is not known. There are no letters in YCAL from Buss to Stein mentioning these paintings.

To Carl Van Vechten
[Rose motto]

[postmark: 16 April 1937]   27 rue de Fleurus
                                                  [Paris]

My dear papa Woojums,

    I have asked Bennett [Cerf] to pass over to you the autobiography as far as it has gotten which is the end of America,[1] I am so hoping that you will be pleased, and then it is to be shown to Thornton [Wilder] and that's all, I do hope you like it and I do hope it makes a lot of money, after having been terribly frugal ever since we have been back we would like to spend a little lots and lots and lots of love

Gtrde.

1. Stein wrote Cerf (undated letter, 1937, Columbia-Random House) that she wanted Wilder to see the typescript of her book *Everybody's Autobiography* but that she wanted Van Vechten to see it first.

[541]

❧

To Gertrude Stein
[Postcard: Unidentified sculpture of a man above an entrance to a
building. Photograph by Carl Van Vechten]

19 April 1937   [101 Central Park West
                                                 New York]

Dear Baby Woojums.

Marie Louise [Bosquet] is on her way to you & she will tell you a
LOT. and Bennett [Cerf] says he has SOME of the mss of Everybody's Autobiography! What a magnificent title & I CAN'T WAIT 'til I see it. Also
I'm in a fever about London. Do send pictures & programmes & clippings,
please in profusion., There is no news. . But our new cook is SWELL and
makes a Grand Cassoulet! next we try Bouillabaisse!
1001 red & yellow roses to you & Mama W!

Papa W!

❧

To Gertrude Stein
[Postcard: Marie Louise Bousquet. Photograph by Carl Van Vechten]

22 April [1937]   [101 Central Park West
                                                 New York]

Dear Baby Woojums.

ask Marie Louise B[ousquet]. to show you the rest of her pictures
which go to her today!
Heard Aaron Copland's opera for High School Children, "The Second Hurricane" hier soir. Not much good.[1]
Love to Mama W & yourself

Papa W.

1. Aaron Copland's *The Second Hurricane,* a play-opera for high school performance, had its
premiere at the Henry Street Music School, New York, with Lehman Engel conducting, on
21 April 1937.

&

To Gertrude Stein
[Postcard: Buon Natale]

27 April [1937]   [101 Central Park West
                                                    New York]

Dear Baby Woojums

Has it occurred to you the CPW not only stands for Central Park West but also for Carlo Papa Woojums! The papers are beginning to write about your Ballet which is tonight!!![1]

[Carl Van Vechten]

1. The Berners-Stein ballet, A *Wedding Bouquet*, had its first performance on 27 April 1937 at Sadlers Wells Theatre, London. The choreography was by Frederick Ashton and the costumes and decor were designed by Lord Berners (executed under the supervision of William Chappell). The role of Webster was danced by Ninette de Valois, Julia by Margot Fonteyn, and the Bridegroom by Robert Helpmann. Stein's dog Pépé was danced by Joyce Farron. The text was sung by members of the Sadlers Wells Opera Company. A *Wedding Bouquet* appeared, for its premiere, on the same program as the ballets *The Rake's Progress*, music by Gavin Gordon, choreography by Ninette de Valois, and *Les Patineurs*, music by Meyerbeer and choreography by Ashton. Constant Lambert was the musical director for all three ballets. In its first season A *Wedding Bouquet* was also performed on 4, 8, and 17 May.

&

To Gertrude Stein
[Postcard: Unidentified Roman Sculpture—Head of a Man.
Photograph by Carl Van Vechten][1]

[postmark: 28 April 1937]   [101 Central Park West
                                                    New York]

Dear Baby Woojums.

I would love and love and love to see the NEW AUTOBIOGRA-PHY but Bennett [Cerf] hasn't shown it to me yet. Please be sure to send me all the clippings & programs of the Ballet last night. I can't wait to hear [about] it! Did Pepe make a succes fou?

l[ove] & k[isses] to both
Papa W

1. This head would appear to be the cast of the Apollo Belvedere that Giorgio de Chirico used in his painting *The Song of Love*, 1914, oil on canvas, 28¾ x 23⅜ inches. Collection of The Museum of Modern Art, New York.

❧

To Carl Van Vechten

[postmark: 29 April 1937]   3 Halkin Street
[London], S.W. 1

My dear Papa Woojums,

It was a success a great success and they gave a big party afterwards and B.W. was on the stage bowing in the best B.W. Fashion and all that was wanted was P.W. to see and there was no P.W. there which was sad but Mama W. said B.W. behaved very satisfactorily, oh I wish you had been there, it was very lovely everything was beautifully done nothing could have been better, they do dance enthusiastically and delightfully and Gerald [Berners]'s music is very interesting and his drop curtain perfectly delightful and [Frederick] Ashton whom I met for the first time is really a genius and we could hardly sleep the night before and not the night after and London is lovely and all we miss is P.W. but we do miss him dreadfully, we go back to Paris and then to Bilignin, have sent 3 programmes and Francis Rose catalogues[1]

lots of love
Gtrde.

1. Stein sent Van Vechten copies of an exhibition brochure, a single sheet folded once to make a brochure 5½ x 4 inches, for *Quelques oeuvres récentes de Sir Francis Rose*, Galerie Pierre, Paris, 27 April to 8 May 1937. Stein contributed a short biographical notice about Rose.

[544]

To Gertrude Stein
[Postcard: Portrait of Leonor Fini. Photograph by Carl Van Vechten]

[postmark: 1 May 1937]

[101 Central Park West
New York]

Dearest Baby Woojums!

Was this the surrealiste card you were asking about? If *so*, it is Leonor Fini. Si non, Dites moi what was on the card please. The reviews came and are very exciting. Thank you, and I'm glad you liked the portrait of M[arie] L[ouise] Bousquet! Mad to see the pix of Wedding Bouquet. No autobiography yet! But SOON! F. Dixon of Flushing writes to ask if I am going to Paris as she wants to send some presents to you & M W I am NOT, but I've written her I can find somebody if she will leave the presence [i.e., presents] with me. M L Bousquet could have taken them![1]

Love & lilies!
!Carlo!

1. I have not been able to locate any of the correspondence between Van Vechten and Dixon. Florence Dixon, who lived in Flushing, New York, had written a fan letter to Stein on 23 July 1933 (YCAL). She was enthusiastic about the excerpts from *The Autobiography of Alice B. Toklas* that had appeared in *The Atlantic Monthly*. Dixon wrote of having read Stein's *Tender Buttons* and of having seen Jo Davidson's bust of Stein in a New York gallery. She attended Stein's lectures in New York (Dixon to Toklas, 13 November 1934, YCAL). In the letters from Dixon to Stein and Toklas that are in YCAL Dixon speaks of collecting presents for them and of her own interest in dogs. I have not been able to locate any of Stein's or Toklas' letters to Dixon. The letters from Dixon to Stein or Toklas that are in YCAL do not go beyond early 1935.

To Carl Van Vechten

[postmark: 3 May 1937]   27 rue de Fleurus
                                                          [Paris]

Dearest Papa Woojums,

Marie Louise [Bousquet] was here all last evening and told us everything and brought me lovely cuff buttons suggested by Papa W. as he would just the thing to give me pleasure, I sent you the first batch of clippings at least some of them there were lots a very good one in the Manchester Guardian but that there was only one copy in the house so I could not take it and it was too long to rewrite,[1] I guess there will be lots of pictures later and as Gerald Berners sends them to me I will send them to you I finished up the Autobiography with a description of our success, and I am just waiting for you to read it I will not be satisfied till you have, I told Bennett [Cerf] to give it to you before anybody, there is as yet only that one copy but when we get to the country there will be another we leave for the country day after to-morrow, are we seeing you this summer are you coming to the xposition if there is one, they perhaps will give the Wedding Bouquet here in Paris in June, and you must photograph Gerald and Pepe the false as you did the true,[2] she was sweet and it is all lovely and we do miss you, and the photo of Marie Louise was a wonder, she was much moved and pleased she had not received hers yet and thanks for George[s Jacques][3] I must write and tell him how pleased I am to have it and what was the surrealist one,[4] what is that it is unbelievable and lots of love always and always, Marie Louise made you and Fania all real

                                                          Lots of love
                                                          Gtrde.

1. Undated clipping from *Manchester Guardian*, YCAL.

2. A *Wedding Bouquet* was not given in Paris in June. Stein is referring to Lord Gerald Berners and Joyce Farron, who danced the role of Pépé in the ballet.

3. Headwaiter at the Algonquin Hotel, New York.

4. Van Vechten's portrait of Lenor Fini. See Van Vechten to Stein, 18 January [1937], for the first portrait of Fini used as a postcard by Van Vechten.

❦

To Gertrude Stein
*[Postcard: Sculpture of Goya in Madrid. Photograph by
Carl Van Vechten]* [1]

13 May [1937]   [101 Central Park West
                                                       New York]

Dear Baby Woojums.

Thanks for the programs, the clips & the Rose catalogue. I am delighted with all this success! and I can't wait till I see this Ballet! O dear,
why can't it be done here? and this is GOYA in Madrid: only it may be
chipped now!
Love to BW & MW!

P W!

Ellen Glasgow was here for [dinner] last night & I asked Bennett [Cerf].
The Atlantic still has the ms. [2]

1. The sculpture, a head of the Spanish painter Francisco de Goya y Lucientes (1746–1828),
is on the north façade of the Prado Museum in Madrid, Spain. It was executed by the Spanish
sculptor Mariano Benlliure (1868–1947).

2. Cerf had written Stein, 22 April 1937 (YCAL), that he was sending parts of *Everybody's
Autobiography* to *The Atlantic Monthly* with the hope that they would serialize it. See Stein to
Van Vechten [19 January 1937], note 2.

❦

To Carl Van Vechten

[postmark: 15 May 1937]   Bilignin par Belley
                                                       Ain

My dear Carl

Here we are getting rested that is to say Gerald Berners has been here
so it has been active but now we are settling down to a country life and the
Tatler the Sketch and Bystander of the 5 and the Bystander of the 12 all

have photographs of us and the Ballet and everything,[1] there is a possibility of it being done in June in Paris, they said that the third performance which was a matinee was just as crowded and enthusiastic as ever and usually matinees at the Sadler's are not, otherwise we are here and writing you more here and this is just to say that because although it is only eight o'clock in the evening we are all asleep, two dogs and us but very loving

Baby Woojums.

1. *The Bystander*, 5 May 1937, had a page of photographs, "Audience for Ballet: A First Night at Sadlers' Wells." *The Bystander*, 12 May 1937, " 'A Wedding Bouquet' The Berners-Stein-Ashton Ballet at Sadlers' Wells," contained six photographs of scenes from the ballet. *The Sketch*, 5 May 1937, "Magnificent Double by Lord Berners' 'A Wedding Bouquet,' " was illustrated by four photographs of Angus McBean. *The Tatler* of 5 May 1937 had a photograph of Stein, Lord Berners, Ramsay MacDonald, and Richard Wyndam at an exhibition of paintings by Captain Richard Wyndam at the Tooth Galleries, London (exhibition 15 April to 14 May 1937).

To Gertrude Stein

20 May 1937

101 Central Park West
New York City

Dear Baby Woojums,

Here are all Florence Dixon's letters which you need not return. The package goes by Bibi Dudensing next week. SO, when you get this will you please drop her a note:

    Madame Valentine Dudensing
    "Low Wood"
    Le Touquet
    P de C
      France

and tell her whether you are in Paris or Bilignin. And she will send you the package.

How are you both? We are well and happy and miss you both. No mss. yet. The Atlantic has not yet returned it.

l[ove] and k[isses]
Papa W!

[548]

I hear Henry [McBride] is going abroad as the Guest of the French government or somebody.

To Gertrude Stein

25 May [1937]   101 Central Park West
                                                     New York City

Dearest Baby Woojums,

Here is more Dixoniana. Your letter came with news about the English weeklies and I have several of them at hand, all that have arrived so far. The rest will be picked up later. Pepe's picture in the Sketch is too adorable. Has anybody thought to paint Pepe in the ballet? I do hope somebody does. Wouldn't I just photograph and photograph were I there!

> *cards and spades to you both!*
> *Carlo Papa W!*

No Mss. Yet.
Henry [McBride] is sailing Saturday.[1]

---

1. Stein used the verso of this letter as part of a draft of a letter. It is possible that Van Vechten's letter and the letter from a Virieu le Grand correspondent arrived in Bilignin on the same day. Page one is written on a single sheet of unlined paper:

> I remember and this was long ago ~~a m~~ they were talking about automobiles and they were saying what one was and what another was and a man there who had had them from the beginning said well all I can say about automobiles perhaps some are better than others but all automobiles are good. That is the way I feel about printing, as long as printing prints words I like them

Page two: written on verso of letter from Van Vechten:

> when they print my words I like it best naturally enough but all words have to be printed and I like it when it is printing. To be sure I do have feelings about margins I do not like big ones, I like little ones, you might say that—that is natural as I like words to be printed and when the margins are big you have

Page three: written on sheet of lined paper:

> less of them, I must say I liked enormously the printing of the Geographical History of America, its about the best printing I have seen of a purely commercial book, but even aside from ~~in~~ with big margins there being less words than with little ones I like the way it looks best with very small ones, I have even dreamed that there might be none, but then it would not be a book, and then ~~I like~~ I made Maurice Darantiere print one with almost none, and

[549]

Page four: written on recto of letter received from a French correspondent from Virieu le Grand, dated 5 June 1937.

> it was a book, Let me see what else about printing when I was very very young my brother and I had a printing press a very little one but we never did get to do any more than print visiting cards I do not think we ever printed any words that were not names and never since then have I done any printing. American books look very different from English and certainly from french ones, I wonder which I like best, naturally American ones.

Always,
Gtde Stein

Stein often wrote drafts of letters, particularly if she was formulating a critical idea or responding to specific questions. These drafts were written in small carnets, the cahiers she used for her compositions, or on loose sheets of paper—often the verso of letters she had received. I have not located the final draft of this letter nor do I know its recipient.

To Carl Van Vechten

[postmark: 2 June 1937]   Bilignin par Belley
                                                           Ain

Dear Papa Woojums

I am sending you this boy's letter because it pleases me so much that they are discovering you, he is not an uninteresting boy he wants to do an anthology of my things and he has some good ideas what do you think about that[1] and what is the autobiography of yours that he talks about, Bennett [Cerf] was to give you the ms. of mine long ago what has happened you were to have it and then Thornton [Wilder] but neither of you have, it bothers me because I will not know until you have had it,[2] we are all peaceful the weather funny but everything else calm, Gerald [Berners] comes next Wednesday again I wish you could be here to meet wth much love

Gertrude.

1. In a letter to Stein, 1 May 1937 (YCAL), Haas proposed the idea of an anthology of Stein's writings. Haas also mentioned to Stein an idea that had often been discussed by Van Vechten's friends, a Van Vechten autobiography.

2. Stein's *Everybody's Autobiography*.

[550]

To Gertrude Stein
[Postcard: Victorian Cushion. Photograph by Carl Van Vechten]

16 June [1937]   [101 Central Park West
                                                 New York]

Did you ever see Basket on a cushion, dear Baby Woojums, or maybe I sent you this before.[1] Pepe in the ballet was ravishing & exactly like himself! Have you got Miss [Florence] Dixon's package? Fania is off tomorrow for a DUDE RANCH in Montana & we both send lots of love to you & Mama Woojums![2]

Papa W

1. See Stein to Van Vechten [26 June 1937], note 1.
2. Marinoff spent a month at the Ox Yoke Ranch, Emigrant, Montana.

To Gertrude Stein

22 June 1937   101 Central Park West
                                                 New York City

Dear Baby Woojums,

At LONG LAST, Bennett [Cerf] let me read the manuscript, over a weekend as the Atlantic had to have it back, and it seems to me that Everybody's Autobiography is one of your finest works. It is not as amusing or as gossipy as the Alice B Toklas opus, but it is much more of an integrated work of art and much more in line with the rest of your work. Don't you agree with me? I think you give the effect of living it as you write it; it all flows with your consciousness and the reader is exhausted[x] by YOUR vitality. I am sure this work will have a most notable success, whatever the press, which is unimportant. I am pretty sure, however, you can count on a good press!

Bennett wants me to illustrate it with photographs. Of course I have hundreds which are suitable, but you may not like the idea at all and if you don't, PLEASE SAY SO. If you do, I think Thornton Wilder and the Kiddie (I don't even know this number's name) ought to be in it and so if you will tell me where I can find the former and will write the latter to write to me and arrange to come to NYC some time, maybe with his uniform, that would be swell.[1]

Fania has gone to a Dude Ranch in Montana for a month, the servants are away, and I am alone in the house. I have taken many interesting photographs lately, Thomas Mann, Thomas Wolfe, and Scott Fitzgerald, among others. I told George[s Jacques] (at the Algonquin) he was in the book and he nearly DIED with pleasure.

my warmest enthusiasm and my heartiest congratulations and lots of love to you and Mama Woojums,

Carlo!

[x]pleasantly!

1. William Garland Rogers was a doughboy attached to the Amherst College Ambulance Unit in 1917 when he first met Stein and Toklas and they christened him "the Kiddie" (see Gallup, *The Flowers of Friendship*, pp. 121–22). Stein and Rogers exchanged a few letters between 1917 and 1919 and then they lost contact.

　　After Rogers read *The Autobiography of Alice B. Toklas* he wrote to Stein again (see Gallup, *The Flowers of Friendship*, pp. 273–74) and reminded her of their meeting and the trip that they had taken to visit various sites around Nîmes, France: Orange, Les Baux, and Arles, among others.

To Carl Van Vechten

[postmark: 26 June 1937]　　　　　　　　　　　　[Bilignin par Belley
　　　　　　　　　　　　　　　　　　　　　　　　Ain]

My dearest Papa Woojums,

That was sweet to send Basket on a cushion,[1] he has poor darling been suffering slightly from an inferiority complex since everybody has been so pleased and occupied with Pepe first on the stage and now on a carpet,

Gerald Berners has just drawn Pepe's head on a carpet for Alice to tapestry, and so Basket says thank you papa Woojums for the kind attention which was much needed and much appreciated. Gerald leaves us to-day I wish you knew each other you would please each other, we now live dreams of the Wedding Bouquet being done by the New York ballet people, Bobsy Goodspeed who is wandering around with Mary Garden in the course of the great many long distance telephones thinks she can persuade an Eddie something who is at the head of it,[2] alas not Eddie Wassermann because if it were he then it would be sure, is he in New York, he has been so sweet to us sending us Camel Pens and postal cards but never an address, Heineman is printing the autobiography in England apparently very enthusiastic, and we are trying to sell it beside as a serial, what has happened to Bennett [Cerf] he is not in love again is he, not a word from him, not a thing about what he is to do with the book or as a serial or anything and whether there are to be photos, nothing not a word, what has happened to him, nothing but good I hope, I have started a pleasing novel called Ida a novel, I think you will like it I hope it goes on and is a novel I always do want to write one so much love and so much much love[3]

Baby Woojums.

1. Note by Van Vechten, 24 January 1941: "a photograph of a Victorian blue velvet cushion with a raised poodle in white kid."

2. Edward M. Warburg, who, with Lincoln Kirstein and George Balanchine, had founded in 1934 the American Ballet (this company subsequently became: the Ballet Caravan, American Ballet Caravan, and Ballet Society; it eventually developed into the New York City Ballet).

3. Stein struggled with *Ida A Novel*, off and on for the next three years.

To Carl Van Vechten

[postmark: 30 June 1937]   [Bilignin par Belley
                                             Ain]

My dear Papa Woojums,

I am pleased you like it, you really truly do like it do you not, I think it is a noble kind of book if you know what I mean, anyway that is the way

I feel about it, I am sending you some suggestions for the illustrations and then will you send some more, the kiddy is Mr. William Rogers, Springfield Union, Springfield, Mass. I am writing him that you will write to him Thornton [Wilder] is already gone, he is to be with us, the first of August, love to you and to you always and always, and I am so glad you do like it and it will be a success won't it, you always know, so much love

Gtrde.[1]

Suggestions.

Frontispiece, Bilignin with me and Basket and the little house, the lovely photo.

Then I think there ought to be the one taken by some newspaper man of you and Alice and me starting on the aeroplane, I think you have one of these, then I think there ought to be a good one of the decor of 4 Saints, perhaps one of St. Ignatius only it would be too many to do a St. Theresa too and you could not do one without the other, one of the ballet, and one of Gerald Berners and me, he can tend to that, and one of the marionette play, the three small photos and then some newspaper ones a page of them, the three heads they did when we came, the little one on the boat when we arrived the kiddy is in that, and you saying goodby to us on the boat, Then I would like the one you took in William and Mary where you can't see me, and the ones of us at Edgar Allen Poe, Bennett [Cerf] suggests 16 pictures, so that leaves about six more, oh yes the one that suggested St. Therese, on the Blvd. Raspail, what else do you think of.

---

1. Note by Van Vechten, 24 January 1941, typed on a pink index card (3 × 5 inches) and attached to this letter:

> When Bennett Cerf got ready to publish Everybody's Autobiography, he asked me if I would illustrate the book with my photographs I agreed with pleasure, provided the idea was satisfactory to Gertrude. I wrote her to this effect. Her reply indicated either that she didn't understand me or that the idea didn't please her. It was as near to a misunderstanding as we have ever been and, fortunately, it was not very near. However, I told Bennett that I wouldn't do the illustrations unless *exclusively my* photographs were used. And he said he wouldn't publish the book with the photographs she had sent over and asked to have him use. I suppose he wrote and cabled her. Anyway, she came round. She started to illustrate the English edition according to her original plan, but eventually they persuaded her to use the American illustrations (mine). Not very difficult, because, of course, she really liked them, ONLY her idea was to make the illustrations more inclusive of the text, a good idea if good photographs had existed of all the subjects she proposed.

[554]

To Gertrude Stein

6 July 1937   [101 Central Park West
                                                New York]

[. . .]¹ You will hear doubtless SOON from Bennett [Cerf].² I think he was waiting to see what the Atlantic would do. You have heard from ME by now. . Fania is on a DUDE RANCH, wandering up and down mountains on bucking bronchos [i.e., broncos]. I am in the City getting eaten (at least my clothes are) by moths. If you want the photographs in my book be sure to send me the kiddie's name and address and write to him too and also Thornton Wilder. . But maybe you won't like the plan at all. It is certainly a nice book WITHOUT photographs and whether they would ADD to it is for Baby Woojums to decide. . If they ARE used I would suggest that my name not be on the title page at all (I should think Bennett would find this sensible) but over a table of photographic contents like this: "Photographs by Carl Van Vechten may be found facing the following pages". NOT ONE WORD from Marie L Bousquet! I'm so sorry to miss meeting Lord Berners. Maybe later. And so glad to have sent a postcard in time to save Basket's FACE.

Love to you both,
Papa Woojums!

1. The top portion of this letter has been torn off.

2. Cerf had written to Stein on 22 April 1937 (YCAL) that he was sending pages from *Everybody's Autobiography* to *The Atlantic Monthly*. On 21 June 1937 (YCAL) Cerf wrote that *The Atlantic Monthly* was going to take only one excerpt from the book. On 29 June 1937 (YCAL) Cerf wrote again to clarify the information.

❧

To Gertrude Stein

10 July 1937   101 Central Park West
                                          New York City

Dearest Baby Woojums,

Of course, you are right about the pictures. They should be all kinds and all sorts and certainly Lord Berners and the Ballet and Florine [Stettheimer]'s set and [Thornton] Wilder and lots of things I haven't taken should be in. . I got carried away by my enthusiasm after Bennett [Cerf] suggested I illustrate the book and wanted to make the pictures the best and most beautiful possible, but YOUR idea is the more appropriate. . But, dear Baby W, I wouldn't want you to use only the pictures of mine you suggest, as they have very little interest as photographs and everybody would say CVV's are the least interesting in the book. So I'm glad it's all settled so far ahead before I really got involved in printing etc. . .

Of course, I love the book. So does Bennett. We had a brief talk before I had really digested your letter, but I told him certainly Baby Woojums way was the BEST. .[1]

Love to you both,
Papa W.[2]

1. When *Everybody's Autobiography* was published, the American and British editions used the same illustrations, photographs by Van Vechten: Stein wearing the dress in which she delivered her American lectures; Stein and Basket and Pepe on the terrace in Bilignin; Lucey Church, near Stein's summer home at Bilignin; W. G. Rogers of Springfield, Massachusetts; Alice B. Toklas at Bilignin; Beatrice Robinson-Wayne as Saint Theresa in *Four Saints in Three Acts*; Stein at the center of a discussion at William and Mary College; Edward Matthews as Saint Ignatius in *Four Saints in Three Acts*.

2. At the bottom of this letter are two drafts of a telegram to Van Vechten. The first is in Toklas' hand: "Happy Book ~~completely exclusively~~ entirely illustrated by Carl." The second draft is in Stein's hand: "Delighted have only Carl photographs ~~pleased~~ Just Carl's photos will be right." See Stein to Van Vechten, 21 July 1937, for the text of the telegram sent.

$\aleph$

To Carl Van Vechten

[postmark: 14 July 1937]   [Bilignin par Belley
                                             Ain]

My dearest Papa Woojums,

Freddy Ashton and the two principal dancers have been staying with us and we had lots of fun, and if you could only have been here to photograph us, we all at last bought ourselves a 35 franc camera and these were my efforts, I wish you had been here to really truly do us, when we were at [Abbaye D'] Hautecombe, Bobby Helpmann, the Bridegroom, by changing his hair and put[t]ing on a filet made himself into Mme Recamier, in the beautiful couch in the Royal Apartments, he was very beautiful, they are a sweet trio and we did enjoy them, and what I liked best is that you have always been the literary idol of Bobby and Willie [Chappell], they knew all your books and they love you and that made us love them just that much more.[1] By this time you have all my ideas about the illustrations and I think it is going to be lovely, the English edition will probably be illustrated too and as soon as I know about that I will let you know, of course I want your name everywhere just as much as possible are you not all of it but of course yes, we are having a very lively summer, Thornton [Wilder] is alas already over here so you cannot take him but he might be back in time, he is to come here the first of August and then I will let you know, Marie Louise [Bousquet] is not a ready writer, we don't hear either but Bobsy Goodspeed says she is a little low in her mind from the letdown after America, Mme Clermont-Tonnerre has written an amusing book about the Eiffel tower and the rest is love[2]

                                             Gtrde.[3]

1. Robert Helpmann, who danced the role of the Bridegroom, and William Chappell, who danced the role of John in addition to being responsible for executing Lord Berners' costumes and decor for A *Wedding Bouquet*.

2. Elisabeth de Gramont, *Mémoires de la tour Eiffel* (Paris: Bernard Grasset, 1937).

3. Enclosed with the letter were four snapshots: Frederick Ashton and Toklas; Ashton, Robert Helpmann, and William Chappell; William Chappell, and Robert Helpmann dressed to resemble an Arab woman.

To Carl Van Vechten

[postmark: 20 July 1937]   [Bilignin par Belley
                                                            Ain]

My dearest Papa Woojums,

Bennett [Cerf] has just written me about the pictures,[1] and now I have one more idea if it pleases you, would it not be a good idea to do a photo of Miss [Florine] Stettheimer and Virgil [Thomson] together with the model of a saint between them or in their hands,[2] do you think it would be nice for you to do it, and one of course of St. Ignatius I must add that to the list, the one I want as the frontispiece is the one you sent me several of, the little house the view of the valley and my sitting on the terrace with a stick and Basket beside me, the one I think the most beautiful photo ever taken. I am getting Georges Maratier to send the one of all of us in the aeroplane and I will try to find the one of you saying good-by but somebody if not can find it in the newspaper of the day after our departure, I think it is going to be lovely just too lovely, I wish you were here to take us all again, how we do wish that, dear dearest papa Woojums, tell Fania to be careful, and you be careful of moths Mike [Stein] used to say that now there are no more candles or lamps sometime the world would be eaten up by moths,[3] lots and lots of love

Gtrde.

1. Cerf to Stein, 9 July 1937 (YCAL), suggested twelve photographs.

2. Note by Van Vechten, 24 July [i.e., January] 1941: "Not as simple as that, Florine Stettheimer always refused to be photographed."

3. See Van Vechten to Stein, 6 July 1937.

Gertrude Stein and Basket I on the terrace at Bilignin, 13 June 1934.
PHOTOGRAPH BY CARL VAN VECHTEN. PRIVATE COLLECTION.

To Carl Van Vechten
[Postal Telegraph]

21 July 1937   Belley

PAPA WOOJAMS ALWAYS RIGHT BOOK ONLY PERFECT WITH PAPAS PERFECT PICTURES ONLY

BABY.

To Carl Van Vechten

[postmark: 22 July 1937]   [Bilignin par Belley
                                                      Ain]

My dearest Papa Woojums,

Never never did it enter my head that you were going to print photographs for all the thousands of volumes which we hope it will be actual photographs I took it for granted that it was going to be reproductions, but we never thought of it being your own photographs printed by your own self if we had of course it would never have been possible that it should be any other ones with yours never but I stupidly thought of them as commercial reproductions being always accustomed to that in books and never never never would I have dreamed that even my own papa woojums would do that for this,[1] I do hope by this time you have forgiven and forgotten and have just gone right on printing just as it was going to be, do send me a wire to say it is alright because I will not be easy in my mind until I hear, you can see how it was not for a moment grasped not by either of us and so of course well of course but now it is alright and now I understand all I did not understand in your first letter and the table of contents and everything of course I understand now and I am so pleased and proud that you will do all of them and each one of them just the way you do even if it goes to hundreds

[560]

of thousands a thing nobody but you in your magnificence could dream of doing and you know now I love you always

Gtrde.

1. Note by Van Vechten, 24 January 1941: "Of course it wasn't my idea or Bennett's to print photographs to go in Eveybody's Autobiography, a fantasy of Gertrude's."

To Gertrude Stein

1 August [1937] 101 Central Park West
New York City

Why, my wonderful Baby Woojums, how did I ever give you that idea? I must have written some very clumsy English. It would be marvellous if we could do it, but I would have to print night and day for eight or nine months and I would have to print over 40,000 photographs and it would cost thousands and thousands! So everything is just where it was: i.e., your original idea is the right one, as it includes Thornton W[ilder] and Lord Berners etc. etc. and if Bennett [Cerf] argues with you remember he argues with me too, as this idea of having Papa W illustrate the book was his, and you must have the book exactly as you like it and so I tell him and tell him. After your sweet cable came I didn't feel sure of exactly what you meant till your letter came and then I couldn't cable you as you asked me to because I didn't want to cable I WASN'T going to print 40,000 pictures and I didn't know what else to cable and tell Mama Woojums if we all lived in the same town none of these things would happen . . .

So I am sending you photo-doodles from Life this week.[1] AND a girl named Margery Sharp has written a novel coming out soon (Little, Brown) called The Nutmeg Tree and it is laid in Belley and there is lots about the Pernollet and the Landscape and Aix[-les-Bains], but not a word about Baby Woojums. Do you know this lady? O yes, she has plenty to say about Brillat-Savarin.[2] Mabel [Dodge] has another one in the fall too: this one about Taos and Tony [Luhan], AT LAST.[3]

About Florine [Stettheimer] and Virgil [Thomson], Virgil isn't here and Florine is NEVER photographed, Hélas! At the moment she is in Canada avec ses soeurs.

At last I heard from Marie Louise [Bousquet], a sensational letter, so sweet! Really if she writes letters like that she should write 'em every day. .[4]

1001 bright stars to you and Mama Woojums and love from Papa Woojums also known as

Carlo!

Did Bibi Dudensing get that Dixon girl's presents to you? What do you think of [Louis] Eilshemius, if any?[5]

1. Van Vechten sent Stein what were labeled as the "thoughtful doodlings of Albert Hirschfeld, New York caricaturist." Hirschfeld had done caricatures transforming Stein into Albert Einstein, Harold Ross into Joseph Stalin, and Mary Pickford into Adolf Hitler, among others. See *Life*, 2 August 1937, pp. 6, 7, 9.

2. Margery Sharp, *The Nutmeg Tree* (Boston: Little, Brown and Co., 1937).

3. Mabel Dodge Luhan, *Edge of Taos Desert; Volume Four of Intimate Memories* (New York: Harcourt, Brace and Co., 1937).

4. This letter is not in YCAL.

5. Louis Eilshemius (1864–1941) was an eccentric painter who lived on East Fifty-seventh Street for fifty years. He went unrecognized until the late 1930s. Van Vechten owned several works by Eilshemius. Van Vechten's "Neglected Genius of Fifty-seventh Street" (*New York Herald Tribune of Books*, 12 November 1939, p. 4), is a review of William Schack's *And He Sat among the Ashes; a Biography of Louis M. Eilshemius*.

To Carl Van Vechten
[Cablegram]

3 August 1937   Belley

ALL UPSET CANNOT SLEEP PLEASE CABLE YOU FORGIVE MAKE MY HAPPINESS BY GIVING ME PHOTOGRAPHS DO KNOW NOW THEY MAKE BOOK

GERTRUDE

❦

To Gertrude Stein
[Telegram]

[postmark: 5 August 1937]   New York

all love to baby Woojums

papa Woojums

❦

To Carl Van Vechten
[Postcard]

[postmark: 17 August 1937]   Bilignin par Belley
Ain, France

Dearest Papa Woojums,

The Kiddy [W. G. Rogers] has come and says you did a photo of him in Central Park and that will be nice and I am as happy as happy can be that all your photos will be there with me, and I just want you alone, I do I do, and I am so happy that it will be all just like that, will Bennett [Cerf] not be in, just as you think best but of course that would please me and a lovely one of Papa Woojums, and a lovely one of every one. I was so happy that we went gambling at Aix[-les-Bains], the first time I had ever been in the inside of one, and I won 4 times on the nose, that is what they told me to say and everything is happy and I love Papa W. enormously

always
B. W.

❧

To Carl Van Vechten
[Postcard: Le Thor Vaucluse)—L'Eglise)

[postmark: 27 August 1937]   [Bilignin par Belley
                                               Ain]

We just had a lovely trip through Avignon and everywhere looking up everybody we knew during the war, St. Remy was lovely how we would like to show it to you and living in a walled town is the most cheerful thing you can do just now, it was lovely so much love from M. W. and B. W. to P. W. now and always[1]

Gtrde.

1. In a letter to Stein, 4 March [1937] (YCAL), Rogers wrote that he and his wife, Mildred Weston, were planning a trip to Europe. In an undated letter, probably in May 1937 (YCAL), Rogers wrote: "[T]here's only one thing I really want. And that is to go back to Arles and Orange and Les Baux with Gertrude Stein and Alice B. Toklas and Mrs. Kiddie." See Van Vechten to Stein, 22 June 1937, note 1.

Rogers and his wife sailed for France on the *Normandie* on 4 August and remained in Europe until 8 September. They spent a few days with Stein in Bilignin and then went on what Rogers termed their "sentimental journey." Rogers wrote of his first meeting with Stein in 1917 and of their 1937 trip together in *When This You See Remember Me: Gertrude Stein in Person* (New York: Rinehart, 1948), pp. 9–19.

❧

To Gertrude Stein
*[Postcard: "Happiness"—painting by Mary Bell. Photograph by
Carl Van Vechten]*

27 August 1937   [101 Central Park West
                                               New York]

Dearest Baby Woojums:

I took the pix to Bennett [Cerf] yesterday & we selected & picked out & chose. Donald [Klopfer] aiding & naturally there had to be some compromises, because we are only using 8, but I hope you will be pleased with the result. The one you like so much comes out too small in a book, but I think you will like the one we have picked instead. . l[ove] & k[isses] to Mama W & you

Papa W.

I am so happy you were *good* damsels at AIX[-les Bains]!

🐿

To Gertrude Stein and Alice Toklas
[Postcard: Portrait of W. G. Rogers. Photograph by Carl Van Vechten][1]

29 August [1937]   [101 Central Park West
                                              New York]

Dear Mama & Baby Woojums.

Love from the "Kiddie" & Papa Woojums

1. This is the photograph referred to in Stein to Van Vechten [17 August 1937].

🐿

To Carl Van Vechten

[postmark: 3 September 1937]   Bilignin par Belley
                                              Ain

Dear Dearest dearest Papa Woojums,

Oh I am as happy as happy can be it is going to be our book, papa Woojums is the only papa Woojums and he is always right, the book is all full of Papa Woojums, as he is always right, and it is going to be a heavenly book, there will be lots and lots of pictures and I just suddenly had a feeling about how beautiful it is going to be, and I am as happy as happy can be,

[565]

the first book illustrated about M. Carl Van Vechten consecration of the loves of Papa Woojums and Baby Woojums, and anything else would be impossible, I know that, I just was off my head on account of the ballet business but that would have been all wrong, Do you realize what a beautiful everyone book it is going to be all you and all me, it makes tears come to my eyes when I think about it and how happy I am, we have been having a very busy summer, quantities of people and for the first time a refrigerator and Alice would love to make you and Fania ice-cream in it, we have a french one now which does not work well but we are going to have a Westinghouse to-morrow, do you remember the lady in Virginia whose father said he sat and let the pine-trees grow, she writes to me that Mark Lutz wants a job in Paris for the autumn, there is of course only one newspaper there now the Herald but as they change their men very frequently I guess there would be no trouble I am writing to him,[1] we xpect to-day the young man Sam Steward who wrote Angels on the Bough,[2] the kiddies have left, we had a wonderful sentimental journey to all the beauty spots we saw together in 1917–18, we had lovely weather and a lovely time and we sang the trail of the lonesome pine together they brought me a copy of it and we even got the french people here including 84 year old Madame Pierlot to join in the chorus,[3] in the mountains of Virginia where Papa Woojums and his ladies were together, well anyway I am happy and you know how happy I am, we also have been seeing a lot of funny french female writers who would amuse you, when Mark comes and you come to see us and Mark we will show them too, oh Carl I am so happy always your own

Baby Woojums.

1. Stein wrote to Lutz [postmark 3 September 1937, NYPL-Berg], repeating the information she had written in this letter to Van Vechten about the possibilities of Lutz finding a job in Paris. Lutz replied to Stein, 18 September 1937 (YCAL), that what Stein had heard was not true, that he did not intend to come to Paris. Mrs. Muncie's letter is not in YCAL, so it cannot be determined whether she was incorrect or whether Stein misunderstood her letter. See Stein to Van Vechten [29 September 1937]. Note by Van Vechten, 24 January 1941: "He didn't."

2. Samuel M. Steward began corresponding with Stein in 1933 when he wrote to inform her of the death of Clarence E. Andrews, a professor of English at Ohio State University. It was Andrews, who had had a brief correspondence with Stein in the 1920s, who had introduced Steward to Stein's writings.

When Stein visited America in 1934–35, Steward unsuccessfully tried to arrange for her to lecture at Carroll College in Helena, Montana, where he was teaching.

Steward had sent Stein his novel, *Angels on the Bough* (Caldwell, Ida.: The Caxton

Printers, 1936). This trip to Bilignin was Steward's first meeting with Stein. See Steward, ed., *Dear Sammy: Letters from Gertrude Stein & Alice Toklas* (Boston: Houghton Mifflin Co., 1977).

3. Stein's favorite song.

To Carl Van Vechten

[postmark: 8 September 1937]   Bilignin par Belley
                                                         Ain

My dearest Papa Woojums,

I am just as happy as happy can be and writing to you on this brand new writing paper to tell you so,[1] oh I am happy and so xcited to know which eight were chosen please please give us the list, Alice and I have been guessing which and we are so xcited, or do you want us to wait and see we will if you think that will be more of a thrill, golly it's hot, but lovely, do you know about Sam Steward the man who wrote Angels on the Bough and then they threw him out of the University of Washington where he was teaching and Loyola at Chicago took him in,[2] well anyway he is staying with us we like him and he is sending you his book as soon as he gets back to Chicago, I think you would like him, the kiddie's picture is magnificent he'll be awfully pleased as we are,[3] they are in London now at a hotel where he says it is very nice xcept if you shave yourself because the light is in one place the mirror in another and the hot water in a third, but that is London oh Papa Woojums I am just as happy as I can be and that is pretty happy

Baby W.

1. A blue paper, 8½ × 11 inches, with the address printed at the top. some of the paper has the address in white type, some in a dark blue type.

2. Steward, who had been teaching at the State College of Washington, Pullman, Washington, had been dismissed because the college president deemed his novel, *Angels on the Bough*, "racy."

3. Note by Van Vechten, 24 January 1941: "W. G. Rogers of Springfield, Mass. whose picture appears in the autobiography [i.e., *Everybody's Autobiography*]."

To Gertrude Stein
[Postcard: Alice Toklas at Bilignin. Photograph by Carl Van Vechten]

16 September [19]37   [101 Central Park West
                                                     New York]

Dearest Baby Woojums. .

The reason I didn't tell you *what* pictures is I *knew* some would be changed because they wouldn't reproduce or weren't the right size or something & sure enough that happened & may happen again! So better [to] be surprised than disappointed! I hope you will be pleased with the *final* layout! Mabel [Dodge] has a new one: "Edge of Taos Desert" all about how she got Tony [Luhan]!

l[ove] & k[isses] to both.
Papa W.

To Gertrude Stein
[Postcard: Beatrice Robinson-Wayne as Saint Theresa in Four Saints in Three Acts. Photograph by Carl Van Vechten]

21 September [1937]   [101 Central Park West
                                                     New York]

Dear Baby Woojums,

Fania is playing Charmian in Antony and Cleopatra with Tallulah Bankhead—Virgil [Thomson] is writing the music for the production.

No more news of the book yet. . The Atlantic sent me an advance copy of the part they are going to publish & I thought this was most skillfully put together.

Lots of love to you both.

!Carlo! and Papa Woojums!

The Legionnaires have been marching all day & you never saw so many people & I [guess we love soldiers?]!

Carlo

To Carl Van Vechten

[postmark: 21 September 1937]   Bilignin par Belley
                                                 Ain

My dearest Carl

Here is Daniel Webster, I think it is quite funny I hope you will like it,[1] it is to be put in the archives, the Yale people have proposed to me to put my original ms. in their care, of course it would be very nice because there they would be safe as the Yale library has a big foundation for original ms. but suppose sometime I should want to sell one, I might need it sometime, I mean I might need to sell, most probably nobody would want to buy anyway it is flattering because they seem to want them,[2] then there has been a comedy of errors, the printer took out of the ms. of Everybody's [Autobiography] all the underlined things which were what the Atlantic was using and I had a fit and then detectively I found out what the matter was and so all these things happen and Daniel Rops[3] was here the french writer and we talked of you and he said he wished you would write some more he said all the french writers liked your things he said il a du talent cette homme, and then he said no wonder he makes such wonderful photographs what wonderful paper he has and then he said once more il a du talent cette homme, everybody is happy and terribly looking forward to November, to see them all dear darling Papa Woojums I love you so I appreciate you so and I do do thank you for everything

Baby W.

1. Enclosed with this letter was the 28-page typescript, with authorial corrections, of Stein's *Daniel Webster. Eighteen in America: A Play*. The piece was published in *New Directions in Prose & Poetry 1937* (Norfolk, Conn.: New Directions, 1937), pp. [162–88]. See Stein to Van Vechten [6 March 1937].

2. For the history of the founding of the Gertrude Stein Collection at the Yale University Library see Donald Gallup, "The Gertrude Stein Collection," in *The Yale University Library*

Gazette (October 1947), 22(2):[21]–32, and Norman Holmes Pearson, "The Gertrude Stein Collection," in *The Yale University Library Gazette* (January 1942), 16(3):[45]–47.

3. Henri Daniel-Rops was the pseudonym of Jean-Charles Henry Petiot (1901–1965). Daniel-Rops was a writer, historian, and teacher. He spent most of his professional career teaching in Paris, but he maintained a country home at Rothonod, a tiny village one kilometer from Belley. Stein had met Daniel-Rops through the Baronne Pierlot, who lived in Béon, not far from Belley.

Daniel-Rops had written Van Vechten on 20 December 1934 (YCAL) asking permission to reproduce photographs of *Four Saints in Three Acts* in the review *Eccleria*, which he edited. Although he read and spoke English, it is possible that he had read only the three Van Vechten novels that had appeared in French translation: *Nigger Heaven*, *Spider Boy*, and *The Tattooed Countess*.

To Carl Van Vechten
[Postcard]

[postmark: 29 September 1937]   [Bilignin par Belley Ain]

Dear Papa Woojums

I am delighted about Fania and Virgil [Thomson] Thornton [Wilder] told us a lot about Tallulah Bankhead and I got awfully interested, and Fania will make a lovely Charmian, and it will be lots of fun,[1] I wish they would do Daniel Webster in Hollywood and then we could come over we are lonesome for you, as it says in the Trail of the Lonesome Pine, I wrote to Mrs. [Lillian May] Ehrman and told her to tell them it was funny like Pinafore, and would they buy it sight unseen,[2] I am writing an American novel called Ida,[3] it begins well, but then it begins to get too funny and one must not be too funny, I have not seen the Atlantic advance yet, the sun is shining and they are picking all the grapes, and then there will be wine, had a nice letter from Mark Lutz, he says it's his brother who is coming not he, the lady whose father watches the pine trees grow got it mixed, we love you more than any tongues can tell

Baby W.

That's a lovely head of Alice is it going to be in and the Saint Theresa.[4] Well I must not ask but it will be lovely and I am so xcited and Papa Woojums is a darling.

[570]

1. Note by Van Vechten, 24 January 1941: "Fania Marinoff played Charmian with Tallulah Bankhead in Anthony and Cleopatra."

2. Mrs. Ehrman and her brother, Ivan Kahn, were still hoping to interest a film producer in Stein's work. See Ehrman to Stein, 11 July 1937 (YCAL).

3. Stein's *Ida A Novel*, published by Random House in 1941.

4. The photograph of Toklas that Van Vechten used as a postcard to Stein, 16 September [1937], was used in *Everybody's Autobiography*. In the book Van Vechten used a different photograph of Beatrice Robinson-Wayne from the one he used as his postcard to Stein of 21 September [1937].

To Carl Van Vechten
[Postcard: Segl-Maria]

[postmark: 5 October 1937]   [Bilignin par Belley
                                                                  Ain]

That is a wonderful photo of the kiddie,[1] it makes him a missing Lincoln and just what is the sadness of America and its [sweetness?] I am awfully interested in it, and trying to do it in Ida, I am awfully xcited about the book, I just can't wait to see it our book and I am so happy

B. W.

1. The photograph of William G. Rogers, "the Kiddie," that Van Vechten used as a postcard to Stein, 29 August [1937], was reproduced in *Everybody's Autobiography*.

To Gertrude Stein
[Postcard: Beatrice Robinson-Wayne as Saint Theresa in Four Saints in Three Acts. Photograph by Carl Van Vechten]

7 October [1937]   [101 Central Park West
                                                                 New York]

Dear Gertrude:

Daniel Webster is here & I must say I LOVE HIM. Maybe Virgil [Thomson] someday will make an opera of this. He ought to! Did I tell you

Fania is playing Charmian in Antony & Cleopatra with Tallulah Bankhead? And Virgil is doing the incidental music. They open Oct. 15 in Rochester & go to Alabama before coming to NYC. . I also recieved Sam Steward's Book[1] and a letter, & a WONDERFUL LETTER from the Kiddie who is *fou* about his pictures.[2] If Thornton Wilder would only come to get photographed he could get in the NEXT BOOK. Really DW & the EIGHTEEN in AMERICA is DIVINE and so are my Baby and Mama Woojums!

> *l[ove] & k[isses] always*
> *Papa W!*

Isn't this a pretty stamp?[3]

1. Steward's novel *Angels on the Bough*.

2. Rogers wrote Van Vechten, 4 October [1937] (YCAL), how pleased he was with the photograph Van Vechten had taken.

3. The stamp was a 3-cent Constitutional Sesquicentennial, 1787–1937, stamp.

❧

To Gertrude Stein
[Postcard: Portrait of Nora Holt. Photograph by Carl Van Vechten]

[postmark: 12 October 1937] [101 Central Park West
New York]

Dear Baby Woojums,

A marvellous postcard from you all about this & that. .[1] Yes, they should do Daniel W[ebster] in Hollywood & they will do it somewhere, I am sure. I met a boy named Dwight Godwin in Harlem last night & he has been studying Ballet at Sadler's Wells & he LOVED & LOVED—the Stein-Berners opus!—[2]

> *Love to both*
> *Papa W!*

[572]

1. Stein to Van Vechten [29 September 1937].

2. A *Wedding Bouquet.*

❦

To Carl Van Vechten

[postmark: 16 October 1937]   Bilignin par Belley
                                               Ain

My dear Papa Woojums

I am awfully happy that you liked Daniel Webster, I have a dream of its being done in Hollywood, with Virgil [Thomson] or Gerald [Berners] or somebody to do the music not xactly an opera, and Freddie Ashton who could make it go funny and real and it would be lots of fun, and give us an xcuse to go to America, to put it on, and it might be a great success, because and this is what because Papa Woojums could tell them just what to do to make it do really something, you see that's what I dream of if you did it, and I think all of us together out there could have a wonderful time and do something, is there any producer, I could write to out there and tell him he ought to have us, you know Carl I do think we could do something there together, I get quite thrilled about it, and Heinemann wants your photos for the book the English edition,[1] and I hope you are pleased with that because I am and I am so happy I am xcited I want to see the book, and I think it would be wonderful if all the Woojums together did Daniel Webster we love you all the time

Baby Woojums.

1. The English edition of Stein's *Everybody's Autobiography.*

To Carl Van Vechten
[Rose motto]

[postmark: 1 November 1937]   27 rue de Fleurus
[Paris]

My dearest Papa Woojums,

Once more at home and waiting to tell you all about, yesterday at the Bromfields [Main Bocher?][1] and I talked about you and Fania and we talked and we talked and when we said good-by I said to him well you are the only person I have ever met who loves Carl almost as much as I do and he does, he says wonderful things about you, we were talking about your sweetness and he said, yes most people you have to take sweet slices of them and slices that are not so sweet, but Carl any slice of Carl has some of that sweetness, and that is rare, yes we did have a nice time talking about you, he was awfully pleased that Fania was going to do Charmian, Thornton [Wilder] is here, some day you will meet and you will understand he has a kind of complex of shyness about photography but once you know each other it will be alright, and surely you will meet over Cleopatra he is awfully fond of Talula [i.e., Tallulah Bankhead], just this now because I have to help making the home beautiful, oh dear we love you so and the book is out tomorrow our book,[2]

lots of love
Baby Woojums.

1. Main Rousseau Bocher, known as Main Bocher (1891–1976), was a fashion designer with salons in Paris and New York.

2. The official publication date of *Everybody's Autobiography* was 2 December 1937.

To Gertrude Stein
[Postcard: Renoir: On the Terrace]

3 November [1937]   [101 Central Park West
                                                 New York]

Dear Baby Woojums

So excited that you want my photographs for London. Bennet [Cerf] is writing of course you can have them. The *Book* should be out soon. My stepmother, age 91, (whom I went out to see, leaving you in Chicago in 1934) just died & I went out again. Illinois & Iowa farms incredibly beautiful! Yes I think Daniel Webster would make a wonderful book for a musical setting and maybe somebody *will* do it. I talk about these things & sometimes they happen. I saw an exhibit of Picasso at Seligman's yesterday & so much belonged or belongs to you.[1] I was quite homesick! Fania & I bought a picture by a new Spanish painter, Emilio Grau-Sala at the Pittsburgh show. He is in Paris (age 25) from Barcelona! Have you met him?

love to both
Papa W.

1. *Twenty Years in the Evolution of Picasso, 1903–1923*, an exhibition at Jacques Seligmann & Co., New York, 16 to 20 November 1937. Of the seventeen works in the exhibition only two had belonged to Stein: *Le Meneur de Cheval, Boy Leading a Horse*, Paris 1905–6, and *Tête de Garçon, Head of a Boy*, Paris, 1905.

To Gertrude Stein
[Postcard: TWA Skysleeper—Over New York Harbor]

9 November [1937]   [101 Central Park West
                                                 New York]

Dear Gertrude

I have a copy of Everybody's Autobiography and it is so beautiful. I hope you will like the pictures, dear Baby W! and your letter is here & how sweet of you & Louis [Bromfield] to talk & talk about Carlo & Fania O dear I wish Thornton W[ilder] would call me up! Leo Stein came to be photographed today. So I guess this is very historical. Is Mike [Stein] ever in NYC or give me his San F[rancisco] address. I might be there some time.

Love to both,
Papa Woojums.

A[ntony] & C[leopatra] tomorrow night opens here.

🦖

To Carl Van Vechten

[postmark: 11 November 1937]   27 rue de Fleurus
                                                [Paris]

My dearest Papa Woojums,

The jacket has come with us and the fetishes but not yet the book, we are so xcited we can hardly wait, but I suppose it just has to come soon now, Thornton Wilder was here and will be here again, he is taking over with him a quantity of my ms. to deposit in the Yale Library, to be safe, with the agreement that if I want to take them out in my life-time I can but at my death they become their property, he says he wants to see you and tell you all about it, he is awfully nice but dreadfully shy, and the other day, well I think he might want some of your ms. for the library, well anyway I suppose you have decided about that, well anyway he wants to meet you and the other day we dined with Elmer Harden and he spoke of you with so much enthusiasm, he said you were so nice to him over there,[1] and I am writing my first book in french,[2] an editor says my french pleases him and I am doing a little book about Picasso in french, he is courageous that editor, and there is a new young painter, who is xciting us all named Toulouse,[3] and I guess that is all xcept lots and lots of love

Baby W.

1. Harden was friendly with Van Vechten's friend Robert Locher. Presumably it was through Locher that Van Vechten and Harden met. See Stein to Van Vechten [5 August 1923].

2. Stein's *Picasso* was part of a series of art books, Anciens et Modernes, published by the Librairie Floury.

3. Robert Toulouse, a French-born painter, whom Stein met through the art dealers Georges Maratier and Edwin Livengood.

❧

To Carl Van Vechten

[postmark: 19 November 1937]   27 rue de Fleurus
                                                Paris

My dearest Papa Woojums

The book has come[1] and we are so xcited, the photographs are wonderful they just are, I think the one of Alice is perhaps the finest photo ever made, not [that] the others are not just as wonderful but Alice and Basket are perhaps the most wonderful, everybody here is crazy about them, I gave Georges Maratier who now has a picture gallery on the rue de Beaune a copy and he had [it] on the table and Picabia is having a show and everybody saw it and everybody was émerveilléed that is all there is to it they just were,[2] I think it is a beautiful book a fascinating book the words and the photographs all mingle together, it is our book and I am so happy I just can't tell you, there is so much to tell you and I will write another letter all about it, soon, and Thornton [Wilder] saw the photos and he is mad about them and everybody is so happy and we say and we say always God bless Papa Woojums,

Baby Woojums.

1. *Everybody's Autobiography.*

2. The exhibition, *Francis Picabia, peintures Dada, paysages récents,* was being held from 19 November to 2 December 1937 at the Galerie de Beaune, Paris. The gallery had recently been opened by Georges Maratier and an American Edwin Livengood. The brochure for this exhibition contained excerpts from statements about Picabia by Stein as well as Marcel Duchamp, André Breton, Jean van Heeckeren, Jean Cocteau, G. Ribemont-Dessaignes, Vivian du Mas, and Jacques-Henri Levesque.

§

To Gertrude Stein
[Postcard: TWA Skysleeper—Over New York Harbor]

[postmark: 25 November 1937]   [101 Central Park West
                                 New York]

Dear Baby Woojums,

I went in to see Charley Towne's portrait yesterday & he is NOT reading a book by GS & that is Henry [McBride]'s blague.[1] As a matter of fact the letters are obscure & you can't see what he *is* reading.

love to both
Papa W.

1. Charles Towne (1877–1949) was a writer and editor. I have been unable to locate the portrait Van Vechten refers to.

§

To Carl Van Vechten

[postmark: 25 November 1937]   27 rue de Fleurus
                                 [Paris]

My dearest Papa Woojums,

We are leaving rue de Fleurus for rue Christine, we are so xcited we can't see, the landlord said he wanted to put his son in and at one o'clock he told us and at 3 we had found a lovely apartment seventeenth century panelling, in the rue Christine ancient home of the Queen Christine daughter of Gustavus Adolphus, and it costs the same as this and it has a terrace roof in front of it, oh well we will be in it the 15 of January, and its address is 5 rue Christine, and we are so xcited, lots and lots of love[1]

Gtrde.

1. The afternoon that Stein had been told by her landlord that she must move, Stein went to visit Meraud Guevara, who was then living on the rue Dauphine. Mme Guevara had been

looking to move and so knew of many apartments in the quarter. It was she who took Stein to see the apartment at 5 rue Christine. (Personal interview with Meraud Guevara, Paris, 29 December 1982.)

To Gertrude Stein
[Postcard: Self-portrait in Top Hat. Photograph by Carl Van Vechten]

1 December [1937]   [101 Central Park West
                                                     New York]

Dear Baby Woojums,

I am so very happy you like the pictures in *your* book I wouldn't have it any other way. . Ask Mama Woojums to write me a letter about it. She hasn't written me *once* since she left America.

Lots of love.
Carlo Papa W.

To Carl Van Vechten
[Rose motto]

[postmark: 8 December 1937]   27 rue de Fleurus
                                                     [Paris]

My dearest Papa Woojums,

I am wanting to hear how our book is going to be liked in America, here everybody is most enthusiastic, the photos are lovely the book is lovely we are lovely oh happy Papa Woojums and Mama Woojums and Baby Woojums we are all just as happy as happy can be as happy more happy than any other three, that is the way we feel about it, I have corrected the proofs for the English edition,[1] I think they have arranged with Bennett [Cerf] about the photos, the last I heard they were arranging and they are quite crazy about them, and I have just finished my first french book, of course Alice has to do the grammar and the spelling and the tenses, but I do think it is going to sound pretty well, we are now selecting the photographs of the pictures to go with it, and then it will go to print, and then day and night we are furnishing our new home, it is 5 rue Christine, and in the spring you will come over and photograph it in and out, that will be such a happiness, we begin moving the 15 of January, and there is so much to do we think we may blow up and burst but we won't we will look forward to making it all lovely to be photographed by Papa Woojums. and the manuscripts I meant for Yale were yours not mine, Thornton [Wilder] is getting all the Americana there is for it, and one of yours would I know delight them, it is lovely Americana, no they have plenty of mine,[2] and Mike [Stein]'s address is 433 Kingsley Avenue Palo Alto. I am so sorry Cleopatra did not last out, send us some photos of Fania in it just the same she must have been charming and my we are xcited lots of love

Grtde.

1. There was one significant error that Stein corrected. In the Random House edition the first sentence of the book reads, "Alice B. Toklas did hers and now anybody will do theirs"; in the Heinemann edition the sentence is corrected to read, "Alice B. Toklas did hers and now *everybody* will do theirs" (emphasis added). In the Vintage paperback edition, issued in March 1973, the sentence is corrected to follow the English edition.

2. Note by Van Vechten, 24 January 1941: "She means the typewritten mss. she had sent me in 1935 which went to Yale in 1940." See Stein to Van Vechten [November? 1935], note 1.

To Gertrude Stein

9 December 1937   101 Central Park West
                                                     New York City

Dearest Baby-Woojums,

How exciting of you to move after all these years! This is the most amazing news in years. I've no doubt the rue Christine will soon become as famous as the rue de Fleurus. I looked it up on the map (I never heard of

[580]

it before) to discover it is near my favorite Quai. You don't tell me what étage: with a terrace it might be rez de chaussez, but penthouses have les terraces aussi. . Well, tell me more, please. .[1]

> *love to both,*
> *Papa W!*

Not a word from Thornton Wilder. Can't you get him to do something about this?

1. The apartment at 5 rue Christine was on the first floor (French style of counting floors, Americans would call it the second floor). The terrace was actually the roof of a garage. The apartment is two blocks from the Quai des Grands Augustins.

To Gertrude Stein

12 December 1937   101 Central Park West
                                    New York City

Dear Gertrude,

Maybe this paper of Mrs Chester Arthur would interest you![1] Anyway it gives me another chance to write to my dearest Baby Woojums! Love to you both from

> *Papa Woojums!*

1. I have been unable to locate the book review by Mrs. Arthur that Van Vechten sent to Stein. See Arthur to Van Vechten, 9 December 1937, YCAL. She thanked him for his kind words about her review and sent him three additional copies.

To Gertrude Stein and Alice Toklas
[Postcard: "Mother and Child"—painting by Mary Bell. Photograph by
Carl Van Vechten]

[postmark: 14 December 1937]   [101 Central Park West
                                                New York City]

Love and Happy Holidays

                                        Papa Woojums & Fania
                                        1937

To Gertrude Stein

17 December 1937   101 Central Park West
                                              New York City

Dear Baby Woojums,

Here is another one of those silly things to amuse you and Mama
W!. Everybody is talking about Baby Woojums' marvellous book and most
everybody likes it. . Virgil [Thomson] and Maurice [Grosser] are sailing in
January after Virgil's new ballet, "Filling Station" is done at the Hartford
Athenaeum.[1] Very excited to see the french book you are doing and also the
English Everybody's [Autobiography]. When will these be OUT?. In a minute I will be addressing letters to 5 rue Christine! How exciting and what a
lovely name for a book!. . We are having a Chinese luncheon party (with a
few Spaniards!) at the Algonquin on Monday: Hilda Yen, the great belle of
China who is over here to learn to fly (she began to learn in Italy and then
they thought she was learning too much and stopped her) and Lin Yutang
and his wife, and Hipolito Hidalgo de Caviedes[x] and the Covarrubii and
Romney Brent. Would that Baby and Mama Woojums would walk in and
Georges [Jacques] would drop DEAD. .

lots of love and merry Christmas to you both from Fania and

                                        Papa Woojums.

[x]who told me a lot about Emilio Grau-Sala!

[582]

1. *Filling Station*, a ballet with music by Virgil Thomson, choreography by Lew Christensen, book by Lincoln Kirstein, and sets and costumes by Paul Cadmus, had its premiere by the Ballet Caravan at the Avery Memorial Theater, Hartford, Connecticut, on 6 January 1938.

To Carl Van Vechten

[postmark: 20 December 1937]

27 rue de Fleurus
[Paris]

My dearest Papa Woojums,

Listen, when we were over at E[dward]. Wasserman's, we saw there a photo of the young Carl and the young Fania and I said did you know them then and he said no but they gave me this photograph when I was going around the world and we were certain that we who did know you then should have one, you are both sweet now but you were both sweet then please can we have one, and the English edition is to have all the photos like the American one they have decided and I am pleased all over, and they that is Daisy Fellowes gave a lovely dinner last night in honor of the book, and I made an answer to the toasts of Louis Bromfield and Bernard Faÿ, and I felt at my most Kate Greenaway as you so lovelily said about me and I wore and Alice wore our lecture dresses and they said we looked very handsome and it brought back such happy days, and I said as far as I can remember in my little speech that America is my country and Paris is my home town and that I wrote Everybody's Autobiography because in America and in France everybody is everybody, and they were all pleased and we were pleased and Papa Woojums is pleased and that makes a happy New Year.[1] Here the book has been completely sold out in all the book stores, but I have not heard anything about America as yet and I had a charming little letter from George[s Jacques] of the Algonquin which was a pleasure, and he was so pleased he said to have his name in a book which was going to be read by millions all over the world I am hoping so,[2] and Alice says she will write to you before we move yes she will, but naturally she is always busy she says she has only written three letters since we came back from America and two of these three were to you and my french book is finished and Madame Clermont-Tonnerre is enthusiastic and so is [Daniel Henry] Kahnweiler and now we hope everybody will be, very soon I will be sending you a copy of it, and how we love Papa Woojums from who all blessings flow yes they do, always and always

Gtrde and Alice.[3]

1. A detailed account of the dinner for Stein is in Wasserman to Van Vechten, 29 December 1937, YCAL.

2. George Jacques, headwaiter at the Algonquin Hotel, New York, had written Stein (6 December 1937, YCAL) thanking her for mentioning him by name in *Everybody's Autobiography*.

3. Both signatures are Stein's.

To Gertrude Stein

23 December 1937

101 Central Park West
New York City

Dearest Baby Woojums,

Thanks so much for sending me your paper on Edgar Wallace which I enjoyed hugely, just as I enjoy detective stories too.[1] And I guess by now you have appeared in every kind of magazine in every possible country. Your bibliography will be an eye-opener to that small part of the public that is yet unaware of your writing. I guess it will even surprise your admirers. To revert to detective stories, have you read The Moonstone, by Wilkie Collins because maybe this is the best one.

love and merry christmas to you both

Carlo Papa Woojums!

1. Stein's "Why I Like Detective Stories," in *Harper's Bazaar* (London) (November 1937), 17(2):70, 104, 106.

[584]

❧

To Gertrude Stein and Alice Toklas
[Telegram]

[postmark: 25 December 1937]   New York

LOVE AND MERRY CHRISTMAS TO BABY AND MAMA WOOJUMS

PAPA AND FANIA

❧

To Carl Van Vechten

[1937][1]   27 rue de Fleurus
                                                 [Paris]

My dear Carl,

This is to introduce Francis Rose but you know all about him so there
is only to say that I know you will like him.

Always
Gtrde.

1. This letter was hand delivered by Rose to Van Vechten.

❧

To Gertrude Stein
[Postcard: Photograph by Nicholas Muray] Carl Van Vechten
Fania Marinoff—July 5, 1923.

29 December [1937]   [101 Central Park West
                                                 New York]

Here you are, Saint Baby Woojums! Is this the one you mean? Sir
Francis Rose is here & has been photographed, but they are not ready yet.

[585]

E[dward] W[asserman] wrote me a long letter about Daisy Fellowes' dinner & said it was the most brilliant fiesta he had ever attended![1] Dying to see the FRENCH BOOK[2] and the English E[verybody's]. A[utobiography].! Did you get a cable on Xmas? Pretty soon I'll be writing to 5 rue Christine!

l[ove] & k[isses] from
Papa W.

1. See Stein to Van Vechten [20 December 1937], note 1.
2. The French edition of Stein's *Picasso*.

☙

To Carl Van Vechten
[Rose motto]

[postmark: 7 January 1938]   27 rue de Fleurus
                                              [Paris]

Dearest Papa Woojums,

You and Fania are so young and tender on the card, thanks so much, some time I would like a big one, of it, would you give it to us for the rue Christine, and Lady Diana Abdy is leaving Wednesday for America, for a fortnight only, she is charming and very lovely and an awfully good friend, it was she who arranged the Oxford lectures and arranged everything with Gerald Berners and I have told her to call you up as soon as she gets there and that you will be sweet to her and you will be, and she ought to make a lovely photograph, I once saw her kneeling on the eye of a white horse and she made the loveliest angel imaginable,[1] and we did get the cable and it pleased us and heartened us all through the cold and the carpenters and the painters and the plumbers, I guess we are very happy but just now we are right in the midst of the push, getting them to get out so that we can get in, and deciding about curtains and what we are to put on the bathroom floor, and oh my, but they all say the worst is when the actual moving commences, well any way you will come and see it and that will be lovely, and everything and all and lots and lots of love

Gtrde.

[586]

1. The exact circumstances surrounding Lady Diana Abdy's "kneeling on the eye of a white horse" cannot be determined. Stein recounts the story in *Everybody's Autobiography*, p. 300, but there is little further information to clarify the incident.

❧

To Carl Van Vechten

[postmark: 20 January 1938]   27 Rue de Fleurus
5 rue Christine
[Paris]

My dearest Carl,

A wonderful country our native land, we are not yet in the rue Christine xpect to by the first of February but to-day a lot of fan mail came straight from Virginia and West Virginia and other places straight unresisted by anybody to 5 rue Christine, now how do they do it, we are not there yet but they are here and here is a letter that will amuse you this is the address

M. Julien Green[1]
Paris
France

and then at the bottom is written

Care of Gertrude Stein if absolutely necessary (and the postoffice sent it here[)].

We we are xhausted not in yet but xhausted, did I tell you that we have the blue pigeon in the grass wall paper in the bed room & the boudoir, do you remember who did it, and it is most xciting,[2] and the piano score of the ballet A Wedding Bouquet is out very well done, printed by J. & W. Chester Ltd. 11 Great Marlborough Street London W.1, and the synopsis is funny, and Marie Murat now Mme de Chambrun has written a book about Queen Christine and she is sending it to us, and I imagine it is amusing, she is,[3] and I guess that is all just now xcept xhaustion and a cold in the head but we will get in, sure she will and we love Papa Woojums so wonderfully much always

Baby Woojums.

I got a lot of Wilkie Collins out of the Church Library at Aix[-les-Bains], of course the Moon Stone when I was young a little frightening, I remember a large fat man who moved easily[4] lots of love

Gtrde.

1. Julien Green (b. 1900), the French novelist, born in Paris of American parents.

2. Note by Van Vechten, 24 January 1941: "The 'pigeons on the grass' wallpaper is the background for several of the photographs I have made of GS. and presented to Yale." Stein first saw and bought a sample of the wallpaper at the shop of the decorator Nancy McClelland on East Fifty-seventh Street, New York.

3. Princess Lucien Murat (Comtesse Marie de Chambrun), *La Reine Christine de Suede* (Paris: Flammarion, 1930).

4. Note by Van Vechten, 24 January 1941: "The Woman in White. [Count] Fosco?"

To Gertrude Stein
[Postcard: Portrait of Cecil Beaton. Photograph by Carl Van Vechten]

[postmark: 26 January 1938]   [101 Central Park West
                                               New York]

Dear Gertrude & Baby Woojums

This will be the first card addressed to 5 rue Christine! Doesn't it seem strange? I'm very excited & wish I could photograph it at once!

I do hope Lady [Diana] Abdy will call up. I would love to photograph her. And I will send you a big one of the picture of me & F[ania] M[arinoff] if you will send it back to me. Otherwise I don't know whatever it is at all! Cecil Beaton got into lots of trouble. Did you hear about it?[1]

Well love & kisses to Mama W and Baby W!

from Fania & Papa W

Dec. '37

1. For Frank Crowninshield's essay, "The New Left Wing of New York Society," American *Vogue*, 1 February 1938, p. 73, Cecil Beaton had provided drawings as a decorative border. Beaton had added tiny written details such as newspaper headlines and book titles to the illustrations. These were written so small as to be almost indecipherable. In two places his drawings used the word "kikes" referring to Jews. On the page of an illustrated journal that he had drawn Beaton wrote, "M. R. Andre ball at the El Morocco brought out all the damn Kikes in town." Someone alerted the columnist Walter Winchell about the illustrations and he broke the story in his column in the *New York Daily Mirror* on 24 January 1938. Winchell's quotes from Beaton's microscopically written sentences created an uproar and many of *Vogue's* advertisers threatened a boycott. Beaton was forced to resign as a contributing photographer and artist on the staff of *Vogue*. See Caroline Seebohm, *The Man Who Was Vogue: The Life and Times of Condé Nast* (New York: The Viking Press, 1982), pp. 209–15.

To Gertrude Stein
[Telegram]

[postmark: 3 February 1938]　　　　　　　　　　　　　　　　New York

LOVE AND SIXTYFOUR KISSES

FANIA CARLO

To Carl Van Vechten
[Rose motto]

[postmark: 4 February 1938]　　　　　　　　　　　　5 rue [Christine
　　　　　　　　　　　　　　　　　　　　　　　　　Paris]

My dearest Papa Woojums,

It is wonderful and yet natural that No nobody else will do should be you. It just would be dearest papa Woojums and our home oh papa papa Woojums it is so lovely and we are so pleased we just can't believe it, sunshine and curtains woodwork and wall paper a terrace and the littlest of little new moons it is lovely, you know Papa Woojums it is funny Everybody's

Autobiography has produced the most completely satisfying fan letters I have ever had, and none of them from women all of them from men who apparently never felt that way before but were just moved I am keeping them all for you for some time when you get here and the English edition is to be out the 18th I will send you a copy with the Picasso book which will be out about the same time, and I am doing an opera about Doctor Faustus for Gerald Berners,[1] and I can't settle down to anything because we love the house so, and sometimes we will love it and papa Woojums together and all our love always

Baby W.

1. Stein's *Doctor Faustus Lights the Lights*, published in her *Last Operas and Plays*, pp. 89–118. Berners was very anxious to do the music for this play, but in December 1939 he confessed to Stein that "all inspirational sources seem to have dried up: I can't write a note of music or do any kind of creative work whatever and it's not for want of trying and I don't believe I shall be able to as long as this war lasts" (See Gallup, *The Flowers of Friendship*, p. 346). Berners never wrote a score for this play.

To Gertrude Stein
[Postcard: Unidentified Mask. Photograph by Carl Van Vechten]

20 February 1938   [101 Central Park West
                                                     New York]

Dearest Baby Woojums!

So excited about your moving. No, I can't remember who did the pigeon wall paper. Maybe I never did know. Here is a fetishe for you. The large fat man in Wilkie Collins is Count Fosco, no doubt, in The Woman in White. I *love* Collins. . I haven't met Thornton Wilder yet. I don't see how he keeps out of my way because he knows everybody I know, anyway he has written a *beautiful* play called *Our Town* and it is a tremendous success.[1] We loved it, and LOVE to Baby & Mama Woojums! Is the English Everybody's Autobiography out yet?

Papa W!

Saw Virgil [Thomson]'s ballet "Filling Station" & it is awfully good. He also has done the music for a film called "The River" which is a sensation![2]

1. Wilder's play *Our Town*, produced by Jed Harris, opened at the Henry Miller Theatre, New York, on 4 February 1938 and ran for 159 performances. In the spring of 1938 Wilder was awarded the Pulitzer Prize for this play.

2. *The River*, 1937, was written and directed by Pare Lorentz; it is a film about the Mississippi River Valley. In 1936, Thomson had done the music for another Lorentz film, *The Plow That Broke the Plains*.

To Carl Van Vechten

[postmark: 21 February 1938]   5 rue Christine
                                                [Paris]

My dearest Papa Woojums

Here we are really and truly here, pretty dead but, and at that moment the hot water did not hot and for a few days since we were deader and we finally concluded that Queen Christine had a jinks against hot water but we finally got the best even of that and so I am going on telling you how pleased we are with the valentine,[1] it gave us a great delight and how delighted I am at the prospect of Four Saints being done again, I do hope it will become a popular opera like Gilbert and Sullivan and then we could do Daniel Webster by the way did Jay Laughlin send you a copy of the New Directions with it in it if not I will send you mine and we are so tired and so happy and so loving P[apa] W[oojums]., Mama and Baby Woojums, and love to Fania and she will love this too both of you will we do.

G[ertrude].

1. Van Vechten had sent Stein a Valentine's Day card (YCAL) inscribed "for Baby and Mama Woojums February 14, 1938" and signed "Papa Woojums!"

❧

To Gertrude Stein
*[Postcard: Detail of fountain at entrance of the Philadelphia Museum of
Art. Photograph by Carl Van Vechten]*[1]

1 March [1938]   [101 Central Park West
                                                 New York]

Yes dear Baby Woojums—

[James] Laughlin (or somebody) sent me New Direction[s] with the
lovely Daniel Webster. O that we could see this masterpiece played! I'm glad
you got your hot water and I'm dying to see Two on the Rue Christine,
which maybe is a good title for you next time!—Fania and I send love &
kisses to both!

Carlo

1. This detail is part of the Washington Monument of 1895 by the German sculptor Rudolph
Siemering. It is a bronze and granite fountain located at the end of the Benjamin Franklin
Parkway, in front of the Philadelphia Museum of Art.

❧

To Carl Van Vechten
[Postcard: Salon de Madame de Maintenon, Palais de Fontainebleau]

[postmark: 12 March 1938]   [Fontainebleau, France]

We think our wood work is a[s] good it isn't of course but we think
it is[1]

B. W.

1. The image on the postcard is of a wood-paneled room in the Palais de Fontainebleau. There
was wood paneling in some of the rooms at 5 rue Christine.

To Gertrude Stein
[Postcard: Detail of fountain at entrance of the Philadelphia Museum of Art. Photograph by Carl Van Vechten][1]

[postmark: 13 March 1938]   [101 Central Park West
                                             New York]

Dearest Baby Woojums!

I can't wait to see 5 rue Christine! It must be wonderful. I *must* make photographs. And I can't wait to see the English Everybody's Autobiography & Picasso & Dr. Faustus is a wonderful idea for a modern opera. . And I am jealous of all the men who are writing you fan letters & l[ove] & k[isses] to both from[2]

Papa Woojums!

1. This is a photograph of a different part of the fountain described in Van Vechten to Stein, 1 March [1938], note 1.

2. Stein mentions fan letters in her letter to Van Vechten [4 February 1938].

To Gertrude Stein
[Postcard: Bryant's Show Boat]

[postmark: 22 March 1938]   [101 Central Park West
                                             New York]

Dearest Baby Woojums

Of course 5 rue Christine is better than anything Madame de Maintenon ever had![1] Much better! I can't wait to see this.

Love to Mama & Baby
Papa Woojums!

1. A reference to the image on the postcard of Stein to Van Vechten [12 March 1938] (see note 1).

To Gertrude Stein

12 April 1938   101 Central Park West
                                                     New York City

Dear Gertrude,

I am absolutely fou about the Picasso book and I have read it twice already. I like everything you say and you very cleverly and clearly separate the periods of his painting, and I guess you write in French as if to the château born! What you say about Spanish painting on the first page and elsewhere, especially about cubism and Spain, is nothing you can argue with and yet nobody has ever said it before and I guess nobody has ever said before that Picasso is not interested in "insides" and "souls", although lots of people complain because they don't find these things in his pictures. . The portrait of GS, dear Baby Woojums, seems to be reproduced better than I have ever seen it before and THAT has a soul and INSIDES TOO and looks more and More like you. . And I loved what you said about creators liking their backgrounds to be Louis XV or whatever and I guess I loved it all.

The moment the book arrived I called up Bennett [Cerf] to ask him if he knew about it and he said very proudly that he held the English version in his hands and had sent a query to Paris about the illustrations.

ONLY in your latest letter you say the English edition of the Everybody's Autobiography is out and you will send that with the Picasso and it didn't come, but I am not worried because obviously it didn't get lost out of the parcel and I guess it will come later.

There is not a lick of news. If you go on the street everybody talks about Austria or China or Spain. I do wish America would get self-centered again. It was nicer then. At that period, also, I think it was considered very bad form to be interested in politics of any kind. Now look at us!

A thousand kisses and four thousand red roses to Mama and Baby W

Papa W!

Enclosed is a photograph of an Eilshemius I recently acquired. Do you like it? The title is: The Demon of the Rocks.[1] And here is a photograph of a small bronze Richmond Barthé did of Fania as Ariel in The Tempest.[2]

[594]

1. Louis Michel Eilshemius, the American painter.

2. Marinoff had played Ariel in a 1916 production of Shakepeare's *The Tempest*. Also in the cast were Louis Calvert as Prospero and Walter Hampden as Caliban. Barthé's sculpture was done after a photograph of Marinoff as Ariel. The sculpture is now in the collection of the American Shakespeare Festival, Stratford, Connecticut.

To Gertrude Stein
[Postcard: Wooden Horse from a Merry-Go-Round. Photograph by Carl Van Vechten]

15 April [19]38
Friday

[101 Central Park West]
New York City

Dearest Baby Woojums

Everybody's Autobiography *in England* has just arrived and is pretty exciting, tho' not as attractive as the American! I am very very glad to have this. I wrote you about the Picasso which is truly marvellous. Happy Easter to Baby & Mama W from

Fania and Papa W!

To Gertrude Stein
[Postcard: Portrait of Ram Gopal. Photograph by Carl Van Vechten]

5 May [1938]

[101 Central Park West
New York]

Dearest Baby Woojums

I was THRILLED by the Italian Autobiography What next! . .[1] On this card is RAM GOPAL, a most beautiful Hindu boy and a Marvellous dancer. . He is coming to Paris soon & I am giving him a letter to you. You

will, I think, find him enchanting. I haven't sent any one to you & Mama
Woojums for months or even years but this is one of the Best ever!

l[ove]. & K[isses].
Papa W!

1. *The Autobiography of Alice B. Toklas, Autobiografia di Alice Toklas,* trans. Cesare Pavese
(Torino, Italy: Giulio Einaudi, 1938).

To Carl Van Vechten
[Postcard: "A wise little owl," Arizona]

[postmark: 10 May 1938]   [5 rue Christine
                                                            Paris]

I have just finished the first Act of Faust, I think you will like it,
when I get some more done I will be sending it along,[1] I do wish you were
here it is such a lovely spring, and we adore our new home and want to
show it to Papa Woojums and Fania always

B. W.

1. Stein's *Doctor Faustus Lights the Lights.* Stein had first mentioned this work to Van Vechten in her letter of [4 February 1938].

To Carl Van Vechten

[postmark: 25? May 1938]   Bilignin par Belley
                                                            Ain

Dearest papa Woojums

We have here a charming neighbor Daniel Rops, a french writer who
is editing for the edition Plon a book about how other races feel about the

white and he wants desperately that you should do the little piece about how American Negroes feel about the whites, he enormously admires your writing and he wants this a lot, he says it would be as short or as long as you like, I could hold out no hopes but I told him I would do my best to persuade you, anyway he is writing to you himself to tell you all about it, you would like both him and his wife, very natural charming people, I told him perhaps you would send him some photos of Negroes including the Four Saints that of course for himself the book is not illustrated, and give him advice but he hopes and we hope that it will be Papa Woojums who will say what the colored in America thinks of the white all our love[1]

B. W.

1. Daniel-Rops wrote to Van Vechten, 20 August [1938] (YCAL), expressing his admiration for Van Vechten's novel *Nigger Heaven*. He asked Van Vechten for a contribution to a volume of essays in a series called *Presences* published by the French publisher Plon. Van Vechten declined to write the essay, and on 17 September 1938 (YCAL) Daniel-Rops wrote Van Vechten expressing regret and asking him to suggest another writer familiar with the race question in America. Whether Van Vechten replied cannot be determined. The volume of essays did not appear.

To Gertrude Stein

[Postcard: Statue of Abraham de Peyster—New York. Photograph by Carl Van Vechten]

20 June 1938

[101 Central Park West
New York]

Dear Gertrude! and Baby Woojums!

So excited about 4 Sts in London.[1] We'll all have to go to that. Why is it that N.Y. Chicago & Hartford are so far ahead of the TIMES? —and I'm dying to know about Faust. Are you going to the country prochainement? Fania is going on a cruise on the "Paris" and will be in Paris for a week about July 27. But you are *sure* to be in Bilignin by then.

Love to you both,
Papa W!

[597]

1. Van Vechten had learned from Virgil Thomson that there was again interest in mounting a production of *Four Saints in Three Acts* in London. Stein had been telephoned on 1 June, just as she was preparing to leave for Bilignin the next morning, by a Mrs. Harry Kaufman, who was acting for Mrs. Dolores Harding in London. Mrs. Harding, a London producer, went so far as to discuss financial terms with Stein and to suggest that Paul Robeson be invited to sing the role of Saint Ignatius (see Stein to Thomson, postmark 1 June 1938 and postmark 4 June 1938, YCAL). Stein waited for word from either Mrs. Harding or Mrs. Kaufman throughout the summer. The planned production never materialized.

To Carl Van Vechten
[Postcard: Belley—La vieille porte]

[postmark: 20 June 1938]

[Bilignin par Belley
Ain]

Dear Papa Woojums,

The opera[1] is finished and Alice will be tapping it now and sending, the theology and the drama will I hope be to you[r] likeing had a funny theological discussion about it with the Haut[e]combe fathers I wish you were here dear papa Woojums, we all do now and always,

B. W.

1. Stein's *Doctor Faustus Lights the Lights.*

﹡

To Gertrude Stein
*[Postcard: Ralph Earl—Portrait of William Carpenter—Worcester
Art Museum]*

3 July [1938]   [Boston, Massachusetts]

Dearest Baby Woojums,

Wandering around the Back Bay for a few days. So excited about
your play & the prospect of 4 Saints in London. How does Bilignin seem
after Rue Christine?

love to Baby & Mama W.
Papa W.

﹡

To Gertrude Stein

17 July [1938]   101 Central Park West
New York City

Dear Baby Woojums!

I loved Dr Faustus Lights the Lights and I am sure it would be sen-
sationally amusing on the stage. The dog and Goethe's last words and the
confusion of Helen of Troy and Margarethe and especially the DOG and
the viper. Who is writing the music for this? I shall read it again tonight. It
seems to me to be written in a new style, a new manner, a new vein, a new
Gertrude. Is this true?

It is VERY VERY HOT here and getting hotter every minute and
sometimes I love it but most times I don't. Fania will be in Paris in a minute but she will miss seeing you and the rue Christine, hélas. I wish I MIGHT
SEE the rue Christine. and I guess I will soon and photograph it TOO.

James Weldon Johnson was killed and he was one of my best friends
and a great man but I don't think you met him.[1] We have new stamps every
hour now and I will always put new ones on your envelope and and and

you will have an excuse to go see that nice priest. How wonderful to argue about ecclesiastical subjects with him. .[2]

Lots of love to you both,

Papa Woojums

Dr Faustus is too marvellous!

1. Johnson was killed in a grade crossing accident on 26 June 1938 while vacationing in Maine.

2. Père Bernardet of the Abbaye d'Hautecombe in Saint Pierre de Curtille, not far from Belley, collected stamps.

To Gertrude Stein
[Postcard: American Eagle—iron relief sculpture over entry way to Arsenal, 830 Fifth Avenue, New York. Photograph by Carl Van Vechten]

[postmark: 19 July 1938]　　　　　　　　　　　[101 Central Park West
New York]

Love to Baby & Mama Woojums because here is a new american Eagle & a new stamp![1]

Papa Woojums

I *love* Dr. Faustus, I can't wait to hear it performed!

1. A three-cent Northwest Territory Sesquicentennial stamp (1788–1938).

To Carl Van Vechten

[postmark: 26 July 1938]　　　　　　　　　　　Bilignin par Belley
Ain

My dearest papa Woojums,

I am so happy that you liked the Faust, I have been struggling with this problem of dramatic narrative and in that I think I got it and I am so

[600]

pleased that you like it. We are awfully upset that we are not seeing Fania but we do believe and seeing will be believing that dearest Papa Woojums will be in Paris and in 5 rue Christine this winter. There has been a complication of Bennett [Cerf] and Batsford did not come to an agreement about the English edition of Picasso and now Scribners is doing it in America instead of Random House, of course I had nothing to with the negotiations which ended so but I am awfully upset about it.[1] I wrote to Bennett suggesting that they print the Faust in a little book, I think it might be popular, what do you think and it might be illustrated by some very clever drawings that a young Turk Abidin Dina made for it just before we left, he only illustrated the first act, if you think this is a good idea and I have referred Bennett to you well we will, dearest Papa Woojums, and it's hot here too, lots hot, and I garden and I have started a novel that Mama Woojums says is early American[2] and we love you oh so much and the stamps are lovely

B. W.

Gerald Berners is to do the music.

1. Donald S. Klopfer wrote to Stein on 24 February 1938 (YCAL) that Random House would be interested in Stein's *Picasso* as a joint venture with Heinemann, the English publisher with whom they had published Stein's *Everybody's Autobiography*. In early May 1938 Cerf had received the French edition of the book and a typescript of the English translation. In the meantime Stein had made an agreement with B. T. Batsford of London to publish the book in England. Cerf wrote to Stein, 17 May 1938 (YCAL), that he thought he could work out an agreement for a joint venture with Batsford. On 13 July 1938 (YCAL) Cerf wrote to Stein that Batsford has made "such an absurd quotation for sheets of your Picasso book that we were forced to turn them down." Cerf also informed Stein that Batsford had cabled him that another publisher, Scribner's, had agreed to meet Batsford's price.

   Stein wrote a long letter to Cerf (? July 1938, Columbia-Random House) in which she carefully recounted the events from her first letter to Cerf about the *Picasso* and her desire to have Cerf publish it. In a letter to Stein of 4 August 1938 (see Gallup, *The Flowers of Friendship*, pp. 330–31) Cerf acknowledged that what had occurred was not her fault. He also declined to publish *Doctor Faustus Lights the Lights* unless there was a Broadway production to stimulate sales.

   In a letter to Stein on 24 August 1938 (YCAL) Cerf admitted that in the handling of the *Picasso* situation, "Random House acted with all the speed and dexterity of a senile hippopotamus. I vote that we forget all about the incident."

2. Stein's *Ida A Novel*.

❦

To Carl Van Vechten

[postmark: 4 August 1938]   [Chambery, France]

My dearest Papa Woojums,

Here I am in a garage waiting for the oil to change into other oil and as it is so hot I just went out and bought what they call a pochette which is this paper and this envelope to write to dear Papa Woojums,[1] I am so pleased you like Dr. Faustus, I am now writing a novel Alice says it is early American[2] anyway I am writing it and it's hot golly it is hot and Alice and the dogs sit still and I sit in the garage, god bless you papa Woojums, and please come and see us soon, so much love

Gtrde.

1. The paper is a lined paper 8 × 6 inches in size.
2. Stein's *Ida A Novel.*

❦

To Gertrude Stein

6 August 1938   101 Central Park West
                                          New York City

Dear Baby Woojums,

I think it would be a good idea to publish the Faust but Bennett [Cerf] thinks it would be better to wait till it is produced and maybe he is right.[1] He seems very hurt about the Picasso.[2] Scribner's of course will do you very well and this should sell. However, I am VERY SORRY the thing happened and don't understand it even when he explains it to me. . As he is your own publisher who has published everything you have asked him to, he should undoubtedly [have] had the first say before an English publisher and if there were an English publisher he should have been instructed that

[602]

no one else but Bennett could publish it here, but maybe all this happened and yet things went wrong. I am sorry if they have gone wrong because I think they were going so RIGHT. But I guess it will all get cleared up.

There is no news here except it is incredibly hot, hotter than I've ever known it to be for four solid weeks and no relief yet. Besides it rains all the time. You have forgotten American hot weather. That is something!

Fania is in Paris this minute, I think, but goes on to London in a day or so (American Express, Haymarket, London) and will sail on the Paris on August 16.

Lots of love to you both,

Papa Woojums

1. In an effort to protect Stein's feelings and her relationship with Cerf, Van Vechten did not tell Stein Cerf's true reaction to her *Doctor Faustus Lights the Lights*. Here, Van Vechten offers substantially the same reasoning that Cerf offered to Stein (see Stein to Van Vechten [26 July 1938], note 1). In a letter to Van Vechten, 4 August 1938 (YCAL), Cerf thanked him for telling him about *Doctor Faustus Lights the Lights* but confessed that he was only "able to stomach" about four pages of the play.

2. Stein's *Picasso* was first published in English by B. T. Batsford, London, in October 1938. The American edition, identical with the English edition, was published by Charles Scribner's Sons on 6 February 1939. The translation from the French text was made by Alice Toklas. Toklas made some alterations in the text while translating it. The manuscript of the translation (YCAL) contains occasional corrections of the translation as well as substitutions of individual words in Stein's hand. A corrected English language edition of this text is printed in *Gertrude Stein on Picasso*, ed. Edward Burns (New York: Liveright Publishing Corp., 1970).

To Carl Van Vechten

[postmark: 15 August 1938]   Bilignin par Belley
                                                              Ain

Dearest Papa Woojums

They have just asked me the William R. Scott publishers to write them a childrens book and I am starting it and I think you'll like it, but will you tell me if it is an all right publisher, it would be rather fun to do, it is called The world is round, do you like the title. But will you tell me if it is a publishing house that is all right. They wrote me a very nice letter about it, the editor is a John G. McCullo[u]gh, he is the one that wrote.[1] Then I am going on writing a long novel so I am busy,[2] and Virgil [Thomson] and the English producer are still communicating, we have now gotten so far as to be discussing an option, so it looks as if something might really happen, and you would come over for it if it did.[3] We have been having a peaceful summer and I have been working a lot, nobody in the house just lots of friends around, and that makes everything peaceful, Gerald Berners is coming next month and that's all, on the other hand I am having wonderful fan letters from all kinds of new and earnest youn[g] men they write very long ones and very interesting ones, some day at 5 rue Christine, I will show you a lot of them, the only thing that bothers me is that Bennett [Cerf] seems upset because they are not doing the Picasso,[4] but they refused the french edition and said they did not want to do the edition and then they refused the conditions of the English edition, I am awfully upset about it, but I had had the impression that they had been a little discouraged at the lack of financial success of Everybody's [Autobiography], by the way they are doing 500 words of it in the Christian Science Monitor, they have just asked permission,[5] I am awfully upset because I am fond of Bennett and I wanted him to be my only publisher and I had nothing at all to do with it it was done through Bennett's London Agent, well anyway you remember the Hockaday school in Texas, well Miss [Ela] Hockaday stayed with us a couple of days, a charming woman and she asked me would Mr. Van Vechten photograph her, I said I could not tell but I could tell him and he would tell her, I think she would love to have you go down and photograph her there in Dallas Texas, and the children are charming, and it would be lovely, her address is Miss Ela Hockaday, Hockaday School, Dallas Texas, and she has just gone home she says they are the only photographs she has ever loved and you are the only Papa Woojums

B. W.

1. John McCullough, an editor at William R. Scott Publishers, wrote to Stein on 2 August 1938 (Columbia-Random House) informing her that his firm was venturing forth for the first time with a juvenile list. He inquired whether Stein would be interested in writing a story for them and what her financial terms would be. Stein consented and wrote *The World is Round*.

2. Stein's *Ida A Novel*.

3. See Van Vechten to Stein, 20 June 1938, note 1.

4. Cerf's letter of 4 August 1938 is in Gallup, *The Flowers of Friendship*, pp. 330–31. See Stein to Van Vechten [26 July 1938], note 1.

[604]

5. The *Christian Science Monitor* had asked for permission to print five hundred words from *Everybody's Autobiography*. The excerpts, however, were not printed.

৯

To Gertrude Stein
[Postcard: Portrait of W. G. Rogers. Photograph by Carl Van Vechten]

22 August [1938]   [101 Central Park West
                                                   New York]

Dear Baby Woojums—

Your sweet little note from the garage while they were changing oil entranced me!—F[ania] M[arinoff] got back last week, very tired, poor devil. She has been everywhere. She found the most Divine venetian candlesticks in Paris. . I am glad you are writing an early american novel and I'm sure it will be extraordinary.

Lots of love to you both.

Carlo. Papa W.

has your villa a name? Why not Villa de la Pierre Rose?!!![1]

1. The house has no particular name and is called the Manoir de Bilignin. As part of the address Van Vechten wrote "Villa de la Pierre Rose."

৯

To Gertrude Stein
[Postcard: Self-portrait in Top Hat. Photograph by Carl Van Vechten]

[postmark: 26 August 1938]   [101 Central Park West
                                                   New York]

Angelic Baby Woojums,

Here is another new stamp (& IOWA this time).[1] A letter from Bennett [Cerf] this morning & he is very loving about *you*. So I guess that is all right.[2] I never heard of Wm. R. Scott & I've enquired of 2 members of the Publishers Ass. & they never did either. But everybody has to begin & look what Donald Evans did! He became a publisher for the sole purpose of doing Tender Buttons![3] O I do hope 4 Sts is done in London & I'm crazy to see what you will do with a children's book.

Love to you both,
Carlo

Fania is back with some venetian candelabra that are killer-dillers.

1. A three-cent Iowa Territorial Centennial stamp (1838–1938). Van Vechten was born in Iowa.

2. Cerf wrote to Van Vechten, 24 August 1938 (YCAL), that he hoped to see him before sailing for Europe on the *Normandie* on 14 September. Cerf also expressed hope that he would see Stein while he was in Paris.

3. Evans had published a number of books of his own and by Louise Norton and Allen Norton under the imprint Claire Marie Publishers before he printed Stein's *Tender Buttons*. See Evans to Stein, 18 February 1914, YCAL.

❧

To Gertrude Stein
[Postcard: Portrait of Robert Hunt. Photograph by Carl Van Vechten][1]

28 August [1938]   [101 Central Park West
                                                   New York]

Dear Baby Woojums!

Why didn't you send Madame [Ela] Hockaday to me on her way through? I would love to photograph anyone by that name. BUT of course I'll NEVER be going to Texas. So write her to come BACK.

Love to you both
Papa Woojums!

1. Hunt was a friend of the poet Witter Bynner.

[606]

❧

To Gertrude Stein
[Postcard: Portrait of Marie Louis Bousquet. Photograph by
Carl Van Vechten]

3 September [1938]   [101 Central Park West
                                                     New York]

O Gertrude & Baby Woojums!

Writing is too difficult for me now & I am too busy & the subject is too controversial, but I have asked a negro friend to do something & maybe she will.[1] Is Daniel [Rops] any relation to FELICIEN [Rops]? I do hope so. *Please let me know!*[2]

No more news now. Here is my Iowa stamp again.[3]

Love to both
Papa W.

When do you go back to the rue Christine?

1. See Stein to Van Vechten [25 May 1938], note 1.

2. Felicien Rops (1833–1898) was a Belgian-French painter and engraver; he was not related to Daniel-Rops.

3. A three-cent Iowa Territorial Centennial stamp (1838–1938).

❧

To Carl Van Vechten
[Postcard: Environs de Belley—Ruines de Château de Beauretour]

[postmark: 7 September 1938]   [Bilignin par Belley
                                                     Ain]

My dearest Carl,

I am writing to Miss [Ela] Hockaday to this effect and who is the dancer with the crossed legs[1] and have just had a lovely letter from Bennett

[607]

[Cerf], he really is sweet and says it was not my fault,[2] and we are so sorry not to have seen Fania and we love you so,

B. and M. Woojums

1. A reference to the portrait of Hunt used by Van Vechten as his postcard to Stein, 28 August [1938]. The note by Van Vechten, 24 January 1941, on this letter: "I must have sent G. S. a postcard of Ram Gopal," is in error. Van Vechten gives the correct information in his postcard to Stein of 16 September [1938].

2. See Stein to Van Vechten [26 July 1938], note 1.

❦

To Gertrude Stein
[Postcard: Winslow Homer, The Gulf Stream. The Metropolitan Museum of Art]

16 September [1938]

[101 Central Park West
New York]

Dear Baby Woojums—

The cross-legged boy is Robert Hunt, a poet, who lives with Witter Bynner, & he is NO dancer.

If there is war you'd better come over here! But I hope there won't be. You will be seeing Bennett [Cerf] soon.

Love to both
Papa W.

When do you go to Paris?

[608]

To Carl Van Vechten

[Postcard: Hauterives (Drôme)—"Palais Idéal" Les trois Géants]

[postmark: 17 ?September 1938]   [Bilignin par Belley
Ain]

This is an xtraordinary place done by a postman when he was not doing his rounds, sometime we want to take P. Woojums there,[1] it is rather wonderful, Daniel Rops found it for us, he is not a relative[2] but they are grateful that he adopted the name and has reminded everybody of it, you would like him and like photographing him and he would like some photos of anything you want to send him including Alice and me, lots of love

B. W.

1. At the end of the nineteenth century the postman of Hauterives, Ferdinand Cheval, returned from his rounds with stones in all sizes and shapes. He used these to build, in his garden, a "palais" inspired by his readings and his dreams.

  Note by Van Vechten, 24 January 1941: "On our motor trip from Paris to Florence in 1913, Mabel Dodge, John Reed, Bobby [Robert Edmond] Jones and I found this fantastic place."

2. Note by Van Vechten, 24 January 1941: "Of Felicien Rops. I had inquired." See Van Vechten to Stein, 3 September [1938], note 2.

To Gertrude Stein

24 September 1938   101 Central Park West
New York City

Dearest Baby Woojums,

Would you and Mama W like to know Lin Yutang?[1] If there is no war (and today looks as if there was going to be) he and his utterly charming wife, Hong (she is really a honey) are in Paris and (save for war) will stay there. If you like the idea I'll send him a letter to you and start things going. If there is a war, what will you do? Stay in Bilignin? That seems too near the Italian border for comfort unless the Italians come over to our side again, as no doubt they will.

our love to both,
Carlo!

1. Lin Yutang, the Chinese writer, whose works include *The Wisdom of Confucius* (1938) and *The Importance of Living* (1938), and Van Vechten had met through Bennett Cerf. Lin's wife's name was Tsuifeng, but "Hong was the name generally used by American friends in addressing my mother" (letter received from Hsiang Ju Lin, 13 January 1982).

To Gertrude Stein
[Postcard: Portrait of Fania Marinoff. Photograph by Carl Van Vechten]

[postmark: 27 September 1938]   [101 Central Park West
                                                 New York]

Dear Baby Woojums,

I have already been to Hauterives & adore it! Is this Postman's Dream near Bilignin? Yes I will send D[aniel] Rops some pictures of you & Alice later.[1] In the meantime I am trying to get a negro lady to write him an article.

love to you both
Papa Woojums!

1. See Stein to Van Vechten [25? May 1938], note 1. Daniel-Rops wrote to Van Vechten on 26 October 1938 (YCAL) thanking him for the photographs of Stein and Toklas. He again asked Van Vechten if he could think of someone to write about the racial situation in America.

≋

To Carl Van Vechten
*[Postcard: Cheval, Facteur en retraite, Auteur du Palais Idéal.
Né le 19 Avril 1836. Hauterives (Drôme)]*

[postmark: 1 October 1938]   [Bilignin par Belley
                                                         Ain]

The war is all over[1] and here we are and it was not very lovely and
they promised to fill our court with Marocains but now everything is lovely
and we would love to see dear P. W. The child's story[2] is about done lots
of love

B. W.

1. Hitler had begun his program of *Anschluss* with the invasion of Austria in March 1938, and
his ultimatum to Czechoslovakia to give up the Sudetenland by 1 October 1938 had brought
Europe to the brink of war. It was temporarily averted by the Munich Pact, signed on 30 September 1938 by Hitler, Chamberlain, Mussolini, and Daladier, which allowed Hitler's army
the right to march into Czechoslovakia.

2. Stein's *The World is Round.*

≋

To Carl Van Vechten

[postmark: 5 October 1938]   Bilignin par Belley
                                                         Ain

My dearest Papa Woojums

We are all for Lin Yutang and his wife Hong, and we will [be] back
in Paris beginning of November and there is no war, at least not here, they
were going to give us 30 Marocains to have their Popotte here in the court,[1]
but the war stopped and they never came, Alice and I all things considered
were quite peaceful until Picabia came, and he was so scared that we thought
he had better go to Paris, farther away from the front, our village was sad
but resigned and then they were so tired having had so much sadness that

[611]

they were even sadder but now already they are beginning to cheer up, and of course you darling you would have seen Hauterives it is only 60 kilometers from here and we will take you again and Gerald Berners has been here, he is a great darling and he wanted Faust to have a longer aria to begin so will you add this to the opera,[2] the child's story is about done,[3] it is pretty and I guess I will be sending you a copy soon and lots of love in peace and in war and always more

B. W.

1. A *popote du officiers*, French for an officer's field mess.

2. Stein enclosed the aria for Faust that now opens her *Doctor Faustus Lights the Lights*.

3. Stein's *The World Is Round*.

To Gertrude Stein

17 October 1938   101 Central Park West
                                                                     New York City

Dear Baby Woojums,

Lin Yutang (you call him Dr. Lin; Yutang is the Buddhistic name, so to speak!) lives at 59 rue Nicolo, Paris XVI. I am writing him today giving him your address and a card of introduction which he may be too shy to send. So, if you don't hear from him presently, DO write asking him and his wife to come to see you. I am sure you and Alice will be enchanted with them both.

In your letter today I at last make out what they were going to put in your courtyard in case of war: Maroccans: I read "manicurists" on your postcard. . and then got as far as "Mexicans." Well, Maroccans would be fun and probably you and Alice would have been raped! I am not surprised Picabia was TERRIFIED. . The opening aria of Faust is most engaging and is Lord Berners writing the music for this? I gave his book The Camel to some one for a birthday recently and now this lady does nothing but read and reread this book. She says it strikes a note she has been looking for for years!

[612]

The Ballet Russe is here and that ALWAYS reminds me of you and Mama Woojums and there is a lovely new ballet (with music by Offenbach) called Gaîté Parisienne which reminds me of Paris in 1907.[1]

Lots and lots of love,
Papa Woojums!

1. The Ballet Russe de Monte Carlo gave the first United States performance of Léonide Massine's ballet *Gaîté Parisienne* (with music from various operettas of Jacques Offenbach and arranged by Maurice Rosenthal) at the Metropolitan Opera House, New York, on 12 October 1938.

To Carl Van Vechten
[Postcard: Brillat-Savarin—Gravure par Bertall]

[? October 1938][1]   [Bilignin par Belley
                                                        Ain]

My dearest P. W.

The vendange is lovely, we eat grapes our grapes everybody's grapes and they are none of them sour,[2] and the World is round is almost done and if the kiddie [W. G. Rogers] asks for it will you send him the Faust, or will you send it to him anyway, and we love you so much, we are hoping to see Bennett [Cerf] on his return from Spain we will not be there before and will hear all about you but we would rather see you

lots of love
Gtrde.

I didn't get this mailed and now The World is Round is done and I hope you will like it.

1. This postcard was enclosed in an envelope.

2. "Gertrude must assuredly have been picking grapes at the d'Aiguy's property at Cerverieu where they had a vineyard surrounding a charming little house about 4 miles from Béon, just outside of Artemare" (letter received from Joan Chapman, 29 November 1981).

❧

To Gertrude Stein

23 October 1938   101 Central Park West
                                                   New York City

Dear Baby Woojums,

I adore The World is Round and like all good children's stories it is good for grownups too. I wish I could try it out on some youngster (I'm sure he would love it) but none is available at this time. You seem to be making experiments in all directions and I don't remember you have ever done anything like this before. Whenever and however it is a huge success. It would be charming to publish it with illustrations of Rose and her Love, of Pepe (who didn't like Rose! There must be some truth in this) of Willie the lion and William, of the Blue chair. Anyway it is most charming and I am letting [W. G.] Rogers borrow it, as you suggest[1] . . . Walter Winchell says Bennett [Cerf] is going to marry a Helen Thompson. Ask him. . Have you met Lin Yutang yet?

Love to all and BOTH!
Papa W!

---

1. Stein's *The World Is Round* was published in two editions. The first, with illustrations by Clement Hurd was published by William R. Scott, New York, on 10 August 1939. The second, the British edition, with illustrations by Sir Francis Rose, was published by B. T. Batsford, Ltd., London in the autumn of 1939.

An abridgement of *The World Is Round* was also published in *Harper's Bazaar*, in both the London and New York editions. The Rose illustrations did not arrive in time to be used by the printers, so George Davis of *Harper's Bazaar* used illustrations by Dugo. *Harper's Bazaar* (New York), 72nd Year, no. 2724 (June 1939), 46–47, 92, 94, 95, 96, and *Harper's Bazaar* (London) (September 1939), 20(6):34–35, 80–82. See George Davis to Stein, 29 May 1939 (YCAL).

❧

To Carl Van Vechten

[Postmark: 15 November 1938]   [5 rue Christine
                                                Paris]

My dearest Papa Woojums,

We had a complete Papa Woojums week, Chinese and Hindoo and all you. Dr Lin and Mrs. L. came to dinner and everybody liked them and we liked them and all had a very good time, and we saw the Hindoo boy and we enjoyed it and then he came here one evening and he was full of you and all you had done for him and there was a great deal of Papa Woojums everywhere and a good time was enjoyed by all.[1] I am glad you liked the World is Round, Francis Rose wants to use it as a film he says it just is a film as it is but that is easy for him to know and not so easy to make the film people know it, however we all live in hope. Paris is very busy and sort of enjoying an armistice buoyancy, we love our flat, and we love Papa Woojums always and always

Baby W.

1. Notes by Van Vechten, 24 January 1941: "Lin Yutang. I gave them a letter to G. S." "Ram Gopal, the dancer."

❧

To Gertrude Stein

[? November 1938]   [101 Central Park West
                                     New York]

Dearest Baby Woojums,

I wish Donald Evans might see the enclosed catalogue![1] I saw a reference yesterday to The Boudoir Companion with a piece called Ida by GS. I hadn't heard of this before.[2] And I hope you and Alice are meeting up with Lin Yutang and HONG and Ram Gopal and Janta![3] many many much love to all!

Papa W!

[615]

1. Stein's *Tender Buttons* was published by Evans' Claire Marie publishing firm in 1914; the price per copy was $1. Van Vechten sent Stein an unidentified booksellers' catalogue that certainly listed a much higher price for the book.

2. Excerpts from Stein's unfinished novel, *Ida A Novel*, were published in *The Boudoir Companion*, ed. Page Cooper (New York: Farrar & Rinehart, 1938), pp. 31–38.

3. Gopal's sister.

To Carl Van Vechten
[Rose motto]

[postmark: 25 November 1938]   5 rue Christine
                                                                [Paris]

Dearest Papa Woojums,

I have not been writing to you lately because Basket died and we like Rose in the story just cried and cried and cried.[1] We are a little better now but it is still pretty bad, and now we do not know quite what to do. The Vet who liked Basket too says we should have another which will never be Basket but some consolidation and it should be as much like him as possible, Daniel-Rops says so too, Pablo [Picasso] says not, he says it would be a torment, just imagine he said if I should die and you went out and got another Pablo it would be alright but it would not be the same, so far we have done nothing but just miss him, little Pepe tries to console us he is very sweet but it isn't the same. Well I do wish Donald Evans might have known, and I did write you about the Boudoir Companion, it must have been one of my most illegible moments but I did tell you,[2] it was the early spring they asked me to contribute and they seem sincerely pleased, Gerald Berners has been over this week, and we have been very busy, English art show at the autumn salon[3] and vin d'honneur and all sorts of things and everybody seems to like the Child's story, I have sold it to Scott, Bennett [Cerf] could not seem to see it,[4] I am afraid Bennett is getting solemn, he is just and sweet and kind but I think he is beginning to believe in the importance of being earnest, and alas, I seem to see its importance less rather than more, had a funny encounter with the real Ernest Hemingway and we loved each other for an hour obstructing traffic on the Faubourg Saint Honoré, he was funny really

[616]

funny, and there is a cinema project, a real one this time and everybody is busy and we love you all the time dear papa Woojums,[5]

Mama & Baby Woojums[6]

1. Rose in Stein's *The World Is Round*.

2. Stein had not written Van Vechten about her contribution to *The Boudoir Companion*.

3. Sir Francis Rose together with Henry Moore, Victor Pasmore, Graham Sutherland, and John Piper were the English artists exhibiting at the Salon d'Automne, Paris.

4. Cerf wrote to Stein, 23 October 1938 (YCAL), that he could not see the book as a juvenile work; he thought it would confuse children and many of their parents as well.

5. Stein had not had word from Ivan Kahn or his sister Lillian Ehrman since 1936 about their efforts to interest a Hollywood studio in her work. Similarly the efforts of Harry Dunham (see Stein to Van Vechten, [25 February 1936], note 1) were not realized. Dunham had last written Stein on 14 February 1938 (YCAL) but had not mentioned the film projects. This may refer to Stein's statement "Francis Rose wants to use it *[The World Is Round]* as a film" (Stein to Van Vechten [15 November 1938]).

6. Both signatures are by Stein.

To Gertrude Stein

2 December [1938]   101 Central Park West
                                                    New York City

Dearest Gertrude,

I am awfully upset about Basket. It seemed to me he was an immortal dog and would be eternal. I always love animals so much more than people and I have a pang whenever I recall any of my dead cats. When they die it is agony and anguish for months. That is why I don't have them any more. There are people who take these things more lightly and get a new dog every time one dies and of course it IS possible to love a new animal, though it never takes the place of an old one. I am so very sorry, sweet Baby Woojums and I know what a heartbreak it is. . I shall look into the Boudoir Companion and I am glad The World Is Round is arranged for. Any publisher YOU choose becomes important on that account. Maybe Bennett [Cerf] is more interested in the Spanish War for the moment than he is in literature.[1] I think The World is Round[x] will be a favorite Child's book and can't wait to find out. I shall send copies to all the children I know. I met [Alexander] Smallens[2] on the street yesterday and he asked "What about the opera Gertrude Stein and [Gerald] Berners are doing? I want to conduct it." I told him I didn't think it was ready yet. The world is dreadfully excited by this. We have a love[ly] new picture of St Cecilia charming the animals, painted by Roelandt Savery (Flemish) circa 1600. We got this at an auction. And I think your picking up [Ernest] Hemingway on the Faubourg St H[onoré] will result in literature on BOTH SIDES.[3] I can't wait to see what you write about this. I'm glad you met all the Orientals and liked them! It seems to me that since there is so much race prejudice one meets more races than one used to. . We had a snow storm the other night with thunder and lightning. Did you ever see anything like that? PLEASE!

  Love to you and Mama Woojums,

         [Carl Van Vechten]

 [x]I dote on this!

---

1. The Spanish Civil War, which had been raging since 1936, was near an end. The Loyalist forces had lost much of the territory they once held. With the fall of Barcelona, in January 1939, the war was almost over. Madrid surrendered in March 1939.

2. The conductor of the 1934–35 performances of *Four Saints in Three Acts*.

3. Neither Stein nor Hemingway wrote about this meeting.

❧

To Gertrude Stein
[Postcard: Kiss Building. Photograph by Carl Van Vechten]

[postmark: 4 December 1938]   [101 Central Park West
                New York City]

Dear Baby Woojums!

  Thornton Wilder & I met at *last* yesterday & had a grand time & I am going to photograph him!—Kitty Cornell was there too & everybody talked about Baby W!

  l[ove] & K[isses] to you both

         Papa W!

[618]

To Gertrude Stein
*[Postcard: Portrait of Carl Van Vechten at the Prospect Park Zoo in front
of the Cheetah Cage. Photograph by Mark Lutz]*

[postmark: 23 December 1938]   [101 Central Park West
                                                 New York]

Dearest Baby Woojums,

I guess I wrote you I had met Thornton Wilder enfin & the Bromfields have been here & we talked endlessly about you and Mama W. They
have become most pro-American. I see you are in the Oxford Dictionary of
American Literature[1] & I *love* Ida!—one of my favorites, please & a merry
Xmas to all from

Fania & Papa Woojums!

1. Stein had been approached by William Rose Benét for permission to include Stein's Choate
lecture, "How Writing is Written," excerpts from *Tender Buttons,* and "The Life of Juan Gris"
in an anthology he was editing with Norman Holmes Pearson. Stein replied, granting permission, on 31 October 1936 (YCAL). Pearson wrote Stein on 31 January 1937 (YCAL) that at
the suggestion of Thornton Wilder he would like to include an excerpt from Stein's "A Long
Gay Book," instead of the *Tender Buttons* excerpts. Wilder had suggested the paragraph beginning "When they are very little just a baby" through the end of the paragraph ("A Long Gay
Book," in *Matisse Picasso and Gertrude Stein,* pp. 25–26). When *The Oxford Anthology of
American Literature,* ed. Benét and Pearson (New York: Oxford University Press, 1938), ap-
peared, only "How Writing is Written" was used (pp. 1446–51). See Stein to Van Vechten [9
November 1936], note 2.

To Gertrude Stein
[Telegram]

[postmark: 25 December 1938]   New York

MOTHER AND FATHER SEND ENDLESS LOVE AND MERRY
CHRISTMAS TO YOU AND MOTHER

CARL VAN VECHTEN

❦

To Gertrude Stein and Alice Toklas
[Telegram]

[postmark: 25 December 1938]   New York

LOVE TO BOTH

FANIA CARLO

❦

To Carl Van Vechten
[Rose motto]

[postmark: 26 December 1938]   5 rue Christine
                                                     [Paris]

Dearest Papa Woojums,

On Christmas day I am wishing Merry Christmas and the happiest of New Years to you and Fania, may you live long and prosper and always be the sweetest dearest onliest Papa Woojums in the world, which you are, we have been having a hectic time with Francis Rose and his troubles but now he is going to have a good show a good show in London, he is to paint some interesting houses in England he has begun to do some successful designing in Paris and he has been separated from entangling alliances and he goes off to England this afternoon and it has been a good two months work, but I guess he is coming out of it all very much alright,[1] and now I am going on with the great American novel which I have begun so often and under such different titles—now I have forgotten just which it is now but I think it is Jenny and Arthur, it was Ida but it is not Ida any longer,[2] and Fanny Butcher sent me Walker Evans' photos of three American houses[3] you know how I felt about them and so I have just been hunting out all those you did of houses in our Virginian trip, we did have a wonderful time, there is snow on the ground here and cold just like it was down there and ice just like it was down there but no alligators and no papa Woojums please

[620]

come and bring an alligator and then it will be all the same and always now dear papa Woojums happy new year to you from[4]

Mama and Baby Woojums.

1. Rose had returned from an extensive visit (1935–38) to the Near and Far East. He spent a great deal of time in 1938 in Paris. The French government organized a retrospective of his work in the Petit Palais, Paris, and he also participated with the English group, which had a section in the Salon d'Automne in Paris. See Stein to Van Vechten [25 November 1938], note 3. Rose's difficulties may have resulted from this exhibition; it is more likely, however, that he had involved Stein in one of his numerous and difficult homosexual relationships.

In 1939 Rose designed the costumes and scenery for Lord Berners' ballet *Cupid and Psyche*, which was presented by the Sadlers' Wells Ballet Company. He also had a one-man exhibition at the Mayor Gallery in London.

2. Stein struggled with various titles for her book *Ida A Novel.*

3. Butcher had sent Stein Walker Evans' *American Photographs*, with an essay by Lincoln Kirstein (New York: The Museum of Modern Art, 1938).

4. Note by Van Vechten, 24 January 1941: "A reference to the alligator in the Franklin Street lobby of the Hotel Jefferson in Richmond." Stein had stayed in that hotel when she visited Richmond, Virginia, in 1935.

To Carl Van Vechten
[Postcard: Two cats in sailboat]

[postmark: 1 January 1939]

[5 rue Christine
Paris]

My dearest Papa Woojums

That is the photograph I like the best of all the ones in print of the Cheetahs, the best of papa Woojums it makes him feel just as if he was here, I wish he was we do, I am once more in the throes of writing the great American novel, now it is called Jenny and Arthur,[1] lots of love on this New Year day,

B. W.

1. Stein's *Ida A Novel.*

≈

To Gertrude Stein
[Postcard: Unidentified building in Boston, Massachusetts Photograph by
Carl Van Vechten]

10 January 1939   [101 Central Park West
                                                        New York]

Dearest Baby Woojums—

Please. Alexander Woollcott called up and he is doing a paper about Poodles & he wanted to know all about Basket & he borrowed your letter about that & *I said he could only use it if he got your permission.*[1] Ethel Waters (Negro) in Mamba's Daughters is our latest sensation and she is a GREAT ACTRESS[2]—and of course we'll all have alligators together again! Wait & see. In the meantime, LOVE to Both—

Papa W

This "fortress" is in Boston!

1. On his Columbia Broadcasting System program of 21 June 1939, Woollcott mentioned Stein in a group of people who owned poodles. The broadcast, titled "Cocaud," after Woollcott's dog, is printed in his *Long, Long Ago* (New York: Viking Press, 1943), pp. 189–94.

2. Ethel Waters, the black actress and singer, played the role of Hagar, the mother of a celebrated radio singer, in the play *Mamba's Daughters*, adapted by Dorothy and DuBose Heyward from the latter's novel of the same name. The play opened at the Empire Theatre, New York, on 3 January 1939. In the *New York Times* of 6 January 1939 (p. 24) nineteen people, including Van Vechten and Marinoff, signed an advertisement praising Ethel Waters' performance and urging readers to go to see the play.

❧

To Gertrude Stein
[Postcard: Portrait of Carl Van Vechten at the Bronx Zoo. Photograph by Mark Lutz]

[postmark: 16 January 1939]   [101 Central Park West
                                                New York]

Dear Baby Woojums,

I'm glad you like the cheetah picture. I do too. Here is another one made in the Zoo. . Jenny & Arthur is a good name for a great American novel, & I am sure it will be.[1] Is this going to be long?—Gertrude Atherton is here & we were talking about you & Mama W today & I wish you & Mama W were here.

*Love
Papa W*

1. Stein's *Ida A Novel.*

❧

To Carl Van Vechten
[Postcard: Photograph of Mango trees—Bulacan]

[postmark: 25 January 1939]   [Paris]

Dearest P. W.

Here we have had a beautiful Chinese dinner and all we want is Papa W. for a truly Chinese [afternoon?] thanks to you.

B. W.

Carl,

We are all here this moment and wish you were among us. Greetings to you both. Expect to see you alligators or alligator pears to Paris.

*[Lin] Yutang
Hong [Yutang]*

[623]

We've had a lovely time with your friends and have been talking about you.

Love from
Baby [i.e., Mama] W.

[signature] *Harriette G. Miller*
[signature] *Harlan Miller*[1]

1. Friends of the Van Vechtens' and the Lin Yutangs'.

To Carl Van Vechten
[Rose motto]

[postmark: 8 February 1939]   5 rue Christine
                                                [Paris]

My dearest Papa Woojums,

This is an additional bit of Faust and there are the catalogues of Francis Rose['s] show and will you give Mark [Lutz] one,[1] and we had a wonderful trip to Bordeaux and we got a very lovely baby Basket and he is not Basket but we make believe he is Basket's boy and Papa W. will take his picture and that will be a pleasure, we had a wonderful trip full of xcitements and now we are back and I am going on with my novel, it goes better in the summer than in the winter, winters seem more occupying than they used to be, and we all send all our love all the time

always
Baby W.

1. The catalogue for Rose's January 1939 exhibition at the Mayor Gallery, London, was a single sheet of paper folded twice to make a triptych, 5 ×7¼ inches. It contained, "Introduction by Gertrude Stein" (p. 5).

🐛

To Carl Van Vechten
[Rose motto]

[postmark: 18? February 1939]   5 rue Christine
                                                  [Paris]

My dearest Papa Woojums,

We have been so busy with the new baby Basket, it takes a lot of time to take a baby Basket in and out and sit with him while he eats a bone so that he does not take it on the bed on the couch, and to see that he does this and not Alice's wool and not my best shoes and poor Pepe was so neglected he just had to get an attack of rheumatism and now we are all petting him, and there is lots going on, the World is Round is getting on, they are trying to find Rose colored paper to print blue on and the Hockaday girls were here and I read it to them and they loved it and they know what children like because they read to their sisters and brothers and they say it will go,[1] and Julian Sawyer says he wants to read Faust so do let him, and Francis Rose is doing Cupid and Psyche a ballet with [Gerald] Berners in London and they are all pleased, and Oklahoma university buys all my books and wants me to contribute to their quarterly[2] and I have and I have changed my car for a new one, hoping The World is Round will make it all easy and we love Papa Woojums and I guess that's all.

Always
Baby W.

1. Elizabeth Jarmon, of the Hockaday School, wrote Stein, 6 February 1939 (YCAL), that she and a Miss Ryan were in Paris and brought Stein greetings from the school. Stein invited them to dinner on 10 February.

2. For a symposium on literary influences in *Books Abroad* (Summer 1939), 13(3):307–8, Stein contributed "My Debt to Books."

To Gertrude Stein

8 March [1939]   [101 Central Park West
                                                   New York]

Dear Gertrude,

Here is how the value of Tender Buttons keeps on rolling along. I'm very curious to see The World is Round on pink paper! Will that be soon now? I hope so. Think of you having a new car! Do you know I've never had any yet! I guess this is something I'm saving for my old age. And a new Basket! Is his name Basket too please? And is he also a white caniche? . . The weather is warm one day and freezing the next, but nobody talks about war any more and maybe the war scare is over. I've noticed they never have wars when people don't talk about them. Do you know a painter named Coutaud and what is his first name?[1]. . Edward Waterboy[2] is here but goes back to Paris samedi on the Queen Mary. .

Love and kisses to Baby and Mama Woojums!

Papa W!

1. Van Vechten had posed the same question to Stein in his letter of 13 April 1936. The painter was Lucien Coutaud.

2. Edward Wasserman.

To Carl Van Vechten
[Correspondence card]

[postmark: 12 March 1939]   [5 rue Christine
                                                   Paris]

Dearest Papa Woojums,

Such a large postal card they give you in France to tell Papa Woojums how much the Woojums love him and they do, and I want to tell you about Serge Roche, who did the furniture which will support the french provisions that are being shown at the fair[1] and you would like him he and his wife are both charming she is not there but he is and I wish you would see him, he has done about the most interesting interior decorating that has been done here and I said you would like him and be good to him, his name is Serge Roche, and he is wonderful with mirrors and I have sold The World is Round to Harpers Bazaar which is very nice,[2] and the Baby Basket is admirable and we love you so and come now do come soon always and always

B. W. and M. W.

1. The New York World's Fair, 1939–40.
2. See Van Vechten to Stein, 23 October 1938, note 1.

To Carl Van Vechten
[Rose motto]

[postmark: 19 March 1939]   5 rue Christine
                                                             [Paris]

My dearest Papa Woojums,

All the old paper is almost gone and then we will have some new but we cannot quite make up our minds just what, it is awful weather cold and cold but we love our place here so that we do not mind, the new Basket eats our handkerchiefs and then races madly around the terrace to have them come out at the other end they get stuck and sometimes there has to be a pull of all of which intimate family life we tell to Papa Woojums. Everybody seems to be xcited about the World is Round, the Harpers people seem to think it will make a very successful film I have kept all the movie rights for myself so I hope somebody will be interested, somebody said Walt Disney but of course I do not know anybody do you know anybody who does, I would like to make a lot of money off of it, now that it is written, I am so glad you like it I do think it kind of lovely, and now another thing, the editor William R. Scott 224 West Eleventh Street and the editor of it John McCullough have found an illustrator, I had suggested Francis Rose but they seemed to want an American, they sent me some of the illustrations by Clement Hurd, they seem sweet but very undistinguished, could you perhaps see them and tell me what you think, I would feel very much better if I knew what you thought.[1] I do not know quite what to say, if you could would you, and I do not know the painter named Coutaud but I will look him up and let you know his first name and lots of love

B. W.

1. For the editions and illustrators of Stein's *The World Is Round* see Van Vechten to Stein, 23 October 1938, note 1.

❧

To Carl Van Vechten
[Postcard: Pont-Sainte-Maxence—Ecole Sainte-Marie du Moncel—Façade
occidental et abbatiale]

[postmark: 22 March 1939]   [5 rue Christine
                                                             Paris]

My dearest Papa Woojums,

Coutaud's first name is Lucien, and can I do anything more about him for you, I know the man who first found him if that is any help,[1] Basket is a poodle a white poodle and very lovely, we are not faithless but we do love him and we do love you always

Gtrde.

1. Note by Van Vechten, 24 January 1941: "I asked about Lucien Coutaud because F[ania] M[arinoff] had bought a painting by this young French artist."

[628]

To Gertrude Stein
*[Postcard: Old Brownstone Façades, West 58 Street, New York. Photograph
by Carl Van Vechten]*

[postmark: 24 March 1939]   [101 Central Park West
                                              New York]

Dearest Baby Woojums,

[Julian] Sawyer came & got Faust—you said he might have it—and
brought it back safely. Serge Roche has *not* turned up yet, but everybody
else has & Hitler is certainly giving us a lot of people![1] We take in Harper's
Bazaar & will watch for your contribution. .
   Happy Easter to you both!

Papa Woojums.

1. A number of European intellectuals and artists had already begun to leave Europe since
Hitler had come to power. Within the next two years, with the help of the American Rescue
Committee headed by Varian Fry, intellectuals and artists such as André Breton, André Masson, Victor Brauner, René Char, Max Ernst, Marcel Duchamp, Fernand Léger, and others
would leave Europe for the United States.

To Carl Van Vechten
[Correspondence card]

[postmark: 31 March 1939]   [5 rue Christine
                                              Paris]

Dearest Papa Woojums,

We are sending you messages by the Chinamen[1] by Nathalie [Barney] by everybody and we wish we could send you messages by yourself,
won't you come over to get them, the Scott people write that they have tried
the World is Round on various groups of children and there is no doubt
about its effectiveness with them, so I am awfully pleased,[2] they are trans-

lating Everybody's [Autobiography] into french and otherwise we are very busy, and also very loving, happy Easter, and April fool's day and everything

B. W. and M. W.[3]

1. Lin Yutang.

2. John McCullough wrote to Stein, 23 March 1939 (YCAL), and reported that they had tried the book out with various and varied groups of children with exciting results. Some of these results were quoted in a press booklet prepared by the publicist Joseph D. Ryle, *Press Book for Gertrude Stein's First Book for Children 'The World Is Round'* (New York: William R. Scott, Inc., 1939), pp. 3–6. The booklet (15 leaves numbered 1–15) also contains excerpts from Stein's letters to the publisher (pp. 11–13) and comments by Stein extracted from letters, p. 6 and p. 15.

3. Both signatures are in Stein's hand.

To Gertrude Stein

5 April 1939
101 Central Park West
New York City

Dearest Baby Woojums,

Thanks for the news about Lucien Coutaud. Does the man "who first found him" know if he has given a one-man show and has he an extra catalogue he can send me or any other data? I would be grateful. The New Basket seems to be lively and lovable and is making great strides in your affection, I can see. I am most curious as to what kind of stationery you will have in the rue Christine. Please send me a very early sheet of this with a NICE letter (as always!). The weather here is as changeable as a wife's mind and I have had a long succession of colds that nothing now will rid me of but a long siege of HOT weather and I am praying for THAT. Fortunately that is ONE thing you may be sure of in New York City . . . A VERY curious coincidence. A man named Leo Stein died in New York. He was president of the Society of the Hard of Hearing and he had a daughter named Gertrude. Was this a relative? . . I KNOW NOBODY at the William R Scott Company. I wrote you I had never heard of the firm. So I can't suddenly ask them to show me some illustrations. Why don't you write *them* to show them to *me* and ask my opinion? It will be too bad, and certainly most unusual, for you to have "undistinguished illustrations."[1] I do HOPE you do sell The World is Round to Disney and I hope you and Mama W will have to come over and stay for YEARS while it is being filmed.

Love to both,
Papa Woojums!

And happy Easter!

1. See Stein to Van Vechten [31 March 1939], note 2.

To Gertrude Stein
[Postcard: Renoir—Boating Party. Phillips Memorial Gallery,
Washington, D.C.]

10 April [1939]   [101 Central Park West
                                                        New York]

Dear Baby Woojums!

Happy Easter to you! So glad the little Shirley Temples like your book. I *love* it I can scarcely wait to possess it in print! The weather is frightfully uncertain & I have a bad cold. Do you know the Baroness Hatvavy of Buda-Pesth?

Love to Both
Papa W

To Carl Van Vechten

[postmark: 28 April 1939]   [5 rue Christine
                                                        Paris]

My dear Papa Woojums,

I hope your cold is getting better and better and no other colds are coming after, I have just had the little Chinese book, with your photo as

[631]

frontispiece,[1] see stamp on this letter they made it for you,[2] it is an awfully cute book, we are reading it with the greatest pleasure, and as you see we can't make up our minds about letter paper yet and have used up all the old, the Scott people now are thinking of doing a preliminary edition of 800 signed copies, I am going to ask them to talk to you, they seem very nice and very enthusiastic, but they wanted the cinema rights but I have kept them, the new Basket is very handsome, we talk to ourselves about it and say he is the son of the other one only he does not resemble him but that is what sons are for, it's cold spring does not seem to be able to come to stay, we won't be leaving for Bilignin until the 20 of May and we do love P. W. and want him all well

Love
B. W.

1. Note by Van Vechten, 24 January 1941: "The book by Lin Yutang's daughters." The book is *Our Family*, by Adel and Anor Lin, with a foreword and comments by Meimei Yutang and introduction by Pearl S. Buck (New York: The John Day Co., 1939). The frontispiece is a reproduction of a photograph of the three Lin daughters by Van Vechten.

2. The stamp on the envelope was a 2-franc 25-centime stamp, "1839 Centenaire de la Photographie 1939," "Arago Annonce la Découverte de la Photographie. Le 7 Janvier 1839."

To Gertrude Stein
[Postcard: Elaborately iced six-tiered Italian cake. Photograph by
Carl Van Vechten]

2 May 1939   [101 Central Park West
                                                 New York]

Dear Baby Woojums!

I loved your Zurburan card[1]. . Here is an Italian cake. The Lin Yutangs are back & we gave them a (partly) Chinese dinner, & tomorrow we are seeing Natalie Barney. My cold is practically gone with the opening of the World's Fair & the warm weather & here is the newest stamp for you.[2] Fania & I send lots of love to you & Mama Woojums!

Papa W

Picasso's Guernica goes on show on Thursday.[3]

[632]

1. In her recent correspondence Stein had not sent Van Vechten a Zurburan postcard.

2. The New York World's Fair, 1939–40, officially opened on 30 April 1939. The fair was organized to coincide with the 150th anniversary of Washington's inauguration as the first President of the United States at Federal Hall in New York City. The stamp on the card was a 3-cent Sesquicentennial of the inauguration.

3. Picasso's painting *Guernica* together with its related drawings and studies was exhibited at the Valentine Gallery, New York, from 4 to 27 May 1939. This was the first showing in America of the painting. The exhibition was presented by the American Artists Congress for the benefit of the Spanish Refugee Relief Campaign. Van Vechten and Marinoff were among the sponsors of the exhibition.

   Picasso had been invited by the Spanish Republican government to paint a mural for the Spanish Pavilion at the Paris World's Fair scheduled to open in June 1937. On 26 April 1937 German planes in alliance with General Franco's anti-Loyalist army had tested incendiary bombs on an unprotected, totally civilian Spanish village, Guernica, killing 2,000 people. Picasso had seen photographic accounts of the bombing in the French newspaper *Ce Soir*. It was from these that he found his theme for the Spanish Pavilion mural. He began his sketches on 1 May 1937, the composition was outlined on canvas by 11 May, and the completed painting was installed in the Spanish Pavilion by mid-June 1937.

To Gertrude Stein
[Postcard: Polar Bear, the Prospect Park Zoo. Photograph by
Carl Van Vechten]

5 May 1939   [101 Central Park West
                                             New York]

Dear Baby Woojums,

   Picasso's Guernica is here & creating vast excitement. Natalie [Barney] came to see me & brought your love. She says she walks with you frequently. Natalie is handsomer than ever & vastly amusing always. I loved the photographic stamp & I can't wait for The World is Round! I haven't heard from [W. R.] Scott. Try to get Thornton Wilder to let me photograph him please!

                                             Love to both
                                             Papa W!

To Carl Van Vechten

[postmark: 12 May 1939]   [5 rue Christine
                                                  Paris]

My dear Papa Woojums,

I have asked John McCullough to call you up and talk to you about the World is Round, they want to do this early special edition, I am not sure about it, and I am asking them to talk to you about it, as I told them I always follow your advice, and also they want to know about publicity and photographs, I said I wanted them to talk to you about that too, in short I want them to talk to you about it all, their address is 224 Eleventh Street, and John McCullough is the one I correspond with, not William R. Scott, I am just a little fussed about it all just now, but I know you will get it unfussed, you know I always do get myself do get myself sort of balled up and then Papa Woojums gets it all all straightened out, and just at present we need straightening,[1] Nathalie [Barney] will be back day after to-morrow and will tell us all about you, the sun is shining and we are so relieved that your colds are all well, you remember the first Negroes we saw in the hospital that scared Alice, when they very black stood in a row and she asked them what was the matter with them and they said, we's colds. We don't want Papa Woojums to be we's colds. Thank you papa Woojums for making the crooked ways straight, it is your way bless you, Baby Basket is getting bigger and better and on the 25 we go to Bilignin but we love our new apt. so we hate to leave it

Always
Baby Woojums.

---

1. McCullough had written to Stein, 20 April 1939 (YCAL), proposing a deluxe edition (350 copies) of *The World Is Round*, signed by Stein and by the illustrator, Clement Hurd. The edition was planned to coincide with the publication of the story in *Harper's Bazaar*. On 26 May 1939 (YCAL) McCullough wrote Stein that he and Clement Hurd had met with Van Vechten and that they had agreed with him not to publish anything during the summer months.

❧

To Gertrude Stein

14 May [1939]   101 Central Park West
Sunday   New York City

Dear Baby Woojums,

I was THRILLED to receive the new photographic stamp (you were the only one who thought of sending it!) and I'm very pleased with the French government to have thought of it. As times get worse at least we can be diverted with stamps and the American government thought of this a few years ago and now we have a new stamp every month and love 'em! . . My cold is gone. Somebody gave me a patent medicine called Brown Mixture and it went right away. . The opening of the new Museum of Modern Art was something: Bobsy Goodspeed, Brancusi, Marsden Hartley, and Anne Lindbergh all in the same room together! Cars were stalled all the way up and down Fifth Avenue as Piccadilly is when there is a Drawing-Room and inside the Museum I discovered that when they are crushed together in a heated room rich people smell a little worse even than poor people. . The show begins with [Albert] Ryder and [Thomas] Eakins and Cezanne and comes down to Miro, Picasso, and even Dali. The arrangement is good and it looks like a smash hit. Sculpture is in the garden and in the basement is a moving picture theatre (for old films) which is most amusing. On the opening night they were showing Theda Bara in A Fool There Was. .[1] Then [Valentine] Dudensing has Picasso's Guernica and when I wandered in the opening day somebody asked me to be photographed and pushed me over next to a nice Spaniard in front of the picture and when it was over we were introduced and it was General Negrin.[2]. There are a lotta important shows here in account of the Fair and I think the two most generally represented artists, curiously enough (I mean in combination) are Picasso and Eakins. . I haven't been to the Fair yet but we expect to go tomorrow if it doesn't rain, which it generally does. Everybody raves about the Fair and says it is beautiful and FUN[x]. . The Lin Yutangs are back and were here for a (partly) Chinese dinner one night. . And I am addressing this letter to Bilignin with the idea that you will be there by the time it arrives!

Lots of love to Baby and Mama Woojums from ton Papa Woojums!

P!

[x]But it is not yet successful.

1. The Museum of Modern Art, New York, had a preview and formal opening of its new building on West Fifty-third Street on 10 May 1939.

2. See Van Vechten to Stein, 2 May 1939, note 3. General Juan Negrin (1891–1956) was the last Republican Prime Minister of Spain (May 1937 to March 1939). After the fall of Madrid, 28 March 1939, he went into exile.

To Gertrude Stein

25 May [1939]　　　　　　　　　　　　　101 Central Park West
　　　　　　　　　　　　　　　　　　　　　New York City

Dearest Baby Woojums,

John McCullo[u]gh and Clement Hurd, the illustrator of T[he] W[orld] I[s] R[ound], came up to see me yesterday and it seems to me, with your usual good fortune you have found some very nice people. You were not very explicit in your letter about what you wanted me to settle and Mr McCullo[u]gh didn't seem to think anything was very wrong. . However. . Clement Hurd had the drawings under his arm and they seem very pleasant and I should think very good for a children's book and I should think all children would like them. They are pretty in blue and white on the pink. I like them and I liked young Hurd. ANYWAY, I said I thought you ought to see the drawings before they were published and I suggested they hold off on their special edition until you had passed on them. They thought this an excellent idea, and Clement Hurd said he even preferred this. . Secondly, I said it was none of my business and I might be wrong, but I thought July was a bad time to get out such a book, when your special friends would be away and could give it no attention (BE SURE to tell them to send a copy to Henry McBride) and when I got through saying this McCullo[u]gh said he was inclined to believe with me that it WOULD be a bad idea. Anyway, there's where we are, I advised them to send you the drawings and I advised them to postpone publication (of the limited edition) till fall. . I didn't tell them definitely to do anything. I think you will find the drawings charming enough and if you agree with me about the fall publication why write or cable McCullo[u]gh that you do, after you have heard from him. But I think he has already decided to wait. So is all this helpful or any good or what you wanted me to do, Mama and Baby Woojums, or does all this mix things up more? I wouldn't know because you didn't tell me exactly what was the trouble.

O yes, he spoke of wanting to come out as soon as possible after the Harper's Bazaar publication and I said I didn't think that made any difference at all. . Especially as they were only printing less than half of the complete thing.[1]

I wish you and Mama were here for the World's Fair. It is very beautiful and it is now fashionable to give dinners in the wonderful foreign restaurants—each foreign building has one—So that one or two nights a week we are invited over to such a repast after which you watch the fountains with flames in the centre or walk about among the artificially lighted tulip beds. We are dining at the opening of the Brazilian pavilion tomorrow night and are a little curious about Brazilian food, as we have never enjoyed any. .

Love and kisses to you both, and five red and white sticks of sugar candy!

Papa Woojums!

I saw Sherwood [Anderson] yesterday and we talked about you and I told him about TWIR.

1. McCullough wrote about this meeting with Van Vechten in his letter to Stein of 26 May 1939 (YCAL). See Stein to Van Vechten [12 May 1939], note 1.

To Carl Van Vechten
[Postcard: Pont-Sainte-Maxence—Ecole Sainte-Marie du Moncel—Les
Combles (Charpente du XIVe Siècle unique en France)]

[before 26 May 1939]   [5 rue Christine
                                                          Paris]

My dear Papa W.

I have just been disqued for a broadcast June 27 Eiffel tower, I hope you will like it, sent out at eleven o'clock evening at Paris, and now it is all warm and soon we will be leaving for the country, I wish you would be here too lots of love[1]

Gtrde.

1. Stein was one of the many artistic and literary personalities who had been asked to participate in the fiftieth anniversary celebration of the construction of the Eiffel Tower. The tower, designed by Alexandre Eiffel, had been erected in the Champ-de-Mars for the Paris exposition of 1889.

Stein's talk, "France and the Eif[f]el Tower," was broadcast on 27 June 1939. The YCAL archives do not have the recording Stein speaks of as having been made; nor have I been able to locate a copy in the archives of the French radio.

The unpublished manuscript of this talk (the last leaf is missing) is in YCAL. It is not listed in either Wilson, *Gertrude Stein: A Bibliography*, or Bridgman, *Gertrude Stein in Pieces*.

The manuscript was written, and presumably the talk was given, in English. It is written in ink on 8½ × 11 inch unlined paper. At the top of the first leaf there is an inscription: "Dedicated to Elizabeth [i.e., Elisabeth de Gramont, Duchesse de Clermont-Tonnerre] who being french has made me love France too. Gertrude. For the Eif[f]el Tower celebration."

The talk begins with Stein recounting being in Paris before the building of the Eiffel Tower and then again while it was under construction. She speaks of Paris as a city that is "xciting and peaceful," qualities that are needed if one is to make literature. She then tells two incidents to define French character: one from her experiences during World War I, the other a recent encounter with a farmer from Bilignin who told her why he felt there would not be a war.

The dedication to Elisabeth de Gramont was appropriate. She had written a book, *Mémoires de la tour Eiffel* (Paris: B. Grasset, 1937).

To Gertrude Stein
[Postcard: Portrait of Carl Van Vechten in Central Park. Photograph by Mark Lutz]

[postmark: 3 June 1939]

[101 Central Park West
New York]

Dearest Baby Woojums

T[he] W[orld] I[s] R[ound] looks pretty sweet in Harper's Baza[a]r. [John] McCullo[u]gh called me again & was vague & I couldn't tell you *what* they are going to do now. But the proofs are here & the type is lovely. I predict a sensation for TWIR.

[638]

A postcard is here from you announcing great events on June 27 but what they are I can't make out AT ALL.

Love to both
Papa W.

❧

To Carl Van Vechten

[postmark: 5 June 1939]   Bilignin par Belley
                                                          Ain

My dearest Papa Woojums,

Here we are and it's nice to be here, the new Basket completely different, every inch a dog, and quite a few inches, just pining to be photographed by Papa Woojums, and [John] McCullough and [Clement] Hurd both were delighted with their visit to you, they both wrote very happily about it, yes you did just what I wanted, you reassured me about the pictures, since then I have seen them and I think they are very charming and go very well with the text and you made them reconsider summer publishing, I did not want to say no to them absolutely, but I wanted them to have your opinion and as it confirmed mine it will make them examine the matter more, and Alice and I giggled a lot about Twir [i.e., The World Is Round], we think it is a lovely name, I have sold the book to Batsford for the English edition, they are bringing it out for Christmas, their idea is a little book to look like a Christmas card, the two editions will be very different,[1] and now I am doing a little operette for a boite de nuit of Agnes Capri, I am doing it about superstitions and in the french language, I don't know how it will turn out, or who is to do the music, I leave that to the Boite de nuit,[2] I wish we were with you eating Brazilian dishes, this stamp is all about it,[3] and now having gardened and all we go to bed, Mama Woojums has a cold like you had a cold but we are hoping that the garden will fix it, lots of love always and always to dear dear Papa Woojums and lots of love to Fania always

Gtrde B. W.

[639]

1. See Van Vechten to Stein, 25 May [1939], note 1.

2. Agnes Capri, a singer with a following among French intellectuals, opened her own *boîte de nuit* in the rue Sainte-Anne, Paris, on 21 September 1939. When Capri approached Stein for a text that might be set to music, Stein had first suggested the Stein-Thomson *Film: Deux soeurs qui sont pas soeurs* or Thomson's *Le Berceau de Gertrude Stein*, eight poems by Georges Hugnet that Thomson had set to music (see Stein to Thomson, postmark 28 May 1939, YCAL). Capri apparently wanted a new work, and so in late June 1939 Stein sent her the typescript of "Les Superstitions" (Capri to Stein, 26 June 1939, YCAL).

In a subsequent undated letter (YCAL) Capri wrote Stein that she had shown the typescript to the composer Georges Auric, who, while he found the piece enchanting, felt that there would have to be some modifications to the text if he were to compose the music for it. Just as Stein had given Thomson a free hand in working with her text, there is no reason to suppose she would not have done the same for Auric. The music was not written and the piece has remained unpublished.

"Les Superstitions" consists of monologues by four characters: L'Araignée (the spider), Le Coucou (the cuckoo), Le Poisson Rouge (the gold fish), and Les Nains (the dwarfs).

The manuscript is written in a French school-children's cahier, similar to the ones Stein used for much of her writing. Whether she was copying into the cahier from another notebook or from some loose leaves cannot be determined, since this is the only extant manuscript of the work. The first part of the cahier contains Stein's French text, with only occasional slips or corrections. The manuscript stops toward the middle of the cahier and then ends on the inside back cover. Toward the middle, several pages after Stein had interrupted her manuscript, the French text has been recopied by Thornton Wilder, who was visiting Stein at the time. Wilder's copy of the manuscript contains occasional corrections of transcription errors in the hand of either Stein or Toklas.

The English translation of "Les Superstitions" was made by Stein in 1940 on sheets of lined paper and follows Stein's French text. There are, however, several parts, particularly in the cuckoo section, where Stein has x'ed out parts of the English translation. The English translation also remains unpublished.

3. The stamp is a 2-franc 25-centime stamp, "Exposition International, New York 1939. Le Pavillon de la France."

To Carl Van Vechten
[Postcard: Titien. Portrait de l'Empereur Charles-Quint á Mühlberg]

[postmark: 14 June 1939]   [Bilignin par Belley
                                                            Ain]

The Spanish pictures are wonderful, we had a lovely time with them would we could see them together,[1] the amusing great event was my broadcasting on the anniversary of the Eiffel Tower to America, I did it on a disk

[640]

and the disk I hope does it to you,[2] had a charming letter from Adel Lin, we did enjoy them thanks to you[3]

Baby W.

1. Note by Van Vechten, 24 January 1941: "The pictures from the Prado in Spain were shown in Geneva during the Spanish [Civil] War."

2. Stein had recorded her talk before the actual date of the broadcast. See Stein to Van Vechten [before 26 May 1939], note 1.

3. Adel Lin had written Stein on 3 June 1939 (YCAL). She thanked Stein for her letter and expressed her appreciation for Stein's comments on the sisters' book, *Our Family.*

To Gertrude Stein
[Postcard: Waterfall on the façade of the Italian Pavilion, New York
World's Fair, 1939. Photograph by Carl Van Vechten]

16 June [1939]   [101 Central Park West
                                                 New York]

Dear Baby Woojums!

This is a part of the waterfall on the facade of the Italian Bldg at the World's Fair & here is our *newest* stamp.[1] I love the French stamps you find to put on your envelopes!

Love to both
Papa W!

I will be 59 tomorrow!

1. A 3-cent 1839–1939 Centennial of Baseball stamp.

[641]

❧

To Gertrude Stein
[Postcard: Parachute Jump, New York World's Fair, 1939]

25 June [1939]   [101 Central Park West
                                  New York]

Dearest Baby Woojums

I'm glad I did all right with your publishers. The World is Round looked very pretty in Harper's Bazaar & will look prettier in a book. Please see that I get the English edition. I also hope I get one of your new discs. I do wish you & Mama W could see the Fair

l[ove]. & K[isses].
Papa W.

❧

To Carl Van Vechten
[Postcard: Van der Weyden dit Roger de la Pasture. La Réposition]

[postmark: 20? July 1939]   [Bilignin par Belley
                                             Ain]

Dearest papa Woojums,

Golly it rains, I really do not believe I have ever seen so much rain, but we like it, I am working not too much, but some, we have lots of passers by, but we would like Carl to come we would when will you, it is a nice fair but it is time to leave it, do come lots of love

B. W.

❧

To Carl Van Vechten

[postmark: 21 July 1939]   Bilignin par Belley
                                            Ain

Dear Papa Woojums,

There is the new Basket and the weather has been tempered to the
unshorn doggie, he is very sweet and leaps up in the air higher than my
head which makes us very proud, it is easy to be proud of a pretty dog, he
has lovely dark eyes, and is very sweet, and Clement Hurd writes me that
Sloan is doing six nursery rugs from the drawings, they will be hand hooked
circular rugs about 3 ft in diameter and will be made of wool and sell from
$12 to $15, he is very pleased and hopes that we will make lots of money
off of nursery specialties as well as the book,[1] the English edition is now
being printed and if I get an xtra set of proofs will send them to you, the
cover sounds very lovely, we are very busy, it is a pleasant and a busy summer, cool but not too cold, no flowers but lots of love to you and to Fania
always, and always

Gtrde B. W.

1. Stein in quoting details from a letter she received from Clement Hurd, 12 July 1939 (YCAL).

❧

To Gertrude Stein
*[Postcard: Empire Clock in the Van Vechtens' apartment. Photograph by
Carl Van Vechten]*

25 July 1939   [101 Central Park West
                                         New York]

Dear Baby Woojums,

Here is strange news indeed about the nut stores. "People have stopped
eating nuts indeed!" I am shocked by the idea.[1] We are having divine weather

this summer and don't expect to leave New York, especially as the Fair is most amusing and we frequently go over for dinner.

Much love from both of us to you and Mama Woojums!

Papa Woojums!

1. Van Vechten sent Stein an unidentified clipping about the Chock Full O'Nuts stores. In 1926 William Black opened a stand that sold shelled nuts. The idea caught on and soon there were several Chock Full O'Nuts stores in the New York metropolitan area. They advertised, "Every kind of nut available." Van Vechten had jokingly mentioned these stores to Stein in the 1920s and the subject became a joke between them. In YCAL there is a fragment of a carton with Chock Full O'Nuts stores advertising on it. When the Depression came, nuts were a luxury item and the stores were converted into coffee shops. See Stein to Van Vechten [29 November 1930], note 1.

To Gertrude Stein
[Postcard: Portrait of Andre Ratoucheff in Morris Gest costume. Miracle Town, Amusement Area, New York World's Fair, 1939. Photograph by Carl Van Vechten]

29 July [1939]   [101 Central Park West
                                                         New York]

Dearest Baby Woojums

Everything is dying here for lack of rain & apparently you are getting too much rain. [John] McCullo[u]gh telephoned he wants to see me (what about?) & is coming tomorrow.

love to you & Mama W
Papa W

This is a Russian midget at the Fair!

❧

To Gertrude Stein
*[Postcard: Portrait of Tsuifeng (Hong) Yutang. Photograph by
Carl Van Vechten]*

[postmark: 31 July 1939]   [101 Central Park West
                                                 New York]

Beloved Baby Woojums!

John McCullo[u]gh came in yesterday and wanted suggestions for
advertising & reviews. I suggested he get the Lin [Yutang] children to review
the book & to get a BLURB from Shirley Temple! He is a very nice fellow
I think you will like him

*love
Papa W.*

Donald Sutherland, who has married a french woman, sent me his
book, Child With a Knife.[1]

1. Sutherland, who was still writing his doctoral dissertation at Princeton University, had married Gilberte De Save de Savigny, whom he met when she came to teach French at his aunt Abbey Sutherland Brown's school in Philadelphia, Pennsylvania. Sutherland had written a novel, *Child with a Knife* (Littleton, N. H.: Courier Printing Co., 1937).

❧

To Carl Van Vechten
[Postcard: Goya y Lucinentes. La Famille de Charles IV]

[postmark: 9 August 1939]   [Bilignin par Belley
                                                 Ain]

Dearest Papa Woojums,

I think your ideas wonderful, hurrah for the review by the Times the
all three of them[1] and the real french Rose is now wearing a Shirl[e]y Temple dress her father bought her,[2] so that would be wonderful, it all will be

[645]

wonderful and I think your photo of the midget one of the best you have ever done, it is a beautiful picture, imagine it rains so hard it is so cold that we have had a fire in the salon all day when I tell the farmers about the heat and draught in America they sigh with envy,

lots and lots of love
B. W.

1. *Our Family*, a book by Adel, Anor, and Meimei Yutang, was reviewed in the *New York Times* on 16 April 1939, p. 9. See Stein to Van Vechten [28 April 1939], note 1.

2. The character of Rose, in Stein's *The World Is Round*, was based on Rose d'Aiguy, the daughter of the Baron and Baroness Robert d'Aiguy, who lived in Béon, not far from Bilignin. Stein also dedicated the book to her.

   At Stein's suggestion Joseph D. Ryle, who was handling the publicity for the book, wrote to the Baroness d'Aiguy for information about her daughter. The reply, 22 May 1939 (YCAL), written from Kebili, Tunisia, makes an interesting comparison with the character Stein developed.

> Rose Lucie Renée Anne d'Aiguy was born in 1928 and is a descendant of an old French Family known since the 14th century. One of her ancestors fought with the French army in the United States for several years under the command of Marchal [sic] Count de Rochambeau during the war of Independance [sic], and her father was made for this reason, a son of the American Revolution.

> She went twice in the South of Tunisia where her father is General Manager of a date palm Company of which her God father, Mr P. C. Merillon, very well known in United States, is the President.

> When Rose was seven she wrote a play in which all the members of her family, the servants and the animals of the house had something to do. Now she is in school in Switzerland. She loves to climb in the trees, read fairy tales and do cooking, but her greatest pleasure is to help the gardener when the hay is cut and ride the old mule when the cart brings it all in the barn.

> Rose has a tender nature and loves to play tricks. She always makes herself beleive [sic] that she beleives [sic] things that she knows well are not true.

> Rose has blue eyes like the blue chair, the blue sky in the morning and the blue shining lake of her country, the Bugey, which was also the country of Brillat Savarin the author of "La Physiologie du Gout."

[646]

To Gertrude Stein
[Postcard: Portrait of Benny Garland. Photograph by Carl Van Vechten][1]

12 August [1939]   [101 Central Park West
                                                      New York]

Dear Baby Woojums!

What a wonderful idea: Sloan's Nursery Rugs after G. S! & what a sweet picture of the new Basket!—I eat *lots* at the foreign pavilions at the Fair: Chile, Venezuela, Cuba, Finland, Denmark! It is fun! & I *am* making some Color Pictures

love to you both from
Fania & Papa W![2]

1. Benny Garland was the child of Pearl Showers' niece. Mrs. Showers was the Van Vechtens' housekeeper.

2. Written and signed by Van Vechten.

To Gertrude Stein
[Postcard: Statue in front of the Polish Pavilion, New York World's Fair,
1939. Photograph by Carl Van Vechten][1]

19 August [1939]   [101 Central Park West
Samedi.   New York]

Dear Baby W!

This is to wish you & Mama W a happy Midsummer Day in the facade of Poland at the World's Fair, & with a *new* stamp[2]

Our love to you both
Papa W

1. The bronze statue, by Stanislaw Kazimierz, represented King Wladyslaw II Jagiello, who defeated the Teutonic Knights in 1410 and founded a mighty Polish dynasty. This statue is now in Central Park, New York.

2. A 3-cent stamp celebrating the twenty-fifty anniversary of the Panama Canal.

❧

To Gertrude Stein
[Postcard: View of New York World's Fair, 1939. Photograph by Carl Van Vechten.]

22 August 1939   [101 Central Park West
                                        New York]

Dear Gertrude,

I have just read The World is Round over again and dear Baby Woojums I have written Mr [John] M[c]Cullo[u]gh: "The World is Round is perhaps the most original child's book, written for grownups to read to each other and their children, since Alice in Wonderland."

Love to you and Mama W.
Papa W!

What a lovely book!

❧

To Carl Van Vechten

[postmark: 30 August 1939]   Bilignin par Belley
                                                    Ain

My dearest Papa Woojums

I am so pleased that you are so pleased with the World is Round, it is a lovely book, I had a nice letter that is card from Adel Lin, what is their present address I think it would be wonderful if they did a review of the book, she says they are xpecting it eagerly, she is an awfully sweet girl,[1] and Bobby Haas said he met the manager of Doubleday Doran in St. Louis and he had seen the book and was mad about it and thought it would be as successful as Ferdinand,[2] that would be nice, but you always know and it is a great comfort, we are in the midst of soldiers and curfew and other things but with it all everybody is peaceful and so are we, everybody is just as nice as they can possibly be, I go on working a little, my Paris book is getting on,[3] and I must send you a copy of the Superstitions to keep which when all is well is going to be sung in a night club in Paris, that will be fun will you come lots of love to you both lots and lots and lots always[4]

Baby Woojums.

1. Adel Lin, one of Lin Yutang's daughters, wrote Stein from Arlington, Vermont (postmark 12 July 1939, YCAL), where she and her family were spending a month living in a log cabin while their father finished a novel.

2. Munro Leaf's *The Story of Ferdinand* (New York: The Viking Press, 1936) was a highly successful children's book. It was made into a film, *Ferdinand the Bull*, by Walt Disney Productions in 1938.

3. Stein's *Paris France.*

4. See Stein to Van Vechten [5 June 1939], note 2.

To Gertrude Stein

13 September [1939]
101 Central Park West
New York City

Dearest Baby Woojums,

Frances Steloff of the Gotham Book Mart is getting out a De Luxe Catalogue and wanted a blurb about you (before the list of your books) signed by me. . Here is what I sent her and I hope it will amuse you:

Gertrude Stein rings bells, loves baskets, and wears handsome waistcoats. She has a tenderness for green glass and buttons have a tenderness for her. In the matter of fans you can only compare her with a moving picture star in Hollywood and three generations of young writers have sat at her feet. She has influenced without coddling them. In her own time she is a legend and in her own country she is with honor. Keys to sacred doors have been presented to her and she understands how to open them. She writes books for children, plays for actors, and librettos for operas. She writes fiction and auto-biography and criticism of painters. Each one of them is one. For her a rose is a rose and how![1]

The Lins are now at the Croydon, 86 Street and Madison Avenue. We had a really wonderful Chinese dinner with them the other night. From the West one hears that Mabel [Dodge] is interested in Krishnamurti.[2] I see I may expect some new mss from you. GOOD! We get no war news at all. So I suppose you don't either. THIS war is being really fought sub rosa. But of course your frenchmen always win.   This time probably it would be safer to blow up Germany from the Rhine to the Baltic.[3]

Fania and I will have been married 25 years on October 21! Isn't that something.

we send love to you and Mama Woojums,

Papa Woojums!

1. Van Vechten's "Gertrude Stein," in *We Moderns: Gotham Book Mart 1920–1940* (New York: Gotham Book Mart, 1940), p. 63. A deluxe edition of this catalogue was for sale at fifty cents. The trade edition was given gratis to clients. The catalogue also contains a Stein letter to "My dear Miss Steloff," postmark 22 October 1939, p. 3, and a list of books by Stein, pp. 63–65.

2. Jiddu Krishnamurti, an Indian religious figure.

3. Shortly before 6 A.M. on 1 September 1939, Germany, without a declaration of war, marched into Poland. England and France, who were committed to the defense of Poland, declared war on Germany on 3 September. The Russian forces entered eastern Poland on 17 September. The last fragment of Polish opposition surrendered on 5 October.

To Carl Van Vechten

[postmark: 17 September 1939]   Bilignin par Belley
                                                       Ain

My dearest Papa Woojums,

I know you have been worrying about us but we are quite alright, just staying here, I have had a radio put in and I get America on it, and they say good morning oh yes good morning, it comes out of Schenectady and otherwise we love France more than ever and they are all sweeter and more wonderful and Alice is nightly proud of being a Pole,[1] and the second day of the war they called me up on the telephone from Paris to interview me about the World is Round, it was strange having a long conversation about that over the telephone at that moment, it was for Time, and I do hope it goes well,[2] we have no plans at present we stay here now and later I do not know probably back to Paris and lots of love to you and Fania

Always
B. W.

1. Toklas' maternal grandfather, Louis Levinsky, was born in 1827 in the town of Exin, in Prussia. He emigrated to the United States, with his brothers John and Mark, in 1848. In 1854 he returned to Europe and there married his cousin Hanchen Lewig (his brother John married her sister Mathilda). Toklas' grandparents returned to the United States in 1855, and it was there, in Brooklyn, New York, that Toklas' mother, Emma Levinsky, was born. In 1856 the Levinskys left by boat for California. They settled in San Francisco in 1869

Very little is known about Toklas' father's origins. Ferdinand Toklas was twenty when he left Poland for the United States in 1865. After a few years in several eastern states, he traveled to San Francisco and there, in 1875, met and married Emma Levinsky. Alice Toklas was born on 30 April 1877 in her grandfather's house, 922 O'Farrell Street, San Francisco.

2. "Rose Is a Gertrude," *Time* (9 October 1939), 34:76.

To Carl Van Vechten

[postmark: 1 October 1939]

Bilignin par Belley
Ain

My dearest Papa Woojums,

Well will we come or not, it is for you to say, [John] McCullough has suggested that we do, and really we might, life is very tranquil here but there is nothing to do to help, everything is so well organised that for the moment we are not needed and we might do good over there, well anyway, I cabled to McCullough that I would consider lecturing a little and reading the World is Round a lot,[1] by the way I have just begun a new child's story about war-time, it begins not badly,[2] but of course we are up against the same proposition, I do not want a strenuous life, a nice quiet one like the last time we were over and I have to earn a good deal of money, because over here well you know it does not cost much and over there the two of us and perhaps this time the two dogs and would you talk to McCullough, and let us know you are our father and our mother and our sister and our brother and our cousins and our aunts dearest Papa Woojums and our protector,

Always
Gtrde B. W.

1. In his letter to Stein, 16 September 1939 (YCAL), McCullough had suggested that Stein consider leaving France and return to the United States for "a flying lecture tour." Stein considered this possibility, but it was too late in the lecture season to arrange a tour.

2. "Helen Button A Story of War-Time" was begun as a separate children's story and then incorporated into Stein's *Paris France*, pp. 80–92 (in Haas and Gallup, A *Catalogue*, this story and *Paris France* are separate entries).

   The story of Helen Button is based on Stein's conversations with Hélène Bouton, a girl of seventeen who lived in the town of Céyzérieu, not far from Bilignin. On 12 September 1939 (YCAL) Bouton wrote Stein in reply to an ad for a servant girl that had appeared in *Le Bugiste*, a local paper. In spite of her age she was hired and remained with Stein and Toklas until they were forced to move from Bilignin to Culoz during the war. (In an interview in Paris, June 1982, Joan Chapman confirmed that the incidents Stein relates in *Paris France* about Helen Button were in fact stories that Hélène Bouton had told Stein.)

To Gertrude Stein

5 October 1939

[101 Central Park West
New York]

Dear Baby Woojums,

Thornton Wilder called up this morning and said he was worried about you. I told him I had just received a letter and that [John] McCullo[u]gh had had a cable, and he was much relieved. McCullo[u]gh called me yesterday and asked if he could come to talk to me about the proposed lecture tour. So he came up to see me yesterday afternoon and I told him a good deal about the last tour but said you might have entirely different ideas about this one and he had better ask you what your terms would be, how many and what kind of people would be invited to listen to you, how long it would take to prepare your lectures, how soon you could get over, etc. I said he had better find out some of these things before he went on making arrangements. So he said he would cable you again. However, he seemed to anticipate no trouble, and he is a nice young man, and I wouldn't be a bit surprised (and how happy!) to see you and Mama W walking down another gangplank! I believe Georges [Jacques] at the Algonquin would turn pink with pleasure!. I suggested a lecture on Picasso would be an idea and I should think you have the material for that in your book, and he seemed to think they would like to hear about the war.[1]. NO letters I have received from Paris have been censored or even opened yet, but for awhile no letters at all came through and naturally we were worried.   You will get wedding cards from FM and CVV maybe in this same mail!

Lots of love to you both, in which Fania joins me!

Papa Woojums

1. McCullough wrote to Stein, 9 October 1939 (YCAL), reporting on his meeting with Van Vechten and Professor Russell Potter of Columbia University. Van Vechten, perhaps remembering Stein's difficulty with lecture agents during her 1934–35 lecture tour, was negative about McCullough's ideas of enlisting lecture agents. McCullough wrote Stein that because of this he was willing to consider doing the necessary work arranging a tour until she and Toklas would arrive. At that point, McCullough felt, perhaps echoing Van Vechten's view, that Toklas would step in and run the tour.

To Carl Van Vechten

[postmark: 23 October 1939]   [Bilignin par Belley
                                                               Ain]

Dear Papa Woojums,

War-time has just brought me this letter paper in Belley and I am writing on it to you,[1] dear Papa Woojums do you think we ought to go to America, will you send us a cable to say what you think, we would feel better about it or perhaps you answered my letter about it by airplane and it will come, Please tell us, the country is cold but we saw wood and could we

bring the dogs, with us, and are you and Fania well and happy and enjoying
your birthdays

lots of love
Gtrde B. W.[2]

1. This letter was written on writing paper that had an embossed decorative border of flowers
with a spray of lilies of the valley and roses pasted on the first page.

2. The envelope of this letter has the seal "Ouvert 6 B 93 Par L'Autorite Miliaire Controle
Postal Militare." From this point until the end of the war, almost all of Stein's letters were
opened by the censors; in none, however, was any part of the text subjected to censorship. In
subsequent notes I have not indicated the letters that were opened by the censors. It is impossible to say whether Van Vechten's letters to Stein were opened, since Stein did not keep the
envelopes.

To Gertrude Stein

24 October 1939   101 Central Park West
                                                       New York City

Dear Gertrude,

When I met the enclosed clip in the paper this morning I nearly died!
Off it goes to Baby Woojums per once![1] And doubtless you've heard from
hundreds of sources that you have a scene on the telephone with the character representing [Alexander] Woollcott in the new Kaufman-Hart play, The
Man who Came to Dinner, in which you ring him (marooned in a small
town in Ohio for Christmas eve) from Paris to let him listen to the bells of
Notre Dame!!![2] You and Alice were the only people in the world we didn't
hear from on our silver wedding anniversity. . So I guess the war has held
up your invitations.[3] We hoped you'd come. . We had 36 people for a sit-
down dinner and Fania wore my mother's wedding dress! It was a most sentimental occasional, and a little tear-making[x].   You ask about lecturing and
I've already talked to [John] McCullo[u]gh and already written you and I've
asked him to let me know what you finally decide.

sprigs of mignonnette to you both, and a bowl of pearls!

Carlo—Papa Woojums.

[x]Fania made a wonderful spontaneous speech!

1. This clipping cannot be identified.

2. George S. Kaufman and Moss Hart's play, *The Man Who Came to Dinner*, opened at the Music Box Theatre, New York, on 16 October 1939 and ran for 288 performances. The character of Sheridan Whiteside, played by Monty Wooley, was based on Alexander Woollcott.

3. An invitation to a dinner on 21 October, in celebration of their twenty-fifth wedding anniversary, was enclosed with this letter.

To Carl Van Vechten
MS. New York Public Library, Manuscripts Division

[postmark: 28? October 1939]　　　　　　　　　　　[Bilignin par Belley
　　　　　　　　　　　　　　　　　　　　　　　　　Ain]

Dearest Papa Woojums,

The invitation came just on the day, and we said we would come with pleasure and eat of the most xcellent dinner and kiss the most xcellent bride and groom and Darby and Joan[1] and yet here we are being snowed on quite heavily to-day although the grapes are not yet all gathered nor the potatoes, nor the wheat, nobody has even asked it to snow heavily before all saints day but they cheer up because they say in the country here that St. Martin has to pasture his donkey yet which means Indian summer, and so as Henry Kahnweiler[2] says to our great astonishment the days pass and pass, but we wish we had passed the silver anniversary with you, if by any chance we do come over will you have another one the way they here always have the fete of the Vogue and then the return of the Vogue lots and lots of love to you both

Gtrde B. W.

1. A jocose term for a deeply attached husband and wife.

2. The picture dealer and art historian.

To Carl Van Vechten
MS. *New York Public Library, Manuscripts Division*

[? October 1939]   [Bilignin par Belley
                                                        Ain]

Very dearest Papa Woojums

Happy happy days to you and Fania, happy happy months and happy happy years dearest both of you we love you so much all of us, including the new Basket who has not seen you but has heard a lot about you and we loved the blurb, Alice said with a sigh, he does write so beautifully when he writes,[1] she did not say she wished he would write more and neither did I because we know Papa Woojums knows best, but we did sigh, and we loved the blurb, and next time you must add sawing wood, that is what I do every day, it's nice to saw wood nice big chunks of wood and pile them up. The last letter was all about possibly going over to America, since then there has been no news xcept that the American Embassy suggests that I could undoubtedly get over[2] but could I get back, and I do not suppose I could earn enough money to come back in clipper ships I would like to do that, did not you get us up there and wouldn't it be fun to go up there all of us just wouldn't it, otherwise there is no news, we are just patiently waiting, when the sun shines we are a little more uncomfortable because it means fighting and when it rains and it does a lot we are a little uncomfortable because it is cold not here because we have lots of coal and wood but out there, your phrase of the war being all fought sub-rosa is wonderful, and everybody is pleased that you say even frenchman [i.e., frenchmen] always win, and so once more the silver wedding bells and all our love all all

always
Gtde Baby Woojums.

1. A reference to the statement about *The World Is Round* that Van Vechten had sent Stein in his letter of 13 September 1939.

2. On 24 August 1939 William C. Bullitt, the American ambassador to France, published the following: "In view of the situation prevailing in Europe it is considered advisable to recommend the American Citizens who have no compelling reason to continue their sojurn here arrange to return to the United States" (YCAL). This statement was reissued on 14 May 1940,

with the advisement that American citizens should congregate in the Bordeaux area in order to return to the United States.

❧

To Gertrude Stein
[Postcard: Fania Marinoff in Carl Van Vechten's mother's wedding dress.
Photograph by Carl Van Vechten]

7 November [1939]   [101 Central Park West
                                                          New York

Dear Baby Woojums,

Almost the moment after I wrote you that we hadn't heard from you at the Anniversary your *wonderful* letter came. Here is FM in my mother's Wedding dress (circa 1861) which FM wore at the Silver Wedding. I am also happy you like the Blurb. It is quite possible I may do a book next year. [John] McCullo[u]gh telephones if you lecture it will probably not be till the fall of 1940.[1] I myself think it would be pretty late to arrange anything now for THIS year. Besides, you'd have to stay here for the duration of the War, once you came.

    Lots of love to you both

Papa W!

1. McCullough wrote to Stein, 5 November 1939 (YCAL), his advice that a lecture tour be postponed until the 1940–41 season.

To Gertrude Stein
*[Postcard: Swimmers at the Aquacade, New York World's Fair, 1939.
Photograph by Carl Van Vechten]*

15 November [1939]   [101 Central Park West
                                                     New York]

Dearest Baby Woojums,

Everybody missed *your* portrait in the Picasso show last night[1] & here is a new stamp for you.[2] Also a glimpse of the Water Ballet in the Aquacade, World's Fair.

LOVE,
Papa W!

1. The Museum of Modern Art, New York, had opened a major retrospective of Picasso's work. *Picasso: Forty Years of His Art*, 15 November 1939 to 7 January 1940. The exhibition was organized by Alfred H. Barr, Jr., in collaboration with the Art Institute of Chicago. The exhibition consisted of 344 works, including *Guernica* and its studies. Barr had approached Stein about the loan of the Picasso *Portrait of Gertrude Stein*. Stein, while not refusing, suggested that it could not be arranged until she returned to Paris in late October. Barr was willing to try to have a special shipment arrangement made for the painting or even to accept it after the offical opening of the exhibition (see Gallup, *The Flowers of Friendship*, p. 340). The outbreak of World War II prevented the shipment of the painting.

2. A 3-cent stamp celebrating the fiftieth anniversary of statehood, 1889–1939, of Washington, Montana, North Dakota, and South Dakota.

To Gertrude Stein

16 November [1939]   101 Central Park West
                                                     New York City

Why, my dear Baby Woojums!

I love your stationery with the rosebuds, but I can't cable you because I don't know what to cable. I have written you all I know about this several times.[1]. [John] McCullo[u]gh tells me that an agent is interested in

[658]

taking you on for lectures in BIG halls, but NEXT year. I am all for that if arrangements are Proper and Secure. Don't do anything without a guarantee. Money in bank, if possible. . But from your letter I gather something is imminent and I don't know what it is so, I can't cable you until I know more about what has happened. If you come now, certainly you will have to stay here for the duration of the war, but we will all love this. . If anything happens within the next few days which gives me an inkling of the new developments you want me to cable about, why of course I'll cable you at once. .

In the meantime LOTS of love,
TO YOU BOTH,

FROM
Papa Woojums.

Maybe you are just asking me if I think you ought to come home to stay? I have read & reread your letter & can't be sure. So if I cabled I might give the wrong impression.—I hope this will be soon enough.

1. See Stein to Van Vechten [23 October 1939].

To Gertrude Stein
[Postcard: Statue of George Washington, New York World's Fair, 1939.
Photograph by Carl Van Vechten][1]

18 November [1939]

[101 Central Park West
New York]

Dear Baby Woojums!

Of course, we will have another anniversary *right away* if you & Mama W come over!

Love
Papa W!

1. This statue was by the sculptor James Earle Fraser.

To Carl Van Vechten

[postmark: 26 November 1939]   Bilignin par Belley[1]
                                                Ain

My dearest Papa Woojums,

It is sad to have the once every ten days or so post come and no letter from Papa Woojums, it kind of does not seem right, please write and write soon, it that is we are like the poilu, we need to get letters.[2] I have just had a cable with very interesting conditions offered by the National Lecture Bureau, what is that is it something good or not, of course that would mean early spring,[3] I am finishing my Paris-France, Batsford's enthusiasm grows and they want it now, the English edition of The World is Round is out, and as soon as I have some copies I will send you one, and please write soon, we are lonesome, we are having lovely weather, and I do kind of like life in the country really do, but do not let another post go without you lots and lots of love

Gtrde.

1. The return address was stamped on the paper.

2. *Poilu* in French means hairy or shaggy. It was a term used for French soldiers in World War I.

3. The cable is not in YCAL. On 15 December 1939 (YCAL) Ford Hicks, manager of the National Lecture Bureau, Inc., of Chicago, Illinois, wrote to Toklas at the suggestion of Samuel Steward. He offered Stein $375 per date and specified that he would try to secure large audiences. On the verso of Hick's letter Toklas drafted a reply setting out some of the details that would have to be arranged if Stein would agree to a lecture tour. One of those details was that colleges unable to pay the large fees should not be excluded from the tour.

To Carl Van Vechten

[postmark: 28 December 1939]

Foyer du soldat[1]
Bilignin par Belley
(Ain)

My dearest Papa Woojums,

Happy New Year happy new year to you and Fania happy happy new year to you both now and always always and now, and do you like our new stamp, we are very busy getting our foyer together, we are making our sport center in the barn and an inside foyer in a large room in the village and there is lots to do, any illustrated American things would be gratefully received by us, they like to look at photographs made in America, and if anybody has any french books, they are not using, I suppose anything is useful, we have gotten a lot of out-door games already, with the aid of some English friends,[2] my book Paris, France is all done, I hope you will like it, it is not long, almost 70 type written pages and now the great question is should it or should it not be illustrated, Batsford thought at first no, and now he kind of thinks yes,[3] well anyway happy new year, I like wintering in the country, I had no idea there would be so much to do, and that I could walk so much as I do, the new Basket jumps and walks, but he does not care for the moon, he says it is too bright, and too unxpected, but anyway happy new year lots of happy new years to Papa Woojums and to Fania from B. W. and Mama Woojums and all love always

Gtrde.

1. The return address was stamped on the paper.

2. Stein's friends the Selby-Bigges who lived in the Château du Chambuet in Yenne.

3. When it was published by B. T. Batsford in April 1940, *Paris France* contained eight illustrations: Juan Gris's painting *Roses* (1914); Elie Lascaux's painting *Le Sacre Coeur*; Picasso's painting *Cafe Interior* (1901); *Prière de Voltaire*, an eighteenth-century script engraving; *Pensée de Rousseau*, an eighteenth-century script engraving; *Landscape Near Belley*, a water color by the Baronne Pierlot; Vlaminck's painting *La Pompe d'Essence*; and Sir Francis Rose's painting *Gertrude Stein at Bilignin*.

To Gertrude Stein

29 December [1939]   [101 Central Park West
                                      New York]

Dearest Baby Woojums!

Why where could all my letters have gone? I have bombarded you with letters and cards and Christmas cards and tried to explain the situation about lecturing, but have had no reply until today when your sweet letter comes, together with that wonderful Prothalamium for Bobolink and Louise.[x1] Who are these sweet people? I don't think I have heard of them but why didn't you do an ode for the Silver wedding of Fania and Carlo? O why didn't you! I am very envious! I can't tell you much about the National Lecture Bureau. I think it is the one [John] McCullo[u]gh went to see (and he said he picked the best one) but you would know about that. Lecture Bureaux are like everything else, good if you are a success, and bad, if you are not a success. I guess you and Mama W could cope with any lecture bureau at all, and how wonderful that you may come over in the spring. If you do come over too you will have to stay here until the war is over because they take your passport away and that will be lovely TOO. . I am sending this by the Clipper and maybe if you came over you would come that way. Only at present it is the long trip to Lisbon. Doris Keane just came over on the clipper and she says it is heavenly and NEVER again will she travel any other way. You start at 8 o'clock in the morning and you lunch in the Azores, and the next morning at dawn you come down for breakfast in Bermuda and then you lunch in New York! Isn't it heavenly! I have had laryngitis for weeks now and finally just gave up and stayed in and stayed out of the darkroom and relaxed and rested and now at last I am getting over it and feel better every minute. Fania has had a healthier winter.   It is the coldest winter we've ever had, as last summer was the hottest.   O yes, when you and Alice come over I'll take your pictures in COLOR please. HAPPY NEW YEAR and LOVE to you BOTH!

Papa Woojums

DYING to see the English WORLD IS R[ound] and PARIS, FRANCE or anything else you do or say.

[662]

Have you seen the Gotham Catalogue, We Moderns, with my blurb? If not, tell me and I'll send you a copy.

    *Sent me by Louise!

1. Stein had written "Prothalamium," a poem to celebrate the marriage of Robert Haas to Louise Antoinette Krause. Haas, with Stein's approval, published the poem, *Prothalamium* (Culver, Ind.: Joyous Guard Press, 1939). See Haas and Gallup, *A Catalogue*, pp. 25–26, for a complete bibliographical account of this poem and its variations of title. See also Wilson, *Gertrude Stein, A Bibliography*, pp. 43–44.

To Carl Van Vechten

[postmark: 10 January 1940]   Bilignin par Belley
                               Ain

My dearest Papa Woojums,

No letter from you, we always xpect one everytime American mail comes and this time there was none. I am sending you the ms. of Paris, France in a day or two, it is all done now and I do hope you will like it. It is so important to know what you think, of course it is just a little short book. About coming over to lecture, you see we are having so many propositions and now [John] McCullough cables that he has two more,[1] they all say they want to give me a great deal of money, which would be agreeable, but they seem not so clear about what I am to do and when, so we talk about it as we sit before the fire and wonder what we will do, but just at present we continue to sit before the fire, we have had quite a bit of winter but so far it does not last very long, we have visits from all the paroissiens[2] of the village, who come and sit before the fire for a formal visit of three hours, in between we meet on the road but we visit sitting down always has to be, and so the time passes, the way it always does in wartime, and we love you Papa Woojums and Fania, and it would be nice to be together it is the one thing that makes the lecture idea not altogether impossible

lots and lots of love
B. W.

1. McCullough to Stein, 4 January 1940 (YCAL).

2. French for parishioners.

&

To Gertrude Stein
*[Postcard: At Ripley Odditorium—Strangest Looking Man—
The Great Omi]*

12 January [1940]   [101 Central Park West
                                                       New York]

Dearest Baby Woojums.

The World is Round (English) with [Francis] Rose's pretty pictures and your lovely inscription has arrived and I am enjoying its wonders all over again.[1] It's just like a new book, please. . Are you coming over? Everybody is asking and I don't know what to tell them. The weather is frightful and I have had laryngitis for WEEKS but I'm getting better. Mabel [Dodge] has started salons again at ONE Fifth Ave and T[hornton] Wilder is performing at the first one.[2]

*Love to both
Carlo.*

I sent you a clip from Robert Haas.
I love the prothalamium!

1. The English edition of *The World Is Round*, published by B. T. Batsford, bore the inscription:

To dearest Papa Woojums

Baby Woojums first baby book; The World Is Round and the World is round. Papa Woojums and Baby Woojums and all the Woojums world is always round and it goes round and it goes round and around.

always and always
to Papa Woojums all
Baby Woojums

2. Mabel Dodge had returned to New York for the winter of 1939–40. She had taken an apartment in the tower at One Fifth Avenue. Invitations were sent out to hear Thornton Wilder elucidate eight pages from James Joyce's *Finnegans Wake* on 12 January 1940.

[664]

To Gertrude Stein

*[Postcard: Swimmers at the Aquacade, New York World's Fair, 1939.
Photograph by Carl Van Vechten]*

20 January 1940

[101 Central Park West
New York]

Dear Baby Woojums,

Hurrah for the Foyer du Soldat! Does this mean you WON'T come over? Robert Haas is writing me often and I *love* the Prothalamium. I sent him some pictures of you which he DOTES on. . We (and Bennett [Cerf]) are dining with Lin Yutang in Chinatown tomorrow. Soon he is going back to China with the children. Very excited about the Paris book! Fania and I send love and kisses, hearts and flowers, to you both!

Papa Woojums!

To Gertrude Stein

3 February 1940

[101 Central Park West
New York]

Dearest Baby Woojums,

Today is your birthday and if you were here we'd be having a big cake for you. No use to cable these days as a cable might not reach you at all and in any case would be sure to be late. Paris, France hasn't arrived yet, hélas. I am dying to see it. May I suggest, now there IS TIME, that you get everything you want IN BLACK and WHITE with these lecture bureaux. I hesitated to say anything that would hold you up before, if you had decided to come over this winter. However this is most important and, if you have a lawyer friend, have him look at the contract carefully. Write the bureau of your preference what you want and ask them to incorporate everything in a sample contract and send it to you and better hurry because there isn't much time, as it takes so long for letters now. Then you and Alice and the lawyer go over the contract with a Fine Toothed comb and see that is Wrong and have it taken OUT. . I think I've asked you lots of times if you know Henry Miller and as you never answer I guess you don't.[1] Anyway he has just been here and he is an odd one. I guess I wrote you about Thornton [Wilder] appearing at Mable [Dodge]'s first evening and now the Baroness d'Erlanger is here. Do you know HER? She is most amusing and loves Harlem, so we get on quite well.[2] She was a great friend of Violette Murat. We have had a pretty Ballet called the Ballet Theatre. . A rich young girl who dances wanted to spend some money and she gave $300,000 and they put on fourteen ballets in four weeks and there was a Negro group and a Spanish group and all the best English dancers came over and it has been most entertaining. To everybody's surprise they did enormous business and turned people away.[3]. It has been Very Very cold for weeks, but I am well again at last and all ready for the warm weather when it does appear. But this has been the coldest winter I can recall.   We have a fireplace here, however, in addition to central heating and keep very warm. So we send love to Mama and Baby W.

Papa Woojums!

Your letters are NEVER opened by the Censor. They recognize Baby Woojums' writing and KNOW it is all right.[4]

1. This is the first time that Van Vechten had mentioned Henry Miller, the author of, among other books, *Tropic of Cancer* (1931), *Tropic of Capricorn* (1939), *Black Spring* (1939), and *The Cosmological Eye* (1939). Van Vechten had photographed Miller.

2. The Baronne Emile d'Erlanger was the daughter of the Marquis de Rochegude. She lived mostly in London, where she entertained on a lavish scale at her house in Piccadilly. The Baronne was a friend of Romaine Brooks, and it was probably she who had introduced the Baronne to Van Vechten.

3. Lucia Chase was the founder of the Mordkin Ballet and was its principal dancer in 1938 and 1939. This company was the foundation of Ballet Theatre Company, now called the American Ballet Theatre. Chase founded Ballet Theatre with Richard Pleasant. The first season, at the Center Theatre, New York, began on 11 January 1940 and ran for four weeks. See the *New York Times*, 7 January 1940, Sec. 9, p. 3.

4. Van Vechten is being playful. Stein's letters were opened, but they were not censored.

❧

To Gertrude Stein
[Postcard: View of Central Park. Photograph by Carl Van Vechten]

6 February [1940]   [101 Central Park West
                                                 New York]

Dear Baby Woojums!

Here are some of the *new* stamps for you.[1] There will be lots more. Paris, France, not here yet. Did you ever get the Gotham Catalogue with *my* blurb?

Love,
Papa W.

1. Stein clipped the stamps from this card.

❧

To Carl Van Vechten

[postmark: 15 February 1940]   Bilignin par Belley
                                                 Ain

My dear dearest Papa Woojums,

No the foyer has really nothing to do with our going over, that is just to occupy the soldiers here and once well started it goes, no the real difficulty is that I am not at all sure I would like lecturing, that is in any large quantity, I would like to go over but to lecture three or four times a week for a number of weeks does not really seem to me as if I would like it, of course we cannot go over without making money and there it is, I dream that Hollywood might do the Autobiography of Alice Toklas, they could make a very good film out of that and then they would pay us large moneys to go out and sit and consult and that would be all new and I would like that and once over there I could lecture or not as I liked, but nobody seems to think that it would be possible, as Bennett [Cerf] has the book now the Autobiog-

[667]

raphy perhaps he could do something but I do not like to ask him, you can always make him do anything you think he ought to do so if you think he ought to do this then you make him, it is just a dream, I would so love to be in America when they are electing a president, that's one thing, the other thing, why did the Lin [Yutang]s not write about the Twir [i.e., The World Is Round], I sent it to them but have never heard a word from any of them and they used to write very regularly before, and also, you may have a visit from a Miss Brown, of the Scott publishing company, there is a child's story incorporated in Paris, France and I have suggested to them that they might do that in a child's magazine before Scribner's do it in book-form and that you would show them the part of the ms. that has it,[1] and Papa Woojums, it is cold and dewy and Pepe sit[s] by the fire and Basket and I are going out to Belley and we think of you all the time and we love you so much, and lots of love,

Gtrde

1. Margaret Wise Brown, editor for children's books at William R. Scott. The story was "Helen Button A War-Time Story." It did not have a separate publication from *Paris France*. See Stein to Van Vechten [1 October 1939], note 2.

To Gertrude Stein
[Postcard: Portrait of Julius Perkins, Junior. Photograph by
Carl Van Vechten][1]

27 February [1940]   [101 Central Park West
                                                      New York]

Beloved Baby Woojums!

Tre Esistenze arrived and was a great surprise![2] Soon you will be translated into Choctaw and Bornean. As it is, your bibliography must be one of the largest and most difficult to make complete there is.   We are having a very cold winter and perhaps it's better you didn't brave American weather this year, but we expect you next. . Lots of love to you both

Papa Woojums!

[668]

1. Julius Perkins, Jr., was the nephew of Van Vechten's cook, Mildred Perkins.

2. *Tre Esistenze,* Stein's *Three Lives,* trans. Cesare Pavese (Torino, Itlay: Guilio Einaudi Editore, 1940).

🐿

To Gertrude Stein

[Postcard: Carl Van Vechten and Fania Marinoff reflected in a distorting mirror. Amusement Center, New York World's Fair, 1939]

4 March 1940   [101 Central Park West
                                                   New York]

Dearest Baby Woojums,

Here are FM and Papa Woojums at the World's Fair and here is an advertisement from the NY Times, March 3, 1940,[1] and here is lots of love to Baby and Mama Woojums!

Papa Woojums

1. The newspaper clipping did not remain with the letter and therefore cannot be identified. There was no advertisement in the *New York Times* on that day specifically related to Stein.

🐿

To Gertrude Stein

19 March [1940]   101 Central Park West
                                                   New York City

Dearest Baby-Woojums,

I LOVE Paris-France, which I ate up at one sitting last night. . For me Paris is smell, and this piece of yours has the true smell of Paris. It has the sounds too. . Somehow, it just IS Paris and it made me feel very nostalgic to read about the way the French ARE. Sometimes they can be most aggravating being that way, but it is nice to read about it afterwards and makes me feel very homesick. . It is so true what you say about Familiarity breeding contempt and usually people are most contemptuous of what ever they are most ignorant of; viz the popular reaction to Picasso's later manner etc. Miss Brown called up and I have already sent her Helen Button in War-Time. But I'm afraid it is too late to do much with this. As Scribner's are publishing the book in April which is just a month from now and most magazines are made up at least two months ahead.[1]. I talked to Bennett [Cerf] about the motion picture possibilities of The Autobiography which are ENORMOUS, but motion picture people are peculiar. You can't approach *them*. They must approach *you*. I think the time to take this up is when you are lecturing in Hollywood. . Of course you both would have to appear in the picture. Even Greta Garbo and Lillian Gish couldn't be you and Alice. I can't wait for this! It will be wonderful!. Bennett says he has part of a novel by you. You haven't written me about this. . The Lin [Yutang]s have gone back to China and maybe they didn't get what you sent them. Their address is American Express Co. Hong Kong. . And about lecturing, I don't know what to say. Maybe you wouldn't like it! you see this time you would be with a professional bureau and the pace would be more strenuous (they think nothing of sending you from New York to Denver) and if you were making money they would want you to lecture every day for MONTHS. But Maybe you would!.[x]. Fania is on an actors' committee that is getting up a big ball for French soldiers and all the time now I take color pictures, but I have no color pictures of Baby and Mama Woojums, which is a source of unhappiness for your loving

Papa Woojums!

[x]like it!

1. See Stein to Van Vechten [15 February 1940], note 1. Scribner's published *Paris France* in April 1940.

To Carl Van Vechten

[postmark: 4? April 1940]   [Bilignin par Belley
                                                              Ain]

My dearest Papa Woojums,

They have just written me that the Yale Library wants to make a show of all my mss. in the fall and I have suggested to them that you might lend them Four Saints and also might give them a complete set of our photos, I am telling you that I suggested it, it would please me a lot to have your photos of us kept with the mss.[1] I think it would be fun, and then they are proposing that I come over and give 15 lectures about France, to biggish audiences that might be a possible solution of the thing,[2] and they seem to think that Alice B. might be done in Hollywood, perhaps we all could go out and act in it all that are spoken of in the book I think it would be fun to have Papa Woojums and all, well anyway spring has come and things do happen, I will be sending you soon the translation of the french Superstitions that I wrote you have the french one haven't you, they are thinking of doing it as a piece of a revue in London which would be fun, I am anxiously waiting to hear how you like Paris, France, I might do a companion piece about the United States of America, it has been suggested but most of all well most of all we love Papa Woojums in the spring time love to Fania always

Gtrde.

1. Through the efforts of Thornton Wilder, Stein had begun, in 1937 to deposit the manuscripts and typescripts of all of her writings in the Yale University Library. In mid-March 1940 (undated letter, YCAL) Thornton Wilder wrote Stein that the Yale University Library, to show its pride in the material she had deposited with them, wanted to mount an exhibition. The exhibition was held from 22 February to 29 March 1941. One of the important byproducts of the exhibition was A *Catalogue of the Published and Unpublished Writings of Gertrude Stein,* compiled by Robert Bartlett Haas and Donald Clifford Gallup. It was the scope of this exhibition, and Yale's interest in Stein's works, that prompted Van Vechten to select Yale as one of the depositories of his varied collections.

2. John McCullough had been actively trying to arrange for a lecture tour. McCullough had been talking with Colstein Leigh, of the Leigh Lecture Bureau, about a tour. Stein must have written McCullough about the letter she had received from Ford Hicks of the National Lecture Bureau (see Stein to Van Vechten [26 November 1939], note 3). McCullough was then ap-

proached by both Hicks and another lecture agent, Lee Kudick. Kudick wired McCullough on 27 January 1940 that he would match whatever Leigh's offer might be to Stein. McCullough sent the wire, including in it the substance of a letter he had received from Kudick to Stein (YCAL). For some reason Kudick withdrew his offer, and McCullough, after considering the two remaining offers, wired Stein on 29 February 1940 (YCAL) that he favored the proposal of Hicks and his eastern collaborator, Elbert Wickes. Stein eventually gave up the idea of returning to the United States.

To Carl Van Vechten

[postmark: 21 April 1940]   [Bilignin par Belley Ain]

My dearest Papa Woojums,

Yes you know about the novel,[1] don't you remember oh about three years ago I told you I was doing a novel about the Duchess of Windsor and it was to be called Ida, I worked at it and then I wrote it over and I have written it over almost three times completely and now Bennett [Cerf] likes it and so I am finishing it for him and he will do it in the fall. I am awfully happy that Random House is doing it, I was awfully unhappy about their not being my publisher but it was not my fault, I wanted them to be and now they are again and I am very happy about it, it is lovely spring weather and I just seem to have forgotten about going over to lecture, I undoubtedly do like writing books better than lecturing, and you never tell about yours, Papa Woojums, is it going on I am so anxious to know, and give our love to Fania and tell her how pleased we are with what she is doing,[2] I do like the french, and I did like everything you said about Paris France

And lots and lots of love always

Baby Woojums.

1. Note by Van Vechten, 24 January 1941: "Of course she had but I had forgotten. In going over these letters I have discovered several references to this book."

The first mention of this novel is in a letter, Stein to Van Vechten [26 June 1937]: "I have started a novel that Mama Woojums says is early American."

The writing of the novel was extremely difficult for Stein and it occupied her on and off for more than three years. In an undated letter to Bennett Cerf (? March 1940, Columbia-Random House) she wrote:

I tell you Bennett I do not know anything about that novel. I have worked at it and written it over and over again and now it is about half or three quarters done and I really do not know a thing about it, usually, you know I know what I know and I put it down but this time I have worked at it until I am all bothered. . . .

Other significant references to the composition of this novel, which is sometimes called "Jenny and Arthur," are in Stein's letters to Van Vechten: [29 September 1937], [26 July 1938], [4 August 1938], [15 August 1938], [26 December 1938], [1 January 1939], [8 February 1939], [21 April 1940], and [20 February 1941].

This is the first mention in these letters of any connection between *Ida A Novel* and the Duchess of Windsor. Stein referred to the connection in her letter to Cerf [? March 1940, Columbia-Random House]. She explained the connection further in another letter to Cerf [? May 1940, Columbia-Random House]: "It was originally inspired by Mrs. Simpson, Duchess of Windsor, and a girl in this village and the two became one and she was called Ida, they are still one and they are going on being. . . ."

In an undated letter to Cerf (? May 1941, Columbia-Random House) Stein asked him to send a copy to the Duchess of Windsor. Cerf replied on 14 May 1941 (YCAL) that he would do so and would let Stein know if she replied. On 13 June 1941 (YCAL) Cerf wrote to Stein that the Duchess of Windsor had acknowledged receipt of the book and had written that she hoped "to emerge from this literary labyrinth with some idea of Ida's thoughts and ways!" The Duchess of Windsor completed her brief note to Cerf by saying, "Will you say to Miss Stein how pleased I am that she should have thought of sending me the book, and how fortunate I think she is *still* to be in her own villa. We had to leave ours and all our possessions last June."

2. Note by Van Vechten, 24 January 1941: "British War Relief work."

❧

To Gertrude Stein

23 April 1940   [101 Central Park West
New York]

Dear Baby Woojums,

In all the trouble you are having these days I worry about you and wonder constantly if you are all right. I hope you are. And one day I began to worry about your paintings, the Picasso portrait etc and have these been put away safely?[1] I am dreadfully excited, of course, about the news of the novel and Bennett [Cerf] publishing it etc and all this is WONDERFUL.[2] Paris-France hasn't come over yet, but I dare say it will arrive soon. Or maybe you can't send it or receive it and maybe I'll have to wait for an American copy. I HOPE NOT. Fania is still sewing for soldiers' wives and babies and they send over packages of garments all the time and then she sells tickets for benefits and she is very good at this and sells lots of them! The Autobiography in the Cinema would be MARVELOUS, with everybody playing his own part! Hollywood would be AGOG. . The idea of leaving a set of photographs with Yale University is a wonderful idea and if they request them I'll be delighted to arrange it, but it would be an awful job to print them just for one show: it would have to be for their *permanent* collection. I have been very busy photographing recently, but mostly Ballet People, and you will LOVE the pictures I am doing in color and when you and Mama Woojums arrive again you must be done in color with all the glory of your waistcoats. Fania is most proud of the waistcoat you gave Her and she wears it Often.[3]

Well, lots of love to you both and La Belle France, and I hope to hear from you SOON.

Papa Woojums!

Did you know [Alexander] Woollcott had had a bad heart attack & is *very* ill?

1. Shortly after England and France declared war on Germany (3 September 1939), Stein and Toklas made a hasty thirty-six-hour visit to Paris to get their identity papers and winter clothing and to arrange for the paintings and valuables in their apartment.

From the time Stein acquired a lease on the house in Bilignin in 1929, she had been in the habit of spending almost six months of the year there. She did not, however, move her paintings with her. In Bilignin she had paintings by Sir Francis Rose, Picabia, and a few other artists. The bulk of her collection, including the paintings by Picasso, Juan Gris, and Cézanne, remained in Paris.

During this visit to Paris Stein tried to place the paintings flat on the floor. She soon realized that there was more wall space than floor space and so she left the pictures in their places. When she returned to Bilignin, she brought back only two paintings, Picasso's portrait of her and Cézanne's *Portrait of Madame Cézanne*. The scene in 5 rue Christine as Stein tried to arrange her pictures is described by Daniel-Henry Kahnweiler in his introduction to Stein's *Painted Lace and Other Pieces*, pp. xvii–xviii.

2. Cerf had written Stein on 2 April 1940 (YCAL) returning the typescript of *Ida A Novel* and asking Stein to go over it for certain corrections. Cerf agreed to publish the novel in a "handsome format."

3. Marinoff gave this waistcoat, together with another given to her by Toklas after Stein's death, to YCAL.

🔆

To Carl Van Vechten

[postmark: ? April 1940]   [Bilignin par Belley
                                                            Ain]

My dearest Papa Woojums,

Am so pleased you liked Paris, France, I never feel comfortable until I have heard from you and now I feel very comfortable,[1] the latest proposition from the Chicago man who seems the most promising lecture man wants only 15 lectures about France and the war to unlimited audiences in Key cities, that sounds better because after that one could do what one pleases, he is also connected with the cinema and seems very taken with the idea of the Auto[biography of] A B. T. as cinema material, in which case we would be over this fall and be photoed in color but then always of course nothing may come of it all,[2] and anyway here we are and though everything is complicated, life is cheerful, we have lots of french soldiers here now including the Legion, funnily enough Picabia's younger son is here quite a nice boy,[3] I wish you were here too, lots of love and lots to you and to Fania

Gtrde B. W.

1. Van Vechten had received the typescript of *Paris France* (see Van Vechten to Stein, 19 March [1940]), but he had not yet received the printed edition (see Van Vechten to Stein, 23 April 1940). This letter responds to Van Vechten's letter of 19 March [1940].

2. A proposal by Colstein Leigh of the Colstein Leigh Lecture Bureau. See Stein to Van Vechten, [4? April 1940], note 2.

3. Picabia's son Gabriel (b. 1911, known as Poncho). He was the son by Picabia's first wife, Gabrielle Buffet-Picabia.

🔆

To Carl Van Vechten

[postmark: 26 May 1940]   [Bilignin par Belley
                                                            Ain]

My dear Papa Woojums,

The child's book is done and I am sending the ms. to you, I am sending one copy to [John] McCullough and one to you and I have suggested to him that you will let each other know which one receives it, and if he has received his, then after you are through with yours will you let the Kiddie [W. G. Rogers] see it, and will you let me know just as soon as soon how you like it, I will be most awfully anxious to know, it has carried me over many anxious days, and I have liked doing it so much, I do want you to like it,[1]

lots of love
Gtrde B. W.

1. Stein's "To Do: A Book of Alphabets and Birthdays," in her *Alphabets & Birthdays*, pp. 1–86.

To Carl Van Vechten

[postmark: 3 June 1940]   [Bilignin par Belley
                                                          Ain]

My dear Papa Woojums,

I am sending you to-day the copy of the child's story To Do and most awfully anxious to know what you think, and then in about a week I will send you the copy of the Novel Ida and will you let Bennett [Cerf] know you have Ida when you have her in case he has not had his. Thanks so much, we are going through some pretty awful days, but we have lots of friends around and we all console each other, do tell Fania how much everybody appreciates what she is doing, we have a friend at Bordeaux and she says they are overwhelmed with all there is to do for the refugees and she tells a touching story of the day of the treason of Leopold, of Belgium,[1] the canteen was full of Belgian soldiers and officers and when they heard the news they all began to cry and the french soldiers consoled them, she said it was terribly moving, do tell me how you like To Do, and lots of love

Baby Woojums.

1. As King and commander-in-chief of the Belgian army, Leopold surrendered to the Germans on the night of 27–28 May 1940. The Belgium government declared his action illegal and moved to London, where it formed a government-in-exile.

[676]

🦨

To Carl Van Vechten

6 July [1940]   Bilignin par Belley
                                                       (Ain)

My dearest Papa Woojums,

Baby and Mama are still here, and it is all over and we are still here and there is so much to tell and we are still here, Mama Woojums made raspberry jam through it all and I cut box hedges and so we got through and all full of love for you, and did To Do ever get there and did you like it, and oh dear so much love to you and Fania[1]

always and always
Baby Woojums

1. The French signed an armistice with the Germans on 22 June and with the Italians on 24 June 1940. American citizens had been warned on 24 August 1939 and again on 14 May 1940 (see Stein to Van Vechten [? October 1939], note 2) to leave France. After consulting with friends, and with the memory of what it had been like to be refugees during World War I, Stein and Toklas decided to remain in France.

🦨

To Gertrude Stein
[Postcard: Portrait of Georges Jacques. Photograph by Carl Van Vechten][1]

29 July [1940]   [101 Central Park West
                                                       New York]

Dear Baby Woojums,

Ida is *here!* I just got Bennett [Cerf] on the phone & *Ida* is *here!* So is Edward Wasserman!

LOVE to Mama & Baby!
Papa Woojums!

[677]

1. The headwaiter at the Algonquin Hotel, New York. This card did not arrive in France until 17 December 1940. See Stein to Van Vechten, 17 December [1940].

⚜

To Carl Van Vechten

[postmark: 27 August 1940]   Bilignin par Belley
                                                               (Ain)

My dear Papa Woojums,

The Woojums family feel most separated and neglected, not a word from Papa Woojums, not one word, since everything happened, not one word, I know you had the ms. of To Do because [John] McCullough has just written that you passed your copy on to him his seemingly having been lost, and now I do not make out very well whether he likes it or not,[1] but most and foremost I want to know how you feel about it, send me by cable or air-mail, a word, we are suffering for a word from you, and tell me if you like it, I myself am attached to it, and I am asking McCullough if he does not want it to send it back to you and will you then give it to Bennett [Cerf], I would like him to see it next,[2] but please oh please Papa Woojums a word by air-mail or cable or something to tell us we are not forgot, as for us life just goes along, it has complications and it has compensations, and that is about all you can say about it, but do write or something please Papa Woojums the neglected Baby and Mama Woojums always loving,

Gtrde.

1. McCullough wrote Stein [7 August 1940, YCAL] that he found that "To Do: A Book of Alphabets and Birthdays" lacked episode and thus it had less appeal than her *The World Is Round*.

2. Van Vechten sent Cerf the manuscript of "To Do." Cerf replied to Van Vechten on 19 November 1940 (YCAL) that he thought that Random House, which was committed to publishing Stein's *Ida A Novel*, could not undertake to publish more than one work by Stein per year. On 9 January 1941 (YCAL), after much prodding by Van Vechten, Cerf wrote him that everyone at Random House was "as cold as a slab of alabaster" about "To Do."

To Gertrude Stein

*[Postcard: Fania Marinoff as Ariel, sculpture by Richmond Barthé.
Photograph by Carl Van Vechten]*

6 September [1940]   [101 Central Park West
                                                       New York]

Dear Baby Woojums,

It isn't that I haven't written, I've written DOZENS of times and ALL
about the book which I'm MAD about but I hardly think it is for les en-
fants. .I hope SOME of my letters get through. I shall get in touch with
[John] McCullo[u]gh and see what he says about passing the mss over to
Bennett [Cerf]. He will be very disappointed because he HOPED you would
make a children's book out of it and I think Bennett has all he can attend
to with Ida.

Bennett, by the way, is getting married again next week to Phyllis
Fraser.[1] We send Love to you both,

Papa Woojums

1. Cerf and Phyllis Fraser, whom he had met at the home of Harold Ross, editor of *The New
Yorker*, were married on 17 September 1940. The ceremony was performed by New York's
mayor, Fiorello La Guardia.

Phyllis Fraser, whose real name was Helen Nichols, had worked in Hollywood at the
R.K.O. Studios as an actress for about two years. She gave that up and moved to New York
and was employed by the McCann-Erickson Advertising Agency at the time she and Cerf met.
Cerf wrote Stein the details of his meeting Phyllis and their marriage in a letter to Stein, 10
October 1940 (YCAL).

To Carl Van Vechten

[postmark: 6 September 1940]   Bilignin par Belley
                                                       (Ain)

Dear Papa Woojums

Gracious goodness, another lot of mail this time boat mail after a
month of not, and not one word from Papa Woojums, I know you are al-

right and had the ms. of To Do, I know that from the Kiddy [W. G. Rogers] and from [John] McCullough[1] but not a word from you, not a postal card not a word, and we do not like it, not at all at all, the Scott people seem to have had a sudden change of heart, sent me my advance money and a cable saying Yes, perhaps the children said it was a child's book even if the adults did not think so, but how can I know anything if Papa Woojums does not say a mumbling word, write, air-mail, boat, cable anything but write do please write.

Always
Baby Woojums.

1. McCullough in his letter to Stein about "To Do: A Book of Alphabets and Birthdays" (see Stein to Van Vechten [27 August 1940], note 1) had written that he read part of the typescript at Van Vechten's.

W. G. Rogers had written Stein [postmark 6 August 1940, at YCAL], thanking her for letting him see the typescript of "To Do" and giving her a brief report on Van Vechten.

To Gertrude Stein

11 September 1940

[101 Central Park West
New York]

Dearest Baby Woojums,

I write and write and cable and cable, but nothing seems to get through. Maybe this will. [John] McCullo[u]gh had TO DO only one night (he borrowed my copy as his never got through) when he wrote his report to you. So now he wants to go over it again and have some children read it. But I agree with him that it is not a child's book (we both, as he says, may be wrong) especially as you say letters M and N are unlucky and half the children who read it will be named Nathan and Mary. . It is too bad he can't talk this thing over with you but that seems impossible just now and you must realize that you are only receiving a very tiny percent of the mail that is being sent to you . . . Bennett [Cerf] is getting married to a Phyllis Fraser on Sept 17 . . We have not met her yet but she is coming here to be photographed with him tonight.

[680]

In view of changing conditions, I am considering presenting your first editions, inscribed, and the periodicals with papers by you to some institution where they would be *kept safely* in vaults. Also, *if you don't object,* your letters. Write me what you think of this. Perhaps you would like to see these in Yale, where your Mss are, but perhaps the N.Y. Public Library which makes equal provision for their care and preservation would make the collection more available to students.

I do hope this letter reaches you. W G Rogers writes you don't get his letters either.[1]

> *Love to you both*
> *Papa W.*

1. Rogers had written to Van Vechten, 9 September 1940 (YCAL), that he had received a letter from Stein, the first in nearly a month. In the letter she expressed her concern at not having heard from Van Vechten in a very long time.

To Carl Van Vechten

[28 September 1940]   Bilignin par Belley
                                                          (Ain)

My dearest Papa Woojums,

What a relief to see your letter with all its pretty stamps, do you know it is the first sign we have had from you since June, and we were peeved, and now it is alright, the history of To Do is mysterious, I had the letter quite promptly from [John] McCullough saying that he did not think it a child's book and as they only do children's books most likely they would not do it, so I wrote to him and said when they had definitely made up their minds they should cable me yes or no, so that I could make other arrangements, his letter was dated 7 August, then sent from New York the 20 of August I received $250 which was their advance and then the first September I had a cable saying Yes letter follows, the letter has not followed, so I do not know what happened, perhaps you do by now, anyway you do not say but I do hope you liked it, and Bennett [Cerf] my gracious not a word from Bennett and I have had letters from him right along, I am writing to him right away to find out about it, who is Phyllis, do tell, and about the things in the vaults, about the letters, I think it might be nicer as I am leaving all my collection of letters to Yale and all your letters to me are in it, that my letters to you should be in the same collection, I would also like the only copies xtant of everything I have done which you have, in typewriting would also go to Yale, but I would like all the first editions and things to go to New York Library, does that seem alright, of course it is all as you think best, Papa Woojums does know best, is the refrain of his devoted family who did every moment mind most dreadfully not having a word from him for all these months and months and months do write a lot and all the time and what has become of Nathalie [Barney] do you know and so much love and write write write to us Baby Woojums and Mama Woojums.[1]

Gtrde.

1. Undated note by Van Vechten written on the envelope: "In this letter G. S. tells me how to dispose of her letters, papers, & books."

This letter was not part of the group of Stein letters that Van Vechten presented to YCAL on 28 January 1941. It remained in his possession until October 1947, when, with the letters he had received from Stein from [18 November 1940] until her death, it was given to YCAL.

Van Vechten arranged that duplicates of Stein first editions not needed by YCAL be given to the New York Public Library. Van Vechten divided his collection of books, manuscripts, letters, and memorabilia representing his wide range of interests among the Yale University Library, the New York Public Library Rare Books and Manuscripts Division, the Berg Collection of the New York Public Library, the James Weldon Johnson Collection of Negro Arts and Letters, and certain specialized collections. See Kellner, *A Bibliography*, pp. [244]-47.

When Van Vechten gave the first group of Stein letters to Yale he attached the following note dated 18 January 1941:

> I first heard of Gertrude Stein through Mabel Dodge who, when she returned to America in 1912, distributed copies of Portrait of Mabel Dodge at the Villa Curonia. Early in the summer of 1913 I went to Paris with Pitts Sanborn. Mabel had invited me to motor to Florence with her, John Reed, and Robert Edmond Jones, but she was considerably delayed in arriving in Paris and in the meantime, through Mabel, of course, I had met Gertrude Stein and Alice B. Toklas. Eventually Mabel arrive[d]. We went to Florence as planned and later I returned to Paris alone.

Van Vechten wrote a second note on the same card also dated 18 January 1941: "The chronology of these letters is approximate as they are not dated, the postmarks are sometimes difficult to decipher. A few may be missing."

To Carl Van Vechten

[postmark: 14 October 1940] Bilignin par Belley
(Ain)

Dearest Papa Woojums

What a comfort, each mail that comes now brings something from Papa Woojums, and golly if you think we liked those days when there was nothing, those long months when there was nothing, well we did not, so keep on writing, I have not heard anything from [John] McCullough, that is I had the money and a cable saying Yes, presumably that they were taking it but nothing else, do let us know why they do not write and what they have decided,[1] I hope you will like Sundays and Tuesdays,[2] and please send us the photo of Bennett and Phyllis [Cerf], and please write all the time, we keep very busy, it is very difficult not keeping very busy as we have to that is I have to go to Belley on foot and we have to find whatever we want when it is there, and now they are all getting in their grapes for wine and we had lots of grapes and I don't know just how but we do seem to be most awfully busy, all the time, and write often and write more often, you do not know what a pleasure your letters are, and love to Fania and lots to Papa Woojums lots and lots and lots,

Baby W. Gtrde.

1. McCullough had written to Stein on 27 September 1940 (YCAL) that he would try to reread the typescript of "To Do: A Book of Alphabets and Birthdays." There was no cable from McCullough. His next communication with Stein was on 15 October 1940 (YCAL), when he returned the typescript of "To Do" and replied that the $250 Stein wrote him about was a mystery to him.

    In an undated letter to Cerf (?November 1940, Columbia-Random House) Stein goes into great detail about the check for $250 she had received from American Express via Marseilles and a subsequent check from American Express via Nice for $243. Stein assumed that the first check, sent from New York on 20 August, was confirmation of McCullough's intentions to publish "To Do." The check, in fact, was sent via Bennett Cerf and represented the money from *The Atlantic Monthly* for her article "The Winner Loses A Picture of Occupied France." The second check, for $243, was sent to Stein on 1 September and represented money earned from Scribner's edition of *Paris France*.

2. "Sundays and Tuesdays" was Stein's original title for the piece printed as "The Winner Loses a Picture of Occupied France," in *The Atlantic Monthly* (November 1940), pp. 166(5): 571–83.

The original title referred to the fact that the German invasion of Poland, which precipitated World War II, and the French declaration of war against Germany had both occurred on Sundays.

Stein, who had become alarmed with the world situation, began to read books of prophecies and astrological predictions. One of these predicted disaster for the Germans on a series of Tuesdays.

≷

To Carl Van Vechten
[Postcard: Patinir, Joachim. Repos pendant la fuite en Egypte]

[postmark: 14 October 1940]   [Biligin par Belley
                                                Ain]

Have just had a letter from [John] McCullough he has not yet tried the ms. on children but he seems to think even if they like it, they could not do it, so I have told him to return the 2 ms. to you, his has probably arrived by this time and would you,[1] I hate to trouble you but would you first let Bennett [Cerf] see it, and then Scribner's, Mr. Gilman Low, and then Harcourt, it would be wonderful if one of them liked it. I can't help thinking it kind of Frank Stocktonish than which I can give myself no higher praise,[2] and you did like it, didn't you Papa Woojums, you did didn't you, because if you did then one of them will, and you did didn't you, autumn has come and Mama Woojums is making nugats and we love you so much, lots and lots and lots of love,

Baby Woojums

1. McCullough to Stein, 27 September 1940 (YCAL).

2. Frank Stockton (1834–1902), American novelist and short story writer.

☙

To Carl Van Vechten

[postmark: 14 October 1940][1]   [Bilignin par Belley
                                                   Ain]

Dearest Papa Woojums,

I just had a letter from [John] McCullough and he has not yet tried it on the children and he seems to think that even if the children like it, they would not want to try it and dear Papa Woojums I hate to bother you you know I do but I do bother you all the same because you are so good, so I am telling him to return the 2 ms. to you, I think by this time he must have had the second one, and will you show it to Bennett [Cerf] and if Bennett says no will you show it to Mr. Wm. Gilman Low III of Scribner's and if he says no, to Harcourt. You do like the book don't you because if you didn't I would know it was no good but you do, and I can't help being sure that the stories are very Frank Stocktonish, and that you know I think awfully high praise to Baby Woojums, please like the book, and think of all those funny stories in it, you do like them, please do, it is getting a little cold and Pepe has his coat on, and Alice a shawl and otherwise everything is as it was, lots of love and more lots and thanks and more thanks always

Baby Woojums.

1. This is the third letter written on the same day. Each was posted separately. The second letter, beginning "Have just had a letter from [John] McCullough," is repeated almost verbatim in this letter. One possible explanation for this is that Stein was deeply concerned about the publication of this book and she wanted to make sure that at least one message got through to Van Vechten.

❦

To Carl Van Vechten
[Postcard: Hauterives (Drôme)—"Palais Idéal" Les trois Géants]

[postmark: 25 October 1940]   [Bilignin par Belley
                                                Ain]

My dearest Papa Woojums,

How are you, autumn has commenced so has sawing wood and Pepe has his coat on, and he and Alice are sitting in the fire, and the garden is being worked over and here we are, what is the news of To Do, Belley has been all xcited because the butchers would not sell meat and were put in gaol, but we all had meat just the same lots of love

Gtrde.

❦

To Carl Van Vechten

[postmark: 14 November 1940]   Bilignin par Belley
                                                (Ain)

My dearest Papa Woojums,

Surely I will do just whatever you want me to do about letters and things but of course as yet none of them are over there, but we will hope that they will all get over there sometime,[1] and I have just had a card from Nathalie [Barney], they are still in Florence seem to be meditating going to Switzerland but do not as yet seem to have made up their mind,[2] I am so pleased you liked about yourself in To Do,[3] I have not heard anything more from [John] McCullough, he said he would have to wait until schools had opened and then settled down before they could try it out on them, of course I would much rather they would do it than anybody else, I cannot really think children would not like it, but then after all children are not always what one thinks they are, we have lots of xcitement, the butchers of Belley, and now the chief judge in Belley turns out to be a charming young man and a poet and we see him a good deal,[4] it is xtraordinary the things that

[686]

can happen in Belley, do congratulate Virgil [Thomson.] for me, I am awfully pleased that everything has happened as it should.[5] Poor Gerald Berners I am afraid will never do the Faust, now, it would be fun if 4 Saints should be done again, I have not had a word from Gerald Berners, if you could find out what has happened to him, it would be nice for us,[6] and Cecil Beaton, it is a lovely evening and I dig in the garden and Alice cooks what there is to cook, and the days pass pleasantly and always we love Papa Woojums and always and best to Fania always

Gtrde Baby Woojums.

1. Note by Van Vechten, 24 January 1941: "I suggested she give *my* part of this correspondence also to Yale Library."

2. Barney to Stein, postmark 25 October 1940, YCAL. Barney and Romaine Brooks spent the war years in the Villa Sant'Agnese, just on the outskirts of Florence.

3. In "To Do: A Book of Alphabets and Birthdays" Stein used specific groups of names beginning with the various letters of the alphabet and told vignettes about the person. Van Vechten was one of the people used to illustrate the letter "V." See Stein's *Alphabets & Birthdays*, pp. 61–65.

4. Pierre Van Der Meulen was the judge in Belley for a few years. Several of his books of poetry were published in Paris by the publisher "Au Divan," 37 rue Bonaparte.

5. Note by Van Vechten, 24 January 1941: "I wrote her that Virgil Thomson had been made music critic of the Herald-Tribune and everybody was talking about him."

   Van Vechten may have written Stein about Thomson's appointment in a missing letter. It is not until 11 December 1940 that it is mentioned in these letters. Thomson had succeeded the late Lawrence Gilman as music critic of the *New York Herald Tribune*. He remained with the paper until 1954.

6. Lord Berners had written Stein more than a year earlier about the problems he was having writing music (see Gallup, *The Flowers of Friendship*, p. 346). When queried by Van Vechten, who was preparing his introduction for Stein's *Last Operas and Plays*, about his failure to write the music for *Doctor Faustus Lights the Lights*, Berners wrote that he was prone to "attacks of melancholia" and that when in this condition, "everything turns to despair" (Berners to Van Vechten, 7 ? 1948, YCAL).

❧

To Carl Van Vechten
[Postcard: Hauterives (Drôme)—"Palais Idéal" La Terrasse—Côté Sud]

[postmark: 18 November 1940]   [Bilignin par Belley
Ain]

My dearest papa Woojums,

Madame Roux came and said letters to give pleasure à Madame but above all one letter with such pretty stamps, that will give pleasure, and the pretty stamps did give pleasure so much pleasure,[1] the man at Scribners is Wm. Gilman Low III send the To Do on to them, will you send it to him directly, happy thanksgiving to you and Fania from us all,

Baby Woojums.

1. Madame Roux was Stein's long-time housekeeper at Bilignin. Since Stein did not keep the envelope, the stamps cannot be identified.

❧

To Gertrude Stein

23 November 1940   [101 Central Park West
New York]

Dearest Baby Woojums,

To Do has come back from [John] McCullo[u]gh at last and I have passed it on to Bennett [Cerf] and now we'll hear what HE has to say. If he doesn't want it, or can't see his way to publish it, or thinks two books would be too many now, I'll follow your instructions and pass it on to the next in line . . . The typewritten manuscripts have directly gone to Yale and will be filed with the other manuscripts and with even more restrictions as I don't want anybody using anything from unpublished manuscripts just yet without YOUR permission.[x] They have instructions always to show the manuscripts to people you and I send out there. . I breathe easier now [that] they are there, because I think they are safer and because it is wonderful to have so much of your work together. . The man who is doing the Bibliography for the exhibition is spending the day examining my collection on Tuesday next. His name is Donald Gallup.[1]. I am printing them a set of photographs[2] and presently, after I have read them and made footnotes, the letters go to them with instructions they are not to be shown until Baby and Papa and Mama Woojums are DEAD. But it is a relief they will be cared for as long as anything is cared for. O yes, McCullo[u]gh says he received the second manuscript of To Do and he wants to keep this for awhile. if this is all right, why no need to do anything. If it ISN'T all right, write him to send the manuscript to me at once. It isn't a matter for me to decide: I told him he could keep it until he heard from YOU. I don't know why he wants to keep it. . Of course, dear Baby Woojums, I Love this book, but I have never thought it was a children's book. . Bennett and Phyllis are very happy and I think this is a most happy marriage. When you come to America you must be photographed in color which is about all I do now, except to get OUR papers in order. Yale wanted a manuscript of mine. As you know I am giving my manuscripts to the NY Public Library, but I am giving Yale the manuscripts of How I listen to Four Saints, printed in the souvenir programs, and to the preface to the Four Saints, printed [in the] book. .

love to you both from Fania and

Carlo

[x] R[obert] B Haas wants to examine some of these & possibly use them in his anthology. I have arranged for the Yale Library to loan them to the University of California Library for his convenience—He will not be permitted to remove them from the Reserve Room. However if he wants to print any unpublished material, *Yale must have your* written consent!

2. Complete—except for the Bad ones!

---

1. A *Catalogue of the Published and Unpublished Writings of Gertrude Stein*, compiled by Robert Bartlett Haas and Donald Clifford Gallup, consists of four sections: "Books and Pamphlets by Gertrude Stein," "Books and Pamphlets With Contributions From Stein," "Contributions to Periodicals," and "A Chronological List of the Published and Unpublished Writings of Gertrude Stein." Donald Gallup was responsible for the first three sections. The fourth section, Haas's checklist, corrected and brought up to date the bibliography Stein had prepared for *transition* (February 1929), 15:47–55.

To Carl Van Vechten

[postmark: 3 December 1940]   Bilignin par Belley
                                                               (Ain)

My dearest Papa Woojums,

The weather is getting cold and I guess it is going to get colder, and when you get away from that fire it is very cold, but we have plenty of wood to burn and we burn it, and I have had the Atlantic[1] and now What are Masterpieces, and Bobbie Haas has made it a very nice book and I am so pleased.[2] And I am wondering if this will get to you for Christmas and we say merry Christmas to you and Fania and love to[o]. I have not heard anything about To Do, have you, but then there has been an election of course, I am very anxious to hear what the children said, and now once more before we go to bed merry Christmas to you two.

Always and always
Baby and Mama Woojums[3]

1. See Stein to Van Vechten [14 October 1940], note 2.

2. Stein's *What Are Masterpieces* was published by the Conference Press on 11 October 1940. The Conference Press consisted, at the time of its founding in 1936, of University of California, Los Angeles, students, Gilbert Harrison, Hal Levy, and Bill Okie. The idea for their press developed while they were working for the campus newspaper. A fourth student who joined in their discussion, William Saroyan, was admitted to the group and the Conference Press was born. The first book they published was Saroyan's volume of short stories, *Three Times Three*.

   The four young men had met Stein in 1935. After hearing Stein broadcast on a Los Angeles radio station, Saroyan telephoned her and asked if they could meet with her. The idea to publish a book by Stein was born at that meeting. In a letter postmarked 1 January 1937 (Columbia-Random House) Stein wrote Bennett Cerf explaining the Conference Press project and asking, as he was her American publisher, his permission. Cerf replied to Stein on 8 January 1937 (YCAL) that he saw no harm in the project if it was limited to this one time. Various problems prevented the book from being issued at an earlier date. The volume contained "Another Garland for Gertrude Stein," a foreword by Robert Haas.

3. Both signatures by Stein.

❧

To Carl Van Vechten

[postmark: 10 December 1940]   Bilignin par Belley
                                       (Ain)

My dearest Papa Woojums,

You have done everything just right and made me very happy, all your arrangements with Yale are perfect and it makes me very happy that everything is together all of us and there are no bad photos, each one was something, I will never forget the book you brought us with all of them in it, there were lots afterwards and the first were wonderful, everybody here the other day was looking at the ones in Everybody's [Autobiography], the french can never believe that photography can be like that, but it is bless Papa Woojums, I am so happy that everything has been so perfectly arranged and Bobby Haas will be so happy, he is working very hard at the anthology, he has taken a year off for it, and the arrangement you have made makes everything possible for him.[1] About To Do[2] I think you are perfectly right, but then you know I am not at all stuck on its being a child's book, I called it a child's book, because it was about alphabets and birthdays but children says Alice have not [i.e., no] monopoly of these things so Mama Woojums has always believed that Papa Woojums was right, and that people will love it but not as a child's book so when you pass it on to Mr. Gilman Low III of Scribners we won't tell him that it is a child's book since Papa Woojums who knows says it is not, and Mama Woojums who knows that Papa Woojums knows says it is not, and Baby Woojums wants everybody to like it, and is not at all keen on children's wanting it not at all not at all. I am writing to [John]McCullough by this air-mail, to tell him to give you the ms. there is no reason why he should keep it, and while one copy is being read, you will have the other one for you, bless you papa Woojums, happy New Year, you are so good you are so sweet you are so dear bless you Papa Woojums and thank you for everything, and happy New Year to you and Fania from us all

                                       Baby Woojums.

1. The anthology Haas planned at this time was never published. Haas did prepare three anthologies of Stein's writings: *A Primer for the Gradual Understanding of Gertrude Stein* (1971), *Reflections on the Atomic Bomb* (1973), and *How Writing is Written* (1974).

2. Stein's "To Do: A Book of Alphabets and Birthdays."

To Gertrude Stein

11 December 1940   [101 Central Park West
                                                     New York]

Dearest Baby Woojums,

Did you know that Virgil [Thomson] is the music critic of the N Y
Herald-Tribune and has made a sensation? Here is his morning's review which
starts off very happily. .[1] Bennett [Cerf] still has TO DO, and, as I wrote
you, [John] McCullo[u]gh is keeping a copy to see what he can think of
doing, until you say take it away from him. So there is still hope on this. I
go on printing pictures of you and Alice for Yale. I'd like to send you a
couple of beautiful prints, but it is impossible to send photographs at the
moment. . There is a rumor which breaks out everywhere that you are in
America. The stupidity of this amazes me because if you were even in Arizona the Sultan of Zanzibar would know about it. Anyway people keep asking me and I keep saying NO. But I hope you may be soon . . . Here is
lots of love to you and Mama Woojums from Fania and

Papa W!

And Merry Christmas and happy New Year! I sent you a Christmas
card. If it reaches you please let me know.

---

1. Van Vechten enclosed a clipping from the *New York Herald Tribune*, 11 December 1940,
p. 24. The clipping, "Good Old France," was Thomson's review of a concert of Robert Casa-
desus at Carnegie Hall, New York. The review began:

> Alice Toklas used to say that French architecture and music, Frenchmen, too, for that
> matter, should mostly be classified as belonging to either the funereal or the casino style,
> but that between the two lay a narrow margin consisting of all that is precious in civi-
> lization. The margin she called simply "Good Old France."

※

To Carl Van Vechten
[Postcard: Hauterives (Drôme)—L'auteur du "Palais Idéal"
et sa Brouette légendaire]

[17 December 1940]   [Bilignin par Belley
                                                      Ain]

My dearest Carl,

A card written July 29 has just come, with a picture of George[s Jacques] of the Algonquin on it, a little late in being delivered but most timely about Greece, do tell him how much we appreciate his country,[1] and bless you Papa Woojums bless you all the time

Baby Woojums

---

1. Greece had repelled an invasion by Italy in October–November 1940.

※

To Gertrude Stein
[Page from Coronet magazine. Photograph "Pigeons, Alas" by Juliette
Lasserre, Paris][1]

[? December 1940]   [101 Central Park West
                                                      New York]

No word from you, dear Baby Woojums for ages! Are you both all right—Love & Merry Xmas

from [yr?],
Carlo!

---

1. *Coronet* magazine (November 1940), p. 47.

❧

To Carl Van Vechten

[postmark: 13 January 1941]   Bilignin par Belley
                                               (Ain)

My dear Papa Woojums,

Nothing from you for a very long time, do write often, you have no idea how we do miss not having a postal card from you at least every week, do do send them, and is there any news about To Do, I had a nice letter from the assistant editor of [John]McCullough about it, she like you said that it was exciting for adults and an occasional child, I imagine she regrets that they did not do it,[1] I do hope somebody will, but I know Papa Woojums will do whatever is best for Baby Woojums, The Yale Library is delighted with your gift, they seem to be awaiting to make a big show and that will be nice, god bless you all and may we have a nice New Year which will include seeing each other, love to you and love to Fania, and always and always,

Baby Woojums.

1. Margaret Wise Brown, children's editor, William R. Scott, to Stein, 28 November 1940 (YCAL).

❧

To Gertrude Stein

15 January [1941]   [101 Central Park West
                                     New York]

Dear Baby Woojums,

I have you in mind constantly because I have been printing pictures of you and Mama Woojums for weeks and now at last they are ready and a box (covered with roses) is being made to hold them and then they will go to Yale. There are over 130 of them! I find one or two which we didn't make much of at the time, that are superb and will undoubtedly be famous in their way. Well, I am to take these and your letters to Yale as soon as the boxes are made. The letters are to be put away until you and I die, but the photographs are theirs' immediately.[1] And [Julian] Sawyer's Bibliography is here[2] and he says tell you he has a copy of it which he is holding for you, but it is impossible, he thinks, to send it just now, but you can tell him what to do. His address is Julian Sawyer, Hotel Sussex, 116 West 72nd Street. It is very handsome and so far I have found only one error, a bad one to be sure. He says I told him that the Portrait of Mabel came out in 1913 AFTER its appearance in Camera Work. I didn't tell him this, of course, and as Mabel gave me a copy in 1912 when she came to this country, it must have been published before this. Did you write this at the Villa in the fall of 1911 and was it published late that year or early in 1912? PLEASE ANSWER THIS.[3] I have no pictures of Phyllis [Cerf] printed at the moment but will make one for you and send it to you soon. A lot of your letters, some seemingly written months ago, came through in a bunch recently. You know by now that [John] McCullo[u]gh isn't doing TO DO, tho' for some reason he is still retaining a mss[x] "to consider." As you instructed I passed the mss on to Bennett [Cerf] and he kept it two months and has just returned it.[4] So I am passing it next to Mr. Gilman Low at Scribner's, as you suggest, and then to Harcourt. Cecil Beaton was here a while ago, but he has gone back to England. I am seeing Anton Dolin the dancer in a day or so and I will ask HIM if he knows anything about Lord Berners. and maybe I'll see somebody else who knows. I haven't heard a word about him. . Life in New York is even a little more exciting than usual with EVERYBODY, except Mama and Baby Woojums, here. I had lunch at the Algonquin today and Georges [Jacques] asked about you and in fact somebody asks about you or talks about you or writes about you every hour. The [Valentine] Dudensings are dining here tonight and Bennett and his wife and McKnight Kauffer and his wife and d'Alvarez and others.[5] We will drink to YOU. IDA is not yet out . . . PLEASE ANSWER MY QUESTIONS ABOUT the Portrait and I'll write again soon and send a picture of Phyllis and tell you what Mr. Gilman Low says. . You are both WOOJUMSES and LOVE

[Carl Van Vechten]

At Christmas I had a lovely letter from Mary Garden who is in Aberdeen, Scotland! I have known her since 1910![6] And I met Baby and Mama

Woojums only THREE years later. It is the anniversary of Sacre du Printemps and Stravinsky is conducting his new ballet, Balustrade here next week![7]

    [x] There are two copies, you will recall.

Fania sends LOVE!

1. On 23 January 1941 Van Vechten wrote to Bernhard Knollenberg, librarian of Yale University Library, that he was ready to give Stein's letters to him to Yale University Library. Van Vechten set out the following condition: "The letters after they are presented, are to be sealed in my presence and with my seal and are not to be examined or opened by anyone until after the death of myself and Gertrude Stein." Van Vechten reserved the right, however, to have access to the letters himself. Knollenberg accepted the terms of Van Vechten's gift. On 28 January 1941 Van Vechten brought to Yale, in specially made slipcases, all but one of the letters he had received from Stein from 1913 until [14 November 1940]. The remainder of the letters Van Vechten received from Stein were presented to YCAL after her death. Van Vechten wrote to James T. Babb, librarian of Yale University Library, to break the seal on the letters on 2 September 1946 (copies of Van Vechten to Knollenberg and Van Vechten to Babb, NYPL-Berg). See Stein to Van Vechten [28 September 1940], note 1.

2. Julian Sawyer's *Gertrude Stein: A Bibliography* (New York: Arrow Press, 1941).

3. Stein's *Portrait of Mabel Dodge at the Villa Curonia* was privately printed for Dodge in an edition of 300 copies by a printer in Florence in October 1912. It was reprinted in *Camera Work*, Special Number (June 1913), pp. 3–5. Van Vechten did not see a copy of the work until he met Dodge, in February 1913.

    The date of composition of this work has traditionally been given as 1911 (see Haas and Gallup, A *Catalogue*, p. 45, number 41, and Bridgman, *Gertrude Stein in Pieces*, p. 336, number 41). This is almost certainly an error. In 1911 Stein and Toklas were staying in the Casa Ricci, a house near Florence that Gertrude and Leo had rented for some years. It was on the return from Italy in 1911 that Stein, with an enormous concentration of energy, rewrote the final 100 pages of her novel, *The Making of Americans*, which culminates in the death dirge of David Hersland. Stein finished this in October 1911.

    Both Dodge, in *European Experiences* (p. 327), and Toklas, in *What Is Remembered* (pp. 75–76), agree that the protrait of Dodge was written while Stein and Toklas were houseguests at the Villa Curonia. From Dodge's letters to Stein in YCAL, it is clear that it was in September 1912 that Dodge was urging Stein to visit her: "well are you coming," she wrote on a Wednesday, early in September 1912. That Stein and Toklas came for a visit is clear from a series of Dodge's letters, written after October 1912, that talk about Stein's visit and Dodge's wish that she would come back. There is no mention of the portrait in the few letters of Dodge to Stein in 1911. Only in November 1912 does she begin mention of it. In a letter [? November 1912], Dodge wrote Stein, "Miss Blood begged a copy of the portrait which I have sent."

    The manuscript of the portrait gives no clue as to its date of completion. The portrait is written in a hard-covered notebook, a schoolchild's cahier that Stein was fond of using for her writing. The notebook was held horizontally and uses almost half of the pages (Stein wrote on only one side of the page). The notebook was reversed and used by Stein for her "Portrait of Constance Fletcher." Fletcher was a friend who was visiting Dodge at the same time.

    From the evidence, then, it would seem that Stein wrote the *Portrait of Mabel Dodge at the Villa Curonia* in late September or early October 1912. The work was then given to a printer in Florence, and presumably Stein corrected the proofs before she returned to Paris at the end of October (see Stein to Van Vechten [17 February 1941]).

[696]

4. Cerf wrote to Van Vechten, 9 January 1941 (YCAL), "I am sorry to say that everybody here is as cold as a slab of alabaster on Gertrude's juvenile."

5. Dudensing was a picture dealer in New York. E. McKnight Kauffer was a well-known designer who worked for Random House at this time. Marguerite d'Alvarez was an opera singer.

6. Garden to Van Vechten, 1 December 1940 (YCAL). This letter is in an envelope postmarked 27 November 1940. Either Garden erred when she dated her letter or the envelope belongs to another letter that is not now in YCAL.

7. George Balanchine had used Stravinsky's Concerto in D for Violin and Orchestra for a ballet, *Balustrade*. The ballet, with decor and costumes by Pavel Tchelitchew, was presented by a company called the Original Ballet Russe at the 51st Street Theatre, New York, on 22 January 1941.

To Gertrude Stein

24 January 1941

[101 Central Park West
New York]

Dearest Baby Woojums,

I LOVE Ida. It is gay and ironic and delightful and in a new vein for you. In the series of letters I have been collating there are many references to this book, sometimes called Jennie and Arthur, and one of these references is worth quoting: "Ida begins to be funny and we mustn't be too funny!"[1] Well, it isn't TOO funny, but of course it is funny. The dog passage is an epic and will be used in anthologies till the end of time. I've discovered that Polybe runs all through the letters too.[2]

Those letters! There are 392 of them! It is a marvellous series and gives your entire professional career (and much else): 27 years of it. They are in a beautiful rose box and I have arranged them chronologically and written notes to them and they are going to Yale this week and they will be sealed and must await *our* deaths until they are opened. There will be more of course and these will be added later and I hope some day you will be able to put my letters to you there too. What a volume they will all make some day. Terrific!

Did you get our Christmas card? In one of your letters you say, "In the next war we'll be in America." That was written around 1918. Well, why aren't you?[3]

And there is a mention of Hart Crane.[x] I didn't remember you knew him. His story fascinates me and sometime we must talk about him.[4] And there is a postcard (early) of Vieu; environs de Belley, Gentilhommière de Brillat-Savarin Why was I never taken there?! . .

I haven't printed Phyllis [Cerf]'s picture for you yet but will. I am also going to make some color pictures[(2)] of the *boxes* of letters and photographs (137!) that go to Yale and I will send you these later. Bennett [Cerf]'s Phyllis is an angel and they are very much in love with each other. In fact she will have a baby in August.[5]

TO DO is back from Bennett and has gone to Scribner's. Mr. Low wrote me a charming note saying of course he'd like to see it.[6] I'll report on this later. [John] McCullo[u]gh still has my copy of this, as you haven't advised me to take it away from him.

Let's write lots more letters for Yale! Now that I have your things out of the way for the time being I am going to work on my own books and manuscripts getting them ready for the NY Library and all the time I am making photographs for various libraries, please!

It is snowing outside but it is warm within. How much we wish we could see you both and we love you very much and kisses and hands across the sea!

LOVE,
Papa Woojums!

[x] When you wrote this I had never heard of Hart Crane.
[(2)] to show the pretty bindings.

1. See Stein to Van Vechten [29 September 1937].

2. Polybe was a dog that Stein had when she lived in Majorca during the early part of World War I. Polybe figures in a number of Stein's works written in 1915–16. In a letter to Virgil Thomson (postmark 12 July 1930, YCAL), who was visiting Majorca, Stein wrote of Polybe, "He used to dance along with the other dogs in the moonlight." See Van Vechten to Stein, 23 February [1923], note 2.

3. This does not appear in any letter written in 1918. Stein wrote this in a letter to Van Vechten postmarked 29 August 1935.

4. See Stein to Van Vechten [17 July 1929], notes 1 and 2, and Stein to Van Vechten [20 February 1941]. Stein had met Hart Crane through Laura Riding and Robert Graves.

5. Cerf's first son, Christopher, was born 19 August 1941.

6. W.Gilman Low to Van Vechten, 21 January 1941.

❦

To Carl Van Vechten
[Postcard: Hauterives (Drôme)—"Palais Idéal" Façade Est—"L'Entrée
du Tombeau"]

[postmark: 24 January 1941]   [Bilignin par Belley
                                               Ain]

Dear Papa Woojums,

The Christmas letter came but not the card but Christmas mail is still coming so we still have hope, had a charming letter from [Donald] Gallup who had such a nice visit with you, he told all about it,[1] lots of love to you both and lots of love dear Papa Woojums from

B. W.

1. Gallup to Stein, 18 December 1940, YCAL.

❦

To Gertrude Stein

31 January [1941][1]   [101 Central Park West
                                               New York]

Dear Gertrude and Baby Woojums!

The mss came back today and goes to Harcourt today. Of course I never told him it was a children's book. I don't think it is. If Harcourt doesn't want it, I have another idea! I dream of Ida and chuckle over her and her playmates in the middle of the night. What a gal! Phyllis [Cerf]'s pictures are not yet printed, but here is a color picture of the cases enclosing the letters and photographs that went to Yale. Hold it by the edges—don't touch the picture itself—to the light with a magnifying glass and you will see the whole thing. The colors are EXACT. It gave me a funny feeling to seal up your letters like mummies! But the Library is MAGNIFICENT and do you know they have ALL the books that were in the Yale Library in 1742. It is

[699]

the only college library that has never had a fire.[2] Love[x] to you and Mama
Woojums

Papa Woojums!

[x] and how!

1. Van Vechten's letter is typed beneath a letter from William Gilman Low III, of Charles
Scribner's Sons, to him (30 January 1941). In returning the manuscript of "To Do: A Book of
Alphabets and Birthdays," Low wrote, "I wish Miss Stein could be persuaded to do another
straight-forward book such as PARIS FRANCE."

2. Van Vechten had visited the library for the first time on 28 January in order to present
Stein's letters to him and other materials to the library's collections.

To Gertrude Stein
[Telegram]

[postmark: 4 February 1941]   New York

Happy birthday and lots of love

Fania and Carlo Van Vechten

To Carl Van Vechten and Fania Marinoff
[Postcard: Environs de Belley—Le Gland]

[postmark: 4 February 1941]   [Bilignin par Belley
                                                      Ain]

My dears,

The snow was gently falling and then your birthday telegram came
and then the snow came out it really did, and now it is still my birthday and
I send you all our love all of it now and always

Baby Woojums

[700]

To Gertrude Stein

10 February [1941]   [101 Central Park West
                                                      New York]

Dearest Baby Woojums!

Harcourt kept the mss. of To Do exactly one day and returned it, saying, "I have your note of the fourth, and the mss. of Miss Stein's To Do: a Book of Alphabets and Birthdays, arrived with it. I have been able to spend an hour over the manuscript immediately. Not only is it somewhat in her difficult style, but it seems to me the idea (sic) isn't sufficient to carry a book. So I am sending the manuscript back to you as you request." I have another idea, as I wrote you, from which something may come. I'll let you know.[1] [John] McCullo[u]gh has returned the manuscript he had and the Yale Show opens on the 22. . I haven't found out anything about Lord Berners yet, but will let you know when I do. . PLEASE TELL ME DID you receive OUR Christmas card?[x] I HOPE SO. No pictures of Phyllis [Cerf] for you yet but will be soon.   You are a woojums of the First Water and so is Mama Woojums and lots of LOVE,

                                                      Papa Woojums.

    [x] And our birthday cablegram?

1. Van Vechten had sent Alfred Harcourt a note on 31 January 1941 asking if he would like to see Stein's new manuscript. Harcourt responded to Van Vechten on 3 February 1941 (YCAL), but he told him "I am a little afraid my interest is personal rather than professional, but do send it over anyway." Van Vechten must have had the typescript hand delivered. Harcourt responded to him, the letter quoted in this letter to Stein, on 5 February 1941 (YCAL). Van Vechten's other idea was to propose the book to the Yale University Press; they, too, rejected the book.

To Carl Van Vechten
[Postcard: Environs de Belley—Pont d'Yenne]

[postmark: 13 February 1941]   [Bilignin par Belley
                                                 Ain]

My dearest Papa Woojums,

The pigeons came and they were pretty pigeons[1] and this is the bridge
that is no more and now we cross on a boat and the Rhone runs fast and is
very lovely and what has happened to To Do and how are you and spring is
here and [we] love you always and always

Baby Woojums

1. A reference to Van Vechten's Christmas card, a photograph of pigeons from a page in *Coronet* magazine. See Van Vechten to Stein [? December 1940].

To Gertrude Stein

14 February [1941]   [101 Central Park West
(St. Valentine's Day)   New York]

Dearest Baby Woojums.

Here is Phyllis Cerf enfin![1] John McCullo[u]gh telephoned me yesterday about his plan for a book and I think it is a "natural" and a marvellous idea and immediately I thought of all the tots in the country beginning
to read *through* Gertrude Stein and I LOVED the idea and I KNEW you
would love it and I suggested the Title:
GERTRUDE STEIN'S FIRST READER
and I hope that's the way it will be and I hope you will write it and PLEASE
DO and everybody will be reading GSFR and it will be ordered by all the
schools and thousands of copies will be sold and the youth of America as
they grow up will take in GS at the breast as they should and from then on

[702]

they will want to read nothing but GS. I DO HOPE IT will all be this way, but maybe you, or the schools, or something, won't want to do it.[2] But I do hope. Anyway here is Phyllis and did you get a Christmas card and a telegram on your birthday?

Please, and LOVE to you and Mama W

Papa W!

1. Enclosed was a photograph of Phyllis Cerf. On the verso Van Vechten wrote, "Phyllis Cerf. *1940* Just *before* they were married."

2. The book was eventually published in 1946 as *The Gertrude Stein First Reader & Three Plays.* The book had decorations by Sir Francis Rose.

To Carl Van Vechten

[postmark: 17 February 1941]   Bilignin par Belley
                                                               (Ain)

My dearest Papa Woojums,

We are so xcited over the over 130 of them and those we have not seen, some day we will see them, happy days,[1] and thanks again to you and Fania for my birthday wishes, it gave us a two delightful times, because first they telephone it letter by letter and then they send it, so we kind of got it twice and we were happy, I am getting a little mixed about the Bibliography, I thought it was Bobby Haas who was doing it and a man named [Donald] Gallup who wrote to me and now it is [Julian] Sawyer, well whoever it is do tell them to send it because books come through alright and I would like to see it.[2] About the Portrait of Mabel I did write it at the Villa when we were there in the fall of 1911[x] and it was printed and the paper chosen and the proof corrected before we left, certainly it was printed within a month of our having been there. And do tell George [s Jacques] how proud we all are of the Greeks, and it is nice to know that he is one of them, we were always pleased and proud of him but now we are pleased of [i.e., and] proud of all of them. I do hope Scribners will do To Do but I am not setting my heart on any one of them, I know you will do whatever is best, I am fond of the book very fond of it and I do hope somebody will do it. I am most awfully looking forward to seeing Ida, do tell us everything that happens, I can't tell you what a pleasure it is to get a letter from you so do write often and more often and so much love, I cannot tell you how much love to you and to Fania, dearest Papa Woojums, the prim roses are out and spring will come, lots of love

Gertrude B. W.

[x]Alice thinks it was 1912 that we were at Mabel's but you would know that by the letters.[3]

1. The photographs Van Vechten had given to YCAL.

2. See Van Vechten to Stein [23 November 1940], note 1. Sawyer's bibliography was a separate project from the Yale catalogue being prepared by Haas and Gallup.

3. See Van Vechten to Stein, 15 January [1941], note 3. Toklas was correct. They had been there in September-October 1912.

To Carl Van Vechten

[postmark: 20 February 1941]   Bilignin par Belley
                                                                    (Ain)

Dearest Papa Woojums

The little photo came and it is as clear as clear[1] and next winter if peace is upon us in the winter evenings Mama Woojums and I will begin to clean up our letters and we will get all yours together and I think I will send them to you direct and then you will make another lovely rosy cover and there they will be side by side forever and that will be nice. Hart Crane was only in Paris a very short time, he came with a letter from [Robert] Graves and Laura Riding and he was fearfully drunk a case like poor [F. Scott] Fitzgerald, and only twice was he sober enough to come to see us, he was very American, intensely so, an old-fashioned American, really more a type of the nineties, than of the 20 century, and Alice says indignantly, if Carl will not stay longer than 48 hours how can he see everything and next time there will be lots to see, lots and lots, oh happy days when you come again.[2]

About To Do I wrote twice to McDougal [i.e., John McCullough] to tell him to return [to] you the ms. and I wrote twice on a postal card to tell you I had, so will you see he does, I am so xcited about your idea, and whatever it is please do it,[3] I know it will be a lovely one and we are really xcited at the idea of Bennett [Cerf] being a papa he will make a nice one but and that is something so different papa Woojums our papa Woojums so much love and more and more and more. I am so xcited about Ida, it has not come yet and I am so pleased you like it. I am working steadily on the new one, Mrs. Reynolds, Ida and Mrs. Reynolds both were each one suggested by somebody in the village, and when you come they will pose for you, Mrs. Reynolds is turning out to be a bit of a mystic, it goes slowly I have about 50 pages done,[4] Ida you know was done over and over again, before it finally became what it is. Oh lots of love dear Papa Woojums and to Fania and lots and lots

always
Baby Woojums.

1. With his letter of 31 January [1941], Van Vechten had sent Stein a Kodachrome slide of the slipcases he had had made for the Stein letters when he presented them to YCAL.

2. See Van Vechten to Stein, 24 January 1941, note 4.

3. See Van Vechten to Stein, 10 February [1941]. In this letter Van Vechten mentions an idea that he has for Stein. The idea is clarified in Van Vechten to Stein, 14 February [1941], where he proposes a Gertrude Stein "First Reader." Stein had not yet received Van Vechten's second letter.

4. Stein's *Mrs. Reynolds* was not published until 1952. The novel is concerned with daily life during the occupation of France. It draws many of its details from Stein and Toklas' domestic life during this period. The preoccupation with prophecies in the novel represents the shared interest of Stein, Toklas, and their neighbor in the nearby village of Chazey-Bons, Elena Genin. Stein and Madame Genin would talk on the telephone several times a day comparing prophecies. Stein was particularly interested in one of Madame Genin's books, *The Gypsy Queen Dream Book and Fortune Teller* published by Herbert Jenkins Limited (letter received from Joan Chapman, 21 February 1983). The Genins did not move into Chazey-Bons until early 1941 and so she could not have been a source of Ida.

&

To Carl Van Vechten
[Postcard: Environs de Belley—Le Rhône et le pont de La Balme]

[postmark: 20 February 1941]   [Bilignin par Belley
                                                 Ain]

Dear Papa Woojums,

Just written you a long letter to tell you how pleased we are with the rosy cover which came out beautifully, and to tell you how happy we are that you like Ida and that please do your idea of To Do whatever you do is lovely and I have written twice to [John] McCullough to return you the ms. and this is the bridge that was blown up and we go across car and all on a boat, and spring has come and lots of love

Baby Woojums

&

To Carl Van Vechten
[Postcard: Environs de Belley—Le Gland]

[postmark: 6 March 1941]   [Bilignin par Belley
                                                 Ain]

Dearest Papa Woojums,

Ida has just come and they have made a lovely book of it, I am so pleased and happy about it and it is funny, funnier than I remembered it, bless you papa Woojums bless you always

B. W.

🐿

To Gertrude Stein

9 March 1941   [101 Central Park West
                                                New York]

Dearest Baby Woojums,

I asked Mrs Geoffrey Toye to find out about Lord Berners and she cabled her husband and the reply came back at once that he is ALL RIGHT at Farthington House, Wantage.[1] . Maybe you won't know that Sherwood Anderson died yesterday (March 8) while on a cruise to South America with his wife. . He was sixty-one years old and he died of an obstruction in the intestines, followed by peritonitis.[2] . . My other idea for To DO was the Yale University Press, but it wasn't a good one. The Yale Press is something entirely aside from OUR friends at Yale and it appears nothing can be done there.[3] . You should be receiving the catalogue of the Yale Show soon, which is more a Bibliography than a catalogue. .[4] My photographs are all over the place and Virgil [Thomson] sent the score of Four Saints. I haven't seen the exhibit yet, but Thornton Wilder has and the Kiddie [W. G. Rogers] has and they will doubtless write you and I suppose soon you'll be getting the Catalogue-Bibliography. I hope you will like the idea of Gertrude Stein's First Reader.[5] To me it sounds like a "natural." Marjorie Worthington was here the other night and asked all about YOU. She brought [Moise] Kisling with her. Do you know him.[6] Be sure to report on the Christmas Card and the birthday cable. It is the only way I have of learning if things get THROUGH and Lots of Love and big HUGS to you and Mama P. [i.e., W.]

Papa W!

Also I sent Phyllis Cerf's pictures!

1. Mrs. Toye was the wife of an English film producer who was associated with Alexander Korda.

2. Anderson and his wife Eleanor sailed from New York on 28 February 1941 on a goodwill tour of South America. Anderson died of peritonitis infection in the Panama Canal Zone on 8 March 1941.

3. Van Vechten had approached Norman Holmes Pearson to try to convince the Yale University Press to publish Stein's "To Do: A Book of Alphabets and Birthdays." Pearson wrote Van

Vechten on 6 March 1941 (NYPL-Berg) that although he would love to see Yale publish something by Stein, he had no influence with the press. "To Do" was eventually printed in *Alphabets & Birhtdays*, vol. 7 of *The Yale Edition of the Unpublished Work of Gertrude Stein*.

4. See Van Vechten to Stein, 23 November 1940, note 1.

5. Stein's *The First Reader* was first published in a French translation by Madame la Baronne d'Aiguy as *Petits poèmes pour un livre de lecture* (Alger, Algeria: Collection Fontaine, E. Charlot, 1944). It did not include the three plays that were added to the English edition, *The Gertrude Stein First Reader & Three Plays*, with decorations by Sir Francis Rose, published in 1946.

6. Marjorie Worthington, the writer and wife of the writer William Seabrook. Moise Kisling (1891–1953) was the Polish-born painter who had settled in France in 1910. Stein may have met him at that time.

To Carl Van Vechten

[postmark: 9 March 1941]   Bilignin par Belley
                                                                 (Ain)

My dearest Papa Woojums,

Phyllis [Cerf] does look sweet and serious, and seems made to be a good wife and mother, I am awfully pleased that Bennett [Cerf] did so well for himself this time, she does really look like a nice wife and a nice mother, thanks for sending it, and I am quite xcited about Gertrude Stein's First Reader only I have not heard anything from [John] McCullough and do not quite know what it is it should be, do you remember that when I was somewhere in the West they gave me a volume a sweet little volume of Reading without tears, and it was wonderful reading, I have just been looking for it but it must be in Paris, but I did think they would like To Do but they didn't, and do I know what the little children do, do, well anyway I know what Baby Woojums does do she does whatever Papa Woojums wants her to do so here goes for a First Reader and a cuckoo, if I get an idea I'll write a page or two and send it on to you, dearest Papa Woojums yes we love you, all of us love all of you, but what does a First Reader do, I remember so well McGuffey and Appleton's Third Reader, I don't seem when I went to school to have had a first and Second Reader, I seem only to have had a Third Reader, perhaps in East Oakland where we were fond of skipping a grade we skipped

Two Readers right away, anyway I will try right away,[1] but would they do
To Do if they had this other one to do, To Do might [be] a fifth Reader,
was there one, I still only remember the Third, well spring is the time for a
first reader and Spring has come. I picked Alice lots of white violets and
pussy willows yesterday, lots of love oh so much from us all to you all, to
you

B. W.

[on back of envelope] Have just done 2 lessons of the first Reader,
will send them soon.[2]

1. Favell Lee Mortimer, *Reading Without Tears; or A Pleasant Mode of Learning to Read* (New
York: Harper, 1857). William Holmes McGuffey (1800–1873) was the author of a series of
books, one primer and six readers, *Eclectic Readers.* The McGuffey system of reading origi-
nated in 1836 and used phonics charts to teach children to sound out words by learning the
pronunciation of each letter of the alphabet. It also used letter grouping recognition. *Appleton's
Third Reader* was part of a series of educational books published by D. Appleton & Co.
    McCullough wrote Stein on 10 February 1941 (YCAL) thanking her for a letter she had
sent on 10 December [1940] and reporting on the project of a first reader that he and van
Vechten had discussed.

2. The first reader consists of twenty lessons (lesson one has a separate "Part Two"). When the
book was published in 1946, Stein added three plays: *In A Garden A Tragedy In One Act; Three
Sisters Who Are Not Sisters A Melodrama;* and *Look and Long. In A Garden* was written for a
fête for neighborhood children in and around Belley. It was first performed on the terrace of
the Château du Béon by Rose d'Aiguy, Mark Godet, and Maurice Godet. Pierre Balmain, who
had been demobilized and was living with his mother in Aix-les-Bains, designed the costumes.
The performance took place in the spring of 1943.

To Gertrude Stein

<table>
<tr><td>[13 March 1941]
Thursday</td><td>[101 Central Park West
New York]</td></tr>
</table>

Sweet Baby Woojums:

Norman Holmes Pearson who is everything at Yale and yet not actually a member of the teaching or library staff, writes me: "Poor [Donald]
Gallup was drafted, and left for Ft Devens on the Thursday morning before

the exhibition opened. . I finished putting it up myself and worked up to within a couple of hours of my wedding on Friday afternoon. I felt a little like a peasant, leaving the fields to get himself wed. And one of the librarians warned me lest I say, 'I take thee, Gertrude,' when the proper moment arrived. The next day my newly acquired wife and my newly acquired daughters and I made a short honeymoon trip to the exhibition room to see how it looked. It seemed fully as scenic a trip as one to Niagara, and much warmer and gayer. So Gertrude and the exhibition will have a particular and unique spot in my memory. Tell her, if you think it will amuse her . . . It was a labor of love for Gertrude on my part and one which it was a privilege to do. ."[1]

Maybe I'll go up next week and I hope to take Mark [Lutz] if he can get away.

So you see I write you nearly every day. . Ida is getting some fine reviews.

Love and kisses to you and Mama Woojums,

Papa Woojums!

1. Pearson to Van Vechten, 1 March 1941, NYPL-Berg. Pearson at this time was working on his doctorate degree at Yale University and was helping with the development of the Yale Collection of American Literature. Pearson was married to Susan Bennett Tracy on 21 February 1941 in New Haven.

To Carl Van Vechten

[postmark: 18 March 1941]   [Bilignin par Belley Ain]

My dearest Papa Woojums

Here it is and do you like it, I will be most dreadfully anxious until I hear whether it pleases you or not, dearest papa Woojums, I am sending you another copy by ordinary mail, and I hope they both reach you and I do so hope that you will like it, the translation of Paris France is going to be printed in Algeria, and I imagine will be out in a couple of months, it will amuse you to have a book of mine printed not in Algerian but in french in Algeria, dearest Papa Woojums I do hope you are liking The First Reader.

Always
Baby Woojums

To Carl Van Vechten

[postmark: 22 March 1941]   Bilignin par Belley
                                               (Ain)

Dearest Papa Woojums,

This is the second ms. copy, and I have just had a nice letter from the librarian of Yale, he says I suppose you have heard from Mr. Van Vechten of his recent superb gifts to us, of your ms. letters from you to him, (Under restrictions specified by Mr. Van Vechten) and photographs which he has taken of you, and then he goes on to tell how sorry he was you would not speak, I would like Papa Woojums to have spoken but Papa Woojums always knows best, and I am full of happiness,[1] and I have had a long letter from [John] McCullough[2] and I have written to him that I am sending you the ms, and that I am very interested in the idea of the first reader and that I am just waiting to know what Papa Woojums thinks and whether you want these, or more of the same or something different, I really like doing them immensely, and I am so xcited about your idea about To Do and what it is, which we do not know, and I ask Alice to guess and she can't guess and neither can I, but it will be satisfying, it is an xciting world and thanks dear Papa Woojums and you know we had the cable and the Christmas card, and Phyllis [Cerf]'s picture, and the pigeons and all our love, in this lovely spring weather to you and to Fania, bless you

Baby Woojums

1. Bernard Knollenberg to Stein, 11 February 1941 (YCAL). Van Vechten had declined to speak at the opening ceremonies of the Stein exhibition. Earlier he had declined an invitation

by William Lyon Phelps, professor emeritus at Yale University, to deliver a lecture on Stein as part of the Bergen Lecture series (Phelps to Van Vechten, 21 November 1940, NYPL-Berg).

2. McCullough to Stein, 10 February 1941 (YCAL).

To Gertrude Stein

27 March 1941   [101 Central Park West
                                                           New York]

Dear Baby Woojums,

The Yale show is just a knockout. It is terrific. I took Mark [Lutz] up there this week and we both nearly died. We felt as if we were in the shrine of Dante or Goethe at the very least. In a beautiful room about 40 feet square on three sides of the wall (windows on the fourth with engraved roundels) and arranged cases. There were also cases in the center of the room. In these were manuscripts, books in several forms, letters, and over all a series of my photographs, about 25 of them, marvellously chosen and arranged.[x] Virgil [Thomson] sent three scores of Four Saints. . and the published score of The Wedding Bouquet was included. . It took about two hours to examine the show thoroughly and they are having it photographed just for YOU and Mama Woojums.[1] . You haven't told me if the Christmas card got through yet, but I KNOW now you got the birthday wire and the color picture of the Yale boxes. And have you received Mrs [Bennett] Cerf's picture?. . There is no news of To Do. That appears to be not very hopeful at the moment. But sooner or later we are sure to find an eager publisher for this. . I do hope you will like the idea for Gertrude Stein's Frist Reader. .Thornton [Wilder] apparently has gone to South America as a good will offering from the government but you doubtless heard from him about the show. I'm so pleased about Mrs Reynolds. Bennett and bride are in Nassau where the Duchess of Windsor lives.[2] I got a letter from the Kiddie [W. G. Rogers][3] and he is mad about the Yale Show and you will hear from him too. . Don't get mixed about the Bibliography. . [Robert] Haas and [Donald] Gallup finally collaborated over the Yale one and [Julian] Sawyer's was done first and is much more elaborate. . I think both of these have been sent you . . . Mabel [Dodge] has come and gone. . She told [Georgia] O'Keefe she wanted to see me, but O'Keefe thought better leave things as they are and only told me after Mabel had gone. The wonderful maps [Miguel] Covarrubias did for the San Francisco Fair are here. . Great twenty foot square murals of the Western Hemisphere: One devoted to races, another to flora, another to fauna, another to habitations, another to locomotion. They are very pretty.[4] . I gave Georges [Jacques] the message about the Greeks and he cried and he said: "It is my greatest pride that I can call Gertrude Sein my friend." You are right and Mama W is wrong about the date of the Portrait because Mabel came to New York early in the fall of 1912: so it must have been 1911 if it was the fall.[5] Lots of love, Baby Woojums and I think your idea of sending my letters to me, when you get an opportunity is a good one and I will put them away in another rosy box, after arranging them and they will go Yale too. LOVE to you both and Fania sends LOVE too and LOVE to you both!

[Carl Van Vechten]

[x] and in mats and with long descriptions type written at the side. Both Pepe and Basket were shown. St Thérèse, St Ignatius, O many of A. B. T. and one of all three of us, also your favorite on the France, the back of your head.

1. The exhibition was held in the Sterling Memorial Library, Yale University, from 22 February to 29 March 1941. Van Vechten visited the exhibition on 24 March 1941 (Pearson to Van Vechten, telegram, postmark 17 March 1941, NYPL-Berg). There is no explanation why Van Vechten waited so long to go see the exhibition.

2. When France fell, in 1940, the Duke and Duchess of Windsor were in their home on the French Riviera. They escaped to Spain and then to Portugal. The Duke had hoped he would be given suitable war work in Britain, but the authorities gave him the governorship of the Bahamas. The Windsors lived in Nassau for five years.

3. Rogers to Van Vechten, 26 March 1941, YCAL.

4. Covarrubias had done six mural-maps, *Pageant of the Pacific*, for the Pacific House in the Golden Gate International Exposition, San Francisco.

5. Van Vechten is incorrect. Dodge came to New York in late December 1912. See Van Vechten to Stein, 15 January [1941], note 3.

❧

To Carl Van Vechten

[postmark: 30 March 1941]   Bilignin par Belley
                                                       (Ain)

My dearest Papa Woojums,

Thanks for getting news of Gerald Berners, I have not had any word from him since the troubles, and I was so upset at hearing of Sherwood [Anderson]'s death. I had had a very sweet letter from him just on the eve of his departure for S. America, and he was looking forward to the trip as going to be so interesting and now he did not have it, I am so awfully sorry for his wife for I think the first time in his marital history he was really happy and suited, dear Sherwood.[1] By this time you will have had my first effort at the First Reader and I am awfully anxious to hear what you will say; everything that is mailed does pretty well come through, sometimes there is quite a long delay, and sometimes it comes through astonish[ing]ly quickly, and the birthday cable was prompt, also Phyllis Cerf's picture, the Christmas card took longer and all were most enthusiastically received.

The only other idea I have about To Do, is to send a copy to Margot Johnson, of the Anne Watkins Inc. 77 Park Avenue New York Telephone Caledonia 5-5576, she seems to want to do something for me, she is the American representative of my English agents, she might have a try,[2] and Bobby Haas in California, might be able to do something with a copy, out there. Did I tell you that they are bringing out Paris France in french in Algeria, would you mind if they used one of your photos, the one of Basket and me in the garden near the little summer-house,[3] the Baronne D'Aiguy has a copy of the photo and she has done the translation, and she would like it, the girls at the Post Office at Belley, get so xcited over your stamps, they try their best to give you new ones in return,[4] we were very xcited over the 13 amendment one, Captain Putz was here when it came, and he would love it,[5] lots of love and lots of thanks dear dearest Papa Woojums, and are you liking the first reader

                                                       B. W.

---

1. The Stein-Anderson correspondence has been collected in *Sherwood Anderson/Gertrude Stein: Correspondence and Personal Essays*, ed. Ray Lewis White (Chapel Hill: University of North

Carolina Press, 1972). Stein is referring to Anderson's letter of 4 November [1940], (pp. 110–11). Anderson wrote about rumors that Stein and Toklas had secretly, and in disguise, arrived in New York. He also reported on his meeting with Maxwell Perkins, Scribner's editor, who had told Anderson about Stein's new book, *Paris France*. This was not, however, Anderson's last letter to Stein. On 26 January 1941 (pp. 113–14), a month before sailing on a goodwill tour of South America, Anderson wrote Stein thanking her for her letter of [? December 1940] (pp. 111–12), in which she praised his novel *Many Marriages*. In his letter Anderson also informed Stein of the sudden death, on 21 December 1940, of F. Scott Fitzgerald. This letter was, for some reason, returned to Anderson. It was remailed on 2 November 1941 by Eleanor Anderson, who described it as "a letter which Sherwood wrote you before we left for South America—I hope that you will get it this time. He spoke of you with affection often" (p. 112).

2. Margot Johnson was the executive vice-president of Ann Watkins, Inc., the American representatives of Stein's English agents, Pearn, Pollinger & Higham Ltd.

Johnson wrote to Stein first on 3 January 1941, establishing the connection with her English agents and telling Stein that they had had no reply from her about the galleys of *Ida A Novel* and had therefore asked Ann Watkins to approach Cerf about the possibilities of an English edition. On 31 March 1941 Johnson wrote Stein and said that when Cerf got back she would speak to him about the children's book. It is not clear from Johnson's letter whether it was *The First Reader* or "To Do." In subsequent letters Johnson concerned herself with placing "To Do." Johnson's letters to Stein are in YCAL.

3. The French edition of *Paris France* used the same photograph by Van Vechten of Stein that had been used as the frontispiece of *Everybody's Autobiography*, Stein in profile wearing the dress she wore when giving her lectures in the United States, 1934–35.

4. One of the girls who worked in the Belley post office was Mlle Bouvier. "Her parents owned a farm not far from Bilignin. Their barn is a landmark, an old Knights of Templars tower" (letter received from Joan Chapman, 5 February 1982).

5. Captain Gabriel Putz was the husband of Marie-Anne du Vachat, the woman who owned the house in Bilignin that Stein and Toklas rented.

To Carl Van Vechten
[Postcard: Environs de Belley—Pont d'Aignoz sur le Seran]

[postmark: 8 April 1941]   [Bilignin par Belley
                                                             Ain]

Dearest Papa Woojums

That was a charming letter of Norman Holmes Pearson, do tell him how much I liked it, and may he be most happily married, daughters and all, and someday we will meet, daughters and all,[1] and I can't wait to get your letter that will tell all about it, lots of love for Easter, always to you and Fania

Tell Mark [Lutz] to write

B. W.

1. See Van Vechten to Stein [13 March 1941]. Pearson's wife had two daughters by a previous marriage.

&

To Gertrude Stein

24 April [1941]   [101 Central Park West
                                                   New York]

Dearest Baby Woojums,

So MUCH has happened! Mr [Bernhard] Knollenberg of Yale wrote me and said Columbia University wanted to borrow the Stein Show and what did I think? And Papa Woojums thought YES on the spot . . Then Mr Adams of Columbia asked Papa Woojums to come up and put it up and I said I would but obviously the person to get was Norman Holmes Pearson who put up the major part of the Yale show, after Donald Gallup was drafted. So Knollenberg said Pearson was writing his doctor's thesis and was very busy. So we telegraphed him. So he came down and put up the show and it is another knockout.[1]. Really, Baby Woojums, I wish you would WRITE Norman Holmes Pearson, 39 Goodrich Street, New Haven, Conn. and tell him how much we appreciate him.[2] I really don't know what we would do without NHP! After Gallup was drafted, he was the only one at Yale who knew all the material and he came in and set up a beautiful show. On this occasion he drove down and set up another beautiful show under entirely different conditions . . . Also he goes back and forth carrying valuable manuscript in his car, so it won't get lost and he adores and dotes on Baby Woojums . . . I am enclosing an invitation for the opening, to which, un-fortunately, I can't go, as I shall be out of town,[x] but I went up yesterday and everything looks as well as it can. . At Columbia the show is giving [i.e., being] given in the Rotunda of the great library which is a room like

[716]

the Pantheon in Paris with an enormous dome . . . The cases are dwarfed by this and there are not so many as at Yale (which is one of the most beautiful and wonderfully arranged libraries in the world) but nevertheless the material is well presented and is most astounding in its cumulative effect. I loaned them several items and there are a great many of my photographs, tho' not as many as at Yale.

THEN the Museum of Modern Art is giving a performance of Four Saints, WITH the ORIGINAL CAST, with either Virgil [Thomson] or [Alexander] Smallens conducting, In CONCERT FORM, i e without scenery or costumes or acting. . It is intended to repeat this performance at Town Hall.[3] Virgil called me up about this and said he would write you. He said, I believe, that the terms would be as usual with you and him. Virgil is now one of the great celebrities here. He has made a knockout as a music critic and is more talked about than [Greta] Garbo. His second string quartet was played at a concert at Town Hall recently.[4] I am going to Four Saints (May 7 is the date) and I'll write you all about it.

THEN The First Reader, Gertrude Stein's FIRST READER with the lovely dedication arrived and I am crazy about it. Of course it may not be at all what they want.[5] I mean we all wrote you *to wait for a model* before tackling this chore, but I guess Baby W was inspired and Could*n't* wait for a model. Anyway, it is *YOUR* first reader and both a child's book and also a wonderful way to *FIRST read* GS . . . So I gave it to [John] Mc-Cullo[u]gh with this advice, last Friday which is just a week ago and I was to hear from him by Monday and I haven't and you know that No gnus is good gnus, SO! Let's hope anyway . . .

And there is the matter of Robert Haas . . . When I gave the mss to Yale it was understood he was to have access to them at the University of California and this was agreed and arranged . . . He had plenty of time to get them there but DIDN'T and has only recently written for them from Pomona College at Stockton where he seems to be now. . Mr Knollenberg the librarian at Yale knows NOTHING about the responsibility of these people and doubts if the mss would be safe in their keeping . . . So he said if they were to go I should take the responsibility of their being lost and of course I wouldn't do that and so here we are at loose ends, so to speak, with Bobby Haas . . . I would suggest he wait either till he can get back to the U[niversity] of C[alifornia] or until he comes east to see these most valuable papers, which NOW could not be replaced.

I have recently had SIX letters or cards from you. Happy Papa W.

Please send me the Algerian Paris-France. BUT YOU HAVEN'T TOLD ME YET IF YOU HAVE RECEIVED the CHRISTMAS CARD, tho everything else seems to have got through. . *Please report on this*, YES OR NO.

The weather is divine, we both have good health and Fania is letting her hair grow grey and is most distinguished . . . We love you both and talk about you a lot.

[Carl Van Vechten]

ˣI have arranged for Prof. John Lyon to write you about it.

1. Knollenberg wrote Van Vechten on 11 April 1941 (NYPL-Berg) enclosing a letter of Mr. Williamson, director of libraries at Columbia University, New York. Knollenberg wrote Van Vechten that he had replied that Yale would be delighted to let Columbia have the material from the exhibition if Van Vechten gave his approval. Van Vechten replied to Knollenberg on 12 April granting his approval.

Van Vechten had been contacted by Charles M. Adams, assistant to the director of libraries, Columbia University. Pearson was persuaded to come to New York and mount the exhibition in one day, 17 April. The exhibition was on view from 18 April until 17 May 1941 in the Low Memorial Library. The official opening was 29 April.

2. Stein wrote two thank-you letters to Pearson, one postmarked 8 May 1941, the other postmarked 23 May 1941 (both YCAL).

3. As part of its "Coffee Concerts," the Museum of Modern Art, New York, presented *Four Saints in Three Acts* on 7 May 1941. The performance was called a public rehearsal and was conducted by Thomson from a piano. Alexander Smallens conducted a concert revival, presented by Louise Crane, at Town Hall, New York, on 27 May 1941.

4. Thomson's *Second String Quartet* was performed at Town Hall, New York, on 20 April 1941.

5. Van Vechten had received a typescript of *The First Reader*, with its dedication, "To Carl Van Vechten who did ask for a First Reader." McCullough eventually decided not to publish the book.

To Gertrude Stein

20 [i.e., 30] April 1941[1]   [101 Central Park West
                                               New York]

Dear Baby Woojums,

Prof. [John] Lyon of Columbia just telephoned and last night was a HUGE success. Bennett [Cerf] spoke and Virgil [Thomson] brought 35 singers and gave all the first act of Four Saints. They did one of your records. [Alfred] Stieglitz on account of his heart hadn't been out one evening for three years, but they got him up to the foot of the stairs leading to the library (they are terrific, you will remember) and he couldn't go farther. . Fortunately he had written out his little talk and Prof. Lyon read that. It seems to have been a very lively and sentimental occasion. . Lyon says he has written you and asked somebody else to too![2] NOW this morning I hear from Mr [Bernhard] Knollenberg that he has discovered Pomona College at Stockton is okay and he is sending the mss out there, SO, we don't have to worry any more about [Robert] Haas.[3]. . This morning the second copy of GERTRUDE STEIN'S READER arrived ([John] McCullo[u]gh still has the first) and your letter, saying at long last that the Christmas card and everything else got through. So the weather is divine and Fania flew to Washington (the first time she has been in the air) this week and is now an *addict* and so she joins us in the CLOUDS.

jonquils, marigolds, lilies of the valley, and forgetmenots to you and Mama Woojums!

Papa Woojums!!

1. The date was a typographical error by Van Vechten. The special Stein evening was held on 29 April. Van Vechten did not attend the ceremony.

2. Professor Lyon's letter is not in YCAL.

3. Haas was teaching at the College of the Pacific in Stockton, California. Knollenberg sent Van Vechten a copy of the letter he had written, 25 March 1941 (NYPL-Berg), to A. C. Gerould informing him that he was willing, with Van Vechten's approval, to have the material Haas needed sent to the University of California at Berkeley.

To Carl Van Vechten
[Postcard: Porte Bonheur (muguets)]

[postmark: 5 May 1941]　　　　　　　　　　[Bilignin par Belley
　　　　　　　　　　　　　　　　　　　　　　Ain]

Dearest Papa Woojums,

Everybody is writing about the show and about the photographs and everybody is so happy about it all and so are we, it does sound lovely as lovely as can be, and now I am waiting to hear about the reader and Bennett [Cerf] says Ida is selling nicely,[1] and we love Papa Woojums so much and there have been lots of lilies of the valley and nightingales and lots of love to you both.

B. W.

1. Cerf to Stein, 25 March 1941 (YCAL).

To Gertrude Stein

8 May 1941
[101 Central Park West
New York]

Dearest Baby Woojums,

Here is the program of FOUR SAINTS and it is to be repeated on May 27 at TOWN HALL. . There was no orchestra. Virgil [Thomson] sat at the piano, and there were no costumes or sets. The work was given like an oratorio but it was very effective indeed and we all cried with joy to hear "How many saints are there in it?" and "Pigeons on the grass alas," once more. And it was wonderful seeing [Edward] Matthews and St Therese and Miss [Altonell] Hines and all the others once more as big as life and looking just the same and so happy to be singing FOUR Saints Once again.[1] . . I saw Henry McBride and his eye shone with pleasure and the whole house was sold out the day the concert was announced . . . [John] McCullo[u]gh called up this morning and he seems to be looking very favorably on the Reader and I am to meet with him and a lady who knows about children and "readers" on Monday and talk over the situation with HER. I HOPE this will lead to something indeed.[2]. Did I tell you Fania now has white hair and looks like a Marquise?

All love to you and Mama Woojums, from us both

Papa Woojums!

BOTH copies of the reader arrived.

[720]

1. Beatrice Robinson-Wayne sang Saint Theresa I, Bruce Howard Saint Theresa II, Edward Matthews Saint Ignatius, and Altonell Hines Commère.

2. McCullough wrote Stein on 11 June 1941 (YCAL) regretting that he could not publish *The First Reader*. He felt, as a result of testing the book out in several private schools, that it was "far too old for a first reader."

To Carl Van Vechten

[postmark: 15 May 1941   Bilignin par Belley
                                                          (Ain)

Dearest Papa Woojums

Your letter all full of xcitements just came, and Alice said the most xciting was Fania's hair, do send us a photo, quick at once, and I did say the Christmas card came, it took longer to come than anything else perhaps because the censor liked to look at it and did not want to part with it but it did come, and it is all so xciting, I just can't wait to hear how the Four Saints sound like an oratorio, I have just written to Virgil [Thomson] care of you, I am awfully pleased that he is so successful, he always said he believed in longevity and he is beginning to have it at last which is a pleasure. And the First Reader you do like it, I know you do, and [John] McCullough is always long-winded, he always has to ask so many people. And you did just right about Bobby Haas, I have not heard from him for a very long time, I think that his father has been ill and I imagine that has changed all his arrangements. I am inclosing a little thing I did of Sherwood [Anderson] for Whit Burnett they are going to do a memoriam for him in Story.[1] The Algerian Paris France will be out the end of this month I think. Mama Woojums has just lost her poppy seeds in many colors that she was going to plant, they were little envelopes in a big envelope and where is it, well anyway the potatoes are growing up and up and that is the principal thing, up and up, bless you papa Woojums bless you bless you, and love to Fania and all the hair, bless you both always all loving,

Baby Woojums.

[721]

1. Stein enclosed a typescript of her "Sherwood's Sweetness," which appeared in *Story* (September/October 1941), 19(91):63. This was an Anderson memorial issue.

To Carl Van Vechten

[postmark: 23 May 1941]   Bilignin par Belley
                                                               (Ain)

My dearest Papa Woojums,

All the Columbians have been writing and they were so sorry and we were so sorry that you were not there because there does seem to have been a nice party and a good time was enjoyed by all. Frances Steloff of the G[otham]. B[ook]. Mart wrote about it too, and she said that the records sell very well to the teachers all over the country, one of whom said that the Picasso record helped the pupils to understand Hiawatha. I liked that.[1] It also made it seem possible that schools would like a Gertrude Stein First Reader and that Papa Woojums like always is right. It would be fun to be read in the schools of the U.S.A. We feel an enormous tenderness these days for the U.S.A. Bless Papa Woojums. I am glad it is alright about the ms. and Bobby Haas, perhaps some day some industrious young man will make duplicate copies of the ms. and there will be less danger in their wandering around, there are so many industrious young men only they will go and be in the army, well there is no hurry, bless Papa Woojums, bless him,

Always
Baby Woojums.

[on back of envelope] Have written to [Norman Holmes] Pearson and all the Columbia professors who took part.[2]

1. Steloff to Stein, 30 April 1941 (YCAL). It was Frances Steloff, owner of the Gotham Book Mart in New York, who, after seeing the Stein exhibition at Yale University, contacted Alfred Barr, Jr., about the prospects of bringing the exhibition to the Museum of Modern Art. When this proved impossible, Columbia University was contacted and agreed to mount the exhibition.

2. See Van Vechten to Stein, 24 April [1941], note 2.

📷

To Gertrude Stein

30 May 1941   [101 Central Park West
                                               New York]

Dearest Baby Woojums,

With all that is going on in the world, it would seem safer to have you HERE, but I guess you have reasons for being THERE. Anyway if you no longer hear from me why you will know I can no longer get letters through. Your letters so far come through in fine style. You were asking about Lord Berners and I've just received word that he is about to have another book published: Far from the Maddening World.[1] Fania went to a "baby shower" for Phyllis Cerf yesterday. . Everybody brought a present for the baby which is not born yet[2] and as soon as I take Fania with grey hair certainly you'll have a picture. MY BOOKS go to the Public Library SOON and then my Negro books to Yale and this is a wonderful collection with pictures and phonograph records and letters included. And then YOUR books to the Public Library. . I hope to live to get all these things and more DONE . . . Four Saints at the Town Hall was a knockout. The Two Saint Theresas were done up in black satin capes with mantillas over their heads, the rest in evening clothes, the chorus in beige uniforms. The orchestra under [Alexander] Smallens was twenty men from the Philharmonic. The performance was terrific, the best I've ever heard of this little masterpiece.[3]. A letter came from you to Virgil [Thomson] yesterday and I have forwarded it to him. By the way Virgil told me the first night he hadn't had time to write you but he was going to NOW. The Askews gave a party after and the Saints came and St Theresa's eyes filled with tears as she recounted how happy it made her to sing in Four Saints.[4] This has certainly been a Stein winter. . I loved your piece about poor Sherwood [Anderson] and thanks for sending it.[5] Did you know Jo Davidson is married again? I've forgotten to whom.[6] [John] McCullo[u]gh still is mooning over the First Reader. He is a Slow Boy. I'll talk to Margot Johnson whom I KNOW presently about To Do. She is a manly and most amusing gal. I photographed her once.[7] Fania is talking about going to Hollywood, but I am so busy photographing dancers and getting my effects ready for posterity I won't have time to go. . I've just run across the name of Jo's new wife. It is Florence G. Lucius and she is a

[723]

sculptress. I hope to receive the Algerian Paris-France soon.[8]. . I am sorry about the poppy seeds and I hope more are available. And I am happy the potatoes are coming up . . . It is Decoration Day and lots of sailors and soldiers and flags, but we are not being BOMBED YET. I dare say that will come later. You are a Baby Woojums and Mama Woojums is a Mama Woojums and I am a Papa

WOOJUMS!!

Fania and I both send heaps of LOVE.

1. Lord Berners' *Far from the Madding War*, with three illustrations by the author (London: Constable & Co., 1941).

2. Cerf's first son, Christopher, was born 19 August 1941.

3. A concert version of *Four Saints in Three Acts* was presented at Town Hall, New York, on 27 May 1941. This performance was presented by Louise Crane. Alexander Smallens conducted a chamber orchestra and a cast of thirty. The cast was the same as the original 1934 production. Beatrice Robinson-Wayne sang Saint Theresa I and Bruce Howard sang Saint Theresa II. Stein wrote Thomson how nice it was that they were going on together again [postmark 15 May 1941].

4. Constance and Kirk Askew. Askew and Thomson had known each other while students at Harvard University. Askew was an art dealer in New York. Their home on East Sixty-first Street in New York was a gathering place for musicians, writers, artists, and filmmakers.

5. Stein's "Sherwood's Sweetness," in *Story* (September/October 1941), 19(91):63. This was an Anderson memorial issue.

6. Davidson's first wife, Yvonne, had died in 1934.

7. Van Vechten and Johnson probably met through William Seabrook in 1936 (see Johnson to Van Vechten, 26 July 1936, YCAL).

8. Stein's *Paris France* (Alger, Algeria: Collection Fontaine, E. Charlot, 1941).

To Carl Van Vechten

[postmark: 31 May 1941]   Bilignin par Belley
                                                          (Ain)

My dearest Papa Woojums,

Thanks for everything, I kind of wish I could have heard the Four Saints, I think it might be very good as an oratorio, and am most anxious to know how it went in Town Hall, because that is a pretty big place isn't it. I was never in it but I remember there was some question of my speaking there and we heard it was enormous so we didn't, do you remember, or something, and it would be wonderful if the First Reader was read in the public schools, I'd like that better than anything, I have been asked to do a little thing in french on the french language, for a new review called Patrie, an official thing under the patronage of Marshal Pétain, and now they have just telegraphed that they want a photo of me so I sent them the frontispiece of Everybody's Autobiography, as everybody always admires that so much, I do not know just how they mean to use it but I thought you would not mind, I like us to be together,[1] and someday when photographs can travel again there are so many new people and more old who are crying for one of me by you, is there any way do you think of sending them. The Yale Library ones have not come yet, and we love you both so much, Alice wants to know what effect Fania's white hair has on her eyes in relation, dear Papa Woojums

always
B. W.

1. Stein's "La Langue Francaise," *Patrie: Revue Mensuelle illustrée de l'Empire*, 10 August 1941, pp. 36–37. *Patrie's* Vichy editor was Jean Masson; the editor in Algeria was Paul Bringuier. Masson had cabled Stein that he had received the typescript on 29 May 1941. On 30 May 1941 he cabled again asking for a photograph (both cables YCAL. They did not use Van Vechten's photograph of Stein. They labeled the photograph they did use, one of Stein at Bilignin, as Stein "dans sa maison de Long-Island, près de New York." The error may have been a deliberate one.

❧

To Gertrude Stein
[Postcard] Fania Marinoff [and] Rollo Peters in The Academy of Music Scene [from] The Streets of New York

[postmark: 2 June 1941]   [101 Central Park West
                                            New York]

Dearest Baby Woojums,

I am sending To Do to Margot Johnson today. I telephoned her & she instructed me to. Good luck to To Do!

l[ove] & k[isses]
Papa Woojums!

[725]

To Carl Van Vechten
[Postcard: Environs de Belley—Le Pont de Lucey]

[postmark: 6 June 1941]

[Bilignin par Belley
Ain]

Dearest Papa Woojums,

the photos have just come of the show and they are perfectly lovely,
we are so xcited, we xamined them carefully with a magnifying glass and
there is one of your photos, we cannot make out what it is, all the others
are very clear, tell us which one that is, and since these photos came through
please send us copies of those we have never seen, please,[1] so much love,
so much to you and Fania, always and always

Baby Woojums.

1. Van Vechten's photographs of the Yale University Library exhibition on Stein.

To Gertrude Stein

16 June 1941

[101 Central Park West
New York]

Dearest Baby Woojums,

With all that is going on in the world, I hate to have you on the
other side of it. But maybe you are happier and more comfortable there than
you would be here. . . . I forwarded John McCullo[u]gh's letter to you, not
very hopefully.[1] If you were both on the same side of the sea perhaps something could be done about this but I doubt it. Said young man is very slow
and plodding and unadventuresome. Of course your instructions were to wait
for instructions before you wrote a first reader, but after all he hasn't sent
you any to this day and probably never will. Well, there are some instructions in his letter but I don't think they will help you much. However, if
you want to try again that is for you to decide. In the meantime Gertrude

Stein's First Reader exists and is a beautiful book! Let's wait a minute or two to see what Margot Johnson can do with To Do. If she is successful with that I'll turn the First Reader over to her. . . . . . Would you mind, Baby Woojums, if I present your first editions to Smith College, instead of the [New York] Public Library!. I don't know that I want to but they are planning (and Mrs Dwight Morrow may give them the money for it) to build a Treasure Room exclusively for books by great women, and it seems to me that even with Jane Austen and Sap[p]ho this room would be very bare without the works of GS and where can we find another complete collection. Also Smith at Northampton is very near Yale at New Haven and the collections could occasionally be exhibited together. But nothing is decided and unless they toe all the marks they won't get the books. But let me know what you THINK, please.[2]

Love to you and Mama Woojums and love to you both and Love,

Carlo

Fania is going to Hollywood (but not to work) this week.

Do you remember Nella Larsen? Her husband has cancer of the spine & we go to see him at Memorial Hospital, but of course, also he is no longer her husband!

1. In his letter to Stein, 11 June 1941 (YCAL), McCullough wrote that after using the material with students it was found that the book was far too adult for a first reader.

2. Van Vechten did not give the Stein books to Smith College. His first editions of Stein were presented to YCAL, and certain duplicate volumes were given to the New York Public Library. Elizabeth Cutter Morrow was acting president of Smith College from 1939 to 1940.

To Carl Van Vechten

[postmark: 22 June 1941] Bilingnin par Belley
(Ain)

Dearest Papa Woojums,

I was delighted with the Town Hall programme, Alice says she would like to have been invited to that Baby Shower, she says she would have seen things she never would have seen the like of, well anyway, I would have liked the Four Saints as an oratorio, I think it was a wonderful idea to do it, and I like your description of Margot Johnson, and hope she will do something with To Do, I guess [John] McCullough must be a Scot on all four sides, and what happened to the lady who knew all about First Readers, Yale must be delighted to get your Negro material, and I guess you are busy, the Yale photographs came through alright, so do send us more, everything seems to come sometime, the sun is shining, shining good and hot, and we needed it a lot, it has been a wet spring, and there is one baby tomatoe already, and lots of raspberries, and we are all very active, vegetables and all are xtremely occupying, and if you get hold of Gerald Berners' book do please send it[1] and lots of love so much lots always from Mama and Baby Woojums to Papa Woojums and Fania,

[Gertrude Stein]

1. The book is identified in Van Vechten to Stein, 16 August [1941], as Lord Berners' *Far from the Madding War* (London: Constable & Co., 1941).

To Carl Van Vechten

[postmark: 4 July 1941]   Bilignin par Belley
                                                          (Ain)

Dearest Papa Woojums,

Anything Papa Woojums says but, I do not like Smith College, I didn't when I was at College at Radcliffe and I didn't at all when I was over there lecturing, so unless Papa Woojums really wants to and if he really wants to it is alright, but unless really it has to be I would rather so much it would be the [New York] Public Library, and I don't like the Dwight Morrow crowd, but whatever you decide is alright with me.[1] And I have not had [John] McCullough's letter but I like the first reader as it is, should it perhaps be shown to Bennett [Cerf] first before it is turned over to Margot Johnson, but all that is for you to decide, McCullough has ideas but he is just perhaps just a bit too Scotch, it is a nice quality but it can be overdone, somebody

[728]

sent me a photo clipping of the cast of Four Saints sitting around the piano and singing and Saint Theresa looks too sweet for words at the piano, it was from the N. Y. Times, and it has cheered everybody up here immensely in these dark days. Our garden is flourishing and it is really hot, and we love you so very much. So far we are happy and comfortable and we are always hoping that we will continue [you?] so. Oh Carl do go on writing often, you do not know what a pleasure it is first seeing your envelopes and then opening them, had a letter from Francis Rose he announces that he has just been made a corporal,[2] so much love to you and Fania

Always
Baby Woojums.

1. Stein's feelings about Smith College were also no doubt colored by her memories of encounters with Smith College students who attended Johns Hopkins University, Baltimore, at the same time as Stein, 1897–1901. These were painful years for Stein as she struggled with her awakening lesbianism. See Leon Katz's introduction to Stein's *Fernhurst, Q. E. D., and Other Early Writings* for an account of this period.

2. Rose had volunteered for the Royal Air Force in October 1940 (Rose to Stein, postmark 5 November 1940, YCAL). He wrote of his promotion in an undated letter to Stein (YCAL).

To Carl Van Vechten

[postmark: 5 July 1941]

Bilignin par Belley
(Ain)

My dearest Papa Woojums,

[John] McCullough sent me a letter all about what the children say,[1] his children do seem to be an awfully priggish lot, I said to him in answer that the trouble was that they knew too much about children, I said what was the use of the children's being children if they knew so much about them, and then he also said you could only use three words for a First Reader, so just to tease him I sent him the inclosed and told him to give you right away the copy of the First Reader if he still had it and also the copy of the Four Little lessons.[2] Even his children though seem to be delighted with the

Play in the First Reader. I imagine that somebody will be able to be very successful with that our book, and that you will find that some one, bless you papa Woojums, I like writing books for you, nothing Baby Woojums likes so much as writing books for Papa Woojums, and Mama Woojums says yes, bless you always

Baby Woojums.

1. McCullough's letter of 11 June 1941 (YCAL) is referred to in Van Vechten to Stein, 16 June 1941.

2. Enclosed with the letter was a typescript with manuscript changes for Stein's "Four Little Lessons A and n." This does not appear in *The Gertrude Stein First Reader & Three Plays*. It remains unpublished (YCAL).

To Carl Van Vechten
[Postcard: Environs de Belley—Château d'Andert]

[postmark: 31 July 1941]   [Bilignin par Belley
                                                             Ain]

Dearest Papa Woojums,

No letter or card from you for two weeks, and that seems a long time, we love to see your handwriting often and often, this is the chateau where there was that crime Balzac wrote about, and I hope the First Reader is finding a home, I always like us to be together we are correcting the proofs for the french Paris France so it will be out in a month or so now lots of love

B. W.

1. In his novel *Une ténébreuse affaire* Balzac makes use of the complicated judicial principles and procedures that he had learned about when he followed, in 1839, the trial at Bourg of a notary, Peytel, who was accused of murdering his wife and his manservant. Peytel was guillotined in spite of Balzac's efforts to save him. Peytel had lived at the Château d'Andert.

❧

To Gertrude Stein

10 August [1941]   [101 Central Park West
                                                   New York]

Dearest Baby Woojums,

Last night I dreamed that you were coming over and cartoonists were doing cartoons in two series to follow your voyage. One series consists of "The Voyage of Miss Stein". . The other was called "Boston Incidents." What all this means I wouldn't know. I have a note from Margot Johnson and "To Do" has been lots of places and isn't sold yet.[1] I don't think it is time to take her another book yet. So, unless you have some definite plan, I think we'd better let the First Reader lie fallow awhile. I don't know the Lady's name who knew all about First Reader, but she was much more encouraging than Mr [John] McCullo[u]gh only she isn't a publisher.[2] Mr McCullo[u]gh just sorta misses taking any kind of a chance. He misses excitement and I guess Mr McCullo[u]gh hardly ever moves very much or says yes or even no with any kind of vitality. If I get hold of [Lord] Berners' book (not yet here) I'll send it to you. It's sure to be here as English mails are perfection.[3] NONE of your letters is ever opened by the Censor and I guess you must have a friend at Bermuda! But I guess this isn't right either, as if you had a friend there, he would open your letters and read 'em with delight . . . Of course if you don't like Smith College, your things won't go there. It's nothing to be decided today anyway, because for the next six months at least I shall be busy giving Negro things to Yale, Melanctha, of course, included. I don't know whether I LIKE Smith College, but I like the New President[4] and I Like Mina Curtiss[5] and it was my idea to start a library there of books by women and name it for my mother and they are terrifically excited and it has practically turned into a building and everything is going to be de luxe and they are getting a new librarian for it. But nothing of Baby Woojums will be sent to Smith without her consent and good wishes, she may rest assured. Tell Alice that Fania's eyes are blacker and she is chicer and more Marquise with white hair. . I'll try sending you some photographs and hope they will reach you. I'll just send them like that and see what happens! YOU tell me when you get them. You ask about one of the photographs Yale sent you. I haven't seen these, so I'm not sure what you want

[731]

to know . . . Fania just got back from California and everybody in USA is wondering if there will be war with Japan and they'd better behave or there will be and the Russians are being most helpful and I'll write you again soon. So here is a picture of Winston Churchill, Tallulah Bankhead's lion cub, please!

Love to you and Mama Woojums,

Papa W!

[on back of envelope] Did I tell you Georges [Jacques] at the Algonquin burns a candle in front of your picture in his room? St. Gertrude!

1. Johnson's letter to Van Vechten is not in YCAL.

2. Possibly Margaret Wise Brown, who was the children's books editor at William R. Scott.

3. Lord Berner's *Far from the Madding War.* See Stein to Van Vechten [22 June 1941], note 1.

4. Herbert John Davis, president of Smith College, 1940–49.

5. Mina Curtiss, American writer and editor. Van Vechten had met her through her brother Lincoln Kirstein.

To Gertrude Stein
["A Little Too Much" motto]

11 August 1941

[101 Central Park West
New York]

Dear Baby Woojums

Here are 18 photographs of *you* which I hope you receive safely with love from

Papa Woojums

Please *date* your letters. It helps as they straggle in *out* of *order.*

To Gertrude Stein
[Postcard: Portrait of Julius Perkins Junior with "Winston Churchill,"
Tallulah Bankhead's lion cub. Photograph by Carl Van Vechten]

16 August [1941]   [101 Central Park West
                                                     New York]

Dearest Baby Woojums.

I have ordered Lord Berners' Far from the Madding War sent to you
& I hope you receive it. It is a charming book and one of the characters
quotes you![1] I sent you a lot of photographs the other day and I hope you
receive them.

l[ove], K[isses]
Papa W.

Please date your letters so I can get the chronology.

1. In Lord Berners' novel *Far from the Madding War* (London: Constable & Co., Ltd., 1941)
Stein is not mentioned by name. There is mention, however, of St. Gertrude, in the chapter
"The Lives of the Saints."

St. Gertrude, she read, although possessed of the greatest natural talents, was penetrated
and entirely filled with the deepest sentiments of her own nothingness. She longed for
death and spent most of her time sighing. In the author's words "The Saint, as a chaste
turtle, never interrupted her sweet sighs and moans" (p. 100).

The novel deals with a university town in wartime. Emmeline, the central figure, is the daughter of a church warden.

To Carl Van Vechten

[postmark: 21 August 1941]   Bilignin par Belley
                                                     Ain

Dearest Papa Woojums,

Have not heard from you for such a long time, do write, I can't tell
you [how] we miss your envelopes and their content when they do not come.

We have now corrected the last proofs of Paris France and it looks as if it was going to be [a] nice looking book and it will be out now very shortly and what is the news of the First Reader, has Bennett [Cerf] seen it and is Bennett a successful father and what are you doing, our news these days is naturally more agricultural than anything else, to-day I gathered apples and pears, we have eaten our first green corn and courgettes have been most delicious, but we want to hear from Papa Woojums we do we do,

Always
Baby Woojums.

To Gertrude Stein

[? August 1941][1]

[101 Central Park West
New York]

Dearest Baby W.

Loved Four Lessons. Report if you get this [Lord] Berners and the photograph I sent you.

Love
Papa W.

1. This letter is written at the bottom of a letter to Van Vechten from John O'Neal, of the Holliday Bookshop, 49 East Forty-ninth Street, New York. O'Neal had written confirming Van Vechten's order to have Lord Berners' book *Far from the Madding War* sent to Stein.

To Carl Van Vechten

[postmark: 2 September 1941]

Bilignin par Belley
Ain

Dearest Papa Woojums,

Well of course if it was your idea to start a library of books by women and name it for your mother I am all for it, of course I am, that is a horse

[734]

of an entirely different color, I thought it was a Morrow idea, and I am not
very keen on them and I was not very keen on the last president but if you
say this one is nice he is nice and that is all there is to that, and would I
like anything better than being dedicated to your mother, you know Papa
Woojums I would not, so go ahead and it will please me every bit.[1] And we
were delighted with the lion cub, I could not get either Basket or Pepe to
look at him, he does look sweet with almost a tear in his eye, everything is
getting most xciting these days, but since trout and ecrivisses and pigeons
keep up and go into our tum-tums we are peaceful, I guess St. Odile is at-
tending to everything alright, did I ever send you a copy of her predictions
that came out so perfectly and have cheered us along ever since the debacle,
if I did not I will and beside all that she is very feminine and it [smiles?]
lovely,[2] we have some nice new neighbors, she half Scotch and half Spanish
and raised in Mexico and he french and writes most interestingly, I will send
you his book, Les Richesses Réelles,[3] I am sorry about the First Reader, have
you shown it to Bennett [Cerf] not so much for him to take it as I always
kind of feel he ought to see anything he thinks to you has been so nice about
everything and is Bennett's baby born, it should have been by now, should
it not, it's kind of late at night and the moon is shining and the rain has
been raining and it's nice to be writing to Papa Woojums, and love to you
so much love and love to Fania, and always

Baby Woojums.

1. Elizabeth Cutter Morrow, who was acting president of Smith College, 1939–40. Stein had
met William Allan Neilson, president of Smith College from 1917 to 1939, when she lectured
there on 10 January 1935.

2. Sainte-Odile was the patron saint of Alsace. Her prophecies of the evils to come from the
Antichrist and from the Danube also spoke of the defeat of the Germans.

3. Elena and Paul Genin, together with Madame Genin's daughter by her first marriage, Joan
Clegg (now Chapman), had moved from Lyon to Chazey-Bons, a hamlet just outside of Belley, in early 1941. They came into contact with Stein and Toklas on their first day there. Madame Genin came upon the name Gertrude Stein in the former owner's telephone book and
asked her husband if he thought it could be the writer Gertrude Stein. A telephone call confirmed Stein's identity and in less than an hour Stein, Toklas, and Basket were making their
way across the valley to Chazey-Bons. Gertrude sat on a sofa as the workmen continued the
moving and questioned Madame Genin about her background, a mixture of Scotch and Spanish (Madame Genin had been brought up in Mexico). Stein and Elena Genin were in daily
contact, sometimes two and three times a day, from 1941 until Stein returned to Paris in late
1944. They spoke about the events of the war and read to each other from books of prophecies.
(Personal interview with Elena Genin, July 1969, author's journal.) Stein speaks of the Genins

in *Wars I Have Seen*. Some elements in the narrative of *Mrs. Reynolds* are drawn from Stein's contacts with the Genins.

Paul Genin had, at the time, a silk factory in Lyon. His book had been published by Sirey in Paris in 1941.

To Carl Van Vechten

[postmark: 9 September 1941]

Bilignin par Belley
Ain

My dearest Papa Woojums,

I know this clipping will amuse you, I will send you a copy of the review when I can get hold of it, as yet I have not seen it, that is not since I wrote it, all in the original french language,[1] autumn is coming on, I am beginning to saw wood again, because it takes an awful lot of wood to keep us well not warm but not too cold in the winter. We have some new pleasant neighbors, but I think I told you about them in our last, I suppose I should really have kept a diary, such wonderful conversations that I have every day, and such nice xpressions, the last one I heard from a farmer about the weather which was uncertain, le temps fait sa tête et il faut travailler autour de la téte, now they are threshing their wheat and soon we will be digging up potatoes, the crops fortunately good, and the First Reader, has Bennett [Cerf] seen it, and is Bennett's baby born, and how we love you and wish we could see you, everybody seems much encouraged and Saint Odille promises a great deal for October, and lots of love to you and to Fania always

Baby Woojums.

1. Enclosed with the letter was a clipping from a local French newspaper, possibly *Le Bugiste*, concerning the review *Patrie*, with references to and quotations from Stein's article. See Stein to Van Vechten [31 May 1941], note 1.

To Gertrude Stein

21 September [1941]   101 Central Park West
                                                          New York City

Dearest Baby Woojums,

The latest is I DON'T THINK SMITH is going to get my books, so we had all that worry for nothing . . . The [New York] Public Library in November is giving a show of my personal books and manuscripts. I wish you and mama W would be here for that. I sent you a lot of photographs, and Lord Berners, but no word that you have received them. In fact no word at all from you for ages. . No news about publishers. None whatever. I loved the Four Little Lessons, but [John] McCullo[u]gh didn't send me HIS copy.[x] In fact I haven't heard from McCullo[u]gh at all again. He probably has gone somewhere to try to understand children. . Airplanes fly over my head every five minutes (we are on the direct route to somewhere) but so far they are good airplanes. Let us hope that none of the woojums family will have any bad airplanes . . . It does seem too awful to think of you on the farm another winter and I hope you are fairly comfortable. . I am very sorry you didn't leave for America long ago. Fania is back from California and working hard at the American Theatre Wing of British War Relief and I am up to my ears in dusty books which go to Yale!

So much much love to Baby and Mama Woojums!

Papa W!

[x]He sent the First Reader back of course!

To Carl Van Vechten

22 September [19]41   Bilignin par Belley
                                                          Ain

My dearest Papa Woojums,

All in two days, the package of photographs, the announcement that we are to have Gerald Berners' book and the lovely photo of the pickaninny and the baby lion,[1] and thanks so much for each and every one, and we are hoping soon for the photographs of Fania, with her new hair, and the book, the envelope of photographs were not even opened by any censors, they all seemed to have intuitively too much respect to dare to look, the last proofs of Paris France are corrected and I hope to be sending you a copy of [it] soon, I am still trying to get you a copy of Patrie with my article on the french language written in the original french, but it seems to be so popular that it is hard to get hold of a copy, I am still trying, the days seem to be so full of people and events and vegetables, and wood, and eggs and other things and now I am trying to get our bicycle made into a tricycle so we can move around a little, that is Alice can, I go as much as 16 kilometres in all directions on foot so I get plenty of variety, and now we have a wood burning taxi so we can move around a bit, and nice new friends so we move around a bit more,[2] but mostly we love Papa Woojums who sends us so much and we love it all, always

Baby Woojums

1. A reference to the photograph of Julius Perkins, Jr., and "Winston Churchill," Tallulah Bankhead's lion cub, which Van Vechten had used for his postcard to Stein, 16 August [1941].

2. Paul and Elena Genin.

To Carl Van Vechten

25 September [19]41   Bilignin par Belley
                                                       (Ain)

Dearest Papa Woojums,

Everything has come xcept the book but that will surely come soon,[1] the photos, the picture of the pickaninny and the lion cub, the account of the book, a copy of Story, with the Sherwood Anderson,[2] and the copy of [William] Seabrook's book about magic, which is awfully sweet. I wonder since he quotes so largely from children's books of me, whether we might have a try at Harcourt Brace with the First Reader add the four xtra lessons

[738]

if you like them, it might please them, particularly on account of Seabrook's book,[3] but of course that is as you think best, the world is full of magic but Papa Woojums' magic works best, we have our potatoes for the winter our wood for the winter and the weather has been lovely, everybody seems to think that things will hum pretty soon, but anyway we have pleasant neighbors. My editors are enthusiastic about Paris France which you will have in about a month now, the American Red Cross wanders along from time to time to make us feel American, and Papa Woojums' letters and postal cards cheer us up, and we love them,

> *lots of love*
> *Baby Woojums*

1. Lord Berners' *Far from the Madding War*. See Van Vechten to Stein [? August 1941], note 1.

2. The Anderson memorial issue of *Story*. See Stein to Van Vechten [30 March 1941], note 1.

3. Seabrooks's *Witchcraft, Its Power in the World Today* (New York: Harcourt Brace and Co., 1940). References to Stein are on Pages 310–13, 359–60, 365. On page 365 he introduces part three of his book with a half-page reproduction of Stein's rose motto, "A Rose is a Rose is a Rose is a Rose." Seabrook calls it, "the sweetest magic circle ever swirled."

To Carl Van Vechten

[postmark: 29 September 1941]   Bilignin par Belley
                                                           (Ain)

Dearest Papa Woojums,

This is the announcement of Paris France and they have just written to ask for permission to use your photo xiii g: 43. for a frontispiece for the edition originale, and I knew you would like it well not perhaps as much as I do but perhaps just as much, I always love us to be together and here we will be and they will send you a copy and they will say the photo is yours, the photo came just in time which is a pleasure, thanks and thanks again, and we are hoping that the ones of Fania in her new hair will come soon, these were not opened by the censor or anything they just came right along, bless you papa Woojums

Always
Baby Woojums.

❦

To Carl Van Vechten

7 October [19]41   Bilignin par Belley
                                                          Ain

My dearest Papa Woojums,

I am pleased that it is going to be New York and not Smith, I always did not like Smith when I was at College [and] when I was over there this last time. It has always seemed to me a very arrivist institution plein de arrivism, and not the gentle Americanism that we love and that all the other colleges had, so I am awfully pleased that it is New York again[1] and so happy about your show, I wish we might be there to see it, and you will tell us all about it and send a lot of photos now they seem to come along so easily, so far the only thing that has not yet turned up is Gerald Berners' book but it will,[2] and you must not worry about our wintering here in the country again, we have plenty of wood and potatoes, and other things, and lots of friends, and everybody is xtraordinarily good to everybody, money is a bit of a nuisance because everything is much more xpensive and we are still on the old xchange, that is the reason I bother you a bit about publishers and have written twice to Virgil [Thomson][3] but we really are quite alright, also we have had to help out English friends,[4] but even so we are quite alright and go on, very completely happy, do you know a man named C. M. de Hauke,[5] he turned up from America, and came to see us one night and said all that he knew about America, but he did not seem to know many people we know xcept Henry McBride, it is lovely autumn now and grapes are plentiful, and

[740]

also hares and little birds, and we are all delighted about the show and bless you Papa Woojums

Always
Baby Woojums.

1. See Stein to Van Vechten [4 July 1941], note 1.

2. Berners' *Far from the Madding War.*

3. Possibly Stein to Thomson, postmark 15 May 1941, and postmark [2? September 1941], YCAL.

4. Possibly Diana Selby-Bigges and her family, who lived at the Château de Chambuet in Yenne in the Savoie.

5. César M. de Hauke, a French-born art dealer.

To Gertrude Stein

19 October [1941]

[101 Central Park West
New York]

Dear and beautiful Baby Woojums,

I am sorry but the enclosed will inform you what has happened to Lord Berners' Book.[1] I'm afraid it will be worse soon, but I hope this letter will get through to you. Also Tommy Driberg of London has been here.[2] People commute here from London and think nothing of it. They come on war business of course, but they come and go frequently. He was here for ten days. Anyway he has seen Berners recently and said that altho' he was living in the country he was engaged in some kind of defense work. Driberg says he knows you and wanted to be remembered. And [John] Mc-Cullo[u]gh has sent me the Four Little Lessons[x], so that's that. I'm glad the pictures came and I'm glad you are using one for a frontispiece and I hope I can get THAT book. Bennett Cerf's father died two weeks ago and you had better write him as he is broken. He adored his father . . . Bennett's father has been going around with a lady for eighteen years but he never dared marry her until Bennett got married, as he had always lived with Ben-

[741]

nett. So a couple of months ago he got married and then he died.[3]. Bennett has bought a house on the east side and moved in, but I haven't the address. Bennett is infatuated with his child. As soon as I have a good photograph of Fania and her white hair I'll send it. So far, nothing is right . . . I'm still working very hard on Negroes for Yale. but this is fun and I'll miss it I guess when Yale gets them all. Prices and taxes are getting very high and soon we'll have no more money, but poor or no we'll always love Baby and Mama Woojums and we send lots of love to them today and always.

[Carl Van Vechten]

I had tea yesterday with Ellen Glasgow on her way back from Maine and we spoke of you.

ˣI loved these & *can't wait* for the French Paris-France!!

1. The enclosure is not at YCAL. Presumably the book never reached Stein.

2. Tom Driberg was a British politician and writer. He submitted columns to Lord Beaverbrook's *Daily Express* from the United States from 13 October to 2 December 1941. Some of these columns were collected in his *Collonade (1937–1947)* (London: Pilot Press, 1949). In his columns Driberg wrote about his experiences in America. Van Vechten is perhaps being glib about the ease of traveling from Europe to the United States. Driberg recounts that he traveled by convoy from England to an unnamed "landlocked Canadian harbor" (p. 198) in an extremely long and uncomfortable journey. Stein had met Driberg in London in 1937.

3. Gustave Cerf died on 2 October 1941, at Lenox Hill Hospital, New York. His widow was Eva Bigelow Cerf.

To Carl Van Vechten

1 November [19]41   Bilignin par Belley
                                                     Ain

Dearest Papa Woojums,

Thanks for letting me know about Bennett [Cerf]'s father, I have just written to him,[1] I am sorry about Gerald [Berners]'s book, but perhaps later on it will come, as books do come through from time to time. Golly it's cold, the November weather has taken to be December, and all the farmers are in despair because they have not yet planted their winter wheat, you see how naturally we have become farmers, and you will be pleased that we are having a turkey for Thanksgiving, those nice new friends of ours, by the way I am going soon to send his new ms. to you, it is called Mon livre de Pourquoi[2] and I would like you to tell me if you think anybody in America would be interested in it, well anyway they have some turkeys and so we are going to have a turkey Thanskgiving and that will be a pleasure. Otherwise our news is everybody's news, and we are very active in the mere business of living, it would be nice if somebody liked the First Reader, well anyway we do the Woojums family does and the Woojums family is very happy and very loving and that is nice,

> *Always*
> *Baby Woojums.*

They are sending you directly a copy de luxe of Paris France, let me know if it gets there, lots of love

> *B. W.*

1. Stein wrote to Cerf, undated letter [? November 1941] (Columbia-Random House), about how much Cerf's father loved him and how pleased he must have been to have seen the birth of a grandchild.

2. Paul Genin's book was published as *Essai sur le chaos* (Alger, Algeria: E. Chalot, 1945). Stein had recommended this book to the reading committee, which consisted of Max Pol Fouchet and Albert Camus. The book contains many ideas and speculations that Genin and Stein discussed during their long walks together during the war years (letter received from Joan Chapman, 19 November 1980).

To Gertrude Stein

21 December 1941

[101 Central Park West
New York]

Dearest Baby Woojums,

I consign this to the air with the hope it will reach you to wish you a merry Christmas (with St Ignatius to help!) but I can no longer be sure of anything as naturally from now on the movements of clippers and ships will be mysterious. I do wish you and Mama Woojums were over here, but wishes are not horses and you and Mama W are certainly not beggars . . . Fania is learning First AID which means lessons all day and is further a captain of the American Theatre Wing on War Relief. I am trying to get my Negro books off to Yale before the bombs fall . . . You wrote a very sweet letter about Smith [College] and the Ada (named after Ada Byron!) Amanda Fitch Memorial Collection of Books by Women. Nothing whatever is decided about this yet, except that the Librarian at Harvard who is a trustee at Smith is much interested. But they have no treasure room as yet and I am fully occupied with the Yale Library at present. . By the way, I've found more items (in storage!) for your collection at Yale and have sent them on. I do wish you and Mama W had been here for my show (of MY books) at the [New York] Public Library. . You received the invitation, I hope. . It is a little like being dead, being all laid out in rows like that, but it is like being an illustrious dead man. I first had the feeling when I saw YOUR show, and I had it again with mine. . The first day was very brilliant and everybody was there from Doris Keane to W. C. Handy (the Negro who wrote the St Louis Blues). Virgil [Thomson] is adding to his laurels as a critic and ALL the orchestras are playing his symphonies etc., as I knew they would. He is on the top of a wave . . . But it is a bad time for publishing. Margot Johnson had almost arranged the publication of TO DO when the war broke out on both sides of us and now nobody knows what any will publish or will want to publish. I do not want to confuse the publishers, so I am saving the First Reader until TO DO is out of the way which it should be soon. Julian Sawyer has now compiled a list of papers and articles etc ABOUT Gertrude Stein, but he is having difficulty at the moment getting THIS published.[1] However I dare say everything will arrange itself. You wrote on November 1 you were sending a copy of the de luxe Paris, France. This has not yet arrived. . I am happy to think of you with a turkey for Thanksgiving. I've just heard from Mary Garden who is in Aberdeen and Mabel [Dodge] sends her usual sprig of sage. . Will be happy to see Mon Livre de Pourquoi, a charming title. And please don't forget to send me the predictions of St Odile and ALL ABOUT HER. I do not know this saint . . . I hope by now you have received my letters about Bennett [Cerf]'s baby boy (Christopher, I think). Anyway he was born in the summer and a letter from you inquires about him as if you had not heard. Believe it or not, I have been too busy to print pictures of Fania with her white hair, but she has changed her appearance

so much since these were taken, rather resembling a Countess of the merveilleuse period now, that I think I shall have to photograph her again. Anyway I'll send something SOON. . You are NOW DATING YOUR LET-
TERS and this is helpful, as Often I can make out nothing from the postmarks
and they often arrive way out of order and I like to keep them in order. . I
have not yet had the copy of Patrie with your article on the French language, either! So love and Kisses to you Both and Fania and I wish you a
very happy New Year! BUT WE WISH YOU WERE HERE.

[Carl Van Vechten]

1. Sawyer's checklist was published as "Gertrude Stein (1874–): A Checklist Comprising Critical and Miscellaneous Writings about Her Work, Life and Personality from 1913–1942," in
Bulletin of Bibliography (January–April 1943), 17:211–12; (May–August 1943), 18:11–13.

To Carl Van Vechten

[25 December] 1941   Bilignin par Belley
Christmas Day   Ain

Dearest papa Woojums,

Had just a letter from Mark Lutz, and he says Carl writes that he is
reasonably healthy these days, that does not mean that you have not been
well, but anyhow it does mean that you are well now and I hope not too
disturbed by everything that is happening, dear me, we thought we had gotten used to everything but when your native land gets into it well your feelings are different, we had a nice Christmas, we all gave all the village children a pretty fête at the home of our new friends the Genins and a good
time was had by all, it really was very pretty and french children do have an
xtraordinary amount of ease and retenue, and then we walked the Bilignin
children home 5 kilometres and everybody was tired and happy. Have you
had your Paris-France it seems to be having a real success I had to sign 18
copies here in Belley, and I get fan letters, and it is all nice but do write

soon we want to know how you and Fania are and we do send you such a lot of love,[1]

Always
Baby Woojums.

1. Lutz's letter is not in YCAL.

2. In a letter to the author, 29 November 1981, Joan Chapman wrote:
    Yes, I remember Xmas '41 party for the village children, with presents, cookies, hot chocolate, a Xmas tree & a lovely *creche* built by Philippe Charveriat cute little wooden houses even a little chateau & a windmill, I think there even was an electric train running through and of course a collection of santas. Gertrude and Alice came to the *cure* and quite a lot of people.

To Gertude Stein

31 December 1941   [101 Central Park West
                                                   New York]

Dear Baby Woojums,

Happy New Year in these dark days! WE WISH YOU WERE HERE. Margot Johnson telephoned me today that Harrison Smith has found an illustrator and agreed to publish To Do, probably in the Spring. . As it would be wellnigh impossible to get a contract to you and back just now, I told her I thought it would be okay with you *(tho I reminded her I had no official authority to do this)* for the Ann Watkins office to sign a contract for you. She is writing you and will also explain why no advance. . There is also talk of his doing the First Reader. As he is editor now of the Sat[urday] Review of Lit[erature] this is all good news, I HOPE. So Happy New Year and Love to you both and I hope this will reach you safely. . Fania sends love too.

Papa W!

Ann Watkins address is 77 Park Ave. NYC.
Harrison Smith's address is 25 West 45 St. N.Y.C.

🙊

To Gertrude Stein

9 January 1942   [101 Central Park West
                                              New York]

Dearest Baby Woojums,

NOW Margot [Johnson] writes me she is trying to get a contract for
To Do through for you to sign and she is sending it in duplicate.[1] I hope all
this happens without a hitch. She is NOW looking at the First Reader! It is
unbearably cold and Fania is busy with first aid lessons and soon will be able
to strap anybody up, no matter how badly splintered. I enclose a clipping
concerning a friend of yours[2]
and my love to both of you,

                                        Carlo (Papa Woojums!)

1. Johnson's letter to Van Vechten is not in YCAL.
2. The clipping did not remain with the letter and therefore cannot be identified.

🙊

To Gertrude Stein
[Postcard: Portrait of Fania Marinoff. Photograph by Carl Vechten]

[early 1942]   [101 Central Park West
                                              New York]

Dearest Baby Woojums.

Here are two pictures of Fania with white hair which I hope you will
receive. I haven't heard from you now in two months—so communication
may be cut off. I *hope* not. We are well & I hope you got the letters and
the contract about your book, "To Do". . I do wish you were over here!

                                        Love to both from Fania
                                        & Papa W!

☙

To Carl Van Vechten
[Cablegram]

[Received in New York, 12 March 1942]   [Belley]

ENCHANTEE   ARRANGEMENTS   POUR   LIVRE   MILLE   RE-
MERCIEMENTS[1]

GERTRUDE STEIN

1. Undated note by Van Vechten: "I think I had been notified by Margot Johnson that Harrison Smith would publish 'To Do' and I had passed the information on to GS. He never did. In 1947 it is still unpublished."
      On 3 September 1943 (YCAL) Johnson wrote Van Vechten that there had been some trouble with the illustrations and that because of the war there were manufacturing difficulties. She hoped that the book would be coming out before the spring of 1944. Further complications developed and Harrison Smith did not publish the book; it was published in Stein's *Alphabets & Birthdays* in 1957.

☙

To Carl Van Vechten

23 March [19]42   Bilignin par Belley
                                                       (Ain)

My dearest Papa Woojums,

      You will have had my cable telling you how happy happy I was about To Do, thanks and thanks again, it took a long time for the letters to come through and all those came on the same day three written early in December and late in December and the last one written in January, it is the first time that we have really felt being separated from our native land, Alice and I both have not liked it, at all, because hitherto, it took a little time to get letters and they did come with a certain regularity but xcepting your three letters and one from Virgil [Thomson][1] for over two months we have not had a word and it is kind of uncomfortable to have America so far away, I hope Fania's strapping up will remain peaceful, but I guess theatre for the boys in blue or whatever color they are now, we do not even hear that, but

[748]

we do not complain, naturally not, only as they all say here now, it is a little long. Here is the prophecy of Saint Odile, the only one that has so far not deceived us, She was an Alsatian saint, and there is something about her blood flaming when France is in danger, I would try to send you a little book about her, but just now books do not get through,[2] we have had nothing since Bennett [Cerf] sent us War and Peace, but that was a great comfort, it took so long to read, and it was so fascinatingly what is going on now in Russia.[3] My book Mrs. Reynolds is going on indeed it is almost done but it cannot quite get done until it that is what Mrs. Reynolds talks about is done, but that has to be done, and so it will all get done, and I am so happy about To Do and I hope they will that is the readers will like it, perhaps it is because America is at war now that a book for children written during that time of terror does appeal to them, bless you Papa Woojums we love you so all of us love you so Mama Woojums and Basket and Pepe and Baby Woojums they all love you so bless you all

Always
B. W.

1. Possibly Thomson to Stein, 5 December 1941 (YCAL). Thomson wrote about the performance of *Four Saints in Three Acts* at the Museum of Modern Art and at Town Hall, New York, in May 1941. He also proposed to Stein that when the war was over they collaborate on another opera.

2. Enclosed with this letter was a one-page typewritten (by Toklas) excerpt from an unidentified source, of a prophecy of Sainte Odile.

3. Cerf wrote Stein on 25 November 1941 (YCAL) that he was sending her Tolstoy's *War and Peace* and Gibbon's *The Decline and Fall of the Roman Empire*.

To Gertrude Stein

15 June 1942

[101 Central Park West
New York]

Dearest Gertrude,

I haven't heard from you in ages and I don't know whether you get my letters or not. Anyway I had a letter and a cable from you not so long ago and two copies of Paris-France (the first and the 4th editions) published in French in Alger. Which naturally I am very happy to have. Margot [Johnson] says To Do is coming out in September and that will be wonderful too. I haven't seen the illustrations but they seem to be pleased with them. NOW I hope we can do something with Gertrude Stein's First Reader. I saw Therese Bonney too and she gave me some news of you but it is rather stale news, However she told me one or two things I was glad to know.[1]. I am working very hard giving my Negro collection to Yale and also in the Stage Door Canteen where I work as a busboy and a captain. This is hard labor as we have on an average of 3,000 soldiers and sailors a night. . Fania got up a dog show and fiesta (where Tallulah Bankhead, Lily Pons, Elsa Maxwell and others showed their dogs) and fiesta for the benefit of this and took in $2200.[2]. Thanks for the prophecies of St Odile and thanks for your letter and cable. I wonder if Bennett [Cerf] has been able to send you Elliot Paul's The Last Time I saw Paris, a duck of a book more like Paris than anything ever written by a Frenchman except perhaps Proust and the two together Proust and Paul give you a pretty complete picture of French life.[3] . . We haven't seen Bennett all winter, nor his wife, nor his baby: we have been occupied and I dare say they have TOO. So endless love from Fania and me to you and Alice and I hope it won't be long before we hear from you again . . . and we wish you were here, but probably you will be some day and LOVE

Carlo!

On the 17 I shall be 62 (count the years!)

Four Saints was done on the air with the original cast and it was wonderful and the words came over better even than they do on the stage![4]

Did you ever receive Fania's picture with white curls?

1. Thérèse Bonney, a journalist, had recently arrived in New York from France. She published an article, with photographs, "Gertrude Stein in France," in Vogue, 1 July 1942, pp. 60–61, 70.

2. The American Theatre Wing had established a center for soldiers where there was food, entertainment, and dancing.

3. Paul's *The Last Time I Saw Paris* (New York: Random House, 1942). Elliot Paul (1891–1959) was a writer and editor. With Eugene Jolas he founded *transition*. There is no evidence that Cerf sent Stein Paul's novel.

4. Alfred Wallenstein conducted *Four Saints in Three Acts* on WOR radio on 4 June 1942. The broadcast was aimed at selling war bonds and had been paid for by the Treasury Department. Virgil Thomson introduced the program.

❧

To Carl Van Vechten

20 June [19]42   [Bilignin par Belley
                                                   Ain]

Dearest Papa Woojums,

Days weeks and months go by and no letter from Papa Woojums, every time the air mail arrives I see an envelope and I say papa Woojums and it isn't, and we are getting kind of worried, do write and write again and again, because the letters do come now and it is a pleasure. May D'Aiguy who translated Paris France has just translated the First Reader and it translates very well into French, the ballad pleases everybody and we have hopes that the little volume might be printed and it will be nice having a little french volume dedicated to Papa Woojums,[1] a Papa Woojums, otherwise there is no news, my book goes on slowly but well, Mrs. Reynolds the weather is lovely the garden by garden we mean vegetables grow happily and we see lots of people and the time passes all too quickly, and we think a lot about our native land these days in whom everybody has so much faith it is very moving, do write now and then do write soon again, have you seen the illustrations of To Do and how are they and do write soon and love to you so much love and to Fania and do write soon,

Always
Baby Woojums.

1. The Baronne Dianne d'Aiguy (called May) lived with her husband Robert, her daughter Rose, her mother-in-law, the Baronne Pierlot, and other members of her family in a château in Béon, not far from Belley. Her translation of Stein's *The Gertrude Stein First Reader & Three Plays* consists only of the first reader (the three plays were added by Stein in 1946). Her translation was published as *Petits poèmes pour un livre de lecture* (Alger, Algeria: Collection Fontaine, E. Charlot, 1944). "A Ballad" is on pp. 49–52 in the English edition and pp. 46–48 in the French edition.

[751]

To Gertrude Stein

20 July 1942

101 Central Park West
New York City

Dearest Baby Woojums,

It is July 20, 1942 and a letter from you dated October 7, 1941, with an announcement of the Alger publication of Paris-France which I have had for some time, has just come in. So you never know what may happen nowadays. I promised you a picture of Fania with white hair and I sent you one some time ago, but you never acknowledged it. So perhaps you never got it. Anyway, here is another. . I am to have a show of Theatre Photographs at the Museum of the City of New York in the fall and I think you will surely be in this.[1] And I continue to shower Yale with gifts concerning the Negro. The Woman's Collection is in abeyance for the Time Being. . I am also making photographs of the Ballet for the Museum of Modern Art.[2] Do you remember Max Ewing? . I am editing HIS effects, letters, etc. for Yale. A most amusing lot of stuff which reached me via his cousin Doris. And the Stage Door Canteen (now with a cooling system) has us both[x] working there two nights a week. It won't be long now before To Do is out and I can't wait and I suppose you know that Therese Bonney had an article about you in Vogue which made everybody homesick to see Baby and Mama Woojums.[3] So lots of love to you both from Fania and

Carlo!

Did I tell you Fania broke her wrist? It is okay again.
[x] F M & C V V.

1. An exhibition, *The Theatre Through the Camera of Carl Van Vechten*, was held from 18 November 1942 to 11 January 1943 at the Museum of the City of New York. The exhibition comprised 104 photographs.

2. In 1945 Van Vechten gave the Museum of Modern Art, New York, a collection of his ballet and dance photographs. In 1942 he gave to the museum the illustrations for a projected edition of *Nigger Heaven* that had been done by E. McKnight Kauffer.

3. See Van Vechten to Stein, 15 June 1942, note 1.

To Gertrude Stein
[Typed on a page from The Playbill][1]

2 August 1942   [101 Central Park West
                                                 New York City]

Dearest Baby Woojums,

This is Papa Woojums luimême in PERSON and not a Shakespearian actor as alleged . . . And also enclosed is an article about the J[ames]
W[eldon] J[ohnson]Collection which tells you about another activity.[2] And
now I am editing Max Ewing's letters for YALE. I recently sent you a picture of FM with white hair. Your latest letter to arrive is dated JUNE 20,
1942 (ALWAYS date your letters, please) which is much nearer home than
the one before. I can't wait to see Gertrude Stein's First Reader in French!
O I do hope it is out SOON.

I haven't seen the illustrations of To Do. Harrison Smith didn't offer
to show them to me and I couldn't ask him. But the book should be out
soon, Very soon. The weather is hot and Fania's broken wrist is all right
and I am working hard for Yale and the Canteen and Fania and I send our
love to you and Mama Woojums!

Papa Woojums!

1. This letter is typed along the sides of an illustration by Don Freeman, "Sketched at the
Stage Door Canteen April 5," on page 11 of an issue of *The Playbill* (a magazine given gratis
in theatres). The illustration depicts "a typical night at the American Theatre Wing Stage Door
Canteen: a noted entertainer singing and probably a Shakespearian actor clearing the tables."

2. Van Vechten's "The James Weldon Johnson Collection at Yale," *Crisis* (July 1942), 49:18–
19. The official opening exercises of the James Weldon Johnson Memorial Collection of Negro
Arts and Letters was held at Sprague Memorial Hall, Yale University, on 7 January 1950.

❧

To Carl Van Vechten

14 August 1942   Bilignin par Belley
                                                             (Ain)

Dearest Papa Woojums,

Your letter just came telling all about your being a busboy, we don't know quite what a busboy is but Margot Johnson has just written that you are dealing out coffee and cocoa so we gather that is what a busboy is,[1] and we are looking forward to being busgirls here very very soon, bless you all, and here inclosed is a translation and printing of the ballad, May D'Aiguy has done it very very well, there is a possibility of the people in Algers who did the Paris-France doing the book, it will be nice to have a french book dedicated to Papa Woojums wouldn't it,[2] and we never did get the photo of Fania with white curls, do try again, make it a post card and it might come, and we are now the age when you feel young and don't count the years, bless us all, had a nice letter from [George W.] Hibbit[t] at Columbia about the broadcasting of Four Saints it seems he made a record of it on a gramophone disk as it came over, he thinks probably WOR, whoever they may be recorded it also, it would be wonderful to have it on a record,[3] otherwise calm xcept that we are having a drought no water at all, unprecedented in this country which usually rains too much, and we are all anxious about winter vegetables, otherwise there are a great many passers-by, and we love you, tell us more about what you and Fania do, lots and lots of love

Baby Woojums

1. Johnson had written to Stein (9 June 1942, YCAL) that the publication date for "To Do" had been set for 15 September. Not until after the war did Stein learn that the book had not been published. Johnson also wrote Stein of Van Vechten's activities at the Stage Door Canteen.

2. Stein's "Ballade," part of *The Gertrude Stein First Reader & Three Plays*, was published in the Baronne d'Aiguy's translation in *Confluences* (July 1942), 11/12:[11]-12. Stein sent Van Vechten the page with the poem. At the top of the page was the inscription, "To Papa Woojums the translation of one of his pieces out of his book, bless him, Always Baby Woojums." See Stein to Van Vechten, 20 June [19]42, note 1.

3. Hibbitt to Stein, 5 June 1942 (YCAL). See Van Vechten to Stein, 15 June 1942, note 4.

※

To Carl Van Vechten

[postmark: 31 August 1942]   Bilignin par Belley
                                                            (Ain)

My dearest Papa Woojums,

Fania's white hair has come as a postal card and we are delighted
with it, it has quite a Cleopatra air, I don't know whether she had white hair
but if she had had white hair that is the way she would have looked I am
sure, thanks and thanks again, and a passing American told us what a busboy is, that he shoves a wagon with the eats it's nice to think of eats, not
that we are hungry, we even went to a barbecue the other evening, a very
small but a whole lamb roasted out of doors,[1] and beside that there is a
drought, no rain for almost 3 months now, unprecedented in this region
and a bit tough on man and beasts. There are two more of the poems of the
First Reader going to be printed in a collection of poetry in 42,[2] and I am
hoping that the whole book will be done soon, I will like a book dedicated
to Papa Woojums done in Algeria. The french are all crazy about it, I have
gotten to be a very popular author over here, I am aching to see To Do, and
we see lots of people, just interrupted to see if I can get the electric stove
going, and back again to send lots and lots and lots of love to Papa Woojums
and Fania

Always
Baby Woojums

1. The barbecue was at the home of Elena and Paul Genin.

2. This project was never realized.

To Carl Van Vechten

4 September 1942   Bilignin par Belley
                                                  (Ain)

Dearest Papa Woojums,

Just had a cable from somebody called William Colt 72 Sixth Avenue saying wish to print few related passages from [The] World [Is Round] in anthologies Carl Van Vechten represent you artistically and financially.[1] I wanted to cable back that Papa Woojums could represent me not only artistically and financially but in every other which a way, but as that would have cost a great deal of money I contented myself in answering yes. But of course it is not necessary that they cable, anybody who wants anything has only to ask you, and you are always the decider, what you say goes, which you and I and everybody knows, golly it is still hot and hotter even if it is the fourth of September, lots of love to Fania and her hair and to Papa Woojums and his hair bless you both

Always
Baby Woojums

1. The cable was probably first read over the telephone to Stein and then a written copy sent to her. Stein has mistaken the name; the cable had come from William R. Scott who had published *The World Is Round*. The cable was received in Belley on 3 September 1942 (YCAL).

To Gertrude Stein

5 October 1942   101 Central Park West
                                                  New York City

Dearest Baby Woojums,

FOUR letters from you more or less ambled in together to make me happy. In one of them you said you hadn't received a picture of Fania with white hair. In another you said you *had* and compared her with Cleopatra

[756]

which ought to make her happy! And DOES. In another you say you have learned what a busboy does, but you really haven't. A busboy is the one who goes around cleaning off tables after people get through eating. There is a tremendous lot of this to do at the Canteen and a tremendous lot of busboys. but Papa Woojums is no longer a busboy. He is a Captain now and has charge of the floor. It is a happy place[x] and a warm place and an amusing place and the soldiers and sailors enjoy themselves HUGELY. I wish you could see it, but maybe you will some day. And I have your letter giving me permission to decide things for you when people are in a hurry and something has to be done quick. I'll use this permission discreetly. Anyway you have Margot [Johnson] too now to look out for you. To Do doesn't seem to be out yet. I loved the Ballade in French and please continue to keep me posted on anything published over THERE. I am very excited about a French book published in Algiers by you dedicated to ME. One of the four letters just received was written on Christmas Day but as it wasn't sent airmail it has just come in . . . Lincoln Kirstein in his Ballet Index (a periodical) is devoting a whole number to my old writings on the Ballet.[1] Remember when we were in a box together at Sacre du Printemps? The Museum of the City of New York is giving me a big photographic show (You will be in it: it is devoted to theatre people but YOU wrote Four Saints) beginning November 17.[2] And a group of Negroes in Harlem is giving a big official dinner for me in November.[3] In the spring Yale is giving a show of my books and manuscripts. Fania has just returned from Washington where she opened another canteen for the American Theatre Wing. You can see our lives our [i.e., are] active. So lots of love and kisses to baby and mama woojums and write soon and often to your loving

Papa Woojums!

[x]The Stage Door Canteen of the American Theatre Wing. Paul Robeson has just done Othello again *most* successfully![4]

1. *Dance Index* was a periodical (1942–49) founded by Lincoln Kirstein and edited by Kirstein, Paul Magriel, and Baird Hastings. Vol. 1, nos. 9, 10, and 11 (September, October, and November 1942), under the title "The Dance Criticism of Carl Van Vechten," reprinted many of Van Vechten's early dance reviews (pp. 144–89).

2. See Van Vechten to Stein, 20 July 1942. This exhibition mounted only 104 of the more than 1,000 photographs that Van Vechten had given to the museum.

3. See Kellner, *"Keep A-Inchin' Along,"* pp. 9–10.

4. Robeson had begun a long tour of Shakespeare's *Othello*, directed by Margaret Webster, with Uta Hagen as Desdemona and José Ferrer as Iago. The tour began on 10 August 1942 at Brattle Hall, Cambridge, Massachusetts. The play opened in New York on 19 October 1943 and ran for 296 performances. Robeson had first done *Othello* in London in May 1930 at the Savoy Theatre.

&

To Carl Van Vechten

15 October 1942   Bilignin par Belley
                                                                (Ain)

My dearest Papa Woojums,

Thanksgiving is coming and we are tremendously looking forward to have lots to give thanks for, and Papa Woojums thanks for Papa Woojums, I sent your article about your collection[1] to Bernard Faÿ, I thought that as the head of the Bibliothèque Nationale he might help you out with Dumas and possibly Pushkin,[2] that is put you in the way of contacts, and in the month of December the First Reader in french is coming out dedicated to Papa Woojums, the first edition is to be an edition of 1500 all numeroted, numbered, and naturally we are all pleased and delighted.[3] We are having a beautiful autumn, Pepe is barking, lunch is on the table and we are all so loving, just as loving as possible and every thought to Fania and to you dear Papa Woojums

Always
Baby Woojums.[4]

1. See Van Vechten to Stein, 2 August 1942, note 2.

2. Faÿ had been appointed director of the Bibliothèque Nationale in Paris on 6 August 1940.

3. The dedication for *The First Reader & Three Plays* is : "To Carl Van Vechten who did ask for a First Reader" (p. [6]). The French translation of the work, *Petits poèmes pour un livre de lecture*, was published on 30 April 1944 in an edition of an unknown number of copies. There were ten copies on *vélin*, numbered 1 to 10, that were published at the same time. The French edition does not have the dedication to Van Vechten.

4. During the night of 7–8 November 1942, Allied armies landed on the south shore of the Mediterranean, in Morocco and Algeria. The Vichy government lost its main elements of independence. The Germans responded by moving their forces into the southern zone on 11

[758]

November. The result was the occupation of all of France (Italian forces were also stationed east of the Rhone). Domestic conditions in France grew much worse, and all contact with the United States was now impossible.

To Carl Van Vechten

[? September 1944]   [Le Colombier
                                                           Culoz, Ain]

My dearest Carl

How are you oh how are you and well I just can't say often enough how are you, almost two years since we have seen your green ink, and your postal cards and now they will commence again, God bless them and you, the last we heard of you was that you were giving food and drink to the troops are you still at [it?], oh we are so happy to have them here, it is a wonder and a delight, we cannot believe we know it is true but we cannot believe it, and how is Fania and how is New York, and how is everything, you will know about us through the newspaper men who have spent three days with us and told us about everything we were so longing to know and now do find some way of sending us word how you are.[1] We are not any longer at Bilignin we are at Culoz, our landlord needed his house and we found this and we were very comfortable,[2] so much to tell perhaps you will come over soon that will be nice Alice will want to add a line she is tapping away at the ms. we had to leave it in writing so the germans would not be able to read it, once more all our love, all, to you both always[3]

Gtde.

1. Eric Sevareid, a news correspondent for CBS, and Frank Gervasi, a journalist with *Colliers*, were among the first Americans to reach Stein in Culoz. Gervasi brought back to the United States a letter from Stein to Bennett Cerf. Enclosed with that letter was this letter to Van Vechten and a letter to William G. Rogers. Cerf forwarded the letter to Van Vechten on 19 September 1944 (YCAL). Sevareid's account of meeting Stein and of the broadcast she made on 4 September 1944 on CBS radio to the United States from Voiron, France is given in his *Not So Wild a Dream* (New York: Alfred A. Knopf, 1946), pp. 457–62. Gervasi wrote of his encounter with Stein in "The Liberation of Gertrude Stein," *Saturday Review of Literature* (21 August 1971, 51:13–14, 57.

2. The house at Bilignin had always been leased from Marie-Anne du Vachat (later Putz), who had inherited it as a very young girl. Captain and Madame Putz served notice that they wanted to take possession of the house. Stein initiated a lawsuit that was heard in Belley on 24 July 1942. Although she lost the suit, she was granted an indefinite extension of her lease. When the French army was demobilized in November 1942, Captain Putz again tried to reclaim the house. A second lawsuit was begun, but Stein and Toklas found another house. The house, Le Colombier, was just outside of Culoz, a town some ten kilometers from Belley. The house belonged to a Madame A. Denis of Massignieu de Rives in the Ain. Stein and Toklas moved into it in February 1943.

3. The book was Stein's *Wars I Have Seen*. Toklas did not add a message to this letter.

To Gertrude Stein
[Postcard]

15 October [1944]

[101 Central Park West
New York City]

Dear St Gertrude and heavenly Baby Woojums!

So happy to get your letter & to know you are okay, and have written a Book. We are all right too & still at 101 Central Park West So love to you and Mama Woojums! from

Fania & Carlo Van Vechten

To Carl Van Vechten
[Radiogram]

[Received in New York
25 November 1944]

Culoz, Ain

JOYOUS DAYS ENDLESS LOVE[1]

GERTRUDE ALICE STEIN

1. Stein had received Van Vechten's postcard of 15 October [1944].

To Gertrude Stein

29 November 1944

101 Central Park West
New York City

Dearest Baby Woojums!

How excited we were to get your radiogram on Sunday. I have not been too sure where you were and sent postcards both to Paris and to Culoz (I wasn't even sure before that Culoz was in Ain).[1] However, it was a long time forbidden to send picture postals to France (and may still be) and I didn't know this rule and sent several picture cards which may reach you just the same in time. It is just now possible to send letters, but no airmail yet. I can't tell you how exciting it was to get the letter you sent through Bennett [Cerf] by the newspaper man, but your radiogram was more exciting still. [W. G.] Rogers, [Julian] Sawyer, so many others are in touch with me frequently about you. There is indeed a Stein Circle that smiles only when you are on the horizon. My latest problem is a Miss Rosalind B Schnitzer, a student at Columbia who wants to examine some of your typed manuscripts for a thesis about you she is preparing. As much of this material is unpublished the Library was a little wary of letting her see it at least without MY permission. . I have instructed her to write directly to you, giving her credentials and her clear intentions and explaining what she wants to look at. And I have instructed Mr Troxell, if her credentials and intentions come up to snuff, to show her a limited amount of material, under supervision, provided she agrees not to copy anything. You can call all this off by cable if you desire. .[2] Florine Stettheimer is dead after a brief illness and her sister Carrie followed her this summer within a month. I have been helping Ettie, the remaining sister, arrange her affairs and one of the things that has resulted is the Modern Museum has promised her a show in the fall.[3] Virgil [Thomson] had some of his portraits performed by the Philadelphia Orchestra recently: he conducted them himself.[4] The enclosed from Time will show you some of my recent activities.[5] Fania, at present, is directing some girls at a Negro High School in Harlem in a performance of Hänsel and Gretel (the opera!)[6] Our canteens go on! The Stage Door is nearly three years old and I have never missed a Monday or Tuesday night. I am one of three people in charge of a service women's tea dance at the Hotel Roosevelt every

Sunday afternoon and I also work at the Merchant Seamen's Club. All these activities are under the protection of the American Theatre Wing. You will probably know of none of these things because I see letters written you early in 1942 were returned . . . I am sending them back to you exactly as they were sent back to me. It may be fun to read all this old news now! Who can tell. Anyway I'll write you more later about the Stage Door Canteen etc. and tell you what has been going on as fast as I think of it. Did you know for instance that Alexander Woollcott had died? I dare say many pleasanter things have happened which I will think of gradually. . In the meantime Fania and I send Love and Kisses to YOU and MAMA Woojums!

Papa Woojums!

My Collection of your inscribed books and periodical appearances is still *intact* will we get anything new for this collection?

1. Only one postcard is in YCAL. It is dated 15 October [1944]. It is addressed to Stein in Culoz, but it also had 5 rue Christine written in in Van Vechten's hand.

2. Rosalind B. Schnitzer (later Miller) was a graduate student at Columbia University. While doing research at Yale University Library for a master's thesis on Stein, she had spoken with Isabel Wilder, Thornton Wilder's sister, and Gilbert McCoy Troxell, curator of the Collection of American Literature. They informed her that she would have to have Van Vechten's and Stein's permission to examine the Stein manuscripts in the Yale Library. Permission was given her to examine various manuscript material but not to copy it. Eventually she was granted permission to print Stein's Radcliffe College themes in her *Gertrude Stein: Form and Intelligibility* (New York: The Exposition Press, 1949), pp. 108–56. See Troxell to Van Vechten, 20 November 1944; Van Vechten to Troxell, 22 November 1944 (carbon); Troxell to Van Vechten, 28 November 1944; Van Vechten to Troxell, 29 November 1944 (carbon); Troxell to Van Vechten, 4 December 1944 (all in NYPL-Berg).

3. The Museum of Modern Art's exhibition in memory of Stettheimer was not held until October 1946. The catalogue essay was written by Henry McBride.

4. Thomson conducted the Phildelphia Orchestra on 21 November 1944 at Carnegie Hall, New York, in his *Suite for Orchestra*, which consisted of five of his musical portraits, some of which had been composed as piano pieces and then orchestrated.

5. The clipping has not remained with the letter. Van Vechten may have sent Stein the article "Not to Newcastle," *Time*, 6 March 1944, p. 75. The article concerns Van Vechten's collections at Yale and Fisk Universities.

6. Marinoff was working with students of Wadleigh High School in New York.

❧

To Gertrude Stein
[Telegram]

[postmark: 29 November 1944]   New York

Highly excited to hear from you
all love carlo fania

Van Vechten

❧

To Gertrude Stein

27 December 1944   101 Central Park West
                                    New York City 23

Dearest Baby Woojums,

I had no sooner received your cable from Culoz than I replied instanter and sent you a fat letter off to Culoz, enclosing all the letters which I had earlier sent to Paris and which had been returned. Now Virgil [Thomson] tells me that he has seen some one who says you are back at the rue Christine.[1] Dear, Dear: I hope all those letters are not lost, but maybe somebody will send them to you from Culoz. Anyway I sent you both another cablegram to Paris, but the cableman didn't like the Mama Woojums and Papa Woojums, so he said he would change this to Father and Mother, which had me in stitches; I explained the relationship as well as I could, so I hope you get the telegram and I'll be glad when airmail will get through to you again. I get airmail letters from soldiers in India in FOUR days sometimes! The war news is frightful for the moment and according to the papers Paris was bombed yesterday; so you will be right in the midst of the battle again. But somehow I am sure you will be all right. Lots of Love and let us hear from you. Fania and I embrace you and Mama Woojums!

Papa Woojums
(Carl Van Vechten)

[763]

1. Stein and Toklas arrived back in Paris sometime in mid-December 1944. It was their friend Katherine Dudley who arranged for a Russian workman, Svidko, to make repairs in the apartment in preparation for their return. In a letter written to Dudley by Toklas from Culoz on 13 November 1944, she said, "For with—as I commenced to say—with all you are doing, we'll be coming back as soon as we can get things in order, in less than a month I hope" (Toklas to Dudley, from a transcript made by Leon Katz). See Dudley to Stein in Gallup, *The Flowers of Friendship*, pp. 370–71.

To Carl Van Vechten
[Postcard]

[postmark: 3 January 1945]
5 Rue Christine 6 Arr.
Paris, France

My dearest dearest Papa Woojums,

happy happy new year to you and Fania, bless you all, and the first letter came to-day the very first which was a wonderful pleasure, here we are in Paris and it seems like it was all a dream and we had just come back from a summer vacation, a funny dream but a dream, and here it is all so natural so natural to be here, and even the G. I[.s] seem always to have been here as part of the Paris landscape, we stop and talk and they photograph me, with themselves and with Basket and we all like it, and Alice says Fania has gotten so plump and pretty, and you are fresh and rosy and bless you both all the time all the time

Mama and Baby Woojums.[1]

1. Both signatures by Stein.

To Carl Van Vechten

[postmark: 6 January 1945]
[5 rue Christine
Paris]

My dearest Papa Woojums,

Just had a letter from a corporal who told us all about you in New York, a nice long letter and it all brought you very near.[1] How we love the

American army we never do stop loving the American army one single minute. I have written something called Yes we are Americans all about the G. I.'s and why they are not like the Dough boys,[2] and Tommy Whittemore will take it over to the agent is she still there,[3] everybody seems to be still there and who do you think turned up last night, [Donald] Gallup who did the show for the Yale Library, I told him all you were doing and he was very pleased, he is [a] major and it is most impressive, to do that so quickly, I have a lot of things for you, there is a french edition just out of the First Reader, and it is lovely in French, I never did see why nobody saw the point of it over there, the french are all pleased with it, and Everybody's autobiography is coming out in french in March, and as soon as I can I will send them to you, was To Do ever done, I never heard, you see the Ballad in the first reader strikes them all as so symbolic.[4] Well Papa Woojums dear papa Woojums isn't it wonderful to write and xpect it to get there so wonderful love to you and Fania from us.

B. W.

1. The letter cannot be identified.

2. There is no such title in the Stein Collection, YCAL. It is possibly a reference to the "Epilogue" to Stein's *Wars I Have Seen*, pp. [247]–59.

3. A friend from Stein's Harvard University-Radcliffe College student days.

4. Stein's *Everybody's Autobiography* was translated by the Baronne d'Aiguy and published as *Autobiographies*, pref. Leonie Villard (Paris: Editions Confluence, 1946). "A Ballad" in the English edition, pp. 49–52; "Ballade" in the French edition, pp. 46–48.

❧

To Carl Van Vechten
[Postcard]

[postmark: 6 January 1945]   5 Rue Christine 6 Arr.
                                              Paris, France

Dearest Papa Woojums,

Your ears must have been tingling, we said so many nice things about you such lovely things. We were with Katharine Cornell, she put us into uniforms and we went in to see her show for the G.I.'s. and we did enjoy it enormously, and afterwards we sat around the fire and we talked about Papa Woojums and she told how you had discovered her, and we told how you did everything for everybody and we said what a wonderful man Papa Woojums is and she is going to tell you all about us and I will send you the First Reader in french by her and bless you and Fania always[1]

Baby Woojums.

1. Stein had met Cornell in January 1935 through Van Vechten. At this time Cornell and her husband, Guthrie McClintic, were touring with the play *The Barretts of Wimpole Street* for the United Services Organization (USO). See Cornell to Stein, 9 January 1945, in Gallup, *The Flowers of Friendship*, p. 373.

Cornell was given a copy of the French translation to bring back to Van Vechten, but it was lost. Through John R. Bianco, Stein mailed another copy to Van Vechten, postmark 11 June 1945. This copy (YCAL) bore the inscription:

To dearest Papa Woojums

I did want you to have the very first one printed and I did send it but anyway here is another one and it is all your book,

Always
Baby Woojums

See Stein to Van Vechten, 12 June [19]45, and Van Vechten to Stein, 21 June 1945.

To Carl Van Vechten

7 February [1945]

[5 rue Christine
Paris]

Dearest Papa Woojums,

Here came your first letter directly to Paris, all of them so far have come up from Culoz, and this one was dated December 27, it is so nice to be in Paris and so nice to have letters from you in Paris, all those back letters have not turned up yet, but they will, it takes some time but they will, the length of time is all very capricious, how we love being in Paris, Basket and I walk and walk and the house is always full of old friends and new G.I.'s. My latest great enthusiasm are some New England M. P.[1] who are guardians of our quarter and come in a bit now and then to sit, bless them all, I have sent you a book by Katharine Cornell, our First Reader and she will tell you all about us and how we do it, I am now doing an article on our arrival in Paris, will send it over by some soldiers,[2] and I am to lecture to a protestant audience in a protestant church in Choisy le Roi,[3] I don't know whether I get into the pulpit or not, and later in Dijon, oh it is nice to be back in Paris, to-day I almost walked to Montmartre, bless you papa Woojums, father Woojums, bless you and all our love to you and Fania always and always

Baby Woojums.

[on back of envelope] The cinema stamp is a lovely stamp.

1. Military Police.

2. Possibly a reference to Stein's "We Are Back in Paris," *Transformation Three*, ed. Stefan Schimanski and Henry Treece (London: Lindsay Drummond Ltd., 1945), pp. 5–9.

3. On Sunday, 4 March 1945, Stein delivered a lecture, "L'Amérique, mon Pays, La France, mon chez moi" in the Salle Paroissiale of the Reformed Church in Choisy-le-Roi, a town just outside of Paris.

To Gertrude Stein

[? March 1945][1]   101 Central Park West
                                                      New York City 23

Beloved Baby Woojums,

I have been reading Wars I Have Seen in the greatest state of excitement, with chills and fever, coos of appreciation, shouts of enthusiasm, bursts of true ecstasy. It is an amazing book in which you have imprisoned your feeling about all the world in the microcosm of a small French village. Never has your "style" been so perfectly wedded to your subject matter or to the effect you planned to make on your reader. The end of course sent me up in an airplane; it explodes like a rocket and fills the sky with showers of pink and blue and silver stars! Dear Baby Woojums your love for America, as expressed in those pages, is as alive as [Waslaw] Nijinsky at top career . . . You DANCE your way out of this superb book and I wish [George] Gershwin were alive to write music about these pages! Some one is sure to do it. Brava, Great Woman, and a couple of Olés! Somebody told me that Richard Wright, the Negro who wrote Native Son, had reviewed the book in last Sunday's PM. I was curious about this review although I didn't expect it to interest me much. To my surprise, it is more understanding than any other review of the book that has yet appeared. I know Bennett [Cerf] will send you some of the reviews, but they may take a long time in reaching you, so I am sending you this by Giovanni Bianco by airmail.[2] He should have it in a week, long before you get this letter. Giovanni, by the way, wrote me a heavenly two-page typewritten letter about you and Alice (apparently at his first visit he spent most of his time with Alive [i.e., Alice] and adored her) and I am so grateful to him that I am sending him a copy of the book.[3] That too may reach him sooner than your copies. In any case, I am happy to have this means of communicating with you by air, and hope if you have anything important to say you will tell him to tell me. A letter and a card are here from you. I can't make out if you have received the letters I have written you, especially one sent to Culoz enclosing two or three 1942 letters to you returned to me when France was occupied. PLEASE REMEMBER TO LET ME KNOW ABOUT THIS. Giovanni sent me a notice of a conference you are giving in the Reformed Church. And of course Kit Cornell called me and told me a lot . . . I am not too sure of your writing but think you write that Donald Gallup is a MAJOR. Let me know if this is true. I am not quite sure which Corporal has written you because I have sent the whole American army so far as I know it STRAIGHT TO 5 Rue Christine! TO DO was NOT done. Harrison Smith agreed to publish it but what happened I don't know. Nor, I think, does Margot Johnson. She still has the First Reader which is a favorite of mine and I am longing to see it in French and all the other things you have. Don't let me miss anything, PLEASE . . . The enclosed will give you some idea of my activities.[4] Gifts shower in for these Collections and I have to arrange and catalogue these and ship them. I photograph as much as ever[x] and was very happy to collaborate with your jacket! and My Canteens! I have never missed a Monday or a Tuesday night[(2)] at the Stage Door Canteen where I am Captain. On Sundays I am one of three people in charge of the American Theatre Wing Tea Dance for Service Women at the Hotel Roosevelt. Some day I will tell you more about this. I haven't missed a sunday in two years (it opened two years ago). And after this is over I go to the Merchant Seamen's Club to work Sunday nights.   Everything is the same except we have no servants. Nobody has. Fania and I scrub floors and make beds and wash dishes and there isn't much meat or butter, but we are well and happy. I communicate frequently with Julian Sawyer and [W. G.] Rogers about you and they have both sent me clippings and advance news about this and that. Everything you say about American soldiers in this war IS true. They are entirely different from the last war. They are the best and most charming soldiers in the world! So Love and Kisses to you and Mama Woojums and WRITE SOON!

Carlo

[x]except at the moment paper and film are very scarce.

[2]for 3 years!

I went to a cocktail party for (of all things!) Marcel Duchamp last week and in the middle of it a man got up and yelled: "I can't stand another second of this. It's just like 1912!" and of course it was except in 1912 cocktail parties were a novelty.

Did you know that Florine Stettheimer died last summer? The Museum of Modern Art is giving her a show next season.[5]

1. In *The Flowers of Friendship* Gallup assigns this letter to "[Feb? 1945]." However, the reference to Richard Wright's review of Stein's *Wars I Have Seen*, "Gertrude Stein's Story Is Drenched in Hitler's Horrors," *PM*, Sunday Picture News Section, 11 March 1945, p. 15, clearly indicates a March date for this letter.

Wright's review was actually a condensed version of an extended essay he had written on Stein (see manuscript, Wright Archives, Yale-JWJ).

Stein had probably first heard of Richard Wright (1908–1960), the black writer, from her friend Max White. White had met Wright at the American Writers' Congress held in New York in June 1937. Both were delegates to the congress. In a letter to Stein, 30 January 1938 (see Gallup, *The Flowers of Friendship*, p. 326). White wrote about Wright, "He says he has been immensely influenced by your writings." There is no indication that Stein had read anything written by Wright before his 1945 review of *Wars I Have Seen*. Wright had probably first read Gertrude Stein in early 1935 (see Michel Fabre, *The Unfinished Quest of Richard Wright* [New York: William Morrow], p. 111).

2. Van Vechten explains the origins of his epistolary contact with Sergeant John R. Bianco, who was attached to the Shaef Mission in France, in his letter to Stein, 21 June 1945. Stein and Van Vechten both referred to him as Giovanni in their letters and it may be that he had anglicized his name when he joined the army. Mail directed to army personnel had a greater priority than civilian mail in the months immediately following the end of the war in Europe. It was for this reason that Van Vechten took to sending his letters and packages to Stein through Bianco. Bianco, because he served as a fleet messenger, was nicknamed Mercury by Stein and Van Vechten.

Bianco probably met Stein toward the middle of February. In a letter to Van Vechten, 17 February 1945 (YCAL), Bianco acknowledged receiving Van Vechten's letter of 6 February urging him to meet Stein.

3. Bianco to Van Vechten, 1 March 1945, YCAL.

4. The clipping referred to may be the article in *Time*, "Not to Newcastle," 6 March 1944, p. 75. See Van Vechten to Stein, 20 November 1944. For a survey of the collections founded by Van Vechten see Kellner, *A Bibliography*, pp. [244]–47.

5. See Van Vechten to Stein, 29 November 1944, note 3.

❧

To Carl Van Vechten

8 April [19]45   5 rue Christine
                                                                     [Paris]

Dear dearest Papa Woojums

What a lunch we had to-day with Giovanni Bianco and his pals and cooked by him and Alice, and provided by them, spaghetti and mayonnaise and crab meat and shrimps and candy and nuts and salad and meat and Alice made ice cream chocolate and oh dear now it is evening and we have to go to bed so full of food, Bianco is great on food Italian food, and he has a pal who is great on Danish food[1] and we have one who is great on Viennese food and the three talk food and Alice talks Jewish and American food and we ate well not all those nations' foods but a jolly good lot of them, just ate and ate, and then one of the boys got a horse cab and took us riding in the Bois de Boulogne, with an independent air, as they used to sing[2] and oh my it was green and there were crowds and it all seemed like the good old days before the first world war, we went around the lake and they were rowing and there were ducks, and there were flowers and dogs and racing at Auteuil, my gracious Papa Woojums can you believe it all, we hardly could and then some other American boys photographed us in the cab and if I can get a copy from them I will send it in my next or by Bianco, but they mostly disappear the boys and there are no photographs, they photograph me on the Champs Elysées or anywhere me and Basket, it's a nice life.[3] I have been lecturing to the American army, they make a lovely audience and then they bring us things so sweetly nice sweet candy, nice boys nice candy, nice Paris, come Papa Woojums come you and Fania, they have a Theater Door Canteen, couldn't you be sent to inspect it, and incidentally us, do come bless you Papa Woojums and Fania and all the nice Americans, god bless them and us, all nice Americans, good-night we are sleepy, so much Bois de Boulogne

Always
Baby Woojums and Mama[4]

1. Mark Hasselriis, a Danish-American soldier and friend of Bianco's.

2. Stein is echoing a line from the turn-of-the-century hit song "The Man Who Broke the Bank at Monte Carlo."

3. The details of this letter are confirmed by Bianco to Van Vechten, "May Day '45," YCAL.

4. Both signatures by Stein.

To Carl Van Vechten

2 May [19]45

5 rue Christine
[Paris]

Dearest Dearest Papa Woojums,

[Giovanni] Bianco will have told you by now more than everything about us and how pleased and happy and touched I was by all you said about the book, and I have sent you a letter for Richard Wright, I was so very much taken with his book Black Boy and I wrote to him about it, you know you sent the review he did of my book and I got one of the soldiers to find me some of his books, the only one they found in the soldiers' library was Black Boy and I am very enthusiastic, and could you send me through Bianco that and all his other books, I do want to read them,[1] you will be pleased that Chaplain Wall of the Penitentiary of Ohio of Columbus Ohio asked for a copy of my book, he says the prisoners want it, they do not care how old a copy it is because they can mend it, I have asked Bennett [Cerf] to send them a copy but perhaps you could too, one does feel for prisoners, all the world has been in prison,[2] I go every evening to see them as they come in, they come in on trucks from the flying fields, and they are tired but so pleased, so pleased, so naturally we have a kind of feeling for even regular prisoners, the war looks like coming to an end and my we will miss the American army when they leave us, they make all our life these days, yes [Donald] Gallup is a major, he comes to see us very regularly and has been most

[771]

awfully sweet, and the other evening Norman Pearson also from Yale came to see us, and we had a very pleasant evening, and they told us all about it. Bianco brings us Mrs Channing Pollock's[3] books that she sends to him and after he has read them he lends them to us and she has rather an amusing taste in novels and do thank her for us, it's funny, that Bianco has such an intimate intermediary and you don't know him. The other evening he found a few too many people here, he said next time perhaps there won't be so many and we can talk about cooking, he also gave us a photo of Fania that we like immensely, he is a funny and very delightful little man, God bless you both and so much love from us both and always for our papa Woojums

Baby Woojums.

1. After reading Wright's review of her *Wars I Have Seen*, Stein read Wright's *Black Boy: A Record of Childhood and Youth* (New York: Harper & Bros., 1945). See Stein to Wright [postmark 26 April 1945], Yale-JWJ.

2. The Reverend K. E. Wall, chaplain of the Ohio State Penitentiary, Columbus, Ohio, wrote Stein on 26 March 1945 (YCAL), that several men had requested that he write for a copy of her *Wars I Have Seen*. See Stein to Cerf, 10 April 1945, Columbia-Random House.

3. Anna Marble Pollock was the wife of Van Vechten's friend Channing Pollock. Although they met in 1901, she and Channing Pollock were not married until 1906. Anna Marble was one of the first women theatrical press agents. Channing Pollock was a press agent, playwright, director, and producer as well as a newspaperman. The Pollocks and Van Vechten first met in 1906. In his autobiography, *Harvest of My Years* (New York: The Bobbs Merrill Company, 1943) Channing Pollock recounts how he first met Van Vechten at a restaurant, the Maison Favre, which was behind the Metropolitan Opera house on Seventh Avenue (see Pollock page 148). In 1948 Van Vechten created The Anna Marble Pollock Memorial Collection of Books About Cats which is administered by the Yale Collection of American Literature.

To Carl Van Vechten
[On last leaf of Galerie Roquépine catalogue of
Riba-Rovira exhibition, 12–30 May 1945]

[postmark: 7 May 1945]　　　　　　　　　　　　　　　[5 rue Christine
　　　　　　　　　　　　　　　　　　　　　　　　　Paris]

My dearest Papa Woojums,

　　　I am sending you two of these for your collections, I think you will like them,[1] life does just seem to move along, I talked again at the Cité

Universitaire for the Librarians, they liked it, and 4 Negro librarians came up and especially thanked me, I do not just know why but they did, my gracious I do like my life with young men and now there are some Russians, well we will miss them all, we surely will God bless you papa Woojums always and always

Baby Woojums.

1. Stein had met the Spanish artist Francisco Riba-Rovira (nicknamed Paco) one day shortly after her return to Paris. She was walking her dog Basket along the quays of the Seine when she saw Riba-Rovira painting. Stein became interested in his work and he painted several portraits of her.

 The catalogue for the exhibition of Riba-Rovira's work, held at the Galerie Roquépine, Paris, from 12 to 30 May 1945, contained an introduction, "Par Miss Gertrude Stein," pp. [3–4].

To Carl Van Vechten

20 May [19]45   5 rue Christine 6 arr.
                      [Paris]

My dearest dearest Papa Woojums,

 Such a nice man turned up, he was from Iowa and his name was Knifey, and you call him Edward VII, and he is really very charming, he spent the evening with us and naturally we did talk a whole lot about you what is more natural than that and he will come to see us if he gets to Paris again and he is going to send me some of his short stories about the War.[1] My how we will miss the American army when it goes away, but we are having it in plenty just now. I am talking out at the biggest hospital next Friday.

 And now we have just come back from the most charming evening with the Glen[n] Miller band who invited us to listen to their concert to the soldiers and we had a lovely time it was beautiful and then after it was over they made me do a few words to the band and it was all so sweet and lovely it just is.[2] I have written a little piece for the New York Times Magazine whatever that is and they are most enthusiastic, as usual it is about the American army bless them.[3] Giovanni [Bianco] is so funny, with only 84 points he is wonderfully funny about it,[4] and Alice is writing a cook book of 100 restriction recipes,[5] well good-night bless you papa Woojums

Always
Baby and Mama Woojums[6]

Love to Fania, bless you papa Woojums. Oh a man named Philip McGregor sang in Magic Flute Dec 41, he came in the other afternoon and sang me Pigeons on the Grass. Nice Americans.

Did Katharine Cornell ever give you the dedicated french first reader I sent over to you by her?

1. Knifey was a nickname for Sergeant Edward G. Darnell. Van Vechten had met him at the Stage Door Canteen. Van Vechten and Stein were in the habit of numbering their friends with the same first names so as to distinguish them.

2. Earl G. Cornwell, a member of Glenn Miller's Army-Air Force Orchestra, had met Stein one afternoon in the Place Vendôme, Paris. He and other members of the orchestra invited her to the concert they were giving in the Olympia Theatre. After the concert Stein gave an impromptu talk. Later that afternoon ten members of the orchestra visited Stein at the rue Christine and held a jam session. See Bianco to Van Vechten, postmark 15 June 1945 (YCAL) and Stein to Van Vechten, 12 June [19]45.

3. Stein's "The New Hope in Our 'Sad Young Man,' " *The New York Times Magazine*, 3 June 1945, pp. 5, 38.

4. In order to be sent back to the United States a soldier needed to have earned 85 points. Points were given for the amount of service time spent overseas, the number of the soldier's dependents, and the time spent in the United States.

5. Toklas never wrote this cook book. She did, however, include a chapter, "Food in the Bugey During the Occupation," in her *The Alice B. Toklas Cook Book*.

6. Both signatures by Stein.

To Gertrude Stein

27 May 1945   101 Central Park West
                                               New York City 23

Dear Baby Woojums,

When I tried to cable the Publications Techniques et Artistiques to be paid for with the enclosed order, the cable company informed me I had to get a Treasury License, and bowled over by so much red tape, I sent an airmail letter to Giovanni [Bianco] with instructions to tell you that this publication may use the picture. Please see that I get a copy of this periodical with your article and if you give them back this slip they should be able to collect the money. .[1] Kitty Cornell cannot find the book you gave her for me: she HOPES it isn't lost and doesn't see how it could be. Is this irreplaceable? I don't seem to know what it is. . I wrote Giovanni to tell you this and to tell you about Miss [Frances] Steloff too. To avoid controversy, I have decided Miss Steloff should write you a letter telling you exactly what she wants and how much she will pay for it and then this will be passed on to you for confirmation. . It is also important to know if there is anything that has to be arranged with the French publishers of A VILLAGE, of which, through some fluke or other, I don't seem to possess a copy. I can't understand this at ALL. Are they épuisé or can I still get a copy? . .[2] Do you need food? Giovanni seems to think you do. I sent two boxes yesterday with some tinned quenelles de brochet. Alice will know how to warm these. They should be served with sauce financière, but I dare say the ingredients of this rich sauce are impossible to come by at the moment. Maybe you can't even get butter. Well, I'm sure you can run up SOMETHING. A card from you has just come to say you are sending the FIRST READER in French by [Katharine] Cornell, but do you mean the mss.? or published? I tremble till I get your reply? Did you get all those past letters returned because there were no boats during the war, which I recently remailed to Culoz? I hope so. I didn't open them to reread them, so I don't know what they say. Do you have somebody to give stamps to in Paris, now that your priest or Abbé is so far away?[3] Have you lectured in Dijon yet? You sent me, through Giovanni, a picture taken at some conference, but it had no caption, and I am not sure what this is. Please explain. You will know more soldiers this time than you did last! We are the same and even more so: no cook, but a cleaning woman twice a week and Fania is a superb cook and makes wonderful Poulet Henri IV and Risotto milanese, which has no peer, and lots of other nice things. . I am taking color pictures of the Canteen, so in years to come I can show you how all this was, and I am dying to take color pictures of YOU. O yes, I sent you two books by Richard Wright as Giovanni says you want them and I am advertising for the third one and you will get that in time and anything else you want. . TWO boxes for you went to Giovanni yesterday . . . . Lots of love to you and Baby [i.e., Mama] Woojums!

Papa Woojums
Carl Van Vechten

There is coffee, tea, and chocolate in the boxes!!

[775]

1. This project was never realized. See Stein to Van Vechten, 12 June [19]45.

2. Steloff wrote to Stein, 29 March 1945 (YCAL), requesting permission to use Stein's A *Village Are You Ready Yet Not Yet A Play in Four Acts* in a volume she was planning to publish. The project was never realized.

3. Stein's friend Père Bernardet of the Abbaye d'Hautecombe.

❧

To Carl Van Vechten

12 June [19]45   5 rue Christine
                                                               [Paris]

Dearest Papa Woojums

So many things to say to you, first about the little First Reader, your book, translated into French and I gave the first copy that came off the press to that faithless woman Katharine Cornell to give to you, it was so much your book, and she took it and put it in her pocket the pocket of her uniform overcoat, and she said then this is for me, no I said I have given you other books this is for Carl please be sure he gets it, it is very important and she said she would. Remind her of the overcoat pocket, it may still be there and I would so very much want to have you have the first copy that came off the press of your book.[1] Then there are the cookies, Giovanni [Bianco] brought the box over, we were all xcited as we unwrapped it and the beautiful box came out with the beautiful cookies, and how we all ate those beautiful cookies. Giovanni telephones daily about the other boxes and the books which have not come yet. We are very fond of him, he is a kind of a sweet baby, all the pretty ways and the desires of a nice baby, you like him better and better, we tease him a lot about his 84 points which should [be] 85, and he telephones a new hope almost every day. We will miss him a lot when he does get his 85 points. Then there is Dick Wright, I am most xcited about his writing, and I have just had a very interesting letter from him, that you sent by Giovanni and at the end he wants to know what I think about jitter bugs, well it just happens that Giovanni and his friend Billy [Cissel] of Baltimore were going to a show to-morrow evening of jitter bugs given for the army and they are taking us, so we will know.[2] We just had a most xciting time with the Glen[n] Miller band, they took us over to hear it with the troops, then I talked to the band afterwards, gave them a little address and they were delighted and then they came over one afternoon ten of them with their instruments including drum and bass viol[in] and played for us in the house here, it was fine and Alice made them chocolate ice-cream supplied by the American army in the shape of chocolate and tinned milk, it was lovely. And Papa Woojums to come back to [the] lovely cookies, no we are not hungry in the starvation sense, no, but in the luxury sense yes, so do not deprive yourself of points in the starvation sense but we do oh how we do appreciate the packages in the luxury sense, those cookies so beautiful to see, so beautiful to eat, the widow of Juan Gris who was here one evening and Alice offered her the cookies, she said with a sigh of satisfaction, at last I know again what chocolate tastes like and in cake, so you see it is like that. Giovanni also gave us the set of photographs of Ethel Waters you sent him, we were very xcited about them, and we liked the account of you in the stage door canteen, and will you give my very great affection to Marian[ne] Moore, I always remember her that night in Brooklyn,[3] oh yes and about that and about Miss [Frances] Steloff, do do whatever you think fit and I hereby authorise you to sign for me anything you think should be signed, why does she not reprint Tender Buttons & Mabel Dodge at the Villa Curonia or both, they would sell now, Alice is selling off at last frantically all the Plain Edition, Galignani sells about 30 a month of them,[4] the army just laps them up, we had a nice long letter from Hunter Stagg,[5] and those people who telegraphed about your photos seem to have disappeared, that does happen in Paris, and a young soldier just came who was sent by a William Alfred who had a letter from you, it is all very complicated, he comes from Syria and Cuba and Los Angeles, so he says,[6] well so much love to you and to Fania, dear dearest Papa Woojums

Mama and Baby Woojums.[7]

1. See Stein to Van Vechten [6 January 1945], note 1.

2. Wright to Stein, 27 May 1945, in Gallup, *The Flowers of Friendship*, pp. 379–81. Wright advised Stein to walk up to some of the black soldiers and ask them about jitterbugs. Among the books Wright sent Stein was Dan Burley's, *Dan Burley's Original Handbook of Harlem Jive* (New York: privately printed, 1944).

3. Marianne Moore (1887–1972), the American poet. Moore wrote an appreciative review of Stein's *The Making of Americans* when it was published. See Moore's "The Spare American Emotion," *The Dial* (February 1926), 80:153–56.

4. The first English-language bookshop on the Continent. It is located on the rue de Rivoli in Paris.

5. A soldier, Boyd Kissinger, who knew Hunter Stagg had written him about meeting Stein. See Stagg to Stein, 3 May 1945 in Edgar MacDonald, "Hunter Stagg: 'Over There in Paris With Gertude Stein,' " *The Ellen Glasgow Newsletter*, issue 15 (October 1981), p. 7.

6. William Alfred (b. 1923), the American poet and playwright. After reading Stein's *Everybody's Autobiography* in 1939, Alfred, then still in high school, wrote Stein a fan letter. A brief correspondence continued until 1941.

    In 1945 Alfred, then in the army, renewed his contact with Stein. There is a letter from Alfred to Stein with the date cut off in YCAL that is probably the letter Stein is referring to. All of Alfred's letters to Stein are in YCAL.

7. Both signatures by Stein.

To Gertrude Stein

16 June 1945

101 Central Park West
New York City 23

Dearest Baby Woojums,

    Your letter of May 2 (Please ALWAYS date your letters) arrived June 16, just one day short of my birthday, which isn't bad, about 6 weeks. The one before this took over two months. Richard Wright's books have been sent to you: Black Boy, Native Son, and Uncle Tom's Children: you should have received them all by now. Also THREE boxes of food, including the quenelles de brochet which I am certain Alice can have fun with. All these through Mercury Giovanni [Bianco] who has turned out to be a honey. Somehow I know these boys I write to quite as well as if I had sat in a New York bar with them for years but this was the only chance for me to have steady epistolatory intercourse with you as Mrs [Channing] Pollock's friend Giovanni was the only one who was stationed in Paris that I could get in touch with. I am now completely in touch with Richard Wright who hitherto was only an acquaintance.[1] He telephones me and he sent me a letter to send to you via Mercury Giovanni and he too is devoted to you.[2] It seems indeed as if the whole American army is making tracks to 5 rue Christine and they must be having the times of their lives. Probably Giovanni doesn't realize yet he is living the kind of life in Paris he will dream about for years and it may never happen again. Have you got any of those old letters I sent to Culoz? You don't mention them. And you haven't yet identified (place and time) a photograph that Giovanni sent me some time back.[3] I haven't given Miss [Frances] Stelloff permission to reprint the Village. I told her to make out some kind of agreement indicating how much she would pay you and I would send it to you to sign (if you cared to). She said she would, but she has done nothing. Perhaps she is communicating with you personally; perhaps she is going ahead WITHOUT permission. In any case I want it distinctly understood I have given her no such permission YET (Giovanni wrote me you said I could do what I thought best about this matter). We had a lunch party yesterday for wounded soldiers at the Stage Door Canteen. It was a jolly party. Wounded men are so much more lively and appreciative of attention than those who have never seen battle. A great many of them could dance, being on the way to recovery or perhaps their legs were spared . . . . Tomorrow my "crew" at the Tea Dance for Service Women is giving me a big party. Did I tell you I had taken over entertainment for this party? Last week I had Paul Robeson and tomorrow Laurette Taylor.[4] This week also we attended the Silver Wedding party of our Pearl Showers (maybe you will remember our second maid?). It was a very hot night but all the women wore long and elaborate dresses and the men were in tails and white ties. Pearl herself (she is near chocolate color) wore a skyblue tulle dress with a satin damask bodice and was smothered in lavender orchids. There was a band, PHOTOGRAPHERS, and a long supper, served for nearly 200 people in a large hall. I've never been to a better party. The principal event, however was something I have never seen before: A REWEdding, a regular service with a minister. Mrs Showers marched in (to Lohengrin) on the arm of her son, while her husband walked in with his daughter[x] and then they replied to questions like this: "After 25 years do you promise to be faithful for the rest of your life, etc?" It was heavenly and Fania cried. Afterwards she told Mr Showers she was very much touched by this beautiful ceremony. His reaction was: "I am devastated." So honey and ambrosia to you and Alice from Fania and

Carlo

You must know by now that Kit [Katharine Cornell] hasn't been able to find the French First Reader. She is most unhappy about it, but there it is.

ˣa most beautiful girl.

You don't say anything about Leroy Hough and Edward VII (Knifey) [Edward Darnell] [5]

1. Van Vechten had met Wright in 1939; he photographed him for the first time on 23 June 1939.

Van Vechten sent Stein Wright's *Native Son* (New York: Harper & Bros., 1940), *Uncle Tom's Children: Four Novellas* (New York: Harper & Bros., 1938), and *Black Boy*, which she had already read.

2. Wright's letter to Stein, 27 May 1945 (in Gallup, *The Flowers of Friendship*, pp. 379–81), had been sent to Stein by Van Vechten through Bianco. See Stein to Van Vechten, 12 June [19]45, note 1.

3. The photograph referred to may be one that Giovanni Bianco sent to Van Vechten after Stein's lecture at the Reformed Church in Choisy-le-Roi (see Stein to Van Vechten, 7 February [1945], note 3. The photograph, probably taken by Bianco, is inscribed by Stein on the verso: "Here we are Major Gallup who did the ms and who introduced me the pasteur Alice just behind me and the flowers the little girl presented, it was a lovely occasion and the sergeant who came sang spirituals." In response to an inquiry Donald Gallup writes: " 'who did the ms' refers to my catalogue, published in connection with the exhibition that Norman Holmes Pearson and I arranged at Yale in February 1941, i.e., it opened on 22 February 1941, two days after I had been drafted into the U.S. Army. The 'sergeant' wasn't a sergeant but a corporal and his name was Clark Rowland" (letter received from Donald Gallup, 20 December 1984). For references to the Yale exhibition of the published and unpublished writings of Gertrude Stein see Van Vechten to Stein, 23 November 1940 and [13 March 1941].

4. Laurette Taylor (1884–1946), the American actress.

5. Soldiers whom Van Vechten had sent to Stein. See Stein to Van Vechten, 20 May [19]45, note 1.

To Gertrude Stein

21 June 1945
101 Central Park West
New York City 23

Dearest Baby Woojums,

I was enchanted to receive the two catalogues of [Francisco] Riba-Rovira. What a charming introduction and how proud this young man must be to have received your accolade! I just telephoned Miss [Frances] Steloff to ask why she hadn't sent me the contract for you to sign in which she

agreed to pay you a small sum for the use of A Village and she said Julian Sawyer had been in with a letter in which you said it was all right for her to go ahead and so she was going ahead . . . So that matter is out of my hands, please. It had been so long since I had heard from her that I suspected something had happened. The new copy of Petits Poèmes is here and I am happy to have this and what a delightful book! Poor Kit [Katharine Cornell] was very distressed that she couldn't find this book. When she returns from her vacation, I'll ask her to look in the pocket of her army coat.[1] If you are "luxury hungry" for cookies that is an easy matter. I can send you more from time to time and more will go to you almost immediately. Rationed and tin foods are more difficult to manage, because they are scarce here too and points are very scarce, but we'll see what we can do. Richard Wright phones he is sending you (via me and Mercurio-Giovanni[)] [Bianco], a book of Harlem Jive which I am sure will amuse you no end and maybe you will begin to talk this way a little. You will find it no end of fun.[2] Wright is also getting for you a book of his that I could not get you, but neither of these book[s] has come through to me yet. When they do, they will go off to you like a shot. You and your Glen[n] Miller Bands and your Jitterbugs are having such a time! Paris will never be the same again and our Wars bring a great deal of pleasure to you one way or the other. Last war it was the Kiddie [W. G. Rogers] and this year it is a whole Regiment of Kiddies.
I am glad Mercurio-Giovanni is proving so satisfactory: I HAD to have somebody to write you through and he was writing Anna Pollock and I asked her for his address, but it might have turned out very differently. Maybe you wouldn't have liked him. Maybe he wouldn't have taken messages and packages back and forth, but he has certainly proved himself a Woojums and should have the Order of Merit and the Cross of Distinguished Service and all the other decorations and a dish of CANNELLONI when he retuns to these shores, a fact which, I HOPE he will not regret all his life thereafter, for somehow I feel he is having the kind of time, knowing you and Alice so intimately, that only comes once or twice during a lifetime. Maybe he'll be sorry when he gets his 85 points, but when he does get them and when he does get to New York, I promise him some Cannelloni (among other nice foods). Fania's Risotto Milanese is really out-of-this-world too. The Marianne Moore you speak of, I am sure, is the POET; MY Marion Moore who works with me at the Canteen and the Tea Dance for Service Women at the Roosevelt [Hotel] is a different one and I don't think you know her. She has nothing to do with Brooklyn. Do you know Lorna Lindsey and do you

know her daughter was killed in Germany and is buried at Berchtesgaden which is ironic. I don't seem to KNOW William Alfred . . . So lots of love to you and Mama Woojums from Fania and

Carlo
Papa Woojums!

1. See Stein to Van Vechten [6 January 1945], note 1.

2. See Stein to Van Vechten 12 June [19]45, note 2. Dan Burley was a young aspiring black reporter when Wright and he first met in Chicago in the 1920s.

❧

To Carl Van Vechten

6 July [19]45   5 rue Christine, 6 arr.
                                                [Paris]

My dearest dearest Papa Woojums,

We had the Quenelles to-day, for lunch, they were delicious, Alice made a real sauce like you said and they were delicious and we blessed Papa Woojums, and all the other things were so more than welcome, and now, Giovanni [Bianco] is gone, we were glad for him but most awfully sad for us, because he is just as nice as he can be and now there have to be new arrangements made. There is lieutenant Jo Barry, and he is writing to you and he is permanent, at least for some time and he will bring us letters and anything else you send, and that will be nice. I have been reading a book that is interesting me a lot, An American Dilemma by [Gunnar] Myrdal, and there he quotes Kelly Miller, his writing sounds interesting, if it is could you perhaps send me a book of his.[1] Giovanni will tell you all about our trip over Germany, I have done an article for Life about it and they are to reproduce the photos, it was most xciting.[2] I have told the Harmonies people to send you a copy of the periodical and I guess they will,[3] by this time you will have had the First Reader book, and the other little french piece I sent you, and I have gotten a copy of the Village for you, that is I have reserved one, as soon as I get it I will send it to you by Jo. It was wonderful in Germany, just living for four days with the American army, the door bell

[782]

rings all day long, one soldier and then another, I must say I do like them all. You are right we do see lots more soldiers this time, thanks for sending me the article in the Times, I had not had a copy, I am glad that I have found a new way, another boy turned up the other day a dark boy from New Jersey, who corresponds with you, but has never met you, lots of love to dear Papa Woojums and to Fania, lots,

> *Always*
> *Baby and Mama Woojums.*[4]

1. Joseph Barry (referred to as Jo or Joe by Stein), an American writer. Stein based her character Jo the Loiterer in her opera *The Mother of Us All* on Barry. While a student at the University of Michigan Barry was arrested for picketing during a prewar political rally. Since there was no charge for picketing, he was arresting for loitering.

    Barry had lent Stein Gunnar Myrdal's *An American Dilemma* (New York and London: Harper & Bros., 1944). In his book Myrdal quotes from various works by Kelly Miller (1863–1938), a black educator and writer who had been a professor of sociology at Howard University, 1890–1926. Miller was called "the father of the Sanhedrin," a 1924 movement that attempted to unite all Negro organizations into one front. Among the works Myrdal cites are Miller's *Race Adjustment: Essays on the Negro in Amerca* (New York: The Neale Publishing Co., 1908) and *Out of the House of Bondage* (New York: The Neale Publishing Co., 1914).

2. Stein's "Off We All Went to See Germany," *Life* (Aug. 1945) 19(6):54–58. The article tells about Stein's trip to Germany, where she and Toklas toured U. S. Army bases. She also visited Salzburg, Austria, and was photographed on the terrace of the Berghof, Hitler's home at Berchtesgaden.

3. Stein's lecture "France Amérique," in *Harmonies*, May 1945, pp. 11–12, 53. Stein had probably sent Van Vechten "La Retour à Paris," *Fontaine* (Apr. 1945), 8(41):163–64.

4. Both signatures by Stein.

To Gertrude Stein

14 July 1945

101 Central Park West
New York City 23

Dearest Baby Woojums,

    With Mercurio-Giovanni [Bianco] gone, I am sending this through Lieutenant [Joseph] Barry[1] and I am also sending the two [Max] Shulman books you asked for through the same source. Regarding Shulman I got the following card from Ted Holliday the bookseller, but you will find plenty about Shulman on the jackets of the books, both of which I take it are slightly autobiographical.[2] I am also sending you (with this) a couple of pages from Esquire which will interest you.[3] You seem to be delving deeply into the Negro problem. [Gunnar] Myrdal indeed! As for Kelly Miller, I don't think he had anything new, and his old books are hard to come by. What especially do you want? There are two packages of books (from Dick Wright) and two packages of food from Fania and Carlo on their way to you via Bianco. I hope these don't get lost now that he has wandered away. Wherever has he gone to? . . . I have taken to going to weddings? Did you ever go to any? I never did before, but I have been to two this month, besides Pearl [Shower]'s wonderful REwedding, of which I am sure I wrote you. Weddings are gay, there is lots of champagne (the best French champagne) and I think I will begin to crash weddings soon! . . . You knew perhaps that the NY Times (curses to them) is tearing down the building harboring the Stage Door Canteen! We have to get out along with our thousands of service men guests at the end of this month and as yet we have no place to go, but maybe some place will TURN UP. Everybody always asks about you and Alice every day and I tell them what a wonderful time you are having with the army and everybody is always excited and everybody says you must be having a wonderful time. So lots of love to you and Mama Woojums and don't let me miss anything.

Papa Woojums!

1. Barry had written Van Vechten, 5 July 1945 (YCAL) telling him that Stein had asked him to replace Bianco as the "address" for Van Vechten's packages to Stein.

2. Stein had head about Shulman from some soldiers. Through Barry she asked Van Vechten to send her Shulman's *Barefoot Boy With Cheek* (Garden City, N.Y.: Doubleday, Doran and Co., Inc., 1943) and *The Feather Merchants* (Garden City, N. Y.: Doubleday, Doran and Co., Inc., 1944). The card from Ted Holliday is not in YCAL.

3. The pages from *Esquire* are not with the letter. They were probably an article by Sinclair Lewis, "Obscenity and Obscurity," *Esquire*, July 1945, pp. 51, 140, in which he mentioned Stein, saying, "Gertrude Stein, the Mother Superior of all that shoddy magic, is still extremely admired even though she is also extremely unread."

❧

To Carl Van Vechten

23 July [19]45[1]   [5 rue Christine
                                                          Paris]

My dearest Papa Woojums,

So much to tell you and you may be getting this by the sweetest man who has done so much to make us comfortable Joel Fisher, and he'll tell you all about a delightful day we are having together. And now for lots of things. Giovanni [Bianco] must be back in New York now, and I hope all those lovely packages catch up with him and then come back again to us, because we do want them dreadfully. I have gotten a copy of the Village for you, the last one that was left, and I'll have Jo Barry send it on to you next week, to-day I had a letter from Knifey Darnell, he thought that he would be gone away and then after all, there he still is in Marseilles, not that I imagine that he is sorry, he is an awfully nice fellow, the other day I met on the street a fellow named Franklin Brewer, who met up with you in the Canteen in Philadelphia, he spent the evening with you, he says you won't remember him, but he never forgot it.[2] He is taking a course at the Sorbonne and we are dining with him Friday evening, by this time you will know all about our trip in Germany, the new Mercury, is Librarian here in Paris and I guess more or less permanent, he is a nice boy,[3] sometimes quite funny, of course not our only Giovanni, Giovanni did grow on one, we were devoted to him, and such a Mercury, give him all and all our love and tell him to be sure to get our packages back, we were so sorry he was leaving on such a sad errand and we do miss him although he did so want to go home, the magazine people who reproduced your photo, have said they have sent you a copy, if not I will make a fuss, dear dearest papa Woojums, I gave some photos of yours away to-day to Joel Fisher, he loved them. Always Papa Woojums

Baby and Mama Woojums.[4]

1. This letter was not mailed. Presumably it was brought to Van Vechten by Joel Fisher, a returning soldier.

2. Franklin Brewer was a technical sergeant in the 333rd Infantry. He had met Van Vechten at the Philadelphia Stage Door Canteen in 1942. Brewer presented himself to Van Vechten as a friend of Prentiss Taylor's, who was a friend of Van Vechten's.

[785]

Brewer and Stein met while she was walking Basket in the Place de Pantheon in Paris. The character of Brewsie in Stein's *Brewsie and Willie* is drawn, in part, from Franklin Brewer. See Brewer to Van Vechten, 30 July 1945 (YCAL).

3. Joseph Barry.

4. Both signatures by Stein.

❧

To Gertrude Stein

10 August 1945   101 Central Park West
                                                       New York City 23

Dearest Baby Woojums,

I have lost track of the packages but from what Giovanni [Bianco] has told me I do not believe you have received them all. Two were sent, for postal reasons, as from Fania Marinoff and Saul Mauriber.[1] You SHOULD have received in the first instance two boxes of cakes (five pounds each) and TWO boxes containing quenelles, tea, coffee, etc. . Giovanni says you only received one of the latter. Then I sent SINCE the first lot, TWO more boxes of cakes. You have never reported as to whether you received Uncle Tom's Children by Richard Wright or the [Max] Shulman books, The Feather Merchants and the other and there are TWO packages of material from Richard Wright you have not yet mentioned. WHY don't you send letters through Lieut [Joseph] Barry, they would reach me sooner! . . . . I was interrupted at this point by the arrival of Essie Robeson whose book on Africa has just been published (the first edition was sold out on the day of publication) and she says Paul is in Paris singing to the soldiers. I do hope you can get together.[2] You will know how to reach him. Kelly Miller's books are mostly out of print, but if you will let me know the title of the one you want, I'll try to get it for you but particular books are as hard to get now as SUGAR or BUTTER.[3] PLEASE AUTOGRAPH THE ENCLOSED PICTURE FOR SGT BILL RANEY and RETURN TO ME. A staff Sgt in Gander, Newfoundland, writes me out of a clear sky: "I have started a collection of first editions of Gertrude Stein's works. Can you help me . . ? When I have completed a Collection of the books I shall start on articles printed in magazines. Of course one can't do much here except by correspondence . . ." etc. I am writing him how to go about all this. Do you want to write him? This is his address: S/Sgt Vernon L Bobbitt,[x] ASN 37,432,672,A Sqd. APO 865, c/o Postmaster, New York. He already has Ida, Picasso, Paris, France 1940, Three Lives, Autobiography of Alice B Toklas, and Everybody's Autobiography.[4]. Giovanni popped in on me and I took him to the Stage Door Canteen and we had a long talk about this and that. He has gone to Buffalo to settle his mother's estate, but I expect him back soon. O yes, Joel Fisher was here too and talked about you with relish and he loves you. And the wonderful lithographs with floral montage came from Germany and they are out of this world and in oval gold frames will look like museum pieces.[5] And your article in Life about Germany was wonderful and here is your interview in the Baltimore Afro-American.[6] And I am most excited to have The Village and hope it is on its way . . . and why doesn't Lieut Barry write to tell me something has COME?[7] I never got a copy of the magazine with my picture of you but perhaps I will, but I did get a letter from Franklin Brewer, whom of course I remember.[8]. . Did you know that Mabel [Dodge] is selling her house in Taos and wants $100,000 for it, all furniture included. Who is "the dark boy from New Jersey" who corresponds with me and who came to see you? What is his name? I don't identify him. . So love and blessings to both of you, from Fania and

Carlo[9]

Very happy we have a new and "permanent" Mercury, but tell him for Gawd's sake to send me some news of you. Giovanni used to write twice a week!

Did you ever get those old letters from Culoz? You never answer questions, so

[x]It seems he is a painter and from Iowa!

The world news is the most exciting the world news has ever been.

1. Saul Mauriber was for many years Van Vechten's photographic assistant.

2. Eslanda Robeson, author and wife of Paul Robeson, had written *African Journey* (New York: The John Day Co., 1945).

3. See Stein to Van Vechten, 6 July [19]45, note 1.

4. While stationed with the air force in Gander, Newfoundland, Bobbitt found a copy of *The Autobiography of Alice B. Toklas*. His wife, who was in New York, was able to obtain certain works by Stein for him. Bobbitt wrote to Van Vechten on 26 July 1945 (YCAL) asking for his advice on how to obtain certain works by Stein. Van Vechten replied on 10 August 1945 (col-

lection Bobbitt) advising him to contact the Gotham Book Mart and Stein directly. Van Vechten also sent him a photograph of Stein and one of Toklas. Bobbitt became head of the Visual Arts Department at Albion College, Albion, Michigan. (Letter received from Bobbitt, 26 January 1983.)

5. Presents Stein had sent Van Vechten through Joel Fisher, a returning soldier.

6. Vincent Tubbs of the *Baltimore Afro-American* had interviewed Stein. The article, "Gertrude Stein Talks for Afro-American," appeared on 28 July 1945 (YCAL).

7. Enclosed with this letter was one addressed "Dear Lieutenant," which was meant for Joseph Barry, whom Van Vechten chides for not writing him news of Stein.

8. Brewer to Van Vechten, 30 July 1945 (YCAL).

9. In Stein's hand at the top of the letter:

> Two Boxes of cake
> 2 boxes of mixed food and all of it was
> marvelous
> coffee marvelous

These are phrases from Stein to Van Vechten, 16[–23] August [19]45.

❧

To Carl Van Vechten

16[–23] August [19]45   5 rue Christine
[Paris]

My dearest Papa Woojums,

    First all the questions, the boxes of cakes and two mixed foods came and were wonderful, the quenelles a dream, Alice says the coffee the best ever simply marvelous, the two books of [Max] Shulman, but alas not the two packages from Richard Wright and not Uncle Tom's children, but I am hoping that they will be returned to Giovanni [Bianco] and they can be sent back, the letters from Culoz all came, they promised me that the magazine the french one was sent, just now everybody is out of town, but I will remind them,[1] the Village has been kept for you, but the shop that has it is closed just at present, it will not be open until September and when it is I will give it to Jo [Barry] to send. Jo is a funny man, a bit timid, he said he thought we wanted a silent Mercury, he is just the other xtreme from Giovanni, I think he would like books, I imagine he would like Nigger Heaven, and did you ever get the french First Reader, that I sent by Giovanni after

Katharine Cornell was unfaithful, [Franklin] Brewer is a nice chap, he will be delighted that you remember him, we see him quite frequently and the inclosed is a description of a talk I gave which did xcite them, they walked me home 50 strong after the lecture was over and in the narrow streets of the quarter they made all the automobiles take side streets, the police looked and followed a bit, but gave it up,[2] I had a letter from the New Foundland book collector and have written to him,[3] I have just begun a GI novel, it begins well, it would be nice if it keeps up like that.[4] There are some funny things going on about my Play, I'll tell you all about that next time,[5] this is our answer to questions and full of love to you dear Papa Woojums, and to Fania, from

Mama and Baby Woojums

Dearest Papa Woojums,

Before your letter got off a whole lot of packages came, that blessed Giovanni managed to get them all to us all the same, two boxes of cookies and such cookies, Uncle Tom's children and I'm mad about it, there is a tremendous mastery in the thing, and also all the newspapers and the 12 million black voices and two more little books,[6] and your Nigger Heaven for Giovanni which I am having Jo Barry send back to you to give to him, I've just read the whole of 12 millions beside the Children of Uncle Tom and I am writing by this same mail to Giovanni and to Dick White [i.e., Wright], I just had to take a day off, not one American soldier have I spoken to to-day, not quite I did talk to one on the street, I kind of wonder sometimes what I will do when they are all gone I talked to another bunch yesterday afternoon and I am doing a kind of novel and it is moving along, just where it will go to I don't quite know but so far it moves,[7] lots of love and so much, and you do send us everything we want, and don't bother about tinned things, the American Aid Society is taking care of us, and anyway food is much easier, lots of love[8]

Baby and Mama Woojums.[9]

1. *Harmonies*: see Stein to Van Vechten, 6 July [19]45, note 3.

2. Enclosed was page 3/4 of *The Stars and Stripes*, Paris ed., Saturday, 11 August 1945. Robert Marshall's article, "Stein Says Americans Lack Spiritual Courage of French" (p. 4), reported on Stein's lecture to 300 soldiers at the University of Paris (Sorbonne) on Thursday, 9 August 1945. The lecture had been sponsored by the Information and Education Division of the U. S. Army.

3. Bobbitt to Stein, 31 July 1945 (YCAL).

4. Stein's *Brewsie and Willie.*

5. The Theatre at the Army University Center at Biarritz had expressed interest in Stein's play *Yes Is For a Very Young Man.*

6. Wright had sent Stein a letter on 23 June 1945 (YCAL), together with a package that included his *Twelve Million Black Voices: A Folk History of the Negro in the United States,* photo direction by Edwin Rosskam (New York: Viking Press, 1941), and a pamphlet *How "Bigger" Was Born* (New York: Harper & Bros., 1940). Also in the package were *Dan Burley's Handbook of Harlem Jive* and a few issues of Father Divine's newspaper *The New Day.* See Wright to Van Vechten, 10 July 1945, Yale-JWJ.

7. Stein's *Brewsie and Willie.*

8. These two letters were mailed together by Joseph Barry.

9. Both signatures by Stein.

To Gertrude Stein

12 September [1945]

101 Central Park West
New York City 23

Dear and Beautiful Baby Woojums,

I am sending this directly through the skies to you, the first I have sent this way: the Post Office tells me I can and I am doing! It is September 12. So PLEASE let me know exactly when it reaches you so that I can compare the time with military airmail.[1] Anyway I can send packages direct to you now as well as airmail as well as regular letters: so everything is the way it was before. Well, not exactly. I dare say air mail will be much improved once it gets to working regularly, as many planes will fly every day and eventually I can get a letter to you in Paris in TWO DAYS. You answered a flock of questions in your latest letter, more than you ever answered before, but one remains unanswered: Did you receive the books that Mrs [Anna] Pollock sent you through Giovanni [Bianco]? They hadn't come when he left but he said that all his mail was being dumped at your door. Anyway Mrs Pollock asks me daily if I've heard from you about these books, so PLEASE let me know. Everything else seems to have come through. A Captain [Irving] Lieberman telephoned me today with messages from you and he is coming to see me tomorrow . . . I may have still more to write you after that. After a month in the country Giovanni is back looking for a job. I haven't seen him but he telephoned me. . Nor have I seen Commander [Joel] Fischer again. You ask if I received the French Reader you sent by Giovanni after Katharine Cornell was unfaithful and I tell you again that I DID receive it and that I am mad about it. This came weeks, even months ago, and I have referred to it several times. I am excitedly waiting for your GI novel and you say something about a play which is not explicit. The newspaper account of your lecture amused me very much. Our Canteen is closing at the end of this month (NEXT MONTH, OCTOBER) and after that I won't have so much to do, but the Roosevelt Tea Dances for Service Women are bound to continue for some time yet and I have charge there of both personnel and entertainment and so that is some job . . . The apartment too is a shambles piled high with material to go to my George Gershwin Collection at Fisk[2] and my James Weldon Johnson Collection at Yale. This all has to be sorted and arranged and listed and packed and it is such a tremendous job that I am doing very little with photographs at the moment and nothing whatever with writing. I have had several offers to write again lately, but I haven't given in to any of them. It seems the GIs on desert isles like my books which were beginning to be forgotten and there is a demand for them again. . The [New York] Public Library is giving me another big photograph show and I am sure you are in this, though I haven't had time to see it yet.[3] . Can Mama Woojums make Risotto Milanese? Fania makes the most divine RM and we just had some for lunch and I like this better than anything, I think. And everybody asks about you and talks about you and I am very proud of you and you will hear from me again soon. Fania and I send lots of LOVE to you and Mama Woojums, and please let me know exactly when this letter gets to you!

Carlo Papa Woojums!

1. Prior to this, Van Vechten had used the Army Postal Service, sending his letters through John R. Bianco or Joseph Barry.

2. In 1946 Van Vechten founded the George Gershwin Memorial Collection of Music and Musical Literature at Fisk University. The collection includes autograph letters, music manuscripts, inscribed books, scores, programs, pamphlets, an archive of Russian music, inscribed photographs from singers and composers, and a selection of Van Vechten's photographs of musicians.

3. To mark the fall opening of the Equity Theatre Library, the Theatre Collection of the New York Public Library mounted an exhibition of Van Vechten's photographs, *Personalities of the Theatre*, at the Hudson Park Branch of the New York Public Library.

To Carl Van Vechten

17 September [19]45   5 rue Christine
                                                                        [Paris]

My dear dearest Papa Woojums,

The twelfth of September letter came this morning, that means just five days, that's pretty good, but don't send packages direct, send them by Jo [Barry], because they do get lost, one of tooth paste and one of kitchen towels sent by kind friends by ordinary post directly have not come, and now I want to tell you how absolutely delighted both Mama and Baby Woojums were about Papa's books, my gracious goodness and I know how terribly pleased Fania is too, all your women folk are delighted, which ones of them are they which they are reading, I do want to know, I am quite sure the [i.e., that] The Tat[t]ooed Countess must be one of them, did I tell you that we saw Rogers do you remember whom we met out there in Wisconsin, he was awfully nice, brought us two wonderful bottles of Rhine wine, and was generally very charming.[1] I am getting I hope the Village to-morrow or the day after and will send it to you through Jo. I did receive Mrs. [Channing] Pollocks books and I have already written to her to thank her. All of Giovanni [Bianco]'s packages have come, the G. I. novel goes on, pretty well I think, the Play In Savoy, was sent by some young actors to Gilbert Miller, but nothing has been heard since,[2] but Papa Woojums we have not had rice for five years, not even black market can produce that, it was rarer even than coffee, but Alice says she makes her own version of macaroni of that ilk, dearest Papa Woojums and dearest Fania, fly over soon,

Always
Baby Woojums.

1. This is not William G. Rogers, "the Kiddie."

2. Stein's play *Yes Is For a Very Young Man*. She had begun writing the play before she returned to Paris in December 1944. The play deals with the divisions of family life during the

occupation. Stein had not yet heard from the Army University Center at Biarritz whether they would do the play. Gilbert Miller was a theatrical producer.

❧

To Gertrude Stein

27 September 1945   101 Central Park West
                                                          New York City 23

Dearest Baby Woojums,

Your letter got back to me on September 24, which is just twelve days to and fro, some kind of record, certainly much better than could be done by airmail before de Wah. However I suspect that this is nothing to what is coming. I dare say the day will soon be here when you can fly to Paris for lunch and get back late at night! Why my pretty pets, to think that you have had no rice! You see you haven't actually told me ever what you need, but Fania has been shopping this morning, now that I have your letter, and some rice and some coffee will go to you tomorrow, Via Mercury Joe [Barry]! I got a long letter from Sam Lerner today full of admiration for the ladies on Christine Street and he informs me, what I had already guessed, that [Franklin] Brewer is Brewsie. . WHO is Willie? I am BURNING to read this GI book, perhaps "looking forward to it eagerly" would be the strongest understatement I ever made. You say you've seen "Rogers"; surely not the Kiddie? At least I have been in touch with him and didn't know he had gone abroad. I've seen Capt [Irving] Lieberman a couple of times: he came here to dinner one night and last Sunday he visited my Tea Dance for Service Women at the Roosevelt [Hotel]. It was the day Josef Hofmann played for us on an imported Steinway and it was a great day.[1] A GI friend came in last night and like all the others nowadays he seemed very depressed. They want to get out of the army but they wonder what in hell they are going to do when they DO get out. They just don't know. Nor does anybody else. Giovanni [Bianco] went right out and got a job. But I don't suppose everybody else will be so lucky. Yes, The Tattooed Countess is one of the books the GI's seem to enjoy and The Blind Bow-Boy is another. There is heavy talk again about dramatizing The Countess (there always has been off and on) and one man even has an idea of making an operetta with a BALLET out of it, using Debussy music. Are you cooking anything with Virgil [Thomson]? The captain [Irving Lieberman] says you are writing another opera together.[2] That would truly be out of this world! In any case I send lots of love to you and Mama Woojums and maybe we'll be flying over for tea soon (not for a cocktail because I am on the WAGON!)

Papa Woojums[3]

1. Josef Hofmann (1876–1957), the Polish-born pianist and composer.

2. The Alice M. Ditson Fund of Columbia University offered Thomson a commission for an opera. Thomson wired Stein and asked if she would be interested in working together again. Stein's reply was positive. When they met in Paris, in October 1945, they worked out several ideas that emerged as the Thomson-Stein opera *The Mother of Us All*.

3. On the verso of this letter in Stein's hand:
> Higham [David Higham, Stein's English agent]
> Copy of
> Paris France
> translation
> Autobiography

To Carl Van Vechten

27 October [19]45

5 rue Christine
[Paris]

Dearest Papa Woojums,

This letter is being taken to you by [Adrian] Hall of the American Embassy, and he will take to you all our love and some dried trompette de la mort, a mushroom from our country which you chop up fine and it takes the place of truffles, and now for our news and there is lots of it. First I have sent the first 2/3 of Brewsie and Wille to Bennett [Cerf], will you get it from him and read it and tell me what you think of it, I am most awfully anxious to know,[1] then you know about the play I wrote for the french resistance which is called, Yes is for a very young man, well there has been a good deal of effort to get it played, the young ones are mad about it, the older ones dubious, but now the young ones have enthused the older ones, and

[794]

the play is to be played by the group of university players at Biarritz and we go down there the 26 of November and stay 10 days to superintend the rehearsal. It will be fun. Two evenings ago four young actors came and read it at the house, and Guthrie [McClintic], Katharine Cornell's husband and a fellow named Dick Worf or a name like that,[2] an awful nice fellow from Hollywood and they all seemed very enthusiastic. I have already told you that the play has been sent to Gilbert Miller by some of the young actors, don't you remember. So you see we have been most awfully busy, and then Virgil [Thomson] wants me to do another opera with him, we have been talking about it, and I have written the prelude and the cast of characters, it is to be around Susan B. Anthony and Daniel Webster, that is if it comes off, I think Susan B. Anthony is a nice character for an opera what do you think and the title is to be The Mother of us all. So if I can only get a little peace and quiet I have lots to do. We have had a perfectly wonderful autumn, just lots of sunshine, Virgil is going back to New York next Monday, there are less and less G. I's around, what seems to be left is mostly colored, and Generals, which is kind of sad, but I suppose that is inevitable, sooner or later they all do have to go home, but we will miss them. Lots of love Papa Woojums to you and Fania from us all,

> *Always*
> *Baby Woojums.*

Jo [Barry] has just come in with rice and coffee, what rice what lovely grains, what a beautiful object is a grain of rice, you betcha.

> *Mama and Baby Woojums.*[3]

1. Stein sent Cerf forty typewritten pages of *Brewsie and Willie* on 21 October [1945] (Columbia–Random House). Cerf answered Stein on 9 November 1945 (YCAL) that he was enthusiastic about the book and wanted her to rush to complete it so that it could be published in the spring of 1946.

2. Richard Whorf, an actor and director, was at this time a reader for the theatre at the Army University Center at Biarritz.

3. Both signatures by Stein.

❧

To Gertrude Stein

19 November 1945   101 Central Park West
                                             New York City 23

Dearest Baby Woojums,

Do you realize we have no Mercury? Joe Barry writes me he is no longer in the army and that he has no address and not to write him until he gets one, but even when he gets one I can't send packages to him as he will no longer be in the army and it would be the same as sending packages to YOU. So Please get a Mercury for US right away.[1] Dick Wright has something waiting to go to you and so has Papa Woojums. You shoulda received THREE packages of coffee and rice in one of which were dishclothes. I hope all three got through. Adrian Hall brought us the Trompettes de la Mort (what a gruesome name for champignons) and the little silver heart and we are very happy to have them, and A Village came through too and I am overjoyed to have this and can't think how I missed having it in the past. Thank you, dear Baby Woojums. I asked Bennett [Cerf] to let me see the mss of Brewsie and Willie and he said he was sending it to the printer as fast as possible but he would let me see the proofs, so I can't report on this. I ran into [W. G.] Rogers at a cocktail party and I told him all your news. He is a sweet man and was enchanted with the idea of Yes is for a very Young Man going on at Biarritz. Is this the play part of which appeared, under another name, in the Saturday Review?[2] I've seen Virgil [Thomson] since he got back and he seems awfully happy that you may collaborate again and Susan B Anthony seems a swell idea. Did you know there were Us three-cent stamps dedicated to her? I'll send you one on a letter if they are still in print. The Mother of us All is a natural for a title. PLEASE send me a couple of programs of the Biarritz performances of the play. Giovanni [Bianco] had a letter to Dick Wright from you and wanted to meet him; so I had them here together with Wright's white wife[3] and two GIs and how Giovanni does chatter, to be sure! Anyway he is very neurotic at present and hates his jobs and wants to get away and I think it is Paris and You and Alice that have made him this way. He burns to get back to it all, and of course that is difficult. Wright's wife is Jewish and very nice indeed and they have a baby. . The Stage Door Canteen has closed and the Seamen's Club closes next week and so now there is only the Tea Dance for Service Women which

[796]

still goes on every Sunday and which I am one of the managers of. But I am very hard at work now organizing the Johnson material described in the enclosed clip and identifying figures in my canteen pictures in color and getting them in definite order.[4] Which reminds me I didn't take color pictures when I saw you last, but I do now, and I MUST get you in color and don't you think it is about time you made another visit to the United States, and everybody asks, "Is Gertrude coming over?" and I always say YES, maybe in the Ides of March . . . and maybe I can bring it about that way. SO, please answer this at once and send me the address of a Mercury where I can address packages, and write me all about the play. Love to you both from Fania and

Papa Woojums!

1. After being released from the army, Barry became public relations director for *Newsweek* in Paris. See Barry to Van Vechten, 15 November [1945], YCAL.

2. Stein's play was originally titled "In Savoy." Under this title a fragment from the play was published in *The Saturday Review of Literature* (5 May 1945), 28(18):5–7. The play was published as *In Savoy or Yes Is For a Very Young Man* (London: The Pushkin Press, 1946). When Lamont Johnson, the actor and director, prepared the play for its premiere at the Pasadena Playhouse, Pasadena, California, 13 March 1946, he asked Stein to make a number of changes in the play, as well as to add some lines and scenes. The complete revised text of this play is in Stein's *Last Operas and Plays*, pp. [1]–51.

The change in title, from "In Savoy" to *Yes Is For a Very Young Man*, was suggested to Stein by the actress Norma Chambers (d. 1953).

3. Wright and his second wife, Ellen Poplar, were married in March 1941. Their first child, Julia, was born on 15 April 1942.

4. The James Weldon Johnson Memorial Collection of Negro Arts and Letters was founded by Van Vechten in 1941. The collection is administered by the Collection of American Literature, Yale University Library. There is no clipping with the letter and it cannot be identified.

To Carl Van Vechten

20 November [19]45   5 rue Christine
                                                          [Paris]

My dearest Papa Woojums,

The rices all the rices and the coffees and the dish cloths turned up, but alas there are no more Mercuries, none, those that are still military can turn into civilian any minute, even if they stay on, I guess we will have to trust to the civilian post, on the whole it comes through fairly well, and what a wonderful collection of stamps, I keep it and show it to everybody and everybody is breathless with delight, I am now putting my mind to the Mother of us all, I have just read a passionately interesting life of her, by Roberta Childe Dorr, I got some floating ideas but they have not quite coalesced,[1] I had a nice long letter from Dick Wright, and sent him some books of mine that he wanted.[2] Did you see what I said of him in the interview in the Chicago Defender,[3] from Giovanni [Bianco], the more you know him the more you like him, at least we were that way, Life is probably going to do a part of Brewsie and Willie.[4] Look up Bill Walton, he took the ms. over for them, we liked him, Alice says how happy she is with all the gifts, she says tell him again, life seems a little quieter, just for a few weeks and then we go to Belgium, lots of love

Baby Woojums.

1. Rheta Lousie Childe Dorr, *Susan B. Anthony, The Woman Who Changed the Mind of a Nation* (New York: Frederick A. Stokes Co., 1928). Stein immersed herself in the subject of nineteenth-century American life. She read widely in the material available at the American Library in Paris and then wrote to the New York Public Library for additional material.

2. Wright to Stein, 29 October 1945 (YCAL).

3. Ben Burns, national editor of the *Chicago Defender*, wrote an article about Stein and her forthright views on the "Negro question" (YCAL).

4. *Life* did not print excerpts from *Brewsie and Willie*.

To Carl Van Vechten

5 December [19]45   [5 rue Christine
                                                          Paris]

Dearest Papa Woojums,

This is Lamont Johnson, and he'll tell you all about us, and all about Yes is for a very young man, and what he is doing, we liked him a lot and hope the play will be a success and I know you will help him all you can, dearest Papa Woojums love to you and Fania[1]

Always

Gtrde

1. The production of Stein's *Yes Is For a Very Young Man* that had been planned for the Army University Center at Biarritz had been canceled. See Gallup, *The Flowers of Friendship*, p. 390. In a letter to Donald Gallup (see Burns, *Staying on Alone: Letters of Alice B. Toklas*, pp. 80–81) Toklas wrote that at first there seemed to be agreement to do the play, with decor by Francisco Riba-Rovira, for ten performances, but when she heard no further news from Biarritz, she telephoned "three times a day for three days." The theatre sent a representative to Paris who told Stein that they had decided to give the play experimental performances without costume and decor—just simply readings. Stein refused and asked for the play to be canceled and for the return of her manuscript.

    Lamont Johnson, the actor and director, was touring as an actor with a U. S. O. company, acting in a play, *Kind Lady*. Johnson met Stein in Paris and after reading the play secured the rights to it. He eventually arranged for its first production at the Pasadena Playhouse, Pasadena, California, on 13 March 1946. Toni Merrill (Mrs. Johnson) and Jane and Robert Claborne, all of whom were members of the touring U. S. O. company and had met Stein in Paris, appeared in the Pasadena production along with Lamont Johnson. See Van Vechten's "How Many Acts Are There in It," in Stein's *Last Operas and Plays*, pp. xii–xvi.

To Carl Van Vechten

[? December 1945]   [5 rue Christine
Just before Christmas.   Paris]

My dearest Papa Woojums,

    Here is Edward Geisler, who was our cavalier, protector and friend on our Belgium trip where we had a really wonderful time and he will tell you all about it and about us, and they used your introduction to Three Lives to make the announcement in Belge, God bless you Papa Woojums and Fania, and we love you always[1]

Baby and Mama Woojums.[2]

[799]

1. Stein gave a lecture, "Que sont nos contemporains," on Friday, 21 December 1945, at 5:30 P.M. in the Salle du Séminaire, Palais des Beaux Arts, Brussels, Belgium.

2. Both signatures by Stein.

❧

To Gertrude Stein

27 December 1945

101 Central Park West
New York City 23

Dearest Baby Woojums,

Bennett [Cerf] says he has written you that he will publish an anthology of Steiniana, including the whole of The Autobiography of Alice B Toklas, and Four Saints, and lots of other things. He has asked me to write an introduction, to select and edit this collection; what suggestions have YOU to make, please? I am advising Wars I have Seen from the point where the Americans come, probably the whole of Tender Buttons, and The Portrait of Mabel Dodge at the Villa Curonia, among other things. T[ender] B[uttons] and the Portrait are so rare now that nobody can see them and everybody wants to and the Portrait opens like a Handel Oratorio on spreading harmonious chords: The Days are wonderful and the nights are wonderful and the life is pleasant! You must let us know what YOU want in this BIG BOOK and also tell me if there is anything you particularly want said in the Introduction.[1]. . There is another matter which I would like to speak about. Some years ago you gave Ann Watkins OR Margot Johnson permission to handle The Gertrude Stein Reader and another book. At your request, I turned the mss over to them. As you know they have done nothing with these. I wish you would have them return the manuscripts to me, as it is possible we might want to use one of these in the Anthology. At any rate, I think they have had them long enough. I don't know exactly whether you wrote to Margot Johnson or Ann Watkins, but Margot has now left Ann and works for the firm of A and S Lyons 515 Madison Avenue. Ann Watkins is at 77 Park Avenue. If you recall which one you wrote to before, write her again, unless you prefer to leave the mss where they are which I think is a bad idea. They should be returned to ME of course. Thank you for the copy of Yank with the interesting interview and I hope SOON to see the proofs of Brewsie and

[800]

Willie![2] Dish towels went to you weeks ago via Mercury [Joseph] Barry, along with flints, coffee and rice. It seems you wanted these all the time but dish cloths are what Barrie [i.e., Barry] asked for and in department store parlance you wash with these and wipe with towels. Mercury Barry writes me he can still receive packages and now I have Mercury St Christopher [Blake] to send things through too. How heavenly it is, all of it: Saints and Gods everywhere in OUR World! You say "Look up Bill Walton" but you don't say HOW or WHERE, so how can I? but I did see Richard Whorf one day here lunching and he had lunched in Paris the day before and WE TALKED of you. Indeed yes, we talked of you. Giovanni [Bianco] is quite neurotic and is giving up his jobs and going to Florida. I think he finds New York too tame after life with you and Mama Woojums . . . A very good friend of mine MAY go to Berlin on an army job and if he does I'll send him to you . . . Christmas is more Christmas than ever now the Wars are over (?) and everybody is behaving more foolishly than ever (real caviare and champagne in streams as broad as the Amazon) again until Wall Street has another crash or New York is crushed by an atomic bomb . . . The last of my canteens (Service Women's Tea Dance at the Hotel Roosevelt every Sunday) closed last Sunday, but I have God's plenty to do and will begin to photograph a little more extensively now that paper is coming back. This afternoon I am photographing the Mexican painter [Rufino] Tamayo and his beautiful wife. So Happy New Year to you and Mama Woojums from Fania and

Papa Woojums!

1. The idea for a volume of selected writings by Stein is first mentioned in Stein to Van Vechten [29 June 1936]. In a series of letters beginning 25 May [1945] (Columbia–Random House) Stein began urging Cerf to republish some of her works. In an undated letter (? September 1945, Columbia–Random House), Stein wrote Cerf, "You see I think some of my books should be treated like classics and left on sale." In a letter of 15 November [1945] (Columbia–Random House) Stein became insistent with Cerf and chided him for not answering her letters about republishing her books.

Cerf had already been thinking of a volume of Stein's selected writings. On 11 December 1945 (YCAL) he cabled Stein, "Keep your pants on letter that will delight you is on way." On 13 December 1945 (YCAL) Cerf wrote acknowledging the receipt of the typescript of *Brewsie and Willie.* He also announced his plans to publish a one-volume edition of Stein's selected writings. The volume, *Selected Writings of Gertrude Stein,* edited and with an introduction and notes by Van Vechten, was published by Random House on 21 October 1946.

2. "Give Me Land," an interview with Stein by Sergeant Scott Corbett, *Yank,* Continental edition (11 November 1945), 2(16):[17].

❧

To Gertrude Stein and Alice Toklas
[Christmas card]

[? December] 1945

[101 Central Park West
New York]

Dear Darlings both and always may the New Year bring you health,
Peace and blessings.
Our Love is ever with you

Carl, Fania[1]

1. Letter and both signatures by Fania Marinoff.

❧

To Carl Van Vechten

[1 January 1946]
New Year's Day

5 rue Christine
[Paris]

Dearest Papa Woojums,

Happy New Year to you and Fania from us both, made happy New
Year because Jo Barry just came in and said that you were going to edit and
introduce the volume Bennett [Cerf] is intending to do for the Modern Library Giants. I am so pleased, nobody could do it like you, you know Papa
Woojums they used your introduction to Three Lives to announce my lecture to the Belgians in Brussells. And now several things. First Bobby Haas
you remember has been working for a number of years now on an anthology
of my work, but I do not think that has anything to do with this. His is a
book intended principally for universities and to be published by some university press, and is to be something that includes unpublished as well as
published.[1] Now as I understand Bennett's idea and that would entirely suit
me would be that it would contain in full all the what might be called most
popular things such as the Autobiography, Making of Americans, that of course

[802]

would not be in full but a fair slice, Tender Buttons, Four Saints, Mabel Dodge at the Villa Curonia, selected portraits from Portraits and Prayers, and some plays of Geography and Plays and I would like some American things from Useful Knowledge, including 4 Religions and sort of end up with the Atlantic Monthly article The Winner Loses, if there is still room one of the Lectures in America. It would be nice to do it chronologically. I do not see much sense in putting in Three Lives since that is the only book on sale of mine at the present moment in America, nor selections from Wars I have seen which must or should be still in print. I have not yet written to Bennett but I am writing to him by this same mail to tell him my pleasure in it and you,[2] bless you papa Woojums, the sun is shining, so brightly on this the first new year of the peace that it cannot help being a pleasure to all concerned, Basket is going to painted by Marie Laurencin,[3] the opera is getting on fine, it is now to be an opera in two acts with an interlude. The first act ends with a magnificent duet between Susan B [Anthony] and Daniel Webster. Tell Virgil [Thomson], I haven't his address

lots of love
Baby Woojums.

1. Haas had been working for some years on the idea of an anthology of Stein's work, "Primer for Reading Gertrude Stein," that would use Stein's writings to explain herself, to explicate her intentions. This anthology was never published. Haas did, however, edit three collections of Stein's works: A *Primer for the Gradual Understanding of Gertrude Stein, Reflections on the Atomic Bomb,* and *How Writing is Written.*

2. Stein cabled Cerf on 4 January 1946 (Columbia–Random House) that she was delighted with the idea for the book and with the idea that Van Vechten should write an introduction.

3. Stein had known the painter Marie Laurencin (1885–1957) since 1907. Laurencin's portrait of Basket II, oil on canvas, 1946, 18 ⅛ × 15 inches, is now in YCAL.

To Carl Van Vechten

26 January [1946]   5 rue Christine
                                                         [Paris]

My dearest Papa Woojums,

I hope I am not bothering you with too many visitors, it seems that I have been sending you a steady stream recently and perhaps you have not

[803]

yet seen them all, but they do want to see you and we think you like to have them tell you about us, the Bill Walton was the New York Life and Time man, and now there is going to be an actress Norma Chambers who was with us New Year's day and read a lot of the opera and then a Captain [Edward] Geisler who was our cavalier in Belgium, and the dish towels, Alice has never loved anything as much, that lovely blue and the lovely flowers that make the blue, Alice has never loved anything more, and the rice, delicious rice, we have not even yet really realized that rice is ours, bless you both, no I have no connection with the Ann Watkins people, they never did anything for me and I dropped the connection, they were no good. I have very good agents here in France and in England[1] and they sell a lot for me and I really make money but I have never really succeeded in having anybody act for me in America, sorrowfully, you will be pleased to know that a lot of my books are going to be translated in Italian and they pay me well,[2] it is pleasant to be well paid these days because life is xpensive. I am delighted about the Omnibus, when you really have made up your mind, let me know but I know that I will be satisfied with whatever you do. You were awfully good to the young lot of Yes is for a very young man, they write passionate letters of enthusiasm and it would be nice if they were successful with it.[3] Basket has just had his portrait painted by Marie Laurencin, very lovely, and we are all very pleased, all the Mercuries are flourishing and everybody loves you, but more than anybody Baby Woojums, love to you both

Always.
[Gertrude Stein]

1. Stein's English agent was Pearn, Pollinger & Higham Ltd. Their American representative was Ann Watkins, Inc. Mrs. Bradley represented Stein in France.

2. The Italian writer Cesare Pavese had translated Stein's *The Autobiography of Alice B. Toklas* in 1938 and her *Three Lives* in 1940. *Wars I Have Seen, Guerre Che Ho Visto,* translated by Giorgio Minicelli, was published by Arnoldo Mondadori in 1947.

3. Lamont Johnson had written of his visit with Van Vechten in a letter to Stein, 1 January 1946 (YCAL). In the same letter he writes of meeting Virgil Thomson, who played the score of *Four Saints in Three Acts* for him. The letter also asks Stein questions about the play *Yes Is For a Very Young Man* and makes suggestions for changes.

❧

To Gertrude Stein

28 January 1946   101 Central Park West
                                                   New York City 23

Dearest Baby Woojums,

Happy Birthday to you! You write me that Joe Barry came to tell you he had heard from me about the Anthology. Didn't you get an airmail letter from me TOO? I wrote YOU directly before I wrote him. Anyway Bennett [Cerf] called me a week ago to go over the books and make my selections and I had lunch with him and this is what we propose to do:

The Autobiography of Alice B Toklas (complete)
The Gradual Making of the Making of Americans (from Lectures in
        America)
The Making of Americans (selections)
Cezanne, Matisse, Picasso, from Portraits and Prayers
Tender Buttons (complete)
Four Saints (complete)
Melanctha (complete) from Three Lives
Portrait of Mabel Dodge at the Villa Curonia
Have They Attacked Mary–He Giggled
Miss Furr and Miss Ske[e]ne and selected plays from Geography and
        Plays
Wars I Have Seen, Pages 194–246: The Coming of the Americans
Lend a Hand or Four Religions (from Useful Knowledge)
The Winner Loses (Atlantic Monthly, November 1940)
As a Wife Has a Cow
Composition as Explanation

Bennett and I both agree that a chronological order will be bad as we want to begin with the Autobiography, but the above order is certainly not even planned. It is only the titles set down. And we simply will not hear of leaving out Melanctha or the end of Wars I have Seen. You see this Anthology is supposed to last a LONG TIME and must have as much of your best work as we can cram in to it and far from damaging the other sales it will add to them. Bennett has a letter from [James] Laughlin of New Directions requesting him to please use Melanctha as it will help the sale of Three

[805]

Lives and I know Dick Wright would be very mad if we left this out.[1] Bennett was planning this book as a surprise for you. He wanted to hand it to you finished on a platter, but you forced his hand and he had to tell you, but don't you think it will be SOMETHING! He thinks that it will do good business for both of you. . . I am happy to be in it, VERY, VERY happy!

Please answer at ONCE, so that I will know you have this.

Fania and I send lots of love to you and Mama Woojums!

Papa Woojums!

1. In 1941 New Directions reprinted the 1933 Modern Library edition of Stein's *Three Lives*.

Wright had written enthusiastically about "Melanctha," one of the stories in *Three Lives*, in his review of Stein's *Wars I Have Seen*, in *PM*, Sunday Picture News Section, 11 March 1945, p. 15. He had also written about it in "Why I Chose 'Melanctha' by Gertrude Stein," in *I Wish I'd Written That*, ed. Whit Burnett (New York: McGraw-Hill, Inc., 1946), p. 234.

To Carl Van Vechten

5 February [19]46

[5 rue Christine, Paris]

Dearest Papa Woojums

Your birthday letter with the full list just came and it does seem absolutely perfect, the only thing I can suggest is that you include some piece of a child's book, either The World is Round or the First Reader, I imagine the World is Round would be the best, and they certainly would give you permission, that is just one side that should be included, otherwise I think your list is perfect, I can't tell you how happy I am that it is you that is doing it, just as happy as can be, Marie Laurencin just made a photo [i.e., painting] of Basket, I will send you a photo of it soon, and we love you both, and it is I hope not too difficult a world with all those strikes, so much love,

Always
Baby Woojums.

❧

To Gertrude Stein

4 March 1946   101 Central Park West
                                                New York City 23

Dearest Baby Woojums,

It is always pleasant to receive presents and I loved getting The White Cow from you which is a beautiful present, both pictures and text.[1]. And Lamont Johnson sent me Yes is for a Very Young Man, but I had no more than time to glance at it before I had to send it off to Paul Feigay, the manager, who BURNED on the other end of the telephone to receive it, read it, and perhaps produce it. He promised to send it back immediately, but he has not done so which may be good for you, but which is bad for ME. Fania had a chance to read it much more carefully than I; besides she is more familiar with reading scripts and understands them better and she thinks it will act like a charm. Somehow I believed in Lamont Johnson (WHY won't he change his name to the more euphonious Johnson Lamont, it would MAKE HIM) when I met him and his enthusiasm thrills me. He sends me letters and telegrams by every post and wires begging me to come out.[2] He wouldn't have to beg me were the OMNIBUS out of the way, but I am working very intensively on that and must get this work finished before I can go ANYWHERE, even to see a play of YOURS. But I am at white heat with excitement about the whole thing. . I haven't heard from Joe Barry in ages and YOU never answer questions; so I don't know whether you get only his letters or the letters I send you direct TOO. You say you dropped the connection with Ann Watkins, but you don't say if you have written her, dropping it, and asking that she return the manuscripts to ME (TO DO and FIRST READER) They were inscribed to me and besides I might want to send them ELSEWHERE if you will definitely cut off with her. Have I ever sent you any of my color photographs? If not I will presently. And next time you come over I'll take YOU and Mama Woojums in color. In the meantime, PLEASE send me a photograph of Marie Laurencin's Basket. . And what happened to St Christopher Baker [i.e., Blake] who wanted to be a Mercury before Joe Barry found out a way he could continue to be THE Mercury. St Christopher just disappeared. In going over the "SOIL" I find

[807]

[Robert] Coady advertised a pamphlet called "How Could They Marry Her"ˣ (limited to 100 autographed copies at $5). Was this really ever published?[3]

Fania wants to send Alice some more towels and probably will one of these days In the meantime Lots of Love to you both,

Papa W!

I'll send you the complete plan of the Omnibus soon.

Edward Waterman is going to Paris in April and Mary Garden and Dick Wright![4] Quel FUN!

Fania sends a kiss!

Are you going south this summer?

ˣby G.S.

1. Stein's *A Book Concluding With As a Wife Has A Cow A Love Story*, illustrated by Juan Gris.

2. Johnson, who had grown up in California, was living at this time in Pasadena, California.

3. Robert Coady and Michael Brenner, who owned the Washington Square Gallery, published a periodical, *The Soil*. Stein's portrait, "Mrs Th----y," was printed in *The Soil* (December 1916), 1(1):16. Their plans for "How Could He Marry Her" did not materialize. The piece was published posthumously in *Envoy* (January 1951), 14:57–71. Coady and Brenner had had other plans to publish works by Stein. See Stein to Van Vechten [23 February 1917], note 3.

4. In his letter to Stein, 27 May 1945 (in Gallup, *The Flowers of Friendship*, pp. 379–81), Wright reveals his motivations for wanting to come to Paris. See also Michel Fabre, *The Unfinished Quest of Richard Wright* (New York: William Morrow and Co. Inc., 1973), pp. 297–98. Wright hoped to find in Paris a city where a black writer would be treated without prejudice.

&

To Carl Van Vechten

9 March [19]46

[5 rue Christine, Paris]

My dearest Papa Woojums,

I always answer questions yes I do, and I am so happy that Fania liked my play and thinks it will act like a charm, sure we get your letters and actually civilian mail now comes more quickly than military. Jo [Barry] is no longer military, Chris [Blake] still is, and says he has written to you. Ann

Watkins says she lost the ms. just how she managed to do that I don't know, but when I asked her to return them she said that they were lost.[1] I don't think the Soil ever published any book, they intended to and then the Irishman that did it up and died and I am quite certain that nothing else was done.[2] I am so happy that you are doing the omnibus, everyday I am happy about it, Nathalie [Barney] and Romaine [Brooks] stayed in Italy all the time and are still there[3] she is talking about coming to Paris next month, it would be nice if it could be you instead of everybody, we have no plans for the summer yet, we have no house and don't yet quite know what we will do, Alice says to tell you all your pretty stamps came in 5 days, which is the quickest a letter has ever come. The opera is almost finished thanks for Susan B's stamp, I will be sending it to you in a couple of weeks to pass on to Virgil [Thomson], Alice says thanks to Fania, here is Marie Laurencin's Basket, bless you both always and always

Baby Woojums.

I haven't a big enough envelope to put in the photo, will send it next Tuesday, Always

B. W.

1. The typescript of Stein's "To Do: A Book of Alphabets and Birthdays."

2. Stein is referring to the co-owners of the Washington Square Gallery, Robert J. Coady (d. 1921) and Michael Brenner (d. 1969). They had planned to issue a signed edition of Stein's "Letters and Parcels and Wool," as well as other works by Stein. See Van Vechten to Stein, 4 March 1946, note 3.

3. Barney and Brooks had spent the war years in the Villa Sant'Agnese on the outskirts of Florence, Italy.

To Gertrude Stein

15 March 1946   [101 Central Park West
Income Tax Day!   New York]

Beautiful Baby Woojums,

I'd like to be able to give you the exact table of contents or the name of the Omnibus we are preparing, but for the last week we have been struggling with the number of words and copyrights involved and until these matters are settled I see no sense in writing you something that would have to be changed later. At the moment I don't know whether we shall have to indulge in adding or subtracting but I will KNOW SOON and I will let you know. Rest assured that the score is practically what we began with, MAYBE a little more! This morning the following came by wire from Lamont Johnson: "Your wire and four harps saw us through to eight curtain calls and mixed reviews come on out the water is boiling." That is all I know about YES so far. Paul Feigay (curses!) still has my manuscript of this masterpiece.[1] Yesterday Captain [Edward] Geisler called and this morning Norma Chambers. She has been sick, she says, and in Virginia. I hope to see them both prochainement. About the opera, Virgil [Thomson] is coming to Paris the end of April but if you can get it over here before then he would be delighted as he could think it over on the journey. Of course, too I am dying to see it. So I hope it comes THIS way, as you promise in TWO WEEKS. I am working very hard on the Introduction. Is there anything special you want said. . ? If there is, please speak up. Ann Watkins saying she lost the manuscripts is something, really something, in fact four and six and a buggy full, n'est-ce pas? I am sending you and Alice more towels with blue leaves by Edward Waterman who goes over in April. He has a brown caniche named Christopher, I am impatient to see Marie Laurencin's idea of Basket. In this letter of yours which has just come you have answered every questions, yes you have, every one, and am I delighted and pleased and enchanted. Here is another question, perhaps not very important. In looking over your letters for the past few years before I wrote my introduction, to see if I wanted to use something (and I did) I ran across five references (in five different letters) to the dedication of the First Reader.[2] You said it was to be dedicated to ME? Did you mean spiritually or did the printer at Algier leave it out or did you change your mind? . . . . . So I am sending you a color photograph I made of ME so you can see what they are like. They are better projected LIFE SIZE on a screen, but they are pretty good this way and I am dying to immortalize you and Alice in Color and as Mae West says so feelingly (or was it Bert Savoy?) you MUST come over. . The world is in a turmoil and most everybody is pretty neurotic but YOU and Mama Woojums and Papa W. So I'll write you more any minute and YOU write ME and Fania and I send love to you both!

P. W!

[810]

F[ania] M[arinoff] is playing The Empress of Austria (Franz Joseph's Frau) in a piece on the Radio Sunday night.[3]

O yes. Richard Wright was here the other night and he said he had sent you Black Metropolis & you had never got it and I said send another through Joe Barry. Is this wrong? and won't you get this?[4]

1. In 1946 Paul Feigay (d. 1983) was beginning his career as a producer of Broadway plays, television, ballet, and sports events.

2. See Stein to Van Vechten, 15 October 1942, note 3.

3. Marinoff played the role of Elizabeth, Empress of Austria, in Maxwell Anderson's play *The Masque of Kings*. The play, part of a series, *Theatre Guild on the Air*, was broadcast on station WJZ, New York, from 10 to 11 P.M., Sunday, 17 March 1946.

4. Wright's Introduction in Horace R. Clayton and St. Clair Drake's *Black Metropolis* (New York: Harcourt, Brace and Co., Inc., 1945), pp. xvii–xxxiv. The book is a study of Chicago's South-Side black ghetto.

To Carl Van Vechten

18 March [19]46

[5 rue Christine,
Paris]

Dearest Papa Woojums

Here is the opera,[1] will you read it and then pass it on to Virgil [Thomson], I guess the play went well, have just had some xcited cables,[2] I am so happy about your doing the Omnibus so happy lots of love

Baby Woojums.

1. Stein's *The Mother of Us All*.

2. *Yes Is For a Very Young Man* was given its first performance at the Pasadena Playhouse, Pasadena, California, on 13 March 1946. It ran until 24 March. Lamont Johnson and his wife had been writing Stein regularly to give reports on the progress of the play.

❧

To Gertrude Stein

26 March 1946   101 Central Park West
                                                       New York City 23

Dearest Baby Woojums,

I think we are now fairly certain what we are going to print in the Collected Gertrude Stein (or whatever it will be called) and so I am sending you the table of contents in the proper order with the advice that you never can tell what publishers will do and that still more *may* be cut out, but I *don't* think so, I really *don't* think so.[1]

The Autobiography of Alice by Toklas (complete)
The Gradual Making of the Making of Americans (Lectures in
          America)
The Making of Americans (selected passages)
Three portraits of painters (Portraits and Prayers)
          Cezanne
          Matisse
          Picasso
Melanctha (complete)
Tender Buttons (complete)
Composition as Explanation (complete)
Portrait of Mabel Dodge at the Villa Curonia
Have They Attacked Mary. He Giggled.
As a Wife has a Cow.
Two Poems:
          Susie Asado
          Preciosilla
Two Plays:
          Ladies' Voices
          What Happened
Miss Furr and Miss Ske[e]ne
A Sweet Tail (Gypsies)
Four Saints in Three Acts (complete)
The Winner Loses (complete)

The Coming of the Americans (from Wars I Have Seen, beginning
  with "Well that was yesterday," on page 194 to the end of the
  book, p. 259)

The World Is Round was ruled out before we began as it is too long complete and it cannot easily be cut. Only yesterday I learned that we would be obliged to take out Lend a Hand or Four Religions (Useful Knowledge). I hope you won't feel too badly about these omissions. There are lots of other things I wanted, O so badly, to include too, but as it is it runs to nearly 300,000 words which seems to be about all we can include at a popular price. Besides an introduction, I am writing short notes to go before each piece and a photograph by me will be used as a frontispiece.

Directly everything was settled, I wrote Bobby Haas immediately and told him I had been invited to edit such a Collection but did not see how it would interfere with HIS plans, but he has not replied. Maybe he is MAD. Personally I think there is room for more than one Gertrude Stein Anthology and if this one is a success, probably Bennett [Cerf] himself will issue another of entirely different material later.

You have still left unanswered the question about Paul Genin's manuscript Mon Livre du Pourquoi which came to me, directed from Bilignin (YEARS ago) in Alice Toklas's hand, only recently released by the British censor. What is this and what do you want me to do with it?

I don't think I told you Mrs [Frank] Case died and that I was one of the ushers at her funeral. She had cancer of the lungs and has suffered needless torture for over two years. We hadn't seen her for a year and a half before she died. Frank is in a very bad way about this because he depended on her for everything.

It is marvellous in Brewsie and Willie how you have got the AT-MOSPHERE and the VERNACULAR. Everybody is patting you on the back even before the book is out. And there is a very nice review of YES est pour un très jeun homme in Time.[2] "Montie" Johnson says he is sending *you* everything and you will find a photograph by me on the cover. Of the program . . Some of the Western reviews were good, some just plain silly. Montie (I do wish this nice boy would change his name!) telephoned and telegraphed and wrote me all the time it was going on and I was very unhappy I couldn't go out, but the Gertrude Stein Omnibus and other duties kept me HERE.

So I send love to you and Mama Woojums and so does Fania and I

[813]

HOPE to hear from you pronto that everything is okay and the Omnibus is already on its way to the PRINTER. Quelle chance, Baby Woojums, and Glory Glory Hallelujah!

Papa Woojums
HIMSELF![3]

1. This list became the contents of the volume *Selected Writings of Gertrude Stein*.

2. "Yes and No," *Time*, 25 March 1946, p. 67.

3. In Stein's hand at the bottom of page 2 of Van Vechten's letter: "110 lines by the author if can manage."

To Carl Van Vechten

1 April [1946]   [5 rue Christine,
                                                      Paris]

Dearest Papa Woojums,

So pleased with all Papa Woojums himself has done, so pleased, we are all pleased, a tear for Four Religions but I know in this world you can't have everything and what you do have is pretty dam good bless you Papa Woojums bless you. About the Paul Genin ms. no that's nothing, it was something then but nothing now, all that is over, we have even lost sight of each other, he was a neighbor and a nice neighbor down there then, but since then, well there is nothing now.[1] I am glad you like Brewsie and Willie, I think it kind of handsome myself, I think I really got them as they were, it was pretty wonderful and I got them, lots and lots of love to you and Fania, dear ones, bless you

Always
Baby Woojums and Mama Woojums.[2]

1. The Genins remained in their home near Belley after the war. They made only occasional trips to Paris in 1945–46.

2. Both names signed by Stein.

[814]

❧

To Gertrude Stein

6 April 1946   [101 Central Park West
                                                     New York]

Chere and Beautiful Baby Woojums,

Yesterday The Mother of Us All arrived and this morning your letter.[1] I read the former and sent it on to Virgil [Thomson]. It seems I never
get really time to read your manuscripts[x] before somebody screams for them,
but I am *sure* The Mother of Us All is perfectly delightful and in a new
manner or at least a new combination of manners. Virgil will like those si-
lences[x(2)] and his own part (I wonder if he will sing it?) . . My favorite part,
after Susan B, is Jo the Loiterer! What a character! Will the Captain sing
this luimême? Well, I can't wait for Virgil to set this and I can't wait to hear
and see it on the stage. I don't think this one can be done with Negroes and
of course Florine [Stettheimer] is no longer with us; so there will be an entirely new setup. I wonder if Mary Garden still has voice enough to sing
Susan B? She would be magnificent in it! . . . . . Now I am worried because
you don't mention the Color Picture of Papa Woojums I sent you air-mail
way back. Did you get this? Anyway here is one of Fania and I can't wait
till I take you and Mama W in COLOR. The other one should have reached
you as I put about forty dollars worth of stamps on it, so many indeed, there
was scarcely room for the address. But you will let me know. I'm glad I
don't have to worry about the Paul Genin mss. .[2] Have you heard from Bennett [Cerf]? The book is to be called COLLECTED WRITINGS OF Gertrude Stein. This is Bennett's title and I think it is a good one, dignified and
completely explanatory. I am calling my introduction A Stein Song, principally because it seems intended to be sung. Like an ODE, perhaps. I hope
you will like it and the notes with which I have prefaced each piece. I am
delighted you are pleased with the contents. . I wanted to put much more
in but we already have nearly 300,000 words which is out of this world. .
Let's have another omnibus in a year or two with MORE GS. . . The
NOTES have gone to the printer together with YOUR copy, and I shall
finish the Introduction in a few days. It is all done now except making the
FOURTH draft with a few final changes. . It is expected to appear (COL-
LECTED WRITINGS) early in September. Brewsie and Willie will be out

[815]

any minute. So you will have to take a lot of boys [i.e., bows] this year, both in the Spring and the Fall. . . . The Metropolitan is having a retrospective show of the taste of 1870:[3] Rosa Bonheur and Cabanel and Bouguereau. I haven't been yet but I'm sure I'll love it. I haven't seen Cabanel's Birth of Venus in fifty years but I shall always remember it as one of my first [SLI?]DES. As for Rosa's Horse Fair! . . Knoedler's is doing something of the sort[4] [word?][5] Have you heard about Peggy Guggenheim's book in which she sets off torpedoes under all the beds she has slept in?[6] The Ballet comes back tomorrow[7] and we are going to a party for [Alicia] Markova and [Anton] Dolin. We expect to give a dinner with the Pearl Bucks, the Lin Yutangs, and the Richard Wrights before Dick sails to Paris. Tomorrow it is also Somerset Maugham. Dish towels I repeat go to you by Edward (I) Waterman. . . . . The weather is warm as warm and spring is here. The park in front of us blooms. I HOPE YOU WILL LIKE what I have written for YOUR book. YOUR OWN BOOK, with as many of my favorites as we could get in. We must have another, later, Baby Woojums, WE MUST. Lots of love to you both. . . . . . .

Papa Woojums!

[x]as many times as I like to

[x] [(2)]They are terrific

O yes, Montie Johnson has written me several times, but I suppose he writes you whatever he has to write. I wish I might have seen YES. My scouts (of which I have many) report the acting was none too hot, especially Mrs. [Jane] Claborne.[8] But TIME came across with a very good review.

---

1. In *The Mother of Us All* it is Susan B. Anthony's fight for women's suffrage that provides a connective tissue to Stein's panoramic overview of nineteenth-century America. Maurice Grosser, as he had done for *Four Saints in Three Acts*, developed a scenario for *The Mother of Us All*.

The opera is a pageant that presents the interaction of people, both historical and fictitious characters taken from many walks of life: Daniel Webster, Lillian Russell, Ulysses S. Grant, John Quincy Adams, and Anthony Comstock mingle with Susan B. Anthony and her companion Anne as well as with the Narrators, Virgil T. and Gertrude S., and two Civil War veterans, Chris the Citizen and Jo the Loiterer (based on Joseph Barry).

2. Van Vechten gave the typescript of Genin's book to YCAL.

3. *The Taste of the Seventies* was an exhibition celebrating the seventy-fifth anniversary of the Metropolitan Museum of Art, New York. The exhibition included Alexandre Cabanel's *The Birth of Venus*, Marie Rosa Bonheur's *The Horse Fair*, and William Adolphe Bougereau's *The Two Sisters*. The exhibition ran from 2 April to 3 September 1946.

4. To mark their one hundredth anniversary, M. Knoedler and Company, a firm of art dealers, mounted an exhibition of paintings that had been purchased by New York's Metropolitan Museum of Art through Knoedler.

5. A cigarette burn in the paper makes it impossible to read this word.

6. Peggy Guggenheim's *Out of This Century: The Informal Memories of Peggy Guggenheim* (New York: The Dial Press, 1946).

7. Ballet Theatre (American Ballet Theatre) opened a season at the Metropolitan Opera House, New York, 7 to 13 and then 21 April to 4 May 1946.

8. Jane Claborne played the role of Denise in *Yes Is For a Very Young Man* at the Pasadena Playhouse.

To Carl Van Vechten

9 April [19]46   5 rue Christine
                                                      [Paris]

My dearest Papa Woojums,

I am so pleased that you liked the Mother of us all. I was pretty pleased with it myself, and Papa Woojums are you sure I did not tell you about your colored photo, there it has been on the mantel-piece side by side with the cover of Brewsie and Willie[1] and admired by all beholders and now Fania has joined too and they do look handsome, we would love to be photoed the same way and also, it is very handsome, do send me the introduction as soon as it is done we are looking forward tremendously to seeing it, yes I think the title is very satisfactory, and everything, I am sorry that they didn't act better in Yes, but then they were the only ones who would act at all, and I did want it acted, they were nice kids, I hope they can go on, so much love. Now they will all be coming I wish it were you,

Always
B. W.

1. The jacket for *Brewsie and Willie* had been designed by E. McKnight Kauffer. The book was designed by Ernest Reichl, who had also designed Stein's *Lectures In America* and *Portraits and Prayers*.

[817]

To Gertrude Stein

17 April 1946

101 Central Park West
New York City 23

Dearest Baby Woojums,

I turned the Introduction in yesterday to Bennett [Cerf] and we also settled on the photographs we are using. For a frontispiece: You and Mama Woojums in the garden at Bilignin (XXXII F 29) and for the jacket head of GS in the garden (XXXII F 12). I cannot send you the Introduction NOW[x] because I haven't a fair copy. Besides I always make corrections in proof and I wouldn't want you to see one thing now and another in print. SO as soon as the proofs are ready, I'll send you the "Stein Song" transferring any changes I make to your set. So far Bennett seems enormously pleased with everything I have done. He was most enthusiastic about the "notes" and now I hope that you will be pleased. Bobby Haas turned up yesterday and I was amazed to find him a pretty young boy with a great deal of charm. He doesn't seem mad either. He showed me his plan for HIS anthology of GS and I like it enormously, but it is scarcely a commercial anthology and he may have to wait for a time to see it in print. Personally I'd like to see all these handsome books ABOUT you in print, Julian Sawyer and the others, whatever their quality, as that would add to the discussion, but nothing could add to your éclat, your superb eminence, or your literary distinction, to say nothing of your charm! Bobby Haas says he is coming back in June and I hope he does because I like him and he adores and worships you. He sighed as he cried "I was born in the wrong time!" He meant he hadn't met you yet. This surprised me considerably because I had always taken it for granted that you knew him. . . I talked with Virgil [Thomson] AT LENGTH about The Mother of Us All, over the telephone, and "sensational" was the word he used. . . He is enchanted with it and I've no doubt it will inspire him to terrific efforts of creation. The BEST part, of course, is Joe the Loiterer and Captain [Joseph] Barry is to be congratulated. That is almost sure to run away with the opera! I mean of course the best part for men. Susan B is a good enough rôle for any star. Virgil thinks Mary [Garden] hasn't voice enough any more for this and at the same time he finds her too sexy. But he'll dig up something tremendous, I predict.[1] This all adds up to a newer and BET-

TER Four Saints. I haven't yet received a photograph of [Marie] Laurencin's Basket. Has this been sent yet? . . . The color pictures I have sent you are originally films to be projected on a screen, life size or bigger. The reproduction processes are still in their infancy and will be improved. The colors on the screen are astonishingly accurate and the portraits appear to be three dimensional . . I have long series of some people and events. Tomorrow night, for instance, I am showing my pictures of [Alicia] Markova (some 361 in the series) in all her dancing roles. Brewsie and Willie apparently will be out in June and Collected Writings of GS in October, but paper, printing, binding, etc. are SLOW nowadays and unpredictable. You never KNOW. So love to you both from Fania and

Papa Woojums!

Your latest reply got back in just a minute over a week from the time my airmail envelope went to YOU!

˟Bennett just called up to say he is very enthusiastic about it!

1. *The Mother of Us All* opened at Brander Matthews Hall at Columbia University on 7 May 1947. The opera was conducted by Otto Luening and was staged by the choreographer John Taras. Dorothy Dow sang the role of Susan B.

❧

To Gertrude Stein

30 April 1946

101 Central Park West
New York City 23

Dearest Baby Woojums,

The Richard Wrights, securing a passport at the very last moment, sail tomorrow (May 1) on the S S Brazil! They are excited. I am sure you will like them. Here are the latest pictures I took of him on March 8, but they were here for dinner one day last week with Pearl Buck and her husband, the Lin Yutangs, Mrs James Weldon Johnson, and Antony Tudor the choreographer. . . which reminds me to ask you if Lord Berners ever finished Faust. . Montie Johnson and his wife[1] and Mrs [Jane] Claborne are here now and they came to see me the other day. They are very sweet people and somehow I feel they are right for your play, no matter what any one says. I am helping them all I can, which isn't much, I'm afraid, because nobody can help anybody much in the direction of the theatre. . As I wrote you some time ago ALL the STEIN book has gone to the printer and proofs, I hope, will begin to come in before long. As soon as I have made corrections, and perhaps some changes, in a set of galley proofs I'll send the introduction along to you pronto, hoping it will please you. . . Virgil [Thomson] read The Mother of Us All aloud to the YES people from Pasadena and they adored it. Everybody agrees so far that Joe the Loiterer is the Part of PARTS. Can Joe [Barry] sing? . . The ballet is here and we go practically every night to see the great [Alicia] Markova and this afternoon we are going for the third time to see the film version of Henry V, by Laurence Olivier. This great film has not yet been released here but occasional private showings are given to special people and we are taking Markova and the Eugene O'Neills today. . So, you'll here [i.e., hear] from me soon and Fania and I send our love to you both,

Papa Woojums!

I HOPE you have the towels that Edward Waterman is bringing you from us. We flew over last week.

1. Toni Merrill, the actress.

To Carl Van Vechten

14 May [1946]   5 rue Christine
                                                                      [Paris]

Dearest Papa Woojums,

They have all come, [Edward] Waterman, the towels, so much thanks, Dick [Wright] and family, Virgil [Thomson], and we have been busy, particularly with Dick and family,[1] saw Virgil at the train where I went to meet Dick and family, and have not seen him since but xpect to soon, Waterman is very happy slightly on the over wt., he does look a little heavy, but so happy, Dick and family are so happy they about are bursting with it, the french have been very good to him, we have been a lot together, I have introduced him to Jo [Barry] and Chris [Blake], and all the young ones, and they get along fine, everybody is pleased, this is just to tell you so, dear papa Woojums, and love to Fania, and everything,

Always
Baby Woojums.

1. Wright and his family arrived at Le Havre, France, on Thursday, 9 May. They reached Paris the next day. Stein had cabled Wright on 8 May 1946 (Yale-JWJ) that she had reserved rooms for him at the Trianon Palace Hotel and that she would meet him at the train station. Stein had also enlisted the assistance of Douglas Schneider, director of the United States Information Service in Paris, in arranging for publicity about Wright to appear in French newspapers. See Schneider to Stein, 4 and 7 May 1946 (YCAL).

To Gertrude Stein

10 June 1946

[101 Central Park West
New York]

Beautiful Baby Woojums,

Here, at LONG enfin, is *your* introduction. I'm sorry you've had to wait a minute but printers take for ever these days. In the meantime it has been WEEKS since you have written; I have heard nothing from or about the Wrights (except a few lines about Julia in a letter from St Christopher and St Stanislas);[1] I have heard nothing from Virgil [Thomson] about how the OPERA is progressing; and Joe the Loiterer hasn't written. I have seen Montie Johnson and his wife and Jane Claborne again. Fania and I went there for dinner one night, Montie cooking. They have Virgil's apartment and are very comfortable and happy. Jane Claborne came in. She is rehearsing (The Man Who Came to Dinner: this is the piece about Alec Woollcott) and will soon go abroad again with it in an USO outfit.[2] Montie has a radio job but he has his eye peeled more and more for possible productions of YES. We like these young people enormously. And I have photographed them. Bobbie Haas writes that he is arriving the end of the week to stay some time.[3] Also I ran into Mrs [William A.] Bradley somewhere or other and we had a long talk and frequently mentioned GS with enthusiasm. I wrote you that Bertha Case died in February. Frank [Case] died last week and I am an usher at his funeral tomorrow at the Church of the Transfiguration (known usually as the Little Church Around the Corner).[4] This is the fourth funeral at which I have officiated since January 1. I think I wrote you that Mrs [Channing] Pollock died. Edward Waterman writes he is seeing you and Mama Woojums.[5] How I envy him! And his descriptions make Paris sound very glamorous indeed. So love and embraces to you both!

Papa Woojums!

You may keep these proofs as I have another set. . .

1. Blake had written Van Vechten on 16 May 1946 (YCAL) reporting on the arrival of the Wrights in Paris. Blake and the Wrights were staying in the same hotel, but they soon quarreled (see Blake to Van Vechten, 5, 6, and 23 August 1946, YCAL). Stanislas was Blake's middle name and Van Vechten had christened him St. Stanislas (see Blake to Van Vechten, 11 March 1946, YCAL).

2. A play by George Kaufman and Moss Hart. In the play the character based on Alexander Woollcott rings up Gertrude Stein every Christmas Eve so he can hear the bells of Notre Dame.

3. Haas to Van Vechten [postmark 5 June 1946], YCAL.

4. Frank Case was the owner of the Algonquin Hotel in New York.

5. Possibly Waterman to Van Vechten, 8 May [1946], YCAL.

❦

To Carl Van Vechten

14 June [19]46　　　　　　　　　　　　　　　5 rue Christine
　　　　　　　　　　　　　　　　　　　　　　[Paris]

Dearest Papa Woojums,

The introduction has just come and it is marvelously balanced, and contains everything, it is perfectly xtraordinary the way you have made it an introduction that all can see, and at the same time an introduction for you and for me, it's made us very happy, it keeps level and it moves around, I don't think anybody has ever handled quotations like that, thanks and thanks again, dear dearest papa Woojums, I have not written for some time first I was waiting for the introduction, then busy with Dick Wright, then had an attack of colitis, then bought a car and then life got complicated, and now the introduction has come, and we have calmed down, Nathalie [Barney] has come too, we had a long long talk about you the other day, Romaine [Brooks] is still in Italy full of complications, but then that is life just now, peace is much more troublesome than war, and then I xpected Brewsie and Willie and it has not come and now I have frantically written to Bennett [Cerf] to know the reason why,[1] and now about the Wrights, it is a long and also complicated story, he interests me immensely, he is strange, I have a lot of theories about him and sometime when it all gets straightened out I'll tell you, of course there was a bit of difficulty on account of the wife and child, she is rather awful, and the child terribly spoiled, and we had finally to sort of give it up, it was too fatiguing, but then in spite of giving it up it just has gone on, he has made quite clear to me the whole question of the Negro problem, the black white the white black, are they white or are they black, is Dick white or is he black, in his particular case it is very interesting, more so than in any of the others I have ever met, well I got to think a lot more before I can say anything, I said to him, your next book can't be Black boy, that is camouflage, you got to find out more than that, I think he knows what I mean. Virgil [Thomson] as yet answers nothing new about the opera, we have cut him out as a character and I think that is right,[2] I have heard nothing from the Montie Johnsons, but I guess they are most awfully busy, thanks again, and so much sun-shine, and we need it, because it rains, of the introduction and love and love and love to you and Fania, from

Mama and Baby Woojums.[3]

1. Stein was extremely impatient to receive copies of *Brewsie and Willie*. On 12 June and then again on 14 and 15 June she wrote Cerf asking him why there was a delay in the publication of the book. (Stein to Cerf, Columbia–Random House). Cerf replied on 19 June 1946 (YCAL) explaining that the delay had been caused by a strike at the bindery. In the same letter he asked Stein to send him two or three pages to be used in the *Selected Writings* that would tell what she thought of the selection and of Van Vechten's foreword.

2. The character Virgil T. remained in the opera. He and the character Gertrude S. are the narrators of the work.

3. Both signatures by Stein.

Gertrude Stein in a small room at 5 rue Christine, April 1946.

🐿

To Gertrude Stein

19 June 1946   101 Central Park West
                                                  New York City 23

Dearest Baby Woojums,

Your letter arrived this morning and made me very happy. You can imagine I was in a sweat until I found out whether or no you liked the introduction. There will be notes too, but the way these are printed I'd vastly prefer you read them when the book comes out. Each Selection is prefaced by a brief note of explanation, dating it, etc. . These are both factual and entertaining. .[x] Bennett [Cerf] (who has gone off somewhere in a SUBMARINE) has surely written you about Brewsie and Willie.[1] This book has been stalled by a binder's strike or something equivalent but now is due on the 15th of July. Selected Writings is due in October. . . I can't make head or tail of what you say of the [Richard] Wrights. As a matter of fact you say you will write more clearly when the complications of describing him clear up a little. I've never seen the baby. I wish somebody would send me Dick's address. He could do it himself but probably won't. I have wanted it several times as I do not think YOU should be bothered with forwarding mail or visitors to him! Get one of the Mercurys to send it to me. I am sorry Virgil [Thomson] has come out of The Mother of Us All. I liked Virgil's part, but Joe the Loiterer is my FAVORITE. Oh, yes, one of the papers says Dick is leaving Paris for Mexico. . . Any truth in that?[2] Has he given any conferences? Were they good? O dear, why doesn't he write me? . Montie [Johnson] telephoned a few minutes ago to say he has been engaged for the first three plays in the summer season at Westport which is nice. I like him so much and also his wife and also Jane Claborne, whose husband has stayed in the West.[3] So I had four birthday parties this year. The Ballet Theatre is going to London tomorrow to appear at Covent Garden. I wish you and Mama Woojums were in London to see Hugh Laing, and the others, but particularly Hugh Laing. So lots of love to both of you,

Papa Woojums!

[x]I hope!!!
Bobby Haas writes he will be in New York this season (summer)[4]

[825]

1. Cerf had cabled Stein on 13 June 1946 (YCAL) about the publication date of *Brewsie and Willie*.

2. Wright remained in Europe until 11 January 1947, when he sailed from Southampton, England, to New York.

3. Robert Claborne, who had played the role of Henri in the Pasadena Playhouse production of *Yes Is For a Very Young Man*.

4. Haas to Van Vechten [postmark 5 June 1946], YCAL.

To Carl Van Vechten

[postmark: 24 June 1946]   [5 rue Christine,
                                                             Paris]

My dearest Papa Woojums,

Bennett [Cerf] asked me to do a little testimonial and here it is and I hope it is alright, dear papa Woojums it is thrilling, these days so far away bless you, love to Fania bless you[1]

Always
Baby Woojums.

1. See Stein to Van Vechten, 14 June [19]46, note 1. Cerf acknowledged receipt of Stein's foreword, which he titled, "A Message from Gertrude Stein," on 27 June 1946 (YCAL). In the Modern Library editions this "message" has always been dated "Paris June 18, 1946." The date does not appear in the manuscript. The idea for including the date was Van Vechten's.

On 4 August 1946 (Columbia–Random House) Van Vechten wrote to Saxe Commins, an editor at Random House, that he was convinced that "A Message from Gertrude Stein" should have a Paris dateline, just as his "A Stein Song" had a New York dateline. Van Vechten suggested that if he did not have the actual date on the piece he should approximate it.

🐉

To Carl Van Vechten

27 June 1946

[5 rue Christine, Paris]

My dearest Papa Woojums

I am sending you in duplicate the changes that Monty [Johnson] has just written to me for, I have sent him a copy but in case it gets lost here is another.[1] They were charming photos you made of Monty, he looks almost like an early renaissance head, very lovely and you want to know about Dick Wright, well it's kind of funny, oh no he is not going to Mexico, he is having a huge success here, being very feted by all the french all the salons and the intellectuals, having a perfectly fine time, and do I like him, well I don't know, there is a strange materialism about him that is not at all Negro, in fact he does not seem to me very Negro, I didn't think his books were but now it is stronger, is it island, or Hindoo, what is it? I have told him that I am meditating about him, but I don't tell him what I meditate, it's a kind of materialism a feeling about money, about women that is not Negro not American. You see I kept saying his books were not Negro, that is what I liked in them so much, but now when he isn't, do I like it so much? I tell you all I think and I tell him or will so that's alright, I have told him some. Dearest Papa Woojums that's the way I feel about it, and in between I read your introduction and it is a comfort to me.

Lots of love
Baby Woojums.

1. The Lamont Johnson–Stein correspondence is all at YCAL. Johnson had suggested certain changes in *Yes Is For a Very Young Man*. Stein's added scene, however, arrived too late for the Pasadena Playhouse production. The first complete production of the play, incorporating all the changes Stein made, was given by the University Players, Princeton University, for two weeks beginning 26 July 1948.

To Gertrude Stein

28 June 1946   101 Central Park West
                                                New York City 23

Dearest Baby Woojums,

Well the "testimonial" arrived and it is beautiful and everybody is crazy about it and Papa Woojums is very much touched and feels very nostalgic and wishes he had a white pleated shirt to put on so that he could look and feel the way he did in 1914[1] and a few minutes later Saxe Commins called to say that the First Reader, published in Dublin, and dedicated to Papa Woojums had arrived, and this is a most complete surprise and I am in tears. . . Are you sending me a copy of this, I hope? Are you sending it quick, I hope? Are you inscribing it, I HOPE. . . . . I can't wait. And Saxe says that Brewsie and Willie is at last printed and I am getting a copy this afternoon! And you will get one as soon as it can be sent to you. You will be interested to know that Selected Works is already completely in galley proofs and that I have corrected all my parts. This is way ahead of schedule but I dare say a printer's or binder's strike can hold us up yet. BUT I HOPE NOT. THIS LETTER IS TO THANK YOU FOR EVERYTHING and to say I HOPE WE'LL be associated always in charming projects of this character, and that I hope I can take some color photographs of you SOON. Montie Johnson, Toni Merrill, and Jane Claborne, dined with us at a Chinese place the other night. He is going into summer stock. We like them a lot. Bobby Haas wrote me he was coming to New York two or three weeks ago and promised to ring me but that is the last I have heard of *that*. So lots of love to you and Mama Woojums and I'm very excited about the future of Selected Works and Brewsie and Willie and the FIRST READER. . . .

Papa Woojums!

Fania is going to Marblehead for a couple of weeks, but I stay here and read proofs and work on my Collections.

1. Van Vechten means 1913. The reference is to the shirt he wore to a performance of *Le Sacre du Printemps* which Stein described in her first portrait of Van Vechten.

To Gertrude Stein

8 July 1946

101 Central Park West
New York City 23

Dearest Baby Woojums,

Brewsie and Willie reads even better the second time. I am tremendously impressed by your ear for the vernacular and hope the future will give us more evidences of this supernal gift. But these boys and girls in their struggle towards truth and solutions for problems are both typical and touching and you have nailed them to the cross to be gazed at and studied permanently and to be worried about and to be loved too. . I won't say it is your best book, but I don't know why not! Your letter with the addition to YES came too and I called the Johnsons at once. Montie had gone to Westport to act in some plays there and Toni wasn't sure whether or not he had received his copy, but I haven't heard from him; so I guess he did. . . I am very much interested in what you write about Richard Wright. . . You see I never think of whether any one is Negro or NOT Negro; I only think of whether I like anybody or not. Or does he interest me? Or do I like his work, and as far as Dick is concerned I answer all these questions in the affirmative. . . but races as races mean very little to me. . . . . I know so many, and I get them all mixed up. . Only Indians stand out like sore thumbs and I knew one splendid Indian who didn't![1] I am working on the proofs of the notes for Selected Writings of Gertrude Stein, and I think these will amuse YOU and educate the others. They are informative, but they are not dull, I believe. That you liked the preface is a great joy to me and everybody else who has read it so far has been most enthusiastic. If I write enough introductions to your work I'll really learn in the end how to write about you to perfection! . . We all loved the "message" you sent us and of course that is going into the book too! In the meantime I burn for the Irish edition of the FIRST READER and I hope you can get me one before I completely burn up! Edward Waterman writes me frequently and usually mentions your name and sometimes even quotes you and that is a pleasure. How does the opera go? I haven't had a line from Virgil [Thomson].

Fania and I send lots of love to you both.

Carlo

[829]

1. It is difficult to know to which "Indians" Van Vechten is referring. He may be alluding to the Indian dancer Ram Gopal and his sister, of whom he took several photographs. He might also be referring to American Indians. During the 1920s he knew Chief Long Lance, a Native American, who lived in Manhattan and who was a popular figure (and not in feathers and warpaint). I am grateful to Bruce Kellner for this suggestion.

To Carl Van Vechten
[Cablegram]

27 July 1946 [Paris]

DEAREST PAPA WOOJAMS

BABY WOOJAMS PASSED SUDDENLY TODAY YOUR LOVING MAMA WOOJAMS

MAMA WOOJAMS.

To Alice Toklas
[Telegram]

[postmark: 28 July 1946] New York

DEAREST MAMMA WOOJUMS

OUR DEEPEST SYMPATHY AND LOVE TO YOU

FANIA AND PAPA WOOJUMS.

Coda

To Alice Toklas

28 July 1946

101 Central Park West
New York City 23

Dearest Mama Woojums,

Your telegram was heartbreaking. It came to me early this morning, brought in by a young girl. I hadn't had the slightest preparation for this. Only Montie Johnson told me a few days ago that some one just back from Paris reported Gertrude hadn't been well. But Baby Woojums' letters to me were full of health and cheer and I am so happy she received the preface to Selected Writings and approved. Also she probably knows that YES is going on this fall, altho Montie only knew himself last Tuesday. But he cabled and wrote at once and we HOPE SHE KNEW.[1] . It is wonderful to remember I have known you both since 1913 without a break. . . but it is horrible to realize that *her* part of the communication can no longer exist. Those who knew her only through the greatness of her work will never know how great she could also be in friendship! . . It seems as if Selected Works had been arranged for by Divinity to appear at the exact moment when they are most needed. . . but much more will eventually be revived. However, I always had it in mind to preserve as much as possible of the most important pieces in this one volume so that any reader might form his own conclusions of her work from a study of this book alone. I hope you will write us as soon as you can to tell us as much as you can. You have our very deepest sympathy and love and if you need assistance on any details of all the thousand and one things that will come up now and in the future you can always turn to Fania and

Papa Woojums!

[833]

1. Lamont Johnson had cabled Stein on 24 July 1946 that arrangements had been completed to present *Yes Is For a Very Young Man* in a New York production. This plan, however, fell through. Johnson and Robert Claborne did not realize their hopes for a New York production until the play opened at the off-Broadway Cherry Lane Theatre, New York, on 6 June 1949. See Gallup, *The Flowers of Friendship*, p. 401.

To Carl Van Vechten and Fania Marinoff

[31 July 1946] Wednesday

[5 rue Christine Paris]

Dearest Fania and dearest Papa Woojums—

When I came back Saturday evening I sent off the wire and put out the envelope and paper and now I'm trying to tell you every thing. For us who loved our Baby Woojums so completely it should be easy to say it all— but the emptiness is so very—very great—and more intensely when I am with you. But there are many many things you must know and gradually you will know them all. Baby told me all over again about a week ago how you had been her most loyal friend from the beginning and how wonderful it was that you had done the perfect introduction. It was one of the three last pleasures Baby was given—it and the two first copies of Brewsie and Willie and the telegram from Montie saying the play was going on. It was a miracle that everything happened in time. I must wait longer but try to tell you at once everything that happened. After the trip to Belgium just before Christmas Baby complained of being tired and said she wouldn't go about so much and we'd see fewer people—it had been too exhausting—the occupation and seeing nearly the whole American army.[1] But in April the doctor said she needed to be built up and then an operation. And Baby said she wanted to feel strong again but refused the operation—and then she felt better but was growing very thin. And finally she consented to go away from Paris to the Sarthe to a lovely house a friend was lending us.[2] But there suddenly the day after our arrival there was a short but very painful attack and when it was over Baby felt better and we stayed on until Thursday when she finally consented to go back to Paris—and we went to the American hospital at Neuilly—both of us full of hope—planning to return to the Sarthe in September.[3] All the great specialists were called and said that Baby must be given a treatment for several days to insure success—and then last Friday morning they refused to undertake it. Tired suffering Baby dismissed them all and said she never wanted to see any of them again. She was furious and frightening and impressive like she was thirty years and more ago when her work was attacked. And then we got Valerie-Radot and Leriche and they consented because she implored them to. And Leriche told me that three years ago the risk would have been very great.[4] And he said never had any one been so sick and not suffered a hundred times more—just two weeks of suffering—that her body was as strong and as sane as her mind. And oh Baby was so beautiful—in between the pain—like nothing before. And now she is in the vault of the American cathedral on the Quai d'Orsay—and I'm here alone. And nothing more—only what was. You will know that nothing is very clear with me—everything is empty and blurred. Papa Woojums—she said it to me twice you are to edit the unpublished manuscripts and I am to stay on here and the Picasso portrait goes to the Metropolitan Museum— and on Sunday Jo Barry takes me down to the Sarthe to bring back Basket and the trunks. There are many things more to tell you but they fade off and perhaps any way I've told you. All the manuscripts and letters got off to Yale three weeks ago—but a lot of printed matter is still here. I'll tell you about that next letter. Later too I'll send the wires and things for Fania and you. And they want photographs for a Homage the good friend Jean Denoël is doing for Fontaine and if it's one of yours he wants he says it is will you forgive me if I give it to him.[5] J[anet]. Flanner said she would keep the French papers—and I'll send you them all. Forgive me and give me a little of the great affection you had for our darling Baby Woojums. Ever your loving but so very loving and lonesome

Mama Woojums

1. Stein had lectured in Brussels, Belgium, on 21 December 1945. See Stein to Van Vechten [? December 1945], note 1.

2. Bernard Faÿ, although in prison, had arranged to loan Stein his house, Le Prieure St. Martin, Luceaux, in the department of Sarthe, France.

3. Stein and Toklas left Paris on 19 July in a car driven by Joseph Barry. After arriving at Faÿ's home, they took a drive to Azay-le-Rideau, where Stein and Toklas once considered buying a home. While there, Stein suffered a severe attack and they took a room at an inn in Azay-le-Rideau. A local doctor informed them that Stein needed to be cared for by a specialist. The next day Stein, Toklas, and Barry took a train back to Paris. At Paris Stein's nephew Allan

Alice B. Toklas at the Cathedral of Chartres, 8 October 1949.
PHOTOGRAPH BY CARL VAN VECHTEN. PRIVATE COLLECTION.

Stein, whom Toklas had telephoned, had arranged for an ambulance to take Stein to the American Hospital at Neuilly.

On 23 July Stein made out her will. She bequeathed "the portrait of myself by Picasso. . . to the Metropolitan Museum of Art in New York City." She gave and bequeathed all her manuscripts, correspondence, and photographs to the library of Yale University. Stein instructed her executors to pay Van Vechten whatever sums of money he, "in his own absolute discretion, deems necessary for the publication of my unpublished manuscripts." The rest and residue of her estate was bequeathed to Alice Toklas:

> . . . to use for her life and, in so far as it may become necessary for her proper maintenance and support, I authorize my Executors to make payments to her from the principal of my Estate, and, for that purpose, to reduce to cash any paintings or other personal property belonging to my estate.

Upon the death of Toklas Stein's estate was to pass to Stein's nephew Allan Daniel Stein and upon his decease to his children.

4. Valery-Radot and Leriche were the two doctors who operated on Stein for cancer at the American Hospital in Neuilly. Valery-Radot was a member of the Académie de Medicine and head of the French Red Cross.

Specific information on the location of Stein's cancer and just how long she was aware of it is difficult to obtain. There is no doubt that the return to Paris, the long visits from American soldiers, and her various speaking engagements tired an already ill Stein. In his introduction to Stein's volume *Painted Lace*, Daniel-Henry Kahnweiler wrote:

> We met again in Paris after the liberation. Then my wife died [15 May 1945], and Gertrude and Alice climbed the four flights of stairs to bid her a last farewell. I cannot say that I suspected the existence of the illness which was wasting Gertrude away, but I remember that this visit touched me very much, for it seemed to represent a great effort for her (p. xviii).

5. Stein had published a number of things in *Fontaine*, a French revue. Denoël was not able to arrange for a memorial issue

To Alice Toklas

4 August [1946]

101 Central Park West
New York City 23

Dearest Mama Woojums,

It was comforting to receive your letter in which in this sad time (which must be an extremely busy one for you) you have set down so much of what happened and how, I am appreciative. I am VERY VERY appreciative too that Baby spoke of my loyalty. In the letter I wrote you last week you will recall I spoke of how wonderful it was that we had known each other, the three of us, for over thirty years without any kind of break! I am so happy too that she got the news about the play. Montie [Johnson] was worried about that; he was afraid she hadn't known until he got Mrs [Jenny] Bradley's cable which told him that she DID know and had replied to his . . Brewsie and Willie, as you know, I am sure, was held up by a binder's strike for two months and just got done in time. Did she ever see the Irish First Reader? I am afraid she didn't, afraid she didn't have time to get it and send me a copy; so I have ordered one from Ireland. . . Will she be buried in Père Lachaise? I have had this hope in mind ever since I learned Baby was lying in a vault at the American Cathedral.[1] But perhaps you have thought of even a better place of repose. . . . I cannot remember the American Cathedral at all and Sarthe, too, is a departement unfamiliar to me, though I think some time or other I must have been in Le Mans. . You write "ALL the manuscripts and letters got off to Yale three weeks ago." Does this actually mean EVERYTHING. . ? Are these letters from all and sundry or special letters or what? I am of course deeply touched that she has entrusted the editing of the unpublished manuscript to me. As you know I gave Yale over 300 of her letters SEALED several years ago. They were not to be opened until her death. If it is all right with you, I see no reason why these letters should not be unsealed now. Write me about this?? I still have a couple of hundred letters from her which will go to Yale later. Everybody has been so kind, so full of feeling. Montie has been wonderful. His GOD has died. He says he has sent you some clippings of Brewsie etc. . . I am honored to have one of my pictures used in the Homage; be sure to send this to me. . . Julian Sawyer telephones that he has loaned his private material for a window at Brentano. . . I am thrilled and thrilled that the Metropolitan gets the Picasso portrait. So I can see it any day and every day. This is a wonderful think [i.e., thing] for Baby to do. Alice, I am reading proofs on the Introduction and Notes and I feel that she saw the manuscript or proofs of A Stein Song and I feel definitely it should be published as she saw it and so we are publishing this note after it: "My introduction to this volume was written, and sent to the printer, a little over three months before Gertrude Stein's death in Paris, July 27, 1946, but I feel that it is wiser, for both sentimental and practical reasons, to let it stand unchanged. C. V. V." Of course you have always had our love as Gertrude had our love (Fania is writing you herself) and if we can help in any way, you know it will make us happy. It is almost a miracle that Selected Writings can come out so soon. Bennett [Cerf] will push it ahead. The play is definite, it appears. Is Virgil [Thomson]'s opera started. . ? I'll be glad to see anything you care to send me; happy to learn anything you care to tell me. . . but I know how much you will have to do. Write when you can. . . . Perhaps Janet [Flanner] too would write me if you asked her to. Or St Christopher [Blake] or St Joseph [Barry]. . . Our love to you always,

Papa Woojums.

We are lonely too. . . . It never occurred to me that Baby could die!

1. Stein was operated on in the late afternoon of 27 July. At 5:30 P.M. she lapsed into a coma. The doctors struggled to revive her, but she was pronounced dead at 6:30 P.M. Stein's body was removed to the vault of the American Cathedral Church of the Holy Trinity in Paris, where it remained until 22 October 1946, when the body was buried in Père Lachaise Cemetery, Paris. Toklas wrote to Van Vechten on 22 October 1946:

> We took Baby from the crypt of the American Cathedral out to Père Lachaise this morning. Dean Beekman whom Baby knew and liked, for years read prayers—three psalms and such parts of the service from the Book of Common Prayer as Baby would have subscribed to—with just Allan and his wife and ten of Baby's intimates there—and then just Allan and his wife and me following to Père Lachaise. (See Burns, *Staying on Alone: Letters of Alice B. Toklas*, p. 24.)

To Alice Toklas

4 August 1946   [101 Central Park West]
                                             New York City

Dearest Alice

I am thinking of the vividness, magnetism, the warmth, the charm of our Baby Woojum's smile, Her beautiful, vibrant rich, lovely luscious voice, Her great and special gift, in the very first moment of meeting her— whether it was a peasant, poet, painter, pauper or prince of making one feel completely at ease, natural. One felt instantly in the presence of a great woman, who at once possessed great knowledge of human frailty, and deep understanding of human quality—and so she helped and inspired people in their search to know and understand themselves. In this crazy cold indifferent, forgetting world it is certain she will be long remembered because she was true a wonder and unique! and which you dear Alice Woojums will remain for always her great glowing spirit, a living presence, a vital force all this you know, dear dear Alice. I repeat these truths because I loved her too, and I share your sorrow and your loneliness.

With my love
Fania

Undated Letters

❦

To Gertrude Stein and Alice Toklas
[Telegram]

[? December 1935–38][1]   New York

LOVE TO BABY AND MAMA WOOJUMS

FANIA CARLO

1. The term Woojums used as a salutation is not found in Van Vechten's letters before 1934. The telegram is addressed to Stein at 27 rue de Fleurus, thus setting a limit of 1938 on the date. In December 1934 Stein was in America.

❦

To Gertrude Stein and Alice Toklas
[Postcard: Ntra. Sa. De La Esperanza]

[? 1940–45][1]   [101 Central Park West
                                                  New York]

Our love always and every blessing [f]or you both this coming year.

Carl and Fania

1. A comparison of the handwriting places this letter in the 1940–45 time period. The card was written and signed by Van Vechten.

[843]

Appendix A:
The First Meeting of Gertrude Stein and Carl Van Vechten

❧

Carl Van Vechten and Gertrude Stein have given similar accounts of how they first unknowingly and then knowingly met.[1] The story of their meeting contains, as John Malcolm Brinnin says, "a series of scenes that Henry James would have been intrigued to elaborate."[2]

Briefly stated, the story goes that Stein attended the second performance in Paris of *Le Sacre du Printemps*. She and Alice Toklas, with their friend Florence Bradley and her sister, shared their box with Van Vechten, whom they did not know at that time. Stein was so impressed by the tall, well-built young man with an elegant, pleated evening shirt that she returned home that evening and composed "One," a word portrait of Van Vechten.[3] When Van Vechten arrived for dinner the following Saturday night, an invitation that followed Stein's receipt of Mabel Dodge's letter of introduction, Stein immediately recognized Van Vechten as the man who had shared her box.

If the account of these two meetings is correct, then Stein and Van Vechten first met without being introduced on Monday, 2 June 1913, at the second performance of *Le Sacre du Printemps*. The dinner party at Stein's residence, 27 rue de Fleurus, would then have occurred on Saturday 7 June.

The correspondence between Stein and Van Vechten makes clear that they did not first meet on the date or under the circumstances that they both described in their writings. The conclusion is supported by Van Vechten's

1. See Gertrude Stein, *The Autobiography of Alice B. Toklas* (New York: Harcourt, Brace and Co., 1933), pp. 167–68, and Carl Van Vechten, "Some 'Literary Ladies' I Have Known," in his *Fragments from an Unwritten Autobiography* (New Haven: Yale University Library, 1955), II, 19–20.

2. *The Third Rose: Gertrude Stein and Her World* (Boston: Little, Brown and Co., Inc., 1959), p. 190.

3. Stein's "One (Van Vechten)," in her *Geography and Plays* (Boston: The Four Seas Co., 1923), pp. 199–200.

[847]

letters to his future wife, Fania Marinoff, by Florence Bradley's letters to Stein, and by the dates of the performances of *Le Sacre du Printemps.*

In New York in the spring of 1913 Mabel Dodge invited Van Vechten, John Reed, and Robert Edmond Jones to motor with her from Paris to Florence. They were to spend the summer at her renaissance Villa Curonia in Arcetri. Van Vechten sailed from New York on the R. M. S. *Mauretania* on 20 May 1913. He arrived in Liverpool on 27 May and spent the night in London. The following day he took the night ferry and arrived in Paris on the morning of Thursday 29 May, the day of the premiere of *Le Sacre du Printemps.*[4]

Mabel Dodge had delayed her departure for Europe in order to help John Reed and Big Bill Haywood organize a pageant to benefit the striking Paterson silk workers on Saturday, 7 June, at Madison Square Garden. Dodge had given Van Vechten letters of introduction to a number of friends, including the one to Gertrude Stein, which Van Vechten sent to Stein the day he arrived in Paris.[5] Stein responded with a letter the next day.

> My dear Van Vechten
> Will you dine with us to-morrow Saturday evening at 7.30. Let me know immediately.[6]

The letter, postmarked 31 May 1913, 7 A.M., arrived at the post office closest to the American Express Company office, rue Gluck, at 7:55 A.M. Van Vechten replied immediately: "I'll dine with you with pleasure this evening.[7]

That Van Vechten was at Stein's house on Saturday 31 May is confirmed by a letter he wrote to Fania Marinoff on Sunday, 1 June (postmarked 2 June 1913).

> Last night [i.e., Saturday 31 May] I had dinner at Gertrude Stein's. She is a wonderful personality. I wish you could meet her. You will sometime. . . .

4. Carl Van Vechten, letter to Fania Marinoff, postmarked 29 May 1913, New York Public Library, Rare Books and Manuscripts Division; hereafter cited at NYPL-MD. The transcription of all letters quoted here has been exact; no changes have been made in spelling, punctuation, or capitalization. Editorial additions have been enclosed in brackets.

5. Mabel Dodge's letter of introduction is printed in *The Flowers of Friendship: Letters Written to Gertrude Stein*, ed. Donald Gallup (New York: Alfred A. Knopf, Inc., 1953), p. 79.

6. Collection of American Literature, Beinecke Rare Book and Manuscript Library, Yale University; hereafter cited as YCAL.

7. YCAL.

She lives in a place hung with Picassos and she showed me some more sketches of his. . . .[8]

Van Vechten's correspondence also confirms that they did not meet on Saturday, 7 June, the date on which, according to their chronology, Stein and Van Vechten said they had their first dinner at 27 rue de Fleurus. Van Vechten's second letter to Stein is not dated, nor has an envelope with a postmark survived. From internal evidence, however, it is possible to date this letter as having been written between 1 and 4 June. The first Paris performance of Mussorgsky's opera *Khovanshchina* was on Thursday, 5 June.

Dear Miss Stein,

I've just been invited to the premiere of *Kovanchina* on Thursday night. Can we change our rendez-vous to another day? [Pitts] Sanborn is going away on Friday for the day and as I want to bring him over perhaps we had better not name a day until later. I'll send you a petit bleu and if you are not free you can let me know.

I want so much to read the plays and Sanborn wants to see those extraordinary Picasso drawings.[9]

On Saturday, 7 June, Van Vechten wrote to Stein asking if he could bring his friend Pitts Sanborn the next day. Stein replied immediately that she was free on Sunday and would expect them in the afternoon.[10]

In a letter written to Fania Marinoff on Sunday, 8 June, Van Vechten wrote:

Last night we [Van Vechten and Sanborn] saw "Julien" at the Opera Comique. It is the successor to "Louise" but it is a colossal bore. This afternoon I am taking John [Pitts Sanborn] to meet Gertrude and see Picasso's extraordinary drawings. . . .[11]

Having established that Stein and Van Vechten met first on Saturday 31 May 1913, it is important to determine which performance of *Le Sacre du Printemps* they attended.[12]

8. NYPL-MD.

9. YCAL.

10. Van Vechten to Stein, [7 June] 1913; Stein to Van Vechten [postmark 7 June 1913], YCAL.

11. NYPL-MD.

12. *Le Sacre du Printemps* had its premiere as part of the *Saison Russe* presented by Serge Diaghilev at the newly opened Théâtre des Champs-Elysées in Paris. The ballet was first performed on Thursday 29 May 1913. There were four subsequent performances: Monday, 2 June; Wednesday, 4 June; Friday, 6 June; and Friday, 13 June. The traditional répétition générale,

In late March 1916 Van Vechten sent Stein a copy of his new book of essays, *Music After the Great War and Other Studies*. In the essay "Igor Strawinsky: A New Composer" Van Vechten wrote of his experiences at a performance of *Le Sacre du Printemps*.

> I attended the first performance in Paris of Strawinsky's anarchistic (against the canons of academic art) ballet, *The Sacrifice to the Spring*, in which primitive emotions are both depicted and aroused by a dependence on barbarous rhythm, in which melody and harmony, as even so late a composer as Richard Strauss understands them, do not enter. A certain part of the audience, thrilled by what it considered a blasphemous attempt to destroy music as an art, and swept away with wrath, began very soon after the rise of the curtain to whistle, to make cat-calls, and to offer audible suggestions as to how the performance should proceed. Others of us, who liked the music and felt that the principles of free speech were at stake, bellowed defiance. It was war over art for the rest of the evening. . . . I was sitting in a box in which I had rented one seat. Three ladies sat in front of me and a young man occupied the place behind me. He stood up during the course of the ballet to enable himself to see more clearly. The intense excitement under which he was laboring, thanks to the potent force of the music, betrayed itself presently when he began to beat rhythmically on the top of my head with his fists.[13]

From Mallorca Stein wrote to thank Van Vechten for his book.

> My dear Van,
>
> Thanks so much for the book. I have been reading it and find you have a charming enthusiasm and know so much and are so conscientious xcept when you say there were three of us in that box instead of four. Now the great ques tion is which one did you leave out.[14]

Van Vechten replied to Stein on 17 May 1916.

> Dear Gertrude Stein,
>
> It's so amusing of you to notice that I wrote there were *Three* in the box. As a matter of fact I left out more than that—a German and his wife—

a dress rehearsal before an invited audience, was held on Wednesday, 28 May. The fullest discussion and documentation of the first performance of the ballet, together with an anthology of the criticism it provoked, can be found in Truman C. Bullard, "The First Performance of Igor Stravinsky's *Sacre du Printemps*," 3 vols. (diss., Eastman School of Music of the University of Rochester, 1971). Bullard also cites critics who reveal that the second performance was marked with incidents similar to those mentioned in the accounts given by Stein and Van Vechten (see note 1). See Bullard, II, 84, 91–92.

13. "Igor Strawinsky: A New Composer," rpt. in *The Dance Writings of Carl Van Vechten*, ed. and intro. by Paul Padgette (New York: Dance Horizons, 1980), pp. 108–9.

14. YCAL.

for instance, entirely. Four seemed *too* many somehow. No-one would ever believe so many sat in a box and I think I decided to leave out Florence Bradley's sister. . . and it wasn't the *first* night of *Sacre* either, it was the second night. But one must only be accurate about such details in a work of fiction. The real point is that in my own consciousness I am not a bit muddled about the *facts*.[15]

That Van Vechten is accurate in this letter about the facts surrounding which performance of *Le Sacre du Printemps* he attended can be confirmed by a letter he sent to Fania Marinoff from Paris postmarked 30 May 1913.

Mike [i.e., Mabel Dodge] gave me several letters—one to Jacques Blanche the painter. I went there yesterday and found his place wonderful. He has asked me to lunch on Sunday with George Moore. I tried to get in to see the Russian dances last night but couldn't so I went to see Polaire at the Folies Bergere. She played "Le Visiteur" which she did in New York last year.[16]

Van Vechten does not mention *Le Sacre du Printemps* to Fania Marinoff until a letter postmarked 4 June 1913.

The other night I saw the Russian ballet and the newest one "Sacre du Printemps" it [i.e., is] the most extraordinary thing I've ever seen on the stage. Both the music and the dancing were of an originality [appealing?]. My darling the French were so startled and offended by this novelty that they hissed it almost without succession. It was impossible to hear the last fifteen minutes of music at all. And how wildly beautiful it was.[17]

There can be little doubt that Van Vechten attended the second performance of *Le Sacre du Printemps* on Monday, 2 June. Stein and Toklas, with Florence Bradley and her sister, also attended that performance, as Stein wrote in *The Autobiography of Alice B. Toklas.*

Florence Bradley, an American actress, had met Stein and Toklas in Florence in the fall of 1912 when they all visited Mabel Dodge at the Villa Curonia. In 1913 Florence Bradley and her sister were living in Paris in an apartment on the rue Humboldt. Although Bradley had seen Stein only a few times during the fall and winter of 1912–13, when she learned that Stein had written some plays she asked to come and read them. Her letter is dated only "Friday," but it was clearly written on Friday, 30 May 1913.

15. YCAL.

16. NYPL-MD.

17. NYPL-MD.

Dear Miss Stein,
We shall be delighted to come on Sunday—am most anxious to read the play!
Saw "Le Sacre du Printemps" last night. Great enthusiasm. It's quite the most
interesting thing I have seen them do. And you—or are you no longer interested.

Yours sincerely
Florence Bradley [18]

Florence Bradley's next letter to Stein is a *carte pneumatique* postmarked 2 June 1913, 14:55.

It is tonight—could get no tickets for Wednesday or Friday, They are in loge
[word?] it—We will go early and do our best for you. So come along at your
ease—to comfort you—we are en face.

In haste
Florence E. Bradley

Monday
Tickets enclosed [19]

This letter leaves little doubt that the invitation was for the performance of *Le Sacre du Printemps* and that Stein and Toklas went to the second performance of the ballet. There they met Van Vechten, whom they
already knew. Whether Bradley also secured tickets for him or whether his
ticket in the same loge was purely coincidental cannot be ascertained. But
it is clear from these letters that their meeting did not happen as Stein had
written in *The Autobiography of Alice B. Toklas.*

In *Everybody's Autobiography* Gertrude Stein said that she wrote *The
Autobiography of Alice B. Toklas* during "a beautiful and unusually dry October at Bilignin in France in nineteen thirty-two followed by an unusually
dry and beautiful first two weeks in November." [20] From various materials
in the Yale archives, it is clear that Stein actually began *The Autobiography
of Alice B. Toklas* in the early summer. Her reference to those six weeks in
the fall is a smooth concealing maneuver. Anyone who has read the book
with a certain amount of care realizes that it was not meant to be read as
history. Stein did not attempt to narrate a carefully documented account of
her life. The writing of *The Autobiography of Alice B. Toklas* represents, like

18. YCAL.

19. YCAL.

20. Stein, *Everybody's Autobiography* (New York: Random House, 1937), p. 9.

[852]

all of Stein's writing, a truth stemming more from the pattern that she weaves out of the facts than from an exact narration of the facts themselves. Out of the various facts of their meetings that are given here, and as they are certain to have taken place, Stein and Van Vechten wove a Jamesian web that served to confirm the importance of their friendship.

As their friendship deepened, the facts surrounding their first two meetings gradually became less important to Stein and Van Vechten. Van Vechten, writing his *Fragments from an Unwritten Autobiography*, did not wish to contradict the legend Stein had created. Perhaps, too, by that time Stein's pattern of the truth had also become part of his own remembrance. As Van Vechten wrote to Stein on 17 May 1916, "one must only be accurate about such details in a work of fiction. The real point is that in my own consciousness I am not a bit muddled about the *facts*."

Appendix B:
An Unpublished Portrait of Carl Van Vechten by Gertrude Stein

Introductory Note

Carl Van Vechten, as part of his efforts to publish Gertrude Stein's works in America, sent a copy of her play *A List* to Edmund Wilson for *Vanity Fair*. Wilson, who had reviewed Stein's *Geography and Plays* in *Vanity Fair*,[1] was enthusiastic but felt that he did not have the space to publish the play in its entirety. He proposed to publish on facing pages an abridged version of Stein's play and excerpts from Avery Hopwood's play, *Our Little Wife*, which had inspired Stein.[2] Stein refused to cut her play, and Wilson wrote to Van Vechten on 6 July 1923, expressing his regret at Stein's decision. When he returned the typescript to Stein on 23 July 1923, Van Vechten also reported that he was having little success in his efforts to convince Alfred Knopf, his friend and publisher, to publish Stein's *The Making of Americans*. The one good piece of news that Van Vechten could report was that his new novel, *The Blind Bow-Boy*, whose publication date was early August, had already sold out its first printing.

Van Vechten's satiric *bildungsroman* begins as a conventional story of a young man, Harold Prewett, who has led a quiet, uneventful life until he is brought to New York by the wealthy father whom he has never met. The father, who wants to counter his son's cloistered education, has provided him with a tutor, Paul Moody. Moody's responsibility is to introduce Harold to New York's most sophisticated and uninhibited society. George Prewett, Harold's father, wants his son exposed to totally free love, sex, and capriciousness. He hopes that after a time in such surroundings Harold will permanently reject the temptations of high living. When Harold finds out his father's true purpose in bringing him to New York, he reacts to his father's

1. See Van Vechten to Stein, 3 May 1923, note 2.
2. See Stein to Van Vechten [6 July 1923], note 3.

[857]

duplicity by opting for the uninhibited set that has provided him with his real education.

Although she had not yet received her copy of the novel, Stein replied to Van Vechten with enthusiasm: "Bully for the boy, I am awfully pleased in your success. It's just the age it should come. I am looking forward to seeing it. I'll have to do another portrait of you, the twenty years after effect."[3] This is the first time a second portrait of Van Vechten is mentioned by Stein.

Van Vechten's reply to Stein of 3 September 1923 expressed his delight at the idea of a second portrait, "twenty years after." Although he had known her for only ten years, Van Vechten must have realized that she was using the term as a literary device. Stein would have been familiar with Alexandre Dumas' novel *Vingt Ans Apres* ("Van" may be a pun on *vingt*); she may also have recalled the chapter "Twenty Years After (1892)" in Adams' *The Education of Henry Adams*. In her reply to Van Vechten (postmark 26 September 1923), written from Nice, where she and Toklas had gone to see Picasso and Juan Gris, Stein included a typescript of "Van or Twenty Years After. A Second Portrait of Carl Van Vechten." It is this portrait that Van Vechten arranged to have printed in *The Reviewer* and which Stein later included in her *Useful Knowledge*, a collection of compositions about American subjects, just as she had included "One. Carl Van Vechten" in her preceding book, *Geography and Plays*.[4]

Amongst the Stein manuscripts in the Yale Collection of American Literature another, hitherto unpublished portrait of Van Vechten was discovered in 1984. This is the one reproduced below. Entitled "And too. Van Vechten. A sequel to One.," the original follows in the same *cahier* as "He and They, Hemingway," Stein's portrait of Ernest Hemingway.

The omission of any reference to this second piece in the much scrutinized *cahier* of the Hemingway portrait is difficult to understand. The appearance of two— or even more—different pieces in a single *cahier* is not unusual. The cover of the *cahier* has phrases from the Van Vechten portrait on it: at the top of the *cahier*, just under the title "He and They, Hemingway," Stein wrote "Does he or he does"; at the bottom there is the phrase "Or does he. He does." Stein tended to fill her *cahiers*. The fact that the Van Vechten portrait appears after the Hemingway portrait need not mean

3. Stein to Van Vechten [5 August 1923]

4. See Stein to Van Vechten [26 September [1923], note 2.

that the two are related. However, the possibility of a connection must be considered.

The portrait of Van Vechten, "And too. Van Vechten. A sequel to One.," immediately follows the Hemingway portrait, which begins on the inside front cover and continues for three pages. The Van Vechten portrait fills the remainder of the *cahier* except for the very last page, which is not used because it was damaged in what appears to have been an accident with sealing wax. Left on the back cover are bits of red sealing wax which burnt a hole in the cover and partially burnt the last page of the *cahier*. The paper surrounding the hole on the back cover has been torn out or cut away.

Establishing the sequence of events that account for this unpublished Van Vechten portrait and for the published one, "Van or Twenty Years After. A Second Portrait of Carl Van Vechten," involves a certain amount of speculation.

There is no typescript of "And too. Van Vechten. A sequel to One." in the Yale Collection of American Literature, and it may never have been typed by Alice Toklas. It does not appear in the bibliography of her writings that Stein prepared for *transition*[5] nor was the work assigned a Haas-Gallup number.[6] Although the file folder for the *cahier* explicitly identifies this piece, neither Richard Bridgman in his revision of the Haas-Gallup listing in his *Gertrude Stein in Pieces*, nor Wendy Steiner in her study of Stein's portraits, *Exact Resemblance to Exact Resemblance*, takes note of this portrait.

Soon after his arrival in Paris, in late December 1921, Hemingway and his wife Hadley met Gertrude Stein.[7] During the eight months that Hemingway was in Europe he and Stein saw each other frequently. Genuine affection and respect are evident in the letters that survive.[8] In August 1923, Hemingway's first book, *Three Stories and Ten Poems*, was about to

5. *transition*, 15 (Feb. 1929), 47–55

6. The standard numbering system used to identify Stein's writings through 1940. The numbering is based on section D of the catalogue of the Yale University Library exhibition of Stein's published and unpublished writings prepared by Robert Bartlett Haas and Donald Clifford Gallup in 1941.

7. The Hemingways arrived with a letter of introduction from Sherwood Anderson, whom Hemingway had met at Y. K. Smith's apartment in the Chicago Near North Side during the winter of 1920–1921. See Gallup, *The Flowers of Friendship*, pp. 142–43; for details of the Anderson-Hemingway friendship see Carlos Baker, *Hemingway: The Writer As Artist* (Princeton: Princeton University Press, 1956), pp. 4–6.

8. Ernest and Hadley Hemingway letters to Stein are in YCAL, Stein's letters to the Hemingways are in the John F. Kennedy Library, Boston, Massachusetts.

be published by Robert McAlmon's Contact Editions. Hemingway was also preparing to leave for Toronto on 17 August to resume working for the *Daily Star*. There is no evidence to indicate when, before his 17 August sailing, Hemingway last saw Stein. It is likely that they saw each other very shortly before his departure. When Stein sent Sherwood Anderson a copy of the Hemingway portrait in February 1924, she wrote that it was "[A] little skit" presented to Hemingway just before he left for Toronto.[9] Perhaps as a parting gift, Stein wrote the portrait, "He and They, Hemingway." She may have read the portrait to Hemingway or given him a typescript of it (however, there is no copy of the work in the Hemingway archives in the John F. Kennedy Library, nor is it mentioned in any of their letters that I have examined).

Stein's use of the pictures, texts, or title on the covers of the French *cahiers* has been well documented.[10] In the newly discovered "And too. Van Vechten. A sequel to One.," there may be echoes of the Hemingway portrait that precedes it in the *cahier*. The "And too" of the title may reflect that this portrait is also in the same *cahier* with the Hemingway portrait. The "And too" also has resonances to the earlier Stein portrait of Van Vechten, including the pun "too" (two) as "a sequel to one." Indeed, throughout this portrait Stein seems to be echoing its connection with the earlier portrait of Van Vechten.

Although their friendship had been firmly established during June 1913, when Van Vechten frequently visited Stein, they had not seen each other since Sunday, 5 July 1914, when Van Vechten and Fania Marinoff came to dinner the evening before Stein and Toklas were to leave Paris. The Van Vechten portrait opens with a series of questions about Van Vechten: "Or does he," "As he was," "Or as he was." The idea of a second portrait, "Now to follow one before the other," is introduced. Stein then plays with the idea of a portrait to follow one, one being the title of the first portrait of Van Vechten and also its numerical identification in relationship to this, the second portrait. Stein's punning is evident in the line "Having or have, halving a halve, having or have." The use of repetition, particularly of words of one syllable, is a device Stein employs to make the reader read word for word:

9. See Stein to Anderson in Ray Lewis White, ed., *Sherwood Anderson/Gertrude Stein: Correspondence and Personal Essays*, p. 36.

10. See Wendy Steiner, *Exact Resemblance to Exact Resemblance*, pp. 111–16. See also Ulla E. Dydo, "How to Read Gertrude Stein: The Manuscript of 'Stanzas in Meditation,' " in *Text: Transactions of the Society for Textual Scholarship*, vol. 1, 1981, pp. 271–303.

As in as in has in has he in, has in as in. As he has in it, has he in it, has he
in as he in as he has in in it. Has he as he has he has he has it in it.

The portrait builds in the manuscript with great intensity. One can
observe Stein working on ideas, rejecting certain beginnings and accepting
others. Near the end of the portrait Stein introduces the phrase, "When this
you see remember me," and adds "and share it." The "this" is probably meant
to refer to the portrait itself, and the "and share it" can possibly be read to
mean and share the feelings I have for you as I write it when you read it.

The bond between Stein and Van Vechten began in 1913 when Van
Vechten arranged for the printing of *Tender Buttons*. It was this simple act
of belief in her talents as writer that bound them into an unbroken friendship that lasted until Stein's death in 1946. It is perhaps this firmly established link that Stein echoes in the final lines of the portrait. She has crossed
out the direct reference to Livingstone in the portrait. Perhaps on reflection
she did not want to direct a reference to the missionary and explorer David
Livingstone and the man who found him in Africa in 1871, the journalist
H. M. Stanley. While one cannot say that Van Vechten "discovered" Stein,
"he always knew, and it was always a comfort," as Stein wrote in one of her
last pieces, "A Message from Gertrude Stein," which appeared in her *Selected Writings*, edited by Van Vechten in 1946. It is also possible that Stein
was punning on "living stone." The word "link" is taken over by the word
"kin," an emotionally charged word which certainly reflects how Van Vechten and Stein thought of each other.

The portrait ends on what seems to be a proverb. A new idea is begun with "Introduce it to me," but this is scratched out. Stein did not use
the last, damaged page of the *cahier* and it is difficult to know whether she
intended to continue the portrait or whether this indeed is the end. The ending
does not seem to resolve the portrait.

It is unlikely that we will ever know why this piece was not typed by
Alice Toklas. From other manuscript notebooks it is apparent that Stein from
time to time tore pages out of a *cahier*, presumably when she was dissatisfied
with the composition or when it contained material that she did not want
preserved or when she needed paper. Whether Stein considered this portrait
unfinished or whether, in the rush to leave Paris in August, Toklas left the
work aside and never returned to type it, we do not know.

Perhaps Van Vechten's letter of 3 September 1923, when forwarded
to Stein in Nice, reminded her of her promise of a second portrait and

prompted her to write "Van or Twenty Years After." The immediate occasion for this second Van Vechten portrait, undoubtedly written in Nice in September 1923 (the *cahier* bears a penciled indication of the month and year in Stein's hand), may have been Van Vechten's letter, but the idea of second portraits seems to have been on her mind. Once "Van or Twenty Years After." was completed, Stein wrote two other compositions that are second portraits: "As a Wife Has a Cow A Love Story," a second portrait of Alice Toklas, and "If I Told Him. A Completed Portrait of Picasso."[11]

Stein's first step as a writer is generally considered to be the completion of her novel *Q.E.D.* in October 1903. (She did write college themes, of course, and as early as 1902 had begun the first, tentative notes for *The Making of Americans*.) By 1923, the date of this portrait of Van Vechten, she had published *Three Lives, Portrait of Mabel Dodge at the Villa Curonia, Tender Buttons, Have They Attacked Mary. He Giggled, Geography and Plays*, and a small number of works in periodicals. After twenty years as a writer, although she must have felt pride in her accomplishment and in the recognition afforded her by friends, she must also have felt continued worry about the difficulties of publication. She had paid for the publication of the volumes of her work, and friends had placed her pieces in periodicals. No publisher had come to her seeking her work.

Also during this period, a different but equally intense involvement with her earlier compositions probably occurred when the French writer, Henri-Pierre Roché (author of *Jules et Jim*), in either late 1921 or early 1922 translated Stein's portrait "Picasso" into French. On 14 February 1922 (YCAL) Roché sent Stein his translation. Three days later he wrote Stein that Jean Cocteau, who had seen a typed copy of the translation when he visited Stein, had telephoned him with the suggestion that the translation should be a little less literal. As a result Roché made some minor revisions which he sent to Stein for her comment. Perhaps in reviewing this translation word by word Stein was led to review her other early work and to reconsider her portraits.

Another development of the same period, early spring of 1923, was that Stein began consciously to channel her energies into elucidating her literary ideas. Although "An Elucidation," announced in a letter in mid-March (Stein to Van Vechten, postmark 15 March 1923), was not published until *transition*, 1 (April 1927), it is one of the first of Stein's attempts to

---

11. Stein's first portrait of Toklas, "Ada," was written in December 1910, her first portrait of Picasso, "Picasso," although frequently dated 1909, was probably written after "Ada."

explore the nature of her compositions and respond to readers' demand that she explain what she was doing.

It should be clear from the various developments discussed above that, although the specific occasion for Stein's writing the two second portraits of Van Vechten was her enthusiastic response to the news about his new novel, the momentum that gave shape to these compositions, and to the second portraits of Toklas and of Picasso as well, had been building for some time.

An Unpublished Portrait
of Carl Van Vechten, 1923

And too.
Van Vechten [now.]¹
a sequel to One—

[Or does he the does.]
Or does he
As he was.
Or as he was.
Or as he does.
Does he.
He does.
I tell you what it is general.
And in general.
Now to follow one
One before.
Before the other.
Now to follow one before the other.
In general
Now to follow one before the other.
And in general.
And in general now to follow one
before the other.

1. The words enclosed in brackets were x'd out by Stein. The first horizontal line was drawn by Stein to indicate a separation between the title and subtitle and the text of the portrait. The short horizontal line at the end of the composition may have been added after Stein x'd out the last line of text in order to mark the end of the portrait. See Stein to Van Vechten [late August 1923] for similarities in phrasing.

Now to follow one before the other and in general.

And I know what it is.

This is what it is.

The man next to him half rose to his feet.

Now to follow one before the other and in general.

And [left him and] I know what it is.

This is what it is.

At the same moment.

This is the same moment.

And in general and now to follow [and] one before the other and this is the same moment.

The same moment and to follow one before the other and in general and at the same moment.

At the same moment and in general and this is what it is and to follow one before the other and this is what it is and in general and at the same moment and the man next to him half arose and at the same moment and this is what it is, and in general and to follow one before the other and at the same moment.

Having or have, halving a halve, having or have.

One before the other or at the same moment, following at the same moment or following one before the other or halving or halve or having or have or one before the other or at the same moment.

As in as in has in has he in, has in as in. As he has in it, has he in it, has he in as he in as he has in in it. Has he as he has he has he has it in it.

So many [sentences] instances make this in three. In three instances. As for instance. This instance as an instance.

For instance.

For instance as this instance as an instance, the instance is, there is an instance, for instance.

[Before.]

[Naturally,]

[Actually, naturally actually, as actually. As to actually, for this]

Actually can sunder, as to the same, actually can sunder and as to the same and actually can sunder and as to the same, the sundered sisters and as to the same. And as to the sundered sisters and as to the same.

[Indicated, as you were, indicated, for as you]

Assuming it to be their name, as an assumption, assuming it to be their name, as a resumption assuming it to be their name and as consumption, assuming it to be their name, consuming, resuming, assuming and assuming and consuming and resuming, assuming it to be their name.

Resuming, assuming consuming. [Consider. Considerable. Consideration.] And to resume and to assume and to refer. Prefer and confer.

Reasonable and said reasonable and fair. If you be not fair to me what care I how fair you be. When this you see remember me and share it. A share to share their share a share. For a share. As for a share.

Now then their link. [with Livingstone.]

Now then their kin.

Now then their link and now and then their kin.

As a kin. [Wait to wait. Weight to weight.] When there was and when there is having it as and having it for, for and [four] three, as they have it for them.

The girl who saved his honor. Honor to them to whom honor is due. Due to you and due.

[Introduce it to me.]

Principal Works
of Gertrude Stein

An Acquaintance With Description. London: The Seizin Press, 1929.

Alphabets & Birthdays. New Haven: Yale University Press, 1957. Intro. by Donald Gallup.

As Fine As Melanctha (1914–1930). New Haven: Yale University Press, 1954. Foreword by Natalie Clifford Barney.

The Autobiography of Alice B. Toklas. New York: Harcourt, Brace and Co., 1933.

The Autobiography of Alice B. Toklas. London: John Lane, The Bodley Head, Ltd., 1933.

Bee Time Vine and Other Pieces (1913–1927). New Haven: Yale University Press. Preface and notes by Virgil Thomson.

Before The Flowers of Friendship Faded Friendship Faded. Paris: Plain Edition, 1931.

Blood on the Dining-Room Floor. Pawlet, Vt.: The Banyan Press, 1948. Foreword by Donald Gallup.

A Book Concluding With As A Wife Has A Cow A Love Story. Paris: Galerie Simon (Daniel-Henry Kahnweiler), 1926. Lithographs by Juan Gris.

Brewsie and Willie. New York: Random House, 1946.

Composition as Explanation. London: The Hogarth Press, 1926.

Descriptions of Literature. Englewood, N.J.: As Stable Pamphlets, 1926.

Dix Portraits. Paris: Editions de la Montagne, 1930. English text with French translation.

An Elucidation. Paris: Transition, 1927.

Everybody's Autobiography. New York: Random House, 1937.

Everybody's Autobiography. London: William Heinemann, 1938.

Fernhurst, Q.E.D., and Other Early Writings. New York: Liveright, 1971. A Note on the texts by Donald Gallup. Intro. by Leon Katz. Appendix, "The Making of *The Making of Americans,*" by Donald Gallup.

Four In America. New Haven: Yale University Press, 1947. Intro. by Thornton Wilder.

Four Saints in Three Acts. New York: Random House, 1934. Intro. by Carl Van Vechten.

The Geographical History of America Or The Relation Of Human Nature To The Human Mind. New York: Random House, 1936. Intro. by Thornton Wilder.

Geography and Plays. Boston: The Four Seas Co., 1922. Preface by Sherwood Anderson.

The Gertrude Stein First Reader & Three Plays. Dublin and London: Maurice Fridberg, 1946. Decorated by Sir Francis Rose.

Gertrude Stein on Picasso. New York: Liveright, 1970. Ed. Edward Burns. Afterword by Leon Katz and Edward Burns.

Have They Attacked Mary. He Giggled. New York: Privately for Henry McBride, 1917. Illustrated by Jules Pascin.

How to Write. Paris: Plain Edition, 1931.

How Writing is Written. Vol. 2, Previously Uncollected Writings of Gertrude Stein. Los Angeles: Black Sparrow Press, 1974. Ed. with preface by Robert Bartlett Haas.

Ida A Novel. New York: Random House, 1941.

In Savoy or Yes Is For a Very Young Man (A Play of the Resistance in France). London: The Pushkin Press, 1946.

Kisses Can. New York: The Banyan Press, 1947.

Last Operas and Plays. New York and Toronto: Rinehart & Co., 1949. Ed. and intro. by Carl Van Vechten.

Lectures in America. New York: Random House, 1935.

Lucy Church Amiably. Paris: Plain Edition, 1931.

The Making of Americans Being a History of a Family's Progress. Paris: Contact Editions, 1925.

The Making of Americans Being a History of a Family's Progress. Abridged ed. New York: Harcourt, Brace and Co., 1934. Intro. by Bernary Faÿ.

Matisse Picasso and Gertrude Stein, With Two Shorter Stories. Paris: Plain Edition, 1933. Also known as GMP.

Mrs. Reynolds and Five Earlier Novelettes. New Haven: Yale University Press, 1952. Foreword by Lloyd Frankenberg.

Narration. Chicago: University of Chicago Press, 1935. Intro. by Thornton Wilder.

A Novel of Thank You. New Haven: Yale University Press, 1958. Intro. by Carl Van Vechten.

Operas and Plays. Paris: Plain Edition, 1932.

Painted Lace and Other Pieces (1914–1937). New Haven: Yale University Press, 1955. Intro. by Daniel-Henry Kahnweiler.

Paris France. London: B. T. Batsford, Ltd., 1940.

Paris France. New York: Charles Scribner's Sons, 1940.

Picasso. Paris: Librairie Floury, 1938. Written in French.

Picasso. London: B. T. Batsford, Ltd., 1938. English translation.

Picasso. New York: Charles Scribner's Sons, 1939.

Portrait of Mabel Dodge at the Villa Curonia. Florence: Privately printed for Mabel Dodge, 1912.

Portraits and Prayers. New York: Random House, 1934.

A Primer for the Gradual Understanding of Gertrude Stein. Los Angeles: Black Sparrow Press, 1971. Ed. Robert Bartlett Haas.

Prothalamium. Culver, Indiana: Joyous Guard Press, 1939.

Reflection on the Atomic Bomb. Volume I of the Previously Uncollected Writings of Gertrude Stein. Los Angeles: Black Sparrow Press, 1973. Ed. with preface by Robert Bartlett Haas.

Selected Writings of Gertrude Stein. 1946; rpt. New York: The Modern Library, 1962. Ed., intro., and notes by Carl Van Vechten.

Stanzas in Meditation and Other Poems (1929–1933). New Haven: Yale University Press, 1956. Preface by Donald Sutherland.

Tender Buttons. New York: Claire Marie, 1914.

Things as They Are. Pawlet, Vt.: The Banyan Press, 1950. See also *Fernhurst, Q.E.D., and Other Early Writings.*

Three Lives. New York: The Grafton Press, 1909.

Three Lives. London: John Lane, The Bodley Head, 1915, rpt. 1920.

Three Lives. London: John Rodker, 1927.

Three Lives. New York: Albert and Charles Boni, 1927.

Three Lives. New York: The Modern Library, 1933. Intro. by Carl Van Vechten.

Three Lives. Norfolk, Conn.: New Directions, 1941. Intro. by Carl Van Vechten.

Two (Gertrude Stein and Her Brother) and Other Early Portraits (1908–1912).

New Haven: Yale University Press, 1951. Foreword by Janet Flanner.
Useful Knowledge. New York: Payson & Clarke, Ltd., 1928.
A Village Are You Ready Yet Not Yet A Play in Four Acts. Paris: Galerie Simon (Daniel-Henry Kahnweiler), 1928. Lithographs by Elie Lascaux.
Wars I Have Seen. New York: Random House, 1945.
Wars I Have Seen. London: B. T. Batsford, Ltd., 1945. Includes an appendix, "The Winner Loses."
What Are Masterpieces. Los Angeles: The Conference Press, 1940.
The World Is Round. New York: William R. Scott, 1939. Pictures by Clement Hurd.
The World Is Round. London: B. T. Batsford, Ltd., 1939. Illustrated by Sir Francis Rose.

Principal Works
of Carl Van Vechten

The Blind-Bow Boy. New York: Alfred A. Knopf, 1923.

The Dance Writings of Carl Van Vechten. New York: Dance Horizons, 1975. Ed. and intro. by Paul Padgette.

Excavations: A Book of Advocacies. New York: Alfred A. Knopf, 1926.

Feathers. New York: Random House, 1930.

Firecrackers: A Realistic Novel. New York: Alfred A. Knopf, 1925.

Fragments From an Unwritten Autobiography. 2 vols. New Haven: Yale University Library, 1955.

In the Garrett. New York: Alfred A. Knopf, 1919.

Interpreters. New York: Alfred A. Knopf, 1920.

Interpreters and Interpretations. New York: Alfred A. Knopf, 1917.

"Keep A Inchin' Along": Selected Writings of Carl Van Vechten about Black Art and Letters. Ed. Bruce Kellner. Westport, Conn.: Greenwood Press, 1979.

The Merry-Go-Round. New York: Alfred A. Knopf, 1918.

Music After the Great War and Other Studies. New York: G. Schirmir, 1915.

Music and Bad Manners. New York: Alfred A. Knopf, 1916.

The Music of Spain. New York: Alfred A. Knopf, 1918.

Nigger Heaven. New York: Alfred A. Knopf, 1926.

Parties: Scenes from Contemporary New York Life. New York: Alfred A. Knopf, 1930.

Peter Whiffle: His Life and Works. New York: Alfred A. Knopf, 1922.

Red: Papers on Musical Subjects. New York: Alfred A. Knopf, 1925.

Sacred and Profane Memories. New York: Alfred A. Knopf, 1932.

Spider Boy: A Scenario for a Moving Picture. New York: Alfred A. Knopf, 1928.

The Tattooed Countess: A Romantic Novel with a Happy Ending. New York: Alfred A. Knopf, 1924.

The Tiger in the House. New York: Alfred A. Knopf, 1920.

Selected Bibliography

Acton, Harold. *Memoirs of an Aesthete.* London: Methuen & Co., Ltd., 1948.

—— *More Memoirs of an Aesthete.* London: Methuen & Co., Ltd., 1970.

Benkovitz, Miriam J. *Ronald Firbank: A Biography.* London: Weidenfeld and Nicholson, 1970.

Bridgman, Richard. *Gertrude Stein in Pieces.* New York: Oxford University Press, 1970.

Brinnin, John Malcolm. *The Third Rose: Gertrude Stein and Her World.* Boston: Little, Brown and Co., Inc., 1959.

Clark, Emily. *Innocence Abroad.* New York: Alfred A. Knopf, 1931.

Coleman, Leon D. "Carl Van Vechten Presents the New Negro." *Studies in the Literary Imagination* (Georgia State Collge) (Fall 1974), 7(2):85–104.

Cunningham, Scott. *A Bibliography of the Writings of Carl Van Vechten.* 1924; rpt. Folcroft, Pa.: Folcroft Library Editions, 1972.

Draper, Muriel. *Music at Midnight.* New York and London: Harper & Bros., 1929.

Dubofsky, Melvyn. *We Shall Be All: A History of the Industrial Workers of the World.* Chicago: Quandrangle Books, 1969.

Fitzgerald, F. Scott. *The Correspondence of F. Scott Fitzgerald.* Ed. Matthew J. Bruccoli and Margaret M. Duggan. New York: Random House, 1980.

—— *The Letters of F. Scott Fitzgerald.* Ed. Andrew Turnbull. London: The Bodley Head, 1964.

Ford, Hugh. *Published in Paris: American and British Writers, Printers, and Publishers in Paris, 1920–1939.* New York: Macmillan, 1975.

Four Americans in Paris: The Collections of Gertrude Stein and Her Family. Catalogue of the exhibition at the Museum of Modern Art, New York, 1970. Articles by Irene Gordon, Lucile M. Golson, Leon Katz, Douglas Cooper, and Ellen B. Hirschland.

Gallup, Donald. "A Book Is a Book." *New Colophon* (January 1948), 1:67–80.

—— "Always Gertrude Stein." *Southwest Review* (Summer 1949), 34:254–58.

—— "Carl Van Vechten's Gertrude Stein." *Yale University Library Gazette* (October 1952), 27:77–86.

—— "Du Côte de Chez Stein." *The Book Collector* (Summer 1970), 19:169–84.

—— "Gertrude Stein and *The Atlantic*." *Yale University Library Gazette* (January 1954), 28:109–33.

—— "The Gertrude Stein Collection." *Yale University Library Gazette* (October 1947), 22:21–32.

—— "The Weaving of a Pattern: Marsden Hartley and Gertrude Stein." *Magazine of Art* (November 1948), 41:256–61.

Gallup, Donald, ed. *The Flowers of Friendship: Letters Written to Gertrude Stein.* New York: Alfred A. Knopf, 1953.

Gelb, Barbara. *So Short A Time: A Biography of John Reed and Louise Bryant.* New York: W. W. Norton & Co., Inc., 1973.

Gilliam, Dorothy Butler. *Paul Robeson; All American.* Washington, D.C.: The New Republic Book Co., Inc., 1976.

Gordon, John D. "Carl Van Vechten: Notes for an Exhibition in Honor of his Seventy-Fifth Birthday." *Bulletin of the New York Public Library* (July 1955), 59:331–66.

Haas, Robert Bartlett, and Donald Clifford Gallup. *A Catalogue of the Published and Unpublished Writings of Gertrude Stein.* New Haven: Yale University Library, 1941.

Hahn, Emily. *Lorenzo: D. H. Lawrence and the Women Who Loved Him.* Philadelphia and New York: J. B. Lippincott Co., 1975.

—— *Mabel: A Biography of Mabel Dodge Luhan.* Boston: Houghton Mifflin Co., 1977.

Hapgood, Hutchins. *A Victorian in a Modern World.* New York: Harcourt, Brace and Co., 1939.

Harris, David. "The Original *Four Saints in Three Acts* (1934)." *The Drama Review* (Spring 1982), 26(1):[101]–130.

Helbling, Mark. "Carl Van Vechten and the Harlem Renaissance." *Black American Literature Forum* (Summer 1976), 19:39–47.

Hemingway, Ernest. *Ernest Hemingway: Selected Letters, 1917–1961.* Ed. Carlos Baker. New York: Charles Scribner's Sons, 1981.

Hicks, Granville. *John Reed: The Making of a Revolutionary.* New York: Macmillan, 1936.

Imbs, Bravig. *Confessions of Another Young Man.* New York: The Henkle-Yewdale House, Inc., 1936.

Katz, Leon. "The First Making of *The Making of Americans*: A Study Based on Gertrude Stein's Notebooks and Early Versions of Her Novel (1902–1908)." Ph.D. diss., Columbia University, 1963.

Kellner, Bruce. *A Bibliography of the Work of Carl Van Vechten.* Westport, Conn.: Greenwood Press, 1980.

—— *Carl Van Vechten and the Irreverent Decades.* Norman: University of Oklahoma Press, 1968.

—— ed. *"Keep A-Inchin' Along": Selected Writings of Carl Van Vechten about Black Art and Letters.* Westport, Conn.: Greenwood Press, 1979.

Kouidis, Virginia M. *Mina Loy: American Modernist Poet.* Baton Rouge: Louisiana State University Press, 1980.

Kreymborg, Alfred. *Troubadour: An American Autobiography.* 1925; rpt. New York: Sagamore Press, Inc., 1957.

Lawrence, D. H. *The Collected Letters of D. H. Lawrence.* 2 vols. Ed. and intro. by Harry T. Moore. London: William Heinemann, Ltd., 1962.

Lueders, Edward. *Carl Van Vechten and the Twenties.* Albuquerque: University of New Mexico Press, 1955.

Luhan, Mabel Dodge. *Intimate Memories.* 4 vols. New York: Harcourt, Brace and Co., 1933–37. Vol. 1: *Background* (1933); Vol. 2: *European Experiences* (1935); Vol. 3: *Movers and Shakers* (1936); Vol. 4: *Edge of the Taos Desert* (1937).

—— *Lorenzo in Taos.* New York: Alfred A. Knopf, 1932.

McBride, Henry. *Florine Stettheimer.* New York: The Museum of Modern Art, 1946.

Mellow, James. *Charmed Circle: Gertrude Stein & Company.* New York: Praeger Publishers, Inc., 1974.

Moore, Harry T. *The Priest of Love: A Life of D. H. Lawrence.* Rev. ed. New York: Farrar, Straus and Giroux, 1974.

Rogers, William Garland. *When This You See Remember Me: Gertrude Stein in Person*. New York: Rinehart, 1948.

Rose, Francis. *Saying Life*. London: Cassell, 1961.

Sawyer, Julian. *Gertrude Stein: A Bibliography*. New York: Arrow Press, 1941.

Schuyler, George. "The Van Vechten Revolution." *Phylon: The Atlanta University Review of Race and Culture* (Fourth Quarter, 1950), 9:362–68.

Secrest, Meryle. *Between Me and Life: A Biography of Romaine Brooks*. London: Macdonald and Jane's, 1976.

Simon, Linda. *The Biography of Alice B. Toklas*. Garden City, N.Y.: Doubleday & Co., Inc., 1977.

Sprigge, Elizabeth. *Gertrude Stein: Her Life and Work*. New York: Harper and Bros., 1957.

—— "Gertrude Stein's American Years." *The Reporter* (11 August 1955), 13:46–52.

Stein, Leo. *Journey into the Self: Being the Letters, Papers, and Journals of Leo Stein*. Ed. Edmund Fuller. New York: Crown, 1950.

Steiner, Wendy. *Exact Resemblance to Exact Resemblance: The Literary Portraiture of Gertrude Stein*. Yale Studies in English, 189. New Haven: Yale University Press, 1978.

Sutherland, Donald. *Gertrude Stein: A Biography of Her Work*. New Haven: Yale University Press, 1951.

Thomson, Virgil. *Virgil Thomson*. New York: Alfred A. Knopf, 1966.

Toklas, Alice B. *The Alice B. Toklas Cook Book*. New York: Harper and Bros., 1954.

—— *Staying on Alone: Letters of Alice B. Toklas*. Ed. Edward Burns. New York: Liveright, 1973.

—— *What is Remembered*. New York: Holt, Rinehart and Winston, 1963.

Tyler, Parker. *Florine Stettheimer: A Life in Art*. New York: Farrar, Straus and Co., 1963.

Unterecker, John. *Voyager: A Life of Hart Crane*. New York: Farrar, Straus and Giroux, 1969.

White, Ray Lewis, ed. *Sherwood Anderson/Gertrude Stein: Correspondence and Personal Essays*. Chapel Hill: University of North Carolina Press, 1972.

Wilson, Robert A. *Gertrude Stein: A Bibliography*. New York: The Phoenix Bookshop, 1974.

Index

Abdy, Lady Diana, 477, 478*n*, 483*n*, 492*n*, 586, 587*n*, 588
Abdy, Sir Robert, 477, 478*n*, 480, 481*n*, 483*n*, 492*n*, 537, 537*n*
Academic Observer, The (Stein issue, Utica Free Academy), 537, 537*n*, 540
"Accents in Alsace" (Stein), 511
Acton, Arthur, 95*n*, 126*n*, 251*n*
Acton, Harold, 126*n*, 250, 251*n*
Acton, Hortense (Mrs. Arthur Acton), 95, 96, 103, 251*n*
"Ada" (Stein), 862*n*
Adams, Charles M., 716, 718*n*
Adams, Henry, 858
Addams, Jane, 403, 404*n*
Addis, Colonel Emmet, 188, 189*n*, 191, 192
Addis, Louise Hayden (later Louise Taylor), 188, 189*n*, 192
Adler, Mortimer, 350, 351*n*, 354, 357
"Advertisement" (Stein), 162*n*
Aherne, Brian, 376
Alastair, 113, 113*n*
Aldrich, Mildred, 155, 180*n*, 267
Alfred, William, 777, 778*n*, 782
Alice B. Toklas Cook Book, The: first idea for book, 505, 506*n*, 507, 521, 524, 526, 774
Alice in Wonderland (Lewis Carroll), 648
Alice M. Ditson Fund (Columbia University), 794*n*
"All About Money" (Stein), 509*n*
Alma-Tadema, Sir Lawrence, 388, 389*n*
Alsop, Joseph Jr., 454, 522, 523*n*, 530, 530*n*
Aman, Jean, 194*n*
Américains d'Amérique (Stein), 273, 273*n*, 274, 278

American Arbitration Society, 412
American Ballet, *see* New York City Ballet
"American Crimes and How They Matter" (Stein), 415*n*, 493
"American Education and Colleges" (Stein), 415*n*
"American Food and American Houses" (Stein), 415*n*, 493
American Fund for French Wounded (A.F.F.W.), 58*n*, 62*n*, 63*n*
American Mercury, The, 93, 94*n*
"American Newspapers" (Stein), 415*n*
American Red Cross, 739
American Theatre Wing (Stage Door Canteen), 737, 744, 750, 750*n*, 752, 753, 753*n*, 757, 761-62, 768, 770, 774*n*, 775, 779, 781, 784, 787, 796, 801
"American States and Cities and How They Differ from Each Other" (Stein), 415*n*
Ames, Georgiana, 494, 495*n*, 497
"Among Negroes" (Stein), 138, 162, 162*n*
"An American and France" (Stein), 475*n*, 493, 520*n*
"An Elucidation" (Stein), 69*n*, 146, 147*n*, 862
"An Icing for a Chocolate Eclair" (Van Vechten), 94*n*
"An Indian Boy" (Stein), 87, 87*n*, 94*n*, 96
"An Instant Answer or A Hundred Prominent Men" (Stein), 161, 162*n*
"An Interrupted Conversation" (Van Vechten), 518*n*
An Intimate Revue (Max Ewing), 320*n*
"And So. To Change So (A Fantasy on Three Careers). Muriel Draper Yvonne Davidson Beatrice Locher." (Stein), 102*n*, 104, 105*n*

GPSR Authorized Representative: Easy Access System Europe, Mustamäe tee
50, 10621 Tallinn, Estonia, gpsr.requests@easproject.com